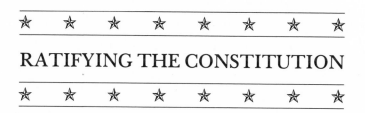

RATIFYING THE CONSTITUTION

RATIFYING THE
CONSTITUTION

Edited by
Michael Allen Gillespie
and Michael Lienesch

UNIVERSITY PRESS OF KANSAS

To Nancy and Ann

Published by the University Press of Kansas (Lawrence, Kansas 66045), which
was organized by the Kansas Board of Regents and is operated and funded by
Emporia State University, Fort Hays State University, Kansas State University,
Pittsburg State University, the University of Kansas, and Wichita State University

The preparation and publication of this volume were made possible in part by
two grants from the National Endowment for the Humanities, an independent
federal agency.

Library of Congress Cataloging-in-Publication Data

Ratifying the Constitution / edited by Michael Allen Gillespie and
    Michael Lienesch.
        p.   cm.
    Originally presented at a conference sponsored by the National
Humanities Center.
    Includes bibliographies and index.
    ISBN 0-7006-0402-2 (alk. paper)
    1. United States—Constitutional history—Congresses.
I. Gillespie, Michael Allen.   II. Lienesch, Michael, 1948–   .
III. National Humanities Center (Research Triangle Park, N.C.)
KF4541.A2R37   1989
342.73 '029 — dcl9   89-30118
[347.30229]   CIP

Printed in the United States of America
10   9   8   7   6   5   4   3   2   1

CONTENTS

v

CONTENTS
vii

FOREWORD

FORREST MCDONALD

The corpus of historical literature on the drafting of the United States Constitution is enormous. That on the ratification of the instrument, though an event of equal importance and far greater drama, is relatively small, despite the abundance of relevant source materials. Indeed, if we leave out of reckoning analyses of *The Federalist* — which, though written as propaganda in support of ratification in New York, is rarely dealt with as such — the present volume is the most extensive treatment of the subject yet undertaken.

The reason for the paucity of historical accounts of ratification is not difficult to explain: the story is one of labyrinthine complexity. The Constitution was ratified by popularly elected statewide conventions, and since North Carolina held two (the first refusing to ratify), there were fourteen conventions. There were, however, far more elections than that. Each state made its own rules about the number, apportionment, and manner of choosing delegates, the result being that the approximately 1,750 men who sat in the several conventions were selected in hundreds of largely uncoordinated elections, mainly by town meetings in New England and by countywide polls elsewhere. Moreover, the process unfolded over a period of almost three years.

Why, one may ask, needed it be so complex? Why did not the Framers leave the decision to the state legislatures, which had ratified the existing Articles of Confederation? Or, better yet, why did they not simply take a popular vote, yea or nay? The answers to these questions may help place the essays in this book in their broad historical and legal contexts.

The complex procedures arose from the ambiguous constitutional relationships Americans had borne one with another since the adoption of the Declaration of Independence in 1776 and the Articles of Confederation in 1781. The authors of the Declaration referred to themselves as "the Representatives of the united States of America," suggesting that the thirteen colonies now regarded themselves as one political entity; but it is to be observed that the word *united* was not capitalized and that the document went on to say that the former colonies "are, and of Right ought to be Free and Independent States" and referred to them as "they," plural. The full title of the Articles was "Articles of Confederation and perpetual Union," again implying oneness, but Article II expressly stipulated that "each state retains its sovereignty, freedom and independence," and Article III described the union as "a firm league of friendship."

The Articles also posed an immediate problem as far as ratification of the Constitution was concerned. Article XIII provided that amendments could be proposed by Congress but would become effective only if they were ratified by the legislatures of all thirteen states. The Framers of the Constitution sought to circumvent that procedure for two reasons. One was that ratification by all thirteen legislatures seemed impossible to obtain (the Confederation Congress had proposed several amendments, two had been approved by twelve legislatures, but none had been ratified by all). The other reason was technical and legal. As James Madison pointed out, if the Constitution were ratified by the legislatures, it would have the force of a treaty among sovereign states; and if it should subsequently be violated in any particular by any state, the others would have justification for dissolving the compact in its entirety.

To "form a more perfect Union," therefore, and to give the Constitution its self-proclaimed status as the "supreme Law of the Land," the Framers carefully crafted a procedure that virtually guaranteed ratification and yet was compatible with the commitments made in the Declaration and the Articles. The Declaration had proclaimed the doctrine of popular sovereignty (governments derive "their just powers from the consent of the governed"); the Constitution would be submitted to the people of the several states in their capacities as citizens of the states, severally. They could not vote as the American people as a whole because the Constitution amended each of the state constitutions, and the people of one state could have no right to amend the constitution of another. The voters would choose delegates to conventions to be gathered for the sole purpose of deciding to ratify or not to ratify. It was provided also that if the conventions of nine states approved the Constitution, the instrument would be binding upon those nine. The others would remain free to join the reconstituted union or not, as they pleased.

To make that procedure valid despite the requirements of the Articles of Confederation, the Framers sent the Constitution to Congress with a request that Congress submit it to the state legislatures, which in turn would be requested to submit it "to a Convention of Delegates, chosen in each State by the People thereof." When Congress and every state did as requested, they in effect amended the amending procedure prescribed by the Articles and thereby legitimated the whole enterprise.

The requisite nine states opted to come under what was called "the new roof" in fairly rapid order, starting with Delaware in December 1787 and finishing with New Hampshire the following June. Opposition mounted as the contests unfolded, however, being expressed largely in the form of a demand for the addition of a bill of rights or for a second general convention to propose various amendments. But on June 25, Virginia became the tenth state to ratify, and New York followed a month later. North Carolina rejected the Constitution in August and did not reverse its position until November 1789, months after the new national government had begun to operate and after the new Congress had approved the Bill of Rights. Rhode Island brought up the rear in May 1790.

Professors Gillespie and Lienesch have devised an ingenious plan of organization for the essays on ratification presented in this volume. The essays are arranged by states, in the order in which the states ratified, but each author, after consultation with the editors, was allowed to develop his story around a particular theme. In that manner the narrative thread is preserved while the authors weave a rich and varied historical tapestry. The reader will come away from this study with an understanding that the ratification of the Constitution was scarcely less miraculous than its drafting.

ACKNOWLEDGMENTS

Bringing together thirteen scholars to write a book about ratifying the Constitution must be a little like bringing together thirteen states to ratify it in the first place. In retrospect, we realize that the process has been both ambitious and, in its successful completion, a little amazing. Most of our thanks must go to the authors of these chapters, who consistently pleased us with their promptness, their scholarly scrupulousness, and their good humor. But even together, the thirteen of us could not have done it alone.

This volume was made possible by two grants from the National Endowment for the Humanities. We wish to thank the Endowment for its generous support and to extend special thanks to John Agresto, Richard Ekman, David Wise, Dorothy Wartenberg, Joseph Phelan, John Alexander Williams, and Alice R. Hudgins for going above and beyond the call of duty in extending their assistance at various stages of the project.

The National Humanities Center sponsored a conference at which the authors were first able to present their research to one another and to the public. We want to thank the Humanities Center and, especially, Charles Blitzer, Val Rogers, Sandra Copeland, John O'Connor, Kent Mulliken, and Wayne Pond for being such gracious hosts.

The North Carolina Commission on the Bicentennial of the United States Constitution was also generous in sponsoring the conference and in providing technical support. Robert Sikorski, associate director of the commission, played a central role in the project at every point, and he deserves special thanks for his many contributions. We would also like to thank Georgia Kebschull for her timely and flawless typing.

Numerous scholars contributed to the project. We thank those who were willing to serve on our advisory board: Peter Fish, Allan Kornberg, and David Price of Duke University, and Donald Higginbotham, Donald G. Matthews, Richard J. Richardson, and John Semonche of the University of North Carolina at Chapel Hill. We offer our thanks also to those who participated in the conference on ratification, contributing their criticism and insightful suggestions: Terry Ball, Eldon Eisenach, Calvin Jillson, Ralph Lerner, Pauline Maier, Stephen L. Schechter, Rob Sikorski, Rogers Smith, and Michael Zuckert. We are honored by the involvement of Forrest McDonald and Wilson Carey McWilliams in this volume, and we thank them for their contributions of the Foreword and the Afterword. We gratefully acknowledge Duke University, which sponsored the project from its inception.

Because we cannot thank our wives enough, we dedicate this book to them.

Chapel Hill and Durham, N.C.   Michael Allen Gillespie
August 1988   Michael Lienesch

INTRODUCTION

MICHAEL ALLEN GILLESPIE AND MICHAEL LIENESCH

It is with some justification that Americans speak of the creation of the United States Constitution as the "miracle at Philadelphia." The events themselves were extraordinary, with fifty-five fabled founding fathers laboring through the long hot summer of 1787, declaiming, debating, disagreeing, and somehow through it all constructing one of the oldest continuously existing constitutions in the history of the world. All things considered—the absence of precedent, the diversity of views, the uncertainty of the times—the outcome does in many ways seem miraculous.

Yet it can be argued that the real miracle of the age was not the Constitution's creation but its ratification. At Philadelphia, fifty-five men, meeting together for three and one-half months, crafted a plan of government. By contrast, in the ratification process, more than seventeen hundred delegates, chosen in town meetings and local elections by tens of thousands of voters throughout the land, came together in the far-flung convention cities of their separate states to debate the new federal government. Their deliberations, taking place not only inside the convention halls but outside as well, in churches and taverns, in letters to the editor and newspaper columns, in whispered conversations and noisy stump speeches, went on intensely for many months and came to a close, with the admission of recalcitrant Rhode Island, only after a period of some three years. Through it all, Americans acquired not only a new Constitution but also, with the recommended amendments that would become the basis of the Bill

1

of Rights, a better Constitution. In the process, ratification inspired some of America's greatest political thinking and writing, including — although by no means limited to — the *Federalist Papers*. It also gave Americans some of their greatest politics.

The significance of ratification was not lost on Americans of the time. When asked late in his life about the meaning of the United States Constitution, James Madison observed that it could be found, not in the deliberations at Philadelphia, where delegates drafted a grand theory of government, but in the debates in the several states, where the theory was explained, interpreted, and tested in the real world of practical politics.[1] For us today, ratification provides a starting point for examining the meaning of our Constitutional republic.

PAST PERSPECTIVES

Under the circumstances, it is lamentable that we know so little about the process of ratification. While studies about the creation of the Constitution abound, books about the ratification of it have been few and far between. Even among recent scholars, with the exception of Robert A. Rutland, few have focused systematically on the process.[2] As a result, studies have tended to follow predictable patterns.

To begin with, ratification has been seen as secondary, an event unimportant in itself. According to most accounts, the federal convention created the Constitution; the state ratifying conventions accepted it. It follows that ratification was a kind of afterthought, an appendix to the act of creation or, at best, an extension of the federal convention. At the Philadelphia convention, great men gathered to change the course of the country; in the state conventions, local politicians and small-minded people came together to prevent those great men from carrying out their higher purpose. At Philadelphia, great words were spoken and great ideas were shaped; in the state conventions, rhetoric was brought to bear, and ideologies were manipulated. Happily, in the end, the champions of the Constitution carried the day, while its blundering and incompetent opponents were vanquished. All told, according to the conventional interpretation, ratification was at best an anticlimax and at worst an embarrassment.

Add to this the fact that ratification has been studied from a variety of perspectives. In relatively recent times, it has been explained by focusing on economic interests, social status, and cultural influences, including ethnicity and religion.[3] It has been described as the product of political ideology, including nationalism, sectionalism, and localism.[4] And it has been depicted in strategic political terms as a conflict between parties and personalities.[5] Notable about these perspectives is that most of the time they have been presented as mutually exclusive, with practitioners not only concentrating on their own explanations but also going out of their way to exclude other explanations.[6] The result has been a sometimes intense intellectual conflict. In the process, the story of ratification has been told all too frequently in tendentious terms or has been lost altogether.

Finally, there are the practical problems. Ratification was an immense undertaking. Occurring simultaneously in thirteen places, it involved thousands of participants and tens of thousands of written sources. Thus, any study of ratification must be a partial treatment. Those who have studied the process as a whole, describing ratification as a continental event, have tended to overlook local issues and prominent state personalities. By the same token, those who have concentrated on the separate states have tended to miss larger trends.

RECENT REINTERPRETATIONS

During the last few years, however, ratification has begun to be reconsidered. To some extent, the attention it has started to receive may be circumstantial, the product of America's recent bicentennial celebration. More important in the long run has been the collection and publication of impressive new reference sources. Probably most significant of all has been the creation of a new set of perspectives that scholars are now bringing to the study of America's founding.

The reference sources are important. Until recently, most studies of the creation and ratification of the Constitution have relied on collections such as Max Farrand's *Records of the Federal Convention*, Jonathan Elliot's *Debates*, and Paul Leicester Ford's *Essays* and *Pamphlets on the Constitution*.[7] In the last few years, however, a rich new reservoir of references has appeared, including the ambitious *Documentary History of the Ratification of the Constitution*, the seven-volume *Complete Anti-Federalist*, and the multivolume *The Founders' Constitution*.[8] In addition, single-volume sources, including Michael

Kammen's *Origins of the American Constitution*, J. R. Pole's *The American Constitution: For and Against*, and Isaac Kramnick's new edition of *The Federalist Papers*, have made many of the ratification materials more widely available.[9]

More important than the sources, however, is a new set of perspectives on the founding. Whereas earlier scholarship had concentrated on the events at Philadelphia, recent studies have taken a greatly expanded view of the Constitutional period by going beyond the creation of the Constitution to consider its ratification and implementation.[10] Instead of concentrating on a few of the leading actors and thinkers of the time, contemporary scholars have looked beyond these to the many less well known but often more prolific politicians and pamphleteers who dominated the politics of the day.[11] Indeed, whereas earlier students had concentrated on the Constitution itself, on its institutions and formal structures, recent ones have gone in search of deeper meanings—the practical problems that made the Constitution necessary, the principles that inspired it, the politics that made it possible.[12] The result has been a new view of the founding, one that considers interests, ideas, and issues and that combines them together into a new kind of political history.[13]

According to this view, ratification was important—a formative act and an essential part of the founding. In the ratification process, the Constitution was not simply accepted but was also explained, interpreted, and, in certain ways, reconstructed. Throughout the state debates, institutions were defined, concepts were clarified, purposes were defended; flaws and weaknesses were pointed out; amendments were recommended. Through this process, the Constitution was given meaning. Thus, ratification should be seen as the original act of Constitutional interpretation. In this regard, it marks, not the end of the founding, but the beginning of American Constitutional history.

At the same time, ratification was complex—a process protean enough to require a multitude of perspectives. Ratification involved interests, including economic, social, and cultural concerns. It involved ideas—the creation of concepts, the discovery of new forms of discourse, the forging of totally new theories of government. And it involved issues, thus testing political power and requiring political strategy. To understand ratification, it is essential to recognize that all of these factors were present at once. In studying ratification, it follows that multiple explanations are necessary, and that no single one will suffice.

Politically, ratification was complex and convoluted. It was a story not of the few but of the many—a multiplicity of actors, interests, and parties. Far from any single national strategy, partisans pursued a multiplicity of state-by-state paths. Much of the time, information was sketchy, and because the mails were slow and travel was hard, coordination between states and regions was difficult if not impossible. At no point was an easy victory taken for granted. For that matter, considering the complexity of the process, it is difficult to describe ratification in terms of winners and losers at all. Instead, it was more a problematic process of conflict and consensus in which compromise and diplomacy were as important as power and political strategy.

Finally, ratification was part of the politics of the period, a set of events that can only be understood in the wider context of the founding and, for that matter, beyond. In each of the states, peculiar histories shaped the process. Unique personalities were involved in major ways. Unpredictable happenings, unforeseen events, and luck all played a role. Above all, ratification was part of a continuing process through which Americans created, constructed, and began the business of living under the Constitution. It is a process that is still going on today.

The essays in this book share this new perspective on the founding. Written independently, they are the product of a diverse group of scholars—six historians and seven historians of political thought. Each concentrates on an individual state; each focuses on a separate major theme or issue; each describes a peculiar political constellation. All of the essays attempt to show the interaction of interests, ideas, and issues. Together, they share an overall commitment to reminding readers that ratification was crucial, that it was complex and problematic, and that it must be understood in context, as part of the continuing story of America's political history.

RECONSIDERING RATIFICATION

When the Philadelphia convention adjourned on September 17, 1787, and forwarded the Constitution to Congress, it set into motion the unprecedented political process of popular ratification. For the convention sent the draft not only to Congress but also to the thirteen existing states, where, according to decisions made at Philadelphia, the plan was to be considered, not by the state legislatures, but by popularly elected ratifying conventions. The result was America's first national election campaign, creating conflict and debate in every state and section, inspiring commentaries and news reports that were published up and down the continent, and leading eventually to the establishment of the first national political parties. It can be argued that it was with ratification that American politics, at least as we know it, began.

Yet ratification was not simply a popular referendum. In keeping with Confederation principles, as well as with existing practices, the thirteen states considered the Constitution more or less independently, deciding in their own separate ways when, where, and how elections would be held, conventions called, and deliberations conducted. Under the circumstances, state and sectional interests, far from being transcended, were constantly being considered, and in many cases they were decisive. Prominent local personalities played important roles. More often than not, outcomes turned on historical happenstance or on seemingly insignificant issues.

In any case, the course of ratification was by no means preordained. The fact that the mails were slow complicated the process. Often the states deliberated with only limited knowledge of debates in the other states. Sometimes they proceeded more or less on their own. The result was a somewhat piecemeal process, in which predictions were impossible and in which the final outcome became apparent only in the end.

Ratification began with the promise of prosperity. Even as the Constitution was being signed, several of the Middle Atlantic states had begun to compete for the honor of being the first to ratify. Prominent among these were Delaware, Pennsylvania, and New Jersey. Eager for economic advantage, these commercial republics, which were closely connected through the influence of Philadelphia, were even more firmly united by the desire for a stronger national economic union. Acting more as a group than independently, they ratified rapidly and with little opposition. Indeed, in Delaware and New Jersey, ratification was unanimous. And even in Pennsylvania, famous for its radical republican tradition, the siren call of commercial expansion seemed strong enough to override opposition.

Appropriately enough, debate over the Philadelphia Constitution began in Philadelphia, where supporters of the Constitution sought to strike while the iron was hot. Taking advantage of the fact that the Constitutional Convention had been meeting upstairs from the state assembly, Pennsylvania Republicans, champions of the Constitution, reported the proposed plan to the legislature almost as soon as it was signed. The political rationale for such speed was the fact that Republicans were comfortably in control of the legislature, and they sought to call a convention before their control could be tested in the next election. Their opponents, confusingly called "Constitutionalists," after Pennsylvania's radically democratic state constitution, sought to slow the process by absenting themselves from the assembly, preventing a quorum, and making it impossible to call a convention. While the Republican sergeant at arms bootlessly chased the opposition up and down the streets and alleys of Philadelphia, a mob of supporters took matters into its own hands, capturing two tardy Constitutionalists in their boardinghouse and carrying them bodily onto the assembly floor. Even at the start, it was clear that ratification would be a highly partisan process.

While Pennsylvanians were at odds, the citizens of Delaware were uniting behind the new Constitution. At issue was the best means for this small state, which had large economic prospects, to attain economic and political independence. With little debate and almost no dissension, commerce-conscious Delaware, which had much to gain from a more efficient economic union, ratified the Constitution on December 7 by a vote of 30 to 0. In his "Independence and the Concept of a Commercial Republic," Gaspare J. Saladino shows the importance of commercial considerations in securing Delaware's unanimous ratification. Reviewing the economic experience of the 1780s, he finds that Delaware was by no means homogeneous in its commercial orientation: different counties had felt differing degrees of prosperity and depression. Saladino relates these competing economic experiences to politics, tracing the connections between economic fortunes and political loyalties, as seen in the conflict between the state's dominant political factions, the Tories and the Whigs. He concludes that the federal Constitution, promising both economic advantages and a certain degree of political equality among the states, transcended these differences and assured speedy ratification.

Back in Pennsylvania, where elections had been held and a convention had convened on November 20, delegates remained divided. In his "Representation and the Meaning of Republicanism," George J. Graham, Jr., describes the divisions and examines the politics that made ratification possible. Graham explains the strength of the Constitutionalist opposition, detailing the strong tradition of popular politics that led many Pennsylvanians to oppose the new government. He also shows how Republicans, led by James Wilson, used a combination of political strategy and political rhetoric to overwhelm the opposition, securing ratification on the twelfth of December 1787 by a vote of 46 to 23. In the end, however, Graham concludes that the political strategy backfired, as the stong-arm tactics of supporters and an apparent Federalist unwillingness to open the plan to sustained public debate left opponents angry and unconvinced. Nevertheless, Graham contends that Wilson's political rhetoric was a significant success in the long run, because his arguments concerning the nature of popular representation would in time prove convincing, perhaps not in Pennsylvania, but throughout the rest of the states to ratify.

The story in New Jersey seemed, on its face, to be similar to that of Delaware. In her "Property and the Price of Republican Politics," Sara M. Shumer considers the absence of opposition in New Jersey, where ratification was effected easily and unanimously, by a vote of 38 to 0 on December 18. Shumer describes the political culture of New Jersey, highlighting a history of widespread popular participation. Focusing on the radical Whig leader Abraham Clark, she analyzes the surprising absence of a democratic opposition to the new Constitution. In Shumer's words (borrowed from Sherlock Holmes), the issue in New Jersey was "why the dog did not bark." She concludes that in order to solve economic problems within the state, and to secure independence from larger and economically threatening neighboring states, Clark was prepared to compromise, by sacrificing political principle in the name of economic necessity. Finally, Shumer considers the compromise and concludes that economic gains sometimes must be paid for at a high political price.

Although economic issues were important in the next three states to ratify (and would play a part in all of the states to follow), social concerns seemed even more significant. In Georgia, Connecticut, and Massachusetts—three states in which social order had recently come under sustained attack—ratification was seen by many as a means to restore stability. Consequently, ratification in these states was less about pursuing prosperity than about securing the social order at home.

Georgia was the first of these to consider the document, which it ratified after only cursory consideration on the last day of December by a vote of 26 to 0. In his "Searching for Security," Edward J. Cashin shows how Georgia's acceptance of the Constitution was in large part a matter of internal security. Threatened on the frontier by Indians and torn by internal sectionalism, seemingly unable to defend itself or its people, Georgia needed help. Thus the decision to ratify was a relatively easy one. Yet, as Cashin shows, ratification of the federal Constitution was inextricably intertwined with the much more problematic process of reforming Georgia's own state constitution. In each case, Georgians came together because of the frontier, united by their fears of Indian invasion and, as Cashin also shows, by their hopes of vast new opportunities in the West.

In Connecticut, the threat to the social order was both internal and external. As Donald S. Lutz describes in his "Achieving Assent and Assuring Control," the state's ancient and politically powerful elite, including its Congregationalist "Standing Order," looked with some concern on the possibilities of popular disorder. Specifically, Connecticut's leaders viewed with apprehension the events in neighboring Massachusetts, where popular protests had erupted recently into the bloody violence of Shays's Rebellion. More generally, they feared the effect that New York's impost and Rhode Island's paper-money statutes would have on their own state's prosperity. Considering the federal Constitution, with its promise of sound economic policies, to be an instrument to ensure stability, Connecticut's elite mounted an extraordinary campaign in the popular press, informing the state's citizens of the benefits of union. The campaign, Lutz argues, was a sweeping success, except in the anomalous case of New Haven, where another kind of social order existed, and in those areas along the Massachusetts border closest to the region that had been the center of support for Shays. On January 9, 1788, the Constitution was ratified by a three-to-one majority of 128 to 40, thus securing Connecticut's solid support not only for the Constitution but—at least for a generation— for the Federalist party as well.

With Connecticut, the first phase of ratification came to a close. By and large, the Constitution appeared to have gotten off to a flying start. The ease of these early successes, however, was something of an illusion. With the exception of Pennsylvania, none of the first states to ratify was particularly powerful. Delaware, New Jersey, and Connecticut were small states, both geographically and demographically, and while Georgia was large in land mass, it was the smallest state in terms of population. Politically, Federalists were still to be tested, having won a close contest only in Pennsylvania, where their tactics had alienated the opposition and raised serious doubts about their dedication to democratic procedures. The early debates in the press had gone well for the Constitution's supporters, but with the appearance of essays by New York's "Cato" and Pennsylvania's "Centinel," and the address of the Pennsylvania minority, thoughtful readers began to consider the other side. As initial enthusiasm waned, opposition grew, and the outcome began to seem less certain.

The first and one of the most decisive tests for the Constitution came in Massachusetts. Badly divided, buffeted by disorder in the wake of Shays's Rebellion, Massachusetts in the 1780s was a politically unpredictable situation. In his "Creating Consensus," Michael Allen Gillespie describes the politics of ratification. Refuting standard interpretations, Gillespie shows that ratification was not brought about by the strategic successes of Massachusetts Federalists. On the contrary, and directly refuting the claims of those such as John P. Roche, Gillespie shows how Federalists failed to realize that consensus provided the basis for a successful ratification strategy.

In part, as Gillespie shows, Federalists were driven by the fear that any compromise would require a second convention, dooming their plans for a strong union. State governments would surely put severe limits on delegates to future conventions; this would weaken their ability to transfer power from the states to the federal government. For many Federalists, it seemed that the Constitution had to be ratified or rejected as it stood. Washington's famous letter urging ratification emphasized the point, asserting that a second convention was not feasible and that Americans must either accept the government proposed or face anarchy.

Gillespie describes a moderate coalition, led by Samuel Adams and

John Hancock, which saw the necessity of compromise. Like most Americans of the day, including most Antifederalists, these thinkers believed that the Articles of Confederation needed to be strengthened but that the proposed plan went too far, threatening state sovereignty. In offering their "conciliatory position"—supporting ratification while insisting on recommendatory amendments—Adams and Hancock provided a solution to the problem. In the process, as Gillespie demonstrates, Adams and Hancock, the aging leaders of the Revolution, helped restore a republican consensus to post-Revolutionary Massachusetts. By abandoning confrontation for consensus, they secured ratification in Massachusetts on the sixth of February 1788 by a narrow vote of 187 to 168.

In Massachusetts, an enormous obstacle was overcome, not only because Massachusetts was a key state but also because, with the idea of recommended (as opposed to conditional) amendments, it became possible to construct moderate majorities favoring the Constitution in the remaining states as well. It must be pointed out, however, that the point was lost on at least some partisans. For example, in New Hampshire, obstinate Federalists refused to compromise, thereby forcing adjournment and the reconvening of a second convention and, in the process, slowing the movement toward ratification substantially. Similarly, in North Carolina and Rhode Island, Antifederalists held the line, and, at least for a time, refused to compromise at any cost. Even so, after Massachusetts, ratification seemed suddenly more possible.

The concerns that dominated the ratification contest in the next three states—Maryland, New Hampshire, and South Carolina— revolved around the relation of the state to the new nation as a whole. One northern, one southern, and one placed strategically in the middle, these three states were among the most distinctive in their political cultures, and they prided themselves on their distinctiveness. Yet in one way they were similar, in that each was troubled by the fear that its own unique way of practicing politics might be lost in a national union. In each case, political principles were very much in evidence. In Maryland, the issue was state size, the time-honored republican precept that freedom could exist only in small and self-contained republics. In South Carolina, the issue was slavery and the peculiar politics that it required. In Congregationalist New Hampshire, the issue was religion—the protection of a Protestant political ethic. In all of these cases, commitments ran deep, and compromise did not come easily. As for ratification, the process slowed at this point, and the politics became painfully protracted.

In his "The Small Republic in the New Nation," Peter S. Onuf describes the situation in Maryland, where a distinctive ethnic and religious culture had created a strong sense of corporate identity. Reinforced by a history of boundary disputes, Maryland tended to see itself as a small and self-contained state with a large commitment to fending off the expansionistic endeavors of its neighbors. Onuf shows how Maryland Antifederalists, led by Luther Martin, drew on traditional republican political theory, with its emphasis on small, self-contained territories, to make their case against the Constitution. At the same time, he goes on to show how their Federalist opponents confronted that case, countering conventional precepts with a reconceptualized theory of an extended union in which western expansion was viewed as a matter, not of state power, but of individual interest. With this conceptual change, Onuf argues, Marylanders were freed to think of themselves, not as a small and circumscribed state, but as a center of regional commerce and a critical link uniting the North and the South in an expanding continental economy. As a result of this reconceptualization, they were able to vote for ratification after only nine days of deliberation, by a vote of 63 to 11 on April 28, 1788.

In South Carolina, as Robert M. Weir describes it, the continuation of slavery was the price for ratification. In his "Slavery and the Structure of the Union," Weir details the potentially divisive differences between low-country and back-country interests in South Carolina politics and suggests that slavery became the means by which those divisions came to be reconciled. Thus, for South Carolinians, slavery was a matter not only of political principle but also of political practicality; it assuaged intrastate sectionalism and created statewide consensus. Under the proposed Constitution, the guarantee of enough southern votes in the Senate to veto abolitionist legislation, the prohibition on the legislative regulation of the slave trade before 1808, and the retention of the police power by the states were strong incentives for South Carolinians to support ratification. After little more than a week of debate, they ratified on May 23, by a vote of 149 to 73. In concluding, Weir considers the ironic results of their thinking, suggesting that for South Carolina, as for the country as a whole, the compromise that allowed the continuation of slavery was in the end a bargain paid for in lost liberties.

In her "Puritanism and the Moral Foundations of America," Jean Yarbrough considers the third of these three distinctive political cultures — Protestant New Hampshire, where moral concerns dominated the debate. In New Hampshire, Yarbrough contends, even practical matters such as the role of the instruction of delegates became matters of principle. The result was that the New Hampshire convention, which was controlled by an uncompromising Federalist faction, broke down, and ratification was almost lost. When the convention reconvened on June 18, Federalists discovered to their chagrin that only a handful of their opponents had been able to convince their constituents to change their instructions. Chastened by the censure of concerned Federalists from around the country, they had no choice but to adopt the conciliatory plan of ratifying while recommending amendents, including a bill of rights to guarantee freedom of conscience, with which they could maintain their Protestant principles while at the same time they could achieve the practical advantages of union. The compromise made possible a narrow victory of 57 to 47, and on June 21, 1788, New Hampshire became the ninth state to ratify.

With New Hampshire, the federal Constitution became law. But ratification was by no means assured, because while the required nine states had ratified, Virginia and New York had not, and no one had any illusion that a federal union could succeed without these two exceedingly powerful states. Together, they contained almost a third of the country's population. Along with Pennsylvania, they constituted the economic, geographical, and political heart of the nation. A union without them would have been no union at all; it would open the specter of two or three regional confederacies. Nor could there be any illusions about easy ratification in these states, where strong opposition parties, led by such charismatic and popular figures as Patrick Henry and Governor George Clinton, were well organized and ready for a fight. Thus, ironically, ratification at this point, although it was already assured, became particularly problematic.

Virginia posed the greatest problem. In size alone it was gigantic, including what is today both Kentucky and West Virginia. In population, it loomed nearly twice as large as the next largest state. Perhaps most important, in its politics, Virginia had long been considered a leader. In particular, Virginia spoke for the South, championing its agrarian economy against the commercial and manufacturing interests of the North, demanding that the Mississippi be open to navigation, and insisting on free markets and free trade. In Virginia, sectional loyalty ran deep.

In "Sectionalism and the General Good," Lance Banning describes the situation in Virginia, where the political elite, while deeply divided on other matters, were united in considering that Virginia spoke for the South. Indeed, as Banning shows, Virginia's ratification can be understood in large measure as a debate over sectional prerogatives, in which both supporters and opponents of the Constitution were seeking to enhance Virginia's self-professed position as leader of the southern states. Concentrating on Antifederalists such as Patrick Henry, George Mason, and William Grayson and contrasting them to Madison, Banning contends that the crucial factor in Virginia was Madison's ability to reconceptualize sectional concerns. By arguing that a consolidated economic union, which would assure the free flow of goods on the Mississippi, would strengthen, not weaken, Virginia's economic power in the region, Madison calmed Antifederalist fears. Indeed, in claiming that with Congress being controlled by agricultural states, Virginia would play the role of leader not only of the South but also of the shipping and producing states, Madison pointed to the possibilities of even more power for Virginia within the union. It was an argument, Banning concludes, that many Antifederalists found convincing, and Patrick Henry's florid rhetoric notwithstanding, Virginia ratified the Constitution on June 25, by a vote of 89 to 79.

New York was next. Under the popular and successful Governor Clinton, New York had achieved an enviable degree of political and economic stability. The policies that made this stability possible, including a profitable state impost tax, were premised on a weak federal government. Having constructed a political coalition dominated by small farmers and western land speculators, for whom the impost meant low property taxes, the practical Clinton had little political incentive to turn over economic power to a central government. At the same time, New York had already become a trading center for both New England and the Middle Atlantic region, and its economic prospects loomed large in the minds of many. In fact, most New Yorkers agreed that their state would be a primary beneficiary of an expanded economic union.

In his "Federalism and the Political Economy of Union," Cecil L. Eubanks describes the calculations that took place in the minds of New Yorkers as they agreed to trade recent prosperity for potential economic power. Describing the background to ratification, Eubanks portrays the politics of New York as a politics of economic power, pitting democratic against aristocratic factions. Concentrating on the essays of "Federal Farmer," published in New York, and on the speeches of Melancton Smith, Eubanks shows how Antifederalists interpreted the new Constitution in these economic terms. Turning to "Publius" and to the speeches of Alexander Hamilton, Eubanks goes on to describe Federalist economic thinking and to show how Hamilton's elitist economics, along with his elitist rhetoric, made for unpopular politics. At the same time, Eubanks also claims that in embracing the concept of an extended republic, New York's Federalists, almost without realizing it, were forced to transcend their classical economics, substituting in its place a terminology that was more appropriate to a modern political economy. In the end, with even Hamilton embracing this new kind of republican economy, Federalists prevailed, and New York ratified on July 26, by a vote of 30 to 27, becoming the eleventh state to ratify.

Within the space of a month, Virginia and New York had ratified, and a stronger union under the Philadelphia Constitution had become a practical reality. There remained only the two recalcitrant rebels, North Carolina and Rhode Island, each with a history of resistance, each having been a thorn in the side of previous attempts at consolidation. Even so, supporters of the new government were surprised at the stubbornness of these states and their determination to resist ratification.

At stake were some unresolved but very important issues. Although North Carolina and Rhode Island have often been seen as insignificant—a kind of anomalous footnote to the ratification process—their resistance did have implications for the shape of the federal union to come. It must be remembered that even after the ratification by New York, the final form of the new system was still to be shaped. Of the eleven states that had ratified, five had attached recommendatory amendments. These amendments differed widely from state to state, and there were vocal minorities within these states that remained convinced that these amendments were not necessary. It remained to be seen whether the Constitution would ultimately be amended so as to address Antifederalist concerns and thereby assure its legitimacy.

North Carolina seemed to see its role as ensuring amendments. Settled on small subsistence farms scattered along a thousand miles of pine forests and sand barrens, North Carolinians practiced a local and provincial politics. In his "Preserving Rights," Michael Lienesch reviews the reasons that they were predisposed to oppose central power and to protect local liberties. Turning to the debates in the state convention, Lienesch contends that the overriding consideration was the protection of rights. In a review of the debates of the convention he describes the comprehensiveness of the concern for rights, the different definitions of rights held by Antifederalists and Federalists, and the prominent part that a proposed bill of rights played in the deliberations. In concluding, Lienesch suggests that while North Carolina's resistance may have been instrumental in ensuring the first ten amendments, it was in the end ironic, because Madison's Bill of Rights failed to secure most of the rights that the North Carolinians had sought to secure. In any case, the first state convention refused to ratify, voting 184 to 83 on the second of August to return the Constitution unsigned.

From the start, North Carolina had been reluctant to separate itself from the ratifying states. As a matter of principle, however, it held out until the First Congress passed a bill of rights and submitted it to the states, at which point North Carolina called a second convention and ratified the original document on November 21, 1789, by a vote of 194 to 77.

Rhode Island was another matter altogether. Acting less out of principle than out of shrewd self-interest, Rhode Island had refused to even call a convention, and in a popular referendum in which Federalists refused to participate, it rejected ratification by a lopsided vote of 2,708 to 237. Throughout the Confederation period, Rhode Island had enriched itself at the expense of other states, by vetoing reforms that would have established a stronger union. The state was dominated by a radical Country faction, which sought to solve the state's financial problems by issuing paper money and then depreciating it. To this end, Rhode Island mandated that the citizens of other states accept Rhode Island paper in payment for debts, while simultaneously requiring that its own citizens be paid in specie. The state also sought to repay both its state debt and its proportion of the national debt in depreciated paper.

In his "Protecting State Interests," John P. Kaminski describes the policies that obstinate Rhode Island followed. He contends that supporters of the Country party, including most Rhode Islanders, saw little advantage to entering a stronger union. By contrast, the members of the Mercantile party, especially Providence merchants, were driven to despair; some even intimated in private correspondence that they would welcome armed intervention by Massachusetts or Connecticut. Finally, when the new federal government passed laws to tax Rhode Island's trade with the other states and when the city of Providence threatened to secede, the ruling Country faction acquiesced. The faction allowed a convention to be called, and it absented enough of its delegates to allow ratification by a slim margin of two votes, 34 to 32 on May 29, 1790. Not incidentally, as Kaminski shows, by the spring of 1790 the state had completely paid off its state debt in depreciated paper money.

With Rhode Island finally in the fold, the first federal union was complete. Ratification had taken almost three years and had required enormous efforts. In the process, however, Americans had not only completed their first national campaign; they had also, in the fullest sense of the word, completed the founding of their nation.

EXPLAINING RATIFICATION

How, then, do we explain ratification? What general conclusions can we draw from the studies of these several states? What did they have in common? What were the different factors that operated in the various states? The essays in this book present no single overriding explanation for ratification. Instead, they explain the process in multicausal terms, citing numerous factors and describing the way in which these factors converged in the context of each of the states.

In the past, depictions of ratification have been far too partial. By and large, they have been told from a Federalist perspective, assuming in retrospect not only the rightness of the Federalist cause but also the resourcefulness of the Federalist politicians who brought it to a successful conclusion. But even in the studies that are more sympathetic to the Antifederalist side, ratification has been described as a military campaign: first the surprise attack, with Federalists striking early to win a series of easy victories; then stalemate, with opposition growing and the early successes slowed; and finally, the last-ditch resistance, as Antifederalists prepared to fight to the end in an effort to defeat the Constitution regardless of the cost. By implication, ratification was a war that took place on a national scale; what happened in the states were only minor skirmishes.

In fact, the essays in this book suggest another pattern altogether. When told from a less partial perspective, ratification emerges, not as a contest between all-knowing supporters and benighted opponents or between a self-interested Federalist faction, on one side, and public-spirited Antifederalist patriots, on the other, but as a more complicated debate in which interests impinged on all sides and in which there were well-meaning patriots in every camp. Most clearly, several of the essays refute the assumption that Federalists were particularly astute as politicians; these essays show that in states such as Pennsylvania, Massachusetts, New Hampshire, and New York, the harsh rhetoric and uncompromising tactics of Federalists in fact almost snatched defeat from the jaws of victory and came close to assuring the rejection of the proposed plan. Indeed, in several states, it was not the Constitution's strongest supporters who saved the day; it was a coalition of compromisers, relying on the power of persuasion and seeking conciliation instead of confrontation.

Thus, the essays in this book suggest a pattern, based less on military power than on diplomatic bargaining and compromise, in which Antifederalists and Federalists attempted, albeit sometimes ineptly, to converge on some common ground of agreement. Ultimately, ratification was not a war, which one side won and the other lost; it was more like a plan for peace, preconditioned by shared frustrations and shared hopes, a process in which, in the end, both sides emerged as winners. Not incidentally, the terms of agreement were struck in the separate states.

Essential elements existed in all of the states. Economic considerations, although they were especially conspicuous in the Middle Atlantic states, were present everywhere. From Delaware to Rhode Island, as the essays in this book show, economic interests played a part in the process. Nevertheless, the authors agree that these interests cannot be explained, following the assumptions of Charles A. Beard, in terms of personal wealth alone. In each case, economic factors are described in context, focusing on the sometimes dramatically divergent economic backgrounds of the several states, as well as on differing economic conditions within them. In every essay, the attempt is made to tie economics to politics. Moreover, the chapters cite not only the connections between economic interests and political positions but also the contradictions, the points — and there were many — at which the actors seemed to transcend their own immediate interests in search of some general good.

The same can be said for social, cultural, and political considerations. In each of the states, there existed distinctive social structures, with their own relationships of authority and deference. Connecticut's "Standing Order" was only one, if an extreme, case. Each of the states can be understood as pursuing its own patterns of political culture. Here again the dissimilarities were striking, as seen in a comparison of abolitionist New Hampshire, with its moralistic Protestant politics, and slave-owning South Carolina, where slavery touched all aspects of life. In every state, unique political relationships were present, including factions, persuasions, and parties that had long local histories even before the Constitution was conceived. By considering Georgia, for example, or by comparing Virginia and New York, the reader will see the significant role that state politics played in ratification.

Throughout the process, ideology was a factor as well. In some of the states, such as North Carolina, ideological factors seemed particularly prominent. In others, including those in which debate was limited, it appeared less important. But political thinking, in the broadest terms, was present in all of the states, and in some it proved decisive. In Maryland, for example, Federalists carried the debate by offering a reconceived concept of union. In Virginia, thoughtful leaders transcended existing sectional loyalties to create a new and more expansive notion of sectionalism. In New York, Antifederalists and Federalists alike found themselves thinking often of the meaning of federalism and of its role in the creation of an expanded republic. Of course, in each of these cases and in all of the states, ideas were inextricably tied to interests and issues, and all of these factors converged within the political process.

At the same time, several considerations were at work dividing the individual states into predictable patterns. The first of these was state size. In the five demographically smallest states, the total vote in favor of ratification was 185 to 79; in the five largest, it was 481 to 435 opposed, counting the first vote in North Carolina. Similarly, in the seven geographically smallest states, the total votes were 537 to 298 in favor; in the four largest states, 290 to 228 against. (The latter totals are arrived at in spite of the fact that Georgia voted 26 to 0 in favor of ratification.) Several factors explain the pattern. Under the Articles of Confederation, small states had in many cases been economically dependent on their larger neighbors. Connecticut, New Jersey, Delaware, and Maryland, for example, were subject to the impost taxes of New York and Pennsylvania. In addition, the smaller states were by definition bereft of western lands. While the cession of some state claims to the Confederation had helped to alleviate the situation, it did not eliminate it, and small states feared a loss of sovereignty relative to their larger counterparts. In general, within the Confederation, the small states lacked power: they were able to act independently to veto legislation, but they had no collective power to legislate. The proposed Constitution, which provided at least partial solutions to each of these problems, found ready support among the small states but some reluctance among the larger ones.

A second major source of division was sectionalism. As a rule, the states tended to be divided into three groups: (1) the northern states, sometimes called the eastern states— Massachusetts, New Hampshire, Rhode Island, Connecticut, and New York; (2) the Middle Atlantic states— Pennsylvania, Delaware, New Jersey, and Maryland; and (3) the southern states—Virginia, North Carolina, South Carolina, and Georgia. In the northern states, the total vote was 436 to 314 in favor of ratification, and in every state except Connecticut the vote was close. Moreover, with the exception of Connecticut, every northern state recommended amendments. In the Middle Atlantic states the story was altogether different: the total vote in favor of ratification was 177 to 34, with no state recommending amendments. In the South, the results were mixed— 347 for ratification to 336 against it—with Georgia and South Carolina ratifying by large margins, Virginia ratifying by the smallest of margins, and North Carolina overwhelmingly refusing to ratify.

The sectional variations were also the product of several factors. To some degree, there was a division between what has been called the center and the peripheries, with the Middle Atlantic states, which were centrally located and strategically placed to take full advantage of a stronger economic union, strongly supporting the Constitution. In these states — New York City might be included as well — commerce and trade, both internal and external, were overriding considerations. In contrast to the agrarian and largely self-sufficient South, these states looked outward on the world, seeking a means to participate in world trade on a footing more equal to England, France, and Spain. Similarly, unlike their New England cousins, who tended to fear the corruption of European manufactures, these Middle Atlantic carrying states were eager to import necessities and luxuries alike, for instead of the dream of a Christian Sparta, it was a vision of commercial empire that danced in their heads.

Sectionalism was also implicated in the issue of the western lands. To most southerners in particular, the new Constitution was a threat to western expansion. Although Georgia was an exception on this count, citizens in the other southern states tended to fear that the northern and Middle Atlantic regions would combine against the South, sacrificing western expansion to the development of a trans-Atlantic trading economy. The Jay-Gardoqui treaty, which many considered to be a blatant sellout of southern interests, was seen as an ominous example of the shape of things to come. In particular, southerners feared that the right to navigate the Mississippi would be sacrificed and that the new government would concentrate its defense expenditures on a navy to protect northern shipping rather than on an army to secure the frontier against Indian attacks.

At the heart of this sectionalism were profoundly different political cultures. In New England, Puritan religion and a long local history of participatory self-government combined to create a strong commitment to state sovereignty and an aversion to centralized control. In the Middle Atlantic states, trade and urban growth, along with the pluralistic combining of cultures, had created an environment of economic freedom and political tolerance that welcomed an expanded national union. In the South, while slavery was important and was absolutely crucial in South Carolina, it was less important than might be expected. Perhaps more significant was the South's social and religious homogeneity, its provincialism, and its deep ideological commitment to individual liberties.

The final, and in many ways deepest, source of division was philosophical. Antifederalists everywhere tended to see the proposed system as a reinstitution of the British colonial government that they had overthrown a few years earlier. The new Constitution promised a capital city far removed from the people, a powerful executive, an aristocratic Senate, and a court system that would be unresponsive to popular will. Assuming, with Montesquieu, that republics could only exist in small states, Antifederalists viewed an extended republic as an invitation to tyranny. By contrast, Federalists in every region saw such changes, however dangerous, as necessary if some semblance of dignity and order was to be restored to the system of state governments that had come into being under the Confederation.

At the same time, there remained room for agreement. The fact was that most Antifederalists admitted the need for change, and most Federalists were committed to retaining republican institutions. In the end, the willingness of partisans in both parties to seek acceptable solutions was instrumental in overcoming what seemed like insurmountable obstacles. In the end, more than any other factor, what brought Americans together was the experience of ratification — the experience of thinking and teaching, of talking together and learning from one another, often confused and ill-informed though it was — through which they discovered a sense of themselves, and thirteen peoples converged into one.

PERPETUATING RATIFICATION

With the entry of Rhode Island in 1790, the first federal union was complete; yet ratification was far from finished. From Vermont in 1791 to Hawaii in 1959, each of the American states has ratified the Constitution upon entering the union. More important, because ratification required reform, it set the stage for a continuing process of Constitutional revision. Thus, in many ways, ratification has remained a part of American politics for the last two hundred years.[14]

Beginning with the Bill of Rights, the process of ratification has been carried on through the act of amendment. So it is that by passing amendments which extended personal freedoms, ended slavery, and opened the political process to all citizens regardless of race or sex, Americans have continued to ratify the Constitution. It is a process that has worked well, for with the exception of the Eighteenth Amendment, which was repealed by the Twenty-first Amendment, the changes have endured and have strengthened the system. Moreover, the process is still going on, in calls such as those to abolish the electoral college, create single six-year terms for the president, and mandate a balanced budget.

In the same way, ratification has continued through the process of Constitutional interpretation. In court decisions and in legal theorizing, judges and scholars have continuously reconsidered the meaning of Constitutional principles, applying timeless precepts to changing realities. In recent times, debate has flourished over issues such as the application of the first ten amendments to the states, the power of the executive in peacetime and wartime, and the existence of a right to privacy. Today, in cases such as those involving abortion, drug testing, and the rights of victims of AIDS, the debate goes on.

Finally, ratification can be seen as continuing in our politics. In our democratic republic, Constitutional change requires public discussion. The Constitution does more than establish institutions; it addresses issues of deep and enduring importance. Thus, as we continue to deliberate among ourselves about the best means to secure the blessings of liberty to ourselves and our posterity, we also become part of the process of ratifying the Constitution.

NOTES

1. James Madison to M. L. Hurlbert, May 1830, in *The Writings of James Madison*, ed. Gaillard Hunt, 9 vols. (New York: G. P. Putnam's Sons, 1901–10), 9:372.

2. Robert Allen Rutland, *The Ordeal of the Constitution: The Antifederalists and the Ratification Struggle* (Norman: University of Oklahoma Press, 1966).

3. Economic interpretations have been dominated by Beard and his critics. See Charles A. Beard, *An Economic Interpretation of the Constitution of the United States* (New York: Macmillan, 1913); Robert E. Brown, *Charles Beard*

and the Constitution (Princeton, N.J.: Princeton University Press, 1956); and Forrest McDonald, *We the People: The Economic Origins of the Constitution* (Chicago: University of Chicago Press, 1958). The most significant study of social status has been that by Jackson Turner Main, *The Antifederalists: Critics of the Constitution, 1781–1788* (Chapel Hill: University of North Carolina Press, 1961). Themes of ethnicity and religion have been treated in several of the best studies of states, including John A. Munroe, *Federalist Delaware, 1775–1815* (New Brunswick, N.J.: Rutgers University Press, 1954); Richard P. McCormick, *Experiment in Independence: New Jersey in the Critical Period, 1783–1789* (New Brunswick, N.J.: Rutgers University Press, 1950); Samuel B. Harding, *The Contest over the Ratification of the Federal Constitution in the State of Massachusetts* (New York: Longmans, Green, & Co., 1896); and Louise Irby Trenholme, *The Ratification of the Federal Constitution in North Carolina* (New York: AMS Press, Inc., 1967).

4. In considering ideological influences, sources are particularly strong. Among the most important are Douglass Adair, *Fame and the Founding Fathers*, ed. Trevor Colbourn (New York: W. W. Norton, 1974); Martin Diamond, "Democracy and *The Federalist*: A Reconsideration of the Framers' Intent," *American Political Science Review* 53 (1959): 52–68; Ceceila Kenyon, "Men of Little Faith: The Anti-Federalists on the Nature of Representative Government," *William and Mary Quarterly*, 3d ser. 12 (1955): 3–43; Forrest McDonald, *Novus Ordo Seclorum* (Lawrence: University Press of Kansas, 1985); Herbert J. Storing, *What the Anti-Federalists Were For* (Chicago: University of Chicago Press, 1981); and Gordon S. Wood, *Creation of the American Republic* (Chapel Hill: University of North Carolina Press, 1969). Best on nationalism is Merrill Jensen, "The Idea of a National Government during the American Revolution," *Political Science Quarterly* 58 (1943): 356–79. Sectionalism is considered in Joseph L. Davis, *Sectionalism in American Politics, 1774–1787* (Madison: University of Wisconsin Press, 1977); Drew R. McCoy, *The Elusive Republic: Political Economy in Jeffersonian America* (Chapel Hill: University of North Carolina Press, 1980); and Peter S. Onuf, *The Origins of the Federal Republic: Jurisdictional Controversies in the United States, 1775–1787* (Philadelphia: University of Pennsylvania Press, 1983). The classic study of the role of local settlement patterns remains Orin Grant Libby, *The Geographical Distribution of the Vote of the Thirteen States on the Federal Constitution, 1787–1788* (Madison: University of Wisconsin, 1894). It should be pointed out that constitutional considerations—the role of state constitutional law—has been a continuing topic of research. See, for a recent example, Donald S. Lutz, *Popular Consent and Popular Control: Whig Political Theory in the Early State Constitutions* (Baton Rouge: Louisiana State University Press, 1980).

5. Studies of political strategy begin with Max Farrand, *The Framing of the Constitution of the United States* (New Haven, Conn.: Yale University Press, 1913), and include William Nisbet Chambers, *Political Parties in a New Nation: The American Experience, 1776–1809* (New York: Oxford University Press, 1963);

Paul Goodman, *The Democratic-Republicans of Massachusetts* (Cambridge, Mass.: Harvard University Press, 1964); Alfred F. Young, *The Democratic Republicans of New York* (Chapel Hill: University of North Carolina Press, 1967); Jackson Turner Main, *Political Parties before the Constitution* (Chapel Hill: University of North Carolina Press, 1975); and Stephen A. Boyd, *The Politics of Opposition: Antifederalists and the Acceptance of the Constitution* (Millwood, N.Y.: KTO Press, 1979). Important articles include John P. Roche, "The Founding Fathers: A Reform Caucus in Action," *American Political Science Review* 55 (1961): 799–816; and Stanley Elkins and Eric McKitrick, "The Founding Fathers: Young Men of the Revolution," *Political Science Quarterly* 76 (1961): 181–216.

6. On the problems posed by these competing perspectives see Richard B. Morris, "The Confederation Period and the American Historian," *William and Mary Quarterly*, 3d ser. 13 (1956): 139–56.

7. *The Records of the Federal Convention of 1787*, ed. Max Farrand, 4 vols. (New Haven, Conn.: Yale University Press, 1911–37); *The Debates in the Several State Conventions on the Adoption of the Federal Constitution . . .* , ed. Jonathan Elliot, 5 vols. (Philadelphia: J. B. Lippincott, 1861–63); *Essays on the Constitution of the United States*, ed. Paul Leicester Ford (New York: Burt Franklin, 1892); and *Pamphlets on the Constitution of the United States*, ed. Ford (Brooklyn, N.Y.: n.p., 1888).

8. *The Documentary History of the Ratification of the Constitution*, ed. Merrill Jensen, John P. Kaminski, Gaspare J. Saladino, et al., 8 vols. to date (Madison: State Historical Society of Wisconsin, 1976–), *The Complete Anti-Federalist*, ed. Herbert J. Storing, with Murray Dry, 7 vols. (Chicago: University of Chicago Press, 1981); and *The Founders' Constitution*, ed. Philip B. Kurland and Ralph Lerner, 5 vols. (Chicago: University of Chicago Press, 1987).

9. *The Origins of the American Constitution*, ed. Michael Kammen (New York: Penguin Books, 1986); *The American Constitution: For and Against*, ed. J. R. Pole (New York: Hill & Wang, 1987); and *The Federalist Papers*, ed. Isaac Kramnick (New York: Penguin Books, 1987).

10. For a recent example see *Beyond Confederation: Origins of the Constitution and American National Identity*, ed. Richard Beeman, Stephen Botein, and Edward C. Carter II (Chapel Hill: University of North Carolina Press, 1987).

11. See, e.g., Bernard Bailyn, *The Ideological Origins of the American Revolution* (Cambridge, Mass.: Harvard University Press, 1967); Lance Banning, *The Jeffersonian Persuasion: Evolution of a Party Ideology* (Ithaca, N.Y.: Cornell University Press, 1978); and Nathan O. Hatch, *The Sacred Cause of Liberty* (New Haven, Conn.: Yale University Press, 1977).

12. See Richard Bernstein, "Charting the Bicentennial," *Columbia Law Review* 87 (1987): 1582–83.

13. See Jackson Turner Main, "An Agenda for Research on the Origins and Nature of the Constitution of 1787–1788," *William and Mary Quarterly*, 3d ser. 44 (1987): 596.

14. The best recent treatment of the Constitution's continuing power to shape popular political thought is Michael Kammen's *A Machine That Would Go of Itself: The Constitution in American Culture* (New York: Alfred A. Knopf, 1986).

PART ONE

THE PROMISE OF PROSPERITY

1
DELAWARE
Independence and the Concept
of a Commercial Republic
GASPARE J. SALADINO

On December 7, 1787, the Delaware Convention ratified the United States Constitution by a vote of 30 to 0, placing that small and often ignored state first among the thirteen states. Delaware's political life had been turbulent since 1776, but on the question of the ratification of the Constitution, the state's two political factions—Whigs and Tories—acted swiftly and unanimously. The state legislature received the Constitution on October 24 and called the state ratifying convention on the tenth of November. The election for convention delegates took place on the twenty-sixth of November; the convention met on the third of December; and it ratified the Constitution on the seventh.

No state acted so quickly and expeditiously. Both Whigs and Tories, often bitter and violent rivals, realized that the strong central government which the Constitution provided was Delaware's best hope for the future. The Constitution would ensure Delaware's independence and sovereignty and would improve its commercial and financial prospects—goals that both factions had desperately tried to attain since the break with Great Britain in 1776.

Thus, Delaware's ratification of the Constitution must be considered in the context of that state's economy and politics since independence. In particular, the ratification can best be understood by concentrating on the issues of economic and political independence, and it must include some consideration of how Delaware's citizens understood the concept of independence itself.

THE ECONOMY

New Castle, Delaware's northernmost county, was the state's commercial center. The Delaware River towns of Wilmington and New Castle, especially the former, were the principal ports; they shipped wheat, corn, barley, rye, flour, lumber, and cattle to the Delaware River metropolis of Philadelphia, the northern states, the West Indies, and Ireland. Almost all foreign imports came from Philadelphia, which controlled much of Delaware's trade. Even the roads, or at least the most important roads, ran in the direction of Philadelphia or to landings on the Delaware River. In 1786, one Philadelphian went so far as to declare that Delaware was part of the "commercial empire" of Philadelphia. So dominant was Philadelphia's control over Delaware that two years later, another Philadelphian asserted that Delaware and New Jersey "are *the least commercial* members of the confederacy."[1]

New Castle was rich for other reasons as well. The flour mills of its Brandywine district, which ground wheat and corn from Delaware and the neighboring states, constituted the state's principal industry—an industry that attained an international reputation for the high quality of its product. Much of the grain supplied to the mills was grown in the rich clay soil of New Castle County by the state's most prosperous farmers, more than two-thirds of whom lived above the subsistence level. The county's farms averaged between one hundred and two hundred acres, and the land was worth more than three times the land in Sussex County because it was so well cultivated and developed.

The farmers in the northern part of Kent County (an overwhelmingly rural county) resembled those in New Castle who engaged in commercial agriculture. The area of Duck Creek, the boundary between the two counties, had several fine granaries, and much wheat and corn was shipped from the adjacent areas. To facilitate the shipment of grain from this area, the legislature in February 1786 passed an act for cutting canals and improving the navigation of Main Duck Creek. Farming in the southern section of Kent County was essentially at the subsistence level, although cattle were raised in the county's marshes and forests and were then driven to the markets of Wilmington and Philadelphia for fattening. Kent County farms were small, and the soil was less fertile than that in New Castle. Dover, the county's principal town, was known primarily as the center of county and state government.

By contrast, Sussex County, the state's most rural county, had more land than the other two counties combined. It also had more people, but it was the state's poorest county. The farms were larger, perhaps twice as big, but they were less well cultivated, and the soil was less fertile. About two-thirds of the farmers were small farmers or laborers, 70 percent of whom owned estates valued at less than £5. Although they produced the same crops that were grown in other parts of the state, a smaller percentage of their produce went to market. As in Kent County, farmers raised some cattle for market, and the abundant forests also yielded a considerable amount of lumber. Lewes, in the southeastern section, was Sussex's largest town and port, but it became less important as the interior of the county was developed.

Although a lack of data makes it difficult to assess the status of Delaware's economy during the 1780s, there apparently was both prosperity and depression. According to people who traveled through the state, New Castle County, especially Wilmington and the Brandywine district, appears to have been better off than the other parts of the state. The mills were so busy that in February 1785 the Whig legislature forced them to set aside days to grind wheat for the public. Other parts of the state were becoming more commercial, too. Nevertheless, in the mid-1780s, citizens from every county petitioned the legislature, asking for an emission of paper money and debtor-relief laws to ease the scarcity of cash and the burden of high taxes. Trade had decayed, and the price of produce was low. Sussex County was especially hard hit and was having the most difficulty in meeting its tax quotas. The state's courts were clogged with debtor cases. An interested observer from New Jersey complained that "the Delay's of Suits in the Delaware State are monstrous."[2]

THE POLITICAL FACTIONS

Between 1776 and 1789, Delaware's political life was dominated by two factions—the Tories and the Whigs. Used before 1776, these labels became synonymous with those who supported independence from Great Britain and those who either did not or were reluctant revolutionaries. Whigs were strongest by far in New Castle County. Ethnically and religiously, this county was more mixed than the two southern counties. More than one-half of the population was Scotch-Irish Presbyterian; a small number of Baptists were also present. Both groups tended to Whiggism. On the whole, Whigs drew their strength from the ranks of the numerous small commercial farmers and from the people living in the towns.

At the same time, New Castle's Tories made up an influential minority. Mostly Anglicans and Quakers, they were the wealthier lawyers, merchants, flour millers, and other businessmen from the Brandywine district, Wilmington, and New Castle, along with the wealthier commercial farmers. Although they opposed British measures, these groups were slow to accept independence. Their orientation was toward Philadelphia, many of whose economic and political leaders were also hesitant to embrace independence. George Read, who voted against independence in the Second Continental Congress but who signed the Declaration of Independence, was the leader of New Castle County's Tories and was the dominant figure in Delaware politics. Called "Dionysius, Tyrant of Delaware," Read took his cue from Philadelphia, especially from the group surrounding Robert Morris. On one occasion, Read wrote: "I have been at Mr. Robt. Morris's Country house with a set of People who think & act alike, some Consolation in these times."[3]

In Kent County, about one-half of the people were Tories. They were Anglicans, Methodists, and Quakers, primarily of English stock, and poor and isolated farmers, particularly in what was called the "forest" in the western part of the county. Some Tories were also influenced by the proximity of Tories in neighboring Maryland. One of the principal Tory leaders was Richard Bassett, who early in the war had led a Tory insurrection. The Whig leaders were Caesar Rodney (until his death in 1784) and Dr. James Tilton, a Scotch-Irish Presbyterian.

In Sussex, considerably more than one-half (perhaps as high as 80 percent) of the people were Tories. As in Kent, these Tories were poor and isolated farmers living in the "forest" in the southwestern part of the county; they came from basically English stock and were Anglicans and Methodists who were influenced by the nearness of the British fleet and of the Tories of adjacent Maryland. Throughout the Revolutionary period there were several Tory insurrections, most notably the Black Camp Rebellion in 1780, and numerous election riots that took place when Whigs sought to uphold laws that disfranchised the Tories. The bitterness of the wartime feelings lingered a long time in this county, where despite their numbers, Tories, who had won some elections early in the Revolution, were not victorious again until 1785.

Between 1776 and 1789, the control of the state legislature swung back and forth from one faction to the other. The Whigs were generally strongest in the lower house, or House of Assembly, while the Tories usually controlled the upper house, or Council. The Tories were victorious in the first state elections in October 1776. Neither party won control in those of October 1777, but the Whigs had definitely made gains, especially in the lower house. The Whigs gained control in October 1778 and held it until the election of October 1781. The Tories regained power in 1781, only to lose out to the Whigs in 1784 and 1785. The pendulum swung back to the Tories in 1786 and 1787. The next year the dominant Tories repealed the acts that disfranchised Tories and became firmly implanted in power. Delaware elected two Tory (or Federalist) senators and one Tory representative in 1788 and 1789. The Federalist party dominated the state's politics throughout the 1790s and was not seriously challenged until the Jeffersonian Revolution of 1800. Nevertheless, Delaware remained solidly Federalist during the first two decades of the nineteenth century, especially in Kent and Sussex counties.

The central issue that divided Whigs and Tories was the part that each had played in the War for Independence. The two factions also split over such issues as debtor legislation, taxation, paper money, representation in Congress by nonresidents, and the manner and extent to which the legislature should encourage the state's economy. In general, both factions supported the strengthening of the central government under the Articles of Confederation, although the Tories pursued this policy more vigorously. Both groups jealously protected the state's sovereignty against the encroachments of Congress, as well as the state's interests in such matters as the disposition of western lands.

THE SEARCH FOR POLITICAL AND ECONOMIC INDEPENDENCE, 1775–87

During the colonial period, Delaware did not have a strong sense of its own identity. Both Great Britain and Delaware's sister colonies generally ignored her separate existence, preferring to think of the colony as an appendage of Pennsylvania.[4] The two proprietary colonies of the Penn family shared the same governor, although each had its own unicameral legislature. Delaware was commonly known as "The Territories of Pennsylvania," or more often as "The Three Lower Counties on the Delaware." The name that appeared on laws and legal documents was "The Government of the Counties of New Castle, Kent, and Sussex, upon Delaware." It came as no surprise, then, that in the new state constitution of 1776, Delaware boldly declared itself "The Delaware State"—a triumphant affirmation of identity and a declaration of independence, rolled into one.

As the American colonies moved toward independence from Great Britain, Delaware insisted upon its equality with the other colonies. The instructions to its delegates to the Second Continental Congress in March 1775 struck a theme that is crucial to understanding Delaware's history for the next fifteen years. The delegates were instructed to urge "decently but firmly" Delaware's right "to an equal Voice in Congress." These instructions were reiterated in March and June 1776.[5]

During the war, this small state displayed a sometimes impetuous independence, both under the Whigs and under the Tories. In 1776, 1777, and 1778 it vigorously protested when Congress sent Continental troops into Delaware to disarm or arrest Loyalists. On the first occasion, the Tory George Read told Pennsylvania delegate Robert Morris: "The insult must not be repeated," while in 1778, President Caesar Rodney, a Whig, complained that Congress's action had "lessoned" the state's governing powers "in the Eyes of the people."[6] In 1779, Delaware charged that Congress's recommendation that Delaware enact price-fixing laws was "an infringement on the rights and liberties of the people."[7] A year later, Delaware refused Congress's request that it renew an embargo on the exportation of provisions.[8] Indeed, in 1781, Virginia's Congressman James Madison would use Delaware's refusal as a reason for Congress to adopt his amendment to the Articles of Confederation giving Congress coercive powers. He reiterated his position in the Constitutional Convention in 1787.[9]

Delaware's strong sense of independence and self-interest were best illustrated by its delay in ratifying the Articles of Confederation. Congress sent the Articles to the states in November 1777, and by July 24, 1778, all states except Delaware, New Jersey, and Maryland had signed the Articles. These three states refused to sign because they believed that the ungranted western lands ought to be held in common by all the states that were defending them "at the common expence" and that the lands should be secured for the troops who served in the war. Delaware's delay prompted its congressional delegate Thomas McKean to write the legislature in January 1779, warning the state that it was in Delaware's interest to ratify at once, for if Delaware ratified "*last*," its action might be interpreted as loyalism and might lead to the use of force by Congress.[10]

On the matter of western lands, Delaware was adamant. In January 1779 a Whig legislature adopted resolutions, probably written by Councillor George Read, that "a moderate extent of limits" be placed on the states claiming lands to the "Mississippi or South Sea," that all states share in the western lands that were ungranted at the start of the Revolution, and that the courts of Delaware were competent to determine all controversies regarding private rights to the soil of Delaware. Read wanted the money from the sale of the lands to go toward paying the public debt, and he feared the power of the large landed states over the small landless ones.[11] In February 1782, Read secured the appointment to Congress of three nonresidents of Delaware who represented land companies based in Maryland and Pennsylvania. The delegates were instructed to protect Delaware's landless claims, as a matter of "the first magnitude"; these instructions were reiterated in June 1783. Virginia's James Madison believed that Delaware looked upon the western lands as "a fund of revenue" and as a means of strengthening the interests of the little states, whereas his fellow Virginian Arthur Lee saw only the influence of the land companies.[12]

To help the state to attain its economic independence, congressional delegates Gunning Bedford, Jr., a Tory, and Eleazer McComb, a Whig, wrote to President Nicholas Van Dyke in June 1783, asking that Delaware make a generous grant of land in Wilmington for the site of the federal capital. Bedford hoped that Delaware would "not loose so fine an opportunity of aggrandising herself." The Delaware delegates took such an active part in the fight over the capital that the Maryland delegates reported that the site "was an object particularly desired by Delaware."[13]

Delaware made one more significant attempt to attain economic independence and to assert its state sovereignty. In September 1785,

Pennsylvania passed a law that raised duties on the vessels of nations that did not have commercial treaties with the United States. Because Delaware imported most of its foreign goods from Philadelphia, these duties raised the prices that Delawareans had to pay. Consequently, in February 1786 the legislature declared that Wilmington and New Castle would be free ports for twenty-five years. Any foreign goods that were imported into these ports would be exempt from duties, and merchants and others who engaged in trade would be exempt from taxes for twenty-five years.[14]

Although the two political factions wanted the state to attain economic independence, they were at odds over how to aid the state's growing debtor class. In June 1785 the Whigs Eleazer McComb and James Tilton, realizing the hostility to paper money that had been caused by its severe depreciation during wartime, tried but failed to get a bank established that would relieve debtors, avoid the depreciation of paper money, and lessen the tax burden.[15] Between May 1785 and June 1787 the legislature received petitions from each county, complaining about the scarcity of money and requesting an emission of paper money. Most of the signers of the petitions were Whigs, although there was strong sentiment for paper money among poor Tories in Sussex County. Other petitions called for the suspension of all executions and prosecutions for debts. In January and June 1786 the Whig-dominated House of Assembly adopted paper-money bills by substantial margins, but the Tory Council, led by George Read, defeated both measures. (Opponents of paper money in the House included the Tories Jacob Broom and Gunning Bedford, Jr.) Tories believed that the depreciation of paper money would endanger the property rights of creditors.[16] In October the Tory Council defeated a bill to suspend executions to recover debts, and both houses ignored the paper-money petitions presented during the first half of 1787.[17]

STRENGTHENING THE CENTRAL GOVERNMENT

On matters concerning the Confederation as a whole, the Tories and the Whigs were often in agreement. On several occasions during the 1780s, the Confederation Congress asked the states to grant it additional financial and commercial powers, and the Delaware legislature acceded to these requests. Congress needed such powers in order to pay the public debt. If Congress had its own revenue sources, it would not have to request money from the states, thereby relieving a poor state like Delaware of a great burden. In February 1781 and April 1783, Congress asked the states to ratify imposts of 5 percent. The latter impost was part of a plan that provided for supplemental funds to be assessed annually against each state. The impost was not to go into effect until these funds had been voted. Delaware ratified the 1781 impost in November 1781 and the 1783 impost and supplemental funds in June 1783.[18] In Congress, the revenue plan of 1783 had been championed by Delaware's delegates. They had also voted for another part of the scheme that called for the creation of a national domain and the sale of lands to pay the public debt. They even supported a measure that would have, if passed, eliminated the twenty-five-year limitation on the impost and supplemental funds and made the revenue "co-existent with the debts."[19]

In April 1784, Congress requested that the states grant it power for fifteen years to prohibit the importation of goods and produce of nations that did not have commercial treaties with the United States. The Whigs, who had returned to power in Delaware in 1784, finally granted this request in February 1786, under pressure from the Tories. They also agreed to incorporate in Delaware the Bank of North America—"a National Bank" that Congress had first incorporated in 1781.[20] In June, again upon a request from Congress, they revised a 1783 act so that the Impost of 1783 could go into effect before all the states voted Congress the supplemental funds.[21]

During most of the 1780s, both factions wanted the state to pay its share of the congressional requisitions, although the Tories were more willing to levy higher taxes to do so. In June 1783, however, the Whigs in the House prevented the Tories in the Council (led by George Read) from raising the amount of the 1783 revenue bill by about 50 percent in order to facilitate the payment of the congressional requisitions.[22] The fight over the requisition of 1785 was especially bitter. The House brought in a bill in January 1786, but the Council adjourned without considering it. Councillor George Reed, who had been asked by the secretary of Congress to use his influence to get this and the earlier requisitions paid, requested that President Nicholas Van Dyke, a Whig, put pressure on the collectors of taxes. Van Dyke replied that his executive powers did not extend that far. In June the Council returned the House bill with forty-nine amendments. The two houses were at loggerheads, and a conference committee finally recommended a bill that became the revenue act of 1786.[23]

In any case, Delaware did consistently support a stronger economic union. In June 1786 it appointed five commissioners to the Annapolis convention to consider the necessity of devising a "uniform system"of commercial regulations for the United States and to report thereon to Congress.[24] The commissioners, all Tories, were John Dickinson, George Read, Richard Bassett, Gunning Bedford, Jr., and Jacob Broom. The convention met in September and recommended that the states meet in convention in Philadelphia on the following May fourteenth to revise the Articles of Confederation. In February 1787 the House and the Council appointed the same delegates who had been sent to Annapolis to the meeting in Philadelphia. Yet the act appointing delegates also included an important proviso: no altera-tion was to be made in that part of the Articles which guaranteed one vote in Congress to each state. George Read, who drafted the act, insisted on this proviso so as to protect the small states against the claims of the large states, especially with respect to the western lands and the payment of the public debt. He did not want Delaware to become "a cypher in the union."[25]

By May 29, all five Delaware delegates to the Philadelphia con-vention were present — an extraordinary performance for a state that had one of the worst attendance records in the Continental and Con-federation congresses.[26] With the exception of John Dickinson, who left because of ill health, the delegates remained until adjournment, and each signed the Constitution. George Read signed for Dickin-son. The delegation played a significant role: Dickinson spoke at least thirty-six times; Read, twenty-seven; Gunning Bedford, Jr., ten; and Jacob Broom, five. Only Richard Bassett was silent.[27]

The delegates insisted upon the equality of the states. So insistent were they that some believed that Delaware was opposed to increas-ing the power of the central government.[28] On May 30, George Read reminded the convention that Delaware's delegates were instructed to oppose any change in the rule of equal suffrage in Congress, and he warned that Delaware would "retire" from the convention if such an alteration were to occur.[29] On June 2, John Dickinson made a proposal that eventually became part of the great compromise on representation in Congress: namely, that each state would have "an equal voice at least in one branch of the National Legislature." A two-house legislature would protect the small states from "the domination of the large States." Dickinson was also a leading advocate of a federal government in which "considerable powers" would be left to the states; the states were "to be left to move freely in their proper orbits."[30] On the other hand, Read believed that the small states would be best protected if all "State attachments" were "extinguished" and if one "great Society" were formed.[31] After the compromise on representation had finally been adopted, Jacob Broom warned the large states against adjourning to reconsider, because that "would be fatal." Gunning Bedford, Jr., attacked the large states for seeking "to aggrandize themselves at the expense of the small." If the large states were to dissolve the Union, Bedford warned, "the small ones will find some foreign ally of more honor and good faith, who will take them by the hand and do them justice."[32]

One of the principal reasons for insisting upon the equality of the states was Delaware's interest in the western lands. John Dickinson hoped that the small states would not be required "to secure the large ones in their extensive claims of territory." George Read asked that "justice" be done on the matter of western lands and that the money raised from their sale "be applied fairly & equally to the discharge of the general debt." He lamented that in the past the large landed states had "injured" the small states, and he asked that all states give up their claims to western land. Gunning Bedford, Jr., also supported the payment of the public debt. He asked the convention: "Where is your plighted faith?" For this reason, Bedford also wanted Congress to have the power to levy an impost.[33]

DELAWARE AND THE NEW CONSTITUTION

The legislative session of May to June 1787 was a short one because "so many distinguished members" were at the Constitutional Convention. Paper-money petitions were presented to the House of Assembly, but on June 8, it tabled them because it had "the greatest

Confidence" that the convention would "in its Superior Wisdom alleviate the distress of the United States as well as put it in the power of this State . . . to make their constituents happy and not to be greviously pressed." Both houses, believing that the convention would finish its work by the end of August, adjourned soon and agreed to reconvene in August to consider "such a system of government as should be recommended by the Federal Convention." No other state legislature made such a provision.[34]

The Constitutional Convention adjourned on September 17, and the response in Delaware to the new Constitution was overwhelmingly positive. Two Philadelphia newspapers, the *Pennsylvania Packet* and the *Pennsylvania Gazette* on September the twenty-fifth and the twenty-sixth, respectively, reported that the Constitution was received with "strong and hearty approbation" and "universal satisfaction." On the twenty-seventh, Jacob Broom of Wilmington found the people "very well satisfied."[35] In early October, 187 inhabitants of New Castle County, George Read's home county, sent five petitions to the legislature, urging an early calling of a state convention and the "speedy" ratification of the Constitution. At the same time, three more New Castle petitions from 140 inhabitants requested that the legislature provide for a cession of land for the federal capital. Congress would benefit because Delaware was centrally located and had "plentiful" provisions, while the people of the state would derive "many advantages" from the capital.[36]

Opposition to the Constitution was virtually nonexistent. Antifederalist William Grayson, a Virginia congressman, heard "of little or no opposition" in Delaware and Maryland. Confederation Secretary at War Henry Knox heard that only James Tilton opposed the Constitution because he had not been appointed to the Constitutional Convention. In fact, Tilton was not a critic of the Constitution, if one believes what he said (writing as "Timoleon") in his pamphlet attacking George Read. Tilton accused Tories of spreading "false and scandalous" rumors that Whigs did not favor the Constitution; he even asserted that "nobody" in the state opposed the Constitution, which he believed had established an effective republican government. When the Antifederalist Richard Henry Lee of Virginia traveled through Delaware, he "harangued the populace" of Wilmington and "distributed many of his inflammatory papers," but to no apparent avail.[37]

The House of Assembly received the eight petitions from New Castle County on the twenty-fourth of October and turned them over to a committee, along with the new Constitution. The committee reported the next day, recommending that an election of seven delegates from each county take place on November 26, and that the state convention meet on December 3. It also recommended that no test oath be required in order to vote, thereby circumventing test laws passed in 1778 to disfranchise Tories. The committee ignored the matter of a cession of land for the federal capital.[38]

Interestingly, the Constitution was considered in a context of extraordinary partisanship. On the twenty-fifth the House Committee on Elections and Privileges reported that there were no election returns from Sussex County, so it ordered an investigation. During its investigation, the legislature learned that threats by Whigs against Tories had delayed the holding of the election in Sussex. President Thomas Collins, a Tory, had gone to Sussex County and had prevailed upon Tory and Whig leaders to agree to a "Union Ticket," to be elected by fifty Tories and fifty Whigs. A large force of armed Whigs was at the polling place in Lewes (a Whig stronghold) to ensure the election of the "Union Ticket"; people were beaten and lives were threatened in the most violent of all elections since the Revolution. A Whig was elected to the Council, and three Whigs and four Tories were elected to the House. The Council and the House read the Tory petitions protesting the election, listened to testimony, and voided the elections. In the Council, George Read prevented James Tilton from recording in the minutes his reasons for dissent.[39]

Yet the Constitution seemed to transcend partisan differences. On the afternoon of November 7, the House recommitted the report of the committee on the new Constitution, and the committee brought in a series of resolutions that the House accepted and sent to the Council on the eighth. The Council heard the petitions from New Castle on the ninth and made several amendments to the House resolutions. The principal alterations were a longer preamble, stating that "great Numbers of the good People" of Delaware supported the Constitution; an increase in the number of delegates from each county from seven to ten; the deletion of the resolution excusing people from taking a test oath; and a resolution providing that a proposition for a cession of land for a federal capital be "recommended to the particular Consideration of the Convention." The resolutions with the Council's amendments were returned to the House the same day and were immediately adopted by the House, which sent them back to the Council on the tenth. On that day the legislature also passed an act providing for a legislative election in Sussex County on the twenty-sixth, the same day as the convention election. The act changed the polling place from the Whig stronghold of Lewes to the home of the Tory Robert Griffith in Nanticoke Hundred, a center of Tory strength.[40]

In the election of delegates to the state convention, Whigs won a majority of seats in New Castle County, defeating two former delegates to the Constitutional Convention, George Read and Jacob Broom, among others. Gunning Bedford, Jr., however, was elected from New Castle, while Richard Bassett won in Kent County. Poor health probably prevented the election of the fifth delegate to the Constitutional Convention, John Dickinson. The Tories were victorious in Kent County because the Whigs stayed away, "not caring by whom the government was ratified." Hence, the Whig leader James Tilton was not elected. Tories in Sussex County used armed force to keep Whigs away from the polling place, and Tories won overwhelming victories in both the convention and the legislative elections. Because there was almost no opposition to the Constitution, it really did not matter which faction won. Nevertheless, Sussex Whigs sent nine petitions, signed by 369 people, to the state convention, asking that it call a new election and decrying the use of armed force in elections. The Whigs asserted that they had stayed away from the polling place in order to avoid bloodshed.[41]

The Delaware convention convened on December 3 at Dover. No journal of the proceedings exists; nor are there any significant sources concerning the debates. The convention refused to invalidate the Sussex election, claiming, according to James Tilton, that it had no such authority and "that, if they had, it would only be wasting time as all were agreed in ratifying the Federal Constitution." On December 4, President Thomas Collins turned over the Constitution and the legislative resolutions to the convention, calling particular attention to the resolution on the federal capital. On the seventh the convention ratified the Constitution unanimously, and all thirty delegates signed the form of ratification. The convention also agreed, by a majority of five to one, to make a cession of land on behalf of the people of Delaware for the location of the federal capital in the state. Delaware had acted so rapidly that the French vice-consul in New York reported that the Delaware Convention "read, accepted and ratified in three hours, without their having the slightest debate on the merit of the question."[42]

DELAWARE'S RATIFICATION

Delaware ratified with such speed for a variety of reasons. Most important, Delaware followed the lead of Pennsylvania, particularly Philadelphia, with whom it had economic, social, and cultural ties. Although Pennsylvania ratified the Constitution five days after Delaware did, it had been known since late September that Pennsylvania would ratify, and it was unthinkable that Delaware would not follow the lead of its powerful neighbor. As Thomas Jefferson noted: "Delaware will do what Pennsylvania shall do." This was particularly true for New Castle County, Delaware's most commercial area. Congressional control over interstate and foreign commerce was most appealing to the commercial interests that were tied to Philadelphia: the merchants of New Castle and Wilmington, the flour millers of the Brandywine district, and the commercial farmers in the environs of these places. There was no surprise in this: as the French vice-consul in New York observed, Pennsylvania had often carried along the votes of Delaware and New Jersey.[43]

Political self-interest also played a prominent role. The Constitution gave Delaware equality of suffrage in the Senate. This concession to the small states was most significant because they were definitely in danger of being overwhelmed by the large states. Some delegates from large states, Nathaniel Gorham of Massachusetts and James Madison of Virginia, were openly hostile in the Constitutional Convention, and there was even a threat of overturning the great compromise on representation concerning Congress. However, the defeat of the large states on this issue continued to rankle many in those states. Interestingly, many of the complaints came from Antifederalists. (Federalists in the large states did not complain because, had a compromise not been reached in the convention, there would have been no new Constitution.) Often the complaints singled out Delaware.

The "Federal Farmer," for example, in a pamphlet printed in New York, opposed the equality of representation in the Senate because it gave Delaware "as much constitutional influence . . . as the largest state in the union." William Symmes, a Massachusetts lawyer, thought that it was "quite ridiculous" that Delaware "should weigh as much in all political debates" as his state. According to Philadephian John Vaughan, Virginia Antifederalist William Grayson, angered by Delaware's and Pennsylvania's ratification of the Constitution, observed that "the example of the Paltry State of Pensylvania & Still more Paltry Estate of Delaware, ought not to bind the Ancient dominion of Virginia." "Brutus," a Virginia essayist, could not understand why Delaware, which paid a sixty-seventh part of the general expenses of the Union, should have the same vote on a money bill as Virginia, which paid one-sixth part. And Patrick Henry, addressing the Virginia Convention, was infuriated that the "two petty states" of Delaware and Rhode Island would be able to "counteract" the influence of Virginia.[44]

Another factor was that some Delawareans were hoping that the federal capital would be located in Delaware. The "Federal Farmer" and "A Columbian Patriot" believed that the Middle Atlantic States (Delaware included) had ratified the Constitution because they had thought that they might receive the advantages of the federal capital. Patrick Henry told the Virginia Convention that this desire "operated so powerfully" in Delaware that the state had adopted the Constitution "without taking time to reflect."[45] In the summer of 1788, when the Confederation Congress was debating the ordinance to establish the new government, Delaware's Dyre Kearney was pushing hard to locate the capital in Wilmington as opposed to Philadelphia. His actions disgusted some Pennsylvanians who dismissed him as "a silly young man" and "a young politician!" Congressman James Madison described Delaware's actions as "absolutely inflexible."[46] In August 1789, John Vining, Delaware's sole representative, presented to the new federal House of Representatives the Delaware Convention's resolution ceding land for a federal capital, and the next month he spoke eloquently for locating the capital at Wilmington. In particular, Vining stressed the economic benefits that would accrue to the state that had the capital.[47]

In general, however, there were the financial considerations. The

Constitution gave Congress control over the national domain, and the money obtained from the sale of land would be used to pay the national debt — two ends for which Delaware had long fought. To reduce the national debt even further, the Constitution gave Congress the power to levy a national impost, a provision that would also benefit Delaware. The money from the impost would go into a common treasury, not into the Pennsylvania state treasury. Speaking to the Connecticut Convention, Oliver Ellsworth said that a national impost was one of the reasons why nonimporting states such as Delaware had unanimously ratified the Constitution. Patrick Henry agreed with Ellsworth. In the First Federal Congress, John Vining insisted that the impost and the collection bills be adopted immediately because, without them, "the wheels of the national machine cannot turn." According to James Madison, Delaware and the other noncarrying states were also favored under the Constitution because it prohibited the exporting states from taxing exports. Madison told the Virginia Convention: "The exporting states wished to retain the power of levying duties on exports, to enable them to pay the expenses incurred." The nonexporting states were afraid that "a contribution" would "be raised of them by the exporting states, by laying heavy duties on their commodities."[48]

Simply put, the new government would be cheaper. Because import duties and land sales would be its principal sources of revenue, the new Congress would no longer have to requisition money from the states. These requisitions had fallen heavily on Delaware. Historian Forrest McDonald, using financial reports made by Delaware's legislative committees, has estimated that between 1781 and 1787, 72 percent of Delaware's expenditures were made for congressional requisitions and other expenses that would be assumed by the new government under the Constitution.[49] After a slow start, Delaware had tried hard (especially in 1786) to meet its share of the congressional requisitions.[50] Between 1782 and 1790 it paid 46.7 percent (or $105,016) of its quota of specie and indents on seven congressional requisitions (1781–88), giving it a fifth ranking among the thirteen states.[51] According to James Tilton ("Timoleon"), "The civil list and requisitions of Congress compose our chief annual expences." Writing as "An Honest Man," Tilton concluded that "the *general federal government*" created by the Constitution would be "*less expensive*."[52]

The state was clearly money poor, a problem that the new government would resolve. One Wilmingtonian, who noted that "Money was never scarcer than now in this Country," believed that the value of lands would "rise immediately on the adoption of the new Federal Government."[53] The scarcity of money would be alleviated somewhat if the new government were to pay the national debt (Continental loan-office certificates), of which over $66,000 was held in Delaware.[54]

And as everywhere else, there was the matter of paper money. Many Delawareans supported the Constitution because it prohibited both the states and Congress from issuing paper money and because it upheld the sanctity of contracts. In the Constitutional Convention, George Read, who, as a member of the Delaware legislature, had helped to defeat the passage of paper-money bills, thought that to give Congress the power to emit bills of credit "would be as alarming as the mark of the Beast in Revelations." While sitting in the state legislature, Read's fellow convention delegates, Richard Bassett, Gunning Bedford, Jr., and Jacob Broom, had also opposed paper-money bills, and as state president, John Dickinson had been no friend to paper money. Advocates of paper money probably did not want to mount an aggressive campaign against the Constitution because the Constitution benefited Delaware in so many other ways. Moreover, if the entire amount of the national debt that was held in Delaware were paid, it would exceed either of the amounts that the paper-money advocates had hoped to raise by their paper-money bills in 1786. In January 1788 the House voted 12 to 6 to accept a committee report recommending that a stay law not be adopted. The committee said that such a law was "a retrospective one" and would "destroy the faith and credit, which ought to be held sacred in all governments." A year later, another House committee refused to recommend the passage of an installment law because it was "repugnant both to the letter and spirit of the new constitution."[55]

The leaders of both political factions and the overwhelming majority of Delawareans, then, fully realized that Delaware's best hope for the future was to be part of the new government under a constitution that would promise Delaware some protection against the large states and would offer it considerable political and economic independence. At the same time, the new government would be more efficient than the Confederation government, and it would "alleviate the distress of the United States." As the citizens of Delaware saw it, the Constitution made real the promise of the Declaration of Independence. The revolution of 1787 followed logically from that of 1776. Delaware was eager to fire the first shot. So it was that the state legislature made every effort to call the state convention at an early date and that the convention acted so quickly and unanimously, thereby bestowing upon this "small State . . . the honor of having given the first signal of a revolution in the general government of the united States."[56]

NOTES

1. The material in this section on the economy is from John A. Munroe, *Federalist Delaware, 1775–1815* (New Brunswick, N.J.: Rutgers University Press, 1954), pp. 21–36, 114–25, 131–41; Jackson Turner Main, *The Social Structure of Revolutionary America* (Princeton, N.J.: Princeton University Press, 1965), pp. 26–27, 32–33; Harold B. Hancock, *The Loyalists of Revolutionary Delaware* (Newark: University of Delaware Press, 1977), pp. 29–32; Peter C. Welsh, "The Brandywine Mills: A Chronicle of an Industry, 1762–1816," *Delaware History* 7 (1956): 23–26; and idem, "Merchants, Millers, and Ocean Ships: The Components of an Early American Industrial Town," ibid., 7 (1957): 327–30. The quoted material concerning the Philadelphia commentators is from the *Pennsylvania Packet* (Philadelphia), 6 March 1786; and "An American" (Tench Coxe), *Pennsylvania Gazette* (Philadelphia), 21 May 1788.

2. Lambert Cadwalader to William Gough, 27 May 1788, Cadwalader Papers, Historical Society of Pennsylvania.

3. The material in this section on political factions is from Munroe, *Federalist Delaware*, pp. 15–21, 43–58, 86–94, 97–103, 109, 198–212, 228–41; Hancock, *Loyalists of Revolutionary Delaware*, pp. 1–11, 29–38, 43, 98–99, 110–17; Harold Bell Hancock, "The Delaware Loyalists," *Papers of the Historical Society of Delaware* (hereafter cited as *PHSD*), new ser. 3 (1940): 1–2, 56–57; David P. Peltier, "Party Development and Voter Participation in Delaware, 1792–1811," *Delaware History* 14 (1970): 77 n; and [James Tilton], *Timoleon's Biographical History of Dionysius, Tyrant of Delaware* (hereafter cited as "Timoleon," *Dionysius*), ed. John A. Munroe (Newark: University of Delaware Press, 1958). For the quoted statement by George Read see Read to Gertrude Read, 14 May (i.e., July) 1776, *Letters of Delegates to Congress, 1774–1789* (hereafter cited as Smith, *Letters*), ed. Paul H. Smith et al., 13 vols. to date (Washington, D.C.: Library of Congress, 1976–), 4:455.

4. John A. Munroe, *Colonial Delaware: A History* (Millwood, N.Y.: KTO Press, 1978), pp. 147–48.

5. For the texts of these instructions, see *Letters to and from Caesar Rodney, 1756–1784* (hereafter cited as *Rodney Letters*), ed. George H. Ryden (Wilmington: Delaware Tercentenary Commission, 1938), pp. 55–57, 72–73.

6. Smith, *Letters*, 9:337 n; Read to Morris, 4 November 1776, ibid., 5:445 n; Rodney to Henry Laurens, 24 April 1778, *Rodney Letters*, pp. 262–63; and Charles J. Truitt, *Breadbasket of the Revolution: Delmarva in the War for Independence* (Salisbury, Md.: Historical Books, Inc., 1976), pp. 75–76.

7. *Journals of the Continental Congress, 1774–1789* . . . (hereafter cited as *JCC*), ed. Worthington C. Ford et al., 34 vols. (Washington, D.C.: Library of Congress, 1904–37), 15:1289–93; and "Minutes of the Council of the Delaware State, from 1776 to 1792," *PHSD* 6 (1887): 508–9 (hereafter cited as *Council Minutes*).

8. Since June 1778, Delaware had levied a series of embargoes, the last of which had expired on 20 October 1780. On its failure to renew see Thomas Rodney to Caesar Rodney, 20 November 1780, *Rodney Letters*, pp. 379–80, 388; and *JCC*, 18:1051, 1062–63, 1075–77.

9. Madison to Thomas Jefferson, 16 April 1781, *The Papers of James Madison* (hereafter cited as *Madison Papers*), ed. William T. Hutchinson, William M. E. Rachal, Robert A. Rutland, Charles F. Hobson, et al., 17 vols. to date (Chicago: University of Chicago Press, and Charlottesville: University of Virginia Press, 1962–), 3:71; and *The Records of the Federal Convention of 1787* (hereafter cited as Farrand, *Records*), ed. Max Farrand, rev. ed., 4 vols. (New Haven, Conn.: Yale University Press, 1937), 1:476, 478.

10. Connecticut Delegates to Governor Jonathan Trumbull, Sr., 15 October 1778, and McKean to Thomas Collins, (8?) January 1779, Smith, *Letters*, 11:58–59, 436–37.

11. *Council Minutes*, pp. 369, 371–73, 377–78, 384, 398–99, 400; Read to Thomas McKean, 4 March 1778, in William Thompson Read, *Life and Correspondence of George Read* . . . (hereafter cited as Read, *Read*) (Philadelphia: J. B. Lippincott Co., 1870), pp. 305–6; *The Documentary History of the Ratification of the Constitution* (hereafter cited as *DHRC*), ed. Merrill Jensen, John P. Kaminski, Gaspare J. Saladino, et al., 8 vols. to date (Madison: State Historical Society of Wisconsin, 1976–), 1:130–35.

12. *Council Minutes*, pp. 710, 715–18, 828, 831, 839–41; John A. Munroe, "Nonresident Representation in the Continental Congress," *William and Mary Quarterly*, 3d ser., 9 (1952): 171–77; Madison to Edmund Pendleton, 23 April and 5 November 1782, Memorandum, 1 May 1782, Madison to Edmund Randolph, 15 October and 5 November 1782, Notes of Debates, 26 February 1783 — all in *Madison Papers*, 4:178, 201, 5:200, 241, 243, 246 n; 6:291; Lee to Samuel Adams, 21 April 1782, *Letters of Members of the Continental Congress* (hereafter cited as Burnett, *Letters*), ed. Edmund C. Burnett, 8 vols. (Washington, D.C.: Carnegie Institution of Washington, 1921–36), 6:331; and *JCC*, 24:381, 25:968–69, 972–73.

13. *JCC*, 24:381, 25:649–50; Bedford to Van Dyke, 4 June, McComb to Van Dyke, 27 and 30 June, Maryland Delegates to the Maryland General Assembly, 3 November, and Thomas Jefferson to the Governor of Virginia, 11 November 1783, Burnett, *Letters*, 7:180, 203, 206, 369, 373.

14. *Laws of the General Assembly . . .* (Oct. 1785) (Wilmington, Del.: Jacob A. Killen & Co., 1786), pp. 4–5 (hereafter cited as *Laws*); Munroe, *Federalist Delaware*, p. 133; *The Statutes at Large of Pennsylvania from 1682 to 1801*, comp. James T. Mitchell and Henry Flanders, 16 vols. (Harrisburg: Harrisburg Publishing Co., 1896–1911), 12:99–104; and *Pennsylvania Packet* (Philadelphia), 6 March 1786.

15. Munroe, *Federalist Delaware*, p. 145.

16. *Council Minutes*, pp. 968–69, 972, 974–75; *Votes and Proceedings of the House of Assembly . . .* (Oct. 1785), (Wilmington, Del.: Jacob A. Killen & Co., 1786), pp. 27, 31, 34, 40, 47 (hereafter cited as *House Votes*); ibid. (May 1786), pp. 6, 9, 10–12; and Munroe, *Federalist Delaware*, pp. 141–43.

17. *House Votes* (Oct. 1786), pp. 6–10, (Jan. 1787), p. 36, and (May 1787), p. 5.

18. *Council Minutes*, pp. 627–29, 666–68, 674, 682, 825, 827, 829, 844–45; *Acts of the General Assembly of the Delaware State . . .* (Oct. 1781) (Wilmington: James Adams, 1782), pp. 3–15 (hereafter cited as *Acts*); *Acts* (May 1783), 16–21; *DHRC*, 1:140–41, 146–48.

19. *JCC*, 24:256–57, 261, 25:924.

20. *DHRC*, 1:153–54; *Laws* (Oct. 1785), pp. 3–4; and *Laws of the State of Delaware* (New Castle: James Adams, 1797), 2:838–40 (hereafter cited as *Delaware Laws*).

21. *JCC*, 30:147; and *Laws* (May 1786), pp. 10–11.

22. *JCC*; 23:660–66; *Council Minutes*, pp. 771, 783–84, 792–96, 808–9; and *Delaware Laws*, 2:776–82.

23. *JCC*, 29:756–71, 776; *House Votes* (Oct. 1785), pp. 21, 23, 34, 36, (May 1786), pp. 22–26, 32; *Council Minutes*, pp. 959, 963, 964–66, 968–70, 974–80, 985–91, 993–95; *Delaware Laws*, 2:852–63; and Charles Thomson to Read, 1 March, Read to Van Dyke, 25 March, and Van Dyke to Read, 7 April 1786, Read, *Read*, pp. 398–406. See also "Timoleon," *Dionysius*, pp. 33–42.

24. *DHRC*, 1:180–85; *House Votes* (May 1786), pp. 8, 13–14, 15–16, 27, 32–33; *Council Minutes*, pp. 969–70, 971–72, 984, 985, 990; and Read, *Read*, p. 430.

25. *DHRC*, 1:203–4; *Council Minutes*, pp. 1001, 1035, 1036, 1038–39; *House Votes* (Jan. 1787), pp. 44–46; and Read to John Dickinson, 17 January and 21 May 1787, Read, *Read*, pp. 438–40, 443–44.

26. E.g., see an abstract of attendance for the period November 1784 to July 1785 in Burnett, *Letters*, 8:175. Not everyone was pleased about Delaware's excellent attendance record in the Convention. Several customers of the *Delaware Gazette* (Wilmington) complained that it was too expensive for a "little and poor state" to maintain five delegates, four of whom also sat in the legislature (*Pennsyl-*

vania Packet (Philadelphia), 29 June 1787, in *DHRC*, 3:mcf (microfiche), doc. no. 6).

27. For a list of the speakers and the number of times that each spoke see *Historical Magazine*, 1st ser., 5, (1861): 18.

28. Farrand, *Records*, 1:242 n, 3:253.

29. Ibid., 1:37.

30. Ibid., 1:86–87, 152–53, 242 n. For more on Dickinson's positions on federalism and the equality of the states see ibid., pp. 42, 136, 2:356, 393.

31. Ibid., 1:202, 424. For more on Read's support of a powerful national government see ibid., 1:136–37, 463.

32. Ibid., 1:167–68, 490–92, 500–502, 531, 570, 2:19. For the hostility toward the small states evinced by such delegates as James Madison of Virginia and Nathaniel Gorham of Massachusetts, see ibid., 1:36, 242 n, 462, 528.

33. Ibid., 1:405, 412, 463, 471, 491, 501, 2:456.

34. *Pennsylvania Packet* (Philadelphia), 2 June 1787; House Resolution Concerning Sussex County Petitions for Paper Currency, 8 June, Legislative Papers, May–June 1787, Resolutions and Reports, Delaware State Archives. This document was called to my attention by Dr. John R. Kern, director of the Delaware Division of Historical and Cultural Affairs. See also *DHRC*, 3:50–51.

35. *DHRC*, 3:52, 13:252.

36. *DHRC*, 3:53–55.

37. *DHRC*, 3:50, 93, 94; and Grayson to William Short, 10 November, and Knox to Nathan Dane, 21 November 1787, in *DHRC*, 14:82, 147.

38. *DHRC*, 3:56–61.

39. Ibid., 62–83.

40. Ibid., 84–91; and *DHRC*, 3:mfc. 23. Despite the Council's action on the test oath, Tories continued their efforts to enfranchise former Loyalists, and by early 1790, voters no longer had to take an oath of allegiance (Hancock, "Delaware Loyalists," p. 43; and Munroe, *Federalist Delaware*, p. 88).

41. *DHRC*, 3:92-104.

42. *DHRC*, 105–13; and Antoine de la Forest to the Comte de la Luzerne, 18 February 1788, in ibid., 16:137.

43. Munroe, *Federalist Delaware*, p. 108; Forrest McDonald, *We the People: The Economic Origins of the Constitution* (Chicago: University of Chicago Press, 1958), pp. 117–19; Jefferson to William Carmichael, 15 December 1787, and Antoine de la Forest to the Comte de Montmorin, New York, 15 December, *DHRC*, 14:446, 481.

44. "Federal Farmer," *Observations Leading to a Fair Examination of the System of Government Proposed by the Late Convention . . .* ([New York: Thomas Greenleaf], 1787), in *DHRC*, 14:32; Symmes to Peter Osgood, Jr., 15 November 1787, ibid., p. 109; John Vaughan to John Dickinson, [post 19 April 1788], Dickinson Papers, Library Company of Philadelphia; "Brutus," *Virginia Independent Chronicle* (Richmond), 14 May 1788; and *The Debates in the Several State Conventions on the Adoption of the Federal Constitution . . .*

(hereafter cited as Elliot, *Debates*), ed. Jonathan Elliot, 2d ed., 5 vols. (Philadelphia: J. B. Lippincott Co., 1941), 3:324 (see also 3:596). See also "A Friend to Good Government," *Country Journal* (Poughkeepsie), 8 April 1788.

45. "Federal Farmer," in *DHRC*, 14:49; "A Columbian Patriot" (Mercy Warren of Massachusetts), *Observations on the New Constitution, and on the Federal and State Conventions* ([Boston, 1788]), in *DHRC*, 16:287; and Elliot, *Debates*, 3:158.

46. Edward Burd to Jasper Yeates, 6 August; William Shippen, Jr., to Thomas Lee Shippen, 5 August; and Madison to George Washington, 14 September 1788 — all in *The Documentary History of the First Federal Elections, 1788–1790*, ed. Merrill Jensen, Robert A. Becker, Gordon DenBoer, et al., 3 vols. to date (Madison: University of Wisconsin Press, 1976–), 1:51 n, 52 n, 138.

47. *Documentary History of the First Federal Congress of the United States of America, March 4, 1789–March 3, 1791*, ed. Linda Grant DePauw, Charlene Bangs Bickford, Helen E. Veit, Kenneth R. Bowling, et al., 7 vols. to date (Baltimore, Md., and London: Johns Hopkins University Press, 1972–), 6:1851, 1861–62; and *The Debates and Proceedings in the Congress of the United States . . .* (1789–1824), comp. Joseph Gales, Sr., 42 vols. (Washington, D.C.: Gales & Seaton, 1834–56), 1:877, 881, 895 (hereafter cited as *Annals of Congress*).

48. *Connecticut Courant* (Hartford), 7 January 1788, in *DHRC*, 15:245; Elliot, *Debates*, 3:158, 483; and *Annals of Congress*, 1:429, 430, 431.

49. McDonald, *We the People*, pp. 119–20. One of the other expenses was the payment of the state's congressional delegates. In the Constitutional Convention, James Madison said that under the new government, small states, such as Delaware, would be relieved of paying their congressional delegates (Farrand, *Records*, 1:319).

50. *House Votes* (Jan. 1787), pp. 27–28.

51. Jonathan Elliot, comp., *The Funding System of the United States and of Great Britain. . .* (Washington, D.C.: Blair & Rives, 1845), pp. 71–72. This percentage is more remarkable when one considers that the legislature did not provide for the requisitions of 1786, 1787, and 1788 (*House Votes* [Jan. 1788], p. 24, and [Jan. 1789], p. 39; and *Delaware Laws*, 2:977–84).

52. "Timoleon," in *Pennsylvania Packet* (Philadelphia), 15 June 1787, in *DHRC*, 3:mcf. 5; and "An Honest Man," *Freeman's Journal* (Philadelphia), 28 November 1787, *DHRC*, 3:76.

53. William Thornton to his parents, 14 April 1788, William Thornton Papers, Library of Congress; see also *House Votes* (Jan. 1788), p. 24.

54. Elliot, *Funding System*, p. 243. Only five of the thirty members of the Delaware Convention held public securities — a total of about $2,311 (McDonald, *We the People*, pp. 120–23).

55. Farrand, *Records*, 2:310; *House Votes* (Jan. 1788), pp. 14, 27, and (Jan. 1789), p. 18.

56. Louis-Guillaume Otto to the Comte de Montmorin, 15 December 1787, in George Bancroft, *History of the Formation of the Constitution of the United States of America*, 2 vols. (New York: D. Appleton & Co., 1882–83), 2:454.

2
PENNSYLVANIA
Representation and the Meaning
of Republicanism
GEORGE J. GRAHAM, JR.

Pennsylvania was the second state to ratify the Constitution. In several important ways, however, it was first. Its election of delegates was the first called and the first held. Its convention was the first convened. Given the strong opposition that existed within the state, Pennsylvania was also the first state in which the Constitution was seriously debated, both in and outside the convention. And it was the first large and strategically important state to ratify, which it did on December 12 by a vote of 46 to 23.

Thus Pennsylvania was, while not the first to ratify, the first real test of ratification. Unlike unanimous Delaware, Pennsylvania was divided on the matter of the new government. On one side were the Constitution's opponents, most of whom were committed to Pennsylvania's radically democratic state constitution of 1776, and who were hence (confusingly) called "Constitutionalists." On the other side, support for the federal Constitution was expressed primarily by those who had originally organized against the state constitution; they were known as "Republicans." The outcome of the contest was largely preordained by the timing of delegate elections, which were held during a period of rising Republican electoral support. In fact, the outcome in Pennsylvania, where at least a significant segment of the population was eager to reap the economic benefits of the new union, was in many ways predictable, almost as predictable as in Delaware.

Yet in Pennsylvania the stakes were higher in that opponents and supporters of the Constitution alike sought to shape the debate over the new document not only within the state but nationally as well. As a result, the Pennsylvania debates took on a special significance, delineating, as it were, the terms of discourse, the grammar, syntax, and vocabulary of ratification. In other words, the Pennsylvania debates were rich in rhetoric. And they were particularly rich in the rhetoric of representation.

PENNSYLVANIA'S POPULAR POLITICS

Even before the Revolution, Pennsylvania's politics had been intense and partisan. Annual elections had been established in 1683 by William Penn's Proprietary Frame of Government, and Pennsylvanians took the principle of popular control seriously.[1] A commitment to representative government was widespread, with those on all sides agreeing that government originated with the people. But the Pennsylvania public was seriously divided over the proper conception of representation, the problem of how the people were to be represented. After 1776, this conflict came to be focused on the innovative state constitution of 1776, the only truly new model of government that came in the first wave of Revolutionary state constitution making.[2]

Throughout the state's early years, the state constitution proved to be a political lightning rod. From 1776 on, Constitutionalists (sometimes also called radicals), supported by popular electoral success, championed the constitution and its radically democratic principles. Anticonstitutionalists, by contrast, made repeated efforts at revision, efforts that failed either because of timing — at one point the British moved on Philadelphia just as James Wilson was about to move on the Constitution of 1776 — or because of the inability of anticonstitutional forces to muster in the Council of Censors the majority required to call a convention.[3]

The divisions over the Constitution were wide and deep; they reflected profound geographical, sociological, and political differences. Specifically, Pennsylvania was divided between Philadelphia, on the one hand, and western Pennsylvania, on the other. This geographical split in turn implied sociological distinctions between urban and rural, merchants and farmers, rich and poor. The differences were deep enough to have become a permanent part of Pennsylvania's politics. Prior to 1776, under the old proprietary system, western counties had been badly underrepresented. Afterward, the 1776 constitution made certain that the western rural counties received more than their share of representatives, thereby providing a counterweight to the growing population of the urban east. In any case, both sides considered themselves disadvantaged, and each was resentful of the other.[4]

To be sure, the distinction between east and west was not entirely clear cut. For one thing, the split was by no means without exceptions: Pittsburgh, for example, was a Republican stronghold. Radicals and conservatives could be found in all parts of the state: James Wilson, leader of the so-called Philadelphia faction, was not a Philadelphian. Merchants and farmers, rich and poor, could be found on both sides of any given issue. In fact, Jackson Turner Main has gone so far as to suggest that the socioeconomic divisions in Pennsylvania were not regional but subregional, dividing the Appalachians and the valleys of the Delaware, the Susquehanna, and the Ohio rivers.[5] Nevertheless, to most people of the time, the main east-west division seemed clear enough, and for all practical political purposes, Pennsylvania was divided down the middle, into eastern and western, urban and rural, rich and poor factions.[6]

Pennsylvania's Constitutionalists, the representatives of the rural west, spoke in the voice of radical democracy. In the Constitution of 1776, they set forth a frame of government that provided all power to the public. This popular power was assured by a unicameral legislature, frequent elections, and an almost total absence of executive power. All deliberations were open and published. While in session, the doors of the legislature were required to be locked open, allowing access by any citizen at any time. All issues were to be voted on in a second term, becoming binding only following a period of open public debate. Limits on officeholding were strict, and rotation in office was required. A unique Council of Censors was to be called every seven years to consider the constitution and how it was being conserved. The council was to be popularly elected. Otherwise, the legislature was the governing body in all things.[7] An early draft of the Constitution of 1776 reflected some of the democratic sentiment that lay behind these measures: "An enormous Proportion of Property vested in a few Individuals is dangerous to the Rights, and destructive of the Common Happiness, of Mankind."[8]

In short, this radical constitution represented the triumph of pure democratic representation. Virtually all of the democratic innovations that could be placed in a Revolutionary-era state constitution were present in Pennsylvania: unicameralism; rapid rotation in and out of office; simple institutions and clear lines of authority, so that the public would know whom to blame for bad decisions; direct access by the public; and egalitarian principles everywhere. As Gordon S. Wood put it, Pennsylvania's pervasively egalitarian constitution marked a revolution in constitution making and "at once brought into question what had been taken for granted in 1776."[9]

By contrast, Republicans spoke with a different voice, one considerably less democratic though no less popular.[10] Pennsylvania's Republicans, after all, while not democrats, were Revolutionary republicans, many of whom, like Benjamin Rush, had impeccable Revolutionary credentials. Although they were opposed to crucial aspects of the state constitution, including annual elections and unicameralism, they were almost without exception enthusiastic supporters of the broader principle of popular power. Thus their support for the federal Constitution, with its longer terms, stronger executive, and more complicated institutional controls, was premised on the assumption that all of these reforms would prove to be no threat to popular sovereignty. Typical of those who made this case was Wilson, who, while at the Philadelphia convention, had been perhaps the most eloquent defender of the principle of popular sovereignty.[11] As a practical matter, Republicans had no other choice. In Pennsylvania, to reject the principle of popular political power was almost unthinkable. For one thing, Pennsylvanians had played a prominent role in the Revolution, and republican memories remained strong. For another, because the two sides that dominated Pennsylvania politics were of roughly equal strength, there was little to be gained by antiegalitarian statements. One might as well announce that one was a card-carrying member of the Philadelphia crowd. Indeed, even to speak of mixed government was to evoke the specter of class politics, and conservatives had nothing to gain by emphasizing class differences. Thus, while conservatives elsewhere were denouncing democracy, Pennsylvania's Republicans were defending it, or at least they were defending the principle of popular sovereignty.[12]

The point should not be overstated. Over time, with a gradual increase of popular support for the Republican side, conservatives went on the offensive, and democratic tenets did come to be tested on a series of issues: the Bank of the United States, test oaths for Quakers, the counting of Philadelphia workingmen for purposes of representation.[13] Yet it should also be said that in each of these cases, Republicans were forced repeatedly to reassert their commitment to the principle of popular sovereignty. Moreover, while their commitments were in large part theoretical, there is no reason to believe that they were any less strong than those of the radicals.[14]

Wilson provides a case in point. His commitment to popular sovereignty was fundamental, a product of his Presbyterianism, the Scottish milieu in which he grew up, and the moral thought of Thomas Reid.[15] For Wilson, public issues were always moral issues, grounded in a deep moral sense, the moral equivalent of first principles. Morality was God given and hence instinctual. In this regard it was the most fundamental of our senses, reaching beyond the physical, the rational, and the emotional.[16] "Our instincts," Wilson declared, "are no other than the oracles of eternal wisdom; our conscience . . . is the voice of God within us."[17] This moral sense was present, or at least potentially present, in all persons, strong or weak, educated or uneducated, propertied or propertyless. "All sound reasoning," he wrote, echoing Reid, "must rest ultimately on the principles of common sense."[18] Because this "common" sense was available to all, even "common" men could act as valuable and responsible citizens of a republic. It was a view of human nature that was neither optimistic, like that of Jefferson, nor pessimistic, like that of his fellow Federalist John Adams, but realistic; and it led Wilson to argue on every occasion for the broadest possible base for the government of the United States and of Pennsylvania.[19]

Yet Wilson's common-sense philosophy did not lead directly to democratic politics. In fact, his conception of popular control was complex and, to some opponents, may have seemed convoluted, because Wilson maintained that direct control was consistent with indirect representation. Citizens had the right to be represented; in fact, they had nothing less than an inherent right to give instructions to their representatives. Representatives were the "creatures" of their constituents and, as such, were strictly "accountable for the use of that power which is delegated unto them."[20] At the same time, these representatives had the responsibility not only to reflect but also to shape public opinion, reaching out to the public through the power of persuasion. Ironically, it was the common sense of the public that allowed representatives to play this role, permitting the creation of "informed" positions through the power of *phronesis*, the public's capacity to grasp the insight of reason. Thus the role of the representative was educative, and his tools were rhetorical. In effect, as Wilson saw it, the role of the representative was to teach. It was a role to which he himself was well suited, having come to politics by way of the classrooms of the University of Pennsylvania.[21]

But Wilson had practiced his persuasive powers in the real world of Pennsylvania politics as well. For example, his *Considerations on the Nature and Extent of the Legislative Authority of the British Parliament* had been a catalyst, a crucial link in the chain of events that had brought about the American Revolution. An important aspect of the tract was its timing, in that the pamphlet had been prepared in 1768 or 1769, but had not been published until late in the summer of 1774, in the midst of the furor over the Coercive and Quebec Acts. The timing was magnificent, not only for swaying public opinion but also for establishing his own reputation as one of America's greatest republican rhetors.[22]

But it would be later in his life, in the debates over the United States Constitution, that Wilson would capture center stage. As a delegate to both the Philadelphia convention and the Pennsylvania ratifying convention, he would be called upon to exercise two kinds of rhetoric — deliberative and justificatory. In the federal convention, he would prove himself adept at deliberation. But it was in the state convention — where he would be called upon to combine deliberation and justification by evoking the power of both rational and emotional *(epideictic)* persuasion — that he would show himself a master of eighteenth-century rhetoric.[23]

THE CONTEXT OF RATIFICATION

Pennsylvania was at the forefront of the ratification process for two reasons. The first was practical, the second symbolic. In practical terms, Pennsylvania was the heart of the new nation both socially and economically. In symbolic terms, it was its political center. During the ratification process, this symbolic status proved to be in many ways the most significant.

No one could mistake the symbolic importance of Pennsylvania in the ratification process. The Constitution had been framed in Pennsylvania, literally downstairs from the sitting session of the legislature. This session, controlled by a majority of Republicans, had for some time been eagerly awaiting the chance to confirm the new Constitution. On September 17, the morning after the Philadelphia convention had adjourned, the assembly had already obtained a copy of the Constitution. Eager to strike while the iron was hot, Pennsylvania's Republicans thought it would be possible to have the state's ringing endorsement in the hands of the Confederation Congress within a matter of days, thus setting the ratification process off to a flying start. By the same token, opponents supposed that a defeat in Pennsylvania would doom the document at its inception.

In fact, the assembly did act in a hurry. On September 28, a motion was put to call a ratification convention to begin on November 20. Alarmed at the motion and fearing certain defeat, opponents absented themselves from the afternoon session, thereby preventing a quorum and forestalling a vote. In response, enraged Republicans, aided by a mob of sympathetic supporters, captured two of the absent Constitutionalists and forced them into the assembly chambers. Following a struggle and amid a good deal of confusion, the motion was made and passed. The message was clear: these Federalists, as they were soon to be called, desired a speedy ratification and were willing to use force to get it.[24]

Republicans were eager to ratify for practical political reasons. For one thing, they were riding the crest of a wave of popularity, having recently experienced a dramatic electoral upturn. For another, by calling for immediate elections, Republicans could more easily mobilize their urban supporters in Philadelphia, while radicals would be left to call out votes where they could amid the scattered communities and far-flung settlements of the west. In addition, an early election seemed strategically sound, fitting well with the take-it-or-leave-it strategy that so many Federalists favored.

Perhaps even more important, Republicans had the advantage of their own ardor. In fact, when it came to the new Constitution, Pennsylvania Republicans were doubly enthusiastic. For more than a decade, conservatives had been chafing under agrarian domination within the assembly, complaining about paper money and easy credit.

In the new national Constitution they saw the solution to some of these economic woes. Even more, however, they saw a chance to strike down their old political nemesis, the radical Pennsylvania Constitution of 1776. With ratification, Republicans saw an unparalleled opportunity to kill two birds with one stone, securing their economic interests within the new nation, while at the same time assuring political power at home.

Under these circumstances, Republicans chose to concentrate on political matters. The choice was salutary, for by focusing on political issues, they gained an immense advantage, countering agrarian charges that the debate was in fact a contest over economics. In this way, as Forrest McDonald has suggested, economic factors were more or less neutralized in the contest.[25]

At the same time, by contesting the Constitution on political grounds, Republicans could take advantage of their greatest strength—the power of persuasion. In other words, they could take advantage of Wilson, their chief advocate for the new Constitution. And here the advantage was great. As the sole participant in the ratification proceedings who had also been a delegate to the Philadelphia convention, Wilson's words carried special weight. In effect, it was Wilson who "delivered" the Constitution to his fellow citizens. In his famous State House Yard speech of October 6, he delivered it in a dramatic way.

THE STATE HOUSE YARD SPEECH

The State House Yard address was the centerpiece of a Saturday evening gathering to select a Republican ticket for the next assembly. The setting was highly partisan. Although the audience gave "claps" and "huzzas" to the suggestion that the new plan of government would "annihilate party," it also (according to a critical correspondent) shouted down with "no, no" a respectable citizen's name because he had hitherto "been esteemed an advocate for the constitution of Pennsylvania."[26] Wilson was among friends and was preaching to the choir.

Yet more than a partisan rallying cry, the address was a kind of preemptive strike in which Wilson defended the Constitution on each of the major points that were likely to prove troubling to Pennsylvania's public. Each potential bone of contention was raised and answered in turn. More to the point, all were answered on Wilson's terms — that is, in the language with which he wished to structure the coming debates. Thus the real audience for the State House Yard speech included not only Wilson's friends but also his enemies and, even more important, the public to which both sides would ultimately appeal.

Wilson began by establishing his own republican credentials. He reminded the audience that he had "received the honor of an appointment to represent you in the late Convention."[27] He further stated that he was coming to them as a delegate, having been summoned to address them by "many gentlemen whose characters and judgments I sincerely respect" (p. 167). In any case, he observed, it was his "duty" to deliver them the Constitution and to "lay before you any information which will serve to explain and elucidate" it (p. 167). Thus, Wilson presented himself as the representative of the people and a servant of them, acutely aware that ultimate power resided with them alone (p. 167).

In the same way, he pictured himself as a public servant. In contrast to those "insidious attempts" being "clandestinely" made to oppose the new system, Wilson came directly to the public, in order to provide them "the impressions of four months constant attention" (p. 167). In this manner, Wilson assumed the pose of a public figure, acting openly and above board, armed only with the power of information. Above all, he depicted himself as a defender of the Constitution. Attempts already had been made, he observed, to "pervert and destroy the new plan" (p. 167). He himself, he stated, was acting only "in its defense" (p. 167). With a single rhetorical stroke, Wilson had reversed the political roles of the two sides. Because state protection was reserved, Wilson could claim for the new Constitution the authority of moderation and stability, while denouncing the opposition as aggressors, attackers, and destroyers. It was a stroke of genius, one from which Antifederalists would never fully recover.

With this, Wilson turned at once to the heart of his argument, the principle of representative sovereignty. When the people had established the powers of legislation under their separate state governments, he argued, they had invested their representatives with every right and authority that they did not explicitly reserve. By contrast, in delegating federal powers, they used another criterion — namely, that authority arose, not from tacit assumption, but from positive grant. "Hence it is evident," Wilson concluded, "that in the former case everything which is not reserved is given, but in the latter the reverse of the proposition prevails, and everything which is not given, is reserved" (pp. 167–68).

The case was deceptively simple: if the power was not granted to Congress, then Congress could not legislate — period. Citing the demand for a bill of rights, Wilson contended that any such statement of rights would be "superfluous" (p. 168). Focusing on the freedom of the press, he contended that the new government placed no restriction whatsoever on the press. Therefore, to reiterate the liberties of the press would be "nugatory" (p. 168). In fact, it might well be dangerous, for "that very declaration might have been construed to imply that some degree of power was given" (p. 168).

Powers that were not expressly stated remained with the state legislatures. Turning to the contention that trial by jury was abolished in civil cases, Wilson took advantage of his "professional experience" to declare the argument "fabricated" and "disingenuous" (p. 168). Noting that the "thirteen separate sovereignties" had differing rules on trial by jury and that the question had proven too complex for the convention to resolve, he cited the wisdom of leaving the situation as it was, " 'as heretofore,' " in the hands of the separate states (p. 169). As to the Supreme Court, he argued, the convention had "fullest confidence that no danger could possibly ensue, since the proceedings of the Supreme Court are to be regulated by the Congress, which is a faithful representation of the people" (p. 169).

Congress could legislate only in the public good. As for the claim that the Constitution created a standing army, Wilson declared it "pernicious" (p. 169). A standing army in peacetime was nothing new. Wilson may have had the Federalist island of Pittsburgh in mind when he pointed to the wisdom of maintaining present fortifications "along the banks of the Ohio" (p. 169). More important, he argued that a republican army posed no threat, existing as it did to protect the people, not to threaten their liberties. Under the Constitution, armies became preservers of the public good: "No man, who regards the dignity and safety of his country, can deny the necessity of a military force, under the control and with the restrictions which the new Constitution provides" (p. 169).

Ultimately, Congress itself was only a reflection of the public. In addressing the contention that the Senate would become a "baneful aristocracy," Wilson denounced it in no uncertain terms: "Perhaps there never was a charge made with less reasons" (p. 169). The Senate's two functions were checked: the House checked its legislative powers; the President, its executive powers. Thus fettered, the Senate could do nothing by itself. Far from being aristocrats, senators should better be seen as democratic delegates. In the organization of the Senate, Wilson saw the potential for "a compromise between contending interests." He explained, in terms that foreshadowed Federalist 10: "And when we reflect how various are the laws, commerce, habits, population, and extent of the confederated states, this evidence of mutual concession and accommodation ought rather to command a generous applause, than to excite jealousy and reproach" (p. 170).

As before, sovereignty resided with the states. The notion that the federal government was intended to annihilate the states was "absurd" (p. 170). Pointing to the fact that presidents were to be elected by electors nominated according to rules set in the several states, that senators were to be elected by the state legislatures, and that members of the House of Representatives were to be elected by the people of the states, Wilson considered the sovereignty of the states untouched. In fact, in many ways the states were strengthened, "bound" together and with the federal government by "indissoluble ties" (p. 170.)

As always, power lay ultimately with the people. Noting the popular fear of the power of Congress to tax, Wilson pronounced it a "visionary evil" (p. 171). On the whole, taxes would come from imposts. In situations of emergency, direct taxation might have to be used. But in either case, taxes would be fair, and states would pay their proper share. More to the point, the power to tax lay only with the people. As Wilson explained, "The interest of the government will be best promoted by the accommodation of the people" (p. 171).

In concluding, Wilson depicted ratification as a struggle between private interest and the public good. Once again he charged that anyone who opposed the Constitution was self-interested, objecting not "because it is injurious to the liberties of his country, but because it affects his schemes of wealth and consequence" (p. 172). By contrast, anyone who supported it, including himself, was following the dictates of reason and common sense:

> I will confess, indeed, that I am not a blind admirer of this plan of government, and that there are some parts of it which, if my wish had prevailed, would certainly have been altered . . . I am satisfied that anything nearer to perfection could not have been accomplished. If there are errors, it should be remembered, that the seeds of reformation are sown in the work itself. . . . Regarding it then, in every point of view, with a candid and disinterested mind, I am bold to assert, that it is the best form of government which has ever been offered to the world (p. 172).

According to reports, the speech had quite an effect. It was frequently interrupted with "loud and unanimous testimonies," and the applause at the end "evinced the general sense of its excellence, and the conviction which it had impressed upon every mind" (p. 172). The speech was reprinted three days later, on election morning, in the *Pennsylvania Herald.* It was reprinted ten times throughout the next month, during the campaign for the convention itself. (In both elections, Republicans won comfortable majorities.) And it was reprinted many times after that throughout the several states. With the State House Yard speech, Federalists had found an "official" position, and the contest over ratification had begun in earnest (p. 131).

THE PENNSYLVANIA CONVENTION

In most ways, the character of the Pennsylvania deliberations was no surprise. Wilson was in charge of the Federalist camp; William Findley, John Smilie, and Robert Whitehill were in charge of the opposition. With the exception of the long-time radical leader Thomas McKean, whose nationalist sentiments drew his support to the Philadelphia Constitution, the partisan divisions followed predictable party lines: Constitutionalists on one side; Republicans on the other.[28] What did seem surprising was the rhetoric. Even before the debates could begin, Wilson was on the floor, delivering a speech that was reported to have "astonished" the convention (p. 339). Indeed, Wilson's address of November 24 attracted attention not only inside the convention but outside as well, where opponents derided it as demagoguery and supporters celebrated it as classical oratory at its best (p. 339). The sympathetic Francis Hopkinson wrote to Thomas Jefferson, "The powers of Demosthenes and Cicero seemed to be united in this able orator" (cited on p. 339).

The convention began by deciding on procedures, and Federalists won the first round. On November 26, McKean moved that the convention consider the Constitution systematically, article by article; and both sides agreed, though they would soon ignore the agreement in practice.[29] More important, when Antifederalists then moved to allow for articles to be voted on seriatim, Federalists protested, with Wilson and Rush contending that the Constitution must be considered as a whole. The point was significant, given that there were a number of issues, including the question of exemption from military service for Quakers, that were of such importance within the state that they might well have doomed the document altogether.[30] In any case, from this point on, the debates tended to consider the Constitution as a whole.

When the delegates turned to the document itself, beginning with its preamble, Wilson struck first. After commenting at length on the wonder of compromise and the marvel of a federal republic that would reconcile diversity of interests among the states, he began to lay out a rhetoric of ratification. Beginning with the preamble, he argued that the people were the sole source of the Constitution, the source of all its power: "But, in this Constitution, the citizens of the United States appear dispensing a part of their original power in what manner and what proportion they think fit. They never part with the whole; and they retain the right of recalling what they part with" (p. 389). In other words, Wilson concluded, the full meaning of "WE, the people," was that the people gave up nothing, and gained everything: "WE reserve the right to do what we please" (p. 389).

All else followed. On issue after issue, in the midst of bitter bickering and partisan politicking, Wilson could be found turning back to the basic assumption that all power remained with the people. In the case of Congress, popular sovereignty was clear. But even in seemingly anti-democratic institutions—in the president, the Senate, and the judiciary—he argued that the ends of popular control had been perfected, or at least had been made as perfect as possible under the circumstances. In fact, it was here that Wilson's commitment to popular power seemed most clear. Presidents were elected by electors; the Senate was a creation of the state legislatures; judges were appointed by the president and senators, who were themselves appointed, at least indirectly, by the people. In each case, the officials had more information, not more power. Moreover, the checks within the constitutional system would constantly bring power back to the ever-present people. In Wilson's eyes, the new Constitution was "not a government founded upon compact; it is founded upon the power of the people. They express in their name and in their authority, "*We the people do ordain and establish,*" etc. from their ratification, and their ratification alone, it is to take its constitutional authenticity; without that, it is no more than *tabula rasa*" (p. 555).

In fact, during the course of the debates, Wilson sounded often surprisingly like his former fellow Pennsylvanian Thomas Paine. Wilson and Paine shared much, including a common faith in the common man's ability to grasp good reasoning and to evaluate it on the basis of primary truths. Like Paine, Wilson saw the people as a whole as the proper source of sovereignty. Like Paine's, Wilson's view of representative government was grounded on the moral wisdom of the public. Like Paine, Wilson claimed that "all authority of every kind is *derived by* REPRESENTATION *from the* PEOPLE, *and the* DEMOCRATIC *principle is carried into every part of the government*" (p. 497).

At the same time, while Wilson's rhetoric was reminiscent of Paine, his principles seemed to point more to Edmund Burke. In particular, Wilson's views on representation were in many ways decidedly Burkean. Representatives did best when they represented, not the immediately perceived interests of the people, but their "true interests" (p. 489). In this sense, representatives were not mirrors of the public but were mediators, reconciling small and short-term interests with the larger and longer-term public good. Representatives could best fulfill this function when serving, not small numbers of citizens, but the public at large, through smaller bodies and larger districts. The Constitutional system, which distanced representatives from the people, allowed representatives the chance to act through their "wisdom and virtue" (p. 489). If this constituted an aristocracy, Wilson argued, then it was an aristocracy of nature, an aristocracy at its best. He summed up: "I apprehend it is of more consequence to be able to know the true interest of the people, than their faces, and of more consequence still, to have virtue enough to pursue the means of carrying that knowledge usefully into effect" (p. 489).

Nevertheless, at almost every point, no matter how Burkean the principles, Wilson relied on Paine's rhetoric. America would never allow an aristocracy. Its genius was democratic. Furthermore, the genius of the Constitutional system was democratic. Observed Wilson, "It is purely democratical; but its parts are calculated in such manner as to obtain those advantages also which are peculiar to the other forms of government in other countries" (p. 579). He concluded his last major speech to the convention with an apt image:

> A free government has often been compared to a pyramid. This allusion is made with peculiar propriety in the system before you; it is laid on the broad basis of the people; its powers gradually rise, while they are confined, in proportion as they ascend, until they end in that most permanent of all forms. When you examine all its parts, they will invariably be found to preserve that essential mark of free governments — a chain of connection with the people (p. 580).

Wilson's rhetoric proved difficult to dispute. While Antifederalists continued to confront the Constitution with charges of aristocratic tyranny, their claims, anticipated by Wilson, sounded somehow hollow. As the convention dragged on, Antifederalist contentions became increasingly extreme. Indeed, by the close of the debates, the Antifederalist cause seemed to consist entirely of symbolism, what we might today call "mere rhetoric." By contrast, Wilson's words, underlined as they were by a clear commitment to popular control, seemed more substantive and sound, in the spirit of eighteenth-century rhetoric.

On December 12, twenty-two days after the convention had begun, Pennsylvania ratified the Constitution by a vote of 46 to 23. The resolution was read at the courthouse to a large body of citizens. Bells were rung, cannons were fired, and the crowd repaired to Mr. Epple's tavern on Sassafras Street, where representatives and citizens together drank thirteen toasts, the first of which was to "The *People* of the United States" (p. 607).

COUNTERATTACK

With ratification in hand, Pennsylvania's Federalists seemed confident that the public celebrations would usher in a grand and glorious consensus on the Constitution. This was not to be. In spite of ratification, opposition remained. In fact, it seemed greater and more determined than ever, spilling over into the public assemblies and eventually out into the streets. Somewhat surprisingly, it was only after ratification that Pennsylvania's Antifederalists really girded their loins, creating their own campaign to challenge the outcome of the ratification process.[31] Ratification was assured, but popular approval was far from being won.

Thus, Antifederalists went on the offensive. The centerpiece of the resistance was the "Dissent of the Minority of the Convention," a broadside that was signed by no less than twenty-one of the twenty-three delegates who had voted against ratification. Published first in December, the "Dissent" presented condensations of preconvention essays and pamphlets that were critical of the Constitution, along with convention speeches by Robert Whitehall, John Smilie, and William Findley. Widely circulated throughout the winter and early spring, not only in Pennsylvania but also in many other parts of the country, it represented a kind of last-ditch effort on the part of Antifederalists to stall ratification, if not by repealing it in Pennsyvlania, then at least by slowing or preventing the process in other states.[32]

Crucial to the dissent was the issue of representation. Citing the secrecy of the proceedings at Philadelphia, the coercion used to capture a quorum, the conduct of the elections, which included numerous irregularities, and the procedures used in the convention itself to dampen dissent, the minority made clear that the process had at no point been accountable to the people. More important, in considering the Constitutional system itself, the dissenters pointed to the lack of popular control. Carefully calculating the size of a quorum in the House and the Senate, they reported that "the liberties, happiness, interests, and great concerns of the whole United States may be dependent upon the integrity, virtue, wisdom, and knowledge of 25 or 26 men" (p. 631). Recalling Montesquieu, the minority pointed skeptically to the notion that three or four million people, spread over an extensive territory and comprising various habits, interests, and opinions, could be condensed into so small a body. Besides, even at its best, the Constitution did not provide fair and equal representation, for several reasons: because the smallest state had as much weight in the Senate as the largest; because exceedingly small numbers of represen-

tatives would be chosen for both branches of the legislature; because
the mode of election and appointment would be under the control
of Congress; and because by the very nature of the thing, only those
of the most elevated rank would be elected, while other orders in society, such as farmers, traders, and mechanics, would be left without
a voice (pp. 630–31). All told, according to the minority, the new system
was "deficient in every essential quality of a just and safe representation" (p. 631).

In effect, the dissenters suggested that the minority inside the convention was in fact the majority outside it. They may well have been
right, because in the wake of the dissent, Antifederalists throughout
the state rose up in arms, called meetings, signed petitions, and at
one point, incited a riot at Carlisle in Cumberland County, where
Wilson and McKean were burned in effigy. As for ratification, none
of this made any difference within the state. It did, however, influence
the ratification process beyond its borders, in that it called into question Federalist motives and tactics. Probably most important, it made
ratification much more problematic and raised the possibility that
the Constitution might be ratified inside the conventions but rejected
outside them.

The Pennsylvania dissent was crucial to the shaping of the Federalist
strategy. If nothing else, it demonstrated that in their rush to ratify, Federalists had failed to take account of continuing popular concerns. In
Pennsylvania, dissent had indeed been stifled. Elections had been hur-
ried; debate had been limited; Antifederalist amendments had been
essentially outlawed. Now, in the wake of victory, Federalists were paying
the price in popular outrage. Indeed, by responding to the dissenters
with personal attacks and narrowly partisan polemics, some Federalists
only managed to fan the flames. Eventually, the attacks became ardent
enough that Benjamin Franklin, the state's elder statesman and its most
prominent champion of the Constitution, called on the newspaper publishers of the state to refuse to publish the diatribes. Interestingly, some
of the state's newspapers, including the one that Franklin himself had
founded, refused to print the call for moderation (p. 645). Clearly, in
the wake of ratification, things had gotten out of hand. For some time to
come, Pennsylvania's politics would be poisonous.

Ironically, Pennsylvania's Federalists had mistaken ratification for legitimation. The irony lies in the fact that Federalists had in their hands the means to secure legitimacy. That tool was the rhetoric of James Wilson. Had they relied on Wilson's words and on the spirit of them, they might well have won a more lasting victory.

Yet the lesson was not lost entirely. After Pennsylvania, Federalists were at least a little chastened. Ratification, it now seemed clear, would require real deliberation, and the people would have to have their say. The new Constitution, after all, belonged to them.

James Wilson had been saying this all along.

NOTES

1. See John Paul Selsam, *The Pennsylvania Constitution of 1776: A Study in Revolutionary Democracy* (New York: Da Capo Press, 1971), p. 191.

2. See Donald S. Lutz, *Popular Consent and Popular Control: Whig Political Theory in the Early State Constitutions* (Baton Rouge: Louisiana State University Press, 1980), p. 14.

3. See Selsam, *Pennsylvania Constitution*, p. 200.

4. See Gordon S. Wood, *The Creation of the American Republic, 1776–1787* (New York: W. W. Norton, 1972), p. 330.

5. See Jackson Turner Main, *The Antifederalists: Critics of the Constitution, 1781–1788* (Chapel Hill: University of North Carolina Press, 1961), pp. 42–47.

6. See ibid., pp. 42–43.

7. See Wood, *Creation*, pp. 87–89.

8. Cited ibid., p. 89.

9. Ibid., p. 237.

10. See ibid., pp. 247–48.

11. See ibid.

12. See ibid., p. 251.

13. See Main, *The Antifederalists*, pp. 42–47.

14. See Wood, *Creation*, p. 251.

15. On Wilson see Geoffrey Seed, *James Wilson* (Milwood, N.Y.: KTO Press, 1978); Charles Page Smith, *James Wilson: Founding Father, 1742–1798* (Chapel Hill: University of North Carolina Press, 1956); and Wilson Carey McWilliams, *The Idea of Fraternity in America* (Berkeley: University of California Press, 1973); see also *The Works of James Wilson*, ed. Robert Green McCloskey (Cambridge: Harvard University Press, 1967).

16. See McWilliams, *Idea of Fraternity*, pp. 197–98.

17. Cited in Smith, *James Wilson*, pp. 321–22.

18. Cited in Seed, *James Wilson*, p. 17.

19. See Smith, *James Wilson*, pp. 321–22.

20. Cited in Bernard Bailyn, *The Ideological Origins of the American Revolution* (Cambridge: Harvard University Press, 1967), p. 171.

21. On rhetoric see Chaim Perelman, *The New Rhetoric and the Humanities: Essays on Rhetoric and Its Applications* (Boston, Mass.: D. Reidel, 1979), p. 16.

22. See Seed, *James Wilson*, pp. 6–7.

23. On deliberative and legitimating rhetoric see George J. Graham, Jr., and Scarlett G. Graham, "The Rhetorics of the Convention and the *Federalist*: Deliberation versus Justification in Founding Discourse," a revision of a 1983 paper presented to the annual meeting of the American Political Science Association; see also the introductory and concluding chapters of *Founding Principles of American Government: Two Hundred Years of Democracy on Trial*, ed. George J. Graham, Jr., and Scarlett G. Graham, rev. ed. (Chatham, N.J.: Chatham House, 1984).

24. For background see Robert Allen Rutland, *The Ordeal of the Constitution* (Norman: University of Oklahoma Press, 1966), pp. 49–65; *The Documentary History of the Ratification of the Constitution* (hereafter cited as *DHRC*), ed. Merrill Jensen, John P. Kaminski, Gaspare J. Saladino, et al., 8 vols. to date (Madison: State Historical Society of Wisconsin, 1976–), 2:54–319; and John B. McMaster and Frederick D. Stone, *Pennsylvania and the Federal Constitution, 1787–1788* (Lancaster: Historical Society of Pennsylvania, 1888).

25. See Forrest McDonald, *We the People: The Economic Origins of the Constitution* (Chicago: University of Chicago Press, 1958), p. 168.

26. Cited from the *Pennsylvania Herald*, 13 October 1787, *DHRC*, 2:175.

27. Cited from the *Pennsylvania Herald*, 9 October 1787, *DHRC*, 2:67. Subsequent citations from vol. 2 of *DHRC* will be given parenthetically in the text by page number.

28. See Seed, *James Wilson*, p. 93.

29. On the convention see *DHRC*, 2:322–616.

30. See Herbert J. Storing, *What the Anti-Federalists Were For* (Chicago: University of Chicago Press, 1981), p. 97.

31. On the postratification period see *DHRC*, 2:642–725.

32. See "The Address and Reasons of Dissent of the Minority of the Convention of the State of Pennsylvania to their Constituents," *DHRC*, 2:617–18.

3
NEW JERSEY
Property and the Price of
Republican Politics

SARA M. SHUMER

The story of the politics of the ratification of the Constitution in New Jersey is a short one. What strikes one immediately is that there was no apparent, or at least no visible, political conflict. At the Philadelphia convention, New Jersey, a small state, had won the equal representation of states in the new Senate, and that seemed to be all that mattered. There were only three articles in state newspapers that opposed ratification, and those were reprints of items written and first published outside the state. Indeed, only three other articles offered any sustained defense of the Constitution, beyond merely announcing its desirability.[1] There is no record of any discord or even any contest in electing the delegates to the state convention, or of any serious debate within that convention, which ratified unanimously, 38 to 0, on December 18, 1787.[2]

Support seemed to be deep and widespread. In the weeks after the document was first received from Philadelphia, popular meetings in six of the thirteen counties passed petitions calling on the state legislature to move quickly in establishing elections for a convention to ratify. The language of these petitions expressed urgency and unquestioning support. Said one: "Nothing but the immediate adoption of it can save the United States in general, and this state in particular, from absolute ruin."[3]

Although the sitting legislature did not in fact act, it was not because there was dissent, but because annual elections were due soon. Held in late October, the elections showed no controversy over the Constitution and returned essentially the same men to office. Almost immediately on returning, both houses of the new legislature unanimously authorized delegate elections. The wording of both resolutions reveals the sense of overwhelming consensus; the original charge was "to deliberate upon, agree to, and ratify." Later this was amended to read "to deliberate upon and if approved of by them to ratify," thus at least admitting the possibility that the convention might come to a negative decision or at least allowing it the right to do so.[4]

The evidence of consensus continued in the election of convention delegates. Elections were held from November 27 through December 1, a short three months after the document had arrived from Philadelphia and only one month after the original call for elections. Throughout that time, there was no recorded educational or electioneering campaign. As was customary in New Jersey, elections were by voice vote in some counties and by ballot in others, and the polling was moved from town to town to allow full participation. Somewhat less customary, there were no charges of fraud. The newspapers entered short notices of the results and of the weather but made no note of debates, of speeches, or of losers or winners, let alone of what anyone had advocated. In this fashion, almost casually and certainly with little deliberation, the people of New Jersey elected representatives to decide what then was seen and now is still seen to be one of the most momentous choices to face the new nation.

The convention itself lasted from December 11 to December 20, giving the people's representatives nine days to debate the advantages and disadvantages of the new Constitution. Throughout, there was little questioning or probing. Delegates gathered on December 11 and 12, offering and receiving their credentials, none of which were challenged. Then, for the next two days, they elected officers and passed procedural rules. On Friday the fourteenth, Saturday the fifteenth, and Monday the seventeenth, they read the Constitution paragraph by paragraph and discussed it. We do not know how long they met each day (although we do know that they started at 10 A.M.), nor do we know what was said, because the official record offers only the scantiest of procedural information. Tuesday morning, after several speeches, "a general review was taken of all the different articles in their relation to each other," the question was put, and the delegates voted unanimously in favor of ratification. It then took them two days to settle their costs and accounts and to have their approval engrossed on parchment. There followed a march to the county courthouse and a public reading, with full pomp and ceremony, to "the acclamations and huzzas of the people."[5] At no point was there any hint of serious disagreement within the convention.

In retrospect it is fair to say that New Jersey moved with a speed and a directness that are awesome given the gravity of the decision. Clearly, in just three days of debate, concerns and fears about the Constitution could not have been fully heard, much less debated, weighed, and settled. The politically interesting questions, thus, become Why was there such unanimity in New Jersey? Why was there so little public debate and discourse, even from those in favor of the new Constitution? More important, Where were those who in other states opposed the new Constitution because they thought that it created a centralized government, taking power away from the people and handing it over to the aristocrats, the men of standing and reputation, the monied men — lawyers, merchants, and large landowners?[6] Where, in other words, were the Antifederalists?

There are of course several possibilities. Perhaps New Jersey was an unusually homogeneous state politically. Perhaps it was a conservative state, or at least was controlled by conservatives. Or as Wood has suggested, perhaps the citizens in New Jersey had matured from the idealism of 1776 to the realism of 1787 and saw the wisdom of a more stable, less democratic government.[7] For us today, this may be the most comfortable and reassuring explanation. Yet none of these answers is satisfactory.

In fact, there were strong reasons for expecting opposition to the new Constitution in New Jersey. The state's constitution encouraged a democratic, participatory style of politics; its citizens had shared in a recent history of active participation; and they had a political leader, Abraham Clark, who acted diligently and effectively in behalf of a conception of republican citizenship quite at odds with that of the new proposed Constitution. All of these factors — participatory institutions and practices, a relatively coherent radical party, and articulate leadership — might well have raised a political force that was jealous of state power, fearful of the loss of power to the central government, and suspicious of a government so remote from the direct influence of the people. The materials were there; the mobilization was not.

To understand why this Antifederalist position never developed —
why, to use the language of Sherlock Holmes, "the dog did not bark"—
we need to look at the politics of New Jersey, past and present, and
at Clark's position within this political context. In doing so, we may
uncover some of the less obvious reasons why citizens of New Jersey
and others who may have preferred a less centralized or a more
democratic government accepted the new Constitution, whatever their
other misgivings.

THE POLITICAL CULTURE OF NEW JERSEY

First of all, we need to understand why the standard explanations
for the total absence of an Antifederalist opposition are inadequate.
New Jersey was far from homogeneous; it was, in fact, severely split
along an east-west axis, following a line from the northwest to the
southeast that corresponds roughly with today's so-called north-south
division. The differences were cultural, religious, and economic, as
well as political, and they were old and enduring. Indeed, as late as
the beginning of the eighteenth century, New Jersey had actually been
two different colonies, called East Jersey and West Jersey, which had
been settled in different ways by different folk and which were governed
independently.

East Jersey had been settled by New Englanders, as well as by people
from Holland, Belgium, Finland, France, Germany, Ireland, Scotland,
Sweden, and Wales.[8] Early on, the religions of the Puritans, Dutch
Reformed, Baptists, and Society of Friends all had significant pres-
ences, and later on, so did the Anglican Church. Diversity among
immigrants was encouraged and supported by a culture of mutual
tolerance and legal guarantees.[9]

West Jersey had begun as a small settlement of Swedes and a
somewhat larger and more significant one of Quakers. It was, in fact,
the first Quaker colony in America, antedating even Pennsylvania.[10]
Soon the population became more diverse, but West Jersey was still
far more homogeneous than East Jersey, remaining a Quaker
stronghold well into the eighteenth century. In general, it was easy
to own land in the West, and the proprietors, who were numerous,
were likely to live on their own land. Although East Jersey had, on
the average, smaller holdings, it was dominated by large and often

absentee landholders. Moreover, East Jersey had experienced long battles over land titles held by small farmers who had been caught in the middle of legal fights among the larger landholders. In contrast to the politically volatile east, the west was more stable, more deferential, and more conservative in its political culture.

Neither developed any great cities or ports, although far more of the population of East Jersey lived in towns with farm holdings outside the town; West Jersey was more uniformly rural. However, neither had a frontier or a hinterland. Indeed, one of the major factors in continuing the differing development of society, economy, and politics in the east and in the west was that the former depended economically and socially on New York City as its metropolitan center, whereas the latter depended on Philadelphia.[11]

The Revolutionary War had further divided the two parts of the state. Although there were differences within each area, West Jersey was far less enthusiastic about independence and the war. In the west, Loyalists and Quaker pacifists, both in and out of the legislature, were opposed. In the east, on the other hand, there was greater and more solid support, and eastern citizens provided greater loans and more men to the effort. The east also suffered great damage during the war, because the route between New York and Philadelphia was the scene of frequent action, coming to be nicknamed "the corridor of destruction."[12] The Quaker west not only loaned less money and sent fewer troops but also, coincidentally, was out of the line of most of the troop movements and the fighting. So, at the end of the war, there were significant political differences concerning taxes, the payment of Continental Congress and state debts, and the need for ready money for rebuilding. The west continued to be the stronghold of conservatives on such issues, while the east was developing a radical republican party.

This sharp sectional cleavage would dominate the politics of the period from 1776 to ratification. Jackson Turner Main has found that in New Jersey the major aligning division was not between "localists" and "cosmopolitans," as elsewhere, but between east and west, with two counties alternating between the sides.[13] Some well-to-do representatives from eastern districts did vote on occasion with the west, and a few delegates of moderate wealth in the west voted with the east.[14] But on the whole, it was the east that supported the more radical positions that favored the debtor class and paper money. Although the towns were in the east and, according to Main, should have been cosmopolitan, the eastern section was still the home of large numbers of small farmers. The west was far more rural and might have been predicted to be more localist in tendency, but politics was shaped there by the wealthy landowners and Quakers.[15] And of course there were no frontier districts in New Jersey; all farmers, whether large or small, were within reach of markets. This would suggest that all of New Jersey should have been "cosmopolitan," but it was not: New Jerseyites sent to their legislature few men of education or cosmopolitan outlook, whether from towns, commercial farming areas, or anywhere else.

What did matter was sectionalism. Throughout the decade of the 1780s, two de facto parties existed in the legislature—the parties of East Jersey and of West Jersey—each of which had considerable coherence and persistence.[16] A combination of past history, culture, including religion and mores, and economics had created sufficiently differing outlooks so that the citizens of the east and of the west consistently elected men of differing political ideologies.[17] Under these circumstances, there was no single political elite or leader to galvanize the state behind a single position. Instead, for many years there had been two rather stable groups of leaders competing. Consequently, if sectional loyalty was to be the cause or the excuse for differences over the Constitution, New Jersey ought to have been deeply divided, with the party of the east espousing the cause of Antifederalism. So the fact that there was no such division requires further explanation.

PARTICIPATORY POLITICS AND REPUBLICAN INSTITUTIONS

The New Jersey Constitution of 1776 established a state government that Thomas Paine would have approvingly called "simple," with the twin virtues that he sought: clear accountability and true responsiveness to the people. As was common in the new states, New Jersey had annual elections, which were held in the fall of each year. The Assembly was composed of three representatives from each of the thirteen counties; and the Council, of one from each. The governor was elected by both houses in a joint session, also annually, and had no power to veto legislation or to appoint officers. All power was firmly located in the legislature. Although it was not unicameral, both houses were elected from the same base, at the same time, and frequently enough to make the power of citizens at the polls a palpable reality. The executive had no independent powers and was fully accountable to the legislature on a regular basis. He might have influence, but he could hardly block a popular legislative majority. All of this contrasted dramatically to the carefully constructed complications of staggered elections, separation of powers, and the checks and balances that Madison and others had built into the new Constitution, hoping to insulate the proposed government from any potential majority or minority faction.

There was a not-so-democratic property requirement for representatives: five hundred pounds of real or personal property for assemblymen and one thousand pounds for councilmen.[18] Although this meant that all representatives had to be men of some property, in practice many middling farmers did serve, especially in the Assembly. Jackson Turner Main has found that from 1779 to 1788, the legislature was composed of some 45 percent farmers, while only 6 percent of large land owners, another 15 percent of professionals, and 14 percent of traders. Perhaps more significantly, he categorized the economic status of 33 percent as moderate, of 23 percent as substantial, and of only 35 percent as well-to-do or wealthy. Surprisingly, 23 percent came from noncommercial subsistence farms.[19]

Suffrage was considerably more inclusive, extending to all "inhabitants" of full age who were worth fifty pounds in either real or personal property. By the mid-1780s, this was the equivalent of approximately one pound in specie, an amount that effectively opened the vote to almost all male adults. Richard P. McCormick has calculated that other factors—such as the refusal of Quakers to take an oath, the remoteness of polling stations for many, especially in West Jersey (although by 1788 there were fifty polling places within the thirteen counties), the reluctance of the Dutch to become active politically, and the lack of organized campaigns—were more responsible for nonvoting than were legal restrictions.[20] Suffrage was so widespread that it even allowed a few women and blacks to vote, at least until 1807, when the word "inhabitants" was changed to "men."

The constitution was radically republican in other respects as well. The judiciary was dependent either on elected officials or on the people directly. The highest court of appeal consisted of the governor and the Council sitting together, and state judges were appointed by the Assembly and by the Council for short terms of five to seven years. Town meetings elected local constables, along with three or four citizens who were authorized to decide on appeals of unjust taxation.[21] In these ways, the people had a powerful direct and indirect involvement with judicial matters, thus making the enforcement of unpopular laws difficult. Of course, the legislature was as unchecked by the judiciary as by an executive.

The citizens of New Jersey also had a tradition of acting "out of doors"—that is, extralegally—which had blossomed during the movement toward independence and the Revolution itself. County Committees of Correspondence had formed in 1774 to protest the closing of the harbor of Boston and had met in July to elect representatives to the First Continental Congress.[22] These same extralegal committees then called for the Provincial Congress which first met in May 1775. This congress, in turn, although wholly extralegal, proceeded to raise taxes and a militia and to enact "a system of annual elections for members of the Provincial Congress, county committees, and township committees." In effect, according to McCormick, "a full-fledged state within a state had come into being."[23] By February 1776, the Provincial Congress was not only operating as a government, punishing those who opposed its authority, but also had changed the suffrage from only landowners to those who possessed fifty pounds of property, real or personal.[24] Thus, with one stroke, they had shifted the political foundations of the state, transforming the substantive meaning of "the people" in the principle that republican government must rest on the consent of the people.

Although the colony was deeply divided over declaring independence, the Provincial Congress that was elected in May 1776 had a clear majority in favor, and on June 22, it authorized the state's delegates to the Continental Congress to vote accordingly.[25] Even before that vote was taken, the Provincial Congress had created a committee to draw up a new constitution, which was reported back and passed into law on July 2. Although the new constitution still referred to New Jersey as a colony and although the Declaration of Independence had not yet been signed, the extralegal Provincial Congress constituted a wholly new government, explicitly overthrowing the royal government on the authority of nothing more than itself and the will of the people, as made known through the May election. As in other states at this time, the people of New Jersey on this occasion demonstrated an awesome self-confidence in their ability to act collectively, without benefit of constitutional checks and balances, a self-confidence in the robustness of democratic citizenship.

The most dramatic example of New Jersey's enduring understanding of republican citizenship lies in the two institutions of petition and nonbinding instructions. We have already noted that the citizens had moved quickly and easily in sending petitions to the state government to establish a constitutional ratifying convention. This continued the tradition of acting out of doors, although, given the lack of controversy, in a mild and nonthreatening manner.

However, the winter of 1785/86 was a different matter. Money—its availability, its reliability and stability—had been a problem in New Jersey, as in other states. Hard currency was scarce; New Jersey had neither ports to collect an impost nor western frontier lands to sell. Thus the state had to raise all money internally, from taxes. The Continental Congress, while requisitioning funds from the states, had been unable to meet even the interest on debts to its citizens. Although New Jersey continued to support the Continental Congress (some New Jerseyites wanted to strengthen its powers to include both raising an impost tax directly and controlling the sale of western lands), the state in 1783 decided to raise its tax quota but to keep it within its own hands, using it to pay off the interest on Continental debts owed to citizens of New Jersey.[26] With hard currency scarce and with previous paper largely recalled, citizens began to have difficulty paying either their taxes or their debts. Consequently, there grew a demand for a new issuance of paper money.

By the summer of 1784, several counties were petitioning the legislature for relief, and in that winter a motion to appoint a committee to bring in a plan failed by only two votes. However, in October 1785, candidates who were committed to the passage of a paper-money bill were elected. The Assembly moved immediately to establish a committee to bring in a bill, and the committee reported back within three weeks. No further action was taken, probably because it was understood that the Council would vote down any such plan.[27] Yet the winter of 1788 saw a rush of political activity. Although previously quiet on the matter, newspapers now printed articles in almost every issue, articulating the political positions of each side. As usual, the conservative side got greater exposure, with four articles against paper money appearing to every one for it.[28]

The people spoke in a different voice. During this same time and before the legislature reassembled in February 1786, the citizens had signed some 140 petitions, listing an amazing 10,217 names.[29] McCormick has estimated that the number of adult males of voting age was about 20,000 and has noted that the elections for the first U.S. Congress brought out an unusually high number of 14,000 voters, due largely to increased organization and electioneering.[30] In this context, the more than 10,000 signatures is extraordinarily high; it attests both to the importance of the issue and to the familiarity of the petition process. The petitions revealed a two-to-one majority for paper money and even showed strong support from the counties of the southwest, where representatives were solidly opposed to any paper-money plan.

On reassembling, the Council narrowly defeated the Assembly's proposal, but a reconsideration was called for May. Further petitions included a more formal one from the town meeting of Newark and from a meeting of delegates called from each ward of Essex County. Finally, a few votes in the Council swung, and the bill passed both houses.[31]

During the 1780s the citizens of New Jersey had petitioned their legislatures frequently on a variety of issues. They assumed this to be an important part of citizenship, considering it their right to tell their representatives what they collectively desired. They acted in semiformal groups, and they also acted through organized political bodies; in both, but particularly in the latter, they acted as a people constituting themselves for public discussion, rather than as individuals. Moreover, it was clear that representatives who defied their constituents in May could expect to be turned out of office the following October on any issue as important as that of paper money.

More than anything else, it was this capacity and habit of combining together to petition their legislature that breathed democratic life into the institutions of the state constitution. For it was this that formed the bond between an active, thinking, debating citizenry and their elected representatives. That bond was at the heart of their claim to self-government. Yet, in approving the new federal Constitution, New

Jerseyites seemed to be ready to compromise this time-honored practice of popular politics. To explain this seeming reversal, other factors must be considered.

ABRAHAM CLARK, RADICAL REPUBLICAN

In Abraham Clark, the party of the east had an articulate spokesman, who defended state sovereignty against encroachments from national power while he still was seeking an effective federal union.[32] While he was New Jersey's representative to the Continental Congress, Clark developed a complex position in defense of his conception of the people's liberties. It was a position that, in some senses, could be considered nationalistic (or, in Main's term, cosmopolitan) and, in others, localistic. He enthusiastically supported and signed the Declaration of Independence and understood the war to be a national effort. From the beginning, he sought to strengthen the Articles of Confederation by giving the Continental Congress an independent source of income. Speaking for New Jersey, he endorsed changes that would permit the national government to collect imposts on foreign goods, regulate foreign trade, and supervise and gain from the sale of the western lands.[33] Moreover, Clark urged New Jersey not to shirk its share of the war effort, either in raising money or in raising troops. Clark's leadership was especially important in the crucial early years of 1776 and 1777, when he served on the Council of the Provincial Congress, where there were others—particularly from the west—who opposed the war and were trying to thwart any efforts to support it.[34]

Although Clark thought the central government needed the resources and power to conduct the war, he also saw the states as independent on all internal matters. His particular concerns were to protect civil authority from encroachments by the military and to protect state authority from encroachments by the national government. Although his own home was sacked and although the British were on his state's soil, he meticulously maintained that certain constitutional limitations were crucial to liberty, lest the tyranny of Britain be merely replaced by tyranny at home.

In this regard, there were two areas that most concerned him. The first rested on the distinction between the Continental Army, which was voluntary and attracted recruits in part on the basis of pay, and the militia, which automatically included all male citizens between certain ages (depending on the state) and whose units were based on town and county musters. The latter, he argued, could not be commanded by any other than officers elected by the troops or, at the higher levels, by those appointed by the state. Particularly important to him was that state militias could not be commanded to fight outside the state by the army, the Congress, or George Washington himself, "without a Subvertion of all Liberty."[35] When the New Jersey militia was ordered into New York, he urged noncompliance. At the same time, he argued that the state's own officers could take the initiative, and in fact, he encouraged them to deploy their troops in support of neighboring states.

The second area concerned the various problems arising from having citizens trade with or actually ally themselves with the enemy. In one early instance, General Washington had issued procedures and penalties to apply to those who had collaborated with the British. Clark was outraged; he was alarmed at the threat to supersede similar procedures and penalties that various state legislatures had enacted.[36] Here, as in other cases, he urged national cooperation, but on the basis of the supremacy of state law and of the state's prerogative to police itself.

In these matters, Clark saw himself as defending the constitutional liberties for which the war was being fought—liberties that lay within the political bodies of the state and townships.[37] To override the actions of state legislatures constituted tyranny, because it would impose upon the people a power external to themselves and their representatives, thus replacing British tyranny with home-grown American tyranny. The Continental Congress needed enough independent power to assure cooperation among the states, especially on issues of trade in which states were clearly interdependent. The states were thusly dependent on each other and had a collective mission and a collective need to cooperate in order to secure the liberties of all Americans; nonetheless, it was the states, not the Congress, that housed the political power of the people.

Just why Clark located America's newly won liberty in the state governments, particularly in that of his own New Jersey, can be most clearly seen by looking at his words and deeds during the paper-money controversy of 1785/86, discussed above. Clark himself spearheaded

that successful drive. Elected to the Assembly in 1784, he had provided leadership on a number of bills to aid those who were most
in distress, by easing bankruptcy laws, simplifying legal procedures,
and seeking to increase the amount of legal tender in the state.[38] He
opposed a paper-money bill that would have been used directly to
pay interest on state debts because it would have aided the monied
men at the expense of the farmers. Instead, his bill made paper money
available to those seeking to borrow, in small amounts of twenty pounds
or more, with moderate interest of 6 percent and with a long-term
repayment plan of one-twentieth each year for twenty years. The
revenue collected from the interest would then be used for payment
of interest on the state debt. Thus, creditors too would benefit.[39]

The example of the paper-money bill suggests that Clark was by
no means a narrow factionalist; rather, he sought policies in the public
interest as defined by his radical-republican principles. Clark maintained that a republic had the positive duty to pursue policies that
would foster equality and prevent the growth of inequality. He saw
the distress of farmers and mechanics neither as their fault (the product of laziness, sloth, or inefficiency) nor as the unfortunate consequence of a neutral market. Rather, he believed that public policies
were at fault, along with the greed of the monied men and the lawyers,
who in differing ways preyed on those of moderate means, used advantage to gain advantage, and, still not satisfied, were "wishing for
greater power to grind the face of the needy."[40] High taxes and hard
money meant that those who were in debt could not pay their debts
and therefore were condemned to long and costly court procedures,
which often forced foreclosure and the sale of their farms for a frac-
tion of their value. As often as not, they ended in debtors' jail.[41] This
led, Clark observed, "to the breaking of families and increase of poverty, and to the promoting of that inequality of property which is
detrimental in a republican government."[42]

Positive policies promoting equality were therefore not only in the
public interest but also essential to the preservation of a republic. These
included laws dealing with bankruptcy, foreclosure, and mitigating
jail terms for those who could not pay their debts, laws that some
Federalists claimed violated their property rights. But Clark, unlike
those Federalists, did not see property as sacrosanct, nor did he see
all legislative efforts at regulation as factional tyranny. The creditor's

rights were created by the legislature: "It is only by their authority that the creditor can recover the payment of his debt." The authority of the people to act through their legislatures was fundamental and entire; the rights of property were secondary and derived from the acts of those legislatures. Consequently, rather than attempting to fragment and frustrate a potential majority, Clark sought ways to mobilize it, thereby empowering the people.[43]

Clark's understanding of republican citizenship can also be seen in his words and actions in support of the paper-money bill. In December 1785, Clark managed to bring a bill out of committee and onto the floor of the Assembly, where he then had it tabled, bringing it forward again in the February sitting. Although there is no written record concerning the matter, it seems likely that his intent was both to avoid a defeat in the Council and to allow time for the people to let their representatives in the Assembly and in the Council know their opinions. To what extent he actively organized the petition campaign is not known, but Clark did take the opportunity to defend his proposal in a series of articles in the *Political Intelligencer*. The essays, signed "Willing to Learn," appeared from December 14 to May 3. He expanded on his position in "The True Policy of New Jersey Defined," a pamphlet published in early February, just before the legislature reassembled.[44] In both places he urged the practice of petitioning and instructing, warning his supporters to get busy because "the opposite party, moneyed-men, merchants and lawyers are very industrious." He ended with a mild but effective threat to his opponents in the legislature, urging his followers to "use humble petitioning only and no doubt you may be heard." "If not" he wrote "our only remedy is the next election of representatives."[45]

Abraham Clark believed in the ability of average citizens to read and listen to arguments, to form an opinion, and then to organize themselves in order to make that opinion heard. Further, he thought it the representative's duty to heed the voice of the people: "No representative can act contrary thereto, without being guilty of a breach of trust, and playing the tyrant."[46] In the case of the paper-money bill, the theory worked. Although the Council, meeting in February, defeated the bill by a vote of 7 to 6, by May the Council had reversed its position, with Governor William Livingston (who was looking forward to his own reelection) leading the way. Clark, the people, and the practice of petitioning had been successful in convincing the legislature to reverse itself within less than a year.

If tyranny is a government that acts contrary to the wishes of the people, as Clark argued, then liberty required both that the people have ways of forming those wishes into public opinions and of expressing them and that they have instituted ways of effectively persuading their representatives to listen to them. Such liberty does not so much require that people be protected from bad government as that they be empowered to enact good self-government. This political liberty, the capacity of the people to act collectively—what Clark called "the people's liberty"—resided for him in the town meetings and the state government of New Jersey. It was not to be found in the proposed federal government. And yet Clark did not oppose ratification. Once again, the question is why?

"THE DOG THAT DID NOT BARK"

New Jersey was one of the five states that went to the stillborn Annapolis convention, and it was probably Abraham Clark himself who urged that a new convention be called with a mandate to go beyond questions of interstate commerce to "other important matters."[47] However, there is no evidence that Clark, or for that matter any representative of New Jersey, ever contemplated that the next convention, the one at Philadelphia, would pursue a total change in the form of government. According to even the most conservative voices in New Jersey, the Articles of Confederation needed strengthening, not abolishing. In fact, the New Jersey Plan, presented by William Paterson, embodied essentially the changes that Clark had been supporting for the previous ten years. Many predicted that as long as the states were given equal power somewhere within the new government, New Jersey would approve. "Give New Jersey an equal vote and she will dismiss her scruples," offered Charles Pinckney as early as June 16, 1787.[48] The cynics proved to be at least partially correct. Equal representation in the Senate may well have been sufficient for conservatives such as Paterson and Livingston, but it should not have been enough for Clark and his supporters.

In fact, following the Philadelphia convention, Abraham Clark was disappointed and apprehensive. During the summer of 1788, he put these misgivings to paper in a private letter, noting that he found the new government to be "more a Consolidated Government than a federal" and therefore "unnecessarily Oppressive, bearing too hard upon the liberties of the people."[49] Yet he never expressed these opinions in public, at least not during the ratification debates; nor did he develop them in anything more than these few cryptic comments. His long political career demonstrates his consistent devotion to defending local authority as the guardian of the people's liberty and his deep belief and faith in effective popular participation as the true substantiation of that liberty. But Clark stood silently by as New Jersey rushed to ratification. Why?

In effect, Clark was caught in a dilemma: he was seeking to create stronger federal power when it came to many economic issues, while still supporting state autonomy on most political matters. In broad strokes, supporters of the Constitution had offered two primary reasons for the new union. The first was economic, including the inability of Congress to raise funds and pay its debts; its incapacity to regulate trade; and its seeming unwillingness to make an equitable disposition of the benefits from the sale of western lands. The second set of reasons were political, centering on the growing concern with popular protest within the states. Shays's Rebellion, along with radical legislation in behalf of debtors, had led persons of property to seek protection by removing powers from the states and by locating them in the central government. Clark found himself in agreement with the new Constitution when it came to the first set of issues; but he remained opposed on the second.

Ultimately, Clark saw New Jersey as caught in the net of economic necessity. Without a port of its own, it depended on the ports of New York and Philadelphia. New York, in particular, raised much of its state revenue from the impost that it collected. New Jersey merchants and consumers, in effect, paid that impost without any benefit to their state. Considerable amount of specie also left the state in pursuit of foreign goods that came in from these ports. Therefore, New Jersey felt keenly the economic interdependence of the thirteen states, as well as its own disadvantage in attempting to stand alone.

At the same time, New Jersey had no western land claims and therefore no access to this ready source of revenue. Moreover, it held 10 percent of the national debt but had only 5 percent of the national population. Having shouldered a disproportionate share of the cost of the war, New Jersey was determined that lands that had been defended by all should be sold and settled for the benefit of all. The state had suffered extensive damage. In desperation, New Jerseyites had withheld their quota to the Congress in order to pay interest directly to their own citizens who held those debts. So they felt caught by extraordinary state costs, including a portion of the national debt; they had a paucity of resources and no direct share in what they perceived as national resources. As Clark had lamented in 1785: "New York and Pennsylvania can raise their Quota of species by State imposts, to which our Citizens by trading with them will contribute . . . , and after all will have the full Quota of this state to pay besides: This is a burden too unequal and grievous for this State to submit to."[50] Clark saw New Jersey's only recourse as the strengthening of the central government. Indeed, he had been fighting for a stronger economic union since 1778. Now that he had finally succeeded in securing a plan, it must have seemed to him absurd and a bit dangerous to oppose the only available alternative to the current disastrous situation.

In order to solve the economic problems of New Jersey, Clark was forced to accept a government that violated his long-cherished political principles, principles for which he had fought and suffered. In effect, Clark was willing to sacrifice political values on the altar of economic necessity. Yet it would be a gross mistake to describe Clark's position as merely self-interested. Obviously, in acquiescing to ratification, he was seeking, not his own economic interests, but those of the state as a whole. Moreover, what he sought for New Jersey was, not privilege or advantage, but economic justice. Only through union would New Jersey have a say in decisions that were then being made solely by the surrounding states.

Perhaps if Abraham Clark had glimpsed the extent to which federal power would come to eclipse local liberty and citizenship and the extent to which the shape of the economic community would come to be determined nationally, not by the state, he might have seen his choice more clearly as the bitter one between prosperity and liberty. If he had, he might have chosen to defend the people's political liberty against the encroachment of economic expediency, as he had once defended it against the invasion of military might.

NOTES

1. For background see *The Documentary History of the Ratification of the Constitution* (hereafter cited as *DHRC*), ed. Merrill Jensen, John P. Kaminski, Gaspare J. Saladino, et al., 8 vols. to date (Madison: State Historical Society of Wisconsin, 1976–), 3:117–97.

2. See *DHRC*, 3:183.

3. "Salem County Petition," October 1787, cited in *DHRC*, 3:137; see also 3:135–37 and 139–40.

4. Proceedings of the New Jersey Legislature, 30 October 1787, cited in *DHRC*, 3:169, 171.

5. From the *Trenton Mercury*, 25 December 1787, cited in *DHRC*, 3:183, 186.

6. Jackson Turner Main, *The Antifederalists: Critics of the Constitution, 1781–1788* (New York: W. W. Norton, 1961), p. 249.

7. Gordon S. Wood, *The Creation of the American Republic, 1776–1787* (Chapel Hill: University of North Carolina Press, 1969), pp. 562–64.

8. See Richard P. McCormick, *New Jersey from Colony to State, 1609–1789* (Newark: New Jersey Historical Society, 1981), p. 37.

9. See ibid., pp. 14–37.

10. See ibid., p. 38.

11. See ibid., pp. 24–35, 40–43, and 38–57; see also Richard P. McCormick, *Experiment in Independence: New Jersey in the Critical Period, 1781–1789* (New Brunswick, N.J.: Rutgers University Press, 1950), pp. 136–37.

12. See McCormick, *Experiment*, pp. 100–01.

13. See Jackson Turner Main, *Political Parties before the Constitution* (Chapel Hill: University of North Carolina Press, 1973), pp. 365–77.

14. See ibid., pp. 156–73.

15. See ibid.

16. See McCormick, *Experiment*, pp. 76–78.

17. See Main, *Political Parties*, pp. 166–73.

18. See Francis N. Thorpe, *Federal and State Constitutions*, 7 vols. (Washington, D.C.: Government Printing Office, 1909), 5:2594–96.

19. See Main, *Political Parties*, p. 159.

20. See McCormick, *Experiment*, pp. 87–89.

21. See Thorpe, *Federal and State Constitutions*, 5:2597.

22. See *DHRC*, 3:119.

23. McCormick, *New Jersey*, p. 116.

24. See ibid., p. 117.

25. See ibid., p. 118.

26. See ibid., pp. 177–78; see also *DHRC*, 3:122.

27. See McCormick, *New Jersey*, p. 193.

28. See ibid., p. 195.

29. See ibid., p. 198.

30. See Richard P. McCormick, *History of Voting in New Jersey* (New Brunswick, N.J.: Rutgers University Press, 1953), pp. 84–85.

31. See McCormick, *Experiment*, pp. 201–2.

32. See Ruth Bogin, *Abraham Clark and the Quest for Equality in the Revolutionary Era* (Teaneck, N.J.: Fairleigh Dickinson University Press, 1982); see also idem, "New Jersey's True Policy: The Radical Vision of Abraham Clark," *William and Mary Quarterly*, 3d ser. 35 (1978): 100–9.

33. See McCormick, *Experiment*, pp. 218–19; Bogin, *Abraham Clark*, p. 119; and *DHRC*, 3:222.

34. See Bogin, *Abraham Clark*, pp. 48–52.

35. Quoted ibid., p. 22.

36. See ibid., pp. 24–25.

37. See ibid., pp. 30–31.

38. Clark consistently defended the rights and interests of the farmers and mechanics, those in debt, and those struggling to survive, although he himself came from a successful farm family, his father having left enough land for farms for his son and two grandsons (see ibid., p. 164).

39. See ibid., pp. 87–117.

40. "A Fellow Citizen" [Clark], *The True Policy of New-Jersey, Defined* (Elizabethtown, N.J.: Shepard Kollock, 1786), p. 37.

41. See ibid., pp. 4–14.

42. See ibid., p. 11.

43. Clark, letter to the *Political Intelligencer*, 3 May 1786, quoted in Bogin, *Abraham Clark*, p. 105.

44. See Bogin, *Abraham Clark*, pp. 93–106.

45. "A Fellow Citizen," *True Policy*, p. 40.

46. Clark, letter to the *Political Intelligencer*, 25 January 1786, quoted in Bogin, *Abraham Clark*, p. 104.

47. See *DHRC*, 3:124.

48. Pinckney to the federal convention, cited in *DHRC*, 3:124–25.

49. Clark, letter to Sinnickson, 23 July 1788, cited in *DHRC*, 3:mcf.181; Clark, deposition, February 1789, cited in *DHRC*, 3:mcf.187.

50. Quoted in McCormick, *Experiment*, p. 237.

PART TWO

RESTORING STABILITY

4
GEORGIA
Searching for Security

EDWARD J. CASHIN

In Georgia, the Constitution was ratified with remarkable dispatch. By chance, the state legislature had been summoned to deal with pressing Indian problems at the same time that delegates William Pierce and William Few had returned to Georgia from Philadelphia with copies of the new Constitution. The assembly immediately called for elections to a state convention. On December 28, the convention met in Augusta and asked Governor George Mathews to send over the copy of the Constitution. The members spent only one day, December 29, in consideration of the document. After a Sunday adjournment, the delegates met on Monday, December thirty-first, and unanimously voted for ratification. The formal resolution was signed on January 2, 1788. Cannons fired thirteen salutes at the Statehouse, and Georgia's two newspapers proclaimed the happy tidings. Thus, Georgia became the fourth state to ratify. Only the distance from Philadelphia prevented an even earlier adoption.[1]

Relatively little can be learned about Georgia's reasons for ratifying by a perusal of the records. The notes of the ratification convention in Augusta were sketchy. Newspaper comment about the new Constitution was rare. Private correspondence touching on the question of ratification was almost nonexistent. In fact, it would be easy to conclude that Georgians were not interested enough or not sophisticated enough to pay much attention to the grand drama of 1787.

Such a conclusion would be wrong. If it was true that Georgians were not wholly attentive to the details of the new Constitution, it was because they were thoroughly involved in two other matters, both of which were threatening the security — in fact the very survival — of the state. The first was the revision of the state constitution, the topic of a decade-long debate; and the second was an Indian war, which was denying to Georgians the prize that they had fought for in the Revolution — namely, the occupation of western lands. The federal Constitution offered a convenient solution to both problems.

GEORGIA'S POLITICS: A BACKGROUND OF CONFLICT

To all appearances, Georgians were almost unanimously in favor of ratification. The only real critique of the Constitution appeared in the Savannah *Gazette* on November 15, 1787. The writer, who signed himself "A Georgian," liked the plan in general but was concerned about the tendency toward an "aristocratical" government. He wondered why the Articles of Confederation had not been retained and strengthened. Compared to the democratic promise of the Declaration of Independence, the new Constitution was "apostasy." Almost immediately, "A Georgian" was taken to task. Addressing his readers as "Friends and Federalists," "Demosthenes Minor" answered the objections point by point in the next issue, while heaping insults upon his victim. When "A Georgian" defended his right as a citizen to express his views, "Demosthenes" replied that "A Georgian" was probably not really a Georgian at all. So went the debate. "A Citizen" wished for more substance and less vituperation in the debate, but no more of either was forthcoming. The final note was sounded by "A Briton" on December 13, 1787, who confessed that he favored the Constitution so that he would no longer be defrauded by paper money. That was the end of public discussion on the subject.[2]

Not even in private correspondence was there real opposition to the Constitution. General Lachlan McIntosh did express misgivings to his friend John Wereat, president of the ratification convention. Concerned about the future of slavery under the proposed union, McIntosh suggested that Georgia try out the Constitution for a period of years before making a commitment to it. Yet McIntosh's letter indicates that even those who hesitated to enter the new union accepted the notion that the majority would rule. Nowhere in Georgia was there any sign of an overt Antifederal campaign.[3]

In fact, Georgians were eager suitors after union. But why they were so willing and why they were so united are not immediately evident. Were Georgians simply not interested in politics? Did they generally speak with one voice? An investigation of almost any one of the ten years preceding ratification would reveal an intense interest in political matters and an equally intense disposition to quarrel. The principal source of factionalism was intrastate sectionalism; the subject of debate was Georgia's Constitution of 1777.

Basic to an understanding of Georgia's internal dissensions is a knowledge of its geographical and demographical differences. Former Governor and Congressional delegate Edward Telfair wrote in 1789, "It is well known that a difference of interest prevails between the upper and lower parts of this state."[4] Sectional divisions were evident in debates concerning Indian policy, land sales, representation in the state assembly, taxation, the emission of paper money, the treatment of Loyalists, and the disposition of confiscated property. In a study of postwar politics, W. W. Abbot has concluded that "an understanding of the whole problem of sectionalism in the 1780's is absolutely essential for unraveling the still un-completed story of political developments in early Georgia."[5]

Georgia was shaped by a volcanic upheaval which formed the Appalachian Plateau and by an ancient ocean which reached to the edge of the plateau. The sand dunes formed by the erosion of the granite rock became a ridge of sandhills marking the fall line of the rivers when the ocean receded. The sedimentary rock of the coastal plain and the swamps of lower Georgia are souvenirs of the prehistoric ocean. The Savannah River rises in the North Carolina mountains and forms the boundary between Georgia and South Carolina. Georgia's first city, Savannah, is located near the mouth of the river. Augusta is situated one hundred twenty miles upriver at the fall line, the head of navigation.

From their origins in 1733 and 1736 respectively, Savannah and Augusta had different interests. Savannah was the link by sea with the mother country. Augusta was, in the words of Georgia's founder, James Edward Oglethorpe, the "Key of the Indian Countrey."[6] Thus, while Savannah looked eastward in search of a thriving mercantilist economy, Augusta looked westward, attempting to create of itself a commercial center for the back country. Yet both cities sought to stake some claim to the tremendous potential prosperity that lay in the west. The result was often conflict.

Throughout the Revolutionary period, the frontier dominated Georgia's politics. At the close of the French and Indian War in 1763, the back country was opened to settlement as far as the Ogeechee River, which roughly paralleled the Savannah River, forty or so miles to the west. Into this region poured thousands of rough newcomers who were more interested in the Indians' land than in their deerskins. The immigrants applauded Governor James Wright's acquisition of new lands in 1773 but were disappointed that he had failed to obtain the strip between the Ogeechee and the Oconee, the next river to the west. When the Creeks went on the warpath in 1774, the settlers hoped that the governor would take advantage of the opportunity to demand possession of the Oconee strip. While Savannah merchants protested the British policies during that summer, the frontiersmen declared their loyalty to the king, who afforded them protection. Yet because the hostilities ended without any concessions, the westerners concluded that the royal government was more partial to the interests of Indian trade than to the settlers' demand for land.[7] Thus the Indian haters of the back country joined the fierce patriots of the Midway district in a radical coalition that took control of the Revolutionary movement.

The handiwork of this frontier coalition was the Constitution of 1777, an embodiment of their democratic ideals. Georgia would be governed by a one-house legislature, which would elect the governor and his council and would appoint county judges as well as a chief justice, who would preside over the county courts in rotation. A controversial provision was the one that provided for the large number of ten representatives from each county. Liberty County, which included three former parishes, received two extra seats. The port cities of Savannah and Sunbury were allowed four and two seats respectively, "to represent their trade."[8] In tracing the rise of the "western members," Harvey H. Jackson has observed that the framers of the constitution were aware that the rapid population of the back country would mean new counties and more western members: "If prewar population patterns held true, and there is no reason to believe Whigs expected otherwise, the constitution of 1777 guaranteed that western members would shape Georgia's political future."[9]

The constitution provided for universal male suffrage, freedom of religion, freedom of the press, trial by jury, and various other rights. Schools were to be erected in each county at public expense. The church was disestablished and entail terminated without prolonged debate. Kenneth Coleman, a historian of the American Revolution in Georgia, has given the radicals credit: they had "overthrown the old order with its aristocratic checks and had established a new one without any checks. They had achieved their revolutionary victory and were ready to enjoy it."[10]

Savannah conservatives disliked the new charter from the moment it was written. John Wereat said that it was drawn up by a cabal of disreputable people "at a nightly meeting in a Tavern." Lachlan McIntosh thought that the framers were multiplying jobs for themselves: "Some I fear lust after the old flesh pott." Joseph Clay expressed concern that conservatives had "lost that influence they otherways wou'd have had and Rule and Government has got into the Hands of those whose ability or situation in Life does not entitle them to it." A Chatham County grand jury complained that there was "no Check on the Assembly." Radicals responded in the same spirit: when their champion, Button Gwinnett, was killed in a duel with General Lachlan McIntosh, Gwinnett's radical followers branded McIntosh and his relatives and friends as Tories and forced McIntosh to leave the state for military service in the north.[11]

The radicals made the most of their political ascendancy. They confiscated the property of Loyalists and enacted generous land-grant legislation. The conservative faction attempted to set aside the constitution in 1779 but failed. George Walton emerged as leader of the back-country party, and John Wereat was spokesman for the Savannah Whigs. By 1779, when both men claimed to be governor, Georgia's politics had been reduced to a state of protracted factional conflict.[12]

The end of hostilities with England failed to produce internal peace in Georgia. On the contrary, the back-country faction in the Assembly was inclined to be severe in its treatment of Loyalists. In 1778, 117 persons were declared guilty of treason, and their property was confiscated. In 1782 the Assembly enlarged the proscription list to include 277 persons, whose estates were used as security for the emission of

£2,000 in paper certificates. Confiscated property could be purchased on credit, with payment being extended over seven years. Many a poor patriot thus became a member of the landed class.[13]

Low-country leaders were more lenient toward repentent Tories. "I agree to forgive everyone now the war is at end," said John Wereat, who assisted Georgia Loyalists in obtaining compensation from Great Britain by evaluating their losses. Joseph Clay was opposed to the confiscation policy on economic grounds, because it was bad for business. He preferred speedy reconciliation and the resumption of trade with England.[14]

By contrast, the back-country leader George Walton was fierce in his opposition to the return of Loyalists and to the repayment of debts due to them. As chief justice, he ruled against a British merchant's right to collect a legitimate debt, regardless of the stipulations of the Treaty of Paris. A letter printed in the Savannah *Gazette* of May 13, 1784, criticized the decisions as being "totally destitute of legal or equitable support." Walton was quick to take up the pen, and under the name of "Brutus," he began a series of nine essays in his own defense. He also used the occasion to attack Governor John Houstoun, who, Walton claimed, had acted unconstitutionally by summoning the Assembly to meet in Savannah.[15]

Walton was answered by John Wereat, writing under the name "Modern Brutus." According to "Modern Brutus," the real reason behind Walton's attacks on Loyalists was that a Loyalist who had loaned Walton money had "had the unheard impudence to ask for repayment," while another had refused to grant Walton further credit in his store. Another writer accused Walton of being under "the most abject influence of party, or which is worse, having an abject party under his influence."[16]

A casualty of the Brutus controversy was the cause of the revision of the state constitution. George Walton had for some time supported revision. In a series of letters in the Savannah *Gazette*, he outlined his reasons. The one-house legislature, according to Walton, gave rise to "dissension, parties and feuds." The delegates were too easily swayed by oratory and factional loyalty. The architects of the Georgia constitution had spent only three weeks at their task, "God knows it was a hasty document." By comparison, it took Massachusetts three years to adopt a constitution. Although it was impolitic to say so in public,

Walton even implied that there were not enough men of ability to fill Georgia's oversized Assembly. Finally, he quoted gentlemen from other states who said flatly that Georgia had the worst constitution in the Union.[17]

Yet when Walton became convinced that Governor Houstoun was in favor of changing the constitution, he reversed himself, commenting that the time was not right for constitutional revision. Georgians had succeeded in repelling the arms of the enemy but not "the agency of their arts." Others agreed. One who wrote as a "Soldier of the Militia" took a belligerent stance: "My countrymen of the West will prove sufficiently prepared for every dark attempt of their private enemies in the cabinet."[18]

Having shelved revision of the state constitution, Walton took up the cause of revision of the national one. In the 1785 fall circuit, he urged that Georgia vote for an amendment giving the Confederation Congress the power to tax. In what seemed to be a factional reflex, a Savannah town meeting objected to the proposed amendment. There followed lengthy public discussion of the merits of the Articles of Confederation. "Agricola" argued that Congress was inadequate to do almost anything. A letter by "T.G." declared that it was obvious that Congress had too little power. Not trusting the back-country-dominated Assembly to suggest needed revisions, he preferred that a special convention be elected for the purpose. On the other hand, "Citizen" criticized the residents of Chatham County and Savannah who found fault with the Articles; in his opinion the national government was as strong as it should be. A "gentleman in the western country" defended the state legislature against its low-country critics.[19]

The low country had another reason to protest. On January 26, 1786, in the absence of the Chatham County members, the legislature had voted to hold its meetings in Augusta, rather than alternating between Savannah and Augusta. As soon as a statehouse could be built at Louisville on the Ogeechee frontier, the legislature would remove to that place. In the meantime, the house appropriated a sum to permit Governor Edward Telfair to transport the state records from Savannah.[20] When the Chatham magistrates refused to cooperate, Governor Telfair issued an order in council on March 17, suspending Chief Justice John Houstoun and eight assistant justices. The order declared that the "leading principles of the Constitution are infringed" and that anarchy would be the result of the court's failure to obey the legislature.[21]

John Houstoun had actually refused to accept the position of chief justice, but he was suspended anyhow. Houstoun declared that the order was nothing more than an act of vengeance. Had he been chief justice, he would have ignored the dismissal. The assistant justices received the thanks of the Chatham Grand Jury for continuing to hold court in spite of the suspension. All of the judges protested that the governor and the Council were deliberately fomenting partisan feelings between the upper and lower counties.[22] Nevertheless, William Few and Abraham Baldwin were retained to assist the attorney general in recovering the state records from Savannah.[23]

After the removal of the records, Chathamites were dealt a worse blow by the legislature. Because of a possible Indian war in 1786, the Assembly authorized the issue of £50,000 in paper bills of credit. The low-country delegates tried to trim the amount to £30,000 but failed. Chatham County residents were furious at the measure that they had so long dreaded. At a mass meeting, mechanics declared that they would not accept the paper. Two weeks later, on September 18, a county meeting was called. According to the *Georgia State Gazette* (Augusta), anger at the issue of paper money ran high. The Chatham Grand Jury joined the protest and denounced the root problem, the Constitution of 1777.[24]

By contrast, the grand juries of upcountry Burke and Richmond counties promised to support the currency. A meeting of Augusta merchants was held on December 2. Abraham Baldwin was named to a committee to bring in a set of resolutions. The committee's report stressed loyalty to the state and the importance of upholding the law. Every citizen was asked to "covenant and agree" to accept the paper money and to bring to the nearest magistrate the names of those who did not do so.[25]

In spite of the spirited declarations of support, paper money depreciated rapidly in 1787. The new governor, George Mathews, denounced "wicked and degenerate" counterfeiters. The Augusta merchants accused planters of refusing to accept paper at the agreed-upon rate of four dollars per hundred pounds of tobacco. The planters answered that they owed money outside the state, where Georgia money was not accepted. Furthermore, Savannah merchants refused the Georgia paper.[26]

CONFLICT OVER THE CONSTITUTION

The year 1787 was crucial, not only because Georgia's delegates helped to draft the federal Constitution, but because defenders of the state constitution agreed to amend that document. In January the legislature began the process in accordance with the method outlined in the constitution itself. The Committee on the State of the Republic was established by the Assembly. Joseph Habersham, Henry Osborne and William O'Bryan—three low-country critics of the constitution— were appointed. George Walton and Abraham Baldwin represented back-country interests on the committee. The committee recommended that the number of county representatives be diminished and the manner of electing the governor be changed. By a resolution of February 2, 1787, the counties were invited to submit petitions in regard to amendments.[27] The request for petitions sparked a year-long discussion in Georgia's two newspapers about constitutional matters. In the Augusta paper, "Curtius" warned that liberty was in danger because of the impending changes. "Cato" replied that revision was "unanimously wished for." "Philanthropos" argued that the preservation of public credit depended on constitutional revision. An Augusta merchant refused to take blame for the depreciation of paper money, pointing a finger at merchants, most of them from Savannah, who had been Loyalists during the war. An anonymous wit summarized all these comments by personifying a six-penny note:

> There's Curtius, the Merchant and good Mr. Cato
> And Grave Georgiensis, all reasoning like Plato
> My fame to establish great thanks to them all
> Perhaps I have stumbled, I hardly can fall
> . . . And now Mr. Printer observe my hard case
> Pray where is the cause of this paper disgrace?
> Would every man act as he ought in his station
> I'd ne'er fall a victim to d— —d speculation.[28]

The Savannah *Gazette* reflected the same intensity of interest in revision. "Philo Patriae" objected to giving the legislature control over the courts. He maintained that the courts were the only protection against creditors. Shays's Rebellion in Massachusetts was an object lesson in what happened when the legislature interfered in court business. "Antonius" and "A Soldier" urged people to sign the petitions being circulated. On the other hand, "Virginius" warned that by their signatures, "you are signing a death warrant to your liberty." To this, "A Soldier" answered, "Shall we say we know we have a bad constitution but are afraid to alter it lest we get a worse one?" After another exchange, the same writer uttered a thought that must have occurred to many Georgians, "If we don't take this chance of changing the Constitution, God knows whether the chance will ever happen again."[29]

Committee member Henry Osborne, who had succeeded Walton as chief justice, campaigned for revision in his circuit of the state. He urged the Richmond County Grand Jury to assist in the amending process: "Our Constitution from experience has been found defective, in consequence of which an alteration has been unanimously recommended by the legislature . . . Your approbation of so salutary a message will tend greatly to promote it."[30]

The same session of the assembly that elected delegates to the Philadelphia convention also launched the revision of the state constitution. In Georgia, there was a clear connection between the two. William Houstoun revealed his attitude when on July 16 the debate at the Philadelphia convention turned to the question of guaranteeing a republican form of government to each state. If this meant guaranteeing the present constitutions, Houstoun was against it. Georgia's constitution was "a very bad one," and he hoped it would be revised, not guaranteed.[31] The fact that they did not have to defend the status quo at home helps to explain the willingness of the Georgia delegates to adopt a new model government in Philadelphia.

Once the federal Constitution had been ratified on January 2, 1788, Georgians could get on with the real work of state reform. By then a majority of counties had returned petitions for revision as required by the state constitution. The Assembly authorized a state convention to be elected as soon as nine states had ratified the federal Constitution. The Assembly then proceeded to elect three delegates from each county to serve in the state convention. Eighteen of the thirty-three delegates had served in the convention that had ratified the federal Constitution.[32]

The state convention met in Augusta on November 4, 1788, and decided to adopt the federal Constitution as a model. As at Philadelphia, the issue of representation almost broke up the convention. The upper and lower counties disagreed sharply on the proper number of delegates from each county. The compromise that was reached was similar to the federal plan. Each county would have one vote in the Senate and from two to five in the House, depending on population.[33]

The governor's authority was greatly strengthened by the power to pardon and veto. Property qualifications for voting and holding office were increased. A seven-year residency requirement for citizenship was added. The new constitution was to be submitted to an elected convention in the same way that the federal Constitution was ratified.[34]

Predictably, there was more of a public reaction to the proposed state charter than there had been to the national one. In fact, criticisms that might have been directed at the new federal Constitution were aimed instead at the state constitution. "A Citizen" thought he discerned "an immoderate lust for aristocratical power." He disliked the property qualification for voting and argued that the seven-year clause would deter people from coming to Georgia. He objected to the bypassing of the old constitution and thought it was a poor excuse to say that the federal Constitution ignored the Articles of Confederation in the same way. "Examiner" accused "Citizen" of trying to alarm the ignorant. "Examiner" explained that drastic measures were necessary because of the deficiencies of the constitution and the failure of previous efforts to revise it. The seven-year wait was necessary in order for aliens to learn about democracy. "Citizen" was defended by an anonymous writer for his noble stand in defense of the former constitution in opposition to the "newfangled plan of government." Under the old charter, every white male person had a chance to become "a dignified character." He liked the large representation in the assembly, and he did not believe that annual elections of two hundred and fifty officials from governor to coroner were too often or too many. The new frame of government, concluded this writer, was part of a plot to establish "that horrid monster" aristocracy.[35]

The ratifying convention met on January 5, 1789, in order to accept or reject the constitution. Instead, it attempted to meet some of the objections by proposing eleven amendments. Property qualifications for holding office were lowered, and those for voting were removed. Yet the Constitution of 1789, with its heightened property qualifications and seven-year-residency requirements, its smaller House, and its stronger Senate, was a clear victory for the low country.[36]

GREAT EXPECTATIONS

From the Georgia perspective, the ratification of the federal Constitution was incidental to the decade-long debate about the proper kind of state government. The question that must be asked is, Why did the back-country defenders of the Constitution of 1777 yield to the low-country clamor for change? The answer lies in the lure of the west and the frustrated expectations of land-hungry Georgians. For if there was one theme that excited and united Georgians, it was the potential of the state's western lands.

Georgia was a virtual empire, stretching from the Savannah to the Mississippi rivers. Unlike the states with claims above the Ohio River, Georgia could not bring itself to give up this territory; not, at least, until some profit could be obtained from it. James Habersham, whose brother Joseph was a member of Congress in 1785, wrote a revealing letter to the exiled Loyalist Thomas Brown, then at St. Augustine, Florida, in which he confessed that Georgians intended to claim the free navigation of the Mississippi by negotiation with Spain if possible or by force if necessary. "The emigrations from the southern states to the waters of the Mississippi are incredible," he added. It was the policy of Congress to encourage this movement. If there were hostilities, "the Spanish and Indian commerce of the Eastern and Western branches of the river will amply repay for the loss of blood or toil in the conquest."[37] In a second letter, Habersham repeated that Georgians were migrating "in shoals" to the west, "the land of promise." These pioneers would constitute a ready army if the United States were obliged to use force to achieve its purposes.[38]

Georgia's interest in settling the west was not limited to covert tactics. When a resident of Natchez, in an early example of "manifest destiny," asked Georgia to establish a government in his district, the Assembly obliged by creating Bourbon County in 1785. The idea that the infant state of Georgia, whose settled area was confined to a forty-mile-wide strip between the Savannah and Ogeechee rivers, would extend its jurisdiction over an area five hundred miles away taxes credibility. Clearly, Georgians lacked the necessary means to oust the Spanish who were in actual occupation of Natchez. Yet Georgians did not lack imagination. This is why, during the Constitutional Convention, Gunning Bedford of Delaware was moved to exclaim: "Look at Georgia. Though a small State at present, she is actuated by the prospect of soon being a great one."[39]

Don Diego de Gardoqui protested Georgia's action to Secretary of Foreign Affairs John Jay. Even though Congress may have secretly encouraged Americans to migrate to Spanish-claimed territory, it was not willing to support Georgia's brash behavior. Congress officially disapproved any attempts by individuals to disturb good relations with Spain. If Georgia was disappointed that Congress did not share Georgia's enthusiasm for expansion, the state was actively annoyed by the proposed Jay-Gardoqui treaty of 1786. John Jay was willing to give up for a time the right of free navigation of the Mississippi in return for trade concessions from Spain. Maryland, Virginia, and the two Carolinas joined Georgia in successfully opposing the agreement. The incident caused Georgians to wonder if their western aspirations would be helped or hindered by Congress. It certainly made no sense to strengthen a union that would frustrate their own best interests.[40]

Ultimately, Georgia's attitude toward Congress depended upon the state's ability to settle lands much nearer than the Mississippi, specifically the strip between the Ogeechee and Oconee rivers. Georgians had vainly struggled for the territory since 1773, when the royal assembly had instructed Governor Sir James Wright to persuade the Creek Indians to cede the region. The Creeks had refused then and had been refusing ever since. Georgians fully expected to claim the area as part of their spoils of victory after the Revolution. In 1783, state leaders invited the Creek chiefs to Augusta to sign away the Oconee strip. Only two chiefs attended the conference and put their names to the treaty. Alexander McGillivray, the acknowledged spokesman for the Creek Nation, denounced the treaty. Nevertheless, Georgia fully intended to pay its war debts by disposing of the lands, and it proceeded to annex them, at least on paper, by establishing the new counties of Washington and Franklin. Until the Creeks permitted occupation of the region, certificates based on future land grants were to be issued and circulated as currency, the value of which varied in proportion to the likelihood of actually possessing the land.[41]

The Creeks were not about to surrender without a fight. Before the war, they had been brought to terms by curtailing their trade. Afterward, McGillivray had taken that weapon away by securing supplies from the trading house of Panton, Leslie and Company, a firm headed by British Loyalists that was based in Florida. In 1785, when the Congress appointed commissioners to treat with McGillivray, suspicious Georgians complained that it was interfering in the state's internal affairs. In fact, McGillivray would have preferred to deal with Congress, rather than with Georgia, but he was deterred from attending the meeting at Galphinton because of the Georgians' insistance on the Oconee as a precondition of negotiations. Only two chiefs appeared, and the congressional commissioners refused to meet with them. The Georgia delegates took advantage of the opportunity to sign another treaty, which repeated the terms of the Treaty of Augusta of 1783.[42]

In March 1786, McGillivray informed the governor of West Florida that Georgians were settling on the Oconee strip and that he intended to drive them away. The Indian raids that McGillivray let loose caused intense anxiety in Augusta. Governor Edward Telfair asked Virginia and South Carolina for help, and he directed Georgia's Indian agents to prevent the Cherokees, Choctaws, and Chickasaws from joining the Creeks. The Assembly, meeting in Augusta in July, was moved to unprecedented exertions. Seventeen forts were authorized along the Oconee, each to be garrisoned by thirty men. Another attempt would be made to lure McGillivray to the treaty table, and this time the commissioners would be escorted by a force of fifteen hundred militia, ready for a fight. These preparations were expensive, and Georgia had no choice but to authorize £50,000 in certificates, backed by the lands under dispute. This emission was repugnant to the low country but was essential to the people of the frontier.[43]

The Georgia commissioners invited McGillivray to a meeting at Shoulderbone Creek on the Oconee in October 1786 and warned him that the state was ready for war. McGillivray replied politely that the Georgians must renounce all pretension to the land under dispute and must draw back within the Ogeechee. McGillivray confided to his Spanish friends that he would not attend the meeting because he had learned that the Georgians meant to take hostages. He was right. A group of Lower Creeks went to the Shoulderbone camp and participated in the ritual repetition of the Treaties of Augusta and Galphinton. Six chiefs were taken back to Augusta as a guarantee that this treaty would be ratified by the rest of the tribe. McGillivray had no intention of agreeing, nor did he show any sympathy for the captive chiefs: "Their detention gives no Concern to us and their friends are Welcome to keep them as long as they chuse."[44]

The truce gave Congress an opportunity to intervene. On October 10, 1786, Congress named James White of North Carolina as Indian superintendent of the Southern District. In a statement of the obvious, it was noted that there was "reason to believe there are animosities between the Indian nations and the inhabitants of the frontiers of North Carolina and Georgia." White's assignment was to investigate the causes for the "uneasiness."[45] At a general conference of the Creeks at Coweta, he learned that the chiefs were overwhelmingly opposed to ceding Oconee and that they were threatening to renew the war if the hostages in Augusta were not released. White sent a request to Governor Mathews to let his captives go. McGillivray told White he was willing to swap the Oconee strip for Georgia territory south of the Altamaha River. White agreed to relay this information to Congress. Nothing came of it, and Indian raids were resumed in April 1787.[46]

The upshot was that Georgians blamed Congress for the new crisis. According to a special state committee, the cause of the hostilities was "the too sudden interference with the treaties of the state by which the minds of the Indians were perplexed and the impression induced that in a war with them they should not have the strength of the Union to fear."[47] In any case, the hostilities, which continued while Georgia's delegates were at work in Philadelphia and lasted into 1788, provided a constant irritant during the ratification of the federal Constitution and the adoption of the new state charter.

By the fall of 1787, Georgia seemed almost unable to defend itself. Even in the face of an Indian war, sectional differences remained evident. A Chatham grand jury handed down a recommendation on October 2, 1787, demanding an investigation to discover whether Indians or whites were the original aggressors. The jurors expressed sympathy for their fellow citizens on the frontier, but they had to "la-ment and execrate" the causes of the trouble; white aggressors should be punished if guilty. Needless to say, back-country Georgians had little use for this low-country notion of justice. Sectional enmity grew even greater.[48]

Having called a meeting of the assembly for September 20, 1787, to deal with the crisis, Governor George Mathews had become exasperated with the laggard low-country delegates who prevented a quorum from meeting. Congress could not help Georgia, whose own government was failing the state. "Such is the situation that we are engaged in a war without the means to prosecute it," he complained, "and a number of the members of the Assembly on this critical and alarming occasion decline rendering their Country any Service or discharging the trust reposed in them by their constituents."[49] A quorum was finally reached on October 18, 1787. The federal Constitution had been published in the Georgia newspapers only a few days earlier. The new charter, with its promise of a stronger, more active, more effective central government, must have seemed like a *deus ex machina* to the governor and legislators. Searching for some kind of security, they promptly called for elections of delegates to a ratifying convention.

THE PRICE OF UNION

The time had come to bury old antagonisms in the promise of a new order of things. It was symbolic that John Wereat, who presided over the convention that ratified the federal Constitution, served as a representative from back-country Richmond County. George Walton, acting as governor in 1789, urged the second state convention to bring the Georgia Constitution into conformity with the federal one. Old Georgians cooperated with new ones to effect the changes. Joseph Clay, one of the most persistent critics of the government under the Constitution of 1777, expressed the general optimism. The Indians, who were not afraid to attack Georgia alone, would be reluctant to engage in a war with George Washington's government. Clay hoped that "the restraining power of the Union" would also check Georgia's impetuous frontiersmen. Clay, the successful merchant, could already see beneficent changes: "The establishment of our new federal Constitution Produces the most happy effects, and gives energy to our laws and the utmost security to our Property and of course must tend to bring an increase in its value."[50]

It was too much to expect that the federal government would satisfy the conflicting interests of Georgians. The back country, in particular, was disillusioned by the Treaty of New York in 1790. Federal officials made much of Alexander McGillivray and the twenty-three chiefs who accompanied him to New York. But McGillivray's only concession was the long-contested Oconee strip. The United States government guaranteed the land west of the Oconee to the Creeks and promised to help the Indians become farmers instead of hunters. In response, Georgians were outraged against the federal government, as outraged as they had been against the royal government years before when Governor Wright had failed to obtain the same Oconee boundary. Believing that the Oconee lands were already theirs according to the Treaty of Augusta, they had expected more from the federal government. Even Joseph Clay, who doubted the validity of Georgia's claim to the Oconee, thought that the administration was wrong to accept McGillivray's assertions without listening to Georgia's claim: "The meanest wretch in the U. States is entitled to a hearing, much less a state."[51]

It could be argued that the back country, which was Federalist during the ratification process, became Antifederalist as the result of the Treaty of New York. As low-country leaders approved the treaty, sectionalism revived. Anthony Wayne sarcastically described the so-called New Creed of Chatham: "They believe in the late treaty with the Creeks—that they believe it to be proper, perfect and right and that implicit obedience and the profoundest respect ought to be paid to it by the people of Georgia."[52] William Few, who by 1791 was a United States senator, expressed the Antifederal position: "Already we begin to perceive the collision of the Government of the United States with that of the individual States, and I am sorry to observe that there are to be found too many public characters that wish to augment and extend the powers of the former over the ruins of the latter."[53]

Georgia's western land was a source of contention with the federal government in another context as well. In 1788, Georgia attempted to give to the United States a strip of land between the Chattahoochee and the Mississippi on the condition that Congress would assume Georgia's debts, which amounted to $171,428. Congress refused the offer because the land was claimed by Spain and was occupied by Indians. In 1789 the Georgia legislature sold 15.5 million acres of western land to three companies, the Virginia Yazoo, the Tennessee Yazoo, and the South Carolina Yazoo companies. When the companies attempted to pay for the land in depreciated Georgia currency, Georgia refused to deliver title to the land. The South Carolina Company brought a lawsuit against Georgia in the federal courts. What followed was a landmark in Constitutional history, when Georgia's refusal to pay any attention to a similar suit, based on a South Carolina citizen's attempt to regain confiscated Loyalist property in Georgia, led to the passage of the Eleventh Amendment to the United States Constitution.[54]

In 1795, after the Pinckney Treaty terminated Spain's claims to the Georgia territory above the 31st parallel, Georgia tried again to dispose of its western lands. This time as much as 50 million acres were sold for $500,000 to four companies. Legislators were bribed by being given stock in the companies. James Jackson resigned his seat in the United States Senate to return to Georgia and organize a reform party that gained control of the legislature in 1796 and repealed the Yazoo Act. Stockholders filed suit against Georgia, and eventually the United States Supreme Court, in another landmark case, *Fletcher v. Peck*, ruled that the repeal was a violation of the federal Constitution in that it impaired the original contract between the state and the Yazoo companies. By that time, 1811, the Yazoo affair was a national *cause célèbre*. It was of less immediate concern to Georgia, because the state had turned over its western lands and all legal entanglements to the United States in 1802.[55]

Still, the Yazoo Acts were only part of the mania for land speculation that coincided with Georgia's entry into the federal union. Under the Constitution of 1777 the land-grant policy had been directed at actual settlement; grants of more than one thousand acres were against the law. Although exceptions had been made prior to 1789, the exceptions became the rule in 1789. Governor George Walton in 1789 signed warrants for fifty thousand acres for one individual; Governor Edward Telfair signed away a hundred thousand acres to another. Governor George Mathews was even more generous in signing grants. Speculators did not scruple at improving plats where no land existed. Between 1789 and 1796, more than three times as much land was granted as existed in the entire state within the Indian line. After these bizarre manifestations of growing pains, Georgia settled down to a praiseworthy if pedestrian policy of land distribution by lottery.[56]

The Georgia experience seems to fit various interpretations of the ratification of the federal Constitution. To the historians of the Progressive Era who saw the ratification movement as a reaction by the creditor elite to democratic agrarian interests, Georgia is a case in point. At the same time, the anti-Beardians who deny that selfish personalty interests dominated the great convention can cite the fact that Georgia delegates were anything but the creditor elite. For the social historians who see the ratification process as a clash between aristocracy and democracy, Georgia offers some appropriate evidence. In short, Georgia is all things to historians, provided that they do not attempt to go into much detail.

Edward S. Corwin's interpretation of the movement to adopt the federal Constitution is perhaps the most apt explanation of the Georgia experience. Corwin has suggested that the desire to change the national government stemmed from dissatisfaction with state governments. More specifically, the pressure to amend the federal Constitution arose out of frustration with state constitutions.[57] In Georgia, there are ample citations to support this position. Pulled apart by the pressures of sectionalism and unable to act together, Georgians sought changes abroad, in their central government, in order to bring about changes at home.

Yet in Georgia there was another factor at work, one that was much more pervasive. Throughout the ratification period, Georgians found themselves seeking security. A poor and relatively weak state, but one with great expectations, Georgia saw the west as both threatening and promising. To secure it would be to secure Georgia, by protecting it from Indian invasions and by opening territories to further settlement. Thus, for Georgians, ratification was a search for security, not only freeing them from very immediate fears, but also opening to them vast new opportunities.

But general interpretations do not entirely explain Georgia's ratification. At some point, personalities are also important. Historians have given too little thought to the man who, more than any other, compelled Georgians to act. In his own way, the Creek chieftain Alexander McGillivray may well have been the most important promoter of the cause of the Constitution in Georgia.

NOTES

1. Julia M. Bland, *Proceedings and the Federal Constitution: Proceedings of the State Constitutional Convention, and Proceedings of the State Legislature with Respect to the Amendments Proposed by the United States Congress on September 25, 1789, March 4, 1794 and December 9, 1803* (Washington, D.C.: Government Printing Office, 1937), pp. 2–8; *The Documentary History of the Ratification of the Constitution*, ed. Merrill Jensen, John P. Kaminski, Gaspare J. Saladino, et al., 8 vols. to date (Madison: State Historical Society of Wisconsin, 1978), 3:269–84; "Material in the Georgia Department of Archives and History relating to the Ratification by Georgia of the U.S. Constitution," microfilm, Georgia Department of Archives and History, Atlanta.

2. *Gazette of the State of Georgia*, 12 October, 15, 22, and 29 November, 6 and 13 December 1787. This newspaper was printed in Savannah. The name of the Augusta newspaper was the *Georgia State Gazette or Independent Register*. In 1789 the name was changed to the *Augusta Chronicle and Gazette of the State*. "A Georgian's" critique has been called "one of the outstanding pieces of antifederal literature" by John Kaminski in "Controversy amid Consensus: The Adoption of the Federal Constitution in Georgia," *Georgia Historical Quarterly* (henceforth cited as *GHQ*) 58 (1974): 244–61.

3. McIntosh to Wereat, 17 December 1787, *The Papers of Lachlan McIntosh, 1774–1779*, ed. Lilla M. Hawes, Georgia Historical Society *Collections* (henceforth cited as GHS *Collections*) 12 (1957): 144–46; Harvey H. Jackson, *Lachlan McIntosh and the Politics of Revolutionary Georgia* (Athens: University of Georgia Press, 1979), 144-46. One author thought that he had discovered an Antifederal movement in Georgia led by a Judge Byron: see Lisle Abbott Rose, *Prologue to Democracy: The Federalists in the South, 1789–1800* (Lexington: University of Kentucky Press, 1968), p. 8. However, the source material that he cites describes events in Pennsylvania, not Georgia; see John Hannum to Anthony Wayne, 1 November 1787, Anthony Wayne Papers, William L. Clements Library, Ann Arbor, Michigan.

4. *Gazette of the State of Georgia*, 1 October 1789. Edward Telfair is identified as the author of a letter signed "A Planter" in the *Georgia State Gazette*, 9 August 1788, cited in *DHRC*, 3:307.

5. William W. Abbot, "The Structure of Politics in Georgia: 1782–1789," *William and Mary Quarterly*, 3d ser. 14 (1957): 59–60. Abbot goes on to say that sectionalism was "surprisingly unimportant" to his study of leadership in the state legislature.

6. Oglethorpe to the Trustees, 8 March 1739, GHS *Collections*, 3:68.

7. For a more detailed treatment of British policy regarding the Indian trade in Georgia see Edward J. Cashin, "Sowing the Wind: Governor Wright and the Georgia Backcountry on the Eve of the Revolution," in *Forty Years of Diversity*, ed. Harvey H. Jackson and Phinizy Spalding (Athens: University of Georgia Press, 1984), pp. 233–50.

8. Kenneth Coleman, *The American Revolution in Georgia, 1736–1789* (Athens: University of Georgia Press, 1958), pp. 79–84. The Constitution is printed in *Revolutionary Records of the State of Georgia* (henceforth cited as *RGG*), ed. Allen D. Candler, 3 vols. (Atlanta: Franklin Turner Co., 1908), 1:282–97.

9. Harvey H. Jackson, "The Rise of the Western Members," in *An Uncivil War: The Southern Backcountry during the American Revolution*, ed. Ronald Hoffman, Thad W. Tate, and Peter J. Albert (Charlottesville: University of Virginia Press, 1985), p. 298.

10. Coleman, *American Revolution in Georgia*, p. 84.

11. John Wereat to George Walton, 30 August 1777, GHS *Collections*, 12:66–74; Lachlan McIntosh to Walton, 15 December 1776, ibid., 12:23–24; Joseph Clay to Messrs. Bright and Pechin, 2 July 1777, ibid., 8:34–36; Alexander A. Lawrence, "General Lachlan McIntosh and His Suspension from Continental Command during the Revolution," *GHQ* 38 (1954): 101–41; George R. Lamplugh, "To Check and Discourage the Wicked and Designing: John Wereat and the Revolution in Georgia," *GHQ* 61 (1977): 295–307.

12. Edward J. Cashin, "'The Famous Colonel Wells': Factionalism in Revolutionary Georgia," *GHQ* 58 (Supplement 1974): 137–56.

13. *RRG*, 1:326–47, 3:59–61.

14. Robert S. Lambert, "The Confiscation of Loyalist Property in Georgia, 1782–1786," *William and Mary Quarterly*, 3d ser. 20 (1963): 89–90.

15. *Gazette of the State of Georgia*, 13 May, 15 July, and 9 September 1784; for a thorough treatment of the "Brutus" letters see Edwin C. Bridges, "George Walton: A Political Biography" (Ph.D. diss., University of Chicago, 1981), pp. 218–24.

16. *Gazette of the State of Georgia*, 2 September and 7 October 1784.

17. Ibid., 22 and 29 January and 5 February 1785.

18. Ibid., 18 November 1784 and 12 February 1785.

19. Bridges, "George Walton," p. 231; *Gazette of the State of Georgia*, 29 September, 6 and 13 October, 24 November, and 15 December 1785.

20. George Russell Lamplugh, "Politics on the Periphery: Factions and Parties in Georgia, 1776–1806" (Ph.D. diss. Emory University, 1973), pp. 150–51; Lucien E. Roberts, "Sectional Problems in Georgia during the Formative Period, 1776–1798," *GHQ* 18 (1934): 213; *Gazette of the State of Georgia*, 16 March 1786.

21. *Gazette of the State of Georgia*, 23 March and 13 April 1786.

22. Ibid., 13 April and 17 October 1786.

23. Ibid., 1 June 1786; Isaac Briggs boasted about his authorship of the "Laureat" piece in a letter to Joseph Thomas, 6 March 1786; he explained the sectional differences, "The U[pper] C[ounty] poeple [*sic*] say that the L[ower]

C[ounty] want to have everything as they please without paying taxes for the support of Government." ("Three Isaac Briggs Letters," ed. E. Merton Coulter, *GHQ* 12 [1928]: 177–84). Briggs decided to become an U.C. person, so he moved to Augusta, where he served as secretary of the ratification convention and, with William Longstreet, took out a patent to invent a steamboat.

24. Lamplugh, "Politics," pp. 168–69.

25. *Georgia State Gazette or Independent Register*, 2 and 9 December 1786 and 10 March 1787.

26. Ibid., 27 January and 10 March 1787.

27. John N. Shaeffer, "Georgia's 1789 Constitution: Was It Adopted in Defiance of the Constitutional Amending Process?" *GHQ* 61 (1977): 329–41. The author concludes that the proper amending process was followed and that contrary to standard accounts, the movement to ratify the federal Constitution delayed rather than accelerated the adoption of the new state document.

28. *Georgia State Gazette or Independent Register*, 3, 10, 24, and 31 March 1787.

29. *Gazette of the State of Georgia*, 5 March, 12 and 19 April, 3 May, 28 June, 5 July, 9 August, and 6 September 1787.

30. *Georgia State Gazette or Independent Register*, 2 June 1787.

31. *Notes of Debates in the Federal Convention*, ed. Adrienne Koch (Athens: Ohio University Press, 1966), p. 321.

32. "Journal of the General Assembly of Georgia," 2 January 1787 to 13 November 1788, pp. 229–67, 300, 393; Lamplugh, "Politics," pp. 194–99; Shaeffer, "Georgia's 1789 Constitution," pp. 335–36.

33. Shaeffer, "Georgia's 1789 Constitution," p. 337; *Gazette of the State of Georgia*, 1 October 1789.

34. Shaeffer, "Georgia's 1789 Constitution," pp. 338–40.

35. *Gazette of the State of Georgia*, 11 and 24 December 1788.

36. Coleman, *American Revolution in Georgia*, p. 273.

37. J.H. to Thomas Brown, 5 August 1785, in Thomas Brown to Vincente Manuel de Zespedes, 18 August 1785, East Florida Papers, microfilm, Florida State University Library, Gainesville.

38. The remark was quoted by Brown to Zespedes, 20 December 1785, ibid.

39. Koch, *Notes*, p. 229; for the creation of Bourbon County see "Journal of the House of Assembly of Georgia," 21 January 1784 to 15 August 1786, p. 174, Georgia Department of Archives and History, Atlanta; William Grayson to William Short, 15 June 1785, in *Letters of Members of the Continental Congress*, ed. Edmund C. Burnett, 8 vols. (Washington, D.C.: Carnegie Institution of Washington 1921–36; reprint Gloucester, Mass: Peter Smith, 1963), 8:141; Coleman, *American Revolution in Georgia*, pp. 261–64.

40. For Georgia's opposition to the Jay-Gardoqui treaty see James Monroe to the Governor of Virginia (Patrick Henry), 12 August 1786, in Burnett, *Letters*, 8:421–25.

41. For a review of Georgia's Indian policy see Randolph C. Downes, "Creek American Relations, 1782–1790," *GHQ* 21 (1937): 142–84.

42. McGillivray to Arturo O'Neill, 10 February 1786, in John Walton Caughey, *McGillivray of the Creeks* (Norman: University of Oklahoma Press, 1959), pp. 102–3; McGillivray reviewed events subsequent to the Treaty of 1783 in his letter to Estevan Miro, governor of Louisiana, 1 May 1786, ibid., pp. 106–10.

43. Coleman, *American Revolution in Georgia*, p. 244, McGillivray to O'Neill, 28 March 1786, in Caughey, *McGillivray*, pp. 104–6; Timothy Bernard to Telfair, 22 August 1786, in "The Unpublished Letters of Timothy Barnard, 1784–1820," ed. Louise Frederick Hays (Works Progress Administration Project 4541, 1939), Georgia Department of Archives and History.

44. McGillivray to Zespedes, 15 November 1786, the Georgia Commissioners to McGillivray, 15 August 1786, McGillivray to Habersham, 18 September 1786, McGillivray to Pedro Favrot, 8 November 1786 — all in Caughey, *McGillivray*, pp. 138–40, 129–31, 135–36.

45. *Georgia State Gazette or Independent Register*, 16 December 1786; *Gazette of the State of Georgia*, 15 February 1787; George Mathews to Daniel McMurphy, 14 February 1787, "Governor's Letter Book, October 20, 1786–May 31, 1789," Georgia Department of Archives and History, Atlanta.

46. McGillivray to O'Neill, 18 April 1787, and Charles McLatchy to John Leslie, 14 May 1787, in Caughey, *McGillivray*, pp. 149–52.

47. Report of the Committee respecting Indian Affairs, 23 January 1787, in "Journal of the General Assembly of Georgia, January 2, 1787–November 13, 1788," pp. 232–35, Georgia Department of Archives and History, Atlanta.

48. *Georgia State Gazette or Independent Register*, 3 November 1787.

49. George Mathews to William Pierce, 16 October 1787, "Governor's Letter Book, October 20, 1787–May 13, 1789," Georgia Department of Archives and History, Atlanta.

50. Clay to James Thomson, 24 April 1790, GHS *Collections*, 8:223–28.

51. Clay to Few, 5 November 1790, ibid., pp. 236–40. The historian E. Merton Coulter writes: "This treaty marked the entry into the heart of Georgia of a gall-like bitterness against the United States government which tinctured her relations with the Federal government in a deep and lasting way." (*Georgia: A Short History*, rev. ed. [Chapel Hill: University of North Carolina Press, 1960], p. 170).

52. Wayne, memorandum on the Old Georgians of Chatham, n.d., Wayne Papers, William L. Clements Library, Ann Arbor, Michigan.

53. Judson A. Dewar, "William Few and Georgia: A Biographical Perspective on the State's History" (Master's thesis, Georgia State College, 1968), p. 190. Abraham Baldwin served in the United States House of Representatives from 1789 until 1799 and thenceforth in the Senate until his death in 1807. He, too, assumed an Antifederal stance. See Patrick J. Furlong, "Abraham Baldwin: A Georgia Yankee as Old Congress-man," *GHQ* 56 (1972): 51–71.

54. *DHRC*, 3:285–90; *Georgia State Gazette or Independent Register*, 19 December 1789 and 20 March 1790.

55. Robert Watkins defended the Yazoo legislation in *Augusta Chronicle*, 7 February 1795; anti-Yazoo protests were printed in the same newspaper on 28 February and 14 March 1795; the repeal of the act is in the same, 27 February 1796. For complete treatment of the episode see S. G. McLendon, *History of the Public Domain of Georgia* (Atlanta: Foote & Davies Co., 1924), pp. 107–63; Lamplugh, "Politics," pp. 343–490; C. Peter Magrath, *Yazoo Law and Politics in the New Republic: The Case of Fletcher vs. Peck* (Providence, R.I.: Brown University Press, 1966).

56. McLendon, *History of the Public Domain*, pp. 40–64.

57. Edward S. Corwin, "The Progress of Constitutional Theory between the Declaration of Independence and the Meeting of the Philadelphia Convention," *American Historical Review* 30 (1925): 511–36.

5
CONNECTICUT
Achieving Consent and Assuring Control

Donald S. Lutz

On January 9, 1788, Connecticut became the fifth state to ratify the United States Constitution. The vote was 128 in favor, with 40 opposed. Not as lopsided as the unanimous votes recorded in the state ratifying conventions of Delaware and New Jersey the previous month, the vote in Connecticut nevertheless reflected what was virtually a foregone conclusion. Connecticut belonged to the Federalists.

Perhaps it is more accurate to say that the Connecticut elite belonged to the Federalists. All but a few of the most prominent politicians in the state supported ratification. The Congregational clergy were overwhelmingly in favor, and the ten major newspapers published in the state became virtual propaganda outlets for the Federalists. Economic elites had a strong commercial orientation, an interest that promised to be aided by a stronger national government. A matter of critical importance was that an existing factional split in state politics between agrarian and commercial interests did not extend into the elite; this permitted the state's political, social, and religious leaders to present a united front.[1]

Among the people at large, a general attitude of localism was perhaps the strongest and most relevant factor. On the one hand, this localism expressed itself in a general distrust of distant government. With a century and a half of virtual self-government, the people of Connecticut could be counted upon to view with deep suspicion anything that threatened local political control. During the war years this had led Connecticut to resist what was viewed as British encroachment on their freedom, to support the weak Articles of Confederation, and to be less than enthusiastic in providing the financial support that the national government required. On the other hand, local control of government meant that the people of Connecticut were overwhelmingly concerned with parochial rather than national issues. The price of nails or the construction of a weir was generally of greater account than events in Philadelphia.[2]

In effect, if changes at the national level did not threaten local government or impinge upon local issues, the natural suspicion of distant government would not be activated. The strong support by state leaders did not so much convince the people of Connecticut to support ratification of the Constitution as it reassured them that there was no cause for concern. Regardless of the formal arguments used, simply to hear or read a state leader's support of ratification conveyed the necessary reassurance. In the absence of a significant split in the leadership of the state and reassured by the elite's vigorous support for ratification, the people of Connecticut pursued their local interests and did not seriously challenge the proratification forces.

THE SOCIAL BACKGROUND OF CONNECTICUT POLITICS

To understand the process of ratification in Connecticut, one must appreciate certain features of the politics it had inherited from the past. When it became an independent state in 1776, Connecticut did not write a new constitution, as almost all the other states did. Rather, like Rhode Island, Connecticut readopted its colonial charter as a working constitution and simply deleted all references to the king. The Connecticut Charter of 1662, although it had been written in England and had been approved by the king, was essentially a ratification of the Fundamental Orders of Connecticut, which had been drawn up jointly by the colonists in the towns of Hartford, Windsor, and Wethersfield in 1639 in order to govern themselves. The readopted charter continued as the state's constitution until 1818, when it was replaced. The new constitution marked the demise of Federalist domination in Connecticut, but in 1788 that demise was still a full generation in the future. The era of Federalist domination from 1788 to 1818 essentially represented an extension of colonial politics, with the same institutions, practices, and influential families in place.[3]

This continuity is illustrated by the gubernatorial election of 1776. In most colonies throughout the colonial era, politics had centered around a struggle between the governor, who was appointed by the Crown, and the legislature, which was elected by the colonists. Rhode Island and Connecticut, however, as a result of their charters of 1663 and 1662 respectively, had governors who were elected by the people. The voters of Connecticut had ousted a Loyalist governor and four of his legislative supporters in the election of 1766 as an aftermath of the Stamp Act crisis—dramatic evidence that elections were an effective means of popular control. Thus, with the onset of the Revolution, Connecticut had a Patriot governor in office, Jonathan Trumbull. He was reelected in 1776 and became the only colonial governor to be retained in office after the outbreak of the Revolution. The extent to which continuity was the order of the day in Connecticut during this time of upheaval elsewhere in America is indicated by the fact that Trumbull's election by the legislature was unanimous.

The mere possibility that a statewide election could be unanimous reflects another important aspect of Connecticut's political system: the mode of elections. The Fundamental Orders established an electoral method whereby each town directly elected its "deputies," with three or four being elected by each town. These deputies, plus the "magistrates" and the governor, when meeting together, constituted the General Court, or legislature. The magistrates were elected by the deputies, and, in effect, so was the governor.[4]

Each voter was to write on a piece of paper the name of someone who he felt was best qualified to be governor. If no nominee received a majority of the votes cast, which was almost certain to happen, the legislature elected the governor from among those names that had in effect been placed in nomination by the electorate. On a statewide basis, there would be relatively few names prominent enough to occur to very many voters, and the requirement that the governor had to have served at least one term as a magistrate helped to ensure that only the most prominent persons statewide had a chance of being elected. The net effect of the electoral system was to place state government in the hands of the most prominent families and to allow these families to retain control. After 1787, because these families were overwhelmingly Federalist, this also meant continued control by Federalists.

During the colonial era there had been some grumbling about the electoral method, but Connecticut's so-called politics of deference prevented widespread discontent. The politics of deference referred to the colonial tendency to defer to the "better sort" in the running of government.[5] However, rule by the better sort had to be continually ratified by the broader population by means of elections, and Connecticut used elections promiscuously. Town officers were elected by the freemen; ministers, by their respective congregations; schoolmasters, by the school committees; inferior militia officers, by the privates; state officers (magistrates), by the deputies; and town representatives (deputies), by the freemen.

Nevertheless, the politics of deference, along with the mode of election, led to the elevation of a narrow cross section of the "better sort." Furthermore, there was an interlocking effect, because the winners at each level were often related by blood, social ties, or political commitments.

The centerpiece to this interlocking elite was the "Standing Order," which referred to the prominent Congregational clergy. Only about half of the churchgoing population in late-eighteenth-century Connecticut was Congregationalist, which amounted to about a third of the population, since one-third were unchurched. Still, the Congregationalists had been prominent in the original settling of both colonies that eventually became Connecticut, and most towns had one or two Congregational clergy who exercised considerable influence over town affairs. Although each congregation was essentially independent, the clergy coordinated their efforts at the state level and formed the "backbone" around which the interlocking elite was built.[6]

Alongside the clergy were the members of prominent families. Among these families, prominence was based in part upon wealth. More important was service, meaning membership on the town council or the board of selectmen. It was not considered unusual that in 1787 both state legislators from the town of Suffield were named Granger, both from Greenwich were Meads, and both from Norfolk were named Humphrey. When it came to marrying off their sons and daughters, these old and established families looked to others of the same standing, which not only produced strong ties among the few families of prominence in a given town, but also linked the establishments of different towns.

In 1787 the Connecticut House of Representatives had members from several different towns with the names Huntington, Wolcott, Wadsworth, Perkins, Parsons, Sherman, Trumbull, Fitch, Ingersoll, Pitkin, Phelps, Griswold, Hillhouse, and Eliott. Other prominent families in state politics included those of Richard Law, Joseph Platt Cooke, John Treadwell, William Samuel Johnson, William Williams, Eliphalet Dyer, and George Wyllys. Together these two dozen or so families—linked by marriage, education, social interaction, economic interests, and long commitment to service in Connecticut politics—dominated state government. From them were drawn, in 1787, virtually all members of the state executive and judicial branches, members of the governor's council (the upper house), members of Congress, and delegates to the Constitutional Convention.

These families were also in the habit of sending their sons to the best colleges, as befitted their social standing, which not only enhanced the level of social interaction among them but also helped to perpetuate their economic security. However, wealth, education, and high social status were not the key factors. One could identify perhaps three hundred families with similar characteristics of wealth, education, and social standing in one town or another. The real key was continuous service to the state through the holding of political office. Once elected to office, the person tended to stay on until old age or death, since the electoral system made it very difficult to unseat incumbents. Thus, the families to first offer service at the state level after 1639 tended to remain prominent in state politics; the number of families prominent in state politics grew only slowly over time; and together these families became a distinct minority of those with similar socioeconomic description. To cite one example, in 1712, Hezekiah Wyllys was elected secretary of the colony (secretary of state), and until 1810 this position was held continuously by him, his son, or his grandson.

By 1787, intermarriage had linked the two dozen family names mentioned earlier into effectively a dozen extended family networks. This "class within a class" was linked to the other several hundred families of similar description by the same ties of marriage, education, and social contacts; but it was distinguished by its "specialization," which was politics at the state level. In any case, Connecticut politics was dominated locally by two or three families out of several hundred of similar description to be found in the state and was dominated at the state level by one or two dozen families out of the three hundred.

The state was effectively ruled by this wealthy, educated, and politically responsible elite, but rule by this select few was underwritten by the general population. In general, the means for popular control were not so much absent as generally not used, although the removal of the governor and four magistrates in 1766 showed that the potential for popular control was in place. Also, in 1783 a "revolt" by the agrarian interest resulted in 60 percent of the legislature's being turned out of office. Yet the 1783 electoral revolt stands in sharp contrast to the civil disturbances in Massachusetts, where similar agrarian disaffection resulted in the courts' being shut down, and eventually led several years later to the armed insurrection known as Shays's Rebellion. The revolt in Connecticut made use of legal electoral means and clearly indicated that the marginal, or peripheral, parts of the state's population could still take advantage of the political process in a way that was not true in western Massachusetts.[7]

Reenforcing the effects of possible revolt by the freemen was a general attitude among those elected to seek the common good. This communitarian spirit was induced by religious belief, supported by the nature of life in small towns, and enforced by social pressure. Connecticut was not only quite homogeneous in the values held by its population; it was also geographically small. Thus, in addition to the threat of removal from office, no matter how distant, there was always the more immediate and real possibility of public disapprobation by one's neighbors. No elected official had to be reminded that regardless of his social rank or inclusion among the elite, a serious breach of public confidence could make for him a hell in a very small place.

The homogeneity in values was matched by economic homogeneity. There was a narrow range of economic interests to be served, and thus there was not as much difference between the rulers and the ruled as social distance might indicate. The most careful analysis of eighteenth-century Connecticut economics to date concludes that the state was composed primarily of the "middling sort," with relatively few that were wealthy or poor. As Jackson Turner Main has put it, the "poor or struggling folk on the tax list were for the most part not truly poor, certainly not permanently impoverished, but striving to reach a happier level at full maturity, and four out of five would succeed."[8] Also, most farmers in Connecticut produced a surplus and were export-oriented, thus creating natural ties of interest with mercantile interests.

Perhaps in no other state were economic interests so homogeneous, so middle class in orientation, and so strongly mercantilist. The nonexporting farmers on the state's economic and geographic periphery constituted a smaller percentage of the population than anywhere else in America. This general and widespread prosperity in Connecticut was a legacy from the War of Independence, when Connecticut had benefited by being able to provide a high percentage of the commodities needed by the American (and in some cases the British) armies, while not having to bear any of the destruction of war.[9]

Rule by the interlocking elite was thus generally benevolent. There is little evidence of an "us versus them" mentality, and those in office, to the extent that they pursued a common agenda, seemed to do so out of the dictates of similar background and values, rather than out of a self-conscious effort to serve their own ends as a class. Indeed, Shays's Rebellion probably failed to spill over into northern Connecticut because the legislature, with the blessings of commercial interests, had voted relief for indebted farmers well before the armed rebellion to the north had broken out. The agrarian faction was thus effectively included in the political process and was rewarded in public policy.

After the adoption of the Constitution and the transformation of those in office to a common defense of Federalist policies, the situation would change. The political elite, now thoroughly Federalist and tied to national politics, increasingly used patronage, legislation, and the electoral system to retain office for other Federalists in the face of an increasing challenge from more democratic elements in the population, especially when these elements coalesced around the Jeffersonians. As might be expected, the democratic impulse was stronger within the agrarian than within the commercial faction.[10] Still, this was in the future, and ratification took place in the context of the more benign political pattern inherited from colonial times. The ratification process revealed the extent to which Connecticut politics was a reasonably fair, consensually operated, and still largely closed shop.

Politics Prior to the Ratification Convention

Both before and after the Revolution, the legislature was the dominant force in Connecticut politics. The governor sat in the legislature and took an active part in proceedings, but his powers were not numerous. Nevertheless, the kind of man who was elevated to the office was guaranteed by the electoral system to be among the most prominent in the state, and the politics of deference, as well as the standing of such men within the interlocking elite, guaranteed that the governor would have considerable influence of a personal nature, if not formal political power.

As evidenced by the dimensions of his reelection in 1776, Jonathan Trumbull was both respected and widely popular, a dominating presence until health forced him to decline further service as governor in 1783. His valedictory speech to the General Court included an extended and forceful plea for strengthening the national government. When the legislature adopted a resolution to commend and thank Trumbull for his services, it was careful not to endorse his proposal for a stronger central government, acting out of what Trumbull later described as jealousy of national powers and resentment toward the Continental Congress over certain financial decisions it had made.[11] Still, Trumbull had made his point. A few months later, in 1784, the highly respected and influential Noah Webster had also argued in favor of a strengthened national government. Although these early efforts at persuasion had produced no obvious results, they demonstrate that leaders in Connecticut were beginning to rethink national government and that the elite was in the process of becoming Federalist in orientation.

Early in 1787, articles began to appear in the Connecticut press favoring the strengthening of national government, and at the spring meeting of the General Court, Governor Samuel Huntington quickly became an open advocate for such a position. Given the nature of Connecticut's interlocking elite and given the central position of the governor in the elite system, it is easy to believe that considerable discussion on the matter had been going on behind the scenes. Debate in the legislature over whether or not to send delegates to the Constitutional Convention revealed, at least initially, an almost even split that tended to follow commercial (Federalist) versus agrarian (Antifederalist) lines, although at least half of the legislators were undecided.

Opposition to sending delegates was headed by Amos Granger of Suffield and prominently included Hosea Humphrey of Norfolk and Daniel Perkins of Enfield. All three of their towns were located hard up against the Massachusetts border, and delegates from all three towns would later vote against the Constitution at the state's ratifying convention. After ratification, Noah Webster contended that the citizens of such remote towns had "rather indifferent" educations and lived in places "remote from the best opportunities of information." This may well have been the case, but as we shall see, Webster's characterization does not provide a complete explanation for opposition to the Constitution. Nevertheless, the arguments used by those who were in opposition at this point reflected considerable fear of a powerful central government that would endanger the liberties of the people. Their arguments also suggested that taking part in the process would implicitly obligate Connecticut to support whatever the majority at the Constitutional Convention decided.

In addition to those from Governor Huntington of Hartford, arguments in favor of sending delegates came from Thomas Seymour and Jeremiah Wadsworth of Hartford, Samuel Davenport of East Haven, Samuel Hopkins of Goshen, John Welton of Waterbury, and Charles Chauncey of New Haven. Delegates from all of these towns to the Connecticut ratification convention would vote for the Constitution. All of these towns were commercial centers and/or were situated on the major river arteries that served the commercial centers.[12]

Not surprisingly, those who favored sending delegates emphasized the flawed nature of the Articles of Confederation, the financial and commercial benefits to be gained from a stronger national government, and the need for greater protection against any foreign invasion of Connecticut. The debate was only beginning, but the geographical pattern, the division of interests, and the central arguments were already in evidence. However, most of the legislators were still unsure, and the early sentiment seemed to be evenly divided, although positions had not yet hardened.

Connecticut finally decided to send a delegation to the Constitutional Convention in Philadelphia, and the three men who composed it were a wonderful reflection of the legislature's state of mind at the moment. Political divisions within the legislature required that the background and politics of these three men be reassuring to both sides.[13] William Samuel Johnson, Oliver Ellsworth, and Erastus Wolcott were the three delegates first elected, but as Wolcott declined, Roger Sherman, in a fateful substitution, was elected in Wolcott's place.

According to the public record, Johnson did not at first favor calling the Constitutional Convention at all. His presence in the delegation had to be deeply reassuring to those who were suspicious of national power.

Ellsworth, by contrast, was on record as favoring the increase of national powers, especially with regard to taxation, and his presence must have been satisfying to the commercial legislative faction. Yet Ellsworth was not a relentless proponent of national power; he was on record as being deeply committed to preserving the identity, influence, and sovereignty of the several states while increasing the effectiveness of national government. That Ellsworth was originally from Windsor, a town in the midst of those communities in extreme north-central Connecticut that harbored great suspicion of distant government, may have helped allay some fears on the part of those who were not entirely in agreement with his tilt toward enhanced national power.

Roger Sherman, the swing vote, was one of the most highly regarded men in Connecticut. Having served prominently at all levels of government, Sherman was the kind of man to whom no one could object. He entered the Constitutional Convention a strong confederationist, yet his extensive national experience had also marked him as a man of national vision. No matter how strong his inclinations toward state sovereignty, it was unlikely that he would abandon the needs of national government for which he had so long labored. Sherman's reputation was enhanced even more at the Constitutional Convention, where he instigated the famous Connecticut Compromise, the inspired innovation that broke a major deadlock, formed the core design for the national Congress, and neatly balanced state and national interests. Of enormous benefit to the Federalist cause was the fact that Sherman, who had widely been regarded as a strong defender of state power, would return to Connecticut a staunch supporter of the Constitution to which he had so heavily contributed (and to which he would thus be considerably attached) and would play a key role in Connecticut's ratification process.

MASSIVE REASSURANCES

Sherman and Ellsworth conveyed a printed copy of the proposed Constitution to Governor Huntington, so that he might lay it before the legislature; and in private correspondence, they urged him to vigorously support its ratification. They also turned to the only medium available for reaching the people at large — the newspapers. Sherman wrote five newspaper essays between September 28, 1787, and the convening of Connecticut's ratifying convention on January 4, 1788. Ellsworth anonymously wrote nine essays under the title "Letters of a Landholder."

Sherman's pieces were not eloquent; rather, they were comprehensive, learned, and most importantly, bore his name. The clear, unwavering support for ratification by a man whose considerable public reputation rested upon his earlier Confederationist stance and upon his pro-Connecticut activities at the national level helped disarm the anxieties among many local leaders. Sherman's reassurances about state representation in the Senate, an institution that he could in truth say he had personally designed in order to protect state interests, carried considerable weight.[14]

Ellsworth's essays, on the other hand, were plain, direct, and practical; they possessed a rhetorical power born of simplicity and passion. Purportedly written by a farmer and addressed to farmers, and thus designed to appeal to agrarian interests, Ellsworth's essays were widely reprinted not only in Connecticut but also in newspapers from New Hampshire to Maryland. It was not uncommon for newspapers simply to reprint items from other papers without attribution, as if written for their paper in the original, and the popularity of Ellsworth's style led his pieces to reach a wide audience.

Nor were these the only two who wrote essays. Connecticut newspapers suddenly found a great deal of news concerning the proposed Constitution, almost all of it positive. The text of the Constitution was printed in full on October 1 by the *Connecticut Courant* (Hartford), which used in its heading the biggest type ever seen in Connecticut newspapers, along with the widely trumpeted news that the state delegations at the Constitutional Convention had voted unanimously in favor of the document. Every petition and letter in favor of ratification was reported, including those in other states. The reporting had all the earmarks of a public-relations effort designed to produce a bandwagon effect.

The New Haven town meeting voted to ask its representatives in the legislature to move speedily on constituting a ratification convention. It was reported that at the recent assembly of the Congregational clergy, virtually everyone had favored the Constitution. The papers reported in detail on Pennsylvania's ratification, and then on the unanimous ratifications in Delaware and New Jersey. October, November, and December saw a drumbeat of positive news on ratification. At the end of October the state legislature voted unanimously to call a ratifying convention, which loosed a spate of letters in support of ratification. It is difficult to imagine a more sustained effort by the media to report the news on an issue, and almost all of it was on one side.

A few essays by Antifederalists were printed, with the *Middlesex Gazette* coming closest to something resembling a balanced presentation. Yet the reporting was so insistent and one-sided that complaints were heard, and at least one newspaper was led to twice print denials that it was biased. The *Middlesex Gazette* alone kept a semblance of balance by publishing several pieces objecting to the proposed Constitution, although this "balance" was only by comparison with the other Connecticut newspapers. In fact, the *Gazette* published a dozen pro-Federalist articles for every one in opposition.

How important were these newspapers in the ratification effort? They were the only medium of political expression that could reach the general public, except for sermons by the clergy. Americans, including those in Connecticut, had been conditioned since the early 1760s to use newspapers as their primary vehicle for political organization. There could have been no American Revolution without the prominent, consistent, and persistent efforts by the clergy and by newspaper editors. Between 1760 and 1790, Americans came to expect the operation of an unfettered press as a bulwark of freedom, and they used the press as an important means for their organizing "out of doors." During ratification, the power of the press persisted and, if anything, grew greater. Ten papers were published in Connecticut; only the two northeastern counties of Tolland and Windham were without at least one. Ninety-eight towns in Connecticut elected a total of 168 voting delegates to the ratification convention. If we array their votes by county and if we note the distribution of papers by county, we find that all fourteen delegates from the seven towns with newspapers voted in favor of ratification. Furthermore, there was a rough correlation between the relative ease that the Federalist newspapers had in covering a county and the level of support that the county gave for ratification. New London County (100 percent of its delegates voted for ratification) was the easiest to blanket, because there were only eleven towns to cover and because the two newspapers neatly bracketed those towns geographically, each paper having to cover only five or six towns. Middlesex County (100 percent for ratification) had one newspaper for six towns. Fairfield County (100 percent) had one newspaper for ten towns. Hartford County (78 percent) had two newspapers for fifteen towns, but unlike New London, here the two newspapers were in the same location. Litchfield County (69 percent) had one newspaper for twenty towns; Tolland County (69 percent) had no newspaper for its nine towns, although four of Tolland's towns were effectively served by papers in neighboring counties. And Windham (68 percent) had no newspaper to serve its thirteen towns (four of Windham's towns were also served by papers in neighboring counties).

In general, the relative impact of Federalist newspapers seems to have been a function of two factors: (1) the ratio of towns to newspapers and (2) the geographical distance between the towns served and the location of the newspaper. The one clear exception to this pattern was New Haven County (43 percent). There, three newspapers served twelve towns, yet the delegates from seven of these towns (Wallingford, Durham, Branford, Guilford, East Haven, North Haven, and Woodridge) cast their ballots against ratification, and the two delegates from Cheshire split. Only New Haven, Milford, Derby, and Waterbury voted in favor of ratification. These last towns, by far the largest in the county, contained almost a majority of its voters. They were also the largest mercantile centers in Connecticut.

Twenty-three of the negative votes came from towns sprinkled along the northern border of Connecticut, especially in the center. Towns within fifteen miles of the Massachusetts border were about as likely to vote against ratification as for it. Put another way, the twenty-four towns closest to the Massachusetts border voted against ratification at twice the state-wide average. These towns were relatively small, isolated, and educationally backward.[15]

Of the remaining seventeen negative votes, thirteen came from New Haven County. These delegates hailed from towns of middling size, which were culturally and educationally advanced and some of which were engaged in commerce, although not on the same scale as the river towns. For example, modest-sized ocean-going ships were built in Guilford's small but safe harbor. The rejection of the Constitution by these towns will require further explanation, because it runs contrary to our expectations.

Except for those towns within fifteen miles of the Massachusetts border and those in New Haven County, only three delegates out of the remaining ninety-one failed to support ratification. The negative votes of the northern border towns, and to a certain extent those from Hebron and Lebanon, can be explained by the absence of connections to the commercial benefits to be had from a stronger central government, by the strength of the local agrarian faction, and by their distance from the Federalist newspapers that conveyed the reassurances of the state leadership. But how can we account for New Haven County?

ANOMALOUS NEW HAVEN COUNTY

For much of the seventeenth century there had been two clusters of settlements in Connecticut, one tied to Hartford, the other to New Haven. Each had developed independently, each was based upon somewhat different political values, and each operated under separate documents of political foundation. By 1662 there were over a dozen towns associated with Hartford in what was known as the colony of Connecticut. These towns included Windsor, Wethersfield, Saybrook, New London, Fairfield, and Norwalk, as well as East Hampton and Southampton on Long Island. The colony of New Haven by 1662 included Milford, Guilford, Branford, and Stamford, plus Southold on Long Island. This meant that the colony of New Haven was surrounded on three sides by Connecticut, and except for the south-central section of Connecticut which formed the colony of New Haven, all the rest of what constitutes the present-day state belonged to the colony of Connecticut.

Neither New Haven nor Connecticut had legal standing in England as colonies, and the restoration of Charles II in 1660 was threatening to both. The civil strife during the Commonwealth era in England had left the colonies without much support or direction, but it had also left them free to run their own governments in Connecticut and New Haven. The restoration of order in England threatened to end this virtual independence. Connecticut sent its governor, John Winthrop, Jr., to negotiate a charter in London. His efforts were wildly successful. Not only did the Charter of 1662 ratify and underwrite the colonial government established by the Fundamental Orders of 1639, it also merged the colonies of New Haven and Connecticut under the Connecticut government. New Haven Colony had a much more restrictive religious basis to its government and culture, so it bitterly resisted joining Connecticut. When it became apparent, however, that the choice was between absorption by Connecticut or by the state of New York, New Haven chose Connecticut. The towns on Long Island were ceded to New York in exchange for a general border settlement.

Thus the colony of New Haven became the county of New Haven within Connecticut. It was the most conservative portion of the united colony, and it was something of an outsider for many years in colonial and state politics. Even though Hartford and New Haven were joint capitals from 1701 to 1784, the governorship was dominated by Hartford for more than a century after unification. The two governors who led Connecticut politics from 1774 until after the ratification of the Constitution, Governors Trumbull and Huntington, both came from Hartford.

The Congregational Church became the established church in Connecticut by the Saybrook Platform of 1708, a move highly satisfactory to the more conservative clergy in New Haven County; but the Great Awakening during the 1730s split the Congregational clergy into orthodox and liberal factions. Orthodox New Haven County found itself surrounded by strong liberal, or "new light," sentiment, both on its east and on its west. Indeed, even within the town of New Haven itself, which was becoming the largest industrial and commercial center in the state, the seminary at Yale had drifted significantly from the old New Haven orthodoxy.

Just how religiously conservative New Haven County was compared to the rest of the state can be illustrated by the figures for church affiliation. New Haven County had the highest percentage of Congregationalists (60% versus 40% statewide), as well as the highest percentage of Episcopalians (30% versus 15% statewide).[16] Estimates at the time consistently showed that other denominations together almost equaled Congregationalists in number, with about a third of the population unchurched; but Congregationalism was still the established church in Connecticut. The Toleration Act of 1784 had somewhat reduced the privileges of Congregationalism, but the Standing Order was essentially intact. Episcopalians were drawn from the most educated and financially secure segments of the population, and they harbored some of the most conservative tendencies, including the remnants of Toryism. For almost three decades, Baptists had been the most consistently reform-minded and nationalist-oriented sect, but they comprised only about 5 percent of those who were churched in New Haven County, as opposed to almost 20 precent statewide. Finally, the more radical denominations, such as the Independents, Quakers, and Universalists, came to 0.5 percent in New Haven County, compared to approximately 8 percent statewide.

New Haven County was, as far as religion is concerned, the most conservative, least diverse, and most provincial part of Connecticut. When one excludes the more cosmopolitan and diverse towns of New Haven, Derby, and Waterbury, the rest of New Haven County was exceedingly conservative — the faithful heir of the old New Haven Colony in both its society and its politics. Although the distinction should not be pushed too far, New Haven County found itself in 1787 a somewhat isolated remnant of a way of life that had once defined a distinct colony. Politically it was outvoted seven to one in the legislature; the governor invariably came from elsewhere; and to the extent that the clergy were involved in the Standing Order, those from New Haven County outside the town of New Haven found themselves fighting a rear-guard action against the more liberal elements of the church. The towns of former New Haven Colony could not win, but they could cast their votes against the recommendation of a state leadership that was at odds with their values and indifferent to their local elites.

Therefore, most of New Haven County found itself ideologically on the periphery of the state's political system. In every other respect the towns of New Haven County had the characteristics of strongly pro-Constitution towns. The tendency toward localism that might have led to negative ratification votes elsewhere in Connecticut was prevented from arising by the reassurances of the state leadership. The same tendency in New Haven County could not be so countered, because its localism was to a certain extent a reaction against the state government as well as the national government. Reassurances by state officials were, instead, unsettling in much of New Haven County.

THE RATIFICATION CONVENTION

Consider the situation of Connecticut voters as they set out to elect delegates to the ratifying convention. The state's leaders, including most of the legislature, had been unified in supporting ratification. Almost everything they had been reading in the newspapers was pro-ratification. Events in other states, especially as reported by the newspapers, indicated a surge in favor of the proposed Constitution. When coupled with events in their own state, at least a mild band-wagon psychology had to be present in many voters' minds. In most parts of the state, those who attended church on Sunday would be exposed to lobbying by the clergy in favor of ratification. Arguments from every quarter promised economic benefits and soothed the innate suspicion of distant government. In addition, those who resided in towns along the borders with Rhode Island and New York had a further incentive to elect proratification delegates.

The Rhode Island problem was acute. In October 1786, that state had passed a law stating that either other states must accept its paper money as payment of Rhode Island's debts or the people of Rhode Island would not pay their debts at all. Rhode Island law at the same time prohibited people from other states from paying Rhode Island creditors with paper money. This was one of several aspects of Rhode Island's behavior that irritated the people of Connecticut, and the irritations fell most heavily upon the people of New London County. Proponents of the Constitution argued that such economic shenanigans would not be permitted if ratification were to take place, an argument that hit home with special force in the valleys of the Thames and Quinebaug rivers. When Rhode Island let it be known early on that it would not even call a ratification convention, Connecticut papers treated the news with scorn. Rhode Islanders were used as models of the kind of people who opposed ratification, and Rhode Island had few apologists in Connecticut in the best of times. Representatives for every single town along the Rhode Island border voted in favor of ratification. In its own way, Rhode Island contributed to Connecticut's ratification of the Constitution.

On the other side of the state, New York presented another problem, in that it was indirectly taxing imports through a state import tax, or "impost." This impost hit Connecticut exports especially hard: newspapers estimated that the people of Connecticut were paying between $40,000 and $60,000 a year into New York State's coffers. By giving the power to pass taxes on imports to the national government, each state's burden would be equalized, and Connecticut would no longer be disadvantaged in the import/export competition. This argument was received warmly in all the towns along the seacoast and major rivers, but nowhere more so than in Fairfield County, which bordered New York and Long Island Sound. As was true in New London County on the other side of the state, every single delegate from Fairfield County voted for ratification in a straightforward demonstration of their constituents' prejudices and interests, and delegates from only one town bordering New York State failed to vote in favor of ratification.

It was no wonder, then, that the overwhelming majority of delegates were proratification. The membership of the convention included the incumbents of the highest offices, as well as many of those who had held the same offices earlier. There were many judges of the courts and ministers of the gospel. The list of those who voted for the Constitution read like a "who's who" of Connecticut. Ellsworth, Sherman, and Johnson, the three men sent to Philadelphia to represent Connecticut at the Constitutional Convention, were also elected to the state ratifying convention. All three spoke in favor of ratification, with Ellsworth being especially active and eloquent. Governor Huntington voted in favor, as did two other members of the prominent Huntington family. Indeed, lest anyone doubt the position of the state's leadership, the last three speakers on the final day of debate were the governor, Lieutenant Governor Oliver Wolcott, and Richard Law, chief justice of the Connecticut Supreme Court. They were all in favor.[17]

The ratification struggle in Connecticut was both an extension of normal politics from the past and a watershed for state politics. Proceeding under the political system that had been inherited largely intact from the late 1630s, the people of Connecticut used their institutions of popular consent to ratify what state elites told them was in their best interests. Most citizens tended to be parochial in their outlook, and to the extent they became interested in the ratification issue at all, it was in terms of how ratification would affect local issues such as Rhode Island's use of paper money in the eastern states, New York's treatment of Connecticut exports, and the like. The broader national issues were raised during the ratification debate, but these issues did not excite the passions nor engage the attention of more than a relative few.

At the same time, the ratification process realigned state political factions. During the 1770s and 1780s the Connecticut legislature had an agrarian faction and a commercial faction of almost equal size, but about half the legislators did not belong to either. With a fairly uniform population in respect to ethnicity (English stock), widespread land ownership, no serious seaboard/back-country conflict, and probably the lowest percentages of extremely rich and extremely poor to be found in any state, the bitterness that was often found in state politics elsewhere was largely missing in Connecticut. When the legislature was first asked to send a delegation to the Constitutional Convention, its response was typical. Members of one faction favored sending a delegation, about as many were opposed, and about half had no apparent opinion.

By the time Connecticut ratified the Constitution, a political realignment had taken place. A majority coalition had been forged, and this coalition thought of itself as Federalist. The three-to-one ratio in favor of ratification roughly reflected the new political alignment among Connecticut elites. The newly dominant Federalist faction then used the existing institutions to reward its own members and to extend its influence into the general population. The Federalist party soon became so entrenched that nearly thirty years passed before the Republicans broke Federalist dominance in the state, an event signaled by the adoption of a new state constitution in 1818. But between 1789 and 1818, as a result of ratification, Connecticut belonged to the Federalists and to the state's extraordinary elite.

Notes

1. There had been a longstanding split between the agrarian and commercial interests in the state which went back to colonial times — a split that was reflected in the legislature by an almost even division between the pronational faction and the prolocalist faction. By the end of 1787 a consensus in favor of the proposed Constitution had emerged among the state's elites, a phenomenon that was noted by most researchers, including the editors of *The Documentary History of the Ratification of the Constitution* (hereafter cited as *DHRC*), ed. Merrill Jensen, John P. Kaminski, Gaspare J. Saladino, et al., 8 vols. to date (Madison: State Historical Society of Wisconsin, 1976–), 3:331–32.

2. The strong tendency toward localism is most fully developed by Milton Watchell Harvey in "The Conflict Between Localism and Nationalism in Connecticut, 1783–1788" (Ph.D. diss., University of Missouri, 1971).

3. The continuity in Connecticut politics between the colonial and early statehood eras is discussed at length by Gideon H. Hollister in *The History of Connecticut; From the First Settlement of the Colony to the Adoption of the Present Constitution*, 2 vols. (New Haven, Conn.: Durrie & Peck, 1855); Richard J. Purcell, *Connecticut in Transition, 1775–1818* (Middletown, Conn.: Wesleyan University Press, 1963); and David M. Roth and Freeman Meyer, *From Revolution to Constitution: Connecticut, 1763 to 1818* (Chester, Conn.: Pequot Press, 1975).

4. The text of the Fundamental Orders of Connecticut can be found in *The Federal and State Constitutions, Colonial Charters, and Other Organic Laws of the United States*, ed. Francis N. Thorpe, 7 vols. (Washington, D.C.: Government Printing Office, 1909), 1:519–23. The text of the 1662 Connecticut Charter can be found in Thorpe and in *Federal and State Constitutions, Colonial Charters, and Other Organic Laws of the United States*, comp. Benjamin Perley Poore (Washington, D.C.: Government Printing Office, 1878), 1:252–57. For a complete discussion of the contents of these two documents and their importance, not only for Connecticut but for American constitutionalism in general, see Donald S. Lutz, *The Origins of American Constitutionalism* (Baton Rouge: Louisiana State University Press, 1988).

5. A good summary of the "politics of deference" and how the concept should be applied in describing colonial politics can be found in John B. Kirby, "Early American Politics — the Search for Ideology: An Historiographical Analysis and Critique of the Concept of Deference," *Journal of Politics* 32 (1970): 808–38.

6. The composition and political role of the Standing Order is discussed in almost every book on eighteenth-century Connecticut politics. In addition to the works by Roth and Meyer, Hollister, and Purcell, one might also consult Alexander Johnston, *Connecticut: A Study of a Commonwealth Democracy* (Boston, Mass.: Houghton Mifflin, 1903).

7. *DHRC*, 3:323.

8. Jackson Turner Main, *Society and Economy in Colonial Connecticut* (Princeton, N.J.: Princeton University Press, 1985), p. 137.

9. Roth and Meyer, *From Revolution to Constitution,* p. 48.

10. Purcell, *Connecticut in Transition.*

11. Bernard C. Steiner, "Connecticut's Ratification of the Federal Constitution," *American Antiquarian Society Proceedings* 25 (1915): 70–73.

12. Discussion on the split in the legislature is taken from Steiner, "Connecticut's Ratification," pp. 76–80.

13. The following description of the three delegates is taken from *DHRC,* 3:327–28; and from Steiner, "Connecticut's Ratification," pp. 80–91.

14. The discussion concerning the role of newspapers in Connecticut's ratification is based upon Judith Maxen Katz, "Connecticut Newspapers and the Constitution, 1786–1788," *Connecticut Historical Society Bulletin,* 30 (1965): 33–44, and upon an examination of the newspapers themselves.

15. The best source on the distribution of the vote for ratification is still Orin Grant Libby's *The Geographical Distribution of the Vote of the Thirteen States on the Federal Constitution, 1787–8* (Madison: University of Wisconsin Press, 1894).

16. Figures on church membership in Connecticut are taken from William Warren Sweet, *The Story of Religion in America* (New York: Harper & Bros., 1930), and from Anson Phelps Stokes, *Church and State in the United States* (New York: Harper & Bros., 1950).

17. The debates during the Connecticut ratification convention can be found in *The Debates in the Several State Conventions on the Adoption of the Federal Constitution,* ed. Jonathon Elliott, 5 vols. (Philadelphia: J. B. Lippincott, 1901), and in *DHRC,* 3:536–62. No formal records were kept during the convention, so what we know about its proceedings is taken from a surviving collection of letters and informal notes about the debate.

6
MASSACHUSETTS
Creating Consensus

Michael Allen Gillespie

On February 6, 1788, Massachusetts became the sixth state to ratify the Federal Constitution. Ratification had not come easily. In the previous five states the proposed plan had been approved expeditiously by large majorities. In Massachusetts there was considerable opposition: by all accounts, a majority of the delegates to the ratifying convention had originally been opposed to the plan. Nevertheless, the convention ultimately approved the new system by a narrow margin.

Federalists roundly congratulated themselves that the first great barrier to the success of the new system had been surmounted. Yet ironically, ratification in Massachusetts was due less to the efforts of these champions of the Constitution than to those of two reluctant ratifiers, John Hancock and Samuel Adams. While a number of factors were important in securing ratification, it was the support of these two old patriots and the "conciliatory proposition" they espoused that carried the day and saved the Constitution.

Why Hancock and Adams supported ratification has never been clear. Both had sincere doubts about the proposed system. Moreover, their support was contingent, hinging upon recommendatory amendments that were intended to limit the federal government in a number of ways. Most scholars have argued that their support was not a reflection of their fundamental political principles but was the result of Federalist manipulation.[1] According to this view, Samuel Adams was fundamentally opposed to the plan but was restrained from openly opposing it by Federalist mobilization of his long-time supporters in

138

favor of the Constitution. Both he and Hancock were then supposedly brought to endorse the proposed system by Federalist promises of electoral support. In essence, according to this view, Hancock and Adams abandoned what they believed to be the long-term good of their country for momentary political advantage.

Such an interpretation calls into question the character of these men. Furthermore, it poses problems for understanding the relationship of the Constitution to the Revolution out of which it arose. That is, it suggests the failure of those whom Pauline Maier called the Old Revolutionaries to carry their principles into the Constitutional era. And it points toward the Federalists, whom Stanley M. Elkins and Eric L. McKitrick have termed the Young Men of the Revolution, as the true founders of American political life.[2]

I want to argue in this essay that this view is wrong: it misrepresents the role played by Hancock and Adams in the ratification of the Constitution in Massachusetts, and it distorts the relationship of the older Revolutionary principles to the newer Constitutional ones. I intend to show that Hancock and Adams favored the Constitution because they believed it was necessary in order to preserve the gains of the Revolution. But their support was tempered by a concern that the new government went too far toward a consolidation of the union and a dissolution of the states, which they regarded as the home of liberty and virtue. While they recognized that a stronger federal union was necessary, they also believed that the Constitution had to be amended to guarantee the continued sovereignty of the states in all internal matters. I will also argue that the Federalists' new understanding of politics led them to adopt a political strategy that alienated potential supporters of the Constitution and nearly brought about its defeat.[3] Hancock and Adams succeeded where the Federalists failed precisely because they did not accept this new view of politics, relying instead upon an older view that dictated a strategy of conciliation.

BACKGROUND: MASSACHUSETTS AS A REVOLUTIONARY REPUBLIC

Massachusetts was a model revolutionary republic. From 1763 on, it had been a hotbed of popular revolutionary sentiment. With the Boston Massacre in 1770, anticolonial resentments had turned to popular outrage, and the result was a widespread commitment to the

Revolutionary cause. Revolutionary sentiment was pervasive enough, in fact, to override some deep historical cleavages — east versus west, agrarian versus commercial interests, conservative republicans versus radicals — that had long lain beneath the surface. But from the early 1770s on, Massachusetts was ruled by a revolutionary consensus. The most conspicuous symbols of this consensus were the two most famous revolutionary republicans, Samuel Adams and John Hancock.

Both have suffered at the hands of their biographers. Adams has been characterized as a rabble-rouser who had a great flair for tearing governments down but little idea of how to build them up.[4] Fortunately, recent scholarship has begun to paint a more convincing picture of Adams as a political thinker who had a positive program for political society.[5] According to this view, Adams was primarily concerned with establishing a moral community of free men — what he sometimes called a Christian Sparta.[6] In this connection he saw himself as following in the long Puritan tradition of his Massachusetts ancestors.[7] At the same time, he had been deeply influenced by the Great Awakening, especially the teachings of George Whitefield, Jonathan Edwards, and others who had emphasized the role of moral education.[8] This Protestant moralism was combined in his thought with the republican philosophy of Shaftesbury, Locke, and Harrington, to form the idea of a moral republic of free men.[9] As Adams saw it, such a republic was not merely an ideal; it was already embodied in the institutions and manners of New England.[10] His belief in this moral community inspired his opposition to Britain. It also guided his ideas about the proper form of constitutional government in America.[11]

A virtuous republic, as Adams saw it, honored not wealth or noble birth, but sobriety of manners, industry, frugality, piety, benevolence, and a willingness to sacrifice oneself for the community.[12] It depended upon political equality, but it was not egalitarian, and it rejected any tendency toward leveling. In fact, the security of property was necessary as an aid to moral worth.[13] While wealth was not in itself blameworthy, avarice was.[14]

Virtue, on the other hand, was good in itself and consequently was the proper end of government. It was also necessary as a means to the preservation of liberty. Without virtue, no free government could endure, for the great passions that virtue restrained would ultimately overturn all checks and balances. Free government always would need to foster virtue. Yet virtue could not be achieved by force or coercion: laws did not make men good but merely restrained them from acting wrongly by inculcating a fear of punishment. The state thus had to establish a system of moral education to form the characters of its citizens. Only from such citizens could virtuous rulers be drawn, and only such citizens would be watchful enough to prevent their leaders from becoming corrupt and tyrannical. Vigilance, however, was only possible in a relatively small republic, and even there it had to be strengthened by frequent elections. Adams regarded the states as the home of liberty and virtue. He also recognized that such small republics could not survive in the face of great nation states. For purposes of defense and commerce, a federal government was necessary.

However, as the pre-Revolutionary period showed so well, such an over-arching government posed great dangers to both freedom and virtue. In Adams's opinion, affluence and the desire for luxury had undermined the virtue of the British and set them on the path toward despotism. This contagion of luxury threatened not only the liberties of the colonies but also their moral fabric, which had been sapped by the introduction of British goods and customs inimical to frugality and industriousness. Adams had hoped that Britons such as John Wilkes would restore the moral fabric of the mother country, but when it became apparent that this was not going to be, he concluded that separation was the only way to preserve the colonies from further infection and to establish a government that would preserve American moral values.[15] Adams hoped to achieve this without bloodshed, and turned to violence only as a last resort. Thus his resistance to Britain and his advocacy of American independence were not expressions of an underlying antipathy to authority; they were the sober responses of a moral patriot to evils that in his view threatened the very fabric of republican political life.[16]

Hancock was a man of a different stamp. Generally seen as a political opportunist more interested in popularity than in political principle, he has yet to receive the extended scholarly reevaluation necessary to restore his character.[17] He certainly desired the acclaim of the public, but he was also sincerely attached to liberty.[18] Like Adams, he believed that freedom was only possible in a moral republic. In his Massacre Day Oration in 1774, he stressed the importance of a righteous government that supported religious institutions and helped to foster strong morals.[19] Reminding his listeners of their Puritan ancestors and calling upon them to unite in defense of their New Jerusalem, he exhorted them to despise the glare of wealth and to honor instead the courage of those who were willing to give up their lives in the service of the community.[20] Like Adams, Hancock advocated frugality and industry, although he did not always live up to these standards himself.[21] He believed that individual rights must be secured from tyrannical intrusions, and he saw representative institutions that were close to the people as the best means to achieve this end. He was not an advocate of social equality. Like Adams, Hancock viewed the community as an organic whole, with every individual having certain duties within this whole.

During the period immediately preceding ratification, both Adams and Hancock occupied positions of authority in Massachusetts. Adams's stock had fallen since 1776, in part because he had spent extended periods outside the state at the Continental Congress, but also because his stern republican moralism was at odds with public opinion. However, he was still president of the state senate. Hancock, on the other hand, was the darling of the multitudes, having served as governor from 1780 until his retirement in 1785. Together, the two represented the triumph of revolutionary republicanism. During the 1780s, however, the old revolutionary consensus had become strained. In 1787, this consensus shattered. The reason was Shays's Rebellion.

SHAYS'S REBELLION AND THE CONSTITUTION

The Critical Period was particularly severe in Massachusetts. Too many people for too little land, a decline in the carrying trade because of British restrictions, and the introduction of low-priced British goods that drove out home manufactures—all had taken a heavy toll on the state's economy. These economic problems were exacerbated by the lack of specie, which fostered a dangerous overdependence upon credit. The downturn in the economy thus led creditors to press debtors for payment in order to satisfy demands being made upon them. Even more burdensome was the public debt.

Massachusetts was worse off than many other states because it had to repay not only its portion of the national debt but also the large state debt incurred during the Revolution. Most of this debt was held by speculators who had purchased it at a great discount. The state's ambitious repayment schedule required a rate of taxation that even in prosperous times would have been burdensome. In conjunction with the economic downturn, the policy became a disaster. Recognizing this, Hancock wisely had never pressed for the effective collection of taxes. His conservative successor, Governor James Bowdoin, however, demanded the immediate payment of taxes that were often several years in arrears. The result was predictable. Many farmers, particularly in the central section of the state, were unable to pay their debts. Their property was seized by the courts for payment, and they themselves were often thrown into prison. Discontent was inevitable, and it crystallized in a series of county conventions aimed at amending the state constitution to redress longstanding grievances.[22]

What began in a peaceful manner ended in violence when redress was not forthcoming. In late 1786, a group of citizens led by Daniel Shays, a former officer in the Continental Army, took up arms against the state.[23] Their main aim was to protect their mortgaged lands, although other demands included paper money and a cancellation of debts.[24] While Shays's Rebellion was easily quelled by the state militia, it sent shock waves through the state and the union.

Within Massachusetts, the rebellion reinforced longstanding sectional cleavages. Since the early 1770s, the central section of the state (with the exception of the Connecticut Valley) had found itself at odds with the coastal region, and especially with Boston.[25] Central Massachusetts, especially the "Tory" county of Worcester, had been the center of support for the Court party during the years before the Revolution and had long been a thorn in the side for both Adams and Hancock.[26] After the Revolution it became the center of the paper-money party and the source of most of the "democratic" objections to the Massachusetts Constitution of 1780. It was also the center of Shays's support.[27]

The immediate effect of Shays's Rebellion was to mobilize voters against the conservative majority that had come to power when Hancock retired.[28] Thus, what the insurgents had been unable to accomplish by force of arms they achieved with votes. Hancock was overwhelmingly returned to office, partly because of the impression that he would be lenient with the insurgents. Many conservatives lost their seats, and were replaced by insurgents or their sympathizers.[29]

The new legislature promptly passed laws to correct many of the problems that had brought on the rebellion, and Hancock pardoned all but nine of the insurgents.

More important, the rebellion polarized the state. For example, unlike Hancock, Samuel Adams did not see the rebellion as a legitimate revolt against tyrannical authority; but saw it as an illegitimate attempt to overthrow a legally constituted, popularly elected republican government.[30] He had no sympathy with the leveling tendencies in this revolt, which he saw as undermining the virtues necessary for good government.[31] Adams accepted the general principle that "no people can be more free than under a Constitution established by their own voluntary compact, and exercised by men appointed by their own frequent suffrages."[32] He thus could argue that "in Monarchies the Crime of Treason and Rebellion may admit of being pardoned or lightly punished; but the Man who dares to rebell against the Laws of a Republic ought to suffer Death."[33]

In any case, Shays's Rebellion set the stage, or at least provided the context, for ratification. On the one hand, leveling tendencies had been let loose, and even the most ardent Old Revolutionaries were alarmed. On the other hand, conservatives had been discredited at the polls. Most troubling, the center had failed to hold, as the revolutionary consensus seemed to collapse. Thus on the eve of ratification, the situation was polarized and politically unpredictable.

The Constitution Arrives

The initial reception of the Constitution in Massachusetts was enthusiastic, and many of its most ardent supporters predicted that it would be expeditiously ratified.[34] Noting the respectable characters of the gentlemen who had compiled the system, Hancock transmitted the proposed plan to the legislature, which voted 129 to 32 to call a convention to consider it. Soon, however, this unquestioning admiration began to wane. With the publication of Elbridge Gerry's objections, profound doubts became evident. Antifederalist polemics in the press, combined with a more thorough examination of the document, solidified this opposition.[35] Finally, the manhandling of the minority in Pennsylvania and the newspaper attacks on Massachusetts Antifederalists reawakened the suspicion, first evoked by the Society of the Cincinnati, that a conspiracy was afoot to establish a more aristocratic government.[36] As a result, when the convention met, the opponents of ratification were clearly in the majority. The Federalists had run an unsuccessful campaign.

Both Adams and Hancock believed that certain alterations in the Articles of Confederation were necessary. Adams recognized that Congress was the only cement that could hold the union together. Unlike his friends Richard Henry Lee and George Mason, he had long favored granting Congress the power to regulate commerce.[37] Adams was particularly concerned that the lack of such power was facilitating the importation of British goods to the disadvantage of home manufactures. Neither Adams nor Hancock, however, favored a truly national government. Indeed, they saw this tendency in the Constitution as a signal defect. Adams wrote to Lee on December 3, 1787, about his concerns:

> I confess, as I enter the Building, I stumble at the Threshold. I meet with a National Government, instead of a Federal Union of Sovereign States. I am not able to conceive why the Wisdom of the Convention led them to give the Preference of the former before the latter. . . . But should we continue distinct sovereign States, confederated for the Purposes of mutual Safety and Happiness each contributing to the federal Head such a part of its Sovereignty as would render the Government fully adequate to those Purposes and *no more,* the People would govern themselves more easily, the Laws of each State being well adapted to its own Genius and Circumstances, and the Liberties of the United States would be more secure than they can be, as I humbly conceive, under the proposed new Constitution.[38]

Adams believed that a stronger central government was necessary, but only for limited national purposes. The states were the true home of liberty and virtue; therefore, they had to remain sovereign.

While Adams and Hancock maintained positions of public neutrality, many Federalists believed they would oppose ratification. Adams was especially suspect. Apparently basing this opinion upon the mistaken idea that Adams was the author of the Antifederalist piece "Helvidius Priscus," Christopher Gore wrote to King on December 30 that "Adams is out full *against* it."[39] At a meeting of the Boston delegates, Adams did criticize the Constitution in the manner of "Brutus" and the "Federal Farmer," but this does not prove that he favored rejection.[40] In a letter to King of January 6, Gore explained that Adams objected to internal taxes and insisted on certain amendments.[41] While the most partisan Federalists viewed this as complete opposition to the plan, it in fact reflected a position between outright rejection and simple ratification.

Hancock had been unable to attend this meeting because of ill health, but he kept abreast of events, one of his chief informants being none other than Samuel Adams. This was astonishing in itself, for Hancock had not spoken to Adams for more than a decade because Samuel and John Adams had supported Washington instead of Hancock for commander in chief of the Continental Army.[42] On his side, Samuel Adams feared that Hancock's high style of life might undermine public virtue, but he never considered himself Hancock's enemy.[43] Their friendship, however, was a thing of the past. Joseph Vinal's extreme surprise when he discovered Hancock and Adams locked in conversation in Hancock's study before the convention is thus understandable.[44] The usual explanation of the ratification overlooks the renewal of this political friendship, assuming instead that Hancock and Adams were brought together by Federalists or that Adams made his peace with Hancock after ratification in order to revive his sagging political fortunes.

Yet it was, in fact, the question of the Constitution that reunited them. Both favored ratification, but only with certain amendments. They did not want to see the Constitution simply ratified or rejected. Federalists, however, were unwilling to accept any amendments, and Antifederalists were unwilling to ratify without amendments. Hancock and Adams found themselves in between, confronted with the problem of bringing the opposing groups together on the basis of consensus. To have publicly adopted such a position at the outset would only have alienated both groups and made compromise impossible. The Constitution could only succeed if Federalists could be convinced that a simple ratification was impossible and Antifederalists could be persuaded that their most extreme fears were irrational. Hancock and Adams thus recognized that only a policy of conciliation and consensus could save the Constitution and that, without it, their hopes for a more powerful federal government would wither and die in the heat of partisan strife.

To some extent, Hancock and Adams were involved in a generational conflict.[45] The Old Revolutionaries were products of a society that looked to the public good first and to private rights and interests second. This notion of an objective public good led them to the position that consensus ought to rule and that those who did not agree were at least potentially subversive. By contrast, most Federalists in Massachusetts, and many Antifederalists as well, were convinced that the public good was little more than the sum of the goods of individuals.[46] Federalists seemed most at odds with the old ways, maintaining that disagreements were inevitable and could be restrained, not by education or morality, but only by institutions that would control the effects of faction by setting ambition against ambition. As a result, few Federalists seemed to be concerned about achieving consensus.[47]

This new style of politics had been evident in Pennsylvania and had become apparent in the preconvention debates in Massachusetts as well. Yet, to many of those who had been brought up under the old colonial system, it served as a reminder of the high-handed actions of Parliament and the Crown. The political manners of certain Federalists in particular had alienated many of those whose votes were needed to secure the ratification and had led to a decline in support for the Constitution during the period before the convention. For ratification to succeed in Massachusetts, a way had to be found to conciliate those who had been alienated and to reconcile the opposing sides. The Old Revolutionaries understood this, and they set out to construct the basis for reconciliation.

THE CONVENTION: THE FAILURE OF FEDERALIST STRATEGY

The convention began on January 9, 1788, and continued until February 7. The debates were one-sided. Almost all of the leading Federalists had been elected as delegates; they included men of great abilities. None of the leading Antifederalists had been elected, largely because they lived in eastern towns that strongly favored ratification. As a result, nearly all of the prestige and talent was on one side of the issue.[48] The result, however, was by no means to Federalists' liking. Their rhetorical skills, which seemingly gave them great advantages in the debate, in fact proved detrimental to their cause, suggesting to their opponents the clever rhetoric of the wealthy and well born.[49] Moreover, Federalists had further hurt their cause by the strident character of their newspaper campaign. While they were much more patient and diplomatic within the convention, which helped to calm some fears, even there they still occasionally tried to over-power the opposition with their rhetoric, invariably to the detriment of their cause.

Adams and Hancock pursued a strategy of conciliation throughout the convention. The strategy was already evident on the first day, when Adams moved that the convention attend daily prayers and that clergy of each denomination officiate in turn.[50] This proposal, which has generally been considered inconsequential, must be understood in the light of Adams's similar motion at the beginning of the Continental Congress, where he, a New England Congregationalist, intentionally urged the members to have an Anglican say the opening prayer.[51] His proposal in the Massachusetts convention served a similar purpose, calming the suspicions of the minority Baptists and Quakers that Con-gregationalist members of the convention were supporting the Con-stitution for sectarian reasons. The gesture was especially important in helping to moderate the differences between the Congregationalists of the east and the Baptists, who were predominately from the cen-tral and Antifederalist section of the state.[52]

After securing a suitable meeting place, the convention began its deliberations on January 14. In a crucial vote that clearly improved the prospects for ratification, the convention agreed to consider the Constitution paragraph by paragraph, rather than as a whole. This procedure prevented a certain and rapid rejection of the plan. On that same day, Adams moved, and his motion carried, that Elbridge Gerry be called to take a seat in the convention in order to answer questions about the deliberations in the federal convention. Winthrop Sargent expressed the Federalist opinion of this proposal in a letter to General Henry Knox: "Sam Adams is an Arch Devil on this occasion."[53] Because the authorship of this motion is not recorded in Elliot's *Debates,* it is generally thought to have been a victory for those Antifederalists who were opposed to the Constitution in any form. Federalists themselves clearly understood it in this manner. Yet, despite his opposition to the Constitution, Gerry was not a die-hard rejec-tionist; he favored ratification with amendments, a position similar to that of Adams and Hancock. Adams's proposal was therefore an attempt, not to undermine the Constitution, but to facilitate a modified ratification.

Federalists were not able to distinguish between these two positions; they believed that amendments would doom the plan as surely as outright rejection. Through a series of maneuvers, they sought to anger and embarrass Gerry in order to drive him from the convention. In this they were successful. Often seen as a Federalist victory, their efforts in fact served to reinforce the impression that they were interested, not in a fair debate, but in aggrandizing themselves.

Discussion of the Constitution, which began on the afternoon of January 14, centered on the question of biennial elections. The debate on this subject was characteristic of the debates as a whole. Federalists presented a variety of abstract arguments for biennial elections. However, they were unable to persuade the opposition Antifederalists, who were unwaveringly attached to the tradition of annual elections in Massachusetts.

Abstract arguments mattered little to the Antifederalists. Few of them were learned men. Yet nearly all of them had taken part in making laws and framing constitutions during the preceding decade. Constitution making was, for them, primarily a pragmatic codification of lessons learned from experience, and their formative experience had been the conflict with Britain. This colonial experience shaped the Massachusetts Constitution of 1780, which was generally regarded as the basis of the people's liberties. Now, it appeared, they were being asked to give up these liberties for a system that in many ways seemed to fly in the face of past experience. So, arguments of a different sort were needed, arguments that appealed more closely to their political experience.

Adams understood this, but many Federalists did not. At one point, after Federalist delegates had explained the potential advantages of biennial elections at some length, Adams rose to ask the simple question "*why* the alteration of elections from annual to biennial was made."[54] Caleb Strong, who had been a delegate at the federal convention, explained that it had simply been a compromise between different state customs. His answer, which was in keeping with the experience of many of the delegates, appealed to their sense of practicality and to their common sense. However, the arch Federalist Fisher

Ames did not understand that this was exactly the sort of argument that would allay the Antifederalist fears and went on at great length and with great vehemence to repeat the potential advantages of such elections. Adams responded that he had asked the question only for purposes of information and that he had heard enough to satisfy himself. The usual explanation of this incident is that Ames intimidated Adams with the force of his rhetoric. Such a conclusion, however, fundamentally mistakes both the character of Adams and the character of the debates. Samuel Adams was not easily intimidated, as many of his contemporaries recognized.[55] More important, it was not Ames's arguments that convinced the opposition; it was Strong's reply. Adams, in this case, understood the language of the people in a way that the Federalist leadership did not.

Adams did not intervene in the debates again until January 24. His long silence is usually explained as a reaction to the meeting of the Boston mechanics, which was organized by Federalists at the Green Dragon tavern, the home of Adams's famed Boston Caucus Club, at which the mechanics announced support for the Constitution. Adams certainly did listen to the voice of the people. Yet a more likely explanation for his silence was the death of his son, who died on January 17 after a long illness brought on by service in the Revolution. The debates during this week were largely a repetition of what had gone before: Federalist arguments that did not allay the suspicions of the opposition. This culminated in the Antifederalist proposal of January 24 to abandon the discussion of the Constitution by paragraphs and turn to a discussion of the plan as a whole in an effort to speed up deliberations on ratification. The success of the motion would almost certainly have led to the rejection of the Constitution. At this point, Adams intervened. Identifying himself with those who had doubts about certain parts of the Constitution, he asserted that he wanted a full examination to remove or confirm them. In any case, "We ought not . . . be stingy of our time, or the public money, when so important an object demanded them; and the public expect that we will not."[56] Adams here probably saved the Constitution from being rejected outright, and he placed the Antifederalists on the defensive by implicitly suggesting that they were putting their private interest above the public good. His intervention was so effective that the proposal was rejected without a return of the house.

On the following day, Adams again opposed the Antifederalist faction, this time arguing against one Major Kingsley, who objected to the use of Shays's Rebellion as proof of the necessity for a stronger government.[57] Kingsley came from Worcester County, the center of Shays's support, and he was objecting to a speech by a delegate from the western part of the state, which had suffered much from the conflict. Adams's interjection here is indicative of his opposition to the insurgency and also of his longstanding conflict with the faction from the central section of the state. This speech throws important light on the question of Adams's supposed opposition to the Constitution. Had Adams been an Antifederalist he would have had to side with the faction that he had always opposed. On the twenty-sixth, Adams again came to the defense of the Constitution, pointing out that the provision for the continuation of the slave trade for twenty years actually opened the door for the eventual annihilation of this practice.[58] Here again his remarks served to defuse what was a potentially explosive issue.

Throughout the course of the debates, Federalists developed strong arguments in favor of ratification. These arguments, however, did not persuade many delegates to change their votes. Cleavages in the state were profound, and the Federalists' strategy at the convention, while more conciliatory than their earlier newspaper campaign, was unable to overcome the cleavages. Federalists began to realize that they could not achieve the simple ratification they desired. Unless an intermediate position could be found that was acceptable to some of the moderate Antifederalists, the Constitution faced certain defeat. But Antifederalists would be suspicious of any Federalist proposal. Thus, Federalists could do nothing to save the Constitution. At this crucial juncture they had no alternative but to turn to Hancock and Adams.

THE CONVENTION: CONCILIATION AND CONSENSUS

On January 31, Hancock appeared for the first time at the convention. He told the delegates that he had been unable to attend because of poor health but that he had kept himself informed of what had occurred. He concluded that "there appeared to him to be a great dissimilarity of sentiments in the Convention. To remove the objections of some gentlemen, he felt himself induced, he said, to hazard a proposition for their consideration."[59] Hancock's absence was in part certainly strategic. The conventional interpretation suggests that he stayed away until it became apparent which side would win and then jumped on the bandwagon. This explanation is dubious, however, because even with Hancock's considerable support, ratification was not assured. It is much more probable that he waited until the most opportune moment to present his proposal for a modified ratification. Of course, many Antifederalists and almost all of the Federalists present had been opposed to such a plan from the beginning. The Federalists in particular had assumed they could achieve a simple ratification by the power of persuasion alone. Only when it became clear to them that this strategy had failed were they willing to listen to arguments for conciliation.

It was at this point that Hancock brought forward his "conciliatory proposition." He suggested that the Constitution be ratified but that certain recommendatory amendments be attached to it "to remove the fears and quiet the apprehensions of the good people of this Commonwealth, and more effectually guard against an undue administration of the federal government."[60] The proposed amendments were generally framed in response to criticisms that had arisen in the press and in the convention debates themselves. The amendments were of three sorts. The first was generally equivalent to the reserve clause. Amendments 2 through 5 and 9 limited Congress's powers to determine representation, levy direct taxes, establish monopolies, and allow officials to accept titles of nobility. Amendments 6 through 8 restricted the federal judiciary by requiring trial by jury in civil cases when such was requested by one or both of the parties and by limiting the jurisdiction of the federal courts in minor civil suits between citizens of different states.

Immediately after the proposition was assigned to committee, Hancock recognized Adams, who rose to speak in support of it. Identifying himself again as one who had doubts about the Constitution, he asserted that Hancock's proposition had removed them. Adams then argued that this proposition ought also to remove the doubts held by others in the convention. Finally, he argued that recommendatory amendments were better than amendments made conditional to ratification or amendments made after ratification. The former were unfeasible, the latter dangerous.

On the following day, Adams was more explicit about the salutary aspects of Hancock's proposition, suggesting that it would secure the essential powers necessary for the federal government without sacrificing the sovereignty of the states. Here he gave great weight to Hancock's proposed amendment to reserve all nondelegated powers to the states. This amendment was crucial to the preservation of liberty, he asserted, because it allowed for frequent elections and thus for "the watchfulness of the people over the conduct of their rulers [which is] the strongest guard against the encroachments of power."[61] He also praised the proposed limitation on internal taxes, although he pointed out the necessity of such a taxing power in time of war. He reasserted that the Constitution, with the proposed amendments, would secure those powers necessary for a federal government, while also preserving the essential sovereignty of the states. He ended by calling upon others to present amendments that would tend to promote unanimity.

Supporters had long maintained that amendments would doom the Constitution because of the difficulties that another federal convention would face. George Washington himself had argued that "if another Federal Convention is attempted the sentiments of the members will be more discordant or less conciliatory than the last, in fine, that they will agree to no genl. plan."[62] Both the Articles of Confederation and the Massachusetts Constitution of 1780, however, had been amended before ratification. In fact, in his "Address of the Convention" in 1780, Samuel Adams had asserted that "it is your interest to revise it with the greatest care and circumspection; and it is your undoubted *right,* either to propose such alterations and amendments as you shall judge proper, or to give it your sanction in its present form, or totally reject it."[63] Proponents of the plan in Massachusetts were thus caught between the desire for unconditional ratification and the tradition of conditional amendments.

The conciliatory proposition provided a solution to this problem. The idea of recommendatory amendments is usually ascribed to the Federalists. The assumption is unlikely. Hancock and his friends were clearly considering the idea in early January, long before Federalists had given it much, if any, thought. In a letter of January 8, Fisher Ames remarked that Hancock told him "that two very respectable States, Virginia and New York, propose a convention to consider amendments. But he is of the opinion that convention is improper.

However, he declares openly for amendments, and a great deal more of the same stuff."[64] In addition, Hancock's advisor, Thomas Cushing, had favored ratification with amendments. Cushing's son-in-law John Avery, who was secretary of the Commonwealth of Massachusetts and was a close friend of Hancock's, wrote in a letter to George Thatcher on the nineteenth of January: "I am seriously of Opinion that if the most sanguine among them who are for adopting the proposed Constitution as it now stands would discover a Conciliatory disposition and give way a little to those who are for Adopting it with Amendments I dare say they would be very united . . . my Wishes are that they may adopt it and propose Amendments . . . . That Amendments should be made, seems to be the prevailing Opinion."[65] It seems likely that the mediator in all of this was James Sullivan, a member of Hancock's Council and a friend of many of the leading Federalists. Indeed, Sullivan may have been the source of the idea. A proposal strikingly similar to the conciliatory proposition was presented by "Hampden" in the *Centinel* of January 26, and "Hampden" was probably Sullivan.[66]

Federalists were anxious to avoid the whole question of amendments. The Federalist Rufus King wrote to James Madison in late January, well after Avery had alluded to the plan of ratification with amendments, that their prospects were gloomy and that they were thinking of recommendatory amendments only as a last-ditch effort.[67] The publication of "Hampden," however, seems to have given them new hope, largely because of its enthusiastic reception. In part this was a reflection of the belief that a basis for consensus had been found. More important was the widespread rumor that tied "Hampden" to Sullivan and hence to Hancock.[68] King was more sanguine on January 30: "I cannot predict the issue but our hopes are increasing. If, Mr. Hancock does not disappoint our present expectations, our wishes will be gratified but his character is not entirely free from a portion of caprice."[69] Nathaniel Gorham wrote to General Henry Knox on the same day, declaring the necessity of compromise: "We cannot gain the question without some recommendatory amendments."[70] When Adams agreed to support this position, it clinched the issue in their minds. "Mr. S. Adams will come out in favor of the Constitution. This and the Governor on the same side will settle the matter favorably."[71]

It has usually been argued that Hancock was persuaded to support the Federalist position by promises of electoral support. This argument derives from the calumnious diatribe written by Stephen Higginson under the pseudonym "Laco," in which Higginson sought to undermine Hancock in the 1788 election. There is in fact some evidence to support these charges. King wrote to Knox on February 1: "Hancock will hereafter receive the universal support of Bowdoin's friends; and *we told him, that, if Virginia does not unite, which is problematical, he is considered the only fair candidate for President.*"[72] However, there are also good reasons to doubt this interpretation. First, Hancock had no need of Federalist electoral support. He had won every election he had entered since 1780 by overwhelming majorities, and he was returned to office in the election following ratification by a 4 to 1 margin over Gerry. In addition, Federalist support of Hancock for president was hardly crucial, since it was generally recognized at the time that he would probably be chosen if Washington were not available.[73] Besides, because of Hancock's distaste for secondary positions, the vice-presidency was not attractive to him.[74] Finally, Gorham had written to Madison on January 27 that Hancock and Bowdoin were the foremost managers of the cause of the Constitution. This was fully five days prior to the date when an offer was supposedly made to Hancock.[75]

The conventional interpretation also has attributed the authorship of the conciliatory proposition to the Federalists, and in particular to Theophilus Parsons. Here again, scholars have relied upon "Laco," who claimed that Hancock read his proposal from a copy in Parsons's handwriting.[76] While the proposal may have been given to Parsons, one of the best legal minds of his day, for final editing, it is unlikely that he wrote it. The similarity to "Hampden" suggests that Sullivan may have been the author. There is also an extant copy with interlineations in Adams's hand, which suggests that he was at least partly responsible for it. According to Benjamin Russell, the copy that Hancock read from had been written by Sullivan.[77] The conciliatory proposition was thus probably a collaboration by those around Hancock.[78] In any case, too much can be made of the authorship of the proposal; the important point is that it was an obvious compromise. John Adams, for example, had suggested such a course of action to Jefferson in a letter of November 10, 1787.[79] James Warren, writing as the "Republican Federalist," had pointed out the dangers of such a path on January 12, 1788.[80] The crux of the matter was convincing the two sides, and particularly the Federalist side, to accept this proposal.

The general response to Hancock's proposition was positive. Federalists welcomed it because it promoted unanimity, although they continued to assert that they would support ratification even without amendments. Die-hard Antifederalists said the amendments were excellent but argued that it was unlikely that they would ever be incorporated in the Constitution. A number of delegates were so torn that they wanted to adjourn in order to resubmit the plan with the amendments to their constituents.[81] Although this is not recorded in Elliot's *Debates*, Adams apparently was the one who skillfully resisted this motion, which was defeated by a vote of 214 to 115.[82] Such a delay may well have derailed the plan, because voters would probably have demanded amendments prior to ratification, as they had in the case of the Massachusetts Constitution of 1780. Again, Adams preserved the fragile coalition that he and Hancock had so skillfully constructed.

On the following day, Adams offered further amendments, but he withdrew them when they did not obtain "the approbation of those gentlemen whose minds they were intended to ease."[83] According to the accepted account, Adams introduced these amendments either to upset the Federalist applecart or because he wanted to gain the same fame that Hancock had won by introducing his amendments.[84] However, Adams had supported this position from the beginning, and he had little desire for fame.[85] More likely, he proposed the amendments for the reasons he himself gave, which were to promote general union and because he felt that they might quiet the fears of a few more delegates and thus increase the likelihood of ratification. The amendments were intended to secure the liberty of the press, the rights of conscience, the right to bear arms, and the right to petition the federal legislature, along with prohibitions against standing armies and unreasonable searches and seizures. The infringement of these rights had been a principle cause of the Revolution. The rights themselves were explicitly secured in the state constitution. Thus, the amendments were apparently designed to give assurance that the Constitution would not negate the work of the Revolution but would instead embody and perfect it.

Nevertheless, Adams's concern with unanimity was poorly understood by many Federalists, who accepted social and political cleavages as natural and who trusted more to institutional arrangements than to civic education and civic virtue to channel and control social conflict.[86] In this respect, Adams has been seen as out of place in a new age of incipient party politics. In particular, he seemed unable to grasp the notion of a loyal opposition, seeing in every division the danger of civil war.[87] But there was a deeper reason for his desire for unanimity, one that grew out of his conception of a moral republic. Adams did not believe that the state should be merely a neutral arbiter of the private interests of competing individuals and groups. Instead, its goal should be the virtuous life. This virtue was good in itself. It was also necessary, the only lasting protection of liberty. The presence of parties proved that the community had failed to unite behind this principle.[88] In addition, this principled motive was tied to the practical concern that greater unanimity was needed to secure ratification.[89] When Adams saw that his proposal was divisive, he withdrew it. Unfortunately, it was revived by another delegate, and Adams was then put in the awkward position of arguing and voting against it.[90] The fact that he did so is evidence of his unswerving support for a modified ratification.

Hancock, who had hitherto spoken only to present his conciliatory proposition, addressed the convention just prior to the vote on ratification. He argued that the plan, if amended, would "give the people of the United States a greater degree of political freedom, and eventually as much national dignity, as falls to the lot of any nation on the earth."[91] He pointed to the universal agreement that a general system of government was necessary. He also admitted that the proposed plan had defects. Arguing that this was not surprising, given the variety of interests and habits of the peoples of the United States, Hancock asserted that the proposed amendments would repair the worst of them. Because they were of general concern and not merely of local interest, the amendments would surely soon be adopted. He concluded with a plea for unity and conciliation. The danger was not that the proposed plan would subvert the people's rights but that the people would subvert themselves by becoming corrupt. As long as they remained virtuous, Hancock declared, their rights would remain secure. Like Adams, he concluded with an appeal for unanimity. To rejoice in a victory over one's fellow citizens in his view was vicious, and it undermined the unity intrinsic to a decent regime. The practical danger of an angry and unruly minority also had to be avoided. (Here the discontent of the Pennsylvania minority was undoubtedly in the back of his mind.) In any case, modified ratification was essential.

RATIFICATION AND ITS AFTERMATH

With the recommended amendments, the Constitution was approved by a vote of 187 to 168. The minority accepted the outcome without complaint; some even pledged to support the instrument and to explain the convention's decision to their constituents. Consensus had been reestablished.

Of course, sectional divisions remained, and the vote generally reflected them. The east voted overwhelmingly for ratification (73 percent to 27 percent), the central section overwhelmingly against it (86 percent to 14 percent), while the west was split and slightly opposed to the plan (58 percent to 42 percent).[92] From a comparison with early reports and previous election returns, it seems that the crucial votes in favor of ratification came from switches on the part of western delegates. Delegates from the central section, that had been the center of support for the insurgency, remained overwhelmingly opposed to a plan which they saw as inimical to their hopes of securing relief from debts and issuing paper money. The westerners were less unalterably opposed. While they had suffered economically in the 1785–86 period, they had also borne the brunt of the recent violence. Thus, they were willing to support the Constitution, if they could be convinced that it was compatible with the preservation of their liberties.

Yet the convention clearly recognized the decisive role that Adams and Hancock had played in uniting the delegates. Federalist opinion was expressed by General Knox in a letter to Robert R. Livingston: "A most perfect union was effected between the friends of Mr. Hancock and Mr. Bowdoin. Handsome things are said of the open and decisive conduct of Mr. Hancock, and also of Mr. S. Adams, notwithstanding his neutrality in the first part of the business."[93] The public gave Hancock credit for securing ratification. In fact a popular ditty, written to the tune of "Yankee Doodle," praised Hancock for saving the Constitution.[94]

In much the same language as he had used in the convention, Hancock reaffirmed his support for the Constitution at the opening of the General Court on February 27. If anything, his assertion of the need for unity was even stronger. He emphasized the necessity of union to deter foreign aggression and internal strife. He also, however, reiterated that geographic and climatological differences, as well as the variety of habits that they produced, proved the necessity for the continued sovereignty of the states. He concluded by praising the conciliatory spirit of the minority and by expressing his hope that the ratification and subsequent amendment of the Constitution would secure American virtue and dignity.[95] Similarly, Adams continued to support ratification, while pressing at every turn for amendments to avoid a consolidated national government.[96]

Adams and Hancock had an explicit vision of the good regime, and within the limits of their political circumstances, they sought to bring it into reality. This vision led them to support independence and Revolution, and it ultimately brought them to support the Constitution with amendments. They envisioned America as a close-knit federation of sovereign republics in which the states would be bound together for purposes of commerce and defense but would be independent and sovereign in realizing their own visions of the good life. As their later political careers indicate, Adams and Hancock believed that the amended Constitution provided the means to bring his vision into reality. Thus, Hancock continued to dominate Massachusetts politics, serving as Governor until his death in 1793. Adams was elected lieutenant governor in 1789, with Hancock's assistance, and when Hancock died, Adams assumed the governorship, which he held until his retirement in 1797.

For Adams and Hancock, Massachusetts remained a sovereign state under the new Constitutional system. Adams wrote to Gerry in August 1789: "The state retains all the Rights of Sovereignty which it has not expressly parted with to the Congress of the United States — a federal Power instituted solely for the support of the federal Union."[97] It was important that this be made clear, he explained in a letter to Richard Henry Lee, so "that the good People may clearly see the distinction, for there is a distinction between the *federal* Powers vested in Congress, and the *Sovereign* Authority belonging to the several States, which is the Palladium of the private and personal rights of the

Citizens."[98] Hancock defended this position in 1792 when he and James Sullivan, then the state's attorney general, were summoned by Associate Justice Marshall Jackson to answer a suit brought in United States Court against Massachusetts by a nonresident. Hancock refused to obey the summons, and he called a special session of the assembly to nullify the pending action. Hancock's speech to the legislature of September 18, 1792, explains his position: "I cannot conceive that the people of this commonwealth, who by their representatives in convention adopted the federal compact, expected a state would be held liable to answer a compulsory civil process of an individual of another state or a foreign kingdom."[99]

While Hancock and Adams were unshaken in their belief that the amended Constitution guaranteed the sovereignty of the states on internal matters, they had reason to doubt that the states would use this independence to establish the sort of moral community that they had envisioned. They were particularly concerned by the growing dissipation and licentiousness of Boston, which in their minds was tied to the growing power of the Federalist party. In his last letter to Adams, written on August 3, 1793, Hancock remarked on this tendency: "My friend, what are we coming to? It is time to step forth and oppose the current of opinions and pursuits that are endeavouring to establish a system foreign to your ideas and mine. . . . I love my country but will not give up its liberties to the last drop of my blood."[100] Both were disheartened by the overwhelming defeat of their attempts to prohibit theatrical performances in Boston in 1792 by a new generation who found such notions old-fashioned.[101] They were likewise distressed to discover that the regulation and restriction of British imports in favor of home manufacturing had not curbed moral laxity. Like most of the Old Revolutionaries, they did not fully realize that the home manufacturing that they favored would eventually produce the same prosperity and luxury as the British commerce that they despised.[102]

Although Adams came to recognize that his Boston would never become a Christian Sparta, he did not give up hopes of an eventual moral regeneration.[103] The French Revolution convinced him that republican principles were gaining ground in the world and that ultimately a sober republican morality would prevail. In this regard, he stressed the importance of moral and political education in a number of addresses to the legislature and in a series of letters to John Adams.[104] As Samuel Adams saw it, the election of Jefferson kindled hopes that this new age was close at hand.[105] He was therefore unwilling to believe that the moral degeneration that he saw would be lasting, hoping instead that it would ultimately be overcome by a more mature people dedicated to a republicanism of freedom and virtue.

The support of Samuel Adams and John Hancock was crucial to the ratification of the Constitution in Massachusetts. The conciliatory proposition that they advocated played an important role in securing the ratification in the remaining states as well. Indeed, this method of ratification was adopted in all but one of those states.

In contrast to the conventional wisdom, the success of the Constitution at this crucial juncture was thus due, not to the youth and vigor of the Federalists, but to the wisdom of two old patriots. Their success was largely the result of their belief in a politics of consensus, which suggested to them an alternative between simple ratification and outright rejection. The conciliatory proposition that they presented, however, was not a compromise between two competing views but a concrete proposal that rested on a comprehensive conception of the appropriate character of a good regime.

The brave new world that was constructed on this Constitutional foundation seems in many respects to bear little resemblance to the virtuous republic of Adams and Hancock. While they may have played an important role in bringing this new system into being, the character that it eventually assumed seems to reflect more fully the Federalist vision of a large commercial republic. Like King Lear, the Old Revolutionaries seem not to have understood the children to whom they left their kingdom.

Such a conclusion, however, rejects the fruitful ambiguity of the American founding. America is not simply the commercial republic, however much this aspect of the regime may have come to the fore in our times. Rather, it contains a variety of possibilities. Among them, in a prominent place, is the idea of the virtuous republic that Adams and Hancock defended. Indeed, it was this republic that Tocqueville saw as the essence of American democracy and as the best hope for democracy in the future. The same idea played a decisive role in

Abraham Lincoln's attempted reformulation of American democracy, and it continues in important ways to inform American life today.

NOTES

1. Most scholars depend upon Samuel B. Harding, *The Contest over the Ratification of the Federal Constitution in the State of Massachusetts* (New York: Longmans, Green & Co., 1896). Harding argued that the contest over ratification was a class struggle, but he retained a strong bias in favor of the Federalists.

2. See Pauline Maier, *The Old Revolutionaries: Political Lives in the Age of Samuel Adams* (New York: Knopf, 1980), and Stanley Elkins and Eric McKitrick, "The Founding Fathers: Young Men of the Revolution," in *The Reinterpretation of the American Revolution 1763–1789*, ed. Jack P. Greene (New York: Harper & Row, 1968), pp. 378–95.

3. Here I argue against John Roche, who sees this caucuslike behavior as the source of the Federalists' success ("The Founding Fathers: A Reform Caucus in Action," *American Political Science Review* 55 [1961]: 799–816).

4. John C. Miller's standard biography, *Sam Adams: Pioneer in Propaganda* (Boston, Mass.: Little, Brown, & Co., 1936), still reflects this view (see p. 344).

5. In *Old Revolutionaries*, Maier has revealed a new Samuel Adams, more akin to the English reformers of 1688 than to the Jacobins of the French Revolution (see pp. 3–51).

6. Herbert S. Allan, *John Hancock: Patriot in Purple* (New York: Macmillan 1948), p. 304.

7. Miller, *Sam Adams*, pp. 7 and 84; William A. Williams, "Samuel Adams: Calvinist, Mercantilist, Revolutionary," *Studies on the Left* 1 (1960): 49.

8. Maier, *Old Revolutionaries*, p. 42.

9. Williams, "Samuel Adams," p. 50; Miller, *Sam Adams*, p. 20.

10. Maier, *Old Revolutionaries*, p. 45.

11. Williams, "Samuel Adams," p. 53.

12. Samuel Adams, *The Writings of Samuel Adams*, ed. Harry Cushing, 4 vols. (New York: Putnam's Sons, 1905–8), 4:226, 343, 352, 359, 371, 377, 387. See Maier, *Old Revolutionaries*, p. 32.

13. Adams, *Writings*, 4: 380.

14. Miller, *Sam Adams*, p. 195.

15. Adams may have seen America as an asylum for mankind in a manner similar to that of Paine: see Bernard Bailyn, *The Ideological Origins of the American Revolution* (Cambridge: Harvard University Press, 1967), p. 143.

16. Maier has made this especially clear in *Old Revolutionaries*, pp. 17–26. She has argued persuasively that for Adams, 1776 was a working out of New England's historic mission (ibid., pp. 272–73).

17. Charles Akers has argued that Hancock has been the chief victim of the modern historiography of the period ("Sam Adams—And Much More," *New England Quarterly* 47 [1974]: 130).

18. This is already apparent in Hancock's stance toward the Stamp Act: see the three letters cited by Allan in his *John Hancock*, pp. 88–89; cf. also p. 253.

19. John Hancock, *An Oration: Delivered March 5, 1774* (Boston, 1774).

20. Allan, *John Hancock*, p. 353.

21. Ibid., p. 300.

22. Stephen E. Patterson, *Political Parties in Revolutionary Massachusetts* (Madison: University of Wisconsin Press, 1973), pp. 218–47.

23. Shays's Rebellion has never received the attention it deserves. See Robert Fear, "Shays's Rebellion" (Ph.D. diss., Harvard University, 1958), and Robert Taylor, *Western Massachusetts in the Revolution* (Providence, R.I.: Brown University Press, 1954), pp. 103–77.

24. William N. Chambers, *Political Parties in a New Nation* (New York: Oxford University Press, 1963), p. 19. The demands of the Shaysites were in part motivated by their perception that speculators who had purchased the state and national debt at a deep discount were unjustifiably benefiting at their expense from its redemption at face value.

25. Oscar Handlin and Mary Handlin, "Radicals and Conservatives in Massachusetts after Independence," *New England Quarterly* 17 (1944): 351; see also Patterson, *Political Parties in Revolutionary Massachusetts*. Patterson does not distinguish between central and western sections of the state, but he comes to many of the same conclusions.

26. Miller, *Sam Adams*, p. 169.

27. Orin Grant Libby, "The Geographical Distribution of the Vote of the Thirteen States on the Federal Constitution, 1787–8," *Bulletin of the University of Wisconsin* (1894–96):52.

28. Robert A. East, "The Massachusetts Conservatives in the Critical Period," in *The Era of the American Revolution*, ed. Richard B. Morris (New York: Columbia University Press, 1939), pp. 349–91.

29. Forrest McDonald, *We the People* (Chicago: University of Chicago Press, 1958), p. 182.

30. Adams, *Writings*, 4:373.

31. Ibid., 2:152; 4:313; Miller, *Sam Adams*, p. 372. On Adams's recognition of the necessity of maintaining the distinction of rich and poor see *Writings*, 4:316.

32. Adams, *Writings*, 4:372–73; cf. also 4:296, 305–6, where he characterizes even county conventions as dangerous.

33. William V. Wells, *The Life and Public Service of Samuel Adams* (Boston: Little, Brown, & Co., 1865), p. 246; *Massachusetts Centinel*, 31 March 1787. Adams took a similar position on the Whiskey Rebellion: see *Columbian Centinel*, 2 April 1794. In a country such as France, revolution might be legitimate; but in republics, respect and obedience were always due to constitutional authorities (Maier, *Old Revolutionaries*, pp. 30, 32).

34. Harding, *Contest*, pp. 16–17.

35. Antifederalists in Massachusetts argued that the states were the home of liberty and therefore were properly sovereign over internal affairs. Thus, while Antifederalists admitted the necessity for the federal regulation of commerce, they wanted no further federal control of their internal affairs. In their view, the suppression of Shays's Rebellion demonstrated the underlying strength of the state government: see "Vox Populi," in *The Complete Anti-Federalist* (hereafter cited as *CAF*), ed. Herbert J. Storing, 7 vols. (Chicago: University of Chicago Press, 1981), 4:41–53. Here they laid great weight on the state's capacity to foster virtue ("John De Witt," *CAF*, 4:16–20) and argued that the difficulties in the state were due to the unregulated self-interest of the commercial republic. In their view, the proposed plan would only augment these difficulties. It not only failed to secure the virtues of the people, but it did not even secure their individual liberties ("Columbian Patriot," *CAF*, 4:270–87). Nor did it guarantee an adequate representation. Massachusetts had not been allotted enough representatives ("Republican Federalist," ibid., pp. 162–90; "Columbian Patriot," ibid., pp. 270–87); qualifications for representatives were not sufficient ("Watchman," ibid., pp. 231–33; "Republican Federalist," ibid.); and they were not sufficiently accountable ("Watchman," ibid.; "Columbian Patriot," ibid.). Checks and balances were insufficient ("David," ibid., pp. 246–49; "Columbian Patriot," ibid.), and the government did not correspond to the genius of the people ("Columbian Patriot," ibid; "Agrippa," ibid., pp. 72–73, 81–87). The lack of such checks and the absence of moral constraints would require the government to use force to maintain order. The government would therefore become tyrannical ("David," ibid.). The supremacy clause, the power to lay internal taxes, and the provision for a standing army, as well as a national administration, were viewed as especially dangerous ("Vox Populi," ibid.; "Poplicola," ibid., pp. 147–50; "Watchman," ibid.; "Agrippa," ibid., pp. 79–81; "John De Witt," ibid., pp. 20–24). This fostered the suspicion that the real aim of the plan was to establish an aristocracy ("Helvidius Priscus," ibid., pp. 151–61; "Columbian Patriot," ibid.; "Republican Federalist," ibid.; "Agrippa," ibid., pp. 106–9). While they did not like the plan, most Antifederalists felt that it could not be safely rejected ("Republican Federalist," ibid.). There was no easy answer. Amendments before ratification seemed illegal ("Bostonian," ibid., pp. 229–30), and amendments after ratification seemed unlikely ("Samuel," ibid., pp. 191–97). On the whole, they thus thought it would be best to adjourn and wait for the decision of Virginia. Alternatively, either a new convention ("Candidus," ibid., pp. 124–37, "Yeomanry," ibid., pp. 223–25) or returning the plan to the old convention with suggested amendments ("Bostonian," ibid.) seemed preferable. Only "Hampden" (ibid., pp. 198–200) argued for recommendatory amendments, the position that ultimately prevailed.

36. Charles Warren, "Elbridge Gerry, James Warren, Mercy Warren, and the Ratification of the Federal Constitution in Massachusetts," *Proceedings of the Massachusetts Historical Society* 66 (1932): 137–55. Warren points out that the

Federalists probably were using their political and administrative positions to prevent the circulation of Antifederalist pamphlets (ibid., p. 155). See also Gordon Wood, *The Creation of the American Republic, 1776–1787* (Chapel Hill: University of North Carolina Press, 1969), pp. 487, 513–14.

37. Adams, *Writings*, 4:286, 311; George Bancroft, *History of the Formation of the Constitution* (New York: Appleton, 1882), pp. 260–61; see also S. Adams to R. H. Lee, 23 December 1784, in *Writings*, 4:308–12. This view was shared by Mercy Warren as well (*History of the Rise and Progress of the American Revolution*, 3 vols. [Boston, Mass.: Manning & Loring, 1805], 3:356).

38. Adams, *Writings*, 4:324.

39. Charles King, *Life and Correspondence of Rufus King* (New York: G. B. Putnam's Sons, 1894), pp. 155, 267. Charles Warren argues that "Helvidus Priscus" was James Warren ("Elbridge Gerry," p. 155). Herbert Storing is more cautious; he points out that both Adams and Warren were suspected of writing the piece (*CAF*, 4:151). In any case, Gore's attribution of the piece to Adams tells us more about the Federalists' fears than about Adams' opinions.

40. King, *Life and Correspondence of Rufus King*, pp. 311–12. The Federalists suspected Adams of helping to circulate copies of *The Federal Farmer* in Massachusetts; see *The Documentary History of the Ratification of the Constitution* (hereafter cited as *DHRC*), ed. Merrill Jensen, John P. Kaminski, and Gaspare J. Saladino, et al., 8 vols. to date (Madison: State Historical Society of Wisconsin, 1976–) 14:156.

41. *DHRC*, 14:156.

42. Allan, *John Hancock*, p. 196; Miller, *Sam Adams*, p. 335.

43. Allan, *John Hancock*, p. 317; Adams, *Writings*, 4:210–12,ood 236.

44. Wells, *Life and Public Service of Samuel Adams*, 3:259.

45. Wood, *Creation*, pp. 606–7, 610.

46. Ibid., p. 612.

47. Ibid., pp. 502–3.

48. Libby, "Geographical Distribution," p. 55; Harding, *Contest*, pp. 59–66; Wood, *Creation*, p. 486.

49. Cf., e.g., the speeches of Randel and Singletary in *The Debates in the Several State Conventions on the Adoption of the Federal Constitution*, ed. Jonathan Elliot, 4 vols. (Washington, D.C.: n.p., 1836), 2:40, 102. As Wood points out, America was actually approaching the point where ability, education, and wealth were becoming liabilities to obtaining public office (*Creation*, p. 493).

50. *Debates*, 2:98

51. Maier, *Old Revolutionaries*, p. 19.

52. Gorham to Knox, 30 October 1787, in E. F. Stone, "Parsons and the Constitutional Convention of 1788," *Essex Institute Historical Collection* 35 (1899): 89.

53. Ibid., p. 92.

54. *Debates*, 2:6.

55. Mercy Warren described Adams as "tranquil and unruffled in the vortex of political altercation; too firm to be intimidated" (*History*, 1:212).

56. *Debates*, 2:96.

57. Ibid., p. 102.

58. Ibid., p. 107.

59. Ibid., p. 122.

60. Ibid., p. 177.

61. Ibid., p. 31.

62. Wells, *Life and Public Service of Samuel Adams*, 3:90.

63. Theophilus Parsons, Jr., *Memoir of Theophilus Parsons* (Boston, Mass.: Ticknor & Fields, 1859), p. 223.

64. Thomas C. Amory, *The Life of James Sullivan* (Boston, Mass.: Philips, Sampson, & Co., 1859), p. 223.

65. George Thatcher, "The Thatcher Papers," *Historical Magazine* 2d ser. 6 (1869): 265.

66. King to Knox, 27 January 1788, in Stone, "Parsons," p. 93. A letter to the rival *Boston American Herald* of 28 January 1788 argued that conditional amendments were not possible (*DHRC*, 14:140).

67. James Madison, *Letters and Other Writings of James Madison*, 4 vols., (Philadelphia: Lippincott, 1867), 1:374.

68. King to Knox, 27 January 1788, in Stone, "Parsons," p. 93.

69. King, *Life and Correspondence of Rufus King*, p. 318. King suggested to Horatio Gates on the same day that "Perhaps we shall adopt and recommend to the Delegates . . . certain alterations" (Winfred E. A. Bernhard, *Fisher Ames* [Chapel Hill: University of North Carolina Press, 1965], p. 62).

70. Stone, "Parsons," p. 94.

71. Dalton to Hodge, 30 January 1788, in Stone, "Parsons," p. 93.

72. King, *Life and Correspondence of Rufus King*, p. 319.

73. Harding points out that this was reported at Boston in the *Massachusetts Centinel* of 9 January 1788 as the opinion of the southern politicians (*Contest*, p. 86).

74. This is made clear by Samuel Otis in a letter to Sedgwick of 13 October 1788, ms. in Massachusetts Historical Society, "Sedgwick Papers," p. 476.

75. Bancroft, *History of the Formation of the Constitution*, p. 258.

76. Wells asserts incorrectly that Colonel May found the paper in Parsons's hand in Hancock's estate when, in fact, May only noted that it was not in Hancock's hand. (*Sam Adams*, 3:259).

77. Amory, *Life of James Sullivan*, p. 223.

78. In Harding's opinion, the suggestion of ratification, with attached amendments by General Heath on the morning before Hancock's proposal, was designed to pave the way for the conciliatory proposition (*Contest*, pp. 87–88).

79. *DHRC*, 14:463.

80. Harding, *Contest*, p. 84.

81. *Debates*, 2:162.

82. Bancroft reports this on the basis of the personal knowledge of John Davis, a delegate to the convention (*History of the Formation of the Constitution*, p. 272).

83. *Debates*, 2:162.

84. Belknap to Hazard, 10 February 1788, in Belknap, "Belknap Papers," p. 17.

85. Adams, *Writings*, 4:226; see also Maier, *Old Revolutionaries*, p. 38.

86. Adams, *Writings*, 4:282.

87. Ibid., pp. 281, 287–88.

88. Ibid., p. 27.

89. See Belknap to Hazard, 3 February 1788, in Belknap, "Belknap Papers," p. 16.

90. Ralph V. Harlow, *Samuel Adams, Promoter of the American Revolution: A Study in Psychology and Politics* (New York: Henry, Holt, & Co., 1923), p. 334.

91. *Debates*, 2:174–75.

92. Libby, "Geographical Distribution," p. 12.

93. *Debates and Proceedings in the Convention of the Commonwealth of Massachusetts Held in the Year 1788*, ed. Branford K. Pierce and Charles Hale (Boston, Mass.: William White, 1856), p. 411.

94. Ibid., p. 332.

95. Ibid., p. 284.

96. James K. Hosmer, *Samuel Adams: The Man of the Town Meeting* (Boston, Mass.: Houghton Mifflin, & Co., 1898), p. 400.

97. Adams, *Writings*, 4:330–31.

98. Ibid., pp. 333–34; cf. also pp. 339, 355, 371, 388.

99. Allan, *John Hancock*, p. 357.

100. Ibid., p. 357.

101. Ibid., p. 340.

102. Miller, *Sam Adams*, p. 198.

103. Adams, *Writings*, 4:124–25, 238, 377–79, 411; Maier, *Old Revolutionaries*, p. 49.

104. Adams, *Writings*, pp. 343, 349, 359, 371, 379, 401.

105. Ibid., p. 409, 411.

PART THREE

THE CONSOLIDATION OF POLITICAL CULTURES

7

MARYLAND

The Small Republic in the New Nation

PETER S. ONUF

When the Maryland ratifying convention met at Annapolis on April 21, 1788, the opponents of the Constitution were badly outnumbered. The Antifederalists' problem was that the Constitution "offered something that nearly every constituency badly wanted."[1] Despite a history of bitter partisanship over paper money and debtor relief, the state's political leadership generally agreed that the proposed system would benefit Maryland. Thus on April 28, after only a few days of discussion, the delegates voted, by a decisive vote of 63 to 11, to ratify. A subsequent effort to recommend amendments made some progress in committee but never reached the convention floor. Afflicted with laryngitis, the Antifederalist leader Luther Martin remained uncharacteristically silent.[2]

Contemporary observers were surprised by this overwhelming decision. Why did the Antifederalists fail to mount an effective opposition? Certainly Luther Martin, a delegate to the Constitutional Convention, believed that the proposed system jeopardized his state's essential interests. Martin had stormed home from Philadelphia, convinced that Maryland and the other small states were doomed to be crushed by their large neighbors under the new federal Constitution. The proposed government was nothing but a "system of slavery," he told the state's legislators in late November. Martin's speech, which was subsequently published in pamphlet form as *The Genuine Information*, touched on a wide variety of Antifederalist themes, but it was most remarkable for its extended analysis of the large-state/small-state con-

171

troversy. Because the principle of the equality of states had been abandoned in regard to the House of Representatives, he explained, the ten small states—including Maryland—would be reduced to "the most abject and servile subjection" to the large states of Massachusetts, Pennsylvania, and Virginia.[3] Yet, no other opponent of the Constitution in Maryland picked up Martin's argument during the ratification controversy.[4] In fact, Martin himself abandoned the issue of state size in subsequent publications, returning instead to the more familiar Antifederalist argument that the "immediate tendency" of the new system would be "to annihilate *all* the state governments indiscriminately"—not just the small states.[5]

The question is why he did this. Apparently, the Constitution's provision for equal representation in the Senate was seen as protecting the vital interests of small states such as Maryland. As a result, most Marylanders, even those who had misgivings about the Constitution, remained unmoved by Martin's dire predictions about large-state domination. Former governor Thomas Johnson, for example, thought the "Scale of power" between "the great and small States" had been "very properly adjusted."[6]

Maryland's Antifederalists generally ignored the issue of size and instead sought to exploit Maryland's position in the sequence of state ratifications—six states already had endorsed the document—to promote the opposition cause elsewhere. A postponed decision in Maryland or a call for amendments could give opponents of the plan a decisive advantage in Virginia. But such cooperation depended on muting objections—such as Martin's—that assumed a conflict of interest between the states or implied that the proposed system would be advantageous to one group of states at the expense of another. With an eye to national developments, Antifederalists tended to minimize the disadvantages of the Constitution that were peculiar to their states and to argue more generally that the "despotic" authority of a "consolidated" national government would threaten every state's sovereignty and every individual's liberty.

Federalists, on the other hand, welcomed the opportunity to defend a constitutional compromise that would incorporate the opposing schemes of representation long advocated by large and small state blocs. The Virginian George Nicholas thought Martin's *Genuine Information* would make good propaganda *for* the Constitution in his state, particularly the parts describing "the advantages which this government gives to the larger states."[7] "Sidney" told "the Working People of Maryland" that he was satisfied that "the small states will watch the large ones in one house" of the new government "and be watched by them in the other." But "Sidney" was not particularly concerned about protecting the corporate interests of small states such as Maryland: "We common people are more properly citizens of *America* than of any *particular state*." The best argument for the Constitution's complicated national legislature was that it would guarantee responsible, limited government by "the wisest and best men."[8]

Historians have long been puzzled by the sudden disappearance of the state size issue that Martin's anomalous performance — and later reversal — so clearly reveals.[9] Antifederalists reputedly anticipated that anxieties about large state domination would fuel "opposition to the constitution" in the "little states."[10] And Marylanders should have been receptive to Martin's arguments: since 1776, their state had led the small, "landless" state campaign against the territorial pretensions of Virginia and the other large, "landed" states; Maryland's statesmen had first developed the arguments about the dangers of disproportionate size later deployed by small-state delegates at Philadelphia.[11] By the time of the ratification debate, however, the issue of state size clearly had run its course. Martin's arguments would fall on deaf ears.

MARYLAND: THE ORIGINS OF A SMALL STATE

Maryland's charter of 1632, granted by King Charles I to Cecilius Calvert, Lord Baltimore, limited the colony's future development within fixed boundaries. For Marylanders, the most obvious and unfavorable comparison would be with their Virginian neighbors, whose 1609 charter opened up a vast hinterland for settlement, with no limits to the west. Sandwiched between the fortieth parallel to the north and the "Old Dominion" on the south, Maryland's western boundary was set at the most distant source of the Potomac River. Even these cramped boundaries proved controversial. Protracted negotiation and litigation with the Penns, proprietors of the new colony of Pennsylvania (1681), was finally resolved in 1769, when the Crown confirmed the Mason-Dixon line — fifteen miles south of the fortieth parallel. Meanwhile, the Virginians asserted that Maryland's western boundary should be fixed at the north rather than the south branch of the Potomac. This interpretation of Maryland's charter, which entailed the loss of considerable territory to the colony, was ratified by the Crown in 1748 but was not acknowledged by Maryland for another half century.[12]

A history of boundary controversies — and of disputes with Virginia over the regulation of tobacco production and of commerce — accentuated Marylanders' sense of their corporate interests and identity. Maryland was founded as a haven for Catholics, and the proprietors' policy of toleration fostered ethnic and religious diversity. The Calverts retained their ownership of Maryland's public lands until the Revolution, even during the period of royal government (1689–1715), and continued to play a dominant role in the colony's political and social life. Maryland thus developed along lines different from those of Virginia, notwithstanding a common dependence on tobacco and slaves and despite innumerable family connections.

Yet, if Maryland's leading men possessed a well-developed corporate consciousness by 1776, it was only after Independence that the state's "small" size would become a compelling concern. Even then, Maryland's population of 233,000 was hardly small in comparison to that of many of the new states. The rapid ascent of Baltimore as a commercial center and the conversion of many planters to wheat production boded well for future economic development.[13] But the necessity of cooperating with the other new states in the war and of establishing acceptable terms of union illuminated Maryland's relative disadvantages. The limited stock of public land was no longer simply the private concern of the Calverts; now the new state's leaders, in comparison with those of better situated neighboring states, would be hard pressed to raise desperately needed revenue from land sales, much less to provide Marylanders with outlets for future settlement or land speculation.

Throughout the colonial period, a colony's territorial extent had been of little consequence as long as its primary political connections were with the British metropolis and as long as there was little need to cooperate with its neighbors. But the prolonged and painful struggle to draft the Articles of Confederation — a struggle in which Maryland played a crucial role — exacerbated interstate conflicts that had been muted or simply did not exist under imperial rule. The relative size of the states became the paramount issue. Marylanders were convinced that the survival of their "small" state depended on making the large states smaller and on preserving the equality of state votes in the Confederation Congress.

American statesmen sought to combine the advantages of local self-government with effective provisions for collective security when they drafted the Articles of Confederation. In 1777, Congressman Charles Carroll of Maryland emphasized how crucial it was to establish the American union on a "rational" foundation that would enhance the "weight & consequence" of the United States and "give great Security to each [state] individually."[14] But the unequal size of the states proved a major obstacle to union. Led by Maryland, the small states refused to confederate until the large states had agreed to curb their western claims. If Virginia and Maryland were already unequal, the development of the West promised to widen the gap between them, thus jeopardizing their continuing union.

Marylanders complained that they were obliged to share the costs of securing the West, by contributing their "blood and treasure" to the common cause, while being excluded from its benefits. The defense of the large states' territorial pretensions constituted a drain on the resources of the entire nation, but when America's enemies were finally subdued and law and order reigned on the frontiers, the fertile western lands would be a limitless source of revenue—for the large states. It was "contrary to all principles of equity on which a Confederation ought to be founded," the Maryland House charged in 1778, that the small, landless states "should be burthened with very heavy expense for the subduing and guarantying immense tracts of country, when they are to have no share of the monies arising from the sale of lands."[15]

Maryland's brief against the landed states was outlined in legislative instructions that were laid before Congress in 1779. After enlisting the small states in their campaign to establish control over the West, the large states would inevitably predominate. "Is it possible," asked the legislature, that they "will use with greater moderation the increase of wealth and power derived from those territories, when acquired, than what they have displayed in their endeavours to acquire them?" Preponderant wealth and power would either lead large states "to oppress by open force their less wealthy and less powerful neighbours" or cause "the depopulation, and consequently the impoverishment," of the small states. Virginia, for instance, "would draw into her treasury vast sums of money" from land sales and so "be enabled to lessen her taxes." As a result, a "disadvantageously circumstanced" state such as Maryland would soon be drained "of its most useful inhabitants, its wealth; and its consequence in the scale of the confederated states would sink of course."[16]

The Maryland instructions suggested that union depended on a balance of state power that was jeopardized by their unequal prospects for economic development. Inequality among the states invited the large states to exploit their superior power at the expense of their small, weak neighbors. When the nominal equality of the states no longer disguised or inhibited these disparities—and when the populous states claimed that equal state voting violated their citizens' right to be "equally" represented—the union would collapse. Then the large states would strike out on their own, annexing their small neighbors or drawing them into regional confederations. Or—and this is what Luther Martin saw happening in 1787—the large states would dictate a new federal compact that guaranteed their superior position.

A theory of union was implicit in Marylanders' concern about the disproportionate size of Virginia and the other large states. State equality, broadly defined, sustained a stable balance that enabled Americans to defend and promote their common interests. The American union therefore constituted an improvement on the European state system only to the extent that the states respected one another's sovereignty and equality and sought to achieve a more perfect balance of power.[17] Before Virginia relinquished its trans-Ohio claims in 1784, the question was whether the tendency of American politics under the Confederation would be toward equality and union or toward inequality and disunion. Even after Congress had gained title to the Northwest Territory, the still vast disparities among the states was a continuing source of concern, and congressmen from small states pressed for further cessions.

The North Carolina delegate Richard Dobbs Spaight—who thought the Virginia cession gave Congress more land than it could "*properly* dispose of for these twenty or thirty years to come"—attributed this agitation to the "envy" of small states that were "so trifling" in size "when compared to the larger ones."[18] Large-state delegations also found that their small-state counterparts continued to resist strong measures against separatists. The "small states appear to wish for every facility to lessen the larger ones," the Virginia delegates concluded.[19]

By keeping up the pressure for territorial concessions and by promoting national control over western development, the small states hoped to counter the tendency toward unequal wealth and power that disparate state size supposedly encouraged. The danger was that as the larger states grew more powerful, their small, circumscribed neighbors would become progressively poorer and weaker, regardless of their supposedly equal rights under the Confederation.

The western land cessions helped to allay anxieties about the disproportionate size of the large states, but they also contributed to an emerging sense that state boundaries were contingent and negotiable. The ceding states agreed to change their own boundaries; then Congress began to project boundaries for new western states, thus inadvertently encouraging separatists to increase their agitation for state divisions. Proposals for redrawing state lines in the East as well as in the West abounded as the sense of imminent crisis grew more pervasive during the mid 1780s. Sectional tensions, exacerbated by the Mississippi controversy, led to talk about breaking up the union and realigning the states.

A general renegotiation of state boundaries may have seemed propitious to some small-state leaders: here, perhaps, was an opportunity to complete the process of equalization that had been begun by the cessions. But jurisdictional upheaval also threatened the very existence of the small states. Would commitment to the principles of state equality restrain the large states from exploiting the possibility—or the reality—of disunion in order to extend their power? Some commentators thought "ridiculously small" states such as Delaware and Rhode Island should simply be eliminated.[20] Would citizens of the small states rise up in defense of their corporate rights?

In the event of disunion, the small states would no longer enjoy the security afforded by a continental balance of power or by the guarantees of state rights that were incorporated in the Articles. The large states would then be able to establish regional dominance and thus—directly by means of annexation or conquest or indirectly by dictating terms of "confederation" to neighboring states—make themselves still larger. Small-state leaders had reason to fear that self-interest would produce factions in their own states that would favor closer alliance or even amalgamation with neighboring large states: merchants would seek commercial concessions, land speculators would seek access to undeveloped public lands, and taxpayers would seek relief. The superior power and resources of large states—and even more of a consolidated national government—undoubtedly appealed to would-be "aristocrats" and ambitious entrepreneurs. But however well "extended dominion" served such interests, "it has always proved incompatible with the preservation of liberties."[21] It would be fatal for Americans to abandon their states, for states alone could preserve a regime of liberty, equality, and union across the American continent.

LUTHER MARTIN'S ARGUMENT

"The principles of the rights of men and the rights of States" once "influenced our conduct," Luther Martin wrote in his *Genuine Information*, but "now [they] seem to be forgotten."[22] By providing for proportional representation in the House of Representatives, the proposed Constitution compromised the equality and integrity of the states and thus subverted the federal balance. The Constitutional guarantee of the corporate integrity of the small states in the proposed Senate was inadequate. Martin insisted that the American states had to become more equal—in every sense of the word, including territorial extent—before the union could be made stronger without jeopardizing republican liberty. The growing inequality of states promoted by the Constitution would subvert the union, he warned, while the dangerous concentration of federal power would destroy individual liberties.

Martin had the conventional wisdom—and the history of the Confederation—on his side: "the best political writers," most notably Montesquieu, had warned that republican government could not survive in large states.[23] But the argument for small states was tempered by the realization that the Americans would have to preserve their independence in a world of great—and despotic—powers. How could they do this without sacrificing the liberty, equality, and independence of their small republican states? The solution, Martin and other defenders of states' rights insisted, was to form a confederation, founded on—and dedicated to upholding—the sovereignty of its member states.[24]

Martin's basic premise was that the states stood toward one another "as individuals in a State of nature." Therefore, "each State is considered equally free and equally independent, the one having no right to exercise authority over the other, though more strong, more wealthy, or abounding with more inhabitants."[25] The proposed system, Martin told the legislature, had been concocted by monarchists and "those who wished the total abolition of State governments," working in unholy alliance with delegates who had wanted to increase the "power and influence" of large states. But principled republicans such as George Mason of Virginia and Elbridge Gerry of Massachusetts had not been seduced by the apparent advantages of the proposed scheme for their states. They recognized that any such departure from federal principles inevitably would "destroy all State governments" as well as the union.[26] The proposed method of ratification was itself a potentially fatal assault on the states. Circumventing the state governments by appealing directly to the sovereign people would only serve "to *weaken* the *bands of society*, to introduce *anarchy* and *confusion*, and to *light* the *torch of discord and civil war* throughout this continent."[27]

Reviewing the history of the Confederation, Martin attempted to show that the union rested on the successful reconciliation of two apparently antagonistic principles. If the small states had secured equal representation in Congress, the large states had succeeded in upholding their extended—and unequal—territorial claims. The American union was premised both on the corporate equality and on the territorial integrity of the states. Martin warned that the proposed Constitution would subvert this original federal compact. For Martin, the very fact that the states were so unequal in extent of territory, population, and potential power made the constitutional guarantee of state equality essential: otherwise, it would be in the power of the largest states "to *aggrandize themselves*, at the *expense of all the rest*." Finally, the small states—and therefore the union itself—would be destroyed.[28]

Supported by only a few other opponents of the proposed Constitution, Martin boldly asserted that the Articles of Confederation were actually working.[29] By securing the essential rights and interests of large and small states alike, Martin argued, the Confederation had abolished force from American politics and thereby had preserved the union. An impartial view of the present situation vindicated the Articles, whatever their defects were in theory. "Was there any *ambitious State or States*," he asked, "who, in *violation of every sacred obligation,* was preparing to *enslave* the *other states,* and raise *itself* to *consequence* on the *ruin* of the *others?*[30]

For Martin, the territorial adjustments of the postwar years constituted a continuing process that promised to perfect the federal compact. The new Constitution would interrupt—and inevitably reverse—this process, thus destroying the union. Citing Article IV, section 3, Martin concluded that the proposed system was "designed to preserve the States their whole territory unbroken, and to prevent the erection of new States within the territory of any of them." This is why Georgia, a lightly populated frontier state with extensive western claims, had joined the large-state coalition and was supporting the new government. Georgia looked forward to the time *"when,* her *population* increase being in some measure *proportioned* to her *territory,* she should *rise* in the scale, and *give law* to the *other States."*[31]

Martin contrasted the probable behavior of Georgia and North Carolina, states that had not yet ceded their western claims, with that of Virginia and the other states that had made cessions to the Confederation Congress. The genius of the existing system, Martin suggested, was that it encouraged large states to make themselves smaller: giving up distant and unenforceable western claims allowed large states to enjoy the advantages of republican government in a more circumscribed territory; by creating a national revenue fund, cessions made Congress stronger and thus better able to secure the territorial rights of its members; and with more modest boundaries, the large states inspired less jealousy from their circumscribed neighbors. Most important, because of equal state voting under the Articles, the large states would not sacrifice any political advantage by becoming smaller; on the contrary, assuming some harmony of interest within its original boundaries, the division of a large state into two or more states would increase its effective voting strength.[32]

Self-interest led the large states to give in to pressure from the small states—and from their own citizens—to curtail their extensive claims. But these incentives would disappear under a system that gave new scope to their imperial ambitions. Thus, Martin's chief concern was not that Maryland and the other small states would forfeit their present political advantage under the Articles. As a relatively populous "small" state, Maryland would be well represented in both houses of the new legislature; in the short run, it would exercise more power in Congress than the "large" state of Georgia. But, warned Martin,

> the States having extensive territory, where lands are to be procured cheap, would be daily increasing in the number of their inhabitants, not only from propagation, but from the emigration of the inhabitants of the other States, and would soon have double or perhaps treble the number of representatives that they are to have at first, and thereby enormously increase their influence in the national councils.[33]

Maryland Federalists impatiently dismissed the claim that the large states would overwhelm the small states: what possible common "interest" would lead states so disparately situated as Massachusetts, Pennsylvania, Virginia, and Georgia to act in concert?[34] The small-state answer to this question, Rosemarie Zagarri has persuasively argued in her work on the question of representation, was that size itself was the issue. Large states would act together to preserve and extend the advantages that came with extensive territory; whether or not they had any *other* common interest, the large states would gain in population, wealth, and power at the expense of the small states.[35]

Martin joined countless other opponents of the Constitution in arguing that republics should be small. Disgruntled frontier settlers certainly endorsed the idea: "as soon as the population increases remote from the seat of government" in the large states, "the inhabitants are urgent for the removal of the seat of their government, or to be erected into a new State."[36] But the large states' determination to preserve their advantages under the new Constitution would lead them to suppress separatist movements; meanwhile, "the hardship, the inconvenience, and the injustice of compelling" them "to remain connected with the old states" would drive frontier people to violent resistance in order "to free themselves from, and to shake off, so ignominious a yoke."[37] Because they would predominate under the Constitution, the large states would be able to consolidate their tenuous hold on distant settlements by calling on the force of the whole union. Thereupon, warned Martin, "the State of Maryland may, and probably will, be called upon to assist, with her wealth and her blood, in subduing" new state movements in all the large states. Force would supersede consent as the basic principle of American politics.

Under the new Constitution, the large states would "have a *motive* for desiring to preserve their territory entire and unbroken, which they *never had before*," Martin explained; they would be able to gratify "*their ambition, in possessing and exercising superior power over their Sister States.*"[38] Of course, Maryland and the other small states would recoil at this misuse of national power, but having ratified the Constitution, they would be bound to submit. Agreeing to the new system, Martin therefore concluded, would be a form of collective suicide, sanctioning a regime of force within and among the states. He asked whether the people of Maryland were willing to endorse the new government, thereby "*giving ourselves masters*" and "riveting our [own] chains!"[39]

Antifederalists were certain that large states and an extended republic would inevitably degenerate into despotism. Luther Martin provided one of the most elaborate accounts of how this would happen. First, recent separatist agitation showed that the large states would have to use despotic force to uphold their claims. Their success in doing so would be made possible by their superior power in Congress under the new scheme of representation. The resultant growth of the large states would enhance this advantage, giving still wider scope to their ambition and further reducing their small neighbors to "servile subjection." The "peace and safety of the Union" depended on dividing the large states, Martin insisted, "since, when their population should become proportioned in any degree to their territory, they would, from their strength and power, become dangerous members of a federal government."[40]

Martin's gloomy assessment of the nation's prospects under the Constitution was grounded in traditional anxieties about the dangers of disproportionate state size for the survival of the union. His *Genuine Information* also presented one of the strongest arguments for the Articles of Confederation in Antifederalist polemics. Besides keeping the peace and eliminating interstate conflict, Martin suggested, the federal compact under the Articles tended to *equalize* the states and so harmonize the fundamental principles of territorial integrity and state equality. Ironically, the very success of the Articles had also dissipated the anxieties about the dangers of size that had once guided Maryland's policy. Martin's tasks, therefore, were to revive the issue of size and to demonstrate the continuing relevance of the old arguments for understanding the essential nature of the new Constitutional regime.

RECONCEPTUALIZING THE UNION

In his *Genuine Information*, Luther Martin developed a powerful argument against the Constitution and for the Confederation. More than any other Antifederalist, he was able to connect the ongoing struggle between large- and small-state blocs under the Confederation to the movement for national constitutional reform. The Confederation had secured the sovereignty of the small American republics and, by encouraging their gradual equalization, had created a progressively more stable and enduring balance of power among them. The federal Constitution, notwithstanding its declared intention of creating a "more perfect union," violated the fundamental principles of union by demolishing state rights and capitulating to the ambitions of the large states.

But Martin's efforts proved unavailing. Most Marylanders rejected his basic assumption that enduring union depended on preserving and perfecting a balance of power among the states. Even Antifederalists seemed ambivalent about the central place Martin accorded distinct state sovereignties in his conception of the American union. They were more concerned with protecting individual liberties or promoting sectional interests. The Antifederalist "Mentor," for example, dismissed the notion that large Virginia and small Maryland were necessarily rivals. The "*real* interests of *the people* of Virginia and Maryland are inseparably the same," he wrote; "their climate and commerce, soil and produce, exports and imports; laws, manners and customs are alike; and if they are wise, they will ever act in concert, on any question that involves their general and mutual interest."[41]

How did Marylanders, including those who opposed a stronger central government, overcome conventional anxieties about the superior power of Virginia and the other large states? The simple explanation is that, notwithstanding their protracted campaign to circumscribe large-state claims, Maryland's leaders did not think it was possible, or even desirable, to work for a perfect equalization of territory. They wanted Virginia to be smaller—and this would make Maryland relatively larger—but they had no intention of extending their own state's jurisdiction to the west. Their working definition of Maryland's corporate interest, even during the western lands controversy, thus diverged significantly from Luther Martin's. While Martin

assumed that territory, population, wealth, and power were interdependent, most Marylanders believed that the state's interests could
be promoted and protected without extending its boundaries. Forgo-
ing direct rule, Maryland and Virginia could both share in the benefits
of western development.

Although Marylanders anticipated many of Martin's arguments in
their campaign against Virginia's western claims, they also advocated
an expansive federal role incompatible with his conception of state
sovereignty. The small states would redress inequalities by asserting
a collective title to the western lands and so strengthen the authority
of the central government.[42] Virginians responded by linking vindica-
tion of their territorial claims to the *defense* of state sovereignty against
Congress's "intolerable despotism." Should Congress once cross "over
the Line of the Confederation, and assume Rights not delegated to
them," no state would be safe from its insatiable "Lust of Power."[43]
As a result, the supposed struggle between small-state defenders of
states' rights and large-state nationalists on which Martin's argument
pivoted in fact had been reversed during the western lands controversy,
as it was at the Philadelphia convention—once the representation issue
had been resolved—and as it would be in the ratification debates.

During the western lands controversy, the small states sought to
establish Congress's jurisdiction in the West so they could share in
the benefits of land sales and economic development. Congress was
also expected to be more sympathetic than Virginia had been to the
claims of private land companies whose membership—including many
leading Marylanders—was concentrated in the small, landless states.[44]
Only by aggressively enlarging the scope of congressional power could
the small states hope to neutralize the relative advantages of the large
states and promote the private interests of their citizens.

The struggle over the western lands transformed Marylanders' implicit definition of state equality. Equality was increasingly understood
in relation to the national government: Would Maryland and the other
small states be protected from disproportionate revenue burdens?
Would their corporate rights and interests be guaranteed? Would they
benefit equally from western development? These questions shifted
attention away from the comparisons between states as distinct political
communities that were central to conventional balance-of-power
thinking.

Before the Constitutional Convention, anxiety about the relative size of the states was most pronounced when disunion seemed most likely: without an effective central government to mediate between the states, differential capabilities would be translated immediately into political advantage; only a balance of power could then preserve the peace. The prospects for union seemed particularly doubtful during the early years of the war, as Congress vainly attempted to hammer out an acceptable confederation. These concerns revived during the postwar period: the "imbecilic" Congress, paralyzed by sectionalism and state particularism, was a weak barrier against anarchy and disunion. At both times, commentators worried about the unstable conditions resulting from the imbalance of state power and proposed radical territorial readjustments. But the survival of the union was never seriously in doubt during the western lands controversy, notwithstanding occasional threats by the large states to withdraw from the union if their jurisdictional rights were not duly respected.[45] While the outcome of the war remained uncertain, no state could afford to betray the common cause.

Marylanders were concerned less about the collapse of the union than about union on acceptable terms. They were determined that the fruits of victory—the vast, incredibly valuable inland empire— should not be unequally distributed. The preservation of their equal status in the union depended on a guarantee of equal opportunities for their own enterprising citizens. Virginians attributed agitation against their claims to the "avidity of the land mongers" who dominated the landless-state delegations.[46] But for Marylanders, the fate of land-company claims raised a question of principle as well as of self-interest. They sought to release economic initiative from conventional jurisdictional limitations, thus enabling small-state investors to mobilize their capital through private land companies and to participate equally in western development. Marylanders were no more driven by self-interest than Virginians were: the novelty of the former's position was their willingness to forgo direct political control. Land-company shareholders were prepared to acknowledge any jurisdiction (including Virginia's) that would recognize their titles. This recognition would neutralize the historic advantage of Virginian investors in the scramble for new lands and thereby minimize the dangerous implications of disproportionate state size.

Virginia ultimately succeeded in rebuffing the land-company challenge, stipulating in the 1784 cession to Congress that private claims not recognized by the state be deemed invalid.[47] At the same time, however, the cession act endorsed the small-state contention that the West should be developed for the "common benefit" of all the states. Congress soon began to formulate a national land policy that would ensure equal opportunity for investors and settlers from all parts of the country.[48]

The way politicians from Maryland defined their state's interests—and their private interests—in the western lands controversy anticipated a new conception of union that transcended the classic balance-of-power paradigm. Although Marylanders saw boundless opportunity for private enterprise and for public land sales revenue to the west, they had little interest in extending their state's jurisdiction. Redrawing boundaries to equalize the states was both impractical and irrelevant to the real interests of their constituents; nor would a greater degree of "equality" (so defined) necessarily guarantee a better balanced, stronger union.

The thrust of congressional policy was to create a common interest in the western lands that transcended state interests. By administering the ceded territory as a national trust and by delaying the formation of new states with their own distinct interests, Congress could counter the centrifugal effects of rapid westward expansion. Equipped with the necessary powers, and commanding the vast resources of the continent, Congress would be able to preserve peace among the states, regardless of discrepancies in size and power.

Maryland's leaders relied on a stronger national government to mitigate inequalities in the union. The western land cessions were more notable for bolstering Congress's sagging prospects than for equalizing state size: even after its cession, Virginia remained disproportionately large. But as long as they were protected by the union, Marylanders had little reason to fear or to envy their large neighbors. The ideological bias toward small-sized republics was reinforced by a growing awareness of a "want of energy" and "vigour" in large states.[49] In large states, separatist movements, partisan conflict, and agrarian discontent demonstrated the liabilities of large size for republican government. "The States that please to call themselves large," Luther Martin told the Constitutional Convention, "are the weekest in the Union."[50]

The controversial question was the impact of disunion on the relative situation of the states. Rejecting Martin's conclusion that a stronger union would exacerbate imbalance and inequality, most Marylanders were persuaded by the Federalist contention that the large states would crush the small unless restrained by a more effective national government. In the event of disunion, they reasoned, the large states would become more vigorous, energetic, and dangerous, discarding their republican governments in favor of the despotic regimes mandated by their extensive territories. Then, of course, Maryland's only hope would be either to strike preemptively before its neighbors' superior power could be brought into play or, anticipating defeat, to negotiate the most favorable possible terms of submission.

A balance of power—and territory—would be desirable in the *absence* of union. But a durable union secured by an effective national government would minimize the importance of achieving such a balance. Marylanders did not therefore naively assume that a strong central government would necessarily uphold their corporate interests and identity. At the Philadelphia convention, resistance to the large-state scheme of proportional representation hinged on this crucial concern. But with the so-called Connecticut Compromise, which guaranteed equal representation in the Senate, most small-state delegates were satisfied that state "equality" was—in this limited, defensive sense—adequately secured under the proposed Constitution. "By this expedient, is safety secured to the lesser states," Alexander Contee Hanson had asked, "as completely as if the senate were the only legislative body?"[51]

But union was more than a contrivance for preserving Maryland's rights against large-state encroachments. Many Marylanders conceived of the union as a regime of harmonious interest and expanding opportunity. From this perspective, state equality meant equal participation in the growing prosperity of the nation as a whole. "Equality," so defined, did not require equal territory, but instead presupposed a complementarity of interdependent interests across the continent. A "Farmer" in Frederick County thus suggested that Maryland could compensate for its small size by encouraging commerce and manufactures: "This state, from its local situation, surrounded and circumscribed in its limits by two powerful sister states, who are possessed of very extensive and fertile frontier territories, has nothing wherein to rival and preserve an equilibrium with its neighbours, but in its commerce and the increasing numbers and industry of its citizens."[52] Achieving this "equilibrium," proponents of economic development made clear, depended less on commercial competition with neighboring states — substituting trade wars for jurisdictional conflicts — than on participating in the general prosperity made possible by interstate cooperation. Such a harmonious regime was implicit in the "Farmer's" prescription for Maryland's economy: commerce could flourish only if enterprising Marylanders enjoyed mutually beneficial trade relations with neighboring states.

The new conception of union — and of Maryland's interest in it — was fully articulated by promoters of the plan to develop the Potomac River as a trade route to the west. One writer proclaimed it a "Work of more political than commercial Consequence, as it will be one of the grandest Chains for preserving the federal Union." Westerners, he explained "will have free access to us, and we shall be one and the same People."[53] Echoing arguments once used by land speculators, spokesmen for the Potomac Company insisted that private and public interests converged in opening the western trade: the "private emoluments" of investors would be matched by "the great advantages that must inevitably flow to our country."[54] "Free access" would make possible the development of reciprocal interests, thus guaranteeing an enduring — and prosperous — union between East and West.

By directing western surpluses to markets in Virginia and Maryland, the Potomac project promised to transform the Chesapeake economy. Alexandria, Virginia, would soon be raised "in importance, and distinction, to an equality at least, with the first commercial cities in the United States."[55] But the entire region would benefit from this "great and important work," the "vast consequences" of which "cannot be elucidated but by time."[56] Thus while Baltimore legislator David McMechen also viewed "a communication and connexion with the Western Country, as a great political object," he predicted that the Potomac route would "introduce an immense source of wealth" to Maryland.[57]

Just as closer economic ties between East and West would benefit both regions and strengthen the union, Maryland and Virginia would be drawn closer by their common interests. Notwithstanding their recent, bitter conflict over the western lands, the two states acted swiftly and harmoniously to organize the Potomac Company in late 1784 and early 1785. Eager to promote their own economic growth, the cities of Winchester, Annapolis, Georgetown, and Frederick joined private investors throughout the region in subscribing more than £40,000 within a few months. When the stockholders first met in May 1785 at Alexandria, George Washington, a longtime proponent of western development, was named company president.[58]

Joint sponsorship of the Potomac Company pointed toward a fundamental realignment in Chesapeake politics. Competition between rival jurisdictions and between allied land speculators had obstructed cooperation: when land was at issue, Maryland's gain was necessarily Virginia's loss. But once the Ohio country came under national control, both states stood to gain equally from the "aggrandizement" of the western trade. "The Friends to American Commerce and American Happiness, will no doubt feel much Pleasure in Contemplating the probable Success" of the Potomac project, the Alexandria newspaper reported after the company's 1786 meeting. This "great national work . . . will serve as a lasting Monument of the Amity and Sisterly Love, with which two States can concur in promoting" the "Happiness" of the entire continent.[59]

Maryland's policy during the "critical period" was to promote regional cooperation by resolving controversial questions with its neighbors.[60] These were concrete steps toward a more perfect union; yet, because interstate compacts violated the Articles of Confederation and because they also seemed to institutionalize the sectional differences that most threatened the American union, most Marylanders eschewed incremental reform and welcomed a radical revision of the federal compact.[61]

Politicians in small states such as Maryland favored a strong central government not simply because of their supposed weakness relative to their large neighbors. They also saw that the nationalization of the West, dismantling of trade barriers, and interstate cooperation in regional development projects could make disparities in state size irrelevant. Prosperous citizens of a small, commercially oriented state such as Maryland were better situated than were poor farmers in a large, relatively undeveloped state, but their prosperity depended on the equal access to the developing hinterland that state mercantilism and disunion threatened to subvert. Marylanders therefore tended to be "nationalists," not because they were indifferent to their state's corporate integrity and welfare, but rather because they recognized that Maryland's prosperity as well as its "equal" standing among the states depended on a much more perfect union.

MARYLAND AND THE CONSTITUTION

"When the convention was appointed," wrote Judge Alexander Contee Hanson, he feared "that the dispute about representation would be the rock, on which the vessel containing all our hopes would be dashed." But when he learned of the "equitable compromise between the larger and lesser states, my anxiety was instantly removed, and my soul enlightened by a sudden ray."[62] The small states certainly had had legitimate concerns about large-state domination. Yet for Hanson, the Connecticut Compromise came like a "sudden ray," removing every shadow of lingering doubt. Now Marylanders could transcend old fears, traditionally centered on the issue of state size, and turn hopefully to the future.

Maryland Federalists predicted boundless prosperity for their state in a harmonious, expanding union. This vision left little room for the destructive competition among states that had crippled the Confederation. "Civis" promised the rapid growth of foreign trade, shipbuilding, manufactures, and commercial agriculture:

> Life and property will be perfectly secure from external attacks, or domestic commotions. — Foreigners of property, mechanics and farmers will emigrate thither, and rapidly increase the value of lands. — Uniform commercial regulations will raise small villages to great towns; and America, from a parcel of jarring contemptible States, will then be a great, free, happy and flourishing empire.[63]

Willingness to embrace this bright prospect depended on being able to extricate hopes from fears and to imagine a future transcending the endless struggle for relative advantage.

Friends of the new Constitution charged that Antifederalists such as Luther Martin, who continued to stir up suspicion and conflict among the states, even after their rights and interests were so equitably secured, remained trapped in a hopelessly outmoded conception of the union. The Antifederalists' "union" remained synonymous with "balance"; anything threatening to shift the present, fragile equilibrium of state power tended inevitably toward "consolidation" and "despotism." But their "discordant" objections to the "proposed government" ("no two sets of objectors, nay no two objecting individuals . . . concur in making the same exceptions") revealed Antifederalism to be no more than an exaggerated expression of — and certainly no solution to — the underlying problems of American politics.[64] In their benighted darkness, opponents of the proposed system would run headlong into anarchy and civil war.

Maryland Federalists granted the necessity of securing the small states' corporate interests and integrity. But certainly those states would be better off under the protection of a powerful national government than if they were left to their own devices in the event of disunion. Federalists rejected Martin's premise that union depended on a balance of power among the states, insisting instead that states' rights would be most secure under a strong central authority. "The idea of a balance has long influenced the politics of Europe," Judge Hanson wrote. "But how much superior to this almost impracticable balance would be a general league, constituting a kind of federal republic, consisting of all the independent powers of Europe, for preventing the impositions and encroachments of one upon another!" Although "a true and perfect confederate government" was "not to be attained" in Europe's present "situation," American voters now had the opportunity to establish just such a scheme. For Marylanders at least, the choice should be clear.[65]

Ratifying the federal Constitution was in Maryland's interest, Hanson explained, even if traditional anxieties about disparities in state size were still justified. Maryland had long refused to ratify the Articles because they contained "no provision, for adjusting the dispute between the United States, and particular states" over the western lands. But under the new system it would be possible to challenge large-state claims in the federal courts; further territorial concessions were therefore more likely. Perhaps North Carolina's decision to withdraw its 1784 cession would be found unconstitutional; certainly Georgia — conscious of the weakness both of its claims and of its defenses against powerful enemies — would agree "to be circumscribed within narrower limits." Hanson and his Federalist colleagues dismissed Martin's contention that large states would dominate the new government: a stronger national government would be less subservient to large-state interests, they argued, and therefore would be better able to secure the rights of small states.[66]

For the most enthusiastic proponents of constitutional reform, the guarantee of states' rights and equality in the union was only the means toward higher ends. The new federal government would not "interfere with the internal police of any individual State," "Uncus" wrote in the *Maryland Journal,* but it also would have — in stark contrast to the Confederation Congress —"full authority to govern the United States" and to "protect the whole."[67] "Hambden" promised Marylanders that the Constitution would "restore order, protect your trade, defend and secure private property, restore mutual faith and confidence, and reestablish your reputation and credit among other nations."[68] Thus the prospects of individual Marylanders depended on the security and opportunity that only a strong union could secure.

The Federalists' appeal to private interest was crucial to the reconceptualization of Maryland's place in the union. Before the Constitutional Convention met, visionary Marylanders were already identifying individual opportunity with the "numberless advantages which divine Providence has really bestowed upon this country." "We shall look to ourselves, to our situation in the scale of nations," a writer in the *Maryland Gazette* (Baltimore) proclaimed, "and a little experience will convince us that, though young, we have great natural strength, abundant resources, and these improveable."[69] Americans had to "improve the bounties of a benign Providence," another writer added, for "our real independence must consist in the exertions of ingenuity and labour."[70] Distinctions among states did not figure in such exhortations. Following the lead of land-company investors, promoters of internal improvements, and merchants who agitated for uniform commercial regulations, these writers looked beyond Maryland's borders. "Providence" would only favor Marylanders if there were no political barriers to participating in national economic development.

Prospects for economic development helped shift Marylanders' attention away from traditional anxieties about state size. A draft for an undelivered defense of the Constitution by Charles Carroll of Carrollton exemplifies this new continental perspective. "Cast, Sir, your eye on the map of our vast domain," Carroll tells an imaginary companion:

> in fancy then ascend the highest ridge of yonder mountains; from their lofty summit contemplate one vast plane sloping from the foot of the Alleghany to ye old Atlantic, and stretching from north to South a thousand miles, watered by mighty rivers precipitating their course eastward, down this declivity to the sea; rivers which now only fertilize and ornament, yet destined soon to waft to ye ports of commerce the varied commerce of the lands thro' which they flow. Turn now, Sir, from this magnificent prospect, and looking westward, view one continued forest, old as creation, reaching from ye same chain of mountains to ye Mississippi. . . . See the wilderness disappears; the fables of Greece are realized. . . . What sources of future wealth and grandeur open upon the imagination![71]

But "what sources of discord too!" if the states failed to perfect their union. Only a strong national government could guarantee that all Americans would share equally in the continent's potentially boundless "future wealth"; disunion would unleash a destructive competition for relative advantage that would subvert these bright prospects, beggaring the states and jeopardizing American independence.[72]

Carroll's vision of continental economic development reflected Maryland's traditional position as a small, circumscribed state. Enterprising Marylanders had long since recognized that their prospects depended on securing an advantageous position in the regional and national economy. Although the western lands controversy and the debate over representation at the Constitutional Convention emphasized the importance of balance in the union and of state equality as defined by Luther Martin in the *Genuine Information*, the tendency of Maryland politics was to play down the importance of distinctions among the states. For Martin and the Antifederalists, this amalgamation of interests and blurring of distinctions would mean the end of state sovereignty and civil liberty. But by distinguishing the interests of the states from those of their governments, Carroll could argue that closer union would benefit both: "Will not the State-governments, as well as the general Government, become more energetic? Will not this energy tend to establish internal peace, useful regulations, ye improvements of our country, and a more flourishing state of commerce?"[73]

Combining a longstanding nationalist tradition with a solicitude for the corporate integrity of the separate states forged through controversies over territory and representation, Maryland Federalists became eloquent proponents of the new federal system. Carroll looked forward to the addition of many more new states to this "most impressive Confederacy";[74] Judge Hanson also anticipated "the peaceable and friendly admission of new states." This faith in the dynamism of an expanding union of states was the political analogue of their vision of continental prosperity. The ultimate size of "a true federal republic," Hanson wrote, *"is neither greater nor less than that, which may comprehend all the states, which, by their continuity, may become enemies, unless united under one common head, capable of reconciling all their differences."*[75]

Only in a "true federal Republic" could Maryland enjoy true equality. Disunion surely meant annihilation, for then the radical imbalance of state power would tell against small states such as Maryland. But the kind of consolidated national government proposed by the Virginians at Philadelphia was equally dangerous: nothing would prevent the large states from tyrannizing over the small. Borrowing a theme from Antifederalist rhetoric, Judge Hanson suggested that inequality would be the premise and tendency of a consolidated continental regime: "In a single government, with a great extent of territory, the advantages are most unequally diffused. As the extreme parts are scarcely sensible of its protection, so are they scarcely under its domination." But "a confederate republic" avoided both extremes. In a union "consisting of distinct states, completely organized within themselves, and each of no greater extent than is proper for a republican form, almost all the blessings of government are *equally* diffused."[76]

Proponents of the new Constitution promised that Marylanders could have it both ways. They could continue to enjoy the benefits of republican government while participating equally in the vast project of developing the continent. For the many Maryland voters with more immediate, concrete interests in supporting the new regime, such rhetoric must have been irresistible.

NOTES

*I wish to acknowledge helpful criticism from Professors Rosemarie Zagarri of Catholic University and Michael Lienesch of the University of North Carolina.

1. Gregory Stiverson, "Maryland's Antifederalists and the Perfection of the U.S. Constitution," a paper delivered at the Conference on Maryland and the Ratification of the Constitution, Washington College, June 1986, p. 11. For earlier efforts to link ratification with class and sectional tensions see Philip A. Crowl, *Maryland during and after the Revolution: A Political and Economic Study* (Baltimore, Md.: Johns Hopkins University Press, 1943), and Jackson Turner Main, *The Antifederalists: Critics of the Constitution, 1781–1788* (Chapel Hill: University of North Carolina Press, 1961), esp. pp. 213–15. Recently, historians have begun to argue that Antifederalists—or, in Edward C. Papenfuse's apt phrase, the "Amending Fathers"—achieved considerable success in shaping the new constitutional order (see Papenfuse, "Completing the Revolution: Defining 'Vox Populi' and the Nature of Representative Government," a paper delivered at the Conference on Maryland and the Constitution, p. 8). In Maryland, Stiverson adds, they succeeded in sustaining "sentiment for amendments . . . under extreme adversity," p. 27. Yet if we need to revise the conventional wisdom on the "rout" of Maryland Antifederalists, it remains true that in seeking to secure personal liberties, they did not challenge the basic structure of the proposed system. With few exceptions—Luther Martin and John Francis Mercer are most conspicuous—Maryland Antifederalists accepted their opponents' nationalist premises and eschewed radical alternatives. My understanding of Maryland politics during the constitutional period relies heavily on the Stiverson and Papenfuse pieces and on Papenfuse's "The Legislative Response to a Costly War: Fiscal Policy and Factional Politics in Maryland, 1777–1789," in *Sovereign States in an Age of Uncertainty*, ed. Ronald Hoffman and Peter J. Albert (Charlottesville: University Press of Virginia, 1981), pp. 134–56.

2. William Tilghman, "Notes of Mr. Chase's Arguments in Convention," Maryland Hall of Records (MdHR P 1592-2). Maryland's archivist Edward C. Papenfuse graciously provided me with a typescript of Tilghman's manuscript notes on the convention proceedings.

3. Luther Martin, *The Genuine Information, Delivered to the Legislature of the State of Maryland, Relative to the Proceedings of the General Convention, Held at Philadelphia* (Baltimore, Md., 1787), in *The Records of the Federal Convention of 1787*, ed. Max Farrand, 4 vols. (New Haven, Conn.: Yale University Press, 1911–37), 3:172–232, at 178. For notes of Martin's original speech see ibid., 3:251–59. *Genuine Information* first appeared in serial form in *Maryland Gazette* (Baltimore), 28 December 1787 to 8 February 1787, and may thus be followed in *The Documentary History of the Ratification of the Constitution* (hereafter cited as *DHRC*), ed. Merrill Jensen, John P. Kaminski, Gaspare J. Saladino, et al., 8 vols. to date (Madison: State Historical Society of Wisconsin,

1976–), vol. 15 passim. The editors' introduction, ibid., 15:146–50, is the best source on the printing history of the pamphlet and on contemporary response to it. For a thorough recounting of Martin's arguments at Philadelphia and in the ratification debate see Paul S. Clarkson and R. Samuel Jett, *Luther Martin of Maryland* (Baltimore, Md.: Johns Hopkins University Press, 1970), esp. pp. 72–112, 135–50.

4. See, e.g., Elbridge Gerry to Vice Pres. of Massachusetts Convention, 21 January 1788, in Farrand, *Records*, 3:263–67; "Centinel" [Samuel Bryan], no. 1, *Independent Gazetteer* (Philadelphia), 5 October 1787, in *DHRC*, 2:158–67, at 165; William Grayson to William Short, 10 November 1787, in *Letters of the Members of the Continental Congress*, ed. Edmund Cody Burnett, 8 vols. (Washington, D.C.: Carnegie Institution, 1921–36), 8:678–80; Joseph McDowell, speech in North Carolina Convention, 28 July 1788, in *The Debates in the Several State Conventions on the Adoption of the Federal Constitution*, ed. Jonathan Elliot, 4 vols. (Philadelphia: J. B. Lippincott, 1876), 4:124. My own research confirms the conclusion of Jensen et al., *DHRC*, 15:146–50, that "no Maryland newspaper appears to have printed a substantial defense of the *Genuine Information.*"

5. Letters of Luther Martin, no. 3, *Maryland Journal* (Baltimore), 28 March 1788, in *Essays on the Constitution of the United States*, ed. Paul Leicester Ford (New York: Historical Printing Club, 1892), pp. 372–77, at 375, emphasis added.

6. Thomas Johnson to George Washington, 11 December 1787, in *DHRC*, 14:404.

7. George Nicholas to David Stuart, 9 April 1788, cited in *DHRC*, 15:149 n.

8. "Sidney," "To the Working People of Maryland," 27 February 1788, in *Maryland Journal*, 27 February 1788.

9. Cecelia Kenyon, "Men of Little Faith: The Antifederalists on the Nature of Representative Government," in *The Reinterpretation of the American Revolution*, ed. Jack P. Greene (New York: Harper & Row, 1968), pp. 526–66, at 533 n; Peter S. Onuf, *The Origins of the Federal Republic: Jurisdictional Controversies in the United States, 1775–1787* (Philadelphia: University of Pennsylvania Press, 1983), p. 172. But see Rosemarie Zagarri, *The Politics of Size: Representation in the United States, 1775–1850* (Ithaca, N.Y.: Cornell University Press, 1987), on the continuing importance of state size in debates over representation.

10. "Antifederal Discoveries," dated Baltimore, 17 March 1788, *Maryland Journal*, 18 March 1788.

11. Onuf, *Origins of the Federal Republic*, chap. 4; Herbert B. Adams, *Maryland's Influence upon Land Cessions to the United States*, Johns Hopkins University Studies in Historical and Political Science, 3d ser. (Baltimore, Md.: N. Murray, 1885), 1:1–54.

12. See the discussion in Lester J. Cappon, et al., eds, *Atlas of Early American History: The Revolutionary Era, 1760–1790* (Princeton, N.J.: Princeton University Press, 1976), p. 89.

13. The best history of revolutionary Maryland is Ronald Hoffman's *A Spirit of Dissension: Economics, Politics, and the Revolution in Maryland* (Baltimore,

Md.: Johns Hopkins University Press, 1973); see also relevant chapters in Norman K. Risjord, *Chesapeake Politics, 1781–1800* (New York: Columbia University Press, 1978).

14. Charles Carroll of Carrollton to Benjamin Franklin, 12 August 1777, *Letters of Delegates to Congress, 1774–1789*, ed. Paul H. Smith, 14 vols. to date (Washington, D.C.: Library of Congress, 1976–), 8:46.

15. Resolves of Maryland House, 30 November 1778, in Kate Mason Rowland, *The Life of Charles Carroll of Carrollton*, 2 vols. (New York: G. P. Putnam's Sons, 1898), 2:11–12.

16. Maryland Instructions, 15 December 1778, laid before Congress 21 May 1779, *Journals of the Continental Congress*, ed. Worthington C. Ford, 34 vols. (Washington, D.C.: Government Printing Office, 1904–37), 14:619–22, at 620–21; see also the Maryland Declaration, 15 December 1778, in William Waller Hening, *The Statutes at Large: Being A Collection of all the Laws of Virginia*, 13 vols. (Richmond: R. & W. & G. Bartow, et al., 1809–23), 10:549–52. For a brief review of the western lands controversy see Onuf, *Origins of the Federal Republic*, pp. 75–102.

17. A Boston newspaper writer explained: "Among confederated republics, the safety and harmony of the whole, depends on a proper equality in the several individuals. The state therefore that wishes to extend its territory to a great degree beyond that of others, is an enemy to the union" ("Remarks relative to the Controversy between Pennsylvania and Connecticut," no. 7, *Independent Chronicle* [Boston], 17 March 1785).

18. Richard Dobbs Spaight to Gov. Alexander Martin, 30 April 1784, in *Letters*, 7:509–10.

19. Virginia Delegates to Gov. Patrick Henry, 7 November 1785, in *Letters*, 8:250.

20. *Cumberland Gazette* (Portland, Mass.), 3 July 1787; Francis Dana to Elbridge Gerry, 2 September 1787, cited in *DHRC*, 13:80 n.

21. *Freeman's Journal* (Philadelphia), 15 June 1785.

22. Martin, *Genuine Information*, p. 186.

23. *Freeman's Journal*, 15 June 1785.

24. On confederations see Emmerich de Vattel, *The Law of Nations, or the Principles of Natural Law Applied to the Conduct . . . of Nations* (translation of the 1758 ed. (Washington, D.C.: Carnegie Institution, 1916), bk. 3, chaps. 47–49. The British radical Richard Price believed that the American confederation could provide a model international organization (*Observations on the Importance of the American Revolution*, 2d ed. [London, 1785]; reprinted in Bernard Peach, ed., *Richard Price and the Ethical Foundations of the American Revolution* [Durham, N.C.: Duke University Press, 1979], pp. 177–224, at 187). For good discussions of contemporary theorizing about international relations see F. H. Hinsley, *Power and the Pursuit of Peace: Theory and Practice in the History of Relations between States* (Cambridge, Eng.: Cambridge University Press, 1963), and Daniel George Lang, *Foreign Policy in the Early Republic:*

The Law of Nations and the Balance of Power (Baton Rouge: Louisiana State University Press, 1985).

25. Martin, *Genuine Information*, p. 183.

26. Ibid., p. 180–81.

27. Ibid., p. 230.

28. Ibid., p. 185.

29. See speeches by Patrick Henry and James Monroe in the Virginia ratifying convention, 9 and 10 June 1788, in *Debates*, 3:151–52, 211–12.

30. Martin, *Genuine Information*, p. 187.

31. Ibid.

32. The division of Massachusetts would "double the state's influence" in Congress, according to "Impartialis," *Falmouth Gazette* (Portland, Mass.), 14 May 1785. See the discussion in Onuf, *Origins of the Federal Republic*, pp. 154–55.

33. Martin, *Genuine Information*, p. 189.

34. Alexander Hamilton speech, 19 June, and James Madison speech, 28 June 1787, both in *Records*, 1:154, 206–7.

35. Zagarri, *Politics of Size*, passim.

36. Martin, *Genuine Information*, p. 196.

37. Ibid., p. 224.

38. Ibid., p. 226.

39. Ibid., p. 230.

40. Ibid., p. 225.

41. "Mentor," 29 March 1788, *Maryland Journal*, 4 April 1788.

42. Opponents of Virginia's claims argued that Congress should succeed to jurisdiction over Crown lands that were not located within clearly established state boundaries. See remonstrance of New Jersey Assembly, 16 June 1778, laid before Congress, 25 June, *Journals of Congress*, 11:650; "Lucius Quintus Cincinnatus," in *The Mote Point of Finance, Or the Crown Lands, Equally Divided*, broadside (Philadelphia, 21 September 1779); Thomas Paine, *Public Good: Being an Examination into the Claims of Virginia to Vacant Western Territory* (Philadelphia, 30 December 1780).

43. George Mason to Thomas Jefferson, 27 September 1781, in Thomas Jefferson, *The Papers of Thomas Jefferson*, ed. Julian Boyd et al., 20 vols. to date (Princeton, N.J.: Princeton University Press, 1950–) 6:120–21. See the discussion in Onuf, *Origins of the Federal Republic*, pp. 87–91.

44. Land-company membership lists are in Jefferson Papers, Library of Congress, Washington, D.C., 7:1164 (Vandalia) and 1166 (Indiana and Illinois-Wabash). The Indiana list was dominated by Pennsylvanians; it included only two or three Marylanders. Illinois-Wabash membership was distributed evenly among residents of Baltimore, Annapolis, and Philadelphia. On western-land speculation in general see Thomas Perkins Abernethy, *Western Lands and the American Revolution* (New York: D. Appleton-Century, 1937).

45. See Madison to Jefferson, 18 November 1781, in *The Papers of James Madison* ed. Robert Rutland et al., 15 vols. to date (Chicago and Charlottesville:

University of Chicago Press and University Press of Virginia, 1962–), 3:308, which suggests that Virginia should not expect "the present Union" to "survive the present war"; see also Madison to Edmund Pendleton, 30 October 1781, and Virginia Delegates to Gov. Thomas Nelson, 23 October 1781, ibid., 3:296–98, 293.

46. Madison to Joseph Jones, 21 November 1780, Madison, *Papers*, 2:191.

47. *Journals of Congress*, 26:111–21.

48. Peter S. Onuf, *Statehood and Union: A History of the Northwest Ordinance* (Bloomington: Indiana University Press, 1987), chaps. 1 and 2.

49. George Read and Roger Sherman speeches at Constitutional Convention, 29 June and 7 July 1787, *Records*, 1:213, 247.

50. Martin speech at Constitutional Convention, 14 July 1787, ibid., 1:290.

51. "Aristides" [Alexander Contee Hanson], *Remarks on the Proposed Plan of a Federal Government, Addressed to the Citizens of the United States of America, and Particularly to the People of Maryland* (Annapolis, Md., 1788), in *Pamphlets on the Constitution of the United States*, ed. Paul Leicester Ford (Brooklyn, N.Y.: privately printed, 1888), pp. 217–57, at 224.

52. "The Farmer to the Inhabitants of Maryland," dated Frederick Co., 12 February 1786, *Maryland Journal*, 17 February 1786.

53. Item dated Alexandria, 15 November 1784, *Virginia Journal* (Alexandria), 25 November 1784. For a similar argument see George Washington to Henry Knox, 5 December 1784, in *The Writings of George Washington*, ed. John C. Fitzpatrick, 39 vols. (Washington, D.C.: U.S. Government Printing Office, 1931–44), 28:3–5.

54. John Fitzgerald and William Hartshorne for Potomac Co. to Editor, 9 February 1785, *Virginia Journal*, 10 February 1785.

55. "Extract of a letter from Alexandria," 25 July 1786, *Freeman's Journal*, 23 August 1786. See also item dated New Haven, 10 March 1785, *Connecticut Courant*, 15 March 1785.

56. "Extract of a letter from Alexandria," 19 May 1785, *Virginia Gazette* (Richmond), 27 May 1785.

57. David McMechen to the Electors of Baltimore-Town, 20 September 1785, *Maryland Journal*, 23 September 1785.

58. Risjord, *Chesapeake Politics*, pp. 241–44.

59. *Virginia Journal*, 17 August 1786.

60. Mary M. Schweitzer, "American Economic Policy and the Movement for a National Constitution," a paper delivered at the Conference on Maryland and the Ratification of the Constitution, Washington College, June 1986.

61. Risjord, *Chesapeake Politics*, pp. 259–66.

62. "Aristides" [Hanson], *Remarks on the Proposed Plan*, in *Pamphlets*, pp. 222–23.

63. "Civis," "To the Independent Electors of Maryland," 26 January 1788, *Maryland Journal*, 1 February 1788.

64. "Federalism," 8 May 1788, ibid., 9 May 1788.

65. "Aristides" [Hanson], *Remarks on the Proposed Plan*, in *Pamphlets*,

p. 248. For a provocative discussion of the balance of power idea by a Maryland Antifederalist see "A Farmer" [John Francis Mercer], no. 7, *Maryland Gazette*, 15 April 1788, in *The Complete Anti-Federalist*, ed. Herbert J. Storing, 7 vols. (Chicago: University of Chicago Press, 1981), 5:64–66. Mercer concluded that the balance had preserved liberty among the states of Europe which, in effect, constituted, "a *great foederal republic*."

66. "Aristides" [Hanson], *Remarks on the Proposed Plan*, in *Pamphlets*, pp. 239–40 n.

67. "Uncus," 29 November 1787, *Maryland Journal*, 30 November 1787.

68. "Hambden," "To the People of Maryland," 8 March 1788, ibid., 14 March 1788.

69. *Maryland Gazette* (Baltimore), 20 March 1787.

70. Ibid., 17 April 1787.

71. Edward C. Papenfuse, "An Undelivered Defense of a Winning Cause: Charles Carroll of Carrollton's 'Remarks on the Proposed Federal Constitution,'" *Maryland Historical Magazine* 71 (1976): 220–51, at 250.

72. Onuf, *Statehood and Union*, chap. 1.

73. Papenfuse, "An Undelivered Defense of a Winning Cause: Carroll's 'Remarks on the Proposed Constitution,'" at p. 247.

74. Ibid., at p. 234.

75. "Aristides" [Hanson], *Remarks on the Proposed Plan*, in *Pamphlets*, p. 248.

76. Ibid., at pp. 247–48.

8
SOUTH CAROLINA
Slavery and the Structure of the Union

ROBERT M. WEIR

On May 27, 1788, a huge parade occurred in Charleston to celebrate the ratification of the Constitution of the United States by the state of South Carolina. The process, to all appearances, had been a straightforward one. The Constitutional Convention in Philadelphia had completed its work on September 17, 1787; by October 4, a copy of the document had been published in Charleston, and on January 19, after four days of discussion, the legislature voted to call a ratifying convention. After the election of delegates in mid April, the state convention met at the Exchange Building in Charleston (the Statehouse had burned on February 5), where it debated the document for two weeks. Then, on May 23, the convention voted by a ratio of 2 to 1 to ratify, thereby making South Carolina the eighth state to do so. Four days later, more than twenty-eight hundred celebrants marched in an imposing procession down Broad and up Meeting streets to Federal Green, where they dined on roasted ox. That evening, according to newspaper reports, "several ships in the harbour exhibited a most beautiful spectacle; their masts, yards, etc. being richly illuminated." Similar celebrations occurred in rural areas of the state. But in the western parts, it was reported, some citizens conducted ceremonies of a different kind. These "had a coffin painted black, which borne in funeral procession, was solemnly buried, as [an] emblem of the dissolution and interment of publick liberty."[1] Not being citizens, slaves did not figure in these reports or, presumably—except perhaps in the preparations and cleanup—in any of the ceremonies.

201

That contemporary accounts failed to mention the slaves is perhaps understandable; that later historians have been nearly as oblivious to the role of slavery in the ratification process is more surprising. There is, to be sure, an extensive literature on ratification in the various states, and some of it deals specifically with South Carolina. Thorough as this coverage has been in many respects, slavery has usually received only cursory mention.[2] In many instances the oversight may not have been serious. But in the case of South Carolina, the omission has jeopardized our understanding of developments; for there, as Frederick Law Olmsted observed in the nineteenth century, "slavery has been longest and most strongly and completely established."[3] Although wrong about the "longest" (Virginia had that dubious honor), Olmsted was correct about the rest. It thus seems inconceivable that South Carolinians would have ratified the Constitution without considering its impact upon their basic institution. To explore the relationship between slavery and the ratification of the United States Constitution in South Carolina is therefore the purpose of this essay.

SOUTH CAROLINA: THE POLITICAL CULTURE OF SLAVERY

Alone among the mainland colonies of North America, South Carolina had a black majority during the eighteenth century. By 1708, slaves had outnumbered freemen, and they would continue to do so until the Revolution. From approximately 3,000 blacks at the beginning of the century, the slave population had climbed to nearly 100,000 on the eve of independence from Britain. Contemporaries estimated that losses during the Revolution had reduced that figure by as much as 25 percent.[4] By 1790, however, natural increase and importations during the 1780s brought the black population up to almost 109,000. Because the net reproductive rate was low, at least until the middle of the eighteenth century, much of the overall increase was due to the purchase of new Africans, and Sullivan's Island in the port of Charleston, where most of them underwent a brief period of quarantine, has been aptly called the Ellis Island of Black Americans. But interruptions in the slave trade caused by prewar embargoes, wartime losses, and expansion of the white population in the western up-country combined to create a large demand for new Africans during the 1780s.

In some ways, the demand for Africans was indistinguishable from the need for any other kind of labor; in other ways, there was a fundamental difference. In the drier areas of the coastal low country and later in the western upcountry, the crux of the matter may well have been simply an abundance of natural resources and a shortage of hands with which to exploit them. Thus, one local entrepreneur doubtless had spoken for thousands of his successors when early in the century he had noted that the timber alone on his land was worth a small fortune, "but I can make little advantage of it till I can compass a good gang of Negroes." Similar thoughts surely lurked in the heads of many an upcountry farmer or planter after the Revolution who dreamed of what his rolling acres could produce. As a result, according to one historian, such men "were consumed by a desire for more slaves."[5] But in the rice swamps of the low country, the situation appeared to be different. There, contemporaries saw black labor as not merely a convenience but an absolute necessity, for the rice fields were reputed to be certain death for whites who tried to work in them. Slaves, it was conveniently thought, could work in such climates with less risk, and modern research does in fact suggest that blacks were more resistant to malaria and yellow fever. In the absence of the blacks, a leading local politician, Rawlins Lowndes, would remind the legislature, "this state would degenerate into one of the most contemptible in the Union." Undoubtedly, Charles Cotesworth Pinckney spoke for almost all South Carolinians when he concurred, noting that "the nature of our climate, and the flat, swampy situation of our country, obliges us to cultivate our lands with negroes, and . . . without them South Carolina would soon be a desert waste."[6]

At the time, however, the state was no desert; rather, it was an oasis of wealth. Historians have tended to substantiate a belief common in the eighteenth century that South Carolinians were the richest of Americans. One scholar has in fact gone so far as to estimate that during the late colonial period, South Carolina enjoyed the highest rate of economic growth of any area in the British Empire, perhaps in the world. Although that claim may be debatable, nine of the ten wealthiest Americans — as measured by the size of their estates recorded for probate in 1774 — were South Carolinians. In one instance, blacks constituted 83 percent of the total personal property, and in most cases, slaves accounted for well over one-half of the inventoried estate.

Rich rice planters of the low country would have had no trouble agreeing with a contemporary's claim that "Negroes were our wealth";[7] nor would most aspiring upcountry men. Many of these, to be sure, were relatively small operators with only a few slaves, if any, but they knew, as well as any large planter, that prosperity and slaves seemed to go hand in hand. For as Charles Cotesworth Pinckney told the Philadelphia convention, the state had recently exported agricultural products worth £600,000 sterling (very roughly the equivalent of $62 million in the mid 1980s), "all which was the fruit of the labor of her blacks."[8] In short, slaves may not have been the present wealth of the upcountry, but they represented the promise of future productivity.

Accordingly, most of the slaves imported during the decade after the Revolution went to the western areas, where by 1790 about one-quarter of all blacks in the state could be found, most of them engaged in the production of indigo and tobacco. Experiments with cotton were just beginning at this time, and only slightly over thirty-three "bags" had been exported during the twelve months ending in November 1787.[9] Nevertheless, many South Carolinians hoped that a satisfactory upland cotton would be found — as would happen after the cotton gin made the production of the green-seed variety economically feasible.

These considerations not only help us to understand why South Carolinians in all sections of the state wanted slaves but also make clear some of the reasons for sectional differences over economic policy during the 1780s. Despite their underlying prosperity, South Carolinians experienced hard times during the 1780s. The disruption and damage caused by the war, the loss of markets (especially in the British West Indies) as a result of independence, and several crop failures because of the weather combined to undermine earnings at the same time that low-country planters were seeking to resume normal operations and upcountry farmers were trying to expand theirs. As a result, the heavy demand for imported goods and slaves led to an increasing burden of debts, which reached crisis proportions in the mid 1780s. The legislature, led by low-country planters and professional men whose own experiences helped them to understand the problems, responded with a limited emission of paper money and stay laws, which temporarily protected debtors against pressure from creditors.

Up to this point, there was relative agreement on appropriate measures. Where eastern and western interests parted company was over the advisability of temporarily restricting the slave trade. During the colonial period, South Carolinians had periodically used this method to alleviate problems caused by an adverse balance of payments. In 1785 the legislature rejected such an approach.[10] Two years later, however, it temporarily prohibited the importation of new Africans. Votes on this question reflected a consistent sectional division, in which representatives from the eastern part of the state usually voted to close the trade; those from the west, to reopen it.[11] This is not to say that rice planters had a moral aversion to the trade; nor at the moment, as Rutledge observed, were they especially afraid of insurrections; they merely could live—at least for the time being—with the supply of slaves they had, which might increase in value in response to the increasing demand from the back country. Westerners, on the other hand, were impatient to get more, immediately. Almost no one, it should be emphasized, regarded this embargo as anything but a temporary economic measure. As first passed, it was part of "An Act to regulate the recovery and payment of debts; and for prohibiting the importation of negroes for the time herein mentioned." Indeed, Charles Cotesworth Pinckney would frankly tell the Constitutional Convention that South Carolinians expected to resume the African slave trade.[12]

South Carolinians had also turned to the Continental Congress for help in solving its economic and strategic problems. Some members of the legislature had viewed the Articles of Confederation, which were submitted to the states for ratification in 1778, as threatening to the state, because "the honor, interest and sovereignty of the south, are in effect delivered up to the care of the north." Nevertheless, South Carolina had approved the Articles, albeit with twenty-one suggested amendments.[13] But the threat of British attack and, ultimately, the British occupation of the state from 1780 to 1782 had chastened the Carolinians, and thereafter they rather consistently supported a strong central authority. Twice during the 1780s they agreed that Congress should have the power to levy duties on imported goods, but the measures had failed because the approval of all the states could not be obtained. Similarly, the South Carolina legislature voted in 1785 to give Congress the power temporarily to regulate foreign and interstate commerce in the hope of forcing Great Britain to make commercial concessions, but that scheme, too, fell through. Moreover, perhaps partly because of their bitter wartime experience, South Carolinians could voice surprisingly nationalistic sentiments. Thus, Charles Cotesworth Pinckney would lecture the local ratifying convention on the Declaration of Independence, which, he maintained, demonstrated that "the separate independence and individual sovereignty of the several states were never thought of by the enlightened band of patriots who framed" it. His cousin Charles, who had long worked hard to replace the Articles of Confederation with something stronger, would remind the Constitutional Convention in Philadelphia that "the idea which has been so long and falsely entertained of each being a sovereign State, must be given up; for it is absurd to suppose there can be more than one sovereignty within a Government." He thought it proper to concentrate "in the Federal Head, a compleat supremacy in the affairs of Government."[14]

Yet South Carolinians also had a history of being fiercely protective of their own interests. Even in regard to such a presumably negotiable matter as who might export what under the "Association" adopted by the First Continental Congress in 1774, South Carolinians had threatened to walk out rather than cut off their exports to Britain, which were destined for reexport to the European continent. The hard line seemed to have worked; South Carolinians had retained the right to ship rice, though in the process they had acquired something of a reputation for protecting their state's position. Nevertheless, in South Carolina the crucial consideration was always slavery. As historians have long suspected, and as Robert A. Olwell has recently demonstrated in detail, the belief that British authorities were tampering with their slaves was a critical element in the willingness of many South Carolinians to revolt in 1775 and 1776. Nor were other Americans to be permitted to do what was denied to the British. "If it is debated whether their Slaves are their Property," John Adams recorded Thomas Lynch as having told members of the Continental Congress in 1776, "there is an End of the Confederation."[15]

Indeed, South Carolinians were so touchy on the question that they could perceive danger — sometimes correctly — even in remote and unlikely places. In the Declaration of Independence, Jefferson's original capstone to the charges against King George III had been a long and eloquent blast against the king who had "waged cruel war against human nature itself, violating it's [*sic*] most sacred rights of life & liberty in the persons of a distant people who never offended him, captivating & carrying them into slavery in another hemisphere, or to incur miserable death in their transportation thither." South Carolinians and Georgians insisted that this section be dropped, and it was. Similarly, when Article 4 of the proposed Articles of Confederation had stipulated that "the free inhabitants of each of these States" would be entitled "to all privileges and immunities of free citizens in the several states," South Carolinians had demanded that it be amended to read "free white inhabitants."[16] A year later, in 1779, an equally revealing incident led to greater long-term effects. Threatened by a British invasion, John Rutledge, who was then governor of the state, had sought help from the Continental Congress, which, he had hoped, would authorize the arming of slaves. Such measures had been taken during emergencies earlier in the century; but this time, one of the prime movers of the idea, Colonel John Laurens, had something larger in mind: namely, emancipation. Service in the Revolutionary army would be a stepping stone to freedom—"a proper gradation between abject slavery and perfect liberty," which would not only prepare a slave to take his place in free society but would also establish his claim to it. The legislature had decisively voted the scheme down twice. From all indications, the chief result—even though the proposal had been suggested and supported by many Carolinians—was considerable resentment and a heightened suspicion of the Continental Congress in South Carolina.[17]

No doubt it could be argued that from the point of view of South Carolinians, some suspicion was justified. During the 1770s and 1780s the abhorrence of slavery was widespread in other states. As a result, the Virginia state legislature had forbidden the slave trade in 1778, and unlike their neighbors in South Carolina, many Virginians hoped that its demise would be permanent. In Pennsylvania, where the Quakers had been agitating against the institution from the 1750s on, the legislature had acted in 1780, thereby making it the first such body in the world to abolish black slavery. Massachusetts followed three years later when Chief Justice William Cushing interpreted the state constitution of 1780, which contained a bill of rights stating that all men were born free and equal, to mean that slavery had been abolished. This ruling made the state "an Assylum of liberty" for blacks who could manage to reach it and a beacon of hope for all who hated slavery.[18] To South Carolinians, however, Massachusetts became a source of considerable irritation when a judge in Boston issued a writ of habeas corpus liberating slaves from South Carolina who had been jailed in Massachusetts by someone acting for their owners. Back in South Carolina, the governor and his privy council impotently fulminated that the actions of the authorities in Massachusetts were "contrary to the Articles of Confederation, and . . . a gross violation of the sovereignty and independence of this State."[19] During the Revolutionary era, every state north of the Mason and Dixon line had taken steps to end slavery; and by the time of the Constitutional Convention, only the two Carolinas and Georgia still permitted the African slave trade.[20]

Given this background, it is scarcely surprising that when the South Carolina legislature voted in 1785 to give Congress power over commerce, it specifically exempted the slave trade.[21] It is also understandable that South Carolinians approached the Constitutional Convention in 1787 somewhat warily, like men walking into enemy country, for the convention was to meet in the Pennsylvania Statehouse — in the very halls, that is, where slavery had received its first serious setback. From this perspective, one can also understand why others at the convention might have regarded the South Carolinians as difficult men, fully capable of disrupting the proceedings.

CONSTITUTIONAL CONSIDERATIONS

How important slavery was as an issue at Philadelphia during the summer of 1787 is a question over which historians have differed. Only a little more than a generation ago, the prevailing opinion was that it was a minor consideration; more recently, social change in our own society has sensitized us to what we had previously overlooked, and we can now see that slavery was an ever-present incubus, dominating some very explicit debates and affecting questions in which the words "slave" and "slavery" were never mentioned. As James Madison, who was a most acute observer, noted, "the States were divided into different interests . . . principally from their having or not having slaves." Accordingly, it is difficult to exaggerate the importance of slavery to the framing of the Constitution; yet, it can be done. The defense of slavery was not what brought South Carolinians, or anyone else for that matter, to Philadelphia; the South Carolinians came, instead, as they repeatedly stated, to establish a national government with enough power to foster overseas trade, pay its (and perhaps the states') debts, protect South Carolina, preserve (but not threaten) the liberty of all free Americans, and generally, in the words of Charles Cotesworth Pinckney, render Americans "secure at home, respectable abroad, and to give us that station among nations of the world, to which, as free and independent people, we are justly entitled."[22] When the pursuit of common goals impinged upon particular interests, as it frequently did, Carolinians were not alone in defending their own turf. What made South Carolinians singular was the nature of what they felt called upon to defend, as well as the tenacity with which they went about the task.

Perhaps the state legislature deliberately selected five large slaveholders from the low country to send as its delegates to the convention, although it would have been difficult to find many politically experienced men with the requisite stature in South Carolina who did not also fit this mold. At any rate, Pierce Butler, Henry Laurens, Charles Pinckney, Charles Cotesworth Pinckney, and John Rutledge were men of varying but considerable ability, all of whom could be exceedingly plain-spoken upon occasion.[23] To a man, they considered the existence of slavery in South Carolina to be an absolutely unnegotiable issue.

Charles Cotesworth Pinckney put the matter very simply in a debate over the slave trade: "S. Carolina & Georgia cannot do without slaves." If those states were denied the right to import slaves, then even though he and "all his colleagues were to sign the Constitution & use their personal influence, it would be of no avail towards obtaining the assent of their Constituents." Given this conviction, whatever anyone thought about the morality of the institution seemed to be irrelevant. The closest that any South Carolinian came in the convention to arguing that slavery was a positive good was when Charles Pinckney stated: "If slavery be wrong, it is justified by the example of all the world. . . . In all ages one half of mankind have been slaves." Rutledge did not bother with even this mild apologia: "Religion & humanity had nothing to do with this question — Interest alone is the governing principle with Nations—The true question at present is whether the Southn.

States shall or shall not be parties to the Union." Or as he said a little later: "If the Convention thinks that N.C.; S.C. & Georgia will ever agree to the plan, unless their right to import slaves be untouched, the expectation is vain. The people of those States will never be such fools as to give up so important an interest."[24] The repeated display of such dogged determination in the defense of an institution which he believed to be indefensible prompted some acerbic words from Gouverneur Morris of Pennsylvania, who observed that "there can be no end of demands for security if every particular interest is to be entitled to it." Implying that it was not just *any* interest they were talking about, Butler testily replied that "the security the Southn. States want is that their negroes may not be taken from them which some gentlemen within or without doors, have a very good mind to do."[25]

The importance of their state, the stature of its delegation, and its unwavering hard line on the question of slavery earned South Carolinians the dubious distinction of being the defenders *par excellence* of slavery. A disgusted Gouverneur Morris proposed that the final document's failure to immediately cut off the slave trade be attributed to the Carolinians and Georgians since it was out of deference to their opinions that the trade was permitted to remain open, at least temporarily. After the convention was over, Edmund Randolph was more specific. "*Even South Carolina*," he noted, was satisfied that the Constitution was not a threat to the institution.[26] The implication, of course, was that its representatives had been the most vigilant and touchy on the issue.

Their vigilance produced success, at least from the point of view of the South Carolina delegation. As Paul Finkelman has recently shown, at least five major provisions of the Constitution explicitly supported the institution, while ten other sections — not to mention that the government created by the document was one of explicitly limited powers — provided "prominent indirect protections of slavery." And as we shall shortly see from the debates in the ratifying convention, the South Carolinians might have added at least two other, less obvious protections to that list.[27] In short, the Constitution was riddled with safeguards for the institution.

At the convention, perhaps the most fundamental and time-consuming debate involving slavery concerned representation and taxation. The South Carolina Constitution of 1778, which was then in force, provided that various areas of the state were to be represented in the local legislature on the basis of wealth as well as population. Coming from an exceptionally wealthy state, South Carolinians maintained that the same principle should apply at the national level, for as Butler phrased it, "money was power." And because slaves constituted much of the productive capital and the most easily ascertainable form of wealth in the area, it therefore followed that they should be represented. Gouverneur Morris was unimpressed; some two months later, he exploded: "Are they men? Then make them Citizens & let them vote. Are they property? Why then is no other property included? The Houses in this City [Philadelphia] are worth more than all the wretched slaves which cover the rice swamps of South Carolina."

But by the time of Morris's philippic the question had already been decided. Thanks partly to the support of the delegates from Massachusetts, especially Rufus King, who said that he "had always expected that as the Southern States are the richest, they would not league themselves with the Northn. unless some respect were paid to their superior wealth," the convention arrived at a compromise. Three-fifths of the slaves—a ratio that had been proposed but never implemented for taxation under the old Confederation—would be part of the basis for determining both representation and taxation for each state under the Constitution. Although Butler repeatedly maintained that all slaves should be counted in the basis for representation, southern delegates on the whole appear to have been more satisfied with the three-fifths arrangement than were many of their northern colleagues. Indeed, they should have been, because they had so far given up little to get it. But as King reminded his colleagues, if northerners expected advantages from their closer connection with the southern states, "they must not expect to receive them without allowing some advantages in return"; and this, he implied, was the time for northerners to make concessions.[28]

In return, what King wanted was, in his phrase, "preferential distinctions in Commerce," which would make the northern states the carriers of the great southern export staples. Accordingly, King and his colleagues were outraged on August 6, when Rutledge offered the report of the Committee of Detail, the draft version of which not only forbade interference with the slave trade but also demanded a two-thirds majority in each house of the legislature in order to pass a "navigation act" that might bar foreign shipping from American ports; furthermore, it banned Congress from imposing a tax on the exports of any state. For King and his compatriots, these provisions were absolutely unacceptable. Counting slaves for representation was, King said, "a most grating circumstance to his mind, & he believed would be so to a great part of the people of America." The two "great objects of the Genl. System" were defense against foreign invasion and internal sedition. But if the slave trade were to be continued and if exports were not to be taxed, one part of the United States would be obligated to defend another part which would be "at liberty not only to increase its own danger [of insurrection], but to withhold the compensation" for the burden of its defense. "There was so much inequality & unreasonableness in all this, that the people of the N[orthern] States could never be reconciled [to it]." He hoped that "at least" some time limit would be placed on the importation of slaves; without it, he could never agree to have them counted in the basis for representation. "At all events, either slaves should not be represented, or exports should be taxable."[29]

After some negotiation, a compromise was reached. According to Madison, "an understanding on the two subjects of *navigation* and *slavery*, had taken place between those parts of the Union." On the one hand, southerners received both their extra representation and their duty-free exports. On the other, they were forced to forgo the unlimited importation of slaves and the requirement of a two-thirds majority for the passage of navigation acts. As Charles Cotesworth Pinckney explained on August 29, "It was the true interest of the S. States to have no regulation of commerce; but considering the loss brought on the commerce of the Eastern States by the revolution, their liberal conduct towards the views of South Carolina, and the interest the weak Southn. States had in being united with the strong Eastern States, he thought it proper that no fetters should be imposed on the power of making commercial regulations." Shortly thereafter, Butler added that although he believed the interests of the "Eastern" and southern states "to be as different [and potentially conflicting] as the interests of Russia and Turkey," he, too, was "desirous of conciliating the affections of the East."

Apparently there was a good deal of conciliation going on; for im-

mediately after the vote to permit Congress to pass commercial legislation by a simple majority, in which the South Carolinians concurred,
Butler moved to add "If any person bound to service or labor in any
of the U—States shall escape into another State, he or she shall not
be discharged from such service or labor, in consequence of any regulations subsisting in the State to which they escape, but shall be delivered
up to the person justly claiming their service or labor." Madison noted
that the provision passed unanimously.[30] As a recent writer has observed, this clause was "added at the last possible moment, without
any serious debate or discussion," or, apparently, "any quid pro quo
for the North." On this vote, "the northern delegates seemed simply
not to understand the import of the issue or were too tired to fight."
Given the widespread fame (or notoriety) of Massachusetts as "the
asylum of liberty," it seems highly unlikely that many delegates did
not understand the issue; nor did northerners such as King and
Gouverneur Morris lack stamina. Instead, the timing of Butler's
motion and the unanimous vote for it suggest that it was part of the
deal between the South Carolinians and the men from Massachusetts.
Indeed, that Madison later seems to have claimed that the fugitive
slave clauses of both the Constitution and the Northwest Ordinance
of 1787 were also the result of a compromise suggests the dimensions
of the package.[31]

One may regard such compromises in varying lights. Some among
the abolitionists of the nineteenth century would maintain that the
resulting provisions made the Constitution "a covenant with death
and agreement with Hell"; more recently, these deals have been termed
"dirty." Yet two points about them should be made. First, as William
E. Nelson has recently argued, the proceedings at the Constitutional
Convention were in a sense fundamentally different from those that
frequently characterize modern democratic politics. The numerical
majority did not ride roughshod over the minority; rather, it sought,
quite consistently, to accommodate the latter's vital interests. Whether
this was the result of political wisdom, folly, or necessity is perhaps
debatable; certainly if it was a mistake, the Constitution is a case—if
there ever was one—of having the sins of the fathers visited upon suc-
ceeding generations. And when one regards the convention in isolation, there is good reason to think, as some historians do, that the
South Carolinians were only bluffing when they repeatedly threat-

ened to walk out if slavery were not protected. But years later, Charles Pinckney, who should have known, recalled that the convention was "repeatedly in danger of dissolving without doing any thing."[32] Reviewing the remarkably consistent pattern of behavior on the part of South Carolinians, which stretched from the first Continental Congress to the firing on Fort Sumter in 1861, one is inclined to believe him.

THE DEBATE BEGINS

Whatever the reasons for their success, the delegates from South Carolina could return home feeling that they had discharged their duty to themselves and their constituents. Nothing in the Constitution stipulated or even implied that the new government could ever emancipate slaves in South Carolina; these bondsmen augmented the voice of free (white) southerners in both the national legislature and the electoral college, in which representation would also be proportional to population; specific guarantees ensured that Congress could not interfere with the slave trade before 1808; and even the states that had abolished slavery would now be required to return fugitive slaves. No doubt Charles Cotesworth Pinckney could speak with conviction when he later maintained that the protections for slavery appeared to be adequate.[33]

Pinckney's remarks may have been designed partly to counter misleading reports that had begun to appear in the South Carolina press that the convention might end the slave trade for twenty-five years. In fact, throughout the ratification period, the actual provisions governing the trade continued to be a source of considerable confusion. In the North, many observers misunderstood the clauses that would temporarily prohibit Congress from interfering with the slave trade; these northerners believed that thereafter, slavery would be completely abolished.[34] To the extent that such erroneous wishful thinking occurred elsewhere, exaggerated fears of the same thing were also rife in South Carolina, where arguments about the Constitution that might be effective in the North could well backfire. Take *Federalist* 42, for example, initially published in New York, in which Madison made these remarks: "It were doubtless to be wished, that the power of prohibiting the importation of slaves had not been postponed until the year 1808, or rather that it had been suffered to have immediate operation." Still, "it ought to be considered as a great point gained in favor of humanity, that a period of twenty years may terminate forever, . . . a traffic which has so long and so loudly upbraided the barbarism of modern policy." Madison's intentions to the contrary, his interpretation would have won few friends for the Constitution in South Carolina. Conversely, "Cato," also addressing the citizens of New York but in opposition to the Constitution, noted that among the most serious objections was the fact "that the slave trade is, to all intents and purposes permanently established."[35]

South Carolinians who were exposed to such conflicting interpretations may well be pardoned if they were somewhat confused. How much of this material they read remains uncertain, however. Partly because the fate of the Constitution in other states was important to South Carolinians and partly because eighteenth-century printers tended to pad their journals with items reprinted from each other, South Carolina newspapers contained much that had originated elsewhere, including the proceedings of official bodies as well as numerous polemics, both pro and con. Contemporaries also indicated that Antifederalist writings from Virginia and Pennsylvania circulated in the upcountry.[36] That most of the published essays failed to mention slavery prominently in either positive or negative contexts suggests that local printers may have screened their borrowings. Whether the materials circulating in the back country dealt more explicitly with the institution is not known; but if they did, condemnations of the Constitution from Pennsylvania and elsewhere might have had a counterproductive effect.

Be that as it may, a leading Antifederalist among South Carolinians, Aedanus Burke, maintained that "the whole weight and influence of the press" was on the side of the Constitution. He complained: "The printers are, in general, British journeymen, or poor citizens, who are afraid to offend the great men, or merchants, who could work their ruin. Thus, with us, the press is in the hands of a junto, and the printers, with most servile insolence discouraged opposition, and pushed forward publications in its favour; for no one wrote against it." Although Burke's complaint was overstated, he was correct in recognizing that most of the local items were written by Federalists. And one of the points that these Federalists sought to make clear for the benefit of South Carolinians was that the Constitution protected slavery and the slave trade. Thus "Civis" published "An Address to the Freemen of South-Carolina, on the Subject of the Federal Constitution," which appeared in the *Columbia Herald* (Charleston) on February 4, 1788, and was later issued in pamphlet form. Noting that one of the current objections to the Constitution was that northerners had "stipulated for a right to prohibit the importation of negroes after 21 years," "Civis" countered that "as they are bound to protect us from domestic violence, they think we ought not to increase our exposure to that evil, by an unlimited importation of slaves." Furthermore, "though Congress may forbid the importation of negroes after 21 years, it does not follow that they will. On the other hand, it is probable that they will not. The more rice we make, the more business will be for their shipping; their interest will therefore coincide with our's." Moreover, he concluded: "We have other sources of supply—the importations of the ensuing 20 years, added to the natural increase of those we already have, and the influx from our northern neighbours, who are desirous of getting rid of their slaves, will afford a sufficient number for cultivating all the lands in this state." Ironically, "Civis" was David Ramsay, a physician and historian who had come originally from Pennsylvania. Something of a closet abolitionist, he was also a member of the state legislature and the ratifying convention; and most important in the present connection, he was an ardent supporter of the Constitution in all his guises.[37]

Unfortunately, the author of "A Dialogue between King *Leo* and His *Servants*," which appeared in the *Columbia Herald* on May 1 and 5, 1788, is unknown; but he was probably a local figure, who obviously possessed a certain imaginative flair. "King *Leo*," it seems, had a dream in which he was told that the "western country," which he had "treated with contempt," would become "a great and mighty empire." He therefore summoned his servant "Pitarto" (William Pitt the Younger), who acknowledged that the "grand confederacy" being planned there "will be a great detriment to us." Accordingly, Pitarto had sent emissaries to sabotage it. "We have directed our emissaries to tell the inhabitants of the southern parts of that country, that their neighbours to the northward will make them pay through the nose for all the produce they carry" and that all the national offices would be filled with northerners. Furthermore, these emissaries were to make clear that if southerners were to resist these oppressions, northerners would "give freedom to their slaves and send a great northern army amongst them, which they will encrease by enlisting the slaves which they shall make free, all which (as they inherit a little of our credulity, and are like us too easily brought to believe what if we had one grain of sense we would see through) we hope they will swallow and digest it as if it was truth." In the meantime, it was obviously in the interest of the "northern parts of this western country" for the southern parts to "have as many slaves as possible, that they may raise more produce and give bread" to the northerners who would be carriers of these products. Notwithstanding this, Pitarto continued, we have "given out, that the northern people will, when the confederation takes place, hinder them from importing any more slaves." His information, Pitarto then assured the King, was that southerners "believe it will prove true."

Although this piece also dealt with other considerations, the writer clearly believed that the putative threat to slavery under the Constitution was a sufficiently significant Antifederalist argument to be worth discrediting. That he sought to do so by tying it to the tail of the British lion suggests not only some of the visceral appeals of the Constitution to South Carolinians but also, indirectly, what they considered to be among the most heinous sins of the British during the war.

Whatever fears South Carolinians may have had on account of slavery and however much some may have sought to capitalize upon rumors, the printed Antifederalist arguments tended to avoid an area in which their case was weak. Thus, a local "Cato," perhaps Aedanus Burke, who wrote one of the more important Antifederalist pieces, had nothing whatever to say upon the subject; in fact, he generally approved of the Constitution but believed that the provisions governing the presidency should be modified to require rotation in office.[38] More thoroughgoing opponents of the Constitution also normally eschewed explicit discussions of slavery, although it was often implicit in their treatment of potential sectional conflict. Indeed, some opponents were sufficiently apprehensive of such conflicts as to resurrect a proposal, which had first been advanced when the Articles of Confederation were under discussion in 1778, for multiple confederations (most commonly, three) in which one of them would consist of the two Carolinas and Georgia, whose common interests were obvious.[39]

Interestingly enough, during the early months of 1788, the discussion about several confederacies involved Federalists as well as Antifederalists, for even the Constitution's supporters needed alternatives in case the document were not ratified. Thus on January 19, Ramsay noted: "It seems to be a prevailing sentiment here that if Virginia & her neighbors should refuse it[,] that we would confoederate with New England. For my part I am fully of that sentiment [and] I would much rather be united with Massachusetts New Hampshire & Connecticut than with North Carolina, Virginia & Maryland. My first wish is union[,] but if that cannot be[,] my second is confoederation with the eastern & middle states." Ten days later, in writing to a correspondent from Massachusetts, Ramsay was more sanguine, but his assessment of the situation still revealed that local politicians were, in effect, playing dominoes with regional interests:

> The sentiments of our leading men are of late much more foederal than formerly. This honest sentiment was avowed by the first characters. "New England has lost & we have gained by the war her suffering citizens ought to be our carriers though a dearer freight should be the consequence." Your delegates never did a more political thing than in standing by those of South Carolina about negroes. Virginia deserted them & was for an immediate stoppage of further importation. The dominion has lost much popularity by the conduct of her delegates on this head. The language now is "the Eastern states can soonest help us in case of invasion & it is more our interest to encourage them & their shipping than to join with or look up to Virginia." In short sir a revolution highly favorable to union has taken place.[40]

SLAVERY AND THE POLITICS OF RATIFICATION

The real basis for Ramsay's belief that the Constitution would be ratified in South Carolina was the recently concluded discussion in the state legislature, where, he had noted, "there appears a great majority for it." Early in January a committee composed of one member from each electoral unit, with Edward Rutledge (John's brother) as chairman, reported in favor of setting a date for elections to the proposed ratifying convention. Instead of considering the question in a narrow sense, a committee of the whole, "by common consent," then discussed the merits of the Constitution in considerable detail over several days. Although the ratifying convention would make the final decision, this preliminary debate was held, as Ramsay reported, "for the sake of informing the country members."[41]

Given the purpose and the length of the discussion, one assumes that it was rather thorough. Yet at least one historian has, quite understandably, termed it "brief." The discrepancy arises out of the nature of the record. The official journal of the house, which was intended to provide only a skeletal record of events, does not contain speeches. Accordingly, the most complete and readily accessible source to date for these discussions has been the nineteenth-century compilation by Jonathan Elliot, who relied on newspapers and other sources for his materials. His work was not flawless, although perhaps he should be excused for circumstances beyond his control. One speech, he noted, was missing, "the reporter of those debates unfortunately not being in the house"; other remarks were omitted *owing to the loss of a note-book in the fire which consumed the State-House.*"[42] Nevertheless, Elliot's accounts are better for the legislature than for the ratifying convention, and taken as a whole, they probably give a reasonably adequate indication of the major elements of the discussions concerning slavery and the Constitution.

The debates in the legislature opened with a lengthy speech by Charles Pinckney, in which he briefly reviewed the problems experienced under the Articles of Confederation and, in more detail, the thinking of the Constitutional Convention in regard to the major provisions of the new Constitution. There followed rather quickly a discussion of the president's treaty-making powers, during which John Jay must have been much on the minds of many legislators. During 1785, while acting for the Continental Congress, Jay had negotiated with a Spanish emissary, Diego de Gardoqui, over rights to navigate the lower Mississippi River. Jay's willingness to trade them away for other concessions that would be more important to the north did much to stimulate southern sectionalism in general and to enrage Charles Pinckney in particular. Furthermore, leading South Carolinians must have been aware of Jay's attempt to abolish the slave trade by treaty at Paris in 1783. Accordingly, although no one appears to have explicitly said so, concern for the safety of the institution doubtless made many agree with Charles Cotesworth Pinckney, who observed that "political caution and republican jealousy rendered it improper for us to vest it [the power to make treaties] in the President alone."[43] Ratification by the Senate would help to protect southern interests.

The first clear-cut mention of slavery came from Rawlins Lowndes, the leading Antifederalist spokesman. His arguments, which ranged from the sound to the specious, were sufficiently provincial to make one sympathize with Ramsay, who privately maintained that Lowndes had "not one foederal idea in his head nor one that looks beyond Pedee," a river near the northern boundary of the state. In fairness to Lowndes, it should be noted that he claimed to be speaking for "a number of respectable members, men of good sense, though not in the habit of speaking in public, [who] had requested that he would state his sentiments, for the purpose of gaining information on such points as seemed to require it."[44] In this case, as elsewhere, Lowndes maintained that under the new Constitution, "the interest of the Northern States would so predominate as to divest us of any pretensions to the title of a republic." To begin with, "What cause was there for jealousy of our importing negroes? Why confine us to twenty years, or rather why limit us at all? For his part, he thought this trade could be justified on the principles of religion, humanity, and justice; for certainly to translate a set of human beings from a bad country to a better, was fulfilling every part of these principles." Harbingers of the nineteenth-century proslavery argument, remarks of this kind appear to have been rare in these debates. Henry Pendleton, a judge who had originally come from Virginia, tactfully rebutted these arguments by noting that only the two Carolinas and Georgia then permitted the importation of Africans and that the state constitution of Virginia forbade it.[45]

Later in the debate, although still in reply to Lowndes, Charles Cotesworth Pinckney elaborated on the provisions governing the slave trade and slavery in general. Regarding "the restrictions that might be laid on the African trade after the year 1808," Pinckney maintained that "your delegates had to contend with the religious and political prejudices of the Eastern and Middle States, and with the interested and inconsistent opinion of Virginia, who was warmly opposed to our importing more slaves." Maintaining that he was as convinced as Lowndes that slavery was essential in South Carolina, Pinckney noted that he and his colleagues "assigned reasons for our insisting on the importation, which there is no occasion to repeat, as they must occur to every gentleman in the house." "A committee of the states," he continued, "was appointed in order to accommodate this matter, and after a great deal of difficulty, it was settled on the footing recited in the Constitution." He added that this arrangement allowed South Carolinians "an unlimited importation of negroes for twenty years," and it might continue thereafter. "We have a security that the general government can never emancipate them, for no such authority is granted; and it is admitted, on all hands, that the general government has no powers but what are expressly granted by the Constitution, and that all rights not expressed were reserved by the several states." In addition, he claimed, "we have obtained a right to recover our slaves in whatever part of America they may take refuge, which is a right we had not before." In conclusion, he maintained: "Considering all circumstances, we have made the best terms for the security of this species of property it was in our power to make. We would have made better if we could; but, on the whole, I do not think them bad."[46]

Most members of his audience seem to have agreed with him, since no one dealt with the subject, except very briefly, thereafter. Robert Barnwell professed to be "particularly pleased with the Constitution" in regard to the slave trade, which was guaranteed for twenty-one years and might well continue beyond that. The eastern states would be the carriers of southern produce and would not want to "dam up the sources from whence their profit is derived." Lowndes wanted to know if anyone could be satisfied with a constitution that did not require that all trials be before "a jury of men chosen from the vicinage, in a manner conformable to the present administration of justice, which had stood the test of time and experience, and ever been highly approved of?" To this, Charles Cotesworth Pinckney raised a question of his own: Would the citizens of South Carolina and Georgia "wish that a cause relative to negro property should be tried by the Quakers of Pennsylvania, or by the freeholders of those states that have not that species of property amongst them?" Lowndes remained unconvinced; he foresaw the doom of the southern states. Believing that people would never "flock here in such considerable numbers, because our country had generally proved so uncomfortable, from the excessive heats," he was certain that the end of the slave trade would mean that "instead of rising in representation [i.e., in Congress, as most of his colleagues believed would happen] we should gradually degenerate." In conclusion, he claimed to wish "for no other epitaph, than to have inscribed on his tomb, 'Here lies the man that opposed the Constitution, because it was ruinous to the liberty of America.'"[47]

A member from the upcountry, who "rose . . . with diffidence," also had strong reservations about the Constitution: "Why was not this Constitution ushered in with a bill of rights? Are the people to have no rights?" There was no bill of rights, Charles Cotesworth Pinckney replied, because "as we might perhaps have omitted the enumeration of some of our rights, it might hereafter be said we had delegated to the general government a power to take away such of our rights as we had not enumerated." He continued, doubtless thinking about the constitution of Massachusetts: "Another reason weighed particularly, with the members from this state, against the insertion of a bill of rights. Such bills generally begin with declaring that all men are by nature born free. Now, we should make that declaration with very bad grace, when a large part of our property consists in men who are actually born slaves."

Very shortly thereafter, the legislature of South Carolina, which had recently decided to move the capital to the interior of the state, voted unanimously to call a ratifying convention and, by the razor thin margin of one vote, to hold it in Charleston.[48] In the meantime, there were to be elections. Representation in the convention was to reflect the composition of the legislature, with some additions from the western part of the state, where new lands had recently been added and where opposition to the Constitution might be strongest.[49] The elections in the low country returned mostly Federalist candidates and, in the upcountry, mostly Antifederalists. Despite the addition of the new western members, the convention, like the legislature, remained malapportioned; and the older, eastern districts retained a majority. Some contemporaries appear to have believed, on this basis alone, that the outcome was a foregone conclusion. Butler, who decided that it was time for a vacation after his labors at Philadelphia, went to the mountains. Lowndes, who normally represented Charleston in the legislature, was not returned by his regular constituency and refused to serve for St. Bartholomews, a rural parish that did elect him. Some upcountry delegates made excuses for not attending—one asked to be excused because there was smallpox in Charleston and he had never had it; and at least seven who had qualified as members of the convention were not there at the final tally.[50] To be sure, smallpox was a dangerous disease, and it was more inconvenient for western members to remain throughout the proceedings, but one suspects that some of them did not want to go on record as differing from their constituents. Others may merely have wished not to take part in something that they disapproved of but could not prevent.

Nevertheless, the convention got down to business on May 13 with 173 members present. Again the record is incomplete; but if the surviving speeches are an accurate indication, the discussions were somewhat different in character from those in the legislature four months earlier. As before, Charles Pinckney led off with a long discussion of the Constitution. This time, however, his approach was more philosophical, and he reviewed the nature of republican government in general, as well as the principles of the Constitution in particular. He also gave a brief summary of conditions in the various states, noting that there was a greater difference between the "inhabitants of the Northern and Southern States" than between the Calvinists and Quakers in Pennsylvania and New York, on the one hand, and the Catholics of Maryland, on the other. "The southern citizen beholds, with a kind of surprise, the simple manners of the east, and is too often induced to entertain undeserved opinions of the apparent purity of the Quaker; while they, in turn, seem concerned at what they term the extravagance and dissipation of their southern friends, and reprobate, as unpardonable moral and political evil, the dominion they hold over a part of the human race." Concluding this section of his speech, he observed that he had "thought it necessary to make these remarks," because it would be "impossible for the house fairly to determine whether the government is a proper one or not, unless they are in some degree acquainted with the people and the states, for whose use it is instituted."

Pinckney's speech set the tone for the convention. Given his comments about the Quakers and slavery, some discussion of the fate of the institution under the Constitution probably became inevitable. But most of the surviving speeches were more in keeping with the rest of his opening remarks, which dealt predominantly with questions of principle and of liberty, unlike those in the legislature, which had been more concerned with interests. In the legislature, it seems, liberty was taken as a given; the question had therefore become, Would this Constitution benefit South Carolina? In the convention, the issue was whether liberty could survive under the new arrangements. (Cynics might have noted that the experienced members of the legislature, who presumably did not need the principles of republicanism explained to them, not only tended to favor the Constitution but were also deeply involved in the market economy that it was supposed to improve. Upcountrymen, who presumably needed an explanation of basic principles and who probably wished to become more involved in that economy, were at the moment doubtless freer to concentrate on those principles and thus were more skeptical of the Constitution.)[51]

Whether because of their commitment to interests or to principles — or both — those who favored the Constitution had the votes; and especially after the news arrived midway in the proceedings that Maryland had ratified, the Antifederalists virtually gave up. Before the final vote, however, the convention appointed a committee to consider possible amendments. Chaired by Edward Rutledge, it quickly (on the same day) reported four. The most important of these, and the one most relevant to the defense of slavery, stipulated that "no Section of the said Constitution warrants a Construction that the States do not retain every power not expressly relinquished by them and vested in the General Government of the Union." The convention immediate ly approved these four additions; handily beat back Antifederalist attempts to add more amendments, including a bill of rights; and voted according to the secretary's tally, 149 to 73 to approve the Constitution. There was neither a great deal of discussion of these amendments nor an attempt to make ratification contingent upon their approval at the national level.[52]

Aedanus Burke, who believed there should have been more changes in the document, was disgusted. Reviewing "the different causes, whereby the new plan has been carried in South Carolina, notwithstanding 4/5 of the people do, from their souls detest it," he offered the following analysis. Antifederalists had failed to organize and prepare; almost "all the rich, leading men, along the seacoast and rice settlements," as well as the professional men and general populace in Charleston, were for the Constitution. So were former Tories and those who had British connections. The press, he maintained (not quite correctly, as we have seen), was "in the hands of a junto." Up to this point, his assessment of the situation was probably sound, but what is one to make of his next point? "*The* principal cause" (italics added) was that the convention was held "in the City, where there are not fifty inhabitants who are not friendly to it. The merchants and leading men kept open houses for the back and low country members during the whole time the Convention sat." He then concluded with the dispiriting impact of Maryland's ratification.

If Burke was right, one is almost tempted to agree in more ways than one with a contemporary characterization of the opposition as "trifling." Yet many of Burke's colleagues were eloquent and deadly serious; perhaps most important to contemporaries, they also represented large numbers of men. "We are not acting for ourselves alone, but, to all appearance, for generations unborn," Alexander Tweed observed. He would listen to the debates and make up his mind accordingly. Patrick Dollard—like Tweed, from Prince Frederick's Parish—also listened and remained convinced that his constituents were right in being "highly alarmed at the large and rapid strides which this new government has taken towards despotism." His neighbors, he continued, said "that it evidently tends to promote the ambitious views of a few able and designing men, and enslave the rest; . . . They say they will resist against it; that they will not accept of it unless compelled by force of arms, which this new Constitution plainly threatens; and then, they say, your standing army, like Turkish janizaries enforcing despotic laws, must ram it down their throats with the points of bayonets."[53]

Neither Dollard's fire-eating speech nor Burke's inadvertent and incongruous characterization of his fellow Antifederalists as essentially frivolous was the only unusual thing about the convention. Several historians have felt that there was something strange in these proceedings, but they have described it in strikingly different terms. In forthcoming essays, James W. Ely, Jr., notes that "the discussions, as reported, seem rather listless" and that the entire convention had "a shadow-boxing quality," while George C. Rogers, Jr., implies that the Rutledges and the Pinckneys managed the proceedings very briskly.[54] The rest of Edward Rutledge's often-quoted summing-up suggests that both assessments are, in some ways, correct: "We had a tedious but trifling opposition to contend with. We had prejudices to contend with and sacrifices to make. Yet they were worth making for the good old cause." What each of these observations, from Burke's to Rutledge's, hints at and what gave the convention its odd character was that it really had two agendas. Its first and obvious purpose was to meet the formal requirement for ratification; the second and at least equally important task was to generate support for the Constitution throughout the state. Given the apportionment of representation in both the legislature and the convention, the formal ratification of the Constitution was probably never seriously in doubt, and the Federalists could doubtless have rammed approval of it through in short order if they had chosen to do so. But the protracted discussions in the Convention were, like the earlier debates in the legislature, designed in part to inform country members while giving them the feeling that they had had their say. Furthermore, it was assumed that the delegates would, in turn, educate their constituents. Accordingly, the convention resolved to print twelve hundred copies of the Constitution, with the proposed amendments, and to distribute six to each member. In short, the real problem for the Federalists was not so much to garner a consensus about the Constitution as to disseminate one; for, as Burke also observed, "the government rests on a very sandy foundation, the subjects whereof are convinced that it is a bad one."[55] Whether those who could do little but be entertained in Charleston went home really converted and, if so, whether they could convince their constituents, only time would tell.

Nevertheless, the protection of slavery in the Constitution bought time for the new government in South Carolina. Had it jeopardized slavery, the Constitution almost certainly would never have been formally ratified by the dominant groups in the state, whose history exhibited an adamant and consistent determination to keep their slaves. Had the Constitution, by some quirk, been ratified without safeguards for slavery, it is at least doubtful that the upcountry would have accepted it. Politicians from that area of the state were the ones who continually pressed for reopening the slave trade; and in 1803 they succeeded, so that South Carolina was, for the next five years, nearly alone among the states in continuing to import Africans. When that trade had been closed in 1787, twenty-one representatives from the upcountry who also served in the ratifying convention voted on both questions. Only five approved the Constitution, but twelve sought to continue the importation of slaves.[56] How willing such men would have been to acquiesce under the new arrangement if it had not protected slavery is of course anyone's guess, but the subsequent history of the state suggests an answer.

Nineteenth-century developments prompt a few additional reflections on eighteenth-century South Carolina, slavery, and the Constitution. First, during the drafting and the ratification of the United States Constitution, something akin to the concurrent majority operated at least at the federal level. John C. Calhoun would later argue that the minority (the South) should have a "concurrent" voice in the decisions of the majority (the North); his assumption — which may have been based partly on the presumed harmony of sectional interests in the politics of antebellum South Carolina — was that the veto power of the minority would force the majority to accept compromise rather than risk disruption or stalemate.[57] At the Constitutional Convention, the need to adopt measures that could obtain their constituents' approval was constantly on the minds of the delegates. Furthermore, all who were there would have agreed that the main purpose of the meeting was to strengthen the union. These two considerations both constrained and empowered the delegates from South Carolina, who gained in leverage what they lost in flexibility.

Thus, when Rutledge reminded the convention that the question before it was not slavery but whether they should have a union, he was not merely threatening to walk out; he was reminding his hearers of their most important area of consensus. Accordingly, it should not be too surprising that one of the final results of the convention was exactly as Charles Pinckney recalled it during the debates over the Missouri Compromise in 1820: "It was an agreed point, a solemnly understood compact, that, on the southern states consenting to shut their ports against the importation of Africans, no power was to be delegated to congress, nor were they ever to be authorized to touch the question of slavery; that the property of the southern states in slaves was to be as sacredly preserved, and protected to them, as that of land, or any other kind of property in the eastern states were to be to their citizens."[58] Charles Cotesworth Pinckney seems to have been able to convey this idea, or something very like it, to his auditors during the ratification debates in South Carolina. At least, after his assurance that "the general government can never emancipate" the slaves, emancipation was a dead issue, and the main focus of attention became the slave trade.

Second, the slave trade was to the eighteenth century what the territories became to the nineteenth — namely, a point of contact, where the convention and the national legislature might be able to do something to limit an institution that they could not otherwise touch. But such a limitation threatened to deprive South Carolinians of a right that they currently possessed; moreover, it was a right that was valued highly by those Carolinians who for other reasons were most apt to be hostile to the Constitution. From this perspective, the persistence of the northern delegates — or perhaps the need to have *their* constituents approve their handiwork — and the problem that faced the South Carolinians when they returned home take on larger dimensions. The potential limitation of the slave trade was more of an achievement than it may appear to have been at first glance.[59] It is also ironic that the Federalists of South Carolina, whose commitment to slavery was unshakeable, played a key role in obtaining approval for one of the first important national limitations on it. Even more ironic, perhaps only the assurance that virtually all South Carolinians shared the belief that slavery must be kept inviolable permitted it to be violated. Finally, the consensus in South Carolina about the necessity, if not the desirability, of slavery frequently served during the debates over ratification, like the threat of disruption at Philadelphia, to prompt discussion of other things. All of which suggests that — Calhoun to the contrary — concurrent majorities may work better at expressing a consensus than in forcing one.

Be that as it may, James Ely has maintained that "the defensive tone adopted by the federalists in explaining the provisions on slavery suggests that insufficient protection of slave property was a major antifederalist argument." The satire involving King Leo and similar items indicate that this may have been true, especially in regard to the slave trade. But one could equally well argue that given the importance of slavery to South Carolinians, the notable thing is how infrequently the Federalists seem to have been called upon to offer evidence for its safety under the Constitution. Were it not for the imperfections in the record, one could be virtually certain that the comparative silence on the subject reflected agreement; everyone knew where all good Carolinians stood on the question of slavery, and they stood together.

As it is, however, something else reveals the power of that consensus with still greater clarity—namely, Charles Cotesworth Pinckney's response when challenged, not about provisions regarding slavery, but about safeguards for liberty. His reply to questions about the omission of a bill of rights or the failure to require trial by jury in every case, it will be recalled, was to invoke slavery. However truthful and accurate his answers may have been, the institution was obviously already beginning to smother concern for the civil rights of whites. That trend would continue until the suppression of free speech and other civil liberties in the name of slavery became almost commonplace in antebellum South Carolina.[60] One accordingly wonders if any of those who staged mock funeral processions in May 1788 realized that they were carrying coffins of liberty that, in reality, contained generations of men, black and white, shackled together.

NOTES

1. *State Gazette* (Charleston, S.C.), 4 October 1787; *Journals of the (South Carolina) House of Representatives, 1787–1788*, ed. Michael E. Stevens, (Columbia: University of South Carolina Press for South Carolina Department of Archives and History, 1981), pp. 318–32; *Columbian Herald*, (Charleston) 7 February, 13 March, and 29 May 1788; *Journal of the Convention of South Carolina Which Ratified the Constitution of the United States*, ed. A. S. Salley (Atlanta, Ga.: Foote and Davis Co. for Historical Commission of South Carolina, 1928), pp. 1–56; Aedanus Burke to John Lamb, 23 June 1788, in George C. Rogers Jr., "South Carolina Ratifies the Federal Constitution," *Proceedings of the South Carolina Historical Association* 31 (1961): 60.

2. Standard general accounts that cover South Carolina include Forrest McDonald, *We the People: The Economic Origins of the Constitution* (Chicago: University of Chicago Press, 1958); Jackson Turner Main, *The Anti-Federalists: Critics of the Constitution, 1781–1788* (Chapel Hill: University of North Carolina Press, 1961); and Robert A. Rutland, *The Ordeal of the Constitution: The Antifederalists and the Ratification Struggle of 1787–1788* (Norman: University of Oklahoma Press, 1966). More specific treatments of South Carolina can be found in Jerome J. Nadelhaft, *The Disorders of War: The Revolution in South Carolina* (Orono: University of Maine at Orono Press, 1981), pp. 173–90; Rogers, "South Carolina Ratifies the Federal Constitution," pp. 41–62; Raymond Gale Starr, "The Conservative Revolution: South Carolina Public Affairs, 1775–1790" (Ph.D.

diss., University of Texas at Austin, 1964); and David Duncan Wallace, *The History of South Carolina*, 3 vols. (New York: American Historical Association, 1934), 2:342–43.

3. Frederick L. Olmsted, *The Cotton Kingdom*, ed. Arthur M. Schlesinger, Jr. (New York: Alfred A. Knopf, 1953), p. 528.

4. Peter H. Wood, *Black Majority: Negroes in Colonial South Carolina from 1670 through the Stono Rebellion* (New York: Alfred A. Knopf, 1974), pp. xiv, 143–44; Julian J. Petty, *The Growth and Distribution of Population in South Carolina*, South Carolina State Planning Board bulletin no. 11 (Columbia, S.C., 1943), pp. 62–63, 48; Robert M. Weir, *Colonial South Carolina: A History* (Millwood, N.Y.: KTO Press, 1983), p. 174.

5. David Ramsay, *History of South Carolina*, 2 vols. (Spartanburg, S.C.: Reprint Co., 1968), 1:272; Petty, *Growth and Distribution*, p. 64; Philip D. Morgan, "Black Society in the Lowcountry, 1760–1810," in *Slavery and Freedom in the Age of the American Revolution*, ed. Ira Berlin and Ronald Hoffman (Charlottesville: University Press of Virginia for United States Capitol Historical Society, 1983), p. 85; Wood, *Black Majority*, p. xiv; Weir, *Colonial South Carolina*, p. 188; H. Roy Merrens, *The Colonial South Carolina Scene: Contemporary Views, 1697–1774* (Columbia: University of South Carolina Press, 1977), p. 18; Rachel Klein, "The Rise of the Planters in the South Carolina Backcountry, 1767–1808" (Ph.D diss., Yale University, 1979), p. 145.

6. H. Roy Merrens and George D. Terry, "Dying in Paradise: Malaria, Mortality, and the Perceptual Environment in Colonial South Carolina," *Journal of Southern History* 50 (1984): 533–50; Wood, *Black Majority*, pp. 88–91; *The Debates in the Several Conventions on the Adoption of the Federal Constitution as Recommended by the General Convention at Philadelphia in 1787 Together with the Journal of the Federal Convention* (hereafter cited as *Debates*), 2d ed., ed. Jonathan Elliot, 4 vols. (Philadelphia: J. B. Lippincott, Co., 1836), 4:272, 285.

7. George R. Taylor, "American Economic Growth before 1840: An Exploratory Essay," *Journal of Economic History* 24 (1964): 427–44; Alice Hanson Jones, *The Wealth of A Nation to Be: The American Colonies on the Eve of the Revolution* (New York: Columbia University Press, 1980), p. 171; *Debates*, 4:273; Alice Hanson Jones, *American Colonial Wealth: Documents and Methods*, 3 vols. (New York: Arno Press, 1977), 3:1959.

8. Max Farrand, ed., *The Records of the Federal Convention of 1787*, (hereafter cited as *Records*), 4 vols. (New Haven, Conn.: Yale University Press, 1966), 1:592. The current value of these exports was estimated by using the current dollar equivalents of the £1 sterling given in Jones, *Wealth of a Nation*, p. 10, and the Consumer Price Index published by the Bureau of Labor Statistics, United States Labor Department.

9. Klein, "Rise of the Planters," p. 137; *Columbian Herald*, 1 March 1788.

10. *Journals of the House of Representatives 1787–1788*, pp. xi–xx; Weir, *Colonial South Carolina*, pp. 146, 165; *Journals of the House of Representatives,*

1785–*1786*, ed. Lark Emerson Adams (Columbia: University of South Carolina Press for South Carolina Department of Archives and History, 1979), p. 336.

11. *Journals of the House of Representatives, 1787–1788*, pp. 232–33; Patrick S. Brady, "The Slave Trade and Sectionalism in South Carolina, 1787–1808," *Journal of Southern History* 38 (1972): 602, 605–6.

12. *Records*, 2:364, 373; Christopher Gould and Richard Parker Morgan, *South Carolina Imprints, 1731–1800* (Santa Barbara, Calif.: ABC–Clio Information Services, 1985), p. 180.

13. William M. Dabney and Marion Dargan, *William Henry Drayton and the American Revolution* (Albuquerque: University of New Mexico Press, 1962), p. 139; Charles Gregg Singer, *South Carolina in the Confederation* (Philadelphia: Porcupine Press, 1976), p. 70.

14. Singer, *South Carolina in the Confederation*, pp. 70, 73–75, 82–87; *Journals of the House of Representatives 1785–1786*, pp. 383, 522; *Debates*, 4:301; Charles Pinckney, *Observations on the Plan of Government Submitted to the Federal Convention* (New York: Frances Childs, n.d.), pp. 12, 27; Mark D. Kaplanoff, "Charles Pinckney and the American Republican Tradition," in *Intellectual Life in Antebellum Charleston*, ed. Michael O'Brien and David Moltke-Hansen (Knoxville: University of Tennessee Press, 1986), pp. 102–3.

15. *Journals of the Continental Congress, 1774–1789*, ed. Worthington Chauncey Ford, 34 vols. (Washington, D.C.: Government Printing Office, 1904), 1:51–52n. 1, 77; Nadelhaft, *Disorders of War*, pp. 21–22; Robert A. Olwell, "'Domestick Enemies': Slavery and Political Independence in South Carolina, May 1775–April 1776," *Journal of Southern History*, forthcoming; *The Adams Papers: Diary and Autobiography of John Adams*, ed. L. H. Butterfield, 4 vols. (Cambridge, Mass.: Belknap Press of Harvard University Press, 1962), 2:246.

16. *The Papers of Thomas Jefferson*, ed. Julian P. Boyd, 20 vols. to date (Princeton, N.J.: Princeton University Press, 1950–), 1:426; Donald L. Robinson, *Slavery in the Structure of American Politics, 1765–1820* (New York: Harcourt Brace Jovanovich, 1971), pp. 82–83; *Journals of the Continental Congress*, 11:652.

17. Robinson, *Slavery in the Structure of American Politics*, pp. 118–22; Robert M. Weir, *"The Last of American Freemen"* (Macon, Ga.: Mercer University Press, 1986), pp. 93–94.

18. Robinson, *Slavery in the Structure of American Politics*, pp. 95–96, 29, 25; *The Federal and State Constitutions, Colonial Charters, and Other Organic Laws of the States, Territories and Colonies Now or Heretofore Forming the United States of America*, ed. Frances Newton Thorpe, 7 vols. (Washington, D.C.: Government Printing Office, 1909), 3:1888–89; William Rotch, Sr., to Moses Brown, 8 November 1787, in *The Documentary History of the Ratification of the Constitution*, ed. Merrill Jensen, John P. Kaminski, Gaspare J. Saladino, et al., 8 vols. to date (Madison: State Historical Society of Wisconsin, 1976–), 14:521.

19. Governor Benjamin Guerard to the House of Representatives, 25 February

1784, with enclosures, Records of the General Assembly, Governors Messages, 1783–85, no. 262, South Carolina Department of Archives and History, Columbia, South Carolina; *Journals of the Privy Council, 1783–1789*, ed. Adele Stanton Edwards (Columbia: University of South Carolina Press for South Carolina Department of Archives and History, 1971), p. 82.

20. Robinson, *Slavery in the Structure of American Politics*, p. 35.

21. *Journals of the House of Representatives, 1785–1786*, pp. 383, 522.

22. Paul Finkelman, "Slavery and the Constitutional Convention: Making a Covenant with Death," in *Beyond Confederation: Orgins of the Constitution and American National Identity*, ed. Richard Beeman, Stephen Botein, and Edward C. Carter II (Chapel Hill: University of North Carolina Press, 1987), p. 220; *Records*, 1:486; *Debates*, 4:308.

23. *Biographical Directory of the South Carolina House of Representatives*, ed. Walter B. Edgar, N. Louise Bailey, and Ivey Cooper, 4 vols. (Columbia: University of South Carolina Press, 1974–81), 3:108–14, 390–94, 525–28, 555–60, 577–81; *Records*, 3:238, 397.

24. *Records*, 2:371, 364, 373.

25. Ibid., 1:604–5.

26. Ibid., 2:415; Edmund Randolph, as quoted in Finkelman, "Slavery and the Constitutional Convention," p. 193.

27. Finkelman, "Slavery and the Constitutional Convention," pp. 190–93. Discussions in the ratifying convention would demonstrate that South Carolinians also construed the provisions regarding the treaty-making powers of the president and the Senate, as well those regarding the adjudication of some legal cases, as protections for slavery.

28. *Federal and State Constitutions*, 6:3252; *Records*, 1:196, 562, 2:222, 562.

29. *Records*, 1:562, 2:181–83, 220.

30. Ibid., 2:449–51, 453–54.

31. Finkelman, "Slavery and the Constitutional Convention," p. 221; *Records*, 2:449; see also Staughton Lynd, *Class Conflict, Slavery, and the United States Constitution* (New York: Bobbs-Merrill, Co., 1967), pp. 185–213; and *Supplement to Max Farrand's "The Records of the Federal Convention of 1787,"* ed. James H. Hutson (New Haven, Conn.: Yale University Press, 1987), p. 321.

32. Finkelman, "Slavery and the Constitutional Convention," pp. 188, 219, 221; William E. Nelson, "Reason and Compromise in the Establishment of the Federal Constitution, 1787–1801," *William and Mary Quarterly* 44 (1987): 458–84; "Missouri Question: Speech of Mr. Pinckney, of South Carolina in the House of Representatives," *Niles Register*, 15 July 1820, p. 350.

33. Finkelman, "Slavery and the Constitutional Convention," p. 193; *Debates*, 4:286.

34. *Commentaries*, 1:180; Finkelman, "Slavery and the Constitutional Convention," p. 215 n. 76.

35. Alexander Hamilton, John Jay, and James Madison, *The Federalist* (New

York: Modern Library, n.d.), pp. 272–73; *The Anti-Federalist Papers and the Constitutional Convention Debates*, ed. Ralph Ketcham (New York: New American Library, 1986), p. 319.

36. *Debates*, 4:318; Steven R. Boyd, *The Politics of Opposition: Antifederalists and the Acceptance of the Constitution* (Millwood, N.Y.: KTO, 1979), pp. 114–15; Rogers, "South Carolina Ratifies," p. 59; Starr, "Conservative Revolution," p. 251.

37. Burke, cited in Rogers, "South Carolina Ratifies," p. 59; *Commentaries*, 4:21–27; *Biographical Directory*, 3:590–94.

38. *The Complete Anti-Federalist* (hereafter cited as *CAF*), ed. Herbert J. Storing, 7 vols. (Chicago: University of Chicago Press, 1981), 5:137–44. Because at the state ratifying convention Burke would offer an amendment to the Constitution that appears to embody some of Cato's suggestions, one might infer that he was Cato. But the scholar who has studied Burke most recently and thoroughly doubts that he was in fact the author. See John Meleney, "The Public Life of Aedanus Burke, Revolutionary Republican in Post-Revolutionary South Carolina" (Ph.D. diss., University of South Carolina, 1988, forthcoming from the University of South Carolina Press).

39. *Morning Post*, 15 and 29 March, 3 April and 10 and 19 May 1788; Starr, "Conservative Revolution," p. 259.

40. Ramsay to John Eliot and Ramsay to Bj. Lincoln, 29 January 1788, *Commentaries*, 3:417, 487.

41. Ibid., 3:417; *Journals of the House of Representatives, 1787–1788*, p. 311; Ramsay, in *Commentaries*, 3:487, 417.

42. McDonald, *We the People*, p. 203; for a useful discussion of Elliot see James H. Hutson, "Riddles of the Federal Constitutional Convention," *William and Mary Quarterly*, 3d ser. 44 (1987): 411–12; *Debates*, 4:300, 316.

43. *Debates*, 4:253–63; Jack N. Rakove, "Solving a Constitutional Puzzle: The Treatymaking Clause as a Case Study," *Perspectives in American History*, n.s. 1 (1984), especially pp. 272–74; "Charles Pinckney's Reply to Jay, August 16, 1786 Regarding a Treaty with Spain," ed. Worthington Chauncey Ford, *American Historical Review* 10 (1905): 817–27; *Debates*, 4:265.

44. For Lowndes see Carl J. Vipperman, *The Rise of Rawlins Lowndes, 1721–1800* (Columbia: University of South Carolina Press, 1978); *Commentaries*, 3:487; *Debates*, 4:287.

45. *Debates*, 4:272, 287; *Biographical Directory*, 3:547.

46. *Debates*, 4:285–86, 296.

47. Ibid., pp. 296, 290, 307, 309, 311.

48. Ibid., pp. 312, 315, 316; *Journal of the House of Representatives, 1787–1788*, pp. 330–32.

49. *Journal of the House of Representatives, 1787–1788*, pp. x, 537; *Debates*, 4:332.

50. Charles W. Roll, Jr., "We, Some of the People: Apportionment in the Thirteen State Conventions Ratifying the Constitution," *Journal of American History* 56 (1969):30–31; Lewright B. Sikes, *The Public Life of Pierce Butler,*

South Carolina Statesman (Washington, D. C.: University Press of America, 1979), p. 51; *CAF*, 5:148–49; *Journal of the Convention*, pp. 9, 39–50.

51. *Debates*, 4:318–32; *Journal of the Convention*, pp. 1–6.

52. Rogers, "South Carolina Ratifies," p. 60; *Journal of the Convention*, pp. 24–39.

53. Rogers, "South Carolina Ratifies," p. 59; *Debates*, 4:333, 337–38.

54. James W. Ely, Jr. "'The Good Old Cause': The Ratification of the Constitution and Bill of Rights in South Carolina," in a collection of papers on the Constitution given at the Chancellor's Symposium on Southern History, the University of Mississippi, 9 October 1987, forthcoming from the University of Mississippi Press; George C. Rogers, Jr., "Ratification Process in South Carolina," a talk given at the annual meeting of the South Carolina Historical Society, Charleston, 5 March 1988.

55. Edward Rutledge to John Jay, 20 June 1788, in *The Correspondence and Public Papers of John Jay*, ed. Henry P. Johnson, 4 vols. (New York, 1896), 3:339; *Journal of the Convention*, p. 54; Burke, cited in Rogers, "South Carolina Ratifies," pp. 60–61.

56. Brady, "The Slave Trade and Sectionalism," p. 602; *Journals of the House of Representatives, 1787–1788*, pp. 252–53; *Debates*, 4:338–40.

57. August O. Spain, *The Political Theory of John C. Calhoun* (New York: Bookman Associates, 1951), pp. 160–61 n. 36.

58. "Missouri Question: Speech of Mr. Pinckey," p. 352.

59. On this point see also William W. Freehling, "The Founding Fathers and Slavery," *American Historical Review*, 77 (1972): 88–90.

60. Ely, "'The Good Old Cause'"; Clement Eaton, *Freedom of Thought Struggle in the Old South*, rev. ed. (New York: Harper & Row, 1964), pp. 27–31, 126, 158, 196–215, and passim.

9
NEW HAMPSHIRE
Puritanism and the Moral Foundations
of America
Jean Yarbrough

On June 21, 1788, New Hampshire became the ninth state to ratify the Constitution, thereby rendering the new federal government effective in the ratifying states, and winning for itself the honor of having been the decisive vote, the "keystone of the federal arch." Being ninth in the federal order, however, was not what New Hampshire Federalists originally had envisioned. When the convention had assembled at Exeter on February 13, they generally had expected that New Hampshire, following in the steps of neighboring Massachusetts, which had ratified a week earlier, would become the seventh state in the federal union. Speedy ratification seemed certain. The state's most eminent political leaders, including Governor John Sullivan, his old rival John Langdon, John Taylor Gillman, Samuel Livermore, Josiah Bartlett, and Thomas Pickering, all stood squarely behind the document. As the convention began its deliberations, Paine Wingate, New Hampshire's representative to the Confederation Congress, and another supporter, confidently predicted that "an adoption [in New Hampshire] is a matter of certainty."[1]

But the Federalists were wrong. Although New Hampshire's most influential statesmen backed the Constitution, a majority of the Exeter delegates did not. Seeking to explain his miscalculation, John Langdon wrote to George Washington: "Contrary to the expectation of almost every thinking man, a small majority of (say four) persons appeared against the system. This was most astonishing."[2] Like other surprised Federalists, Langdon blamed the upset on demagogues and small-minded politicians who, in the months preceding the convention, had canvassed the back country, inflaming the people against the new government. "Just at the moment that the choice for members for our convention . . . took place, . . . a few designing men . . . frightened the people out of what little senses they had. This induced them to choose not only such men as were against the plan, but to instruct them positively against receiving it."[3]

Thus a large number of delegates arrived at Exeter with instructions to oppose the Constitution. After ten days of discussion, some of them became convinced that opposition was a mistake, but because they could not in good conscience disobey their instructions, they agreed to vote with the Federalists for an adjournment until June. In the meantime, they would try to persuade their towns to change their instructions or to release them from these "shackles" altogether.

By the time the Convention reassembled at Concord on June 18, Maryland and South Carolina had voted in favor of union, raising the total number of ratifying states to eight. On June 21, 1788, adopting the strategy of the Massachusetts convention, which was to ratify with a series of recommendatory amendments, New Hampshire became the ninth state to ratify the Constitution.

Although the history of these events is readily available, any attempt to examine more closely the issues underlying the ratification debate in New Hampshire is frustrated by the convention's failure to keep a record of its proceedings.[4] Yet though we cannot know what was said inside the conventon walls, we can, through a reading of contemporary newspapers, correspondence, town histories, and state papers, gain some insight into the issues that divided Federalists and Antifederalists. In addition to New Hampshire sources, the debates taking place in the Massachusetts newspapers are also helpful, because ties between the two states were close, and Massachusetts newspapers circulated widely in New Hampshire.[5] Finally, the Connecticut newspapers provide another source, especially for those New Hampshire towns that were located along the Connecticut River, whose settlers were originally from Connecticut and felt an affinity with those towns downriver.

In what follows, I will argue that the ratification debate raised three important issues concerning the moral meaning of republicanism. The first was the issue of instruction, which forced New Hampshirites to consider what the purpose of an elected delegate should be: Should he simply transmit the views of his constituents, or should he be free to follow the dictates of his own reason and conscience? The question of instruction, on which the ratification of the Constitution in New Hampshire nearly foundered, raised this issue in its most radical form and tested the limits of Federalist statesmanship.

In addition to this procedural issue, which in New Hampshire turned out to be a matter of principle as well, delegates disagreed on two other issues — namely, religion and slavery, both of which were rooted in a distinctively New England view of the moral foundations of republican government. In New Hampshire there was general agreement that republican government required a virtuous citizenry and that this virtue was best instilled by Protestant Christianity. This belief found its greatest expression in the New Hampshire Constitution of 1784, which expressly declared that republican government depended upon "morality and piety, rightly grounded on evangelical principles." Unlike Antifederalists elsewhere, who attacked the Constitution for failing to guarantee religious freedom, New Hampshire Antifederalists objected to the absence of a religious test for officeholders. Because New Hampshire Antifederalists believed that republican government was rooted in a shared religious morality, they feared that the new government lacked a proper moral foundation and therefore would, through example, subvert those foundations in the states.

Then there was the question of slavery. Although the Constitution's toleration of slavery did not directly affect manners and morals in New Hampshire, Antifederalists saw these compromises as fatal to republican institutions. As Antifederalists understood it, republican government required more than an accommodation and balance of interests; republicanism rested upon a shared moral horizon, which was impossible for the new nation to construct, given the presence of the slaveholding South.[6]

Finally, in common with Antifederalists everywhere, those from New Hampshire opposed the Constitution because it did not contain a bill of rights. Only the last-minute decision of the second convention to recommend twelve amendments helped to win over the more moderate opponents. Yet a close look at these amendments and at their subsequent history in the First Congress suggests that on fundamental political questions, Federalists and Antifederalists in New Hampshire were not so far apart. Unlike the more radical nationalists in other states, New Hampshire's Federalists supported many of the amendments that sought to reduce the scope of federal powers.

In what follows, I shall argue that the issues that divided New Hampshire Federalists and Antifederalists were rooted in the religious and political culture that they shared.[7] Whereas Antifederalists rejected the Constitution because they saw that their Puritan morality could not be extended throughout the United States, Federalists, while accepting that morality as the basis of the New Hampshire republic, sought a different moral foundation for the extended republic.[8] In the last analysis, what separated the two sides in New Hampshire was not so much a different conception of the structure and powers of government, as a disagreement over the moral foundation of republicanism in America.

THE PROBLEM OF INSTRUCTION

On February 13, 1788, 113 delegates assembled at Exeter to begin their deliberations. Because the state's most conspicuous political leaders were arrayed on the side of the Constitution, the Federalists expected an early victory. But what Antifederalists lacked in influence and ability, they made up for in numbers. In the remote northern and southwestern parts of the state, independent-minded farmers had seen no need for a greatly invigorated central government and had therefore instructed their delegates to vote against it. According to one contemporary account, "upwards of forty towns" instructed their representatives to oppose the Constitution.[9]

Drawing on town records, Orin Grant Libby has found that fifteen towns or "classes" of towns took a direct vote on the question of ratification.[10] In almost every case, the town expressly instructed the delegate to vote against the Constitution. In addition, twenty-six towns appointed committees to consider the Constitution and to advise the delegate on how to vote. In nineteen of these twenty-six towns, the committee voted to oppose the Constitution. Yet these figures do not reveal the full strength of the towns' opposition, for in other cases, there are only records that committees were appointed, but there are no records of their decision.[11]

The practice of instructing representatives in writing had a long history in New England, dating back to the colonial period. Indeed, the right of instruction, together with the theory of representation that underlay it, was explicitly sanctioned in the New Hampshire Constitution of 1784. On the assumption that representatives are merely "the substitutes and agents" of the people, Part I, Article 32, declared that "the people have a right . . . to assemble and consult upon the common good, [and] give instructions to their representatives."[12]

As the delegates at Exeter were to discover, however, the principle of instruction presented a problem, because it did not permit a delegate to disregard his instructions, even though he may have been persuaded to do so during the course of deliberation and discussion. His job was simply to mirror his constituents' views, even if he no longer held them himself. According to contemporary reports, a number of Antifederalist delegates found themselves in precisely this dilemma.[13] As John Langdon explained to Rufus King: "After spending ten days on the arguments [,] a number of opponents came to me and said they were convinced, and should be very unhappy to vote against the Constitution which they (however absurd) must do in case the question were called for."[14]

In the face of this dilemma, the Federalist response was to seek an adjournment so that the instructed delegates might "return home to their constituents, acquaint them with the conviction that had arisen in their minds, and of the arguments which had produced it — and to prevail on them to annul their instructions, which bound them to act contrary to their opinions."[15]

Although New Hampshire's Federalists sought to put the best possible face on the decision to adjourn, those who were further removed from the conflict regarded the action as a major setback. Not only did it check the momentum for ratification: it also bolstered Antifederalist morale in Virginia and New York, states that were crucial to the ratification drive and in which opposition to the Constitution was already powerful.[16]

In light of these difficulties, it is worthwhile considering if the New Hampshire strategy to adjourn was well advised. There was, after all, another alternative: to adopt the Massachusetts strategy of recommendatory amendments. At the Massachusetts convention, Antifederalists were also bound by instructions, but these delegates could be persuaded to vote their consciences because Federalists were willing to compromise on the all-important question of amendments. Because wavering Antifederalists could use this concession to defend their action to their constituents, they could more easily be persuaded to disregard their instructions.

If Federalists had been willing to give them something in return, more moderate Antifederalists might also have been persuaded to vote "the clear conviction of [their] own minds."[17] Indeed, some Antifederalist leaders apparently saw instruction as a bargaining chip for securing a bill of rights. Thus "A Farmer" advised: "Let each town, or district, qualified by law to send a member, give him instructions to insist upon the additions of a Bill of Rights to the Constitution, and to have such amendments made in it, as shall effectually secure it on all sides."[18] And in one of the very few instances where we know anything about the substance of a town's instructions, the Marlborough Committee instructed its representative "to Accept or Reject the New Proposed Federal Constitution—if you can have our Bill of Rights secured to us and a Firm Test of the Protestant Religion secured secured to us, etc. it will be satisfactory. Otherwise Reject the whole."[19]

Yet, unlike their Massachusetts counterparts, New Hampshire's Federalists were unwilling to compromise on the amendment issue, and so they were forced to seek an adjournment in the hopes of obtaining new instructions. But because Federalists only managed to secure the release of one or possibly two delegates from their instructions during the interim — too few to tip the balance in their favor — they ultimately were forced to adopt the Massachusetts strategy. And as we shall see, because the two sides were much closer on the substance of the amendments than Federalists and Antifederalists elsewhere were, it is questionable whether their decision to adjourn was worth the risk.[20]

THE ROLE OF RELIGION

Today it is difficult to appreciate the objections to the absence of a religious test for federal officeholders. But New Hampshirites had no doubts about it. Politicians and clergy alike agreed that religion and morality were the mainstays of republican government. In contrast to Jefferson's Virginia, the Puritan statesmen of New England expected government to use its power to support religion, which in turn would preserve political institutions from the corruption and decay inherent in human nature.[21]

Like the Massachusetts Constitution of 1780 on which it was modeled, the New Hampshire Constitution of 1784 included an explicit statement about the religious foundations of republican politics. "Morality and piety," it said, "rightly grounded on evangelical principles, will give the best and greatest security to government and will lay in the hearts of men the strongest obligations to due subjection." To this end, the constitution called for religious instruction, because "a knowledge of these is most likely to be propagated through a society by the institution of the public worship of the Deity, and of public instruction in morality and religion." Indeed, New Hampshire went even further, by insisting that the state *support* the cause of religion: "Therefore, to promote these important purposes, the people of this state have a right to impower and do hereby fully impower the legislature to authorize from time to time, the several towns, parishes, bodies-corporate, or religious societies within this state, to make adequate provision at their own expense, for the support and maintenance of public protestant teachers of piety, religion and morality." In addition, the constitution required the chief officeholders of New Hampshire to be "of the Protestant religion."[22]

At the same time, however, the New Hampshire Constitution declared the right of conscience to be "inalienable," and it guaranteed that members of one sect would not be compelled to support another. As these Protestant statesmen understood it, there was no contradiction between the right to conscience and the compulsory support for religious instruction. Freedom of conscience extended only to belief, not to support. In their minds, the Constitution of 1784 achieved two necessary public purposes: it protected religious liberty; and at the same time, it provided essential support for religious institutions. This interdependence of religion and politics is what lies at the heart of New Hampshire's objections to Article VI of the federal Constitution.

New Hampshire Antifederalists offered several arguments against the absence of a religious qualification for federal officeholders. First, "A Friend to the Rights of the People" observed that the failure to include a religious test was contrary to good policy. Religion was necessary in order to keep public officials honest. "When a man has no regard to God and his laws nor any belief of a future state: he will have less regard to the laws of men, or to the most solemn oaths or affirmations."[23]

Second, it was also bad policy, because it would undermine the religious convictions of the common people. "A Customer" warned that if "our great folks are not obliged to make a declaration on that score; and if the lower class, who are desirous to imitate those who move in a higher sphere, should once be made to believe it unfashionable, we may turn our clergy a grazing—and employ our time, that heretofore has been employed in politicks and religion, to the pursuit of wealth, to enable us to pay our debts, and support the dependants on government in the style of the great men of the east."[24]

Finally, New Hampshirites feared that the federal Constitution's indifference to religion might somehow—just how was a bit vague—undermine public support for religion in their own state. In an essay printed in the *Freeman's Oracle*, "A Friend of the Republic" warned: "Consider for God's sake gentlemen, the sacredness of your office and the magnitude of your trust, your country [New Hampshire], its Religion, and Laws are in your hands: if you adopt this Constitution, you overturn the whole at once."[25] On the floor of the convention itself, Deacon Matthias Stone worried that "if this Constitution was adopted that Congress might deprive the people of the use of the holy scriptures—that pearl of a great price—that inestimable jewel—."[26]

Of course, the objections to Article VI went beyond New Hampshire alone. Throughout New England, the absence of a religious test prompted broad reflections on the proper relationship between religion and politics in a republican government. According to Charles Turner of Massachusetts, religion was central in forming the character of the people, and in preserving free institutions. In an argument that anticipates Tocqueville's discussion of religion, Turner observed that as America became more commercial, only "the prevalence of Christian piety and morals" would save the republic from "slavery and ruin."[27] Although Turner did not expect Christianity to arrest the development of commerce, he believed that only a stern religious education could keep its excesses in check.

In the same way, the anonymous Massachusetts writer "David" concluded that there were political advantages to be gained from a state's involvement in "religious concernment." According to "David," every state must choose one of three means of controlling the turbulent passions of mankind. A state may punish offenders, reward virtuous actions, or predispose the people in favor of virtue through the public support of religion. Because "David" believed that the third method was "most probable" in theory, as well as "most successful" in practice, he concluded that "religion is a proper subject for publick protection and encouragement."[28] In this, "David" shared the widespread Antifederalist distrust of institutional checks to control human nature. But he added to it a distinctive New England jeremiad, by insisting that men could only be saved from corruption by the restraints of religion.

Whatever the theoretical merits of this argument were, there was no way to implement it in practice. What "David" had in mind was public support along the lines of the Massachusetts and New Hampshire constitutions, with their provisions for public funding of the ministry. Yet even in the eighteenth century, such a solution was unworkable, because the country already contained a multiplicity of religious sects and because the states treated church-state relations in various ways. In this respect, it is interesting to compare "David's" arguments with those of Turner, noting the differences in their recommendations. No less than "David," Turner believed that Christian morality provided the only true foundation for republican government. But whereas "David" sought to amend the federal Constitution along the New England model, Turner held that the Constitution gave Congress the power to find a solution. Accordingly, he urged the new Congress, "in one of their first acts, in their first session, most earnestly to recommend to the several states in the Union the institution of such means of education as shall be adequate to the divine, patriotic purpose of training up children and youth at large in that solid learning and in those pious and moral principles, which are the support, the life and soul, of republican government and liberty, of which a free Constitution is the body; for as the body without the spirit, is dead, so a free form of government, without the animating principles of piety and virtue, is dead also, being alone."[29]

Even if Turner was right in asserting that the task of forming the character of a free people was "more blessed" than the act of founding a government, his argument was unlikely to mollify those Antifederalists who believed that the Constitution vested too many powers in the federal government and that education was the sole prerogative of the states.[30] In any case, it is surprising that most of the clergy in predominantly Congregationalist New Hampshire supported the Constitution, including Article VI, and a few actually violated the longstanding tradition against clerical involvement in politics by seeking election to the convention. From the roll-call vote on ratification, it appears that four ministers and one deacon favored the Constitution, while one minister and three deacons opposed it.[31]

It was chiefly the Reverend Samuel Langdon who defended the absence of a religious test, going so far as to call Article VI "one of the greatest ornaments of the Constitution." Responding to Deacon Stone's speech against this provision, the Reverend Mr. Langdon "took a general view of religion as unconnected with and detached from the civil power—that it was an obligation between God and his creatures, the civil authority could not interfere without infringing upon the rights of conscience."[32]

But what were the grounds for this separation? In his study of religion and government in American constitutional history, Mark de Wolfe Howe has discussed two different principles—one ecclesiastical, the other political—on which separation can be defended. The first, or ecclesiastical principle, which was developed by Roger Williams as the basis for Rhode Island's policy of toleration, insists that religion and politics be separated so as to preserve the purity of religion. When the church becomes involved in worldly affairs, its own religious principles are likely to become corrupted. The second, or secular principle, which was elaborated upon by Thomas Jefferson, seeks to protect politics from the manipulation of corrupt clerics. It separates church and state for the sake of political and religious liberty.

Interestingly, the Reverend Mr. Langdon's argument belongs to the second tradition. In his response to Deacon Stone, Langdon warned that if church and state were united, ecclesiastical rulers would become "the supreme head, dispensing laws to Kings and emperors." It was to protect the liberties of the people, rather than to preserve religion from worldly corruption, that "religion must stand on its own ground."

Although Langdon's concern was to guarantee political and religious liberty to the people, his conception of liberty of conscience was not so broad as it might first appear. Like many Protestant clergymen, Langdon fervently hoped that under the new Constitution, Roman Catholicism would not "gain ground" and that it might soon sink "like a mighty millstone never to rise again." For the citizens of New Hampshire, liberty of conscience was essentially a Protestant concern, although in fairness it should be said that since New Hampshire was a predominantly Protestant state, the illiberal implications of this position might not have been so readily apparent.

Moreover, Langdon spoke approvingly of the New Hampshire Constitution for having "guarantied to us the free exercise of our religion," and this despite its provisions for public support of the ministry and a religious test for state officeholders. Thus, although Federalists and Antifederalists disagreed over whether religion should, or even could, provide the moral foundation for republican government in a territory as religiously diverse as the United States, New Hampshire's Federalists were willing to accept religion as the cornerstone of their state government or, at the very least, to recognize its political utility. This partial agreement with their opponents is what separates New Hampshire Federalists from their counterparts outside of New England.[33]

THE SIN OF SLAVERY

Given the central importance of instruction to New Hampshire's ratifying convention, it is surprising that the more general questions about the nature of representation and its relation to free government, which so enlivened the debates in Virginia and New York, played a relatively minor role in New Hampshire. This may be because when New Hampshirites reflected upon the larger questions of freedom and tyranny, the institution they thought about first was not representation: it was slavery. Significantly, the one speech recorded in Elliot's *Debates* is Joshua Atherton's passionate denunciation of this "peculiar institution." And even if, as Walker suggests, Atherton, the Amherst delegate, did not actually write the speech until later, he was the acknowledged leader of the opposition, and the ground that he chose was slavery.[34]

What makes the debate over slavery so interesting is that it touched no concrete economic or social interest; it was, pure and simple, a matter of moral and religious principle.[35] By 1787, slavery was no longer an issue in New Hampshire. From the beginning of the Revolutionary era, the number of slaves in New Hampshire had declined dramatically. In 1775, the census reported 657 slaves (up from 633 in 1767), but by 1790, only 158 slaves remained, and in 1800, the number had declined to 8.[36] Without ever having been formally abolished, slavery died a natural death in New Hampshire.

Nor was opposition to slavery limited to Antifederalists. At the Philadelphia convention, the New Hampshire delegate John Langdon had strenuously supported giving Congress the power to prevent the increase of slavery. Despite the rapid decline of slavery in his own state, Langdon did not believe the states could be trusted to stop the slave trade on their own. As he put it, "He c[oul]d not with a good conscience leave it with the States who could then go on with the traffic, without being restrained by the opinions here given that they will themselves cease to import slaves."[37]

However, since at Philadelphia, Federalists had lost on this issue, at Exeter they had to justify the Constitution's compromises regarding slavery. In general, the Federalist position was that the Constitution compared favorably with the Articles of Confederation on this point. Reiterating the argument of Federalists at the Massachusetts convention, James Neal observed: "In the Confederation there was no provision whatever for its [slavery] being abolished; but this Constitution provides that Congress may, after twenty years totally annihilate the slave trade, and that, as all the states, except two, have passed laws to this effect, it might reasonably be expected that it would then be done. In the interim, all the states were at liberty to prohibit it."[38] Because the Constitution greatly increased the scope of federal powers, Federalists concluded that they had done all they could reasonably do, given the prejudices of the southern states, to place slavery on the road to extinction. Thomas Dawes, also of Massachusetts, summed up the Federalist position when he remarked: "We may say that, although slavery is not smitten by an apoplexy, yet it has received a mortal wound, and will die of a consumption."[39]

Although compromise was the crux of the Federalist argument, supporters did not always limit themselves to prudential considerations. Some, such as General William Heath, while they recognized the evil of slavery, sought to minimize the moral implications of their assent:

> Two questions naturally arise: If we ratify the Constitution,
> shall we do anything by our act to hold the blacks in slavery?
> Or shall we become the partakers of other men's sins? I think,
> neither of them. Each state is sovereign and independent to
> a certain degree and the states have a right, and they will
> regulate their own internal affairs as to themselves appears
> proper; and shall we refuse to eat, or drink or to be united
> with those who do not think or act, just as we do? Surely not.
> We are not, in this case, partakers of other men's sins, for in
> nothing do we voluntarily encourage the slavery of our
> fellowmen.[40]

Unlike Dawes, General Heath had no illusions about the future of
slavery in the southern states. But because he had absolved the North
from all moral responsibility, and because he was convinced that there
was nothing more the free states could do, he supported the
Constitution.

Although General Heath's speech was not central to the Federalist
position, it is important because it brings us to the heart of the Antifederalist view of slavery. Whereas Federalists were satisfied that the
Constitution did not in principle condone slavery—in fact went out
of its way never to mention the word[41]—and that it had taken positive
steps gradually to end slavery, Antifederalists saw the Constitution's
provisions as so much obscurantism and hypocrisy. Thus, "A
Gentleman" objected to the great lengths to which the Framers had
gone to avoid mentioning the word "negro."[42] Apparently unconvinced
that the Constitution's silence might be interpreted as an unwillingness
to sanction slavery, Antifederalists regarded these subtleties as sheer
casuistry; for them, the issue was open and shut: there could be no
compromise on the moral foundation of republican government.

Despite northern toleration of slavery under British rule, Antifederalists insisted that in founding their own government, the states
must act according to conscience. Moreover, Antifederalists rejected
the suggestion that each state was an independent and autonomous
moral community. According to "Phileleutheros," the Constitution
bound the states together into one national community. If New Hampshire were to consent to join this "more perfect Union," it must be
on grounds that were morally acceptable and consistent with the principles of free government.[43]

Writing in the *New Hampshire Gazette*, apparently in an effort to influence the vote in New Hampshire after the vote in Massachusetts had been taken, the Massachusetts Antifederalists Consider Arms, Malichi Maynard, and Samuel Field elaborated on these fundamental principles: "Every man is the sole proprietor of his own liberty, and no one but himself hath a right to convey it unless by some crime adequate to the punishment, it should be made forfeit, and so by that means becomes the property of government."[44] Turning from the individual to civil society, they reminded their readers that the sole purpose of government was to secure each individual's natural and indefeasible rights "and not to be made an engine of rapine, robbery, and murder." Because slavery so clearly violated "the plain and simple ideas" of free government, Antifederalists could not in good conscience support the Constitution.

But it was not simply that slavery was inconsistent with the principles of republicanism. If they joined with the slaveholding South, New Hampshire Antifederalists believed they would indeed become "partakers" in the slaveholders' sins. As Joshua Atherton put it in his speech before the New Hampshire ratifying convention, "The idea that strikes those, who are opposed to this clause, so disagreeably, and so forcibly is . . . [if we ratify the Constitution] that we become *consenters to* and *partakers in*, the sin and guilt of this abominable traffic, at best for a certain period, without any positive stipulation that it should even then be brought to an end."[45] Unlike the unnamed Portsmouth delegate to whom he was responding, Atherton did not believe that through the Constitution "an end is to be put to slavery." On the contrary, Antifederalists feared that the compromises in the Constitution would gradually weaken the opposition to slavery altogether. Thus, commenting on the twenty-year ban on regulating the slave trade, Consider Arms predicted: "By that time [1808] we presume that enslaving the Africans will be accounted by far less an inconsiderable affair than it is at present."[46] Indeed, anticipating the "positive good" arguments of George Fitzhugh, "A Gentleman" went further, warning: "That man that will give his vote to import *africans* for the space of 21 years, to drag out a miserable life in *slavery,* will vote to enslave the *Americans* at the end of that period."[47]

In these predictions, Antifederalists proved to be more correct than Federalists, for the Antifederalists understood that the moral foundations of republican government could not rest on the opposing principles of slavery and freedom. Still, the Federalist defense of the Constitution on prudential grounds had something to recommend it, for it is hard to see how New Hampshire's refusal to join the Union would have helped the slaves. Indeed, Atherton's speech suggests that he was more concerned with preserving the moral integrity of New Hampshire than with the abolition of slavery: "We do not think ourselves under any obligation to perform works of supererogation in the reformation of mankind; we do not esteem ourselves under any necessity to go to Spain or Italy to suppress the inquisition of those countries, or of making a journey to the Carolinas to abolish the detestable custom of enslaving the Africans."[48] As Atherton pointedly stated, his purpose was simply "to wash our hands clear of it." And although this policy might satisfy the moral and religious sensibilities of New Hampshirites, it promised no relief to the slaves.

Still, not all Antifederalists saw the split between morality and politics in such absolute terms. Consider Arms and his associates questioned whether the North really needed to compromise on slavery in order to secure ratification. In their calculation, only the two southernmost states would have refused to ratify and they could have been forced by economic boycotts to join the Union without slavery.[49] It is questionable however, whether Arms's head count was correct; refusal might well have pushed a majority of the southern states into the opposition,[50] thereby defeating the Constitution. Although this defeat would not have disturbed moralists such as Atherton, it certainly would have refuted Arms's more prudential argument.

That slavery should have played so crucial a role in New Hampshire's ratifying convention can largely be attributed to the distinctive moral and religious tradition of New England. Indeed, for Antifederalists especially, the moral and religious issues were linked, since it was religious convictions that led them forcibly to oppose slavery on moral grounds. As Herbert J. Storing has persuasively argued, many northern Federalists also opposed slavery, but their belief that republican government was held together by interests made it easier for them to compromise on the issue.[51] By contrast, Antifederalists insisted that republican government must rest on a common moral and religious foundation, and nowhere was this assumption as explicit as in Puritan New England.

FEDERALIST VICTORY

On June 18, 1788, the New Hampshire ratifying convention reassembled, this time at Concord, to continue its consideration of the Constitution. In the four-month interim, the Federalist-controlled press had launched a full-scale propaganda campaign, while newly converted delegates had sought to persuade their constituents to alter their instructions or to unfetter them altogether. Yet in only one town, Hopkinton, did this strategy succeed and its delegate, Lt. Joshua Morss, vote in favor of ratification.[52] Perhaps more important to the final outcome was the fact that five Antifederalist delegates who had attended the first convention did not return to Concord. Although the reasons for their absence have never been satisfactorily explained, it does suggest that Federalists may have succeeded in converting some of their opponents, who then had absented themselves when they could not change the opinion of their towns.[53]

By this time, the drama of ratification had reached its climax. Maryland and South Carolina had recently ratified, raising the number to eight, just one state short of the required number. The Virginia ratifying convention had been in session since June 6, while New York had convened its assembly on June 17. The race to ratification was on. And on June 21, 1788, just four days after it had begun, the New Hampshire convention voted to accept the Constitution.

In part, the Federalist success belongs to Judge Samuel Livermore who, during the last two days of the convention, persuaded his rural colleagues that the Constitution would secure the northern borders of the state against British invasion. But this local issue cannot be separated from Livermore's decision, which was supported by John Langdon, to propose a series of recommendatory amendments in the hope of conciliating more moderate Antifederalists throughout the state.

On the third day of the convention, after two days of "general discussion," a committee of fifteen, chaired by John Langdon and including Samuel Livermore and John Sullivan, as well as the Antifederalist leader Joshua Atherton, was appointed "to consider and report upon such articles as they shall think proper to be proposed as amendments to the Federal Constitution, and lay the same before this Convention." By that third afternoon, the committee, composed of eight Federalists and seven Antifederalists, had reported to the convention: it recommended twelve amendments, the first nine of which were nearly identical with those adopted by the Massachusetts ratifying convention under the leadership of Theophilus Parsons and John Hancock.

Whereas New Hampshire Federalists now embraced the Massachusetts strategy of recommendatory amendments, Antifederalists looked toward New York, where opposition leaders, with the question still before them, had insisted that merely recommendatory amendments were useless. Writing to the New York Antifederalist John Lamb, Joshua Atherton requested a copy of that state's amendments, which, unlike the Massachusetts ones, made ratification contingent upon their acceptance. "Could our Convention receive your Resolution not to adopt, without the necessary Amendments, before they have proceeded too far, together *with your Amendments,* I have not the least Doubt but a great majority would immediately close with your views and wishes."[54] But the list did not arrive, and Atherton, apparently without a plan of his own, lost on two key votes—to make the amendments obligatory and to adjourn the convention. Sensing victory, Federalists called the "main question" the next morning, whereupon the Constitution was accepted by a vote of 57 to 47, with 4 delegates not voting.

This time the Federalist strategy was to isolate the hard-core Antifederalists by winning over the more moderate opponents with a series of recommendatory amendments. In general, Antifederalists believed that a bill of rights was necessary for two reasons: to provide greater security to individual liberties and to limit the powers of the federal government. The proposed amendments, put forth by a Federalist majority, were nearly evenly divided between these two categories. The first five sought to revise the powers and the structure of the federal government in order to preserve the autonomy of the states. Thus, the list of amendments began with the standard provision that "all powers not expressly and particularly delegated . . . are reserved to the several states to be by them exercised."[55] The amendments then sought to erect barriers against congressional tampering with federal elections and to limit Congress's power to tax. Significantly, these last two amendments were not incorporated into the Bill of Rights, while the first was decisively weakened by deleting the phrase "expressly and particularly" and by adding that these powers were reserved either to the states or to the people. Yet, as in the debates over the Bill of Rights in the First Congress, the line between Federalists and Antifederalists was not so sharp. Samuel Livermore, New Hampshire's most outspoken representative and one of the principal drafters of the state's amendments, supported all these so-called Antifederalist measures.

The last seven of New Hampshire's amendments dealt primarily with individual rights. Articles VI through XI reiterated common law—procedural rights in civil and criminal cases—a major Antifederalist concern. Here it is noteworthy that although the New Hampshire convention largely adopted the Massachusetts amendments wholesale, they did make important changes in Article VII, which related to the jurisdiction of the federal courts in common-law cases.

The last three amendments were New Hampshire's own contributions. They restricted standing armies in times of peace, protected the right to bear arms, and secured freedom of conscience, while prohibiting Congress from making any laws "touching religion." In view of the importance of religion at the New Hampshire convention, this last provision requires some discussion. At first sight, the amendment would appear to be the contribution of Federalists, since it was they who, in their defense of Article VI, linked the absence of a religious test with freedom of conscience, while their opponents sought to preserve the ground of republican morality. But if the section on freedom of conscience reflects Federalist concerns, the second half of the amendment, prohibiting Congress from enacting laws "touching religion," may well have been the work of Antifederalists, because it seems to bar the federal government from interfering in New Hampshire's religious establishments.

The New Hampshire amendments are important, not only for what they contained, but also for what they omitted. Most striking, they made no provision for the more political rights of association, free speech, and press. Yet "A Farmer," writing in the only New Hampshire paper that would publish Antifederalist arguments, regarded these rights as "essential to a free people."[56] So did the New Hampshire Constitution of 1784, which stated that the liberty of the press ought "to be inviolably preserved." Nor did the protections against unreasonable searches and seizure, self-incrimination, and cruel and unusual punishment find their way into the New Hampshire amendments.

One possible explanation is that although Federalists supported the amendments at the ratifying convention, they remained unconvinced that such guarantees were really necessary. Tobias Lear, the New Hampshire Federalist who served as George Washington's secretary, expressed this opinion in his letter to the general immediately after the Concord vote. These amendments, he explained, "were drawn up more with a view of softening and conciliating the adoption to some who were moderate in their opposition, than from an expectation that they would ever be ingrafted into the Constitution."[57]

In this respect, it is instructive to compare the New Hampshire recommendations with the actual Bill of Rights, adopted in 1791, and to consider the opinions of New Hampshire's most outspoken representative, Samuel Livermore, in this debate.[58] As in the state ratifying conventions, it was Federalists, under the leadership of James Madison, who led the fight for the Bill of Rights. Madison's explicit purpose was to provide greater security to individual rights, while simultaneously warding off more radical proposals to revise the structure and the powers of government.

At first, Livermore was not convinced that a bill of rights was necessary. Like Tobias Lear, he apparently regarded the states' recommendatory amendments as nothing more than a ploy to secure ratification. As Livermore observed when Madison first introduced the subject, "He [Livermore] was well satisfied in his own mind, that the people of America did not look for amendments at present; they could never imagine it to be the work of the First Congress."[59] Undeterred, Madison pressed the issue, both because he was now convinced that the federal government might, through its implied powers, encroach upon individual rights and because he wished to avert a call for a second constitutional convention, which would seek more drastic limitations on federal powers. Livermore soon came around, speaking in favor of several proposals to secure individual rights. He regarded what became the Fifth Amendment protections as "very essential," and he spoke in favor of "freedom of conscience." Only on the question of cruel and unusual punishment did the New Hampshire congressman reveal a certain "puritanical" streak: "No cruel and unusual punishment is to be inflicted; it is sometimes necessary to hang a man, villains often deserve whipping, and perhaps having their ears cut off; but are we in future to be prevented from inflicting these punishments because they are cruel?"[60]

From the perspective of national powers, even more significant was Livermore's support for Madison's proposal to extend certain prohibitions to the states. On this all-important question, Livermore had "no great objection to the sentiment, but thought it not well expressed. He wished to make it an affirmative proposition; 'the equal rights of conscience, the freedom of speech and of the press, and the right of trial by jury in criminal cases shall not be infringed by any state.'"[61] But Livermore was not a reliable nationalist. Although he apparently saw no problem with extending certain protections of the Bill of Rights to the states, he also fought for the New Hampshire amendments, which sought to limit national powers. Defending a proposal similar to the one adopted by New Hampshire to limit Congress's power over congressional elections, he observed that "this was an important amendment, one that caused more debate in the Convention in New Hampshire than any other whatever."[62] And on another amendment, to limit Congress's power of raising taxes, he "thought this amendment of more importance than any yet obtained. . . . It had been supposed that the United States would not attempt to levy direct taxes; but this was certainly a mistake. He believed nothing but the difficulty of managing the subject would deter them."[63]

Finally, Livermore supported retaining the word "expressly" in the Tenth Amendment. Failing on each of these issues, an obviously frustrated Livermore declared to Congress that "unless something more effectual was done to improve the Constitution, he knew his constituents would be dissatisfied. As to the amendments already agreed to, they would not value them more than a pinch of snuff; they went to secure rights never in danger."[64]

The statement is revealing, for it suggests that the rift between Federalists and Antifederalists in New Hampshire was not as wide as it was in other states, such as New York and Virginia, where more radical nationalists directed the drive for ratification. And despite Livermore's gloomy prediction, New Hampshire voted on January 25, 1790, "to accept the whole of said amendments, except the second article, which was rejected." Ironically, it was Livermore's great opponent, Joshua Atherton, who correctly perceived the mood of the

New Hampshire voters. Writing to his Antifederalist ally John Lamb in New York, Atherton observed that the people's view of the Constitution seemed to be: "it is adopted, let us try it."[65]

In 1788, principle and practicality went hand in hand for New Hampshire. With the revised federal Constitution, New Hampshire could look forward to freedom at home, including moral and religious freedom, and to unity abroad, in a stronger federal union. Indeed, as New Hampshire's Daniel Webster would argue a generation later, liberty and union were, in New Hampshirites' minds, one and inseparable. And so they would remain until the Civil War shook these moral foundations to the ground, and Abraham Lincoln built them back up again.

NOTES

1. Cited by Lawrence Guy Straus in "Reactions of Supporters of the Constitution to the Adjournment of the New Hampshire Ratification Convention — 1788," *Historical New Hampshire*, p. 47.

2. Ibid., pp. 38–39; see also Langdon to Rufus King, 23 February 1788, in Joseph B. Walker, *Birth of the Federal Convention* (Boston, Mass.: Cupples & Hurd, 1888), p. 29.

3. Straus, "Reactions," p. 39.

4. Walker, *Birth*, pp. 112–14. Jonathan Elliot's *Debates in the State Conventions on the Adoption of the Federal Constitution* (hereafter cited as *Debates*) contains only one entry for New Hampshire, a speech by Joshua Atherton opposing the Constitution because of its provisions on slavery. Although Atherton's opposition to slavery is not in question, historians have suggested that the speech itself was written later, since no report of it before 1827 can be found. In addition to Atherton's remarks in Elliot's *Debates*, the New Hampshire historian Joseph B. Walker has discovered a second speech by General John Sullivan, in which he defends the jurisdiction of the federal courts in disputes between different states. But this speech, although authentic, is unlikely to shed much light on the larger questions involved in the ratification controversy.

5. See, for example, John Sullivan to Jeremy Belknap, 26 February 1789, in Sullivan, *Letters and Papers*, ed. Otis G. Hammond, 2 vols. (Concord: New Hampshire Historical Society, 1930–39), 2:566–67.

6. Herbert Storing, *What the Anti-Federalists Were For* (Chicago: University of Chicago Press, 1981), p. 100.

7. In stressing the religious and political traditions of New England, I explicitly reject the argument of Nathaniel Joseph Eiseman, in "The Ratification of the Federal Constitution by the State of New Hampshire" (Master's thesis, Columbia University, 1937), who seeks to explain the New Hampshire ratifying convention in terms of economic and social factors, especially the division between poor farmers advocating paper money and rich commercial interests promoting hard currency. For a persuasive critique of this position as it relates to New Hampshire, see Forrest McDonald, *We the People: The Economic Origins of the Constitution* (Chicago: University of Chicago Press, 1958), esp. pp. 239–51. Also see Jere R. Daniell, *Experiment in Republicanism: New Hampshire Politics and the American Revolution, 1741–1794* (Cambridge, Mass.: Harvard University Press, 1970), esp. pp. 216–17; and Albert Stillman Batchellor, "A Brief View of the Influences That Moved in the Adoption of the Federal Constitution by the State of New Hampshire" (Concord, N.H.: Rumford Press, 1900).

8. I am indebted to Herbert Storing for this basic point, although in his attempt to delineate the general lines of Antifederalist thought, he does not consider regional differences.

9. Jeremy Belknap, cited by Robert A. Rutland in *The Ordeal of the Constitution* (Norman: University of Oklahoma Press, 1965), p. 118.

10. Orin Grant Libby, *Geographical Distribution of the Vote of the Thirteen States on the Federal Constitution, 1787–1788* (Madison: University of Wisconsin, 1894); see also Eiseman, "Ratification," pp. 27–36.

11. Eiseman, "Ratification," pp. 27–36, esp. p. 36.

12. *The Federal and State Constitutions, Colonial Charters, and Other Organic Laws of the United States*, ed. Francis N. Thorpe, 7 vols. (Washington, D.C.: Government Printing Office, 1909), 4:2451.

13. The precise number is in doubt. Jeremiah Libbey, relating information that was given to him by John Pickering, reported 11, while John Sullivan estimated the number to be "about 30": see Eiseman, "Ratification," p. 57; and Sullivan to Belknap, 26 February 1788.

14. John Langdon to Rufus King, 23 February 1788, cited by Walker in *Birth*, p. 29.

15. Cited by Libby in *Geographical Distribution*, pp. 73–74.

16. George Washington to General Knox, 30 March 1788, cited by Straus in "Reactions," p. 39; see also, Washington to John Langdon, 2 April 1788, cited by William F. Whitcher in "New Hampshire and the Federal Convention," *Granite Monthly* 11 (1888).

17. From the Election Sermon preached to the Legislature, delivered by the Rev. Samuel Langdon, cited by Eiseman in "Ratification," p. 68.

18. In *The Complete Anti-Federalist* (hereafter cited as *CAF*), ed. Herbert J. Storing, 7 vols. (Chicago: University of Chicago Press, 1981), 4:209.

19. Eiseman, "Ratification," p. 31.

20. Only Rutland considers the Federalists' options, but he blames Atherton for not having been willing to compromise. Yet later on, somewhat inconsistently,

Rutland suggests that it was in fact the Federalists who learned to compromise. Cf. Rutland, *Ordeal*, pp. 120 and 213.

21. On this general point see Mark de Wolfe Howe, *The Garden and the Wilderness: Religion and Government in American Constitutional History* (Chicago: University of Chicago Press, 1965); see also Stephen Botein, "Religious Dimensions of the Early American State," in *Beyond Confederation*, ed. Richard Beeman, Stephen Botein, and Edward C. Carter II (Chapel Hill: University of North Carolina Press, 1987), pp. 315–32.

22. *Constitutions*, 4:2454.

23. in *CAF*, 4:242; see also the speech by Deacon Matthias Stone in the *American Herald* (Boston), 3 March 1788.

24. *CAF*, 4:202.

25. *CAF*, 4:244.

26. *American Herald*, 3 March 1788.

27. *Debates*, 2:171–72.

28. *CAF*, 4:247–48.

29. *Debates*, 2:172.

30. It apparently satisfied Turner, however, for he voted in favor of the Constitution.

31. In Massachusetts, the vote was even more lopsided: 13 clergy supported the Constitution, while only 3 opposed it (*Debates*, 2:178–81).

32. *American Herald*, 3 March 1788.

33. In this respect, consider the designation of April 10, 1788, by the Federalist President John Sullivan as a "Day of General Humiliation, Fasting and Prayer" to try to build support for the Constitution; consider also the reference to God in the official ratification statement of New Hampshire.

34. Batchellor, "Brief View," p. 33.

35. On the widely known disposition of the North toward slavery see the remarks of Charles Pinckney at the federal convention, in *Records of the Federal Convention of 1787*, ed. Max Farrand, 4 vols. (New Haven, Conn.: Yale University Press, 1911–37), 3:253–54.

36. Everett S. Stackpole, *History of New Hampshire*, 2 vols. (New York: American Historical Society, [1916]), 2:255–56.

37. in *Records*, 2:373.

38. *Debates*, 2:107. Although the New Hampshire Antifederalist position is known, there is little available for the New Hampshire Federalists. Accordingly, I rely on the Massachusetts Federalists, who were compelled to respond to the same objections against slavery. These views were widely circulated in the Federalist press of New Hampshire.

39. In *Debates*, 2:40–41. For New Hampshire, see Atherton's reference to the Federalist position, ibid., p. 203.

40. Ibid., p. 115.

41. See the important discussion by Herbert Storing in "Slavery and the Moral Foundations of the Republic," in *The Moral Foundations of the American*

Republic, ed. Robert H. Horwitz (Charlottesville: University Press of Virginia, 1979), pp. 214–33.

42. *CAF*, 4:12.

43. *CAF*, 4:269.

44. *CAF*, 4:261.

45. *Debates*, 2:203; see also "Phileleutheros," in *CAF*, 4:269.

46. *CAF*, 4:262.

47. *CAF*, 4:12.

48. *Debates*, 2:204.

49. *CAF*, 4:261.

50. See, e.g., Washington to Langdon, 2 April 1788, cited by Whitcher, "New Hampshire."

51. Storing, *What the Anti-Federalists Were For*, p. 100.

52. Libby reports that Salisbury also changed its instructions, but Walker, drawing on private correspondence and the failure of the town's delegate to vote, doubts this. See Walker, *Birth*, p. 17.

553. See the discussion in Eiseman, "Ratification," p. 70.

54. Cited by Rutland in *Ordeal*, pp. 211–12.

55. A list of the amendments can be found in Walker, *Birth*, pp. 49–51.

56. *CAF*, 4:206–7.

57. Tobias Lear to George Washington, 22 June 1788, cited by Eiseman in "Ratification," p. 80.

58. Despite considerable opposition to the Constitution in New Hampshire, the state's first congressional delegation was entirely Federalist. John Langdon and Paine Wingate were chosen to serve in the Senate, while Nicholas Gilman, Samuel Livermore, and Abiel Parker won seats in the House. In the debates on the amendments, Gilman and Parker remained largely silent.

59. *Debates and Proceedings in the Congress of the United States*, 42 vols. (Washington, D.C.: Gales & Seaton, 1834–56), 1:465.

60. Ibid., p. 783.

61. Ibid., p. 784.

62. Ibid., p. 797.

63. Ibid., p. 804.

64. Ibid., p. 804–5.

65. Cited in *Documentary History of the First Federal Elections*, ed. Merrill Jensen and Robert A. Becker (Madison: University of Wisconsin Press, 1976), p. 770.

PART FOUR

THE SEARCH FOR POLITICAL SOLUTIONS

10
VIRGINIA
Sectionalism and the General Good

LANCE BANNING

In Massachusetts, the elite was so one-sidedly in favor of the Constitution that their eloquence became a problem. At the state convention, Rufus King complained, particular objections to the Constitution could be answered. The really baffling difficulty was the opposition's fixed "distrust of men of property or education."* Every effort to respond to that served only to confirm that all the lawyers, judges, clergymen, and merchants favored the reform, that it was "the production of the rich and ambitious."[1]

James Madison, to whom King wrote, may have recalled his letter wryly when Virginia's state convention met. In the Old Dominion, voters sent their customary representatives to the convention. The private circumstances of the gentlemen on one side of the argument were not extremely different from the circumstances of the other.[2] Yet the gentlemen were as divided as the people. As the meeting came to order, the Federalists were marginally more optimistic than their foes, estimating a majority of three or four. But they were neither certain that they had the votes nor confident that they could hold them in the face of the forensic talents and behind-the-scenes stratagems of their opponents. Most of all they feared the magical effects of Patrick Henry's tongue, together with concerted efforts, in the hall and out, to play upon the members' "local interests."[3]

*When quoting from contemporary sources, I have expanded abbreviations and have modernized punctuation and spelling wherever this seemed helpful for twentieth-century readers.

Eight states had ratified the unamended Constitution when
Virginia's state convention met. No one doubted that the national
decision was at stake. If Henry and his allies could persuade the wavering or undecided members to demand amendments, other states would
follow suit, the ratification process could be stalled, and constitutional
reformers might be forced into a second general convention. In order
to accomplish all of this, all Henry and the others had to do was to
provoke more doubts than Federalists could put to rest. This they
sought to do, in no small part, by meeting the proponents of reform
on grounds of fundamental Revolutionary theory. From one perspective, then, this state convention brought together nearly every public
man of major influence in Virginia for a brilliant and dramatic
recapitulation of the larger national debate. With stirring speakers
on both sides, the shorthand record of the confrontation is a classic
illustration of the way in which Federalists successfully rebutted a persuasive case that constitutional reform might undermine the
democratic Revolution.[4]

Neither side, however, argued solely in such terms, nor is it possible to fully comprehend this theoretical dispute without considering the "local interests" that concerned both sides. Henry swore that
he was motivated by the purest patriotic motives, but Federalists believed that he was moved primarily by his profound suspicion of the
North, that recent happenings had predisposed him to denounce
whatever issued from the federal convention, even that he really hoped
to break the Union.[5] And although it seems unlikely that the aging
hero really did prefer a separate southern confederation, the Federalists
were probably correct about the rest. Certainly, the disaffection of
Virginia's two nonsigning members of the Constitutional Convention
can be traced beyond dispute to state and regional considerations much
like Henry's. It is obvious, in fact, that opposition leaders in Virginia
saw the Constitution as oppressive and undemocratic, not least because they judged it dangerously unfair to their constituents and
region.

What is not so obvious — and yet is no less worth remarking — is the
very great extent to which Virginia Federalists were deeply influenced
by the same concerns that moved the opposition. In Virginia, as in
every other state, the ratification contest pitted nationalists against
particularists. Here, however, it is scarcely less revealing to approach

it in the light of state and sectional considerations that were vital to Federalists and Antifederalists alike. This is necessary, in the end, even to define these terms. For *all* Virginia politicians were particularists in the sense that their perspectives, hopes, and fears were shaped by calculations and concerns arising from their regional position and the state's historical relationship with other members of the Union. The ratification contest in Virginia was a close one, from this point of view, principally because the customary leaders of the Union's largest state — as homogeneous a group as any in the country — were divided very evenly and sharply over questions of the state's essential interests. Why they were and how their disagreement was related to their theoretical division are the subjects of this chapter.

VIRGINIA: STATE, SECTION, AND NATION

Virginia's delegation to the Constitutional Convention was the most distinguished of the dozen to appear. It would have towered higher still if Richard Henry Lee and Patrick Henry had accepted their appointments. Lee believed that service at the federal convention was incompatible with membership in the Confederation Congress, which might be called upon to act on the convention's recommendations. Henry pleaded uncertain health and straightened personal finances. Legend has it that he later said he "smelt a rat," which would accord with the suspicions of the other members of the delegation. Madison and Edmund Randolph feared that Henry's sympathies — by no means "anti-federal" through most of his career — had shifted so decisively in 1786 that his refusal to attend the Philadelphia convention augured a determination to resist whatever it proposed. They blamed the recent argument in Congress over the terms of a projected treaty with Spain.[6]

The sectional collision sparked by John Jay's effort to conclude a treaty with Spain is described in every standard study of the background of the Constitutional Convention.[7] Instructed to resolve outstanding boundary disputes, to secure free navigation of the Mississippi River (which Spain had closed to American commerce in 1784), and to obtain a commercial treaty if he could, Jay, the Confederation's secretary for foreign affairs, had found the Spanish envoy, Don Diego de Gardoqui, willing to concede commercial privileges only if the states would agree to forgo the navigation of the Mississippi for a term of twenty-five years. On May 29, 1786, believing that these terms would mean significant relief for the depressed economies of the commercial states and that they only asked the Union to forbear a while from pushing its insistence on a claim that was of no great present consequence to the United States, Jay moved for new instructions that would free him to conclude the pact. Led by Massachusetts, whose representatives were eager to assist their struggling fishermen and shippers, seven northern states approved the change in Jay's instructions; but every state from Maryland to Georgia stood immovably opposed. With nine votes necessary to complete a treaty, the impasse was complete, and the resulting talk of separate regional confederations was a major influence, soon thereafter, on the call from the Annapolis convention for a meeting capable of full examination of the defects of the union.

New Englanders were understandably infuriated by the stubborn southern stand on the Jay-Gardoqui negotiations. In order to protect their speculative interests in the West, it seemed, the southerners were selfishly denying needed succor to the desperate people of the northern ports. Privately, some eastern politicians wondered whether there was any value in a continued union with the south.[8]

To southerners, of course, the selfishness seemed altogether on the other side. Jay and the New Englanders appeared to them to be insisting, in a time of perfect peace, on a concession that would sacrifice the vital interests of their section — and the future greatness of the union — for the sake of privileges that Spain would probably concede without a treaty. As Virginia's William Grayson put it, "the occlusion of the river" would indeed "destroy the hopes of the principal men in the southern states in establishing the future fortunes of their families." But this would hardly be the only consequence of denying the westerners a convenient outlet for their produce. The closing of the river, Grayson said,

> would render the western country of no value and thereby deprive the U.S. of the fund on which they depended to discharge the domestic debt,. . . separate the interest of the western inhabitants from that of the rest of the union and render them hostile to it, [and] weaken if not destroy the union by disaffecting the southern states when they saw their dearest

interests sacrificed and given up to obtain a trivial commercial advantage for their brethren in the east.[9]

The proper policy for the United States, as Grayson saw it, was to
grant an independent revenue to Congress, together with the right
to regulate the country's trade, and then to force a Spanish recognition of the right to navigate the river. But the southern states would
never grant these necessary powers, Grayson warned, if the northern
ones persisted in their present conduct.[10]

Southern outrage over northern actions in the Jay-Gardoqui matter simply cannot be explained as nothing more than a result of a
determination to protect investments in the western lands. To sympathize with southern feelings, which were nowhere more acute than
in Virginia, we must realize that as of 1786, the West was everywhere
perceived as an extension of the South. Western settlement was still
almost exclusively on lands southwest of the Ohio. Settlers in Kentucky or in Tennessee were often literally the kin or former neighbors
of important southern families,[11] and a great deal more than family
ties and family fortunes seemed at stake in their continued membership in the American union. For years, Virginians had identified the
economic future of their commonwealth with improvements that
would make the Chesapeake the entrepôt for European imports to
the West.[12] More recently, as population had moved increasingly into
the old Southwest, it had become increasingly apparent that admission to the Union of new southwestern states could fundamentally affect the federal balance, guaranteeing southern dominance within
the federation or assuring the emergence of a national majority whose
agricultural character and interests would accord with Virginia's
republican ideals. All of this seemed threatened by the Jay-Gardoqui
treaty.[13]

James Monroe, who took a central part in the congressional proceedings, probed the implications in a deeply troubled missive to
Governor Henry. After blasting Jay's intrigues with eastern congressmen, Monroe warned Henry that the creation of a separate northern confederacy was being talked about "familiarly" in Massachusetts.
Massachusetts congressmen, he thought, might have no other object
than to further such a scheme, calculating that the southern opposition would inflame the northern states. On the other hand, he added,

a Spanish treaty on these terms was plainly a transparent eastern ploy
for permanent ascendancy within the Union. A lengthy closure of
the Mississippi would "break up" the western settlements and either
"prevent any in future" or assure that the westerners would find it
in their interest to separate from the confederation. Emigration from
the older states would be abruptly checked, new states would not be
added to the Union, and "the vacant lands of New York and Massachusetts" would appreciate in value and desirability. "In short,"
Monroe concluded, the Jay-Gardoqui project was designed to keep
"the weight of government and population" in the East; and if the
men behind it could not succeed at that, they would not hesitate to
use their failure to destroy the Union.[14]

Believing that a fracture of the Union was an urgent danger, Monroe
was most concerned to caution Henry that Virginia must do everything
within its power to prevent the middle states from joining in a partial northern league. To Madison, he wrote that it would be as well
to go to war at once as to permit Pennsylvania and New Jersey to form
a separate confederation with New England and New York.[15] Obviously, not all Virginians drew the lesson that the South could not afford to strengthen federal powers. Madison believed that thoughts
of separate regional confederations would be silenced only if the central
government were armed with the authority to act upon New England's
suffering and to compel the Spanish to respect the Mississippi claim.
It is clear, however, that if northern readiness to close the Mississippi
was in fact the leading cause of Henry's deep distrust of federal reform,
then Henry was more singular in his conclusions than he was in his
alarm.[16]

For Madison, perhaps for most Virginia public men, the Jay-
Gardoqui crisis and resulting talk of fragmentation of the Union
became the final impetus for the decision to support a constitutional
convention. Virginians played the leading role in bringing a successful
meeting into being. Yet Madison was no less angry than his fellows
over northern conduct on the Spanish treaty, no less conscious of its
implications.[17] He certainly agreed with Grayson and Monroe that
constitutional reform would be defeated in the South unless the Jay-
Gardoqui project could be squelched, and he immediately set out
to do just that.[18] Because of their political and personal connections
with Kentucky and the West, of which the commonwealth had always

been the patron and protector, all Virginia politicians shared in the anxiety provoked by the congressional proceedings, and all of them embarked on constitutional reform with vivid memories of the crisis. No other episode of the confederation years engendered such intense and uniform emotional revulsion. No incident suggested so convincingly how chronic differences between New England and Virginia could suddenly erupt in pressing dangers.

Patent differences of economic interest between the planting and commercial states do not require extended comment. The South exchanged its staple goods for foreign luxuries and manufactures. On the simplest calculation — and some contemporaries reasoned little further — southern interests called for open markets and free trade. Discontent with British domination of the region's commerce did encourage many southerners to argue that the South should join New England in a transfer to the federal government of power to retaliate against the Europeans' navigation laws. Beyond that, though, the interests of the regions seemed as different as their cultures. If the federal government were granted the authority to regulate the country's trade, southern shipping costs would almost certainly increase as a result of northern protectionist demands. Independent federal revenues, another need that few denied, had always posed another puzzle. With slavery concentrated in the South and regional economies so different, the confederated states had never reached agreement on a mix of revenues that might bear equitably upon the different sections. Southern ownership of vast tracts in the West and different sectional experiences in managing the Revolutionary debt were other obvious foundations for persistent disagreements with the East. Accordingly, although the Old Dominion and the Bay State had cooperated closely in the movement for American Independence, it is also true that from the start, and with increasing frequency by the middle 1780s, the most persistent coalitional division in the federal legislature had always been between New England and the South. Virginia was the natural, normal leader of the southern coalition, as Massachusetts was the natural leader of New England.[19]

To understand Virginia's leading role in constitutional reform, together with the fierce internal disagreement that ensued, it will be critical to bear in mind the range and depth of sectional disputes that culminated in the Jay-Gardoqui crisis. It will be useful, too, to recognize that the Virginians paid a standing price for their accustomed leading part in federal affairs. The Old Dominion occupied about a fifth of the United States in 1786. Its size, its age, its uniform commitment to the Revolution, and, of course, the unexampled talents of its leaders had always given it a full, if not a disproportionate, influence on its sisters. Inevitably, the obverse of that influence was the jealousy of smaller states and frequent conflicts with the North. Thus, eight years of war, accompanied or followed by extended controversies over peace terms, western cessions, a location for the seat of federal government, and the navigation of the Mississippi River, had instructed every public man of stature in Virginia in the benefits of union *and* in the suspicions, difficulties, and resentments that the relationship entailed.[20]

Like every other state, Virginia had a separate history, a unique position in the Union, and a special set of state and regional concerns. These produced no uniform conclusions when Virginians were confronted by the complex issues of constitutional reform, and there is no neat way to type the individual decisions that resulted. Former congressmen and men with no significant experience outside the state, former continental officers and men without a military background — individuals who *should* have thought alike or *should* have split into opposing camps — made various decisions. Every one of them, however, understood the world with minds that were conditioned by their Chesapeake location and Virginia's proud, yet problematical, relationship with other states. And so, although it will not solve the mystery of individual choice, it proves instructive to inquire how the Virginians got from common starting points to different endings. The records of the state and federal conventions will permit some interesting conclusions.

REFORMING THE CONSTITUTION: TWO VIRGINIA VIEWS

At the Constitutional Convention on September 17, three delegates refused to sign the finished plan. Two of these were prominent Virginians. Edmund Randolph, former congressman, long-time attorney general of the state, and heir to one of its outstanding family names, had recently succeeded Patrick Henry in its highest office.[21] George Mason, planter-statesman, was the major architect of the Virginia

Constitution and the author of its widely influential Declaration of Rights.[22] At the opening of the convention, both Virginians had supported the replacement of the old confederation with a federal republic.[23] Throughout the long, familiar argument between the small and larger states, both men had spoken repeatedly, and often quite effectively, for large-state, nationalist positions.[24] For both, the process culminating in decisions not to sign originated with the small-state triumph of July 16 and flowed from an unshakeable anxiety about the future of self-government, Virginia, and the South within a system dominated by the smaller, northern states.[25]

The sectional considerations that were near the heart of the Virginians' discontent became apparent in the days immediately preceding the decision to accept the Connecticut Compromise. With several delegations seeking to increase their representation in the lower house or to reduce the seats allotted to their rivals, remarks by several members made it clear that North/South issues were involved. The members of the Constitutional Convention generally assumed, as most contemporaries did, that population growth was fastest in the South and West, which would eventually possess more people than the North and East. Randolph's motion for a periodic census, which would force the national legislature to adjust proportionment to changes in population, therefore led to sharp exchanges on the previous decision for a partial representation of the southern slaves and on the terms on which new states might be admitted to the Union.[26] Mason summarized the southern point of view when he delivered one of the earliest of the convention's several ultimata. The North, he said, was undeniably entitled to preponderate at present, but without provisions that would guarantee that this preponderance would change as population shifted; "he could neither vote for the system here nor support it in his state."[27]

The northern attitude toward slavery was not his major worry. Mason was concerned, as grew increasingly apparent, with familiar economic differences between the planting and commercial states, with the position of Virginia, and with the specter of minority control. With the passage of a compromise between the big and little states, the South would be outnumbered slightly in the lower house and even more unfairly in the Senate. In order to preserve the Union, Mason would accept a temporary disadvantage in the lower house,

and yet he knew that an equality of voting in the Senate would prolong the northern domination of that branch. A periodic census, the
liberal admission of new states, and an exclusion of the Senate from
the power of the purse thus struck him as the minimal securities required in order to protect the planting states from the resulting risks
to their essential interests, as well as to assure majority control.[28]

Minimal securities, moreover, were not, on further thought, enough.
As Randolph said, soon after the decision of July 16, the small-state
victory on the construction of the Senate "had embarassed the business
extremely." All the powers granted to the central government thus
far "were founded," he remarked, "on the supposition that a proportional representation was to prevail in both branches of the legislature."[29] All had to be reviewed in light of the decision that the
states would vote as equals in the second house; and by the time of
the report of the Committee of Detail, both of the eventual nonsigners
had become extremely anxious. For both, a powerful, reeligible executive had been a constant worry. For both, however, commerce and
taxation were undoubtedly the principal concerns.

The Committee of Detail assumed responsibility for much besides
a careful ordering of the convention's previous decisions. Among its
many contributions, it incorporated several demands that delegates
had warned would be conditions for their states' consent. Southerners
had been especially insistent on this subject, and the committee made
provision for all their ultimata: requirement of a two-thirds vote in
Congress for the passage of commercial regulations; prohibition of
a tax on exports; and a ban on any federal interference with the slave
trade. Northerners were outraged, and the numerous concessions to
the South became the focus for a sectional dispute that raged through
much of August. This was finally resolved by the convention's second
famous compromise — between the Deep South and New England.
In exchange for a confirmation of the ban on export taxes and a temporary prohibition of restrictions on the slave trade, South Carolina
voted to forgo the two-thirds rule on commerce. This bargain was
unquestionably the act, when linked with the convention's alteration
of the clause concerning money bills, that prompted the Virginians'
declarations that they would not sign.[30]

On August 22, Mason angrily denounced the slave trade, insisting
that the common interests and security of all the states were threatened

by the practice and that the efforts of the upper South to halt it would be futile if the lower South were to continue to import new slaves and to supply the West.[31] Although he favored the prohibition of a tax on exports, which seemed certain to be levied mainly on the southern staples, Mason also bitterly condemned the other half of the convention's second bargain, protesting that majority control of commerce would deliver southerners, "bound hand and foot," into the mercies of the "Eastern States."[32] Randolph fervently agreed: "There were features so odious in the Constitution as it now stands that he doubted whether he should be able to agree." Rejection of the two-thirds rule, he warned, "would complete the deformity of the system."[33] Mason seconded this warning two days later, "declaring that he would sooner chop off his right hand than put it to the Constitution as it now stands."[34]

These declarations, together with the final motions of the two Virginians, leave no doubt that it was the conjunction of their sectional concerns with their republican convictions that led to their decisions not to sign. On September 7, Mason urged the revival of a privy council as an instrument to aid and check the single national executive. He was unwilling to confide extensive powers of appointment to the president alone, for he already feared an elective monarch; yet neither was he willing to accept so many links between the chief executive and an objectionable Senate, whose members' lengthy terms would make them relatively independent of the people.[35] For Randolph, too, it was the combination of a powerful, reeligible executive, a malapportioned Senate, and the sometimes-hazy grant to a majority in Congress of powers that could be manipulated to the disadvantage of the planting states that touched the quick of his dissent. Convinced that nothing less than radical reform could meet the Union's needs, he had, he said, "brought forward a set of republican propositions as the basis and outline of reform. These republican propositions had, however, . . . been widely and . . . irreconcilably departed from." Thus, he could no longer lend his aid to "a plan which he verily believed would end in tyranny."[36]

The convention made a series of attempts to reconcile its three dissenters. It decided that all money bills must originate in the lower house, whose ratio of members to the people it decreased. It ruled that two-thirds of the Congress, rather than three-fourths, would be enough to override a presidential veto. It transferred from the Senate

to the lower house the power to select the president whenever an electoral majority should fail to appear. Still, the delegates would not
reinstitute the two-thirds rule on navigation laws or listen seriously
to Mason's argument that two-thirds should be necessary to adopt commercial regulations until 1808 (by which time, he may have hoped,
the South would have its reinforcements from the West).[37] The delegations also brusquely and unanimously declined to add a bill of rights.[38]
All three dissenters, in return, resisted the majority's appeals to leave
their doubts within the hall. Mason wrote at once to Richard Henry
Lee, who mounted a resistance in the Continental Congress and soon
was writing letters of his own, several of them meant for publication.
The veteran congressman explicitly concurred in Mason's published
explanation of his views.[39]

Mason, Lee, and Randolph, like Grayson and Monroe, were gen-
uinely anxious to preserve the Union. All but Mason had significant
experience in federal offices. Each was willing to accept a sweeping
constitutional reform. There was not a full-fledged localist among
them. All of these men, however, were compelled to judge the Constitution as Virginia fathers of a new republic; and for all of them,
to different degrees, provincial and republican commitments joined
to generate profound anxieties about the unamended plan.

Mason's pamphlet, which became a starting point for Antifederalists
throughout the country, put their fears succinctly. The crusty author
powerfully denounced the failure to include a bill of rights. He emphasized his principled objections to a government that seemed profoundly flawed in its essential structure, not his sectional concerns.
Still, no power troubled Mason more than the majority's ability to
regulate the country's trade, through which "the five Southern States,
whose produce and circumstances are totally different from that of
the eight Northern and Eastern States, will be ruined." And it was
hardly incidental that the snowy-haired Virginian placed such heavy
stress upon the faulty character and swollen powers of the Senate,
wherein the sectional imbalance would be greatest. Members of the
upper house, he pointed out, would share the power of the purse,
although "they are not the representatives of the people." This violation of a basic Revolutionary maxim, together with the numerous
"alarming" links between "that branch . . . and the supreme Executive," had always struck him as a fundamental danger, possibly be-

cause this was the point at which his Revolutionary principles fused most completely with his sectional concerns. "This government," said Mason, "would commence a moderate aristocracy" and would inevitably become more thoroughly aristocratic or monarchical with time. And while he did not say so, it is plain that Mason thought that this "corrupt, oppressive aristocracy" would prove the more "tyrannical" because it would commence a northern one.[40]

What a contrast to the views of the Virginia signers! Where, indeed, could we discover such a striking difference? Mason feared that constitutional reform would end in the revival of hereditary rule and, in the meantime, work the ruin of Virginia and the South. James Madison believed, no less sincerely, that the Constitution was a necessary, "democratic" remedy for democratic ills.[41] He also thought, which is more relevant to this discussion, that the plan was in the interests of Virginia. Why he did—and why, in the event, first Randolph, then a slight majority in the Virginia state convention, took his side—can tell us much about the Federalist victory in the state. And this will be more certainly the case if we begin by recognizing that the sympathies and reasoning of Madison and Mason, who had often been close allies, were by no means as antithetical as may at first appear.[42]

James Madison was not insensitive to the concerns that troubled his nonsigning colleagues. At the peak of the collision with the smaller states, Mason had declared that he would "bury his bones" in Philadelphia before consenting to a failure of the meeting.[43] Madison was more inclined than either of his friends to risk a small-state walkout from the Constitutional Convention rather than accept state equality in the Senate, which all of them condemned for sectional as well as democratic reasons.[44] No delegate insisted so repeatedly that the essential differences within the nation were between the North and the South, the carrying and the producing states, not between the small states and the large ones.[45] Throughout the Constitutional Convention, Madison's Virginia background and perspective strongly influenced his positions. On balance, these distinguished him as clearly from his northern allies as from the dissenters in his delegation. They also help explain why the Virginia Federalists were not to be defeated by appeals to southern interests.

Attitudes toward the executive are an instructive illustration. At the beginning of the Constitutional Convention the major architect of the Virginia Plan shared much of his Virginia colleagues' deep distrust of an "elective monarch." As he listened to the arguments of Wilson, Hamilton, and Morris, Madison's opinions changed; and in the aftermath of the decision on the Senate, his willingness to strengthen the executive grew even more pronounced. Sectional concerns were a significant consideration. The appointment of judges by the Senate, he remarked, would "throw the appointments entirely into the hands of the northern states." He therefore moved that they should be appointed by the president, with the concurrence of a portion of the Senate, a plan he also came to favor where treaties were concerned.[46]

Madison remained more wary of a strong executive than were the members from the Middle states. Late in the convention, for example, he supported Mason's motion to revive a privy council, which could check the head of the executive without recurring to the senate. But Madison's attempt to balance his unceasing worry over possible encroachments by the lower house with his residual concerns about an overpowerful executive and a Senate dominated by the smaller, northern states became especially apparent when he moved to give the Senate, acting without executive concurrence, the power to conclude a treaty of peace.

Madison's intentions were transparent here, as were the reasons for his speedy second thoughts. War, he reasoned, was a certain and familiar instrument of magisterial ambition. He therefore wished to make it easy to make peace, and the convention followed him at first by making a majority of senators sufficient for such treaties. Two southerners, however, quickly moved a clause providing that a two-thirds vote should still be necessary whenever territory was involved. Doubtless recollecting his determined wartime efforts to protect Virginia's western claims and with the Jay-Gardoqui battle surely also in his mind, Madison confessed that it had been too easy to make treaties, despite the nine-states rule. Joining the majority to overturn his earlier proposition, he followed with an unsuccessful motion that a quorum of the Senate should consist of two-thirds of all its members.[47]

Madison, in sum, was not less dedicated to a limited, republican regime than were the other members of his delegation. He was not less conscious of the differences between the North and South, and he certainly had no intention of delivering the planting states into the hands of a commercial faction.[48] Nevertheless, he did define essential southern interests in a different fashion, and the difference throws as bright a light on subsequent Virginia disagreements as does any other fact.

Consider Madison's position on a tax on exports, where he stood at odds with every other speaking member from the planting states. Export taxes, he insisted, had been fertile sources of contention when levied by the several states. In federal hands, however, they would prove much more than a convenient, painless source of revenues. Export taxes could be used both to encourage native manufacturing and shipping and to force the European powers to concede more "equitable" commercial regulations. "The Southern States," he said, "being most in danger and most needing naval protection," which might be paid for by these taxes, "could the less complain if the burden should be somewhat heaviest on them." "Time," in any case, would "equalize the situation of the states."[49]

Madison had not decided to support a sweeping constitutional reform until experience convinced him that the states' attempts to force the British to dismantle their restrictions on American trade were not just futile but were also an increasing danger to the Union. While the "interfering" efforts of the different states engendered bitterness between them, he observed, all grew more disgusted with a general government that could do nothing to relieve their plight.[50] By the time of the convention, Madison was absolutely dedicated to a general power over commerce, which could be used to force the British to relax their navigation laws. As he conceived it, this was necessary both in order to preserve the Union and in order to create the economic basis for a sound republican society in the United States—one in which American producers would have outlets for their agricultural commodities and could avoid the overcrowding and intensive economic growth that might endanger their ability to sustain a healthy civic life.[51] He therefore struggled to the last to save a federal tax on exports, and he parted from most southerners again to argue strongly for majority control of commerce.[52]

Madison's political economy should not be seen as narrowly and strictly southern, anticipating as it did a future in which Virginia would become a shipping as well as a planting state, together with a present in which sectional abuses of the power over commerce would be made improbable by the complexity of the federal government, the presence of an agricultural majority in inland regions of even the most commercial states, and the rapid addition of new states from the West.[53] Nevertheless, Virginia's economic difficulties during the postwar years entered heavily into his thinking, as did the military situation of the South. Madison admitted that the price of an American navigation act would be a temporary rise in southern shipping costs, but he insisted that the costs would be a fair exchange for benefits received. As before, he emphasized, above all else, the southern need for the protection that would be afforded by an increase in the Union's maritime capacities. "He stated the vulnerable situation of [all the southern states] and of Virginia in particular."[54]

Even as a Revolutionary youth, while bragging of his neighbors' prowess with their rifles, Madison had been acutely conscious of Virginia's vulnerability to foreign and domestic dangers. The War for Independence had confirmed his fears and held, he thought, no clearer lesson for the South. Penetrated everywhere by navigable rivers, having no ships of their own, and always faced potentially with an internal danger from their slaves, the southern states were desperately exposed to British naval power and could look for succor only to their stronger northern sisters. Postwar British dominance of southern trade and postwar conflicts with the northern states, to which the South's extensive commerce would be easy prey in case of a collapse of the confederation, were other indications of the section's inability to stand alone. Of all essential southern interests, then, as Madison perceived it, none was dearer than the Union. Of all potential perils to Virginia's or America's commitment to the democratic Revolution, none thrust deeper than the danger that the Union might collapse and that each state or each of the resulting small confederations would have to treat its neighbors as potential foes. If the United States should ever replicate the fractured politics of Europe, Madison believed, then every state or every small confederation would eventually be governed in the European way. None would lose their liberties more quickly than Virginia and the South.[55] Thus, the sectional disputes and regional considerations that affected all of the Virginia framers pulled in two directions, not just one. Although they heightened the suspicion of the North, they also strengthened an awareness of the indispensability of union. At the Richmond ratifying convention, many delegates would be affected simultaneously by both of these concerns, and both of the opposing trains of thought that had been represented at the Constitutional Convention would have a major influence on the course of the deliberations.

DEBATING THE CONSTITUTION: THE VIRGINIA CONVENTION

The earliest reactions to the Constitution in Virginia were overwhelmingly enthusiastic. Fairfax County voters ordered Mason to support the submission of the plan to a ratifying convention and made it clear that he would not be representing them when it assembled.[56] Randolph fretted over mounting pressure to explain why he had not united with the signers.[57] The legislature called unanimously for a full and free convention. Elections would be held in April, and the meeting would convene in June.[58]

As everywhere, however, opposition to the Constitution mounted over time, and it was obvious before the spring elections that the state was thoroughly divided.[59] Madison, whose relatives and friends insisted that his presence in his county was essential to assure his own election, was dismayed by the unusual division of the state's great men, on which he blamed the close division of the voters. Reading the returns, leaders on both sides considered the decision thoroughly in doubt. Many thought the outcome might depend on the Kentucky representatives, whose views were less well known but who were thought to be especially offended by the northern willingness to close the Mississippi. It was the westerners that Madison particularly mentioned when he worried over Antifederalist appeals to "local interests."[60]

On June 3, 1788, as soon as the convention had completed its preliminary business, George Mason moved a full consideration of the Constitution, clause by clause, before a question should be taken. Suspecting that the Federalists might have a small majority, he feared that they might muscle a decision through before the opposition could develop its appeal for previous amendments and a second general convention. Madison immediately agreed to this procedure, less because he doubted that he had the votes than because he was determined to avoid a lasting alienation of the losers.[61]

Mason's motion, it is sometimes said, was a severe strategic blunder, since no one was a match for Madison in clause-by-clause examination of the Constitution. In fact, however, the convention followed this procedure very loosely during its first eight days. Henry smattered the proposal with repeated and often devastating scatter shots, which were directed less at the particular provisions of the plan than at its fundamental thrust and nature. The Federalists were forced to meet the legend on this mixed terrain. With help from Madison, George Nicholas, and Henry "Light-Horse Harry" Lee, Edmund Randolph took the point, announcing that he still retained the reservations that had led him to refuse to sign but that the unconditional approval of eight states had simplified the question. Virginians, Randolph said, had only to decide between the Union and disunion, to which he never would agree.[62]

Under Henry's inescapable direction, the early arguments went quickly to the fundamentals. Insisting that a "splendid," "energetic" government was "incompatible with the genius of republicanism," Henry warned that failure to include a bill of rights, together with the faulty structure and indefinite authority of the new government, put all the people's liberties at risk.[63] The Federalists, revealingly, conceded that a splendid government was not a proper object for the nation.[64] They nonetheless insisted, first, that this was not the sort of government they had in mind and, second, that the federal features of the Constitution would provide effective safeguards against consolidation. The new regime, they argued, was perfectly republican in structure. Indeed, the compound government erected by the Constitution would offer more security for liberty than any simpler system.[65]

The federal power of direct taxation and the smallness of the House of Representatives were special topics for dispute, as Antifederalists developed their concerns about consolidation and irresponsibility to popular control. So, unavoidably among Virginians, were equality of voting in the Senate and the power of congressional majorities to regulate the country's trade.

Here, of course, the opposition touched on just those "local interests" that Madison most dreaded; and on the fourth day of debates, Henry interjected the alarming issue of the Spanish treaty.[66] As speakers turned increasingly to a consideration of Virginia's role and future in a strengthened union—a debate that reached its climax when Henry called directly on the former members of the Continental Congress for information about the Mississippi — Madison's initial optimism noticeably cooled.[67]

The fear of northern domination of the South, which had assumed so critical a role at Philadelphia, was naturally expressed with even less restraint at the Virginia state convention. Antifederalists returned time after time to the inadequate securities against a gradual "annihilation" of the states, to the certainty that a consolidated government could not care fairly for the great diversity of interests in the country, and to the likelihood that from the first, Virginia's interests would be sacrificed to the demands of the commercial states.[68] "I hope my fears are groundless," William Grayson said, "but I believe it as I do my creed, that this government will operate as a faction of seven states to oppress the rest of the union."[69]

Commercial regulations seemed an obvious example. "The interest of the carrying states," Grayson hardly needed to remark, "is strikingly different from that of the productive states." The former would "assuredly unite," and the condition of the latter would be "wretched." Virginia's agricultural commodities would be carried only on the northerners' conditions. "Every measure will have for its object their particular interest."[70]

Direct taxation posed another danger. Suppose, suggested Grayson, that northerners should lay a tax on slaves. They would neither help to pay this tax nor be accountable to Virginians for their conduct. "This total want of responsibility and fellow-feeling," Grayson said, "will destroy the benefits of representation."[71]

Mason certainly agreed. While it had been the power over commerce that had most alarmed him at the Philadelphia convention, it was now the "ruinous" potential of direct taxation that troubled him the most. The federal government, he reasoned, would undoubtedly impose such taxes as would be the most productive and the easiest to collect, probably the kinds of taxes that had been suggested in Robert Morris's recommendations of 1783. Poll taxes would be an obvious recourse, although no tax was more oppressive to the poor. Land taxes were another, although a tax on land could only operate unequally within a nation where land values varied so enormously by region. Madison had argued, it was true, that changes in population were already working to remove the federal majority into the South and West. Several Antifederalist speakers had agreed. "A very sound argument indeed," said Mason, "that we should cheerfully burn ourselves to death in hopes of a joyful and happy resurrection."[72]

Death might certainly result, Patrick Henry added, from yet another difference between the North and South. Federal authorities would obviously construe the Constitution as they pleased, and they would readily discover an implicit power, in time of war, to "liberate every one of your slaves." Much as he deplored this institution, Henry said, he recognized "that prudence forbids its abolition." But "the majority of Congress is to the north, and the slaves are to the south." If urgent national necessity should combine with antislavery feelings, a sectional majority, "who have no feeling of your interests," would "certainly exercise" this power.[73]

Fantastical imaginings, the Federalists responded — and, in truth, this was the politician speaking, not the prophet. The former governor himself was less concerned with antislavery sentiment than with the hazy powers of the new regime, and there is nothing in the record to suggest that Henry's warning had significant effects or that the worries that would dominate a later generation were already much at work in 1788.[74] Not slavery, but the Mississippi, was the issue that transfixed contemporary minds and seemed to demonstrate most graphically why sectional aggressions would undoubtably result from differences between the regions.

Virginia Antifederalists were eager, not simply to contrast the voting strengths of North and South, not merely to remind the delegates of inconsistent regional desires, but to produce persuasive evidence of a prevailing northern disposition to take advantage of their numbers. For this purpose and because both sides believed that westerners might hold the balance in the meeting, Antifederalists returned repeatedly to the congressional proceedings of 1786, emphasizing that the Constitution's alteration of the nine-states rule was just the sort of opening the East would seize. Federalists replied with evident alarm, insisting that the larger powers of the reconstructed government would guarantee that southern senators would always be alert and present in their seats, so that the two-thirds rule would still require nine states for the conclusion of a treaty. But the anxious tone of Federalist replies suggests that Antifederalists were gaining, and Henry probably expected to assure his triumph when he called for a full discussion of congressional proceedings on the Mississippi. Hugh Blair Grigsby tells us that the hall was overflowing when the congressmen delivered their responses, many thinking that the Antifederalists might move immediately for a decision as soon as this discussion was concluded.[75]

Henry Lee led off, satisfied to stress that the majority in Congress had never planned a permanent surrender of the American claim to a right to navigate the Mississippi.[76] Monroe and Grayson followed with fuller narratives of the congressional transactions, emphasizing that a seven-state majority had certainly—and, in their view, unconstitutionally—approved a change in Jay's instructions that would bind the nation to forgo the navigation for a generation's time. This "temporary" sacrifice of southern interests, they insisted, would devastate the West as certainly as would an absolute surrender of the claim, and neither congressman saw any indication that the northern states were willing to abandon the disgraceful project. Both believed that northerners intended not only to advance their economic interests but also to "depress the western country, and prevent the southern interest from preponderating." Both maintained that a surrender of the Mississippi would be more likely if two-thirds of a quorum of the Senate was sufficient to conclude a treaty.[77] The Federalists were in a desperate position by the time Monroe concluded his remarks, and Madison responded with a brilliant demonstration of the legislative talents that so often made him first in any public meeting he attended.

Madison did not dispute the facts that Grayson and Monroe had just presented, nor did he deny that southerners were right about the critical importance of the Mississippi, which he knew he had a reputation for defending. Rather, he disputed Antifederalist impressions of the "disposition" of the North, together with opponents' judgments of the relative positions of commercial and producing interests in the reconstructed Union. And he roundly disagreed with their assessment of the nature of the most important threats to western and Virginia interests.

If economic interests were the sole consideration, Madison maintained, the eastern states would shortly recognize that none had more to gain from opening the Mississippi, for the carrying trade would rise or fall with the productions of the West.[78] These kinds of interest, though, were simply not the sole consideration. Emigrations to the West were rapidly increasing from New England, as well as from the South, and this would quickly have the same effects on northern sentiments as it already had on southern.[79] Individuals might still be hostile to the West, but under the new Constitution it would be "the sense of the people at large" that would "direct the public measures." Commercial needs, accordingly, would have *less* influence in the new regime than in the old one. Sending representatives from the interior of the northern states, as well as from the South, the "landed interest" would control the House of Representatives from the beginning, dominate the elections of the president, and grow more western in its character and sentiments with every passing year.[80]

The Mississippi, Madison concluded, could not be more endangered if the Constitution were approved. If senators attended to their duty, nine states would still be necessary to conclude a treaty, while the president's dependence on the agricultural majority for his election would assure additional protection for the South and West. Moreover, it should never be forgotten, Madison reminded the convention, that the weaknesses of the confederation had "produced" the Jay-Gardoqui "project." Resolutions that the nation had a *right* to navigate the Mississippi had "re-echoed," he declared, "from every part of the United States," but they would prove as "fruitless" in the future as they had in past until "a change takes place which will give energy to the acts of the government." A stronger system would remove temptations to exchange the nation's general interests for temporary, partial ones. And only by adopting such a system could "the people of [the western] country" win "an actual possession of the right, and protection in its enjoyment."[81]

If there was one decisive day at Richmond, June 13 was probably that day. Madison's rebuttal of his colleagues' fears was quickly seconded by Nicholas, whose repetition of its central points was all the more effective because he spoke as one who was already planning to remove to Kentucky. The two of them did not decisively defeat the opposition. There is no conclusive evidence that any votes were changed.[82] Yet subsequent proceedings do suggest that Madison and Nicholas successfully defused the issue, robbing it of much of its potential to impinge on other matters or to occupy the members out of doors. On the morrow the convention turned with a renewed determination to a clause-by-clause discussion, and Madison began to dominate proceedings, much as Henry had been able to direct the earlier debates. During the convention's final days, the Antifederalists increasingly despaired.

The Reasons for Ratification

It was not enough, of course, for Federalists to argue that the right to navigate the Mississippi had been threatened by the weaknesses of the existing system and might be most effectively asserted by a stronger new regime. Other federal powers also seemed to be compelling threats, and it is clear that Madison did not convince most delegates that the "producing" interests would control the reconstructed federal system.[83] But Madison and Nicholas accomplished something hardly less important in the argument about the Mississippi. They showed the wavering and undecided members why Virginians might conclude that even local interests might be best advanced within a stronger system. They did so by advancing elements of the extended reasoning that Madison had offered in *The Federalist* and at the Constitutional Convention: reasoning that clearly seems responsible for Randolph's change of course; and reasoning that may have seemed decisive, now, to others in the hall.

Newly sensitized to fundamental differences between New England and the South, which had erupted in so frightening a form when Jay had asked for new instructions, all Virginia leaders read the Constitution partly for the ways in which it would affect their region. Never more distrustful of the North, most of them concluded that the plan contained inadequate securities against manipulation of the larger powers of the new regime by northern politicians, who had recently revealed their sectional designs and who were commonly suspected of being disillusioned with the Revolution.[84] The structure of the Senate seemed unduly advantageous to the smaller northern states, as did the Senate's special powers. The federal government was granted several powers subject to abuse and likely to result in sectional collisions. While most Virginia politicians readily conceded the necessity for federal reform, most therefore wanted constitutional amendments that would guarantee additional protection for their state, together with a bill of rights. The central question for the state convention, then, was whether such amendments would be made conditions for

Virginia's ratification or whether they should be entrusted to the action of the first federal Congress.

Antifederalists advanced a simple, yet compelling, case for previous amendments. As Henry put it, "I should . . . take that man for a lunatic, who should tell me to run into the adoption of a government avowedly defective, in hopes of having it amended afterwards." "Do you enter into a compact first, and afterwards settle the terms?"[85] As Henry saw it, Virginia was at peace, confronted by no peril more apparent than the dangers to its vital interests and to liberty itself that were inherent in the unamended Constitution. Time was on the Old Dominion's side. The need for constitutional reform was felt most urgently in the commercial North and East, although the South and West, which were becoming stronger year by year, were being asked to shoulder all the risks. Given these conditions, Virginia could afford a year or two's delay in putting a new government into effect. The ratifying states would be compelled to grant the safeguards it required.[86]

Several serious miscalculations, Federalists replied, were hidden in the Antifederalist position. Wherever there was power, Madison admitted, there was always the potential for abuse. But wherever "power can be *safely* lodged, if it be *necessary*, reason commands its cession." "We are reduced to the dilemma of either submitting to the inconvenience or losing the Union."[87] Clause by clause, the little general and his allies countered every opposition worry, always arguing that every delegated power was at once essential and invariably accompanied by multiple securities against misuse. The central government created by the Constitution, they repeated, was carefully restricted to responsibilities that the separate states could not effectively discharge. The powers of the states, internal checks and balances, and the predominating influence of the agricultural majority would all combine to guard against a dangerous consolidation or against misuse of governmental powers by the North. Federal powers would be delegated, Madison insisted, to representatives "chosen for short terms,. . . responsible to the people, and whose situation is perfectly similar to their own. As long as this is the case," he reasoned — and it would be the case as long as the people retained sufficient virtue "to select men of virtue and wisdom"—"we have no danger to apprehend."[88] Virginia's most essential interests, like liberty itself, would actually be less at risk in an enlarged, compound republic than in the current, feebler system.

Of all the Antifederalist miscalculations, however, none seemed greater to the Federalists than the excessive confidence with which the opposition talked about amendments and denied the urgency of the existing moment. The ratifying states, the Federalists maintained, would not reverse their stands "to gratify Virginia."[89] If the Old Dominion did succeed in blocking the reform, opponents of the Constitution in the different regions of the country would never reach agreement on the changes they desired.[90] The present moment, then, might really be the last for making needed changes in the context of a general confederation. And a general union of the states was simply not less necessary for the South than for New England.

The old confederation, Edmund Randolph cried, was gone. "It is gone, whether this house says so or not. It is gone, sir, by its own weakness."[91] "Could I . . . believe that there . . . was no storm gathering" and that previous amendments could be really be secured, "I would concur" with Henry's plan, "for nothing but the fear of inevitable destruction would lead me to vote for the Constitution in spite of the objections I have."[92] But to insist on previous amendments at this point could only prove "another name for rejection." "If, in this situation, we reject the Constitution, the Union will be dissolved, the dogs of war will break loose, and anarchy and discord will complete the ruin of this country."[93]

"Is this government necessary for the safety of Virginia?" Randolph asked. He was willing for the outcome to depend on a considered answer to this question, and he answered it himself as Madison had answered fellow southerners at Philadelphia or earlier within the current meeting. Vulnerable to Indians or foreign enemies by land and sea, internally endangered by its large slave population, Virginia had no navy, Randolph said, no military stores. All her patriotic efforts in the War for Independence would have been to no avail without assistance from the other states. But if the Union should collapse,

> those states, then our friends, brothers, and supporters, will . . . be our bitterest enemies. . . . The other states have upwards of 330,000 men capable of bearing arms. . . . In case of an attack, what defense can we make? . . . Our export trade is entirely in the hands of foreigners. We have no manufac-

tures. . . . Shall we form a partial confederacy? . . . Partial
confederacies will require such a degree of force and expense
as will destroy every feature of republicanism. . . . I believe
that, as sure as there is a God in heaven, our safety, our
political happiness and existence, depend on the union of the
states. . . . In union alone safety consists. . . .[94]

At the Constitutional Convention, Edmund Randolph had been
first to plead for a procedure under which the Constitution would
be offered to the people of the states, the state conventions would propose amendments, and a second general convention would complete
the plan of constitutional reform. Now, at Richmond on June 25,
he had the final word:

> *I went to the federal Convention . . . I refused to subscribe,
> because I had, as I still have, objections to the Constitution,*
> and wished a free inquiry into its merits. [But] the accession
> of eight states reduced our deliberations to the single ques-
> tion of *Union or no Union.* . . . When I see safety on my right,
> and destruction on my left, . . . I cannot hesitate to decide
> in favor of the former."[95]

In the Old Dominion, as in other evenly divided states, a vital handful of the silent, back-bench delegates appears to have agreed. A motion to insist on previous amendments was defeated by a vote of 88
to 80. Virginia ratified the Constitution by a margin of 10 votes and
recommended numerous amendments to the first new Congress.[96]

The Proponents of the Constitution surely would have lost at Richmond if the opposition had been able to convince a scattering of
doubtful delegates that the reform would undermine the democratic
Revolution. They would have failed as certainly if Antifederalists had
offered a superior analysis of state and southern interests, for the
records of the state convention show that these considerations entered
heavily into the views of every speaking member. But the interests of
Virginia were a complicated matter, and a dedication to republican
ideals could call as plainly for immediate approval of the Constitution as for previous amendments. Thus, on both essential points, the

Federalists debated their opponents to, at worst, a draw. They probably preserved and may have slightly widened the narrow margin they
began with.

This result does not suggest that the proceedings of the meeting
offer little insight into the opinions of the silent delegates and voters,
whose reasoning determined the decision. If the arguments at Richmond changed few minds, they do permit a number of instructive
inferences about the patterns of Virginia thinking, and they do suggest some further observations on the reasons for, and the conditions
of, the federal triumph.

Virginia's close division on the Constitution does not lend itself convincingly to any of the most familiar explanations of the ratification
contest. It was not essentially a function of conflicting economic
interests, class divisions, or contrasting localist and cosmopolitan perspectives. It did not pit radicals against conservatives or younger men
against their seniors. Among the state's most influential men, it pitted unionists against particularists only in a complicated sense, and
one that only partly overrode their shared commitments and
agreements.

Among Virginians whose ideas we can directly reconstruct from
private correspondence, public writings, and the records of the state
and federal conventions, none disputed the necessity for constitutional
reform. Just as clearly, none believed that constitutional reform was
worth the sacrifice of liberty or of the vital interests of Virginia and
the South. Rather, men of comparable experience and intellect, responding to the same alarms and sharing many common values, were
compelled to solve a very difficult equation when presented with the
Constitution. Regional disparities, the history of sectional disputes,
the current disposition of the North, and even the condition of the
Revolutionary enterprise in both the Old Dominion and the nation—
all had to be considered in order to determine where Virginia's interests lay. Several speakers at the state convention candidly confessed
that they could see no easy answer and could judge the Constitution
neither altogether good nor altogether bad. Many silent delegates and
many voters, I suspect, were swayed by all of the concerns the speakers
voiced and made their individual decisions in related ways.[97]

Virginia's leaders had reacted with intense and virtually unanimous alarm to the sectional crisis of 1786. Patrick Henry may have been the only one who silently resisted the conclusion that the Union must be strengthened (or who flirted later with the thought that separate regional confederations might be preferable to a proposal that appeared to strengthen it too much).[98] Confronted with the unamended Constitution, nonetheless, several former nationalists were seized by much the same anxieties as those that captured Henry. Commercial regulations could be made, they saw, and federal taxes levied, by congressional majorities whose sympathies and interests seemed as incompatible with theirs as Parliament's had been. Recent history showed, they thought, that sectional temptations would result in sectional abuses; it even seemed to warn that influential eastern politicians might prove eager to employ the great and often dangerously ambiguous authority of the new government in ways that would be consciously intended to produce additional consolidation and a permanent subjection of the South and West. Virginia's liberties and interests, they concluded, simply could not be entrusted, even temporarily, to northern politicians.

On the other side, James Madison was probably unique in his conviction that Virginia's economic interests would be safe because an agricultural, republican majority would use the Constitution from the start to foster a political economy in which the interests of the shipping and the producing states would harmonize and gradually converge. But Madison and other Federalists could offer a persuasive case that the debilities of the Confederation were themselves the leading cause of the closure of the Mississippi and of the eastern economic suffering that had produced the recent sectional collision. They could argue that opponents of the Constitution, even in Virginia's own convention, would never reach agreement on the changes they required. And finally—what may have been the margin—they could demonstrate effectively that both Virginia and republican self-government, as most Virginians tended to define it, were incalculably more vulnerable to a collapse of the confederation than the Antifederalists were willing to admit. They carried the convention and the state, I would suggest, because the calculations that persuaded Edmund Randolph influenced others too. Virginians did not vote to sacrifice their liberties or local interests to larger national needs. Rather, a majority may have decided that the interests of Virginia, which included its survival as a liberal republic, were inseparable from the perpetuation of the Union. Randolph clearly did, and Randolph's tortured course may have epitomized the ratification contest in the state.

If this was so, however, there are grounds for yet another, final observation. The majority at Richmond voted, as their governor preferred, for subsequent amendments that would guarantee additional protection for Virginia's special interests, as well as for the liberties protected by its Revolutionary charters. As Patrick Henry feared, James Madison proved instrumental in defeating substantive reductions in the commerce and taxation powers of the new regime, even as he led the first new Congress in the preparation of the Bill of Rights. Virginia's second-most-important nationalist continued to believe that federal navigation laws, together with a federal power of direct taxation, were indispensable to the regime's success. He also thought that they were in the interests of his state, and his positions at the state and federal conventions should suggest that this had never seemed to him a merely incidental point.[99] Madison transcended the particular in ways that periodically exposed him to the deep distrust of some Virginians. Still, his concept of the Union was indelibly conditioned, as was theirs, by his Virginia background and perspective. He supported constitutional reform in part because he was more fearful than his foes about Virginia's fate outside the Union. But he supported it, as well, because he was more confident than they that a majority of agricultural producers would direct the new regime and keep the central government within its chartered limits. When that faith was tested, it is not surprising that his vision was to prove as incompatible as theirs either with a consolidated system or with eastern domination of the reconstructed union.

The Constitution split Virginians sharply and in truly fundamental ways. While he was not a vengeful man, Henry died without forgiving Madison for the defeat of 1788, and Randolph's promising career was wrecked by his reversal during that year.[100] In hindsight, nonetheless, the record of the ratifying contest speaks as clearly of the commonalities among Virginians as it does of their dissensions. They disagreed about Virginia's interests or, at least, about the most effective way that these could be secured. But in their general association of the interests of producers with the interests of republics, their

shared commitment to the West, their uniform denunciations of consolidation, their dislike of government "splendor," and their settled,
common fears of standing armies, public debts, and magisterial ambitions, it is easy to detect the themes that would unite the great
majority again behind the Resolutions of 1798 and the distinctively
"Virginian" policies of the "Dynasty" years. In these agreements, too,
it may be possible to see that it was not expediency alone, or even
mainly, that explains why Madison continued at their head.

NOTES

1. King to Madison, 20 and 27 January 1788, in *The Papers of James Madison*,
ed. William T. Hutchinson et al., 15 vols. to date (Chicago: University of Chicago
Press, 1962–), 10:400, 436–37. See, similarly, the often-quoted complaint of Antifederalist delegate Amos Singletary about "these lawyers, and men of learning and moneyed men, that talk so finely, and gloss over matters so smoothly,
to make us poor illiterate people swallow down the pill," in *The Debates in the
Several State Conventions on the Adoption of the Federal Constitution . . . ,*
ed. Jonathan Elliot, 5 vols. (Washington, D.C.: Government Printing Office,
1888), 2:102.

2. The most extensive and quantitatively sophisticated argument to the contrary concedes that differences of wealth, occupation, education, and the like,
"account for only a tiny portion of a delegate's voting behavior" (Norman K.
Risjord, *Chesapeake Politics, 1781–1800* [New York: Columbia University Press,
1978], p. 316). Risjord's discussion (pp. 293–317) of the ratification contest in
Virginia builds on his "Virginians and the Constitution: A Multivariant Analysis,"
William and Mary Quarterly, 3d ser. 31, (1974): 613–32; Norman K. Risjord
and Gordon DenBoer, "The Evolution of Political Parties in Virginia, 1782–1800,"
Journal of American History 60 (1974): 961–84; Gordon DenBoer, "The House
of Delegates and the Evolution of Political Parties in Virginia, 1782–1792" (Ph.D.
diss., University of Wisconsin, 1972); and Jackson Turner Main, *Political Parties before the Constitution* (Chapel Hill: University of North Carolina Press,
1973). All find a slight, though significant, correlation between support for the
Constitution and wealth, continental military service, higher education, and
the like. Contrast Robert E. Thomas, "The Virginia Convention of 1788: A
Criticism of Beard's *An Economic Interpretation of the Constitution," Journal
of Southern History* 19 (1953): 63–72; and Forrest McDonald, *We The People:
The Economic Origins of the Constitution* (Chicago: University of Chicago Press,
1958). McDonald argues (p. 268) that economic and occupational differences
fell into "no meaningful pattern whatever" and that the property holdings of
delegates on opposite sides "were virtually identical except that more small
farmers from the interior supported ratification than opposed it."

3. Madison to George Washington, 4 June 1788, and to Tench Coxe, 11 June 1788, in *Papers of James Madison*, 11:77, 102. For estimates by Antifederalist leaders see *The Papers of George Mason, 1725–1792*, ed. Robert A. Rutland, 3 vols. (Chapel Hill: University of North Carolina Press, 1970), 3:1040, 1044–46; William Wirt Henry, *Patrick Henry: Life, Correspondence, and Speeches*, 2 vols. (New York: Charles Scribner's Sons, 1891), 2:342–43.

4. I have discussed the meeting from this point of view in "'To Secure These Rights': Patrick Henry, James Madison, and the Revolutionary Legitimacy of the Constitution," in *To Secure the Blessings of Liberty: First Principles of the Constitution*, ed. Sarah Baumgartner Thurow, (Lanham, Md.: University Press of America, 1987), pp. 280–304. Nearly every great Virginian who desired a seat was present at this meeting. Washington avoided it, although his known support was probably more useful to the Federalists than any other influence. Thomas Jefferson, who was claimed by both sides, was serving as the Union's minister to France. The only other notable exceptions were Richard Henry Lee, who disliked the Richmond climate, and his brother Arthur, who withdrew from the elections in favor of another Antifederalist candidate.

5. See Madison to Edmund Randolph, 10 January 1788, Edward Carrington to Madison, 10 February 1788, George Nicholas to Madison, 5 April 1788, and Madison to Jefferson, 22 April 1788, in *Papers of James Madison*, 10:355 and 494, 11:9 and 28.

6. Madison to Washington, 7 December 1786, Randolph to Madison, 1 March 1787, and Madison to Jefferson, 19 March 1787, ibid., 9:200, 301, 319.

7. I have relied especially on the excellent discussions in H. James Henderson, *Party Politics in the Continental Congress* (New York: McGraw-Hill, 1974), pp. 387–94; Jack N. Rakove, *The Beginnings of National Politics: An Interpretive History of the Continental Congress* (New York: Knopf, 1979); and Edmund Cody Burnett, *The Continental Congress* (New York: Macmillan, 1941), pp. 654–59.

8. See Charles Thomson's report of the speech by Rufus King, 16 August 1786, *Letters of Members of the Continental Congress*, ed. Edmund C. Burnett, 8 vols. (Washington, D.C.: Carnegie Institution, 1921–36), 8:429; Burnett, *Continental Congress*, p. 657.

9. Thomson's "Minutes of Proceedings," 16 August 1786, in *Letters of Members*, 8:427–28.

10. Ibid., pp. 429, 438; see also Charles Pinckney's speech of 16 August in *Journals of the Continental Congress*, ed. Worthington Chauncy Ford et al., 34 vols. (Washington, D.C.: Government Printing Office, 1904–37), 31:935–48.

11. N.b. Madison's reference to the westerners as "bone of our bones, and flesh of our flesh" (to Lafayette, 20 March 1785, in *Papers of James Madison*, 8:251).

12. An open Mississippi, it was generally assumed, would be the natural outlet for western exports, but it would still prove most convenient for the westerners to get their imports along the Potomac and Ohio route. Interestingly, Virginia's ultimatum during the congressional proceedings would have accepted closure

of the river to American imports for a time in exchange for its opening to western exports: see the motion of the Virginia delegates in *Letters of Members*, 8:440–42.

13. Points in this paragraph are powerfully developed by Drew R. McCoy in "James Madison and Visions of American Nationality in the Confederation Period: A Regional Perspective," in *Beyond Confederation: Origins of the Constitution and American National Identity*, ed. Richard Beeman, Stephen Botein, and Edward C. Carter II (Chapel Hill: University of North Carolina Press, 1987), pp. 226–58.

14. Monroe to Governor Henry, 12 August 1786, in *Letters of Members*, 8:422–25.

15. 3 September 1786, *Papers of James Madison*, 11:113–14; see also 9:104.

16. Henry's sparse surviving correspondence does not clearly confirm the contemporary analysis, but none of his biographers has doubted that his contemporaries were correct. For this and Henry's generally nationalistic course before the incident see Robert Douthat Meade, *Patrick Henry* (Philadelphia: E. B. Lippincott, 1957–69), and Richard R. Beeman, *Patrick Henry: A Biography* (New York: McGraw-Hill, 1974).

17. Letters to Monroe, 21 June 1786, to Jefferson, 12 August 1786, to Monroe, 5 October 1786, to Washington, 7 December 1786, in *Papers of James Madison*, 9:82–83, 96–97, 140–41, 200.

18. To Monroe, 21 June and 15 August 1786, ibid., pp. 82–83, 107.

19. In addition to Henderson and the other sources cited in note 10 see Joseph L. Davis, *Sectionalism in American Politics, 1774–1787* (Madison: University of Wisconsin Press, 1977).

20. See, further, Thomas Perkins Abernathy, *Western Lands and the American Revolution* (New York, Russell & Russell, 1959; originally published in 1937); Peter Onuf, "Toward Federalism: Virginia, Congress, and the Western Lands," *William and Mary Quarterly*, 3d ser. 34 (1977): 353–74; idem, *The Origins of the Federal Republic: Jurisdictional Controversies in the United States, 1775-1787* (Philadelphia: University of Pennsylvania Press, 1983); and Lance Banning, "James Madison and the Nationalists, 1780–1783," *William and Mary Quarterly*, 3d ser. 40 (1983): 227–55.

21. A modern biography is John J. Reardon's, *Edmund Randolph: A Biography* (New York: Macmillan, 1975).

22. Robert A. Rutland, *George Mason: Reluctant Statesman* (Williamsburg, Va.: Colonial Williamsburg, 1961); Helen Hill Miller, *George Mason: Gentleman Revolutionary* (Chapel Hill: University of North Carolina Press, 1975).

23. See Randolph's speech of 29 May, introducing the Virginia Plan and arguing that nothing less than a complete reconstitution of the central government could meet the nation's needs, along with Mason's early effort to distinguish a "national" government from one purely "federal," in *The Records of the Federal Convention of 1787*, ed. Max Farrand, 4 vols. (New Haven, Conn., 1966 [1937 ed.]), 1:18–23, 34. References to proceedings in the convention are to Madison's notes.

24. See, for example, Mason's defenses of the popular election of the lower house on 6 June and 21 June, their joint defense of a provision requiring an oath from state officers to support the federal Constitution and federal laws, Randolph's comparison of the Virginia and New Jersey plans on 16 June, and Mason's speech of 20 June on the powers of the convention and the impracticability of Paterson's plan (ibid., pp. 133–34, 359, 203, 255–56, 338–40).

25. It is clear that both of the eventual nonsigners swallowed the convention's central compromise with deep reluctance and only on condition that the upper house should be denied a role in framing money bills: see Madison's explanatory note of 5 July and Mason's remarks of 6 July, together with Randolph's alternative proposal for conciliating the smaller states, ibid., 1:526 and 544, 3:55–56.

26. The complicated maneuvers on these subjects occupied the delegates from 9 through 14 July, the days immediately preceeding the critical vote on the upper house.

27. Farrand, *Records*, 1:578–79.

28. By the terms of the committee report of 10 July, the states from Maryland south—the states, not incidentally, that had opposed the change in Jay's instructions—would be outnumbered 36 to 29 in the lower house, but they would be outnumbered 8 to 5 in an equally apportioned senate. It should be recognized that the "large-state" coalition was primarily southern in its composition.

29. Farrand, *Records*, 2:17.

30. On 8 August, Mason said that giving equal powers over revenues to a branch whose members' terms would be of long duration—one that the convention currently intended as the locus of the powers over treaties and appointments—could only tend toward aristocracy. He and Randolph were outvoted in the delegation by Madison, Washington, and John Blair, who cast Virginia's vote with the majority to strike the clause denying the Senate a role in shaping money bills. On 9 August, Randolph moved to reconsider. Both he and Mason warned that they might retract their approval of the Connecticut Compromise unless the Senate was denied an equal power over the purse. Correctly estimating his colleagues' growing discontent, Washington changed sides on 13 August, and Virginia voted for Randolph's motion. In the end, nevertheless, the convention proved willing to concede no more than a clause requiring that money bills must originate in the lower house, which struck the two Virginians as no concession at all.

31. Farrand, *Records*, 2:370.

32. 29 August, ibid., p. 451.

33. Ibid., pp. 452–53.

34. 31 August, ibid., p. 479. On the same date, Mason prepared a list of changes he considered necessary and solicited the Marylanders' aid in securing them. These included more explicit definition of the powers of the national government, a two-thirds rather than three-fourths vote to override a presidential veto, a two-thirds requirement for navigation laws, a money-bill clause, a

prohibition of "perpetual" taxes, and executive ineligibility for a second term. See ibid., 4:56–57.

35. Ibid., 2:537.

36. Speeches of 10 September, ibid., pp. 560–61, 563–64.

37. Motion and speech of 15 September, ibid., p. 631.

38. Proceedings of 12 September, ibid., pp. 587–88.

39. Lee to Mason, 10 October 1787, in *Papers of George Mason*, 3:996–99, including "the greatness of the powers given, and the multitude of places to be created, produces a coalition of monarchy men, military men, aristocrats, and drones whose noise, imprudence, and zeal exceeds all belief, whilst the commercial plunder of the south stimulates the rapacious trader." For Lee's objections more generally see the letters to Samuel Adams, 5 October 1787, to Randolph, 16 October 1787, to James Gordon, Jr., 26 February 1788, and to Edmund Pendleton, 22 May 1788, in *The Letters of Richard Henry Lee*, ed. James Curtis Ballagh, 2 vols. (New York: Macmillan, 1911–14), 2:444–47, 450–55, 460–63, 470–74. Although I am aware of the counterarguments by Steven R. Boyd and Walter H. Bennett, I agree that Lee was not the "Federal Farmer": see Gordon S. Wood, "The Authorship of the *Letters from the Federal Farmer*," *William and Mary Quarterly*, 3d ser. 31 (1974): 299–308.

40. "Objections to the Proposed Federal Constitution," available in Farrand, *Records*, 2:637–40; *Papers of George Mason*, 3:991–93. For its circulation see the editorial note in the latter, p. 993.

41. The phrase was used in Madison's speech of 6 June, in Farrand, *Records*, 1:135. And see, of course, Madison's numbers of *The Federalist*.

42. On Madison's and Mason's views of one another—even in the aftermath of the ratification dispute—see the touching exchange between Mason and Jefferson in *Papers of George Mason*, 3:1224.

43. 5 July, Farrand, *Records*, 1:533.

44. Madison's note on the large-state caucus of 17 July (ibid., 2:19–20) leaves no doubt on this point when read in light of the earlier positions of all three men.

45. See, especially, the speeches of 28 and 30 June, ibid., 1:446–49, 486–87.

46. 21 July, ibid., 2:80–81.

47. Proceedings of 7 and 8 September, ibid., pp. 540–41, 547–49.

48. For more on these points see Lance Banning, "The Practicable Sphere of a Republic: James Madison, the Constitutional Convention, and the Emergence of Revolutionary Federalism," in *Beyond Confederation*, pp. 162–87.

49. Speeches of 16 and 21 August, Farrand, *Records*, 2:306–7, 361.

50. Banning, "James Madison and the Nationalists," pp. 252–54.

51. On this point see particularly Drew R. McCoy, *The Elusive Republic: Political Economy in Jeffersonian America* (Chapel Hill: University of North Carolina Press, 1980), chap. 3.

52. When the southerners secured the ban on federal export taxes, Madison moved to permit them on a two-thirds vote, "a lesser evil than a total prohibition" (21 August, ibid., p. 363). The convention did, of course, forbid state ex-

port taxes, which he had denounced as inequitable to New Hampshire, Connecticut, New Jersey, Delaware, and North Carolina, all of which had seen their exports taxed at ports in neighboring states.

53. See Madison's speech of 29 August, ibid., pp. 451–52, and, more fully, McCoy, "James Madison and Visions of American Nationality."

54. Madison's speech of 29 August.

55. See especially Madison's speech of 29 June, Farrand, *Records*, 1:464–65, and *Federalist* 41. But Madison's association of southern weaknesses, the collapse of the confederation, and an end of republican liberty went back at least as far as 21 February 1783: see *Papers of James Madison*, 6:272.

56. *Papers of George Mason*, 3:1000–1001. Mason supported a ratifying convention in any case, and he easily won election from neighboring Stafford County, where he also owned property.

57. Randolph to Madison, 29 October 1787, *Papers of James Madison*, 10:229. Randolph's letter to the speaker of Virginia's House of Delegates was not published until January 1788. Primarily a defense of his conduct and an argument for previous amendments, the letter contained substantive objections that were much the same as Mason's, although couched in more moderate terms. Randolph called equal suffrage in the Senate and majority control of commerce the "most repugnant" features of the Constitution, but he also objected strongly to indefinite presidential reeligibility, "ambiguities of expression," and the uncertain boundary between state and federal powers (Farrand, *Records*, 3:123–27).

58. The ratifying process would be cheaper if elections were held concurrently with the usual election of the state assembly and the convention scheduled just before the legislative session, but the late date would also make it possible to watch the other states. The legislature appropriated funds for a delegation to a second general convention and couched the resolution for a ratifying convention in language that left this possibility open.

59. As everywhere, although there were numerous exceptions, the least commercial portions of the state (the Southside) tended to oppose the Constitution, the most commercial portions (e.g., the Northern Neck) tended to approve it, and the central Piedmont was divided. Full discussions of this pattern and of the ways in which it followed and departed from familiar intrastate divisions can be found in the sources cited in note 3 above. For a full discussion of the spring elections, Antifederalist strategy, and Antifederalist contacts with opponents in other states see also Steven R. Boyd, *The Politics of Opposition: Antifederalists and the Acceptance of the Constitution* (Millwood, N.Y.: KTO Press, 1979), pp. 101–10, 124–35.

60. For Madison's analysis and worries over the Kentuckians see his letters to Jefferson, 9 December 1787, to Randolph, 10 January 1788, to George Nicholas, 8 April and 17 May 1788, and to John Brown, 9 April 1788, in *Papers of James Madison*, 10:311–13 and 355, 11:12 and 16–17.

61. The best short narratives of the convention include DenBoer, "The House of Delegates and the Evolution of Political Parties in Virginia," chap. 6; David

John Mays, *Edmund Pendleton, 1721–1803: A Biography* (Cambridge, Mass.: Harvard University Press, 1952), pp. 217–72; and Jackson Turner Main, *The Antifederalists: Critics of the Constitution, 1781–1788* (Chapel Hill: University of North Carolina Press, 1961), pp. 223–33. The fullest is still Hugh Blair Grigsby's *History of the Virginia Federal Convention of 1788 . . .* ([Richmond]: Virginia Historical Society, *Collections*, vol. 9–10, 1890–91).

62. Elliot, *Debates*, 3:23–29. A handful of speakers carried almost all of the burden for both sides. Speaking almost every day and often rising several times, Henry was a genuine colossus for the opposition, although he was very capably assisted by Mason and Grayson. The Federalists distributed the weight more evenly, with Randolph, Madison, Lee, George Nicholas, and Edmund Pendleton all speaking often. Monroe and John Marshall entered the lists more briefly and infrequently for the opposing camps, but both were quite effective when they did so.

63. See especially Henry's speech of 5 June, *Debates*, 3:43–64, quotation at 53–54.

64. Ibid., pp. 81 (for Randolph) and 135 (for Madison).

65. See especially the 5 June speeches of Madison and Randolph, ibid., pp. 65–97. See also pp. 536–37.

66. 7 June, ibid., p. 141.

67. Compare the 13 June letters to King and Washington, in *Papers of James Madison*, 11:133–34, to those cited in note 2.

68. See especially Mason's eloquent initial speech (*Debates*, 3:29–34), in which he warned that a concurrent power of direct taxation would entail a competition which the central government would certainly win and that the federal taxes would be levied "by those who have neither knowledge of our situation, nor a common interest with us, nor a fellow-feeling." Note also that Monroe's rather restrained opposition to the Constitution also focused on the power of direct taxation and the likelihood of a competition for revenues that would destroy the states (ibid., 207–22).

69. Speech of 11 June, ibid., p. 282. This speech is the single best source for Grayson's distinctive view of the Constitution as "too weak for a consolidated and too strong for a confederated government."

70. Ibid.

71. Ibid., p. 285.

72. Speech of 11 June, ibid., pp. 264–67. Mason did not belabor the obvious: poll taxes might include a levy on slaves; and southerners, including Madison in 1783, had always fiercely and successfully resisted a tax on acreages of land, while New Englanders had always blocked a tax on assessed values. For Henry's and Grayson's agreement with Madison that the population of the South would soon outnumber that of New England see ibid., pp. 57, 292.

73. Henry's speech of 24 June, ibid., pp. 589–90.

74. These remarks came late in the convention, when the Antifederalists plainly feared defeat. Moreover, Henry did not envision a civil war over slavery but

a national response to manpower shortages such as those experienced during the War for Independence. See also Madison's brusque demolition of such concerns, ibid., pp. 621–22.

75. *History of the Virginia Convention*, 1:230–33.

76. *Debates*, 3:333–34. Privately, Lee had been the only Virginia congressman who had been willing to accept Jay's proposal. Although he had sided with the rest of the delegation in public, his personal views may have cost him his seat at the next election.

77. Ibid., pp. 334–44; quotation from Monroe, p. 340, but compare Grayson, pp. 340, 343. For more on Monroe's reaction to the Constitution, which was so mixed that Madison counted him a Federalist until shortly before the convention met, see Monroe's draft of a letter to his constituents, in *The Writings of James Monroe*, ed. Stanislaus Murray Hamilton, 7 vols. (New York: G. P. Putnam's Sons, 1898), 1:307–43.

78. *Debates*, 3:345.

79. Ibid. Compare the speech of Madison on 12 June, p. 312, and of Nicholas, p. 240.

80. Ibid., pp. 346–47; see also 12 June, pp. 312–13, in which Madison insisted that New Jersey, Connecticut, Delaware, and New Hampshire should not be seen as carrying states.

81. Ibid., p. 348. Madison did not suggest that Washington would doubtless win the first presidential election, but he knew that this would naturally occur to all his hearers. He did say, truthfully, that if he were at liberty to mention all the circumstances in his knowledge, he could convince the house that "this project will never be revived in Congress." On the superior security of the Mississippi under a stronger regime see also the 10 June speeches of Nicholas and Marshall, pp. 223–24, 231, 238–41.

82. Patricia Watlington, in *The Partisan Spirit: Kentucky Politics, 1779–1792* (New York: Atheneum, 1972), pp. 149–56, argues that the Kentucky delegation had an Antifederalist majority of 11 to 3 at the beginning of the meeting and that it voted 10 to 3 against ratification. The trans-Allegheny counties in present-day West Virginia sent 4 delegates, all of whom were probably Federalists from the beginning.

83. Among the alterations recommended by the convention were a two-thirds vote in Congress for passage of commercial regulations, a requirement of two-thirds of the whole Senate for passage of commercial treaties, a requirement of three-fourths of the whole number of both houses for ratification of treaties that ceded territories or navigational claims, and a provision that would make it possible for states to raise their share of direct taxes in advance of federal collection.

84. Virginia's fears of promonarchical sentiments in New England should not be lightly discounted. See, for example, *Papers of James Madison*, 9:286, 291–92, 295, 299.

85. *Debates*, 3:176, 591.

86. Speech of 24 June, ibid., pp. 594–96. Compare Grayson, pp. 614–16. Edward Carrington conveyed an important truth before the convention when he wrote to Madison that Henry would try to force amendments no matter how many states had previously ratified, believing "that the other states cannot do without us" (*Papers of James Madison*, 10:383).

87. *Debates*, 3:394, 95, italics added.

88. Ibid., pp. 90, 536–37.

89. Randolph, ibid., p. 68.

90. Madison, 24 June, ibid., pp. 617–19.

91. Ibid., p. 84.

92. Ibid., pp. 596–97.

93. Ibid., p. 603.

94. Speech of 16 June, ibid., pp. 71–80; ibid., pp. 85, 80. Defending the power of direct taxation as indispensable in time of war, Madison had "beg[ged] gentlemen to consider" that "the Southern States are most exposed" (Speech of 11 June, p. 251; repeated, p. 621). Contrast Henry's insistence that Virginia could defend itself, if necessary, against the whole weight of the rest of the Union or any foreign threat (ibid., pp. 57, 141–47, 150–56). Contrast also Grayson's often-quoted mockery of the dangers that Virginia might face from its neighbors (ibid., p. 277).

95. Ibid., pp. 652, 66.

96. For the recommended amendments see ibid., pp. 657–61.

97. Some delegates or voters may have made decisions for reasons that were not discussed in the debates at Richmond and were very seldom mentioned in public writings or private correspondence. The evidence for this is slight, but because some interpreters are inclined to emphasize the hidden motives, other issues bear a mention. Randolph once attributed much of the opposition to a fear that the new government would force a payment of the British debts. Madison twice ascribed some of the opposition to a fear of a revival of the Indiana Company claim, and on 17 October, wrote to Jefferson that "the articles relative to treaties, to paper money, and to contracts created more enemies than all the errors in the system . . . put together" (*Papers of James Madison*, 10:230, 11:18 and 133.

98. In the convention, even Henry frequently admitted the necessity for change. His letter to R. H. Lee, 15 November 1788, is the only evidence I know of that he may have given a passing thought to a separate regional confederation. This letter does appear to hint that if the First Congress should deny "substantial amendments," North Carolina and Virginia's Southside might form a separate government under which he might seek shelter (see W. W. Henry, *Patrick Henry*, 2:428–30).

99. Thus, Madison consistently supported direct federal taxation partly because he reasoned that an exclusive reliance on import taxes would overburden the South: see especially his speech of 11 June in *Debates*, 3:247–61, and the

letter to George Thompson, 29 January 1789, in *Papers of James Madison*, 11:436–37.

100. For Henry on Madison see Spencer Roane to William Wirt, in W. W. Henry, *Patrick Henry*, 2:517–18.

11
NEW YORK
Federalism and the
Political Economy of Union
CECIL L. EUBANKS

The New York State ratifying convention convened on June 17, 1788, almost nine months after the Confederation Congress had sent the new Constitution to the states. During that time, eight states had assembled conventions and had voted in favor of ratification, and two more states, New Hampshire and Virginia, had conventions in session and would ratify before New York would take its final vote. Despite the fact that Federalists constituted a minority in the New York convention — they were outnumbered 46 to 19 — the Constitution was ratified, on July 26, 1788, by a close vote of 30 to 27.

The ratification controversy in New York focused on immediate economic and political issues that involved the power of the national government to enact and to enforce taxes. However, deeply embedded in those concerns over the nature of national and state power were class antagonisms that had existed in New York since its colonial settlement. In this essay those antagonisms will be examined in the context of the political discourse surrounding ratification in New York.[1]

Although the combatants in the New York ratification controversy did not always divide along clear, well-defined social and economic distinctions, it is possible to see in their discourse two distinct and essentially class-based views of republican government.[2] Moreover, in the subtleties and complexities of these views, two contrasting conceptions of political economy can be discerned. Finally, in this discourse, one can witness the transformation of the language of republican virtue into a language of self-interest and, thus, the transformation of a political vision dominated by concerns about virtue to one concerned with commerce and empire. First, however, it is necessary to examine briefly the historical grounding of this discourse.

COLONIAL NEW YORK

New York's geography, along with its initial patterns of settlement, made it a large, isolated, sparsely settled, and vulnerable colony. Claimed by the Dutch in 1609 and seized by the British in 1664, New York was a vast wilderness. Bounded on the North by Canada, the colony was dominated by rugged forests and the largely uninhabitable Adirondack Mountains. The western part of the state extended to the Great Lakes, with the area beyond Lake Oneida and the Mohawk River being populated by Indians who tenaciously defended their hunting lands and made colonial settlement there a slow and dangerous process. The southeastern section of New York was, of course, its most vulnerable and most promising area. The three coastal islands of Richmond, Manhattan, and Long Island would become centers of conflict with the British and centers of commerce with the world.[3]

The settlement of the Hudson River Valley by the Dutch aristocrats, who carved out large landed estates, had a significant impact on the character of New York politics. Large numbers of immigrants avoided New York, preferring Pennsylvania and the New England states, where independent freeholding was preferable to the prospect of tenancy under a manor lord. The consequence of this pattern of settlement was to leave New York rather sparsely inhabited in comparison to surrounding colonies.[4] More important, it would be the source of conflict over rents and the manorial system for generations.[5]

At the same time, it should be noted that while the large manors existed primarily along the northeastern shore line of the Hudson River, extending from Westchester County northward, the southern part of the state, the richest and most densely populated, was largely devoid of the manorial system. Long Island, in particular, consisted of settlements based on either a congregational system or on the Dutch "Freedom and Exemptions" system, both of which allocated land in small tracts.[6]

Furthermore, although the vast majority of New Yorkers engaged in agriculture — primarily wheat, lumbering, fur trading, and horse to breeding—the major source of income as early as the 1780s came from commerce. The port of New York exported goods from New York farms, as well as from neighboring states, to the West Indies and to southern colonies; and it imported goods from Europe for New Yorkers, as well as for citizens of neighboring states. This led to a sizeable industry for New York merchants and shipowners, and it created the great center of commerce, New York City. It also set into place an enduring sociopolitical division of sentiment in the state between the rural upstate sections and the more cosmopolitan commercial centers of the southeast.[7]

REVOLUTIONARY POLITICS

Prior to the Revolution, the politics of New York was dominated by wellborn holders of landed estates, the "great families" of Dutch aristocrats—the DeLanceys, Livingstons, Schuylers, and Van Rensselaers, who had been granted immense tracts of land in the Hudson River Valley.[8] From 1752 to 1775, the conflicts between the Livingston and Delancey families often overshadowed struggles between Loyalists and Patriots and between tenants and lords of the manor. During the Revolution, however, old political alliances had begun to break apart, and new ones had begun to emerge. The Livingston party of landed interests came under the leadership and direction of a new generation of conservatives. James Duane, Philip J. Schuyler, John Jay, Robert R. Livingston, Jr., and Gouverneur Morris were the most prominent of these new leaders; and all of them were associated by birth or marriage with the "great families" of New York. Into their ranks they recruited such notable New Yorkers as William Duer, Egbert Benson, and Alexander Hamilton. Ever cautious, they assumed as their role the maintenance and direction of a conservation revolution, attacking social radicalism and maintaining their vested interest in a propertied aristocracy.[9] Largely from the more established and wealthier urban and commercial southern counties of the state, including New York City,[10] these "conservative Whigs" were frustrated aristocrats who were to become nationalists and Federalists.[11]

At the same time, an opposing coalition of moderate "popular Whigs" began to take shape. Largely representative of the embattled yeoman and tenant farmers of the state's northern counties, they also received considerable support from the rising bourgeoisie of the south. Although they did not possess large landed estates, the popular Whigs tended to hail from respectable families. Led by George Clinton, Melancton Smith, and Abraham Yates, they and their constituents bore the brunt of New York's political and military leadership during the war.[12] Supportive of the Revolution and suspicious of national power, these popular Whigs were to become Antifederalists.

The politics of New York State during the Revolutionary period was of course more complex than any dichotomous division between popular and conservative Whig parties. It consisted of conflicts between the northern middle-class Patriot counties and the southern Loyalist counties, between rural interests and commercial interests, and between those who advocated state sovereignty in the context of a national confederation and those who supported a stronger central government that would have direct and coercive power over individual citizens of all the states. A great many of these disputes, however, took on the character of a conflict between popular and conservative Whigs, later between Clintonians and anti-Clintonians, and ultimately, between Antifederalists and Federalists. Because the conflicts included fundamental disagreements about the role of popular representation in a republican government, they were often perceived as class divisions.[13] Indeed, one observer has aptly characterized the controversies as "the politics of opportunity" versus "the politics of privilege."[14]

The republicanism of the popular Whigs was localist in character and middle class in orientation. Suspicious of centralization and aristocracy, popular Whigs embraced the virtues of freedom, independence, industry, and frugality. Arguing that citizens must be provided the opportunity to advance their "lives, liberties, and estates," they called for roughly equal access to land, education, and government.[15] Despite New York's wartime difficulties, the popular Whigs objected, for political as well as economic reasons, to national efforts to fund the debt or to tax imports. A republic of small homogeneous communities, in which all of the citizenry was *actually* represented, was best suited, they believed, to their future political and economic well-being.[16]

By contrast, New York's conservative Whigs were men of property and privilege who, in Alexander Hamilton's words, wanted a "government of the union able to protect them against domestic violence and the depredations which the democratic spirit is apt to make on property."[17] Anxious over the endangered rights of property, fearful of levelers, and suspicious of office-holders who had no significant stake in the community, they preferred a republic more distant from the mass of the citizenry and more representative of those who possessed a clear vision of the public good, a republic in which a natural hierarchy of virtue and wisdom would exist and would be empowered to govern. Nurtured by wartime frustrations over the lack of national power, they now sought a government, a national government, capable of paying the debt of the Union and of "regulating, protecting and extending the commerce of the Union."[18] Having fought a successful revolution, they were now intent on building an empire.[19]

These differences in republican philosophy would figure prominently in the intense political battle over the ratification of the Constitution in New York.[20] But their immediate impact was felt in the controversy over the political and economic issues of the Confederation period in New York.

THE CONFEDERATION IN NEW YORK

The Revolutionary War had a profound impact on the politics of the state of New York. During the war, New York had been in constant peril. Occupied by British troops and often the site of military engagements, the state had consistently sought assistance from the national government and had just as consistently failed to obtain it. Prior to the peace, New York had petitioned on at least two occasions for a strong national government. In 1780, Alexander Hamilton and George Clinton, representatives of two decidedly different constituencies in New York politics, agreed that the Confederation Congress needed to have more power. With support from both Hamilton and Clinton, New York's delegates to the Hartford convention had been specifically instructed to empower Congress to "exercise every Power which they may deem necessary for an effectual Prosecution of the war."[21]

In early 1781, Congress had requested permission from the states to assess a 5 percent import duty. The proceeds from this tariff were earmarked to pay off the national war debt, both principal and interest. New York's legislature quickly agreed to the proposal, as did those of eleven other states. Rhode Island refused, and the weakness of the confederation was exposed once again.[22] Thus, in July 1782, with British troops occupying New York City and with the state in the midst of economic chaos — the Continental Army remained unpaid, and the public debt continued to increase — the New York legislature called for a national convention to amend the Articles of Confederation and to give Congress the power to tax. Again the resolution was ignored.

Nevertheless, once the war had ended, many New Yorkers became convinced that they had paid their share of the war effort and were now entitled to pursue a policy that would best meet the needs of the state. With the strong support of Governor Clinton, a program was initiated that consisted of three major components: the enactment of a state impost; the sale of state lands, both unsettled and former Loyalist estates; and modest taxes on real estate and personal property.[23]

Under Clinton's plan, New York's approval of the federal impost of 1781 was rescinded, and a state impost was enacted. The impost quickly became the major source of state revenue, producing from $100,000 to $225,000 annually, or approximately one-third to one-half of the state's income. Not coincidentally, the burden of the impost fell upon outsiders, on goods imported for citizens of Connecticut, New Jersey, Vermont, Massachusetts, and even some of the southern states. The state impost allowed the Clintonians to reduce the state's dependence on property taxes and thereby to enhance their own political support with those partisans they had long championed, the yeoman farmers.[24]

A second important aspect of the Clintonian recovery plan was the sale of Loyalist lands, which had been confiscated after the evacuation of British troops in 1783. Approximately $4 million was raised as a result of the sale. This policy effectively alienated nationalists in the state, including Hamilton and Livingston, who in addition to fearing a violation of the treaty of peace, regarded the policy as a dangerous assault on property rights. In addition, the sale of unsettled land, while it represented an even greater potential bonanza to New York, raised difficult issues of territory and state sovereignty. Significant portions of land, including that which was known as Vermont, had either been claimed by New Hampshire and Massachusetts or were regarded as national territory. Because it had failed to convince Congress of the state's legitimate right to these lands, New York's ability to stake a claim to them seemed to be dependent upon its own power, presumably under arms, to seize control of the lands.

Thus New York's postwar economic policies required a weak Congress. A strong central government would no doubt result in a loss of land, a repeal of the impost, and perhaps a limitation on the sale of Loyalist property. If that were to occur, the only remaining significant source of revenue to pay off the state's debt would be a tax on personal property, which was political anathema to the Clintonians.[25]

Despite the exigencies of the depression in 1785–86, New York had become a creditor state by 1790. In fact, with the assistance of a paper-money bill, the state impost, and revenue obtained from the sale of state lands, it had become one of the wealthiest states in the confederacy, with holdings in federal securities of more than $2.8 million. Governor Clinton was acutely aware of the importance of commerce to his state. In 1785 he advocated giving Congress the power "to restrain trade with countries without commercial treaties with the United States."[26] Because of the state impost, any stimulation of trade would result in more revenue for New York. Thus, in an ironic twist, New York, with Clinton's approval, joined Virginia in calling for the Annapolis convention. And at Annapolis, it was one of New York's commissioners, Alexander Hamilton, who offered the resolution calling for the convening of the Philadelphia convention to consider larger matters touching on trade and commerce, namely the revision of the Articles of Confederation.

While New York was making its remarkable recovery, the Confederation was attempting to solve national economic problems. Eventually, Congress passed a second impost in 1783; and by 1786, all of the states except New York had accepted it. The Clintonians, led by Abraham Yates, engaged in a public campaign to persuade New Yorkers that the national impost would result in a dangerous concentration of power in the Congress and would inevitably lead to the demise of the power of the states. In May 1786, the New York legislature, which was dominated by Clintonians, agreed to the national impost, but only if New York were to retain the right to control the collectors of the revenue and to pay the impost revenues in the state's paper money.[27]

The Confederation Congress was not sympathetic to New York's provision. On two occasions it requested Governor Clinton to call a special session of his legislature to reconsider New York's provisional acceptance of the impost, but Clinton refused. When the state legislature finally met in regular session in January 1787, the Hamiltonians immediately tried to censure Clinton, but failed by a vote of 39 to 9.[28] The legislature considered the impost once again but refused to remove the condition that would allow the state to control the collectors. This refusal was tantamount to a veto of the national impost.

Clearly, the Clintonians were extraordinarily ambivalent about the power of the Confederation government during the war years and afterward. From their perspective, the Confederation Congress had failed to support New York's claims to the Vermont lands. It had proven ineffective in forcing the British to evacuate New York forts. Moreover, the peace treaty with Britain, drafted by John Jay, recommended that Loyalist lands be restored to their former owners. Finally, by 1786, efforts on the part of the Confederation Congress to fund the debt and to assume the power of taxation of imports had come to be regarded with considerable suspicion. New York's own impost was a major source of revenue, and to abandon it to the national government would cause property taxes to be raised within the state.[29]

Yet during the war years and afterward, New York was dependent upon the Union. Although the state was often disappointed with Congress's failure to act, New York could not afford to leave the Union. With the Atlantic on the east, Canada to the north, and the states of New Jersey, Connecticut, and Massachusetts all displeased at being victimized by the impost on the south and southeast, the borders of the state seemed all too vulnerable.[30]

Equally clear was the growing disenchantment of the conservative Whigs, not only with the Confederation, but with the Clintonians as well. New York conservatives did not have to be convinced about the impotency of the Confederation government during the war. In the years thereafter, they had become increasingly wary of what John Jay characterized as the "insecurity of property," as well as the inability of the national government to tax. Jay feared that republican government was endangered on the one hand by those who had little if any respect for property and on the other by those whose commitment to republican principles was waning. What he and his fellow conservatives such as Robert R. Livingston were seeking was a commitment to a republican government that would balance "democratical" and "aristocratical" elements at home and, at the same time, balance state and national powers within the Union.[31]

Clintonians were suspicious of such conservative motives. Supportive of some enhancement of national economic power, especially on matters of trade and commerce, which would be to New York's benefit, the Clintonians were uneasy about enhanced national political power. Their opposition to the impost of 1783 was based largely on the fear of a too-powerful national government. Abraham Yates, who led the fight against the impost, expressed the fears of many Clintonians when he argued that granting Congress the power to collect taxes would "swallow up the legislatives of the particular states."[32] When the Confederation Congress attempted to get New York to call a special session to reconsider its stance on the impost, Governor Clinton and his New York colleagues clearly resented this intrusion into New York's political institutions. It was not surprising that in its regular session, New York's legislature voted not to rescind its action. Despite its growing reputation for being Antifederalist, the same legislature voted to call for a general constitutional convention, but with the express understanding that the purpose of the convention was to amend the Articles of Confederation.[33]

THE CONSTITUTIONAL DEBATES

In March, New York began the process of selecting delegates to the Philadelphia convention. Robert Yates, John Lansing, Jr., and Alexander Hamilton were chosen. Yates was a justice of the New York Supreme Court, and Lansing was mayor of Albany. Both were sympathetic to the rights of the states. With typical insight, James Madison wrote to George Washington that Yates and Lansing would be "much linked to the antifederal party here, and are likely of course to be a clog on their Colleague."[34] Yates and Lansing consistently voted on the opposite side from Hamilton, especially on whether the convention had the power to write a new constitution with a more powerful national government, as Hamilton would have preferred, or whether it only had the power to revise and amend the Articles of Confederation, as Yates and Lansing insisted. Both Yates and Lansing left quietly in early July, and largely because it appeared that the convention would propose a strongly centralized national government, they did not return.[35]

Hamilton was the strongest nationalist among the group: he was well known for his June 18 speech before the convention, in which he outlined his own plan for the new government, which included an executive, senate, and supreme court that would be chosen for life and in which the state governors would be appointed by the national executive. His support for this radically national government, so obviously contemptuous of the rights of the states, would haunt him later as he defended the Constitution of 1787 in the *Federalist* essays and in the New York convention. He left the Philadelphia convention near the end of June, and he returned at a later date to serve on the convention's Committee of Style. He was the only New York delegate to sign the Constitution.

When news reached New York that more than a revision of the Articles of Confederation was taking place in Philadelphia, the public debate over the Constitution began. In New York, as in Pennsylvania, supporters of the Constitution accused its opponents of having Shaysite or Loyalist sympathies. Worse, they implied that the opposition was only interested in the protection of their state-held offices. Taking the lead in New York was Hamilton, who initiated the debate with a slashing personal attack on Governor Clinton. According to Hamilton, Clinton had, "in public company . . . reprobated the appointment of the Convention, and predicted a mischievous issue of that measure." Arguing forcefully for a more powerful general government, Hamilton asserted that the governor had acted hastily and had had no warrant to prepossess "the public mind against the hitherto underdetermined and unknown measures of a body to whose councils America has . . . entrusted its future fate." But Hamilton's most serious charge was that Clinton had been guilty of exhibiting a "greater attachment to his *own power* than to the *public good*."[36]

Thus the debate began. The *New York Journal* defended Clinton and charged that those who questioned his political motives were guilty of "high treason against the majesty of the people." The writer, identified as "a republican," raised suspicions that would become crucial to the New York debate, lifting the lid off the long-simmering stewpot of class antagonism. Thus, Hamilton was attacked for being among those who formed a "certain lordly faction" in New York, "composed of men, possessed of an insatiable thirst for dominion, and who, having forfeited the confidence of their fellow-citizens, . . . reprobate our laws, censure our rulers, and decry our government, thereby to induce the necessity of a change, that they may establish a system more favorable to their aristocratic views."[37]

The public debate in New York was one of the most prolific in all of the states, and it produced some of the best commentary on the Constitution. Opinions were expressed in pamphlets, broadsides, and, profusely, in newspapers. The newspapers of New York were predominantly Federalist, especially in the northern part of the state and in the cities, most notably New York City. Three New York City newspapers were strongly Federalist: the *Daily Advertiser*, the *Independent Journal*, and the *New-York Packet*. The *New York Journal* was strongly Antifederalist.[38] Initially, they were filled with essays and published speeches from other states, including, on the Federalist side, ones by "An American Citizen," "A Countryman," "Landholder," James Wilson, and John Sullivan and, on the Antifederalist side, "Centinel," "An Old Whig," "Cincinnatus," Elbridge Gerry, George Mason, and Richard Henry Lee.[39] From the middle of October 1787 to the conclusion of the New York ratification convention in July 1788, the newspapers ran essays, speeches, satire, letters, poems, fillers, and convention debates. Extended essays that were produced in New York included, for the Federalists, ones by "Caesar" and "Publius," while the Antifederalists responded with "Cato," "Brutus," and the "Federal Farmer."[40] As John Kaminski has observed, "Nowhere else were the people as well informed about the Constitution as in New York."[41]

The ratification controversy in New York mirrored disputes that had long existed in New York politics. The Federalists were the party of the "commercial and professional classes of New York City," who because of background and interests had much in common with the large landholders of the state. By comparison, the Antifederalists — the party of Governor Clinton — tended to be made up of small farmers whose loyalties were radical or popular Whig in character.[42]

Antifederalists were, in fact, politicians of a different sort from their Federalist counterparts. The conventional impression, which many of them held themselves, was that they were less politically skilled. Gordon Wood refers to them as "politicians without influence and

connections, and ultimately politicians without social and intellectual confidence."[43] Melancton Smith and Abraham Yates of New York
were among these "new politicians" who "had bypassed the social
hierarchy in their rise to political leadership" and who "lacked those
attributes of social distinction and dignity that went beyond mere
wealth."[44] They were never identified as "gentlemen," as was, for example, Chancellor Robert Livingston. Thus, the move for a new constitution was viewed with suspicion by these new politicians, not only
because of their local attachments but also because of their mistrust
of the Federalist desire to establish a system that would entrench
aristocratic privileges. Antifederalists were obsessed with this fear of
an aristocracy in their midst, and there is no better, no more powerful evidence of their obsession than the debates that swirled inside
and out of the ratification convention in New York.

What was particularly galling to Antifederalists was the fact that
the great majority of the people seemed to defer to the power, prestige,
and influence of the "enlightened few." Clearly the people must be
awakened and warned. In attacking the so-called natural
aristocracy—or, more properly, its right to govern exclusively—
Antifederalists were attacking a classical conception of society that
was organic, hierarchical, and naturally elitist, while pursuing another
classical concept—namely, that of the small, homogeneous, and participatory community of yeoman farmers. This explains, in part at
least, their belief that the middling class, uncorrupted by the Old
World influences of wealth and status, was more capable of discerning the public good.

An early exchange between "Cato" and "Caesar" reflected these class
antagonisms. Beginning on September 27, 1787, a series of seven essays
entitled "Cato" appeared in the *New York Journal*.[45] In "Cato's" fourth
letter, he wrote that the new Constitution, particularly in its executive
power, was likely to establish *"an imperfect aristocracy* bordering on
monarchy,"[46] and in his first letter he challenged his readers to reflect
on the Constitution with care and candor and to see whether or not
it contained the "influence of a powerful few" and the danger of "a
standing army."[47] "Caesar" responded to "Cato" with two letters that
reinforced Antifederalist fears of an arrogant aristocracy at work. Addressing himself to "Cato's" contention that all power is derived from
the people, "Caesar" responded: "For my part, I am not much at-

tached to the *Majesty of the multitude*, . . . The science of Government is not easily understood. . . . If truth . . . is permitted to speak, the mass of the people of America . . . cannot judge with any degree of precision, concerning the fitness of this New Constitution."[48]

The two most impressive sets of essays to emerge during the New York ratification controversy were the Antifederalist *Letters from the Federal Farmer to the Republican* and *The Federalist.*[49] The *Country Journal* (Poughkeepsie) first published the initial five letters in the "Federal Farmer" series in November 1787. Although they were not reprinted in newspapers in any great quantity, it is estimated that thousands of the series were sold in pamphlet form, and at least four editions were published. The authorship of the "Federal Farmer" letters is under considerable dispute. They were long attributed to Richard Henry Lee, but it is now generally agreed that Lee did not write the letters. Who did write them remains unsettled, however.[50] Whoever wrote them is said to have produced "the best of any thing that has been written" in opposition to the Constitution.[51]

The "Federal Farmer" began with the assertion that all orders of society must be represented by the powers of government. The new system of consolidated government, "so unnaturally divided between the general and state governments," made representation of the people "very uncertain." It could not hope to "preserve the rights of all orders of men in the community."[52] This should not be surprising in view of the make-up of the Philadelphia convention itself. Although composed of men of ability and integrity, it was disproportionately representative of the aristocratic parts of the community and, by contrast, was not sufficiently representative of the democratic parts of the community. The result of this representation was a "strong tendency to aristocracy . . . in every part of the plan."[53]

The argument proceeded to elaborate on the extended republic thesis. "Federal Farmer" was convinced that "one government and general legislation alone never can extend equal benefits to all parts of the United States." There were simply too many different laws, customs, and opinions in the several states that would be invaded by the uniformity required in the proposed consolidated plan. Free and equal representation in the legislature was crucial to free and good government, but representation for the "Federal Farmer," meant actual not virtual, representation. "A full and equal representation, is that which possesses the same interests, feelings, opinions, and views the people themselves would were they all assembled."[54] Every order of man must have a share in the community; merchants, traders, farmers, and mechanics should all be able to bring their best-informed men to the legislature. That legislature must, of course, be rather large in order to achieve this goal. It was inconceivable to the "Federal Farmer," as well as to most Antifederalists, that a representative legislative body that contained fewer persons than the total of state senators in the United States could adequately represent those states.

In the third letter by the "Federal Farmer," these speculations on representation ventured into the arena of class. He tended to view society in terms of its democratic element and its aristocratic element. One portion of the latter, the natural aristocracy of wealth and ability, was and ought to be represented in this new government. The great body of people, however, the middle and lower classes, would not be adequately represented in the democratic branch, the House of Representatives. "Federal Farmer" proposed to ensure the democratic character of the House by making two fundamental changes, both of which are indicative of his representative philosophy. First, he would make the House larger. One representative for every fifty thousand inhabitants was an absurdly low figure upon which to base representation of the democratic element of the community. Second, and perhaps more important in the long run, "Federal Farmer" would not permit Congress to regulate elections. If the states were allowed that power and if they acted on the principle of representing all parts of the community, he argued, they would divide themselves into districts, confine the choice of representatives to those who have a permanent interest and residence in the district, and provide that the representatives elected would have a majority of the votes in that district in order to be elected. The principle of a single-member district with majority rule would make possible a more accurate representation in the House of Representatives.

Although "Federal Farmer" acknowledged the existence of a natural aristocracy and the need for it to be represented in the general government, his sympathies were clearly with the yeoman middle class. There are, he asserted in the fifth letter of his essay, "two fires, between which the honest and substantial people have long found themselves situated." The conduct and views of these two "fires," or "unprincipled parties," were a constant danger to the people. That danger had culminated in the present plan of government. "One party is composed of little insurgents, men in debt, who want no law, and who want a share of the property of others." The other party is "composed of few, but more dangerous men . . . [who] avariciously grasp at all power and property." This party of aristocrats and monarchists posed a danger to free and equal government. "Between these two parties is the weight of the community; the men of middling property, men not in debt on the one hand, and men, on the other, content with republican governments, and not aiming at immense fortunes, offices, and power." The present constitutional crisis had been precipitated by the actions of these two fires, to the detriment of both the middling class and republican government. In 1786 the insurgents, "levelers" and "Shaysites," had "invaded the rights of others, and attempted to establish governments according to their wills." This assault in turn had encouraged the aristocrats and monarchists to take the political field and, with the "tongue and the pen," to endeavor "to establish in a great haste, a politer kind of government."[55]

"Federal Farmer's" analysis of the forces behind the Philadelphia convention was based on a set of fundamental propositions concerning the character of republican government. This Antifederalist essayist was obviously a believer in the principle of limited government and checks and balances. Typical of most Antifederalists, he supported more limitation on the power of government. Representation, especially in the House of Representatives, must be actual, a mirror of the constituency. Finally, a conception of civic virtue was inherent in the "Federal Farmer's" view of republican government, and it bore some resemblance to the classical Aristotelian vision. The middle class — the yeomen — was best suited to know and to practice this virtue. As "Federal Farmer" bluntly stated, the levelers and the aristocrats were "really insignificant, compared with the solid, free, and independent part of the community," the yeomen.

On the other side was the *Federalist*, published under the pseudonym "Publius" and consisting of eighty-five essays written by Hamilton, Madison, and Jay. They were published in the New York City press from October 27, 1787, to May 28, 1788, and then in a two-volume edition, the first volume of which appeared on March 22, 1788, and the second, on May 28. Although they received national attention and were believed to be the very best of all the Federalist writing on the Constitution, their role in the ratification controversy was not as significant as has been imagined. The essays were judged to be lofty in manner and argument; they were not designed to appeal to the good sense of the common man.[56]

Federalists were understandably reluctant to confront directly the arguments based on class antagonism; instead, they preferred to stress the need for order and stability, which would lead to American prestige abroad and economic prosperity at home. But ultimately they could not resist the challenge. Writing on behalf of "Publius" in *Federalist* 35, Hamilton answered the charges of the Antifederalists and of "Federal Farmer" in particular. Limiting his class analysis of American society to three groups, Hamilton asserted that the landholder would certainly be able to "know and feel whatever will promote or injure the interest of landed property." Similarly, the merchant would "understand and be disposed to cultivate the interests of the mechanic and manufacturing arts to which his commerce is so nearly allied." But, the "man of the learned profession" was the one who would be neutral in the rivalry between the "different branches of industry" and who would be an "impartial arbiter between them." Hamilton's faith in the "learned profession" was furthered by his representative philosophy, which he expressed in the rhetorical question "Is the man whose situation leads to extensive inquiry and information less likely to be a competent judge [of the people and their dispositions] . . . than one whose observation does not travel beyond the circle of his neighbors and acquaintances?"[57] Clearly not. Thus the harmony of a society could be assured if the "natural aristocracy" were to be allowed to govern, to represent, virtually, society's interests. Hamilton would later pursue his defense of this view of society and of the need for leadership in his discussions of the executive power and of the judiciary.[58]

The authors of "Publius," especially Madison and Hamilton, were ultimately at odds on this matter. For although Madison also justified rule by the elite, he did so in a way that inevitably destroyed the foundation of the classical and organic vision of society that Hamilton held. In *Federalist* 10, Madison argued that government would "refine and enlarge the public views by passing them through the medium of a chosen body of citizens, whose wisdom may best discern the true interest of their country and whose patriotism and love of justice will be least likely to sacrifice it to temporary or partial considerations."[59] However, Madison was more willing to abandon the classical conception of society for a mechanistic one, in which classes would become interests and factions and the mechanisms of representation and government would ensure that a natural aristocratic elite would govern, despite the egalitarian impulses of American society and the local loyalties of the Antifederalists.

Hamilton put the matter more bluntly in *Federalist* 71, when he observed that "the people commonly *intend* the public good." But their passions, the "wiles of parasites and sycophants," and the "artifices of men who possess their confidence more than they deserve it" lead them to error. They do not always "*reason right* about the *means* of promoting" the public good. Thus, "the duty of the persons whom they have appointed [was] to be the guardians" of the public good.[60] Such unabashed elitism disturbed Antifederalists everywhere, but especially those in New York. It led "Federal Farmer" to conclude that "every man of reflection must see, that the change now proposed, is a transfer of power from the many to the few."[61]

Hamilton's classical aristocratic views combined a justification of elite rule with a view of society that was both hierarchical and organic. The organic interdependency that existed between all of the elements of society make virtual representation by an aristocratic elite both possible and desirable. Hamilton's defense of noblesse oblige, as well as his attraction to the British system, was well known. Indeed, he may well have been a liability in the New York convention, despite his erudition and oratorical skills. As Charles Tillinghast wrote, no doubt speaking the mind of many New York Antifederalists: "You would be surprised did you know the Man, what an *amazing Republican* Hamilton wishes to make himself be considered. *But he is known*."[62]

THE RATIFICATION CONVENTION

On January 11, 1788, the New York legislature achieved the quorum necessary to consider the new Constitution. Governor Clinton transmitted the Constitution to the state legislature, along with the resolutions of the Constitutional Convention and the Continental Congress and a letter of opposition by former delegates Robert Yates and John

Lansing, Jr. Clinton told the legislature that he would have no more to say on the matter. After some debate, particularly on whether the legislature should append the call of a ratifying convention with a statement of disapproval, which was defeated, the New York Assembly resolved on January 31 to call an election of delegates, to begin on April 29, for a convention to meet in Poughkeepsie on June 17, 1788. The next day, after a similar debate, the state senate agreed to the Assembly's resolution. Somewhat surprisingly, the election of delegates to the ratifying convention was open to all adult males (voting for state offices had property qualifications attached). Federalists proposed the change because they hoped that it would add supporters to their ranks. Some Antifederalists opposed it, but quietly. As descendants of the popular-Whig persuasion, they did not wish to give the impression of being against universal male suffrage.[63]

It appeared that Federalists and Antifederalists alike favored postponing New York's consideration until the middle of June. Federalists wanted more time in order to convince a populace that they assumed was against the proposed Constitution. Perhaps the required nine states would ratify by June, and New York would be placed in the awkward position of having either to ratify or to secede. Furthermore, the debate in New York, which Federalists expected would be strongly in opposition to the Constitution, taking place as late as it did, would not have a negative effect on other states' consideration of the Constitution. Antifederalists hoped that another state, perhaps Virginia, would disapprove of the Constitution, thereby relieving New York of the burden of being first. Moreover, the Antifederalists were by no means certain of victory. They needed time to organize their forces and to formulate amendments to the proposed Constitution.[64]

In the elections for delegates, which were conducted primarily at the town and county levels and with considerable vigor, Antifederalists won an impressive victory. Of the sixty-five delegates who were chosen, forty-six were Antifederalists and only nineteen were Federalists. These figures are slightly misleading, however. Many Antifederalists recognized the need to alter the Articles of Confederation, so they did not favor the outright rejection of the new Constitution. They merely wanted amendments, or failing that, they were willing to settle for conditional ratification and perhaps a second convention.[65]

The New York convention met on June 17, elected Governor George Clinton as its president, chose to have its deliberations open to the public, and selected a committee to determine its rules for conducting its business, and then adjourned. Debate began on the nineteenth of June.

Robert R. Livingston was the first delegate to speak. Emphasizing the peace and stability that would result from the new Constitution, he spoke in favor of ratification. At the conclusion of his address he offered a resolution to the effect that the proposed Constitution should be considered clause by clause, before any vote would be taken on it or on any amendments that might be proposed during such debate. The resolution passed, and the convention adjourned for the day. There was discontent among some Antifederalists, who feared what the Federalists welcomed — namely, that a long delay might cause the country delegates to leave early in order to tend to their farms. They also feared that the delay would give time for New Hampshire and Virginia to ratify. Most Antifederalists, however, supported the clause-by-clause consideration.[66]

Two speakers dominated the convention — Melancton Smith and Alexander Hamilton.[67] In a series of exchanges during the first two weeks of the convention, they gave voice to very different philosophies of republican government, which were reminiscent of the debate between "Federal Farmer" and "Publius." On June 20, Smith opened the debate on the general issue of representation in an extended republic. It simply was not possible for the will of the community to be represented adequately in such a fashion. Smith was clearly advocating the small republic and, with it, the notion that the states were the true repository of the people's liberties.

In the course of responding to the issues of number and representation, Smith developed a theory of republicanism that was shared by many Antifederalists. Representatives should "resemble those they represent. They should be a true picture of the people." Size was important, as was composition. The extensive political and commercial expertise of those who had achieved a refined education must be balanced against the "common concerns and occupations of the people."[68]

It was natural for a society to divide into classes. If the legislature were kept small, people of education, wealth, and birth would accede to importance in it and would dominate it, and those who were accustomed to "walk in the plain and frugal paths of life" would not be adequately represented. Hence a larger legislature was needed so as to allow for the calm and sober influence of the "substantial yeoman." Smith offered poignant testimony to his faith in yeoman sensibilities:

> The same passions and prejudices govern all men. The circumstances in which men are placed in a great measure give a cast to human character. Those in middling circumstances have less temptation; they are inclined by habit, and the company with whom they associate, to set bounds to their passions and appetites . . . they are obliged to employ their time in their respective callings; hence the substantial yeomanry of the country are more temperate, of better morals, and less ambition, than the great. (p. 247)

In short, the best possible security to liberty was a representative body composed of the yeomanry, whose interests were the interests of the community. "When the interest of this part of the community is pursued, the public good is pursued, because the body of every nation consists of this class, and because the interest of both the rich and the poor are involved in that of the middling class" (p. 248).

Hamilton felt compelled to confront the class argument that Smith had raised. In so doing, Hamilton wove together three separate arguments, not all of which were consistent. Smith's aristocracy was a phantom. All men of distinction were aristocrats. But to see in them, in officeholders, the specter of perpetual rank was mystifying. The people have the right to elect the most meritorious representatives if that is their choice. If they confuse wealth with virtue, they will be wrong, but no amount of tinkering with the size of the legislature will remedy this fact.

On the matter of size, Hamilton returned to the extended republic thesis, arguing again that in large districts, corruption is more difficult, intrigue is less likely, and factions are less possible. Indeed, Hamilton argued, in the extended republic, wealth would have less influence, not more. "In a small district," he reasoned, "the people in the vicinity of a great man are more immediately his dependants" (p. 257).

Hamilton's third argument was in reality a defense of aristocracy. He attacked the Antifederalist notion, as expressed by Smith, that in the middle class, the yeomanry, there was superior virtue. "Where does virtue predominate?" If there were any differences to discern between classes of men on the question of virtue, the advantage lay with the wealthy. The vices that they possessed, which were typical of their class, "are probably more favorable to the prosperity of the state than those of the indigent, and partake less of moral depravity" (p. 257). The differences between classes on the matter of virtue were differences in kind, not in quantity. Each class had its own peculiar set of vices, although Hamilton did not identify the particular vices of the wealthy. Whatever the class, Hamilton again contended, "the true principle of a republic is that the people should choose whom they please to govern them" (p. 257).

There seems to be little doubt that Hamilton was being circumspect in his defense of aristocracy at the New York convention by emphasizing instead the extended republic thesis of Madison. Federalists were weary of defending themselves against the Antifederalists' attacks that the Federalists were aristocrats. Thus, Hamilton's republican rhetoric placed confidence in those whose substance and leisure allowed them, not luxury, but the luxury of pursuing a public life devoted to the common good.

If Hamilton was prudent in his arguments, Chancellor Livingston was not. On Monday, June 23, Livingston, turning his attention toward Smith's earlier pronouncements on class, challenged Smith's assertion that the rich are more intemperate than the poor or the middle class. "Is there less intemperance in feeding on beef than on turtle? or in drinking rum than wine?" (p. 276). At the same time he argued that the rich were less unfeeling than the poor, less occupied by their own "cares and distresses," and therefore able to feel more sympathy for others. If a government was to be composed of classes other than aristocrats, where could they be found? "Why, [we] must go out into the highways, and pick up the rogue and the robber; [we] must go to the hedges and ditches, and bring in the poor, the blind, and the lame" (p. 277). Livingston concluded his attack on Smith with an unconvincing appeal to a universal aristocracy. In terms of wisdom and virtue, "We are all equally aristocrats" (p. 278).

Smith had not intended to pursue this debate on class any further, but Livingston's ridicule could not go unanswered. In his response, Smith asserted that human beings are influenced by different interests and different prejudices. Ambition happens to be one of the peculiar passions of the rich and the great. In order to have a truly representative government, the middle class must be a substantial part of that government. More important, Smith offered the classic Antifederalist view of direct representation: "Representation from the United States could not be so constituted as to represent completely the feelings and interests of the people; but . . . we ought to come as near this object as possible" (p. 281).

In the debate in New York about the nature of the Senate, the length of terms of office, and eligibility for reelection, these contrary philosophies of representation surfaced again. John Lansing argued in favor of an amendment that would enforce rotation in office. Limiting their terms and requiring senators to be subject to recall would ensure that they would be dependent upon the state legislatures and therefore their constituencies, and it would "oblige them to return, at certain periods, to their fellow-citizens, that, by mingling with the people, they may recover that knowledge of their interests, and revive that sympathy with their feelings, which power and an exalted station are too apt to efface from the minds of rulers." The design of representation should always be that the "sense and spirit of the people's interests and feelings should be carried into the government" (pp. 293–94). And while it might sometimes be necessary for the smaller interests of the states to be sacrificed to the larger interests of national unity, state sovereignty ought never be subordinated.

In the midst of the debate on limited tenure and recall of senators, Hamilton arose to give a lengthy discourse on the nature of government and the nature of the Senate. There are two principles at work, he argued, in the formation of government. Both are legitimate. One is the "zeal for liberty," which occupied the attention of the states in forming a government after the Revolution, as rightly it should have. Yet that same zeal, when excessively pursued, endangers the other principle, the "principle of *strength* and *stability* in the organization of government and *vigor* in its operation." The smaller and more permanent Senate would provide that stability, as a check on the fluctuations of the popular assembly. Hamilton was suspicious of the people's ability to "possess the discernment and stability necessary for systematic government." Popular assemblies, both ancient and modern, had been "frequently misguided by ignorance, by sudden impulses, and the intrigues of ambitious men" (pp. 301–2). The proposed resolution would take away stability in government; it would deprive the Senate of its permanency and make it subject to those impulses and intrigues which are typical of popular assemblies and which it was specifically designed to correct.

Hamilton distinguished between the real and the apparent interests of states, and in so doing, he capsulized the arguments between Federalists and Antifederalists on the issue of representation. For Smith, "the nearer the representative is to his constituents, the more attached and dependent he will be" (p. 315). For Hamilton, "every petty district is not the government" (p. 318). The particular interests must be sacrificed to the general interest.[69] It is clear that for Hamilton, the purpose of the Senate, as proposed by the Constitution, was to protect Congress from factions that might arise as a result of state prejudices. "We are," he said, "attempting, by this Constitution, to abolish factions, and to unite all parties for the general welfare" (p. 320).

By contrast, Smith was fearful that the power of Congress to intervene into the regulation of the times, places, and manner of elections would result in at-large elections. Thus, like "Federal Farmer," he proposed that each state be divided into districts. The system of single-member districts was entirely consistent with his theory of representation. At-large elections could easily result in the overrepresentation of one particular part of a state, and the rest of the people of that state would not be represented.

RATIFICATION AND REPUBLICAN POLITICAL THEORY

The debates in the New York convention—which were largely between Smith and Hamilton and which ranged widely over issues of confederation and union, small and extended republics, social class and political economy—were, more fundamentally, discussions about the possibility of discerning the public good. Was there a structure, a process, or a citizenry capable of knowing the common good? Could that structure, process, or citizenry be trusted to bring about the common good? These were questions about republican virtue, and they had become critical to eighteenth-century republican discourse. At stake in the debates were the conflicting claims of the classical and modern worlds.

Both Hamilton and Smith were searching through these worlds for solutions to the problems of republican governance. That they would each discover a sometimes bewildering combination of inconsistencies should come as no surprise.[70]

One classical definition of virtue was Aristotelian. Virtue was the wisdom acquired through education and the rational pursuit of the good life, which meant the good life in the public realm. This view was closely associated with the notion of a hierarchical, organic society and a mixed government of democratic, aristocratic, and monarchic elements. It was the view of republicanism with which Hamilton had so often been associated. In the New York convention he departed from this concept of virtue — at least to some extent — partly, no doubt, because of its negative association with British politics and partly because of the influence of David Hume. Like Hume and Madison, Hamilton agreed that the power of self-interest was prevalent in all human beings and that reason was and ought to be the servant of passion. Thus, Hamilton initially denied that wealth should be equated with virtue, and because of the omnipresence of self-interest and factionalism in all human beings and at all social levels, he embraced Madison's extended republic thesis. If virtue cannot be guaranteed in the citizenry, the structure of the extended republic and the process associated with conflicting claims of self-interest would protect the common good. Nonetheless, Hamilton could not completely relinquish his aristocratic notions, for he concluded that although all people are possessed of the vice of self-interest, the vices of the rich are "more favorable to the prosperity of the state." In short, in his attempt to reconcile a classical vision of virtue with modern claims about human nature, Hamilton combined a modernist psychology of the primacy of self-interest and passion with a classical aristocratic conception of honor and noblesse oblige.

Yet, Hamilton added a significant and clever emendation to Madison's extended republic thesis. A republic, Hamilton argued, must have sufficient power to protect itself. All republics, small and large, are forever subject to the corrupting influence of internal factions and the designs of foreign regimes. Thus, they must be possessed of the requisite power to protect themselves against these dangers. Local interest must always succumb to national interest. Parties and factions must be limited to the legislature, especially the House of Representatives. This line of reasoning elucidates Hamilton's continuing interest in building strong national institutions, such as the presidency and the Supreme Court, and in developing a powerful foreign policy, the foundations of which would be an extensive commercial empire.

A more typical eighteenth-century definition of virtue, with intellectual roots in the thought of Machiavelli, Harrington, and Montesquieu, insisted simply that virtue was a passion for the public good that thrived in small, homogeneous communities of social equality. Although this perspective also accepted the modern view of human nature as essentially self-interested, it retained the classical ideal of a public-spirited society. In effect, it assumed that public spirit had to be socially constructed, that there existed in human nature no natural and rational impulse toward the public good.

Machiavelli and Montesquieu both insisted that a republic was possible only if private fortune, selfishly pursued in the context of social equality and frugality, could be transformed into a passion for the common good. In order to illustrate his meaning, Montesquieu used the monk as a prototypical example of one whose denial of the ordinary passions leads to a passion for the order of the monastery. "The more austere it is, that is, the more it curbs their inclinations, the more force it gives to the only passion left them."[71]

In one sense, Melancton Smith and the New York Antifederalists embraced Montesquieu's vision of republican virtue by emphasizing the simple life of industry and frugality, which they felt resided in the middle class. They insisted, as Montesquieu did, that such a life was more prevalent in a small republic. Indeed, many Antifederalists claimed that the misfortunes of the Confederation had occurred because a life of frugality had been abandoned for a life of luxury, both in the private and in the public realms. They called, therefore, not for a change in government, but for a renewed commitment to the values of industry and frugality.

Smith and his fellow Antifederalists were also drawn to the vision of simplicity and republican virtue that Thomas Jefferson espoused, which emphasized independence and an agrarian society. Independence was conducive to virtue. "Dependance [sic] begets subservience and venality, suffocates the germ of virtue, and prepares fit tools for the designs of ambition." Manufacturing must be resorted to as a matter of necessity, not choice. "Let our workshops remain in Europe" was Jefferson's cry.[72] Although the New York Antifederalists did not entirely share Jefferson's antagonism toward manufacturing, especially local manufacturing, they certainly shared his views on the attractive simplicity of the small community and the morality of those who pursued the simple life. Smith made this clear in his defense of the superior moral virtues of the yeomanry. Yet Smith and the Antifederalists in New York were not satisfied to leave the fate of the republic in the hands of a supposed virtuous yeomanry. Because of the universal persistence of self-interest, they insisted on structural checks upon all government, such as frequent elections, rotation in office, a bill of rights, and the independent power of their small republics, the states.

In both perspectives on virtue—the Hamiltonian vision, influenced by Hume, and the Antifederalist viewpoint, influenced by Montesquieu—there is the strong suggestion that civic-mindedness may be the by-product of self-interest, not a substitute for it. But neither side could fully relinquish its view that public-spiritedness, or republican virtue, could be located in human beings, either in the rich and wellborn, as in the case of Hamilton, or in the middling class, as in the case of Smith. Yet, as both parties subsumed different views of privatized self-interest into their classical conceptions of virtue, they moved steadily into a world in which virtue would be altogether abandoned and in which process, structure, and self-interest would prevail.

The Ratification of the Constitution

The news of Virginia's ratification reached Poughkeepsie on July 2. That information signaled a dramatic change in the proceedings of the New York convention. During its first two weeks the convention had painstakingly debated only the first eight sections of Article 1 of the Constitution. During the next five days of meetings, the balance of the Constitution and proposed amendments were considered without comment from the Federalists. Because the Constitution had already been ratified, the Federalists no longer had need for delay. Clearly, they had adopted a new strategy.[73] Now they could wait to see how the Antifederalists would respond.

Left to their own devices, the Antifederalists drafted fifty-five amendments and began to display less hostility toward the new Constitution, discussing not rejection, but the proper form of ratification.[74] Should amendments be a prior condition of ratification? or Should the Constitution be ratified with the proviso that subsequent to its ratification, amendments would have to be considered within a specified time? On July 10, after two days of caucusing, the Antifederalists agreed to a package of explanatory, conditional, and recommendatory amendments, proposed by John Lansing. The bipartisan informal committee selected to consider these amendments could not agree on a compromise because John Jay, now the Federalists' floor leader, insisted that the Federalists would not accept any form of conditional ratification. Finally, on July 11, 1788, Jay moved that the Constitution be adopted, without condition, but with this proviso: the parts of the Constitution that were considered to be doubtful ought to be explained, and the amendments that were deemed to be useful ought to be recommended. Lansing's explanatory and recommendatory amendments were acceptable, but his conditional amendments were not.

Jay's motion was debated for four days, whereupon Melancton Smith moved an amendment to it: ratification ought to be conditional nevertheless, until such time as a convention would be called to propose amendments. This was a concession for the Antifederalists, but it was not a sufficient one for the Federalists. Smith's resolution also contained some explicit limitations on national power, such as restrictions on the power of Congress to regulate elections for senators and representatives, a prohibition of excise taxes, and a ban on all direct taxes unless and until requisitions had been made but had failed in execution (*Debates*, 2:411). Governor Clinton addressed the convention in support of Smith's compromise, but the Federalists were insistent that no conditional ratification was acceptable to them or to the Congress.[75]

Much to the surprise and consternation of his Antifederalist colleagues, Smith then announced that he did not believe conditional ratification would be acceptable to Congress, and he would not vote for it. New York could not afford to be excluded from the Union. More surprising still, Smith and Judge Zephaniah Platt of Dutchess County then proceeded to introduce still another ratification proposal. New York would ratify the Constitution, but only after first declaring it defective and upon the subsequent condition that the state would withdraw from the Union if Congress within four years did not call a constitutional convention to correct those defects.[76]

Smith's new plan both baffled and angered Antifederalists, who adjourned in order to caucus and arrive at some agreement on their strategy. Meeting in caucus, they then defeated Smith's proposal, and he withdrew his plan. On Saturday, July 19, John Lansing moved to postpone the consideration of the several propositions before the convention so that it could consider a conditional ratification, with a bill of rights attached and with other amendments proposed. This motion carried, and a tedious debate ensued on the various amendments proposed. Then, abruptly, on Wednesday, July 23, Samuel Jones, an Antifederalist from Queens County, moved that the words "on condition" in the form of ratification be replaced with "in full confidence."

Smith spoke eloquently in support of Jones's amendment. Although Smith thought the Constitution was radically defective, he had become convinced that the defects could be corrected by the amending process that the Constitution itself provided. With the Constitution now assured of ratification, Smith and a number of his Antifederalist colleagues were convinced that New York's failure to join the Union would surely result in civil strife and the possible secession of the southern counties. By late June, this fear of the consequences of New York's failure to ratify had begun to plague Smith. In a letter written to Nathan Dane of Massachusetts shortly after the news of New Hampshire's ratification, Smith expressed his anxieties: "The most I fear is that there will not be a sufficient degree of moderation in some of our most influential men, calmly to consider the circumstances in which we are, and to accommodate our decision to these circumstances."[77] Smith was prepared to abandon the strategy of conditional amendments.

Alexander Hamilton's impressive rhetoric, particularly during mid July, in which he reminded the opposition that the choice now was whether New Yorkers wished to enjoy the benefits of union or assume the risks of independence, may have been influential in convincing Smith of the wisdom of abandoning the strategy of conditional amendment.[78] But what ultimately convinced Smith to support unconditional ratification was a letter from James Madison to Alexander Hamilton, responding to Hamilton's suggestion that perhaps Smith's "subsequent conditions" were acceptable. On the contrary, Madison responded, "the Constitution requires an adoption *in toto*, . . . any condition whatever must viciate [*sic*] the ratification."[79]

Although Hamilton did not read this letter to the convention until July 24, Smith had seen it before then. Indeed, he had obliquely referred to it on July 23, in his speech before the convention supporting the Jones amendment, in which he admitted that "reasonings . . . from persons abroad" (i.e., Madison) had led him to conclude that conditional ratification of any kind would be unacceptable to the nation and dangerous to the interests of New York. Thus, Smith and eleven of his Antifederalist colleagues joined the nineteen Federalist delegates to pass Jones's amendment by a vote of 31 to 29. On the next day, John Lansing moved a resolution that would have reserved New York's right to withdraw from the Union unless proposed amendments were submitted to a general convention. This motion was defeated, 31 to 28.[80]

The Committee of the Whole agreed to the report in the form of the Jones amendment and unanimously agreed to a circular letter that would be sent to the various state legislatures, recommending a general convention to consider proposed amendments.[81] On Saturday, July 26, 1788, the New York convention ratified the Constitution by a vote of 30 to 27.[82]

How was ratification possible in New York, given the considerable odds against it? In retrospect, the outcome was not as surprising as it might seem. A number of political and economic factors explain the final vote for ratification.[83]

To begin with, Federalists and Antifederalists in New York were never very far apart. Both desired a political community that could provide some consistency in trade and money matters along with uniform protection of the rights and property of the people and mutual recognition of the laws of the individual states. The Articles of Confederation had been woefully lacking in accomplishing these ends. On this point, all were agreed. The issue facing both parties was, not whether reform was needed, but how much reform was required. Even so perceptive a critic as "Federal Farmer" admitted that the Confederation was "defective" and "not well administered." Like that of so many Antifederalists, his view was that the Constitution should be adopted with a few essential alterations. Thus, New York Antifederalists were not unalterably opposed, as the debates may have suggested. They feared national power, to be sure, but many of them favored ratification, with appropriate amendments and perhaps a second convention.

Then there was the matter of strategy. Antifederalists were divided and unable to agree on strategy. Many had difficulty deciding whether to reject outright, to delay, or to force the amendments and then to ratify. Their confusion contributed to their political weakness in the ratifying convention.

The Federalists' strategy, by contrast, was more successful. Their tactic of delay was particularly effective. When New Hampshire and Virginia announced favorable votes on ratification, Federalists emphasized the dangers to New York if it should fail to ratify, particularly if the southern counties of the state should decide to secede, join the new union, and leave the northern part of the state separated and vulnerable. Ratification became an infinitely more pleasant prospect than the threat of civil war, disunion, and isolation. Of course, failure to join the Union would also mean forfeiture of federal monies and protection, as well as the loss of the benefits of New York's impost.

Political skills contributed as well, both inside and outside the convention. Within the convention's walls, the influence of Melancton Smith, as floor leader, and of Samuel Jones, who clearly saw the need for compromise, brought crucial votes from Dutchess and Queens counties. John Jay's considerable patience and prestige were important, both during the public debate and in the convention, particularly during its latter days. Hamilton's tireless arguments before the convention and his persuasive politics during adjournment surely made a difference, even though his manner and reputation may have been counterproductive at times.

Above all, in New York the Federalists were uncharacteristically conciliatory in admitting that some amendments, particularly those securing certain rights of the people, were appropriate additions to the Constitution and would be forthcoming in the First Congress.[84] Some Antifederalists, including Melancton Smith, eventually concluded that these amendments were more likely to be promulgated from within the Union than from without. Hence their willingness to recommend — not require — amendments.

Outside the convention, newspapers supported the Federalist position. As more and more states ratified the Constitution, public sentiment for approval seemed to increase. This was especially true in New York after news had reached the state that New Hampshire and Virginia had ratified. Antifederalists who expected to continue political careers in New York must have considered the future implications of their stance against a popular Constitution.[85]

All told, the power of events and the expediency of self-interest were major reasons for New York's approval.[86] Nonetheless, there were still significant differences in political philosophy between the Federalists and the Antifederalists. Given what the future held for the further development of the American republic, those debates may have been the last full consideration of two classical views of republican government.

In New York, both Antifederalists and Federalists embraced a hierarchy of human motivations. In both philosophies of government there was an assertion that the human mind is possessed of reason, prudence, and passion. They disagreed on the mixture of these elements, particularly among the classes of society. For Federalists, a small aristocracy possessed reason, which is to say wisdom and virtue. Enlightened self-interest was the basis of appeal for a larger group of citizens, while the masses were largely motivated by passion. Antifederalists were at once more skeptical and more democratic. Human beings were, to be sure, motivated by passion and self-interest. There was a universality to human avarice. But if there was any virtue or wisdom to be found in society, it was best to look for it in the common sense of the common man.[87]

When these abstractions were put into practical theory, Federalists saw the judiciary as the repository of conscience, the executive as the seat of energy and unity, and the Senate as the home of wisdom and stability. The Federalists' goal was to strengthen these elements of government and to limit the self-interested passion of popular assemblies, such as state governments and the House of Representatives.[88] This propensity for regarding reason, energy, and unity as virtuous was precisely Hamilton's position in the public debate and at the ratification convention. It was essentially the argument of those who possessed aristocratic sensibilities, and were fearful of the fickleness of popular will.

Antifederalists, by contrast, following the lead of Montesquieu and clinging to their more pessimistic view of human nature, saw the middling class, the yeoman farmer, as the personification of frugality and industry, virtues essential, they thought, to a republican government. Only a small homogeneous community could possess the similarity of habits and manners necessary for the development of this civic virtue. The bonds of political obligation could not be extended indefinitely.[89]

Both visions, then, possessed a classical dimension. Both embraced a conception of civic virtue in representative government. Antifederalists looked to the integrated community of political participation and to the virtues of the simple agrarian life. Federalists desired a world of hierarchy and the virtues of a natural aristocracy. Nevertheless, crucial to the ratification controversy in New York was the fact that this discussion of the nature of republican government was inextricably bound to differing conceptions of federalism. And ironically, both Antifederalists and Federalists embraced versions of federalism that ultimately negated their respective classical visions. Antifederalists insisted that classical republicanism was compatible only with small, homogeneous, and autonomous communities — the states. In this insistence they were espousing a notion of government closer to the spirit of the Greek model of the polis. The great challenge that the New York Antifederalists faced — during the Revolution they had become only too conscious of this task — was how to provide security for these communities, both economically and politically. In other words, Antifederalists recognized the need for more national consolidation, although they were reluctant to abandon their classical vision of the small republic. In truth, the internal political and class divisions of New York gave additional impetus for more consolidation. New York was hardly a uniform community of virtue. Yet if the small republic could no longer be regarded as the "pre-condition of the good life," it could at least preserve autonomy, allow for representation by a virtuous citizenry, and protect republican freedom. Martin Diamond has argued that most American Antifederalists tended to emphasize the small republic as a defense against despotism and to ignore the virtuous aspects of the small republic. This may have been true nationally, but it was clearly not the case in New York. There, the Antifederalists were keenly aware of what was at stake in the transformation from a confederacy to the compound or extended republic of Madison. For them, the federalism of the extended republic might be able to provide for the common defense, but whether it could retain the civic virtue of good republican citizenship was questionable.[90]

Thus, New York Antifederalists, like Antifederalists elsewhere, could admit to the need for greater consolidation of power. In the process, they attempted, with some success, to retain a considerable degree of state sovereignty. Indeed, the very act of ratification was based on a partial desire to retain New York's integrity as a political community. In doing this, they would continue to enjoy the advantages of national economic expansion.

At the same time, New York Federalists, with the able assistance of David Hume and James Madison, were providing a solution for securing a stable regime, the extended republic. The extended republic thesis justified a large consolidated union as a protection against despotism. Federalists often spoke of this extended republic in terms of classical mixed government. Hamilton in particular embraced this theory. Yet in truth, the new federalism espoused by Madison—a compound republic of economic factions extended over a large territory, with thirteen semisovereign political communities and with a variety of indirect elections designed to filter and refine public opinion—rendered obsolete the theory of classical mixed government.[91]

What happened in New York was a transformation of political terminology. Under the rubric of the extended republic—or the new federalism—the language of the ratification controversy would eventually become archaic. Henceforth, political discourse in New York and in America would begin to assume the form of Hamiltonian nationalism, political as well as economic, versus Jeffersonian market liberalism. As the American conception of political reality gradually moved from virtue to commerce,[92] what remained in both the descendants of the Federalists and of the Antifederalists—the Hamiltonians and the Jeffersonians—bore little resemblance to their classical roots. There was, after all, no classical language for understanding a commercial system or for comprehending a life of economic self-interest.[93]

The particularistic individualism of the Antifederalists and, later, the possessive individualism of the Jeffersonians came to be dominated more and more by the image of the market, not only for the purpose of securing profit, although undoubtedly that was important, but also as a natural means for the free, rational, self-interested human being to act out a life of productivity with minimal compulsion. Market liberalism endorsed limited government and greater empowerment to citizens, and it encouraged voluntary associations and "extensive networks of free exchange."[94] In short, it provided a meaning and an identity for human endeavor. As Joyce Appleby has noted, "emerging individualism had become the instrument of progress," and the undeveloped resources of the United States were ready made for such a philosophy.[95] Paramount among those resources was the state of New York.

Whereas the Antifederalist-Jeffersonian discourse emphasized individualized productive commerce, the Federalist-Hamiltonian nationalists became preoccupied with the vision of a powerful commercial state. As Hamilton so often reminded those around him, "the prosperity of commerce is now perceived and acknowledged by all enlightened statesmen to be the most useful as well as the most productive source of national wealth."[96] Hamiltonian nationalism asserted the prominence of trade, urbanization, public credit, standing armies, and sovereign national power. Commerce was not just a means for acquiring wealth; it was also a way of building an empire.

Although they would ultimately be at odds, these two philosophies of commerce coincided and prospered for a time in New York. The funding of the national debt was greeted warmly by Federalists and Antifederalists alike. The Clintonians supported charters for state banks, large grants of land to speculators, and the public building of roads. The Clintonians' programs were designed to encourage "aspiring entrepreneurs," thereby avoiding burdensome taxation of the yeomanry.[97] Hamiltonian measures benefited the wealthy citizens of New York, to be sure, but the state treasury also held federal securities, and it invested in banks. Smaller investors, among whom were many former Antifederalists, were rewarded as well. The emphasis on commerce worked to the advantage of both farmers and merchants. And national military power was successful in defeating the Indians, restoring the New York forts to American soil, and protecting the shipping industry.[98]

Despite the fact that these two political philosophies would become organized into two contending political parties—the Federalists and the Democratic-Republicans—it is significant that in their respective visions of commerce, they both dreamed of empire. Under the leadership of Thomas Jefferson, the Democratic-Republicans would speak of the growth of westward expansion as an opportunity to continue the movement of the agrarian philosophy westward and, thereby, to create an "empire of liberty"[99] while Hamilton and the Federalists looked to the sea, to national power through a connection with Europe, to a grand commercial empire that would eventually become the center of power in the Western Hemisphere.

George Washington visited the state of New York in 1784, and as he considered its vast acreage and inland waterways, he realized its great commercial possibilities. Prophetically, he called the area the "seat of Empire."[100] For with New York's ratification, in which Americans discovered a modern language for their politics, a new nation was finally created. And in New York, the Empire State, a republican empire was conceived.

NOTES

1. The prevailing paradigm in this regard is that of J. G. A. Pocock, to whom I am greatly indebted. See *Virtue, Commerce, and History: Essays on Political Thought and History, Chiefly in the Eighteenth Century* (Cambridge, Eng.: Cambridge University Press, 1985). I am also indebted to and agree with Isaac Kramnick, who argues that a particular political discourse is not likely to be as hegemonic as Pocock suggests. Kramnick contends that a variety of " 'distinquishable idioms' coexisted in the discourse of politics in 1787–1788": see *Isaac Kramnick* "The 'Great National Discussion': The Discourse of Politics in 1788" *William and Mary Quarterly*, 45, no. 1 (January 1988): 4–5.

2. The role of social class in the ratification disputes in New York remains a hotly disputed issue. For contending interpretations see E. Wilder Spaulding, *New York in the Critical Period, 1783–1789* (New York: Columbia University Press, 1932); Jackson Turner Main, *The Antifederalists: Critics of the Constitution, 1781–1788* (Chapel Hill: University of North Carolina Press, 1961); Staughton Lynd, *Anti-Federalism in Dutchess County: A Study of Democracy and Class Conflict in the Revolutionary Era* (Chicago: Loyola University Press, 1962); and Linda Grant De Pauw, *The Eleventh Pillar: New York State and the Federal Constitution* (Ithaca, N.Y.: Cornell University Press, 1966). It should be noted that the primary materials on New York are so numerous and so scattered that it will be some time, if ever, before the authoritative interpretation of the ratification is written.

3. De Pauw, *Eleventh Pillar*, p. 4.

4. The first federal census of the state, taken in 1790, listed a population of 340,120. Virginia, Pennsylvania, North Carolina, and Massachusetts had larger populations. See United States Bureau of the Census, *Heads of Families at the First Census of the United States Taken in the Year 1790: New York* (Washington, D.C.: Government Printing Office, 1908), pp. 9–10; and De Pauw, *Eleventh Pillar*, p. 5.

5. De Pauw, *Eleventh Pillar*, p. 5; see also Spaulding, *New York in the Critical Period,* and Irving Mark, *Agrarian Conflicts in Colonial New York, 1711–1775* (New York: Columbia University Press, 1940).

6. De Pauw, *Eleventh Pillar*, p. 6.

7. Ibid., pp. 6–8.

8. Ibid., pp. 5–7; and Spaulding, *New York in the Critical Period*, pp. 77–80.

9. Alfred F. Young, *The Democratic Republicans of New York* (Chapel Hill: University of North Carolina Press, 1967), pp. 6–22.

10. John P. Kaminski, "New York: The Reluctant Pillar," in *The Reluctant Pillar: New York and the Adoption of the Federal Constitution*, ed. Stephen L. Schechter (Troy, N.Y.: Russell Sage College, 1985), pp. 48–49.

11. Young, *Democratic Republicans*, pp. 5–6.

12. Ibid., pp. 6–22.

13. As I mentioned earlier in the text, it is difficult to substantiate completely the socioeconomic dimensions of these class distinctions. What is more compelling are the statements of the combatants themselves, which reveal, as I will show, a strong sensitivity to class issues.

14. George Dangerfield, *Chancellor Robert R. Livingston of New York, 1746–1813* (New York: Harcourt, Brace, 1960), p. 88 n, cited in Young, *Democratic Republicans*, p. 54.

15. The unmistakably Lockean character of this pronouncement was typical of its author, Governor George Clinton; see Charles Z. Lincoln, ed., *Messages from the Governors*, 11 vols. (Albany, N.Y.: J. B. Lyons Co., 1909), 2:255–56, 16 January 1786.

16. Young, *Democratic Republicans*, pp. 33–58.

17. Alexander Hamilton, "Conjectures about the New Constitution," probably 17–30 September 1787, in *The Papers of Alexander Hamilton*, ed. Harold C. Syrett and Jacob E. Cooke, 27 vols. (New York: Columbia University Press, 1961), 4:275–76.

18. Ibid.

19. Young, *Democratic Republicans*, pp. 59–82.

20. Kaminski, "New York: The Reluctant Pillar," pp. 49–50.

21. Ibid., pp. 50–51; and De Pauw, *Eleventh Pillar*, pp. 3–17.

22. Kaminski, "New York: The Reluctant Pillar," p. 51; and De Pauw, *Eleventh Pillar*, pp. 32–34.

23. Kaminski, "New York: The Reluctant Pillar," p. 52.

24. Ibid., pp. 52–53.

25. Ibid., pp. 53–54.

26. Ibid., p. 55.

27. Kaminski, "New York: The Reluctant Pillar," pp. 56–57; and De Pauw, *Eleventh Pillar*, pp. 33–43.

28. Kaminski, "New York: The Reluctant Pillar," p. 57.

29. Young, *Democratic Republicans*, pp. 56–58.

30. De Pauw, *Eleventh Pillar*, pp. 16–17.

31. Young, *Democratic Republicans*, pp. 81–82.

32. Abraham Yates, *Political Papers, Addressed to the Advocates for a Congressional Revenue, in the State of New-York* (New York: Shepard Kollock, 1786), p. 19, cited in De Pauw, *Eleventh Pillar*, p. 35.

33. De Pauw, *Eleventh Pillar*, pp. 36–43.

34. Letter to George Washington, New York, 18 March 1787, in James Madison, *The Papers of James Madison*, ed. Robert A. Rutland, 15 vols. (Chicago: University of Chicago Press, and Charlottsville: University Press of Virginia, 1962–85), 9:315, cited in Kaminski, "New York: The Reluctant Pillar," p. 61.

35. Kaminski, "New York: The Reluctant Pillar," pp. 59–63; and De Pauw, *Eleventh Pillar*, pp. 57–66.

36. "Alexander Hamilton Attacks Governor George Clinton," *New York Daily Advertiser*, 21 July 1787, in *The Documentary History of the Ratification of the Constitution* (hereafter cited as *DHRC*), ed. Merrill Jensen, John P. Kaminski, Gaspare J. Saladino, et al., 7 vols. to date (Madison: State Historical Society of Wisconsin, 1981), 13:136–38. This piece was, at first, anonymous. It was later identified as having been written by Alexander Hamilton.

37. "A Republican," *New York Journal*, 6 September 1787, *DHRC*, 13:139–40.

38. Because of the amount of Antifederalist literature pouring into to his offices, Thomas Greenleaf, its printer, changed its publication from a weekly to a daily.

39. "An American Citizen," Tench Coxe, *DHRC*, 13:247; "A Countryman," Roger Sherman, ibid., 14:106; "Landholder," probably by Oliver Ellsworth, ibid., 13:561; "Centinel," Samuel Bryan, ibid., 13:326–28; "An Old Whig," possibly by George Bryan, ibid., 13:376; and "Cincinnatus," Richard Henry Lee or his brother Arthur, ibid., 13:529–30.

40. "Brutus," published in the *New York Journal* between October 1787 and April 1788, cited in *Pamphlets on the Constitution of the United States*, ed. Paul Leicester Ford (New York: Da Capo Press, 1968), pp. 117, 424. Ford attributes its authorship to Robert Yates, but Herbert Storing contends that there is no evidence to support or to refute this. See Herbert J. Storing, *The Complete Anti-Federalist* (hereafter cited as *CAF*), 7 vols. (Chicago: University of Chicago Press, 1981), 2:358.

41. Kaminski, "New York: The Reluctant Pillar," p. 72; and De Pauw, *Eleventh Pillar*, pp. 91–105.

42. Storing, *CAF*, 6:3.

43. Gordon S. Wood, *The Creation of the American Republic, 1776–1787* (New York: W. W. Norton: 1972), p. 486.

44. Ibid., p. 487.

45. Although he agrees that considerable doubt exists as to the authorship of the letters, Storing thinks that Governor George Clinton is probably the author; see *CAF*, 2:103. Linda De Pauw disagrees; she argues that the most probable author is Abraham Yates: see *Eleventh Pillar*, pp. 283–92.

46. Storing, *CAF*, 2:116.

47. Ibid., p. 105.

48. Caesar II, letter to the *New York Daily Advertiser*, 17 October 1787, *DHRC*, 13:396–97. The authorship of "Caesar" is also open to debate. Paul Leicester Ford argues that Alexander Hamilton wrote the essays, while Jacob E. Cooke disagrees. See Cooke, "Alexander Hamilton's Authorship of the 'Caesar' Letters, *William and Mary Quarterly* 17 (1960): 78–85.

49. Kaminski, Storing, and De Pauw all agree on this, and the independent observer cannot but conclude likewise. Storing, however, makes a good case that the "Brutus" series, which has long been neglected, deserves equal consideration: see *CAF*, 2:358.

50. William W. Crosskey, in *Politics and the Constitution*, 2 vols. (Chicago: University of Chicago Press, 1953) 2:1299–1300, may have been the first to doubt Lee's authorship. Herbert Storing, *CAF*, 2:215, and Gordon S. Wood, "The Authorship of *The Letters from the Federal Farmer*," *William and Mary Quarterly* 31 (1974): 299–308, are in agreement with this suspicion. Robert H. Webking, in a more recent essay, "Melancton Smith and the *Letters from the Federal Farmer*," *William and Mary Quarterly* 44 (1987): 510–28, argues that Melancton Smith wrote the letters.

51. Virginia Federalist Edward Carrington to Thomas Jefferson, New York, 9 June 1788, *Commentaries*, 2:75, 18 n, cited in Kaminski, "New York: The Reluctant Pillar," p. 71.

52. "Letter from the Federal Farmer to the Republican," *CAF*, 2:223–24.

53. Ibid., p. 228.

54. Ibid., p. 230.

55. Ibid., p. 253.

56. Despite the importance of *The Federalist*, especially to later generations, it appears that a more significant piece of Federalist writing, for the purpose of persuading the public to support ratification in New York, was John Jay's *An Address to the People of the State of New York*. Samuel B. Webb, writing to Joseph Barrell, argued that it "had a most astonishing influence in converting anti-federalism to a knowledge and belief that the new Constitution was their only political salvation" Samuel B. Webb to Joseph Barrell, New York, 27 April 1788, Webb Family Collection, Yale University (cited in Kaminski, "New York: The Reluctant Pillar," p. 72). Jay's pamphlet was answered by Melancton Smith in an essay entitled *An Address to the People of the State of New-*

York: Showing the necessity of making Amendments to the Constitution, proposed for the United States, previous to its Adoption, published on 17 April 1788. Both pamphlets can be found in Ford, *Pamphlets on the Constitution*, pp. 67–86, 87–115.

57. *The Federalist Papers* (New York: New American Library, 1961), p. 216.

58. See especially, *Federalist* 68 and 78.

59. Ibid., p. 82.

60. Ibid., p. 432.

61. "Letters from a Federal Farmer," p. 251. See Gordon Wood, *Creation of the American Republic*, pp. 471–518, for a lengthy discussion of these sentiments.

62. Charles Tillinghast to John Lamb, 21 June 1788, John Lamb Papers, N.Y. Historical Society, cited in Robin Brooks, "Alexander Hamilton, Melancton Smith, and the Ratification of the Constitution in New York," *William and Mary Quarterly* 24, no. 3 (July 1967): 349.

63. Kaminski, "New York: The Reluctant Pillar," pp. 73–77.

64. Ibid.

65. De Pauw, *Eleventh Pillar*, p. 176.

66. Kaminski, "New York: The Reluctant Pillar," pp. 101–2.

67. For a discussion of their relative influence in the convention see Bower Aly, *The Rhetoric of Alexander Hamilton* (New York: Russell & Russell, 1965), and Brooks, "Alexander Hamilton, Melancton Smith, and the Ratification of the Constitution in New York," pp. 339–58.

68. Jonathan Elliot, ed. *The Debates in the Several State Conventions on the Adoption of the Federal Constitution*, vol. 2: *The Debates in the Convention of the State of New York* (Philadelphia: J. B. Lippincott, 1941), p. 245 (hereafter cited in the text by page number or referred to in the notes as *Debates*).

69. For a discussion of Hamilton's philosophy of the general interest see Cecilia Kenyon, "Alexander Hamilton: Rousseau of the Right," *Political Science Quarterly* 73 (1958): 161–78.

70. In portions of the following argument, I am greatly indebted to Gerald Stourzh, *Alexander Hamilton and the Idea of Republican Government* (Stanford, Calif.: Stanford University Press, 1970). See especially pp. 38–75.

71. Baron de Montesquieu, *The Spirit of the Laws*, ed. Franz Neumann, trans. Thomas Nugent (New York: Hafner, 1949), bk. 5, chap. 2, pp. 40–41, cited in Stourzh, *Alexander Hamilton and the Idea of Republican Government*, p. 65.

72. Thomas Jefferson, "Notes on the State of Virginia," in *Writings* (New York: Library Classics of the United States, 1984), pp. 290–91.

73. De Pauw, *Eleventh Pillar*, pp. 217–28.

74. Ibid., pp. 218–19.

75. Ibid., pp. 221–26.

76. Kaminski, "New York: The Reluctant Pillar," p. 109; and De Pauw, *Eleventh Pillar*, p. 226.

77. Melancton Smith to Nathan Dane, 28 June 1788, Nathan Dane Papers, no. 7532, bk. 52, Beverly Historical Society, Beverly, Massachusetts. Cited in

Brooks, "Alexander Hamilton, Melancton Smith, and the Ratification of the Constitution in New York," p. 347.

78. For a discussion of Alexander Hamilton's rhetoric and its influence in the New York convention see Bower Aly, *The Rhetoric of Alexander Hamilton* (New York: Russell & Russell, 1965).

79. Madison to Hamilton, (20 July 1788), in *Papers of Alexander Hamilton* 5:184–85; cited in Brooks, "Alexander Hamilton, Melancton Smith, and the Ratification of the Constitution in New York," p. 355.

80. Kaminski, "New York: The Reluctant Pillar," pp. 108–114; and De Pauw, *Eleventh Pillar*, pp. 227–43.

81. De Pauw argues that the ratification was equivocal, almost conditional. The Constitution was ratified "in full confidence" that a list of "recommendatory" amendments would be considered in good order. The word *condition* had been dropped from the ratification, but the Federalists agreed to the circular letter: see *Debates*, 2:413–14. Hamilton suggested this strategy, and Jay drafted the letter. The invitation to "sister states" to call a new convention for the purpose of considering amendments so frightened Madison that he introduced the amendments himself, in Congress, thus defusing the amendment controversy. It should be noted, however, that Madison favored a bill of rights as well; see De Pauw, *Eleventh Pillar*, pp. 257–64.

82. Kaminski, "New York: The Reluctant Pillar," pp. 111–14; and De Pauw, *Eleventh Pillar*, pp. 241–45.

83. Kaminski, "New York: The Reluctant Pillar," pp. 114–17; De Pauw, *Eleventh Pillar*, pp. 241–64; and Main, *Antifederalists*, pp. 250–57.

84. Young, *Democratic Republicans of New York*, pp. 111–15.

85. Ibid., pp. 110–11.

86. Kaminski, "New York: The Reluctant Pillar," pp. 114–15; De Pauw, *Eleventh Pillar*, pp. 246–54; and Main, *Antifederalists*, p. 257.

87. I am indebted to Daniel W. Howe, "The Political Psychology of *The Federalist*," *William and Mary Quarterly* 44 (1987): 485–509, for this discussion.

88. Ibid.

89. For an interesting discussion of these issues see Howe, "Political Psychology of *The Federalist*"; Douglass G. Adair, " 'Experience Must be Our Only Guide': History, Democratic Theory, and the United States Constitution," in *The Reinterpretation of Early American History*, ed. R. A. Billington (San Marino, Calif.: Huntington Library, 1966), pp. 129–48; and Jean Yarbrough, "Representation and Republicanism: Two Views," *Publius* 9 (1979): 77–98.

90. Martin Diamond, *The Founding of the Democratic Republic* (Itasca, Ill.: F. E. Peacock Publishers, 1981), pp. 124–30. I am indebted to Diamond for the development of this argument on the relationship between republicanism and federalism. See also Martin Diamond, "The Ends of Federalism," in *The Reluctant Pillar: New York and the Adoption of the Federal Constitution*, ed. Stephen L. Schechter (Troy, N.Y.: Russell Sage College, 1985).

91. Douglass Adair, "That Politics May Be Reduced to a Science: David Hume,

James Madison, and the Tenth *Federalist*," *Huntington Library Quarterly* 20 (1957): 343–60.

92. See J. G. A. Pocock, "Virtue and Commerce in the Eighteenth Century," *Journal of Interdisciplinary History* 3 (1972): 120–23.

93. The debate over the nature of classical republicanism and its influence in the founding period is both interesting and controversial. See especially Joyce Appleby, "Republicanism in Old and New Contexts," *William and Mary Quarterly* 43 (1986): 20–34; Lance Banning, "Jeffersonian Ideology Revisited: Liberal and Classical Ideas in the New American Republic," ibid., pp. 3–19; and James T. Kloppenberg, "The Virtues of Liberalism: Christianity, Republicanism, and Ethics in Early American Political Discourse," *Journal of American History* 74 (1987): 9–33.

94. Appleby, "Republicanism in Old and New Contexts," p. 32.

95. Ibid., p. 34.

96. *Federalist Papers*, p. 91.

97. Young, *Democratic Republicans of New York*, p. 231.

98. Ibid., pp. 573–74.

99. Stourzh, *Alexander Hamilton and the Idea of Republican Government*, p. 191.

100. David M. Ellis, James A. Frost, Harold C. Syrett, and Harry J. Carman, *A Short History of New York State* (Ithaca, N.Y.: Cornell University Press, 1957), p. 4.

PART FIVE

THE RATIONALE OF RESISTANCE

12
NORTH CAROLINA
Preserving Rights

MICHAEL LIENESCH

Apparently some friends of the Constitution were surprised to learn that on the second of August 1788 the delegates to North Carolina's convention had responded to the new federal system with a resounding refusal to ratify. Buoyed by a rapid succession of summer victories and believing that North Carolina would follow in line with her big sister Virginia, who had ratified a few weeks earlier, Federalists throughout the country swallowed hard when they heard the reports from Hillsboro. It had been "generally expected," Madison confessed to Jefferson, that North Carolina "would in some form or other have fallen into the general stream." The event, he reported with characteristic understatement, "has disappointed us."[1] Others were more forthcoming in expressing their sense of shock: "good God what can they promise themselves!" exclaimed an astonished James Gordon in a letter to Madison.[2] Almost immediately, the surprise turned to outrage and scorn: Federalists everywhere denounced this unfathomable decision. North Carolina, observed one angry New Englander, "hath gone a whoring after Strange Gods."[3]

They should not have been surprised. From earliest times, by geography and demography, in economics and social structure, North Carolina had been predisposed towards a politics of resistance to distant power and protection of local liberties. The colonial history of the state had been characterized by almost continuous conflict between imperial representatives and an activist lower house of the legislature.[4] With the Mecklenburg Resolves of 1775, North Caro-

343

linians had become some of the earliest subscribers to the cause of colonial rebellion; and in the state's Constitution of 1776, they had sought to create a government, in the words of one set of delegate instructions, "as near a simple democracy as possible."[5] After the War, they had continued in the same tradition, resisting power and protecting their rights, especially when it involved the collection of taxes. In this context it was perfectly predictable that a majority of the convention's delegates, on leaving for Hillsboro, would make solemn promises to their fellow citizens that "the preservation of [their] civil and religious rights and liberties" would be "the ruling principle of their conduct."[6]

In the ratification convention itself, the delegates often referred to their rights. Indeed, during two weeks of debate and through well over two hundred pages of reported proceedings, the concept of rights was pervasive, appearing repeatedly and in many different variations. These included civil, political, universal, and human rights; rights of "the people"; rights of "my country"; "the rights of this state"; "the rights of individuals"; along with substantive "rights," such as the freedom of religion and the right to a free press, to jury trial, and the like.

Partisans on both sides made use of the concept. Yet much of the time they interpreted it in very different ways. Specifically, Antifederalists tended to describe rights as communal and constitutive. That is, they spoke of rights as belonging to citizens, not as individuals, but as parts of larger publics — as citizens of communities, states, or nations. Moreover, Antifederalists assumed that rights were essential to the very existence of these publics, that rights defined the purpose of these publics, which was to secure freedom, meaning the rights of people to rule themselves. Federalists, on the other hand, were inclined to speak of rights as individual and inherent, adhering to citzens as persons, and existing largely to protect private liberties, especially the rights of conscience.

Furthermore, during the course of the convention, these concepts changed. In general, as the debates proceeded, Antifederalist readings of rights gave way to Federalist ones. By the close of the convention, however, for Antifederalists and Federalists alike, the meaning of rights had undergone a radical revision. Thus, the North Carolina debates can be seen, at least in part, as a conceptual contest, a debate over definitions, and ultimately, a struggle to determine the "real" meaning of rights.[7]

PRECONDITIONS TO A POLITICS OF RIGHTS

In 1788, North Carolina was the fourth-largest state in land mass, extending some nine hundred miles from the Atlantic Ocean to the Mississippi River, a vast expanse of tidewater lowlands, piedmont forests, and rolling ranges of mountains. Off the Atlantic coast lay a line of narrow islands and treacherous sand bars, so that along three hundred miles of coastline, there was only one serviceable port. Inland, wide sounds, a succession of rapid rivers, and long stretches of forest made travel slow even at the best of times. Settlements were scattered; even individual residences were sometimes ten to twenty miles apart, a hard day's journey on horseback. Isolated not only from the rest of the country but also from one another, the residents tended to turn inward, building strong family ties and local loyalties. The result was often a profound provincialism. Writing in the mid 1780s, one traveler described the extreme insularity of the people: "They could not tell me the name of the place, county, or parish they resided in, nor any other place in the adjacent country."[8]

At the same time, North Carolina was the fourth-largest state in population, which consisted of almost 400,000 people, a mottled mixture of Anglo-Saxon, Scotch Highland, Scotch-Irish, and German immigrants, in addition to their African slaves. Most had arrived quite recently, by way of the Middle Atlantic states: heavy emigration had begun in the early 1700s and continued with the arrival of large numbers of Scoth-Irish even in the mid 1750s. Religiously, the state was a haven for dissenters; it had relatively few Episcopalians but large numbers of Presbyterians, Baptists, Lutherans, German Reformed, Quakers, and Moravians. As to slaves, their numbers tended to be small, at least in comparison to Virginia and South Carolina, so that throughout the early period, blacks constituted slightly more than 20 percent of North Carolina's total population. All told, the population was remarkably heterogeneous, an awkward amalgamation, according to one Anglican missionary, of "many sorts of People, of various nations and different opinions, customs, and manners."[9]

Economically, North Carolina was a land of small farmers. Throughout much of the state the soil was poor, consisting of heavy red clay or barren sandhills, which made large-scale commercial agriculture impossible. With only one working port, what little trade there was tended to be overland through Virginia and South Carolina. Ownership of property was widespread, although most freeholders owned small amounts of land and few if any slaves. A chronic shortage of currency, made worse by frequent issues of paper money and rampant inflation, hindered the development of a commercial economy. Counterfeiting complicated the economic problems, as did the widespread embezzlement of taxes by local collectors. In any case, small-scale subsistence farmers found a haven in North Carolina, while larger landholders, along with those engaged in business and the professions, discovered the going to be particularly tough. As another mid-eighteenth-century traveler put it, it was "a fine country for poor people, but not for the rich."[10]

In terms of social structure, this was a gangling and hopelessly unsophisticated society. Arriving late, settling in scattered communities, and drawing on a diversity of ethnic and religious loyalties, North Carolinians had from the start no natural social elite. Even in the older tidewater regions, plantation society was relatively new, in addition to being less economically secure than in other parts of the South. The low percentage of slaves and the absence of slave rebellions contributed to the weakness of what little tidewater aristocracy there was. Towns were small and scattered, merchants and traders were relatively few, and professionals consisted of a handful of circuit-riding preachers and lawyers. (Although lawyers were "bad everywhere," commented Virginia's Richard Henry Lee, Carolina's were "worse than bad.")[11] Newspapers were published sporadically; schools were almost nonexistent; educated people were the exception, illiteracy the rule. Culture consisted of religious revivals, shooting and boxing matches, and cockfighting, and rum was usually in great supply at all of them. According to the revivalist Charles Woodmason, "The Manners of the North Carolinians in General, are Vile and Corrupt—The whole Country is a Stage of Debauchery Dissoluteness and Corruption."[12]

The politics that followed was predictable enough. Parochial, highly partisan, with partisanship rooted in strong local loyalties, and dominated by a tradition of dissent and popular protest, North Carolina's early political life was a rough-and-tumble operation. During much of the colony's earliest history, there had been continuous conflict between local elites, mostly concerning land patents and the control of local offices, in which no single family or group could effectively gain control.[13] By the mid-eighteenth century, with the creation of more and stronger institutions, factionalism had given way to sectionalism, with northern and southern interests—the older and the newer regions of the tidewater—doing battle over representation in the legislature.[14] During the prewar period, the sectional rivalries had shifted to a confrontation between east and west, which became entangled with popular protests over taxation and official corruption and came to a head in the Regulator riots.[15] In any case, long before the Revolution, North Carolinians had had plenty of practice at addressing petitions, closing down courts, and terrorizing tax collectors, to say nothing of abusing their colonial rulers. As Governor George Burrington had complained to his superiors at the Board of Trade, "All the Governors that ever were in this Province lived in fear of the People . . . and Dreaded their Assemblys."[16]

With independence, the pattern persisted. As early as 1776, Thomas Burke, one of the state's representatives to the Continental Congress, was criticizing the Articles of Confederation and insisting on the insertion of an article that would guarantee to each state all powers not specifically delegated to Congress. Even so, the North Carolina Assembly at first balked at ratification, choosing to accept only certain of the articles. In 1783, at the close of the war, the Assembly refused to endorse ratification of the Treaty of Paris and opposed, in particular, a provision allowing for the restoration of confiscated property to former Loyalists. Throughout the postwar period, North Carolinians continued an old tradition of failing to meet requisitions to the national treasury, resisted congressional pressure to cede their western lands, protested the Jay-Gardoqui treaty, and opposed Indian treaties entered into by United States commissioners. Under the circumstances, it was hardly surprising that almost before the ink was dry, they would be criticizing the new Constitution as "destructive" of their "inestimable rights."[17]

As to ratification, opponents had the upper hand from the start. An alliance of aging war heroes (Thomas Person, Griffith Rutherford, Joseph McDowell, William Lenoir, Joseph Graham), powerful political leaders (Willie Jones, Judge Samuel Spencer, Timothy Bloodworth), and popular religious leaders (Elisha Battle, David Caldwell, William Lancaster), along with lesser public officials (the Federalist Archibald Maclaine complained that the other side had captured "every public official, except the Clerk of the County Court"), Antifederalists constituted a formidable opposition.[18] Particularly powerful in the piedmont and in the west, popular among small farmers, assured of strong support from Baptists and other dissenting sects, they were without any doubt the majority party in the state.[19] (Thomas Person may have been exaggerating, though probably not by much, when he told Gen. John Lamb that "nine tenths of the people of this State are opposed.")[20] Moreover, Antifederalists were active early, so that even in the Assembly elections of 1787, pro-Constitution candidates were already being beaten, and at least one, the prominent Federalist William Hooper of Orange County, was being beaten up, having his "eyes blacked" in a particularly contentious campaign.[21] Above all, the Antifederalist forces were committed. As Timothy Bloodworth vowed on the eve of the convention, they would work "with pure melting ardor" to defeat the Philadelphia Constitution.[22]

By contrast, Federalists had a hard row to hoe. Although the socioeconomic boundaries were blurred, and people of considerable status and wealth could be found on each side, Federalist leaders were drawn disproportionately from the ranks of relatively large landholders (Whitmell Hill, John Gray Blount), merchants (John Steele, Stephen Cabarrus), and especially lawyers (Maclaine, John Sitgreaves, James Iredell, William Richardson Davie, Richard Dobbs Spaight).[23] Strong only in the old Albemarle regions of the tidewater and in the coastal towns, with no solid base in any of the religious groups, Federalists saw themselves as representing the "respectable *Planter*, . . . the *Merchant*, . . . the hardy *Mariner*, . . . the valuable *Artisan*, . . . [and] those of the learned professions."[24] In preconvention contests, they had suffered significant losses, with some of the state's most prominent Federalists having been defeated, while others chose not to run at all because the opposition was so strong.[25] In the elections to choose convention delegates themselves, the trend continued and worsened, with leaders such as Alexander Martin and William Blount, both delegates at Philadelphia, being defeated at the polls. At one point, some local Federalists became desperate enough to incite a riot at one polling place, at which they knocked the sheriff of Dobbs County senseless and made off with the ballot box.[26] The tactics did not help; Federalists were destined to be a distinct minority at Hillsboro, an embattled but virtuous elite, as they seemed to style themselves, looking down with disdain on the misguided many, that "set of fools and knaves," as Maclaine called them, "in every part of the State, who seem to act as by concert; and are uniformly against any man of abilities and virtue."[27]

The proceedings at Hillsboro followed in kind. From the start it was clear that Antifederalists, with more than twice the number of Federalists and with a working majority of one hundred, controlled the convention. Ably led by the shrewd and politically experienced Willie Jones of Halifax, long a leader in the General Assembly, they overwhelmed the opposition on every crucial vote.[28] At the same time, Federalists tended to dominate the debating. With Iredell speaking frequently, and Davie playing a prominent role ("the great cannon from Halifax," as one opponent called him, "will discharge fire-balls among us"), and with Maclaine taking the low road ("I never heard, in my life, of such a silly objection"), they held the floor much of the time.[29] What followed was an acutely partisan contest. Interspersed with splenetic invective ("horrid ignorance," "totally mistaken," "trivial, ill-founded objections," "too absurd to merit a refutation"), including highly personal attacks ("opprobrious epithets," "indecent scurrility"), the convention degenerated at least once into a shouting contest ("a very warm altercation," as the convention clerk politely put it) and came close to dissolution on at least three out of its twelve days.[30] In the end, however, the votes were, with one insignificant exception, exactly as they had been at the beginning. As Timothy Bloodworth confessed to the convention—and he spoke for Antifederalists and Federalists alike—the debates had "gone in at one ear, and out at the other" (p. 143).

In fact, however, the debates at Hillsboro did make a difference. For while the political lines held fast, the philosophical positions changed. Predictably enough, in their championing of a lost cause, Federalists had to make certain concessions. More surprisingly, although they controlled the convention, Antifederalists found themselves on the defensive in the debates; they were forced to answer the arguments of their Federalist foes and to retreat as a result, step by step, in an increasingly problematic defense of their principles.

By the close of the convention, they were taking positions not only different from but also inimical to those they had held at the start. In short, Antifederalists won the political battle, but they lost the philosophical war. The conflict over the concept of rights testifies to their failure.

THE RIGHTS OF REPUBLICANS

In the beginning, Antifederalists seemed remarkably sure of themselves. No sooner had the convention opened and the Federalist James Galloway had moved that the Constitution be considered clause by clause, than Willie Jones was on his feet, offering the Antifederalist alternative — namely, that the question of ratification be put at once, thereby saving the state and themselves a good deal of money and time. When Iredell protested, Jones was magnanimous: he consented to a full and fair hearing. After all, he, not Iredell, had the votes. Moreover, as soon as the convention convened in earnest on the next morning, Antifederalists were on the offensive: the Reverend David Caldwell proposed that the discussion begin with a statement of principles — the "rules or maxims," as he called them — which constituted "the fundamental principles of every free government" (p. 7).

In listing these principles, the Reverend Caldwell began with one of the oldest and most honored of Anglo-American political precepts — that government is a compact between rulers and ruled, an agreement by which the rulers received certain powers and the people retained certain liberties, or rights. This assumption had been confirmed by Magna Carta, clarified and detailed in the English Bill of Rights of 1689, and incorporated into American law through the colonial charters and early bodies of liberties.[31] In North Carolina, the principle had been in operation since the late seventeenth century; it had been established in the early charters and reiterated in proprietary decrees, legislative statutes, and local custom.[32] Inherent in all of these was the assumption that rulers and ruled were always at odds, that the power of the rulers was potent, and that the freedom of the people was fragile. In order to secure that freedom, there had to be rights, and those rights had to be inviolable. As Caldwell put it, "Unalienable rights ought not to be given up, if not necessary" (p. 9).

At the same time, Antifederalists were eager to set forth the first principle of American republicanism — that through these compacts, the people retained the right to rule themselves. Here they drew on the more recent tradition of American self-government. Along with most of the early state constitutions, North Carolina's Constitution of 1776 began with the statement that all political power was vested in and derived from the people only. In order to govern themselves, the people offered certain powers to their representatives. At the same time, they specifically retained certain powers of their own, as a people, which they also called rights, including the right to free elections, jury trials, and the like. As Antifederalists saw it, even in a republic, rulers and ruled were at odds. Said William Goudy in endorsing Caldwell's motion, "Power belongs originally to the people; but if rulers be not well guarded, that power may be usurped from them" (p. 10). In proffering powers to their representatives, the people needed to be particularly cautious. Goudy continued, "If we give away more power than we ought, we put ourselves in a situation of a man who puts on an iron glove, which he can never take off till he breaks his arm." In short, even in a republic — perhaps especially in a republic — rights had to be protected. Warned Goudy, "Let us beware of the iron glove of tyranny" (p. 10).[33]

Finally, Caldwell and his Antifederalist colleagues offered one other premise — that compacts should not only be lawful and mutual, but also "plain, obvious, and easily understood" (p. 9). Here they made a point that was of particular importance in North Carolina — that compacts specified rights. In beginning their Constitution of 1776 with the lengthy Declaration of Rights, North Carolinians had followed in the footsteps of most of the other American states.[34] But their declaration was unusual, not only for its length (twenty-five articles), but also for the fact that it included virtually all of the other liberties listed in all of the other state constitutions combined.[35] Even so, the Declaration of Rights was more than just a list of liberties; it was also a statement of intentions, of goals to pursue, a set of "oughts" rather than a set of "shall nots." Beyond this, it articulated, or constituted, a common cause or purpose to which republicans could commit themselves. For North Carolinians it was their most fundamental document, a kind of sacred text, from which all else followed. Antifederalists argued that any constitution should begin with such a declaration. It was in this spirit that the redoubtable Thomas Person, long a leader of North Carolina republicans, insisted that they begin their deliberations by placing "on the table" not only Caldwell's principles but also "the Declaration of Rights, Constitution of the state, and the Confederation" (p. 12).

In responding to these arguments, Federalists were, at least at first, put on the defensive. Having carried the day on the crucial point of considering the Constitution clause by clause, they seemed taken aback when Caldwell reclaimed the initiative by calling for a statement of principles. Iredell made the practical point that it would take as much time to consider principles as it would to consider the Constitution itself. As an alternative, he repeated the case for treating the Constitution clause by clause, not as a package of principles, but as a set of procedures, or operating rules. Nevertheless, Federalists seemed to realize that principles were, in one way or the other, the heart of the matter and that it was now up to them to demonstrate, in Iredell's words, the superiority of their own "much nobler principles" (p. 9).

Iredell began by calling into question Caldwell's first principle — that government was a compact between rulers and ruled. In other countries, he argued, government may have been the creation of such a compact. In America, however, government was the product entirely of the people. He had only to remind the convention delegates of the recent Revolution: "The people are known with certainty to have originated it themselves" (p. 9). It followed that traditional Anglo-American assumptions about the rights of Englishmen had no place in their discussion. The Reverend Caldwell, Maclaine declared flatly, had "taken his principles from sources which cannot hold here" (p. 10).

With this, Federalists turned to the matter of self-government, the right of the people to rule themselves, a principle that they embraced eagerly. In America, Iredell reiterated, the people had created their own goverment. As a result, those in power were the people's "servants and agents" (p. 9). Maclaine added that rulers were elected only temporarily; they could be removed at any point and others put in their places. In any case, he argued, the people had little to fear from those in power: "We shall have no officers in the situation of a king" (p. 10). Indeed, citizens were served best when they afforded their leaders more power, not less. Under these circumstances, rights seemed somehow secondary. As Federalists saw it, the people had one right, preeminent and preemptory, from which all others followed: the right to rule themselves. Thus they saw rights, not as limiting those in power or as protecting the people, but as empowering them. Said Maclaine: "The people here are the origin of all power. . . . We do not bind ourselves" (p. 10).

As to declaring principles and specifying rights, however, Iredell and his fellow Federalists remained reticent. Iredell himself announced that he, for one, had "no manner of objection to the most explicit declaration that all power depends upon the people." At the same time, he made it clear that such a statement alone would not "strengthen their rights." At the very best, he observed, "it may be the means of fixing them on a plainer foundation" (p. 11). Federalists had no intention of beginning their convention (let alone their Constitution) with any statement of rights. For them, the listing of liberties could only limit the power of those who governed and, by extension, the power of the people. Concluded Davie, "It will be wrong to tie any man's hands" (p. 12).

After some discussion, it became clear that Antifederalists were not prepared to press the point. One of their own leaders, William Lenoir, announced that while he agreed with Caldwell's principles, he was unwilling to be bound by them. When the Federalist James Galloway echoed these sentiments, the issue lost the appearance of a partisan test, and the convention voted to proceed without a statement of principles. Antifederalists did not seem to notice that they had been beaten before they had even begun to fight.

THE RIGHTS OF THE PEOPLE: STATE, SECTION, AND NATION

Even before the reading of the first clause of the Constitution, the debate in North Carolina had heated up. After the reading of the preamble, things got hot in a hurry, as Antifederalists found cause for concern in the opening phrase "We, the people." Again the Reverend Caldwell spoke first, pointing out that the Constitution was created neither by the people nor by their elected representatives. Touching on the concept of direct representation, Caldwell contended, at least implicitly, that the role of representatives was to serve as delegates, not only conveying the opinions of those who had elected them, but also carrying out their express instructions. However renowned, the delegates to the convention at Philadelphia had been granted no such power to speak for the people, to "use their name, or to act for them. They were not delegated for that purpose" (p. 16).

At issue was more than the styling of one phrase, for in North Carolina the concept of representation had been for decades a matter of conflict. From the time of the colony's first charter, the assembly had been at odds with the royal governors, and throughout a long series of struggles involving issues of apportionment, franchise, and the control of elections, it had become particularly powerful.[36] The situation had been complicated by longstanding sectional rivalries, the upshot of which was that North Carolina's colonial politics had been dominated by discussions concerning the rights of the people to be represented.[37] Even before 1765 and the Stamp Act, North Carolinians had made clear their position on taxation and representation, which was that only their own assembly had the right to impose taxes on them.[38] Having looked so long to the legislature to express the popular voice, North Carolinians had tended to equate their own rights with the rights of their representatives, considering that the assembly effectively constituted "the people." With this in mind, Antifederalists began to sink their teeth into the Constitution's first article, and for the rest of the day they condemned the proposed powers of Congress in detail, affording special attention to its power to control the time and place of its own elections. The angry Joseph Taylor asked: "Did the people give them the power of using their name? This power was in the people. They did not give it up" (p. 24).

Relying on this concept of representation, Antifederalists drew a clear connection between the people and the state of North Carolina. Here several factors were involved. For one, North Carolinians preferred to think of themselves as North Carolinians, their first and, for many, their only loyalty being to their state, which they also referred to as their "country" (Taylor, p. 24). Throughout the debates, when speaking of North Carolina they used terms that suggested commonality and strong state ties: "our situation," "our country," or simply, "us" (Taylor, p. 24). By contrast, when they spoke of the United States or its representatives, it was almost always "them" (Taylor, p. 24). Nor were they too tolerant of divided loyalties. Observed Taylor, "I am astonished that the servants of the legislature of North Carolina should go to Philadelphia, and, instead of speaking of the *state* of North Carolina, should speak of the *people*" (p. 24).

Beyond that, Antifederalists seemed comfortable in considering themselves secondly as southerners. Taylor was typical: "We see plainly that men who come from New England are different from us" (p. 24). Throughout the second and third days of the convention, their sectionalism surfaced in references to the ratio of slaves to citizens in federal representation. On the third day, it was present in the debates over federal powers of taxation and the regulation of trade. Finally, when the convention reconvened on Monday morning to consider the problem of ratifying treaties, Timothy Bloodworth—who for years had been a champion of southern rights to navigate on the Mississippi and an ardent foe of the Jay-Gardoqui treaty, which had seemed to threaten those rights—made clear that the most critical problem to be faced by any constitutional revision was sectionalism, "the jarring interests of the Eastern, Southern, and the Middle States" (p. 135). Nor did the issue disappear, for throughout the duration of the convention, Bloodworth remained a presence, pointing balefully, like some Southern Cassandra, toward the more powerful, more populous North: "They will always outvote us" (p. 185).

Ultimately, Antifederalists saw the proposed federal system as a threat to their freedom. For them, the rights of the people were inseparable from the rights of their states. By extension, the rights of the states were implicated in the rights of their sections. As North Carolinians and even as southerners, they saw themselves as bearing certain rights. As Americans, they considered themselves to be relinquishing rights, especially the right to govern themselves. Assuming that freedom could thrive only close to home, in small states, Antifederalists were predisposed to be wary of distant and extensive government, including that of the United States. The new Constitution, Bloodworth concluded, would require "a total repeal of every act and constitution of the states. . . . It will produce an abolition of the state governments. Its sovereignty absolutely annihilates them" (p. 179).

In replying, Federalists worked from a very different definition of "the people." Maclaine began by announcing his astonishment at Antifederalist ojections to the Constitution's preamble. Clearly, he admitted, the Constitution was not the product of the people, since it had been the creation of a select group of "gentlemen" (p. 16). Nevertheless, while not of the people, the Constitution was, he said, "intended . . . for the people, at a future day" (p. 16). What Maclaine had immediately in mind was the fact that the people were to ratify the document, so that only "when it is adopted, it is the act of the people" (p. 16). In a larger sense, however, he was articulating another concept of representation, one in which leaders would rule in the interest of the ruled, not so much acting at the latter's behest by following their instructions, as acting in their interest more broadly defined, by acting for their benefit, as defined by the leaders themselves. Davie proceeded to elaborate on the concept: he entered into a lengthy defense of the Constitution, along with a lengthy criticism of the Confederation, and ended by calling on the convention's delegates to consider themselves bound, not by their constituents, but by their consciences. He summed up with a textbook definition of indirect representation: "I hold my mind open to conviction" (p. 23).

With this competing concept of representation, Federalists could sever the conceptual connection between the people and the lower house of the legislature. Here Davie was remarkably candid. To his mind, he confessed, it was a "radical vice" of the old system that it "legislated on states, instead of individuals" (p. 21). Following a line that he had seen Madison pursue at Philadelphia, Davis argued that all confederated governments — what he called all "merely federal" governments — were "short-lived" (p. 22). In fact, he went well beyond Madison to contend that the principle of state sovereignty was itself open to question. That states should reserve all popular power, he concluded, was a "solecism in politics" (p. 72).

Throughout the convention, Federalists showed a striking tendency to speak of themselves as citizens, not of North Carolinia, but of "the Union" or of "the United States" (Iredell, p. 35). In general, they spoke of state interests as something small and petty—"local and particular," as Iredell put it—in contrast to "the general interests of the United States" or "the general sense of all America" (p. 38). State sovereignty was seen as a problem; federal power, as a solution. When they used the term "the people," Federalists used it most often, and most comfortably, to describe "all the people of America" (Maclaine, p. 47). As for North Carolina itself, they seemed to express surprisingly little loyalty. At times the state seemed almost an embarrassment to them, as when Governor Samuel Johnston called the state's performance in financial matters "disgraceful and humiliating" (p. 89). Indeed, Johnston showed almost shocking contempt for his fellow North Carolinians, denouncing them at one point as "swindlers" (p. 89).

As to sectionalism, Federalists were equally disdainful. As far as Maclaine was concerned, sectional prejudice was beneath contempt. The people of New England were no different from the people of North Carolina. Besides, northerners were not to legislate for southerners: "We are to be represented," Maclaine reminded the delegates, "as well as they" (p. 25). Throughout the end of the week, Federalists developed their case. Referring to the events at Philadelphia, Davie recalled that northern representatives had made concessions on the issue of slavery. Governor Johnston came down from the chair to describe the common commercial interest in sound money that tied the sections together. Responding to Bloodworth, Iredell pointed to the shared stake in protecting themselves from foreign invaders and internal insurrections. Federalists did not deny that sectionalism was significant. The Constitution, confessed Spaight, who had also been present at Philadelphia, had been "a compromise between the Eastern States and the Southern States" (p. 101). Yet by compromising, the delegates had transcended sectional interests, and had transformed sectionalism into nationalism with visions of what Iredell called "the rising glory of America" (p. 98).

As the debates proceeded, Federalists seemed to become increasingly confident in equating the people, not with the separate states, but with the United States. By Tuesday morning, Davie was referring to the states in the most contemptuous terms, denouncing the "contracted and narrow-minded regulations of the individual states, and their predominant disposition to advance the interests of their own citizens to the prejudice of others" (p. 157). By contrast, he described the federal union as the true body politic: "The people of the United States have one common interest; they are all members of the same community" (p. 157). Significantly, Davie's remarks came in a discussion of judicial power, in which he suggested that the federal government had become the true protector of the rights of the people, who, he concluded, "ought to have justice administered to them equally in every part of the continent, in the same manner, with the same despatch, and on the same principles" (p. 158).

Yet, Federalists had taken an even more sizeable step toward redefining the meaning of "the people." For from this point on, they would speak of the people, not in the singular, but in the plural, as "citizens of the United States" (Davie, p. 159). More important, Antifederalists would as well. Hesitantly, almost hypothetically, Antifederalists had begun to accept the Federalist argument: if there were to be a national government, reasoned Judge Samuel Spencer, and if that government were to deal directly with citizens, then those citizens should have rights, not as North Carolinians, or as southerners, but as Americans. "The expression, 'We, the people of the United States,' shows that this government is intended for individuals," Spencer told the delegates, conceding a point that Antifederalists would never have conceded before; "there ought, therefore, to be a bill of rights" (p. 153).

THE RIGHTS OF CITIZENS

With the reading of Article III of the Constitution late on Monday afternoon, Antifederalists took the offensive once again. But even as the debate commenced, it seemed a kind of last stand. In speeches that were longer and more passionate than before, their leaders drew a line beyond which they would not retreat. That line was the bill of rights, intended, said Judge Spencer, "to secure to every member of the society those unalienable rights which ought not to be given up to any government" (p. 137).

For Antifederalists, some statement of rights was essential. In making the point, their opening came with the reading of Article III of the Constitution, which deals with the power of the federal courts, especially in cases involving citizens from different states. Here, Antifederalists raised a series of objections involving federal jurisdiction, the power of the state judiciaries, and the connections between federal and state courts. But at the center of their concerns lay the absence of a federal bill of rights. In theory, Antifederalists assumed that citizens were protected by the rights granted to them in their respective state declarations of rights. As a practical matter, however, different states granted different rights, with some states having chosen not to include in their constitutions any formal declaration of rights at all. More important, as a matter of principle, Antifederalists maintained that wherever there was power, there ought to be some statement of rights. Since the time of Magna Carta, said Spencer, such a bill of rights had been, for free people, a "necessity" (p. 138).

Antifederalists insisted that rights be explicit, and absent from the Constitution was any express federal right to trial by a jury of one's peers. Antifederalists expressed astonishment at the abandonment of this oldest of common-law rights. General McDowell, the aging hero of the Revolution, seemed particularly effective in reminding the delegates that they had fought a war to win such liberties. When Federalists responded that they had not intended to abandon jury trials, that they had merely not insisted on them, Antifederalists were not impressed. The issue involved more than any single right. At least for Judge Spencer, the heart of the matter was that constitutions were meant to limit powers and to secure rights. In limiting powers and securing rights, explicit statements were preferable to implicit understandings. Implicit rights were no rights at all. "I know it ought to be so, and should be so understood," he told the delegates, "but, sir, it is not *declared* to be so" (p. 137).

In general, Antifederalists insisted on the principle of specificity. True to their Anglo-American heritage, they believed that freedom demanded a government of laws, not of men. Schooled in republican skepticism, they put little faith in their elected representatives, regardless of the latter's reputations. As for their leaders, McDowell observed, they had no reason to rely on their "virtue and wisdom" (p. 150). Surprisingly, in considering their fellow citizens, they seemed to put equally little faith in the people. Said McDowell, "The depravity of mankind militates against such a degree of confidence" (p. 150). Yet as a rule, their concern seemed to be less with representatives and with their fellow citizens than with future representatives and future citizens. Here the issue was interpretation. Although they did not use the term, Antifederalists were the strictest of strict constructionists. Said Spencer, "it is necessary that it should be expressly declared in the Constitution, and not left to mere construction and opinion" (p. 152). McDowell said it more simply: "I wish to see every thing fixed" (p. 150).

At first, Federalists tried to sound surprised. The very notion of a bill of rights, they argued, was out of place in a free republic. At best, a statement of rights could only be redundant. At worst, it might prove harmful. Thus the less said, the better. "As to a bill of rights," Davie would tell the convention, "it is unnecessary to say any thing" (pp. 159–60).

Nevertheless, Federalists were compelled to make the case against the addition of a bill of rights. Iredell led off; once again he took Anglo-American assumptions to task. A bill of rights may well have been appropriate in England, he argued, where the absence of a written constitution left powers unclear and rights open to usurpation. By contrast, a bill of rights was inappropriate in America, where written rules provided for precise limits to power and for the protection of rights. "Had their constitution been fixed and certain," he told the convention, referring to the English, "a bill of rights would have been useless, for the constitution would have shown plainly the extent of that authority which they were disputing about" (p. 148). In addition, returning to a point he had made at the beginning of the debates, Iredell pointed out that the rights of Englishmen were secured by compact, having been wrestled from the rulers by the ruled through a long series of struggles. The rights of Americans required no such compact; they resided in the people by virtue of their victory in the War, through which they had won, once and for all, the right to govern themsleves. "Of what use, therefore, can a bill of rights be in this Constitution," Iredell asked, "where the people expressly declare how much power they do give, and consequently retain all they do not?" (p. 148). Englishmen were ruled by rulers, Americans by themselves. It followed that in England, the bill of rights was necessary and proper. In America, Iredell concluded, it was "not only useless, but absurd" (p. 149).

Replying to Antifederalist demands for explictly enumerated rights, Federalists turned the doctrine on its head, arguing that the only powers were explicit powers and that the only rights were implicit rights. Here, Iredell seemed to have his friend James Wilson in mind, arguing, as Wilson had at Philadelphia, that because all power resided in the people, they retained all rights not expressly relinquished to their rulers. Under these conditions, to enumerate rights was redundant. In fact, it was dangerous, for to list some would be to omit others. Consequently, concluded Iredell, a bill of rights could only serve as "a snare rather than a protection" (p. 149).

To secure their freedom, Federalists looked to other sources. The Constitution itself provided checks. Its enumeration of powers, Iredell argued, was "clear and plain" (p. 172). Federalists thought that official oppression would be rare. Governor Johnston, in particular, stressed the point that the people would choose virtuous and wise leaders. "If not," he observed, "it will be our own fault" (p. 150). Still, should oppression occur, the system was self-sustaining, for the people would retain the ultimate redress. Although it seems highly ironic, Federalists relied on the right to revolution. "That power which created the government," said Iredell with some portent, "can destroy it" (p. 130).

Although Federalists made some plausible points, their case was not convincing, and Antifederalists were not moved. Federalist leaders seemed to sense the direction of the debate. Maclaine continued to denounce the opposition for its "doubts and fears" (p. 172). But others, led by Iredell, took another tack, so that in turning to a discussion of the Fifth or the amendment Article, they became uncharacteristically compliant. The Constitution, they admitted, was probably not perfect. It was, however, perfectible. In fact, according to Iredell, "one of the greatest beauties of the system" was that it could be "altered with as much regularity, and as little confusion, as any act of Assembly" (pp. 176, 177).

In effect, Federalists had left open the door to a bill of rights. Indeed, by Wednesday morning, the last full day of the convention, it was Federalists who had become the protectors of rights, by resisting the calls of certain Antifederalists for the establishment of test oaths and a state-sponsored religion, and by championing the cause of religious freedom. Yet the rights that they were seeking to protect were the rights not only of citizens but also of persons, not only of Christians and Jews but also of "pagans and Mahometans," all of whom, Iredell argued, reserved rights of "conscience" (pp. 194, 198).

In insisting on a bill of rights, Antifederalists had made their point unmistakably. No one seemed to notice that in making it, they had strayed from their original assumptions, the first principles with which they had started. For where before they had considered rights to be civil and political, the product of law and politics, arrived at through compacts between rulers and ruled, they now described them as inherent in individuals. As Spencer told the convention on Tuesday morning, rights were gifts from God; they were the product of nature, not of law or politics. In this sense, they were in the most sweeping sense "the rights of individuals" (p. 153). Where before they had considered bills of rights to be packages of political principles, educating and inspiring citizens, they now were describing them as lists of personal liberties, those "human rights," as Spencer called them, "that ought not to be given up, and which ought in some manner to be secured" (p. 153). Above all, where before Antifederalists had considered rights to be preeminent, the very prerequisites of freedom, they were now describing them as somehow secondary—less a precondition than a product of their politics—"secured to individuals in consideration of the other rights which they give up to support society" (Spencer, p. 154).

AFTERMATH: NORTH CAROLINA AND THE BILL OF RIGHTS

Throughout the last two days of debate, Antifederalists held the line, insisting that without a bill of rights, the Constitution could never be ratified. Repeatedly they made the case, with Lancaster, Lenoir, and McDowell lining up to provide a virtual laundry list of liberties, summarizing those that had been mentioned before, and adding at least one other—the right to a free press. By this time, their remarks were sounding all too familiar, the repeating of rights having taken on an almost ritualistic quality. Finally, late on Wednesday afternoon, Willie Jones arose, breaking his self-imposed silence, to call the question of ratification. In his hand he held a declaration of rights, along with a set of twenty-six amendments, all of which, he insisted, citing his friend and mentor Thomas Jefferson, should be included in the Constitution, not after ratification, but before. In the meantime, North Carolina would remain outside the union. Jones himself presumed that it would take about eighteen months to have the amendments ratified. But he had "rather be eighteen years out of the Union," he announced, "than adopt it in its present defective form" (p. 226).[39] Interestingly, in calling the question, he referred to one final right, the "right to reject" (p. 225).

After some confusion, Federalists reacted first with anger, then with resignation. Clearly their opponents had the votes. Indeed, they did not disagree when Jones observed that throughout the entire convention, "no person had changed his opinion" (p. 217). Nonetheless, they were angry, and the final hours of the debate rapidly devolved into a flurry of what Johnston called "illiberal and ungenerous insinuations" (p. 227). Willing as they were to consider a bill of rights, Federalists continued to argue that it should be added after ratification. They found it hard to accept the fact that they could not convince their counterparts of the rightness of ratifying, then amending. To do it otherwise, Johnston counseled, would result in "no possible good" (p. 225). When Iredell called for postponement, and his motion was defeated by voice vote, he could see that the handwriting was on the wall. The debate, he announced, "is now at an end" (p. 241).

On the final vote, Antifederalists carried the day comfortably, with a hundred votes to spare (184 to 83), and the convention had come to a close. In another sense, however, the battle had only begun. Having been beaten badly inside the convention, Federalists turned outside, to the court of public opinion, where they had held certain advantages from the start. Controlling most of the state's newspapers, they let loose with an unprecedented barrage of criticism, denouncing the "strange, imprudent, and outrageous proceedings of the late Convention at Hillsborough."[40] Probably more important, in preparing their propaganda, Federalists pointed to changing conditions, to the advantages that were becoming available to the state from federal navigation and tariff laws, to the need for federal protection from the threat of Indian uprisings in the West, and to the payment of Loyalist land claims by the British government, lessening old fears that the federal government might move to seize lands confiscated during the Revolution. Throughout, they stressed the advantages of joining the union and the disadvantages of going it alone and being "served up as sauce for Rhode-Island."[41] Above all, however, Federalists held in their hands a trump card, which was Madison's willingness to press the Congress for a bill of rights. When Madison gave notice in May 1789 that he would submit amendments to Congress early in the next session, Federalists expressed relief. Davie wrote to Iredell, "Nothing ever gave me so much pleasure."[42] By the following November, when the second convention had convened at Fayetteville, "rank anti's" had become "perfect fed's"; an "amazing change" had taken place "in the sentiments of the people."[43]

At Fayetteville, North Carolina became the twelfth state to ratify the Constitution. Overwhelmed in the voting, Antifederalists barely put up a fight. Willie Jones was conspicuously absent. After all, by late 1789, the Constitution seemed inevitable. At the same time, the addition of a bill of rights, in some form, seemed also a foregone conclusion. Thus, while not embracing the Constitution, its former opponents did not stand in its way, choosing instead, as one Federalist described them, to "acquiesce cheerfully."[44]

In a way, they themselves had been at least partly responsible for this inevitability. Willie Jones's twenty-six original amendments (twenty had been borrowed from Virginia, six added by North Carolina) had been heavily weighted to considerations of political power, designed as they were to limit the control of the federal government over elections, the terms of representatives, ratios of representation, the power of the courts, control of state currencies, and the like.[45] By contrast, James Madison's twelve proposed amendments were almost exclusively designed to provide for the protection of personal rights, especially the rights of conscience. Of the ten that were finally adopted, only the tenth reserved certain powers to the states.[46] Yet Antifederalists could hardly criticize them. After all, Antifederalists were the ones who had insisted on a bill of rights. Moreover, during the course of the convention, Antifederalists had become champions of those very same individual rights. In the end, seeming less convinced than resigned, they saw the rights of conscience as the best of a bad bargain. For North Carolina's Antifederalists, Madison's bill of rights was, as one said, "a matter of necessity rather than choice."[47]

Yet the bargain they had struck, in which ratification was traded for rights, was in the end a costly one. From the close of the final convention, rights belonged to the people, not in their collective capacity as citizens of a republic, but as individuals, as persons, and ultimately as property holders. And so commenced the long decline of Antifederalism in North Carolina. As eighteenth-century republicanism gave way to nineteenth- and twentieth-century liberalism, the liberty-loving patriots of the Revolution were replaced by the rights-conscious secessionists of the Civil War and by the proponents of states' rights and massive resistance in the era of the civil-rights movement. Already in 1790, the Antifederalist William Dickson had shown the change when he had written in a letter to the Reverend Robert Dickson that it had become clear to him and to the "Southern people" that the North would now attempt "to liberate and emancipate the slaves."[48] For Dickson, rights had become synonymous with the rights to own property and slaves: "If divested of their negroes," he ended his letter, "their lands will become useless or rather burdensome to them . . . and the most opulent and considerable families would in a short time be reduced to indigence and extreme poverty."[49]

NOTES

1. James Madison to Thomas Jefferson, 23 August 1788, *The Papers of James Madison*, ed. Robert A. Rutland et al., 15 vols. to date (Chicago: University of Chicago Press, and Charlottesville: University Press of Virginia, 1962–), 11:238.

2. James Gordon, Jr., to Madison, 31 August 1788, ibid., 11:246.

3. Jeremiah Hill to George Thatcher, 29 August 1788, cited in Robert A. Rutland, *The Ordeal of the Constitution* (Norman: University of Oklahoma Press, 1966), p. 281.

4. See Jack P. Greene, "The Role of the Lower Houses of Assembly in Eighteenth-Century Politics," in *The Reinterpretation of the American Revolution*, ed. Jack P. Greene (New York: Harper & Row, 1968), pp. 86–109.

5. *North Carolina Colonial Records*, ed. William L. Saunders, 14 vols. (Raleigh: P. M. Hale, 1886–1914), 10:870, cited in Louise Irby Trenholme, *The Ratification of the Federal Constitution in North Carolina* (New York: AMS Press, Inc., 1967), p. 38.

6. *Pennsylvania Gazette*, 7 May 1788, cited in Robert A. Rutland, *The Birth of the Bill of Rights* (Chapel Hill: University of North Carolina Press, 1955), p. 184.

7. For a statement of this theoretical perspective, see my *New Order of the Ages* (Princeton, N.J.: Princeton University Press, 1988), pp. 3–14..

8. J. F. D. Smyth, *A Tour in the United States of America*, 2 vols. (London, 1784), 1:104, cited in A. Roger Ekirch, *Poor Carolina* (Chapel Hill: University of North Carolina Press, 1981), p. 29. See also Trenholme, *Ratification*, pp. 11ff.

9. John MacDowell to the Secretary of the Society for the Propagation of the Gospel, 17 April 1760, *North Carolina Colonial Records*, 6:236, cited ibid., p. 30. See also Trenholme, *Ratification*, pp. 20ff.

10. "Journal of a French Traveller, 1765," *American Historical Review* 26 (1920/21): 738, cited ibid., p. 27.

11. Lee to William Lee, 19 June 1771, *The Regulators in North Carolina*, ed William S. Powell et al. (Raleigh: State Department of Archives and History 1971), p. 482, cited ibid., p. 25.

12. Charles Woodmason, *The Carolina Backcountry on the Eve of the Revolu tion*, ed. Richard J. Hooker (Chapel Hill: University of North Carolina Press 1953), pp. 80–81, cited ibid., p. 28.

13. See ibid., pp. 51–85.

14. See ibid., pp. 86–111.

15. See ibid., pp. 112–60. See also Jack P. Greene, *The Quest for Power* (Chape Hill: University of North Carolina Press, 1963), pp. 39–45.

16. Burrington to Board of Trade, 20 February 1732, *North Carolina Co lonial Records*, 3:338, cited in Greene, *Quest*, p. 41. See also Hugh T. Lefle and William S. Powell, *Colonial North Carolina* (New York: Charles Scribner Sons, 1973), pp. 113–28.

17. "An Essay on the Constitution proposed to the People of the U.S., By th Federal Convention," *Martin's North Carolina Gazette*, 19 December 1787. Se also Trenholme, *Ratification*, pp. 40ff.

18. Maclaine to James Iredell, 15 January 1788, *Life and Correspondence o James Iredell*, ed. Griffith J. McRee, 2 vols. (New York: D. Appleton & Co. 1857–58), 2:216. See also Trenholme, *Ratification*, pp. 100ff.

19. See Henry G. Connor, "The Convention of 1788–'89 and the Federal Con stitution. . . ," *North Carolina Booklet* 4 (1904): 10.

20. Person to Lamb, 6 August 1788, in "News, Letters and Documents Con cerning North Carolina and the Federal Convention," ed. William K. Boyd *Historical Papers* 14 (1922): 80.

21. See Trenholme, *Ratification*, p. 102.

22. Bloodworth to Lamb, 28 June 1788, "News, Letters and Documents," p. 7

23. See Trenholme, *Ratification*, pp. 147ff.

24. "Alonzo," letter to the *State Gazette of North Carolina*, 27 March 1788

25. See Trenholme, *Ratification*, pp. 101–03.

26. See "The Convention Election Riot at Kinston, 1788," in "News, Letter and Documents," pp. 75–76.

27. Maclaine to Iredell, 29 August 1787, *Life*, 2:178.

28. On Willie Jones (whose name was pronounced like Wylie) see Trenholme *Ratification*, pp. 129ff.

29. William Porter to the convention, *The Debates in the Several State Con ventions on the Adoption of the Federal Constitution*, ed. Jonathan Elliot, 2c ed., 5 vols. (Philadelphia: J. B. Lippincott, 1861–63), 4:94; Maclaine to the con vention, *Debates*, 4:37. Hereafter, most citations of vol. 4 of the *Debates* wil be given parenthetically in the text by speaker and page number.

30. Maclaine to the convention, *Debates*, 4:43, 4:45, 4:47, 4:64; Davie t the convention, ibid., 4:103, 4:247.

31. See Forrest McDonald, *Novus Ordo Seclorum: The Intellectual Origin of the Constitution* (Lawrence: University Press of Kansas, 1985), pp. 9–55.

32. See ibid.; Greene, *Quest*, pp. 39–45; and Ekirch, *Poor Carolina*, p. 51.

33. See also Walter F. Pratt, Jr., "Law and the Experience of Politics in Late Eighteenth-Century North Carolina," *Wake Forest Law Review* 22 (1987): 587–94.

34. Rob Sikorski has pointed out to me that in framing the Declaration of Rights, North Carolinians referred to the constitutions not only of other states, but also of private organizations, including churches and fraternal groups.

35. See Rutland, *Birth of the Bill of Rights*, pp. 57–60.

36. See Charles Lee Raper, *North Carolina: A Study in English Colonial Government* (New York: Macmillan, 1904), pp. 85–100.

37. See Ekirch, *Poor Carolina*, pp. 86–111; Lawrence London, "The Representation Controversy in North Carolina," *North Carolina Historical Review* 11 (1934): 255–70; and Michael A. Gillespie, "The Question of Representation and the Rejection of the Constitution in North Carolina," unpublished paper.

38. See Raper, *North Carolina*, pp. 125–47.

39. It should be noted that by the time of the convention, Jefferson had recanted this strategy: see Trenholme, *Ratification*, p. 182.

40. "A Citizen and Soldier," in "To the People of the District of Edenton," 1788, in *A Plea for Federal Union*, ed. Hugh T. Lefler (Charlotte: University of Virginia, 1947), p. 43.

41. Letter to the *State Gazette of North Carolina*, 17 April 1789, cited in Trenholme, *Ratification*, p. 241.

42. Davie to Iredell, 4 June 1789, *Life*, 2:260.

43. Letter to the *State Gazette of North Carolina*, 1 October 1789, cited in Trenholme, *Ratification*, p. 212; Charles Johnson to Iredell, 23 November 1789, *Life*, 2:273.

44. William J. Dawson to Iredell, 22 November 1789, *Life*, 2:272.

45. See Trenholme, *Ratification*, pp. 184–86. North Carolina Federalists concurred in six of these amendments. See ibid., p. 187.

46. For background on the bill of rights see Edward Dumbauld, *The Bill of Rights* (Norman: University of Oklahoma Press, 1957), pp. 3–56; see also Richard E. Ellis, "The Persistence of Antifederalism after 1789," in *Beyond Confederation*, ed. Richard Beeman, Stephen Botein, and Edward C. Carter II (Chapel Hill: University of North Carolina Press, 1987), pp. 297–300. Ellis points out that Antifederalists unsuccessfully attempted to strengthen the tenth amendment: see ibid., p. 299.

47. William Dickson to Rev. Robert Dickson, 28 December 1790, in *The Dickson Letters*, ed. James O. Carr (Raleigh: Edwards & Broughton, 1901), p. 38.

48. Ibid.

49. Ibid., p. 39.

13
RHODE ISLAND
Protecting State Interests

JOHN P. KAMINSKI

On May 29, 1790, Rhode Island ratified the Constitution and, after a year of separation, rejoined the Union. Controlled by an agrarian Country party since May of 1786, Rhode Island steadfastly opposed the Constitution until its large wartime debt had been redeemed with depreciated state paper currency. The Country party's radical fiscal policies divided the state and alienated Rhode Island from the other states, keeping the state aloof from federal affairs for over three years. "Obstinate to the last," Rhode Island held out. Yet ironically, in looking out for its own self-interest, it increased the power of the federal government and strengthened the union.

THE SETTING: ECONOMIC ANXIETIES

After the American Revolution, Rhode Island's economy was in serious straits. In addition to the extensive destruction on the islands, the war had saddled Rhode Island with a large public debt. Before the Revolution, the colony had rarely collected an annual revenue larger than £2,000. After the war, the annual interest payments due to state public creditors amounted to more than £10,500. The tax necessary to raise such a revenue fell heavily on ordinary citizens because, unlike other states, Rhode Island had no western lands and few confiscated Tory estates that could be sold to ease the tax burden. To make matters worse, much of the public debt had gravitated into the hands of wealthy speculators. A lopsidedly unfavorable balance of trade also contributed to the economic problems, as specie was shipped out of the state to pay for imports. Although farmers were unable to obtain hard currency for their produce, the state and private creditors insisted on payment in specie. Thus, at a time when the state was being forced to increase taxes, the circulating medium of exchange seemed to contract, making it difficult if not impossible for many Rhode Islanders to pay their taxes and private debts.

Rhode Islanders hoped to solve their economic problems by reestablishing their lucrative prewar commerce. They were suspicious, however, and felt threatened when Congress proposed an amendment to the Articles of Confederation giving it the power to levy a tariff to raise revenue earmarked to pay the national debt. Some Rhode Islanders thought it would make Congress too independent of the states; others did not want to see the federal debt (much of which, like Rhode Island's state debt, had been purchased by speculators at extremely low rates) paid at face value. For these reasons, most Rhode Islanders opposed the impost, and Rhode Island refused to ratify it—the only state to withhold its assent. Thus, because the Articles of Confederation required unanimous approval by the states, the impost was defeated. Rhode Island's lone dissent made it the whipping boy of the Confederation, as all of the country's economic ills were attributed to Rhode Island's refusal to conform.

Rhode Island merchants soon realized that Congress needed the power to regulate commerce. The Mercantile party, in control of the state government until the spring of 1786, granted Congress the power to regulate commerce in 1785 and approved a second federal tariff in 1786. The state even appointed delegates to attend the Annapolis convention in September 1786 in order to consider granting Congress additional commercial powers. It appeared as if the black sheep of the American flock was back in the fold.

The short postwar period of prosperity in Rhode Island was followed by a deep economic depression. Farmers, who had been encouraged to produce more to feed the troops during the Revolution, had purchased additional land to increase their harvests. The market for these crops disappeared as the armies left the state, but the farmers' debts did not disappear, and farmers faced bankruptcy and foreclosure proceedings. The state soon became divided into two hostile factions. A merchant-creditor faction, dominant in the coastal towns, opposed debtor-relief measures, preferring instead a strengthened central government that could encourage economic recovery through the regulation of commerce. The second faction, centered in the interior towns, supported debtor relief from the state legislature.

Ideologically these two factions disagreed on little except the means to restore economic equilibrium to the state. Here they disagreed heartily. The debtor-relief faction advocated state paper money that would be loaned on real estate collateral. This fiscal measure had frequently been used with success during colonial times, but the disastrous experience with state and continental currencies during the Revolution was fresher in the minds of fiscal conservatives. An overwhelming fear of uncontrollable inflation caused many in the merchant-creditor faction, along with many Rhode Islanders in general, to oppose a new emission of paper money, no matter how serious the state's economic plight.

The struggle over paper money began in early 1784 when the towns of Westerly and Hopkinton petitioned the legislature for a state currency. These requests were summarily rejected. In February 1786 the Assembly rejected another appeal for paper money from ten of the state's thirty towns. The strong public demand for relief, however, forced the legislature to request the towns to consider paper money and to give their assemblymen instructions. This action was immensely important, for the town meeting was the seat of political power in Rhode Island. If enough towns favored paper money, the legislature would be obliged to enact some sort of fiscal relief. Twenty-seven towns instructed their assemblymen to support paper money, but despite this overwhelming endorsement, the Assembly again defeated the paper-money proposal in March 1786 by a vote of 43 to 18.

Proponents and opponents of paper money realized that the state's future fiscal policy depended on the upcoming elections in April. Consequently, a concerted effort was made to convince the public of the virtues and vices of paper money. William Ellery of Newport, a signer of the Declaration of Independence, ominously wrote that "we have been for many years free from party strife. This paper frenzy is like to kindle a war which may last for years."[1]

THE "REVOLUTION" OF 1786

The state election of 1786 was nothing less than a revolution. The Country party, running on the pledge "To Relieve the Distressed," elected a new governor and deputy governor and won control of both houses of the legislature. William Ellery lamented: "Paper money has carried all before it."[2]

The new Assembly met in early May and immediately suspended the collection of the last tax. Before the end of the month, the legislature authorized the emission of £100,000 of paper money to be loaned for fourteen years to any Rhode Islander who owned real estate worth double the value of the amount borrowed. Four percent annual interest was to be collected during the first seven years; thereafter one-seventh part of the principal was to be repaid annually. The money was declared legal tender. Creditors who refused a tender in paper money were liable to forfeit the debt to the state, while the obligation on the debtor was eliminated. Never before had such a radical legal-tender provision been established.

Almost immediately insults and ridicule were hurled upon the state. A correspondent from Hartford styled the act as "the most extraordinary that ever disgraced the annals of democratical tyranny." The writer lamented "the depravity of human nature" that could "sanctify such palpable fraud and dishonesty, by a solemn Act of legislation."[3] "Rogue Island" was charged with committing a crime against its people and the other states, while a Bostonian maintained that "Fool-Island" had demonstrated that it was incapable of governing itself "and therefore one of the Sister States must take them into her care and protection."[4]

By mid June £40,000 of paper money had been loaned, but the opposition persisted. Consequently the Country party decided to take drastic action. At its June session, the legislature passed a Penalty Act: anyone who refused to accept the currency at face value was subject to a £100 fine for the first offense, half going to the state and half to "the Person who shall inform." A second conviction carried the same fine and disenfranchisement. Despite the Penalty Act, the opposition to paper money continued. Country party leaders admonished farmers to withhold their produce from Providence and Newport—the heart of the opposition. The shortage of foodstuffs caused uneasiness in the towns, and open violence occurred in Newport. A correspondent charged that "the country people, influenced by a few designing worthless characters, are determined, by starving us out, as they style it, to compel us to swallow the paper money."[5] Only the timely intervention of the governor, the council, and a few influential citizens prevented a major conflict.[6] The governor, because of "the great Uneasiness now prevailing," called a special session of the legislature to consider the matter.[7]

The governor set the tone of the special session that convened on August 23 when he condemned the machinations of "a Combination of influential Men" who were attempting to defeat the intent of state laws. "The public Good must be the Pole Star—the Legislature must be wise—and the Executive decisive."[8] The legislature responded with an amendment to the Penalty Act aimed at producing swift and final action. The most odious provision of the act, according to the minority, provided that all paper-money cases were to be tried in special courts without juries and without the right to appeal.[9] The legislature also passed an act providing that Rhode Island's share of the congressional requisition could be paid in paper money.

On September 13, 1786, delegates from Providence County towns met at Smithfield to consider the merchants' continued opposition. The delegates attacked the subversive tendencies "of the mercantiled Interest" and proposed that the legislature consider several plans, one of which called for a state-trade system that would have effectively eliminated the merchant class. The proposal called for the state to own all stores, ships, wharves, shipyards, and the like. A state commission would send ships on fishing and mercantile ventures while severely limiting the importation of luxuries. The Smithfield Convention recommended that the legislature "take the lead in this business . . . in such manner, and under such regulation, as they in their wisdom shall think most convenient for the welfare, advantage, and well-being of the State."[10] The governor, at the request of the convention, called a special session of the legislature to meet on October 2 to consider the proposal. On September 28, Noah Mathewson reported that "a State Trade is now proposed & should it be adopted, would complete the mad system."[11]

Shortly after the Smithfield Convention adjourned, the state Superior Court considered a test case under the provisions of the second Penalty Act. In the case of *Trevett* v. *Weeden*, the defendant allegedly refused paper money at par in his butcher shop. The defense attorney argued that, according to the second Penalty Act, a special court (not the Superior Court) should hear the case and that the Penalty Act itself was unconstitutional because of the no-jury provision. Four of the five justices ruled that their court had no jurisdiction in the case. Despite the court's disclaimer of authority, it ruled the Penalty Act unconstitutional.[12]

At about the same time, the Country party suffered another rebuff. On September 18, Congress resolved that Rhode Island could not use its paper money to pay its continental taxes.[13] Country party leaders swallowed this bitter pill, but they would remember this congressional intrusion later when more important fiscal matters arose.

In this atmosphere of discontent the special session of the legislature met on October 2. A bipartisan committee recommended that all penalty acts and the tender provision be repealed. Country party leaders rejected the report and introduced a bill that would require everyone in Rhode Island to take an oath supporting paper money. Any citizen who refused would be disenfranchised; any lawyer who refused would be disbarred; any merchant who refused could not send or receive vessels; and any government official who refused would be turned out of office.[14] This "Test Act" was so controversial that the legislature sent it to the towns for their consideration. When the legislature reconvened on October 30, it found that only three towns favored the bill. The legislature then decisively defeated the measure, but a motion to repeal the tender provision was postponed to the next session.

The defeat of the Test Act worried Country party leaders, who feared their opponents more than ever. In December the legislature reconvened and repealed the two penalty acts. However, it strengthened the tender provision by making it easier for debtors to force creditors to accept a paper tender. The legislature also put severe limitations on mercantile credit instruments and promissory notes, proposed the repeal of Newport's city charter, and passed an excise tax, which fell heavily on the larger towns. Finally, the legislature voted to redeem one-quarter of the state debt with paper money. To some, these measures were still too limited. The *Providence Gazette* of January 6, 1787, reported that a bill introduced in the December session would abolish all debts and would distribute all property equally every thirteen years among heads of families.

Whether or not such a leveling bill was introduced in the legislature is uncertain. It might have been a Country party attempt to intimidate its opponents, or perhaps a Mercantile party plant to embarrass its opponents. Whatever the motivation, the newspaper report of the bill contributed to the mounting fear of Rhode Island's leveler tendencies—fear not only within the state, but nationwide. Within two months of its publication, the alleged bill was reprinted in at least eleven newspapers from Vermont to Georgia.

Much ado was made about the fraudulent abandonment of debts under the legal-tender provisions of the paper-money act. In reality, however, relatively few debtors took unfair advantage of the tender. More often the tender provision forced all Rhode Islanders to accept the currency and thus to absorb a sort of hidden tax as the money continued to depreciate.

Far more important was the redemption of the state debt. In March of 1787 a legislative committee estimated that the state debt amounted to almost £160,000, or nearly $545,000. This public debt was composed of two types of securities—£107,000 in six percent notes and £53,000 in four percent notes. Both kinds of securities had become concentrated in the hands of speculators. The legislature authorized the redemption of all of the state's six percent notes with paper money in four equal installments beginning at once.

With fiscal policy as the overriding issue, both parties readied themselves for the April state elections. The Country party "carried all before them" in the election with majorities of two to one in most contests. The Country party took the landslide victory as an endorsement of the proposed redemption of the state debt with depreciated paper money—money that had fallen to only one-sixth its face value. Consequently, additional acts were passed redeeming the balance of the six percent notes in quarterly installments in June of 1787, February of 1788, and May of 1788. Any public creditor who failed to submit his certificates to the treasurer within six weeks for payment of a quarter part of the face value in paper money would forfeit future claims on that quarter part of the securities.[15] The legislature ingeniously financed this redemption plan by levying taxes payable in paper money immediately after each quarter of the debt was paid. Thus a ready supply of paper money was available for the next quarter's payment. The result was that the six percent notes were redeemed with no excessive amount of taxation.

In October 1788 the legislature provided that the first quarter of the four percent notes should be redeemed. Opponents attacked this the four percent notes should be redeemed. Opponents attacked this second "procrastinated payment," which would be dragged out as long as possible in order to go back to the voters repeatedly with a "popular" program.[16] Country party leaders discredited this criticism by providing in December 1788 that all of the four percent notes should be redeemed in full in March of the following year. When March arrived the legislature, demonstrating its professed sense of fairness, extended the payment period to September for both the four and six percent note holders. Few public creditors took advantage of the extension. In fact, less than ten percent of the public debt was redeemed. Those public creditors who refused paper money once, refused it a second time.

The funding of the state debt with depreciated currency had drastically changed the fiscal situation of Rhode Island. By the end of 1789 the entire state debt had been either redeemed or forfeited. State expenses had been reduced to less than £10,000 annually, forty percent of which was paid by the interest on paper-money loans. With the state in such healthy fiscal condition, the Country party was willing to compromise. In September of 1789 the legislature temporarily repealed the tender provision until the next session a month later. In October the legislature made real estate and certain personal property payable for debts. The act also officially admitted that paper money had depreciated. A scale of depreciation set the final ratio at fifteen to one—fifteen dollars of paper was equal to one dollar of gold or silver coin. Rhode Island had completed the most extensive fiscal program in the country. By paying the public debt in depreciated currency, the Country party had indirectly redistributed the state's wealth. Had the redemption of the state debt not occurred, the gulf between the most wealthy speculators and the state's farmers would have widened significantly. Rhode Island's fiscal policy prevented this polarization and thus alleviated some of the farmers' hostilities that elsewhere erupted in violence; but, at the same time, Rhode Island had alienated its public creditors, the Confederation Congress, and its sister states.

RHODE ISLAND AND THE CONSTITUTIONAL CONVENTION

By 1787 the struggle in Rhode Island over paper money had become enmeshed in national issues. On February 21, 1787, Congress officially called a general convention to revise the Articles of Confederation.

One of the most important reasons for calling this convention was to give Congress power to restrict the radical policies of state legislatures. The policies of Rhode Island stood out above all others. Rhode Islanders knew that the proposed convention would consider measures antagonistic to its paper money and the impending redemption of its state debt with depreciated currency. After all, hadn't Congress already chastised Rhode Island in 1786 when it refused to accept the state's currency in payment of the congressional taxes? Therefore Country party leaders were suspicious of any attempt to broaden federal power at the expense of state sovereignty.

Soon after it convened in mid March 1787, the legislature read the congressional resolution calling the Constitutional Convention. A motion to appoint delegates to the convention was rejected by a two-to-one majority. When the new legislature met for the first time after the spring elections, assemblymen from Newport and Providence urged the appointment of convention delegates. Surprisingly, the Assembly agreed to the appointment by a majority of two of the seventy assemblymen. The measure, however, was killed when the Upper House, seemingly in a well-orchestrated Country party scenario, defeated the appointment by a two-to-one majority.[17]

In response to their state's isolationist policy, a committee of twelve merchants and tradesmen of Providence wrote a letter to the Constitutional Convention. "Deeply affected with the evils of the present unhappy times," the committee expressed the hope "of the well inform'd throughout this State" that Congress might be given additional powers over commerce and taxation. The committee asked that Gen. James M. Varnum, who carried the letter to Philadelphia, be allowed a seat in the convention "when the Commercial Affairs of the Nation are discuss'd."[18] The convention read the letter on May 28 but refused to allow General Varnum to sit as an informal delegate.

When the state legislature reconvened in mid June, the Upper House reversed its previous action and agreed to send a delegation to Philadelphia. The Assembly, however, on June 16, rejected the measure by a majority of seventeen.[19] Two days later, General Varnum wrote the president of the convention:

The measures of our present Legislature do not exhibit the real character of the State. They are equally reprobated, &

abhor'd by Gentlemen of the learned professions, by the whole mercantile body, & by most of the respectable farmers and mechanicks. The majority of the administration is composed of a licentious number of men, destitude of education, and many of them, Void of principle. From anarchy and confusion they derive their temporary consequence, and this they endeavor to prolong by debauching the minds of the common people, whose attention is wholly directed to the Abolition of debts both public and private.[20]

The response to Rhode Island's boycott of the convention was unanimous. A southern correspondent in the *Newport Herald* of April 12 hoped "when the convention meets in Philadelphia, that measures will be taken to reduce you to order and good government, or strike your State out of the union, and annex you to others; for as your Legislature now conducts, they are dangerous to the community at large." The *Pennsylvania Herald* of June 9 reported that the convention had resolved that "Rhode-Island should be considered as having virtually withdrawn herself from the union, and . . . upon no account shall she be restored to her station." By contrast, the May 19 *Massachusetts Centinel* maintained that Rhode Island's failure to appoint delegates was "a circumstance far *more joyous than grievous*; for her delinquency will not be permitted to defeat the salutary object of this body." In Virginia, William Nelson, Jr., hoped that Rhode Island "may not again attempt to shew, how the machine may be retarded, by one of it's most trifling wheels refusing to perform it's office."[21] William Grayson, a Virginia delegate to Congress, charged that the "cry" in Rhode Island "is for a good government, after they have paid their debts in depreciated paper: —first demolish the Philistines (i.e., their Creditors) & then for *propriety*."[22] On September 2 Francis Dana, a Massachusetts delegate to the Convention who was unable to attend because of illness, wrote his fellow delegate Elbridge Gerry that Rhode Island's "neglect will give grounds to strike it out of the Union & divide their Territory between their Neighbours."[23]

Because of this universal condemnation, the governor called a special session of the legislature to meet in mid September to appoint convention delegates. Instead, a joint legislative committee drafted a letter to Congress explaining why the state refused to send delegates. The letter, adopted on September 15, acknowledged that "many severe and unjust sarcasemes [had been] propagated against us" for refusing to send a delegation to Philadelphia. The legislature, however, maintained that it could not constitutionally appoint such a delegation because a state law provided that only the people could elect delegates to a convention intended to amend the Articles of Confederation. Nevertheless, the legislature intended to join "with our Sister States in being instrumental in what ever may be advantageous to the Union, and to add strength and permanance thereto, upon Constitutional principles." An official protest from the Newport and Providence assemblymen stated that "the Legislature have at various times agreed to Conventions with the Sister States" without violating "the Rights and Liberties of the Citizens of this State."[24] The letter and the protest were sent to Congress on September 17, the day that the Constitutional Convention adjourned. Congress read the Rhode Island communications on September 24.

THE STRUGGLE TO CALL A STATE CONVENTION

On September 28, Congress sent the Constitution to the states, recommending that they call special conventions chosen by the people to consider the new form of government. The previous day the Constitution had been printed for the first time in Rhode Island by the Providence *United States Chronicle*. On November 3 the state legislature ordered one thousand copies of the Constitution printed and distributed to the towns. The Assembly, however, rejected a motion calling a convention to ratify the Constitution. The pattern was set for the next two years.

The Constitution fared badly in Rhode Island for several reasons, foremost among which was the states' rights philosophy of most of the inhabitants. Because of its religious and economic unorthodoxy, Rhode Island for years had been maligned. Occasionally proposals were made to obliterate it as a political entity. Such suggestions increased because of the state's opposition to the new Constitution. These proposals merely strengthened the Country party's resolve to maintain its opposition to the Constitution.

Many Rhode Islanders opposed the Constitution because they believed it threatened their fiscal system. Generally the Country party favored paper money and opposed the Constitution, while the Mercantile party opposed state currency and supported the new government. Since the Constitution banned state paper money and protected the sanctity of contracts, there was some doubt about the effect ratification would have on the money in circulation and the public-debt redemption program. Would all money have to be recalled immediately? Could the state debt still be paid in depreciated currency? What measures could the legislature enact to support the currency? These were critical questions that no one could answer with complete assurance.[25]

The new year 1788 started optimistically for the Mercantile party. On January 1, the town of Little Compton instructed its assemblymen to "use their utmost Endeavours" to obtain a state ratifying convention.[26] Sixteen days later news arrived in Rhode Island that Georgia and Connecticut had ratified the Constitution, followed a month later by news of Massachusetts' accession.

When the legislature convened on February 25, the minority demanded a state convention. Four days later such a measure was defeated 43 to 15. Country party leaders proposed that the Constitution, like any other controversial issue, be submitted to the towns where the freemen could express their opinions directly. Such a referendum was approved on March 1 by a vote of 42 to 12. The legislature defeated a minority amendment to the referendum asking the freemen to instruct their assemblymen on the advisability of a state convention.[27]

The Rhode Island referendum was held on March 24, 1788, when the Constitution was rejected by a vote of 2,711 to 239. Only two of the thirty towns supported the Constitution—Bristol and Little Compton. Federalists in Newport and Providence boycotted the referendum so as not to expose their real statewide weakness. Providence, with about five hundred freemen, voted 1 to 0 against the Constitution, while Newport, with three to four hundred freemen, voted 10 to 1 against it. Newport, Providence, and Bristol instructed their assemblymen to try to get a state convention called to consider the Constitution.[28]

The legislature met in late March. On April 2 the Assembly rejected a motion calling a state convention by more than a two-to-one majority. The referendum was tabulated and a letter was prepared to Congress informing it of the results which were based "upon pure Republican Principles." Although the Constitution had been overwhelmingly defeated, the Assembly believed that it contained some necessary provisions that could be adapted to the Confederation government. Rhode Island, the letter indicated, would be willing to grant Congress the sole power to regulate commerce, but the Constitution as a whole was dead.[29]

As the April statewide elections neared, Rhode Islanders faced a clear decision. They could support either the Mercantile party and the new Constitution or the Country party and its fiscal policies. The election resulted in another landslide victory for the Country party. William Ellery lamented: "We are like to have much the same administration this as we had the last year. Indeed there is no probability that any material alteration will take place until our State debt is paid."[30] When a proposal was made for a state convention in the Assembly on June 14, the house brushed it aside without even taking a vote.

On June 26, news arrived in Rhode Island that New Hampshire had ratified the Constitution—the ninth state to do so. Soon a new government would be organized and Rhode Island would not be included. On July 5, news of Virginia's ratification was received. On July 28, William Ellery wrote his frequent correspondent Benjamin Huntington expressing the opinions of many Rhode Islanders: their state would "stand out as long [as] it can; but if New York accedes, it will, it must soon come in. If it should continue to be obstinate to the last; it is not invincible. It may be annihilated, and divided."[31] Ironically, the next day news arrived that New York had ratified the Constitution. Despite Ellery's predictions, the Country party was not ready to give up its fight—the state debt had not yet been completely redeemed.

The legislature met again in late October 1788. Federalists hoped that a convention would be called. Peleg Arnold, one of the state's delegates to Congress, wrote the governor that a convention could consider the Constitution "and make its objections to the particular parts that are incompatible with a good system of government, and make known to the states of the Union on what terms the State would join them."[32] Despite this appeal, the Assembly, for the fifth time, defeated a motion for a convention by a vote of 40 to 14. On the same day the Assembly rejected a motion to repeal the tender provision on state paper money.

On the last day of the session, Country party leaders agreed to send the towns' copies of New York's proposed amendments to the Constitution and its Circular Letter calling for a second general convention of the states to consider amendments to the Constitution. The towns were asked to instruct their assemblymen whether Rhode Island should comply with the Circular Letter and appoint delegates to the proposed general convention.[33]

Nine towns voted to send a delegation to a second convention, five voted to call a state convention, and sixteen did not instruct their assemblymen. The Assembly ushered in the new year on January 1, 1789, by rejecting another motion for a state convention by a vote of 34 to 12.[34]

By March of 1789 Rhode Island Federalists were more alarmed than ever before. The new federal Congress was scheduled to convene on March 4, and their state still had not called a convention to consider the Constitution. On March 10, a Providence town meeting instructed its assemblymen to seek a convention, asserting that "a new Era in the Political Affairs of this Country has taken Place"— an era that saw Rhode Island "stand perfectly alone, unconnected with any State or Sovereignty on Earth."[35] Unless the legislature called a convention to ratify the Constitution, the state was doomed. On March 13, the Assembly again rejected a motion for a convention.[36] The Country party had not yet "extinguished the State debt," therefore ratification would have to wait.[37]

Two weeks after this latest defeat, twelve prominent Rhode Island Federalists wrote President George Washington asking him and Congress to make a public appeal to Rhode Islanders. Only in this way could enough upright men be elected to the legislature in April to pass a convention bill.[38] Washington, however, was not inaugurated until after the state elections. Jeremiah Wadsworth of Connecticut advised Rhode Island Federalists to make public, "Manly" overtures to Congress requesting that body to use force, if necessary, to command obedience from the recalcitrant state. If public overtures were considered too dangerous, secret remonstrances should be submitted. Wadsworth also added that Connecticut recruits might be sent to assist Rhode Island Federalists in their struggle.[39]

The Country party again easily won control of the legislature at the April elections. In May the Assembly postponed consideration of the convention question until June. The legislature then provided that Rhode Island would comply with the provisions of Congress's expected tariff. Federalists attacked this "sham acquiescence" that was obviously an effort to appease Congress and avoid economic sanctions.[40] When the legislature reconvened in June, the Assembly again defeated the call for a convention and the repeal of the tender provision.[41]

By September 1789 the entire state debt had been paid or forfeited. Country party leaders realized that Rhode Island would have to ratify the Constitution soon if they wanted to maintain political power within the state. A prolonged delay might result in congressional military or economic intervention. In either case, Federalists would blame the Country party. But how could the Country party embrace the new form of government after having denounced it for two years? Simply put, the Country party had to find a way to ratify the Constitution without appearing inconsistent, at the same time not giving credit to its opponents. Since the Country party controlled both houses of the legislature and the executive offices, it would be difficult to obtain ratification without appearing to repudiate its two-year stand. An ingenious plan was needed.

On September 15, 1789, a special session of the legislature convened. Two days later, at the request of Country party leaders, the legislature passed an act requiring the towns to hold meetings on October 19 at which the freemen would be asked to vote on whether or not the legislature should call a convention.[42] On September 19 the legislature approved a letter to Congress assuring it of Rhode Island's friendship and praying that discriminatory measures not be enacted against the state. A week later Congress recommended twelve amendments to the Constitution to be considered by the state legislatures.[43] Then another special session of the Rhode Island legislature ordered that 150 copies of the amendments—the future U.S. Bill of Rights—be printed and sent to the towns for consideration. When the regular session of the legislature convened on October 26, it was thought that a majority of the assemblymen favored the call for a convention, but enough towns had instructed their delegates against the measure that it was defeated for the ninth time.[44]

The year 1790 looked ominous for Rhode Island. North Carolina had ratified the Constitution in November of 1789, leaving Rhode Island alone out of the Union. Congress had previously set January

15, 1790, as the date when economic sanctions against Rhode Island would commence if the state had not yet called a convention to ratify the Constitution. No one knew what else Congress might do, but Federalist James Manning of Providence believed that the federal government would "address our feelings, as they cannot operate on our reason."[45] Federalists in the large towns went so far as to ask President Washington if he and Congress would protect their towns if they seceded from the state and joined the Union.[46]

When the legislature reconvened on January 11, it was believed that the Assembly was equally divided and the Upper House slightly opposed to calling a convention. On Friday, January 15, the Assembly narrowly passed a convention bill by a vote of 34 to 29. The following day the Upper House defeated the measure 5 to 4. The Upper House wanted to resubmit the question to the freemen in their towns, but the Assembly rejected this idea. The Assembly passed another convention bill, which the Upper House rejected at 10:00 P.M. on Saturday. In an extraordinary Sunday session on January 17, the Assembly passed its third convention bill by a vote of 32 to 11. When the Upper House considered this bill, it was split 4 to 4—one of the members had left for home the previous day. The governor, a Country party man but a friend to the Constitution, then cast the deciding vote in favor of the convention. On Monday the act was sent to President Washington along with a resolve asking Congress to suspend its discriminatory measures against Rhode Island.[47]

Convention Politics

The election of the seventy convention delegates occurred on February 8. The most optimistic Federalist reported that opponents of the Constitution had a majority of six delegates. More pessimistic Federalists feared the majority was as high as seventeen.[48]

The convention assembled on March 1 at Little Rest in South Kingstown, a Country party stronghold. The convention read the Constitution and considered it "Generally." A committee drafted and reported a bill of rights and amendments to the Constitution. Federalists wanted to vote on the Constitution, but Country party leaders opted for one more delay. On March 6 the convention voted 41 to 28 to adjourn without taking a vote on the Constitution. The delegates agreed to reconvene eleven weeks later in Newport. Deputy-Governor Daniel Owen, the president of the convention, admitted privately that the adjournment was necessary to ensure a Country party victory in the April elections. In the interim, the proposed bill of rights and amendments could be considered by the freemen in their town meetings on election day, April 21.[49]

During the week that the convention met, Country party leaders held secret "nocturnal caucuses." On March 6, after the convention adjourned, a final caucus occurred at which a slate of candidates for state offices was adopted. Governor John Collins was dropped from the slate and replaced by Deputy-Governor Owen. This unexpected switch was, in reality, a carefully planned strategy. Even though the Country party controlled both houses of the legislature, they had maneuvered the voting so that all the attention and opprobrium was focused on the governor's casting of the vote that enabled a convention to be called. Collins, an ardent paper-money man, had few friends among Federalists. But as a friend of the Constitution, he was considered expendable by the Country party. Consequently, Collins was dropped from the Country party slate and was personally blamed for calling the convention. In this way the Country party escaped responsibility for calling the convention but denied Federalists the credit (if there was going to be any credit). Thus, even though the Country party–dominated legislature had called a convention, the Country party could still run in the April elections as opponents of the Constitution. John Collins would serve well as a sacrificial lamb. Two weeks later, Owen resigned from the slate and was replaced by Arthur Fenner of Providence, described as "a violent Anti."[50] The Country party again won control of the Assembly, although only with a majority of five, and of the Upper House.

Some adamant Country party Antifederalists spoke of circumventing the convention by having the legislature at its May session resubmit the Constitution directly to the people. Enough Country party members sided with Federalists to thwart such action. William Ellery reported "that the Antis, in private conversations with the Feds, have talked more favorably respecting an accession to" the Constitution. A resubmission to the people, however, was almost tantamount to rejection. Such a proposal, therefore, frightened Country party leaders almost as much as Federalists. Most legislators believed that ratification was near, and they wished to do nothing to jeopardize the chances of adoption.[51]

For months, Rhode Island Federalists had advocated that Congress pass restrictive legislation that would affect Rhode Island's commerce. Finally, on May 13, 1790, the U.S. Senate took decisive action, passing a bill to boycott Rhode Island. No American ships could enter Rhode Island, and no Rhode Island ships could enter the United States. The same restrictions applied to commerce by land. Violators would be punished with forfeiture, fines up to $500, and imprisonment for six months. To add more pressure on Rhode Island, the Senate bill demanded that the recalcitrant state pay Congress $25,000 by December 1, 1790, in payment of Rhode Island's share of the expenses of the old government. When newly elected Governor Fenner heard about the bill, he immediately wrote President Washington saying that there was no reason for Congress to pursue such actions. "Many persons of influence who have heretofore opposed the Adoption of the new Constitution here, have withdrawn their opposition." Surely the state would ratify the Constitution at the next session of the convention.[52] Rhode Island Federalists were not so confident. A Providence town meeting instructed its convention delegates to meet with delegates from Newport and other towns if the convention failed to ratify the Constitution. The delegates were empowered to apply to Congress for protection if and when the towns seceded from the state.[53]

RHODE ISLAND IN THE UNION

The convention met on Monday, May 24, in Newport. For several days little of real importance occurred — a few amendments to the Constitution were proposed and accepted, but the opponents of the Constitution put forth only token opposition. Federalists, however, were still fearful. Newport delegate Henry Marchant wrote that "we had an anxious arduous & distressing week. Nor were we much encouraged in Success till within a few Hours of the Question being taken. For when we met at the beginning of the Week they were twelve Majority against Us."[54] Finally, on May 29, the important question was called. Four Country party Antifederalists were absent. The tense roll call was taken and the Constitution was ratified 34 to 32, after which a proposed bill of rights and amendments were also accepted.[55]

Immediately after the convention adjourned, President Daniel Owen sent word to President Washington that Rhode Island had ratified. Two weeks later, Congress acted to put several federal laws into effect in Rhode Island. The state was back in the Union. President Washington congratulated Rhode Island "upon this event which unites under one general government all the branches of the great American family."[56]

For the next sixteen years, until his death, Governor Arthur Fenner molded a nonpartisan coalition in state government that generally presented a united front on national issues. The cooperation of old enemies was perhaps best illustrated when former Country party leaders worked successfully to have Congress assume much of Rhode Island's state debt that had either been forfeited or had been redeemed with depreciated paper money. The small portion of the state debt not assumed by the federal government was then funded by the state legislature. Thus, in the final analysis, Rhode Island public creditors were not permanently hurt by the events of 1786–89. The financial burdens on debtors and taxpayers had been eased during those difficult years, but in the end, the public creditors got paid in full and the state benefited.

Rhode Island, the smallest state in the Union, played a major role in the drafting and ratification of the Constitution. Its immediate importance was as a symbol of the pervasive problems under the Articles of Confederation.

It was Rhode Island that rejected the Impost of 1781, thus dooming it. The fact that Virginia rescinded its ratification of the impost on December 6, 1782, and New York repealed its ratification on March 15, 1783, went virtually unnoticed. Symbolically, it was more effective to say that the smallest state thwarted the will of the other twelve states.

Rhode Island's solitary boycotting of the Constitutional Convention also served to set the state apart as the "unhappy, fallen, lost sister."[57] Federalists used Rhode Island's refusal to appoint Convention delegates as a justification for the Constitution's provision giving Congress power to regulate federal elections — one of the Antifederalists' most objectionable provisions of the Constitution. If a state failed to elect federal senators and representatives, as Rhode Island had failed to appoint convention delegates, Congress would, out of self-preservation, have to step in and provide for an election.

Finally, the radicalism of Rhode Island's fiscal policies was a godsend for Federalist propagandists. Just as proponents of a stronger central government used Shays's Rebellion to convince Americans of the necessity of a constitutional convention to revise the Articles of Confederation, so too was Rhode Island's experience used. Shays's Rebellion was, in fact, quashed by the state militia. How, it was asked, could the constitutionally elected state government of Rhode Island, radical as it was, be controlled under the Articles of Confederation? The answer was simple — it couldn't be controlled. Furthermore, what happened in Rhode Island could happen in other states. Therefore a constitution had to be established that would protect life, liberty, and property from the ravages of uncontrollable state governments. Thus the symbol of Rhode Island was powerful. According to Oliver Ellsworth, writing as "Landholder," "the little state of Rhode-Island was purposely left by Heaven to its present madness, for a general conviction in the other states, that such a system as is now proposed is our only preservation from ruin."[58]

Tiny Rhode Island stood as a symbol of its own self-preservation. Whatever its reasons, it held to the principle that its own interests came first. Yet ironically, in the very process of preserving its interests, Rhode Island promoted federal power, and in the end, strengthened the union.

NOTES

1. William Ellery to Benjamin Huntington, Newport, 11 April 1786, Thomas C. Bright Autograph Collection, Jervis Library, Rome, N.Y.

2. Ellery to Huntington, Newport, 25 April 1786, Huntington Autograph Book, Jervis Library, Rome, N.Y.

3. *United States Chronicle* (Providence), 1 June 1786.

4. "Jonathan," ibid., 25 May 1786.

5. "Extract of a letter from a gentleman in Providence, R.I., to his friend at the southward, dated 1 July 1786," *New Jersey Gazette* (Trenton), 28 August 1786.

6. John Brown, *Providence Gazette*, 8 July 1786; *New Haven Gazette*, 27 July 1786; *Newport Mercury*, 7 August 1786.

7. *United States Chronicle*, 17 August 1786.

8. Ibid., 7 September 1786.

9. *Providence Gazette*, 2 September 1786.

10. Ibid., 30 September 1786; "W.B.," *United States Chronicle*, 21 September 1786.

11. Noah Mathewson to Noah Webster, 28 September 1786, Webster Papers, New York Public Library.

12. James M. Varnum, *The Case, Trevett against Weeden* (Providence, 1787); *United States Chronicle*, 5 October 1786.

13. *United States Chronicle*, 12 October 1786.

14. Ibid.

15. Extensions were frequently granted. See *Newport Herald*, 22 November 1787.

16. Ibid., 6 November 1787; *Daily Advertiser* (New York), 15 December 1787.

17. *Newport Herald*, 22 March and 10 May 1787.

18. 11 May 1787, Brown Misc. Papers, John Carter Brown Library.

19. *Newport Herald*, 21 June 1787.

20. Newport, 18 June 1787, *The Records of the Federal Convention of 1787*, ed. Max Farrand, rev. ed., 4 vols. (New Haven, Conn.: Yale University Press, 1937), 3:47–48.

21. William Nelson, Jr., to James Madison, New York, 7 May 1787, Madison Papers, Library of Congress.

22. William Grayson to James Monroe, New York, 29 May 1787, Monroe Papers, ser. 1, Library of Congress.

23. L. W. Smith Collection, Morristown National Historical Park, Morristown, N.J.

24. RG 360, Papers of the Continental Congress, item 64:600–603, National Archives.

25. William Ellery to Benjamin Huntington, Newport, 30 September 1788, Huntington Autograph Book.

26. Papers Relating to the Adoption of the Federal Constitution, 56, Rhode Island State Archives.

27. *Newport Herald*, 6 March 1788.

28. Providence Town Records, 24–26 March 1788, 2:4766–67, 4785, Rhode Island Historical Society; Newport Town Records, 24–28 March 1788, 1:146–49, Newport Historical Society; Bristol Town Meeting, [24] March 1788, Papers Relating to the Adoption of the Federal Constitution, 109, Rhode Island State Archives.

29. John Collins to the President of Congress, 5 April 1788, Letters from the Governor, 4:76, Rhode Island State Archives; *Newport Herald*, 10 April 1788.

30. William Ellery to Benjamin Huntington, Newport, 22 April 1788, Thomas C. Bright Autograph Collection.

31. Newport, 28 July 1788, Thomas C. Bright Autograph Collection.

32. Letters to the Governor, 20:117, Rhode Island State Archives.

33. *Newport Herald*, 6 November 1788.

34. Ibid., 8 January and 14 May 1789.

35. Providence Town Records, City Clerk's Office, Providence City Hall.

36. *Newport Herald*, 19 March 1789.

37. William Ellery to Benjamin Huntington, Newport, 10 March 1789, Ellery Letters, Rhode Island State Archives.

38. Rhode Island Gentlemen to George Washington, Providence, 27 March 1789, RG 59, Misc. Letters, Department of State Records, National Archives.

39. Jeremiah Wadsworth to William Arnold, Esq. & Messrs. Brown & Francis, Hartford, 19 April 1789, Letters of Members of the Continental Congress, ed. Edmund C. Burnett, 8 vols. (Washington, D.C.: Carnegie Institution, 1921–36), 8:819 n.

40. *Newport Herald*, 14 May 1789; William Ellery to Benjamin Huntington, Newport, 14 May and 15 June 1789, Ellery Letters, Rhode Island State Archives; Ellery to William Duer, Newport, 21 May 1789, Duer Papers, B. V. 2:49, New-York Historical Society.

41. *Newport Herald*, 18 June 1789; *United States Chronicle*, 18 June 1789; William Ellery to Benjamin Huntington, Newport, 15 June 1789, Ellery Letters, Rhode Island State Archives.

42. *Newport Herald*, 24 September 1789.

43. Letters from the Governor, 4:77, Rhode Island State Archives.

44. *Newport Herald*, 5 November 1789.

45. James Manning to Timothy Green, Providence, 9 December 1789, Timothy and Timothy R. Green Papers, Duke University Library.

46. Jabez Bowen to George Washington, Providence, 15 December 1789, RG 360, Papers of the Continental Congress, item 78, 10:613, National Archives; William Ellery to Benjamin Huntington, Newport, 17 April and 3 May 1790, Ellery Letters, Rhode Island State Archives.

47. *Newport Herald*, 21 and 28 January 1790.

48. Jeremiah Olney to Alexander Hamilton, Providence, 12 February 1790, Olney Papers, Rhode Island Historical Society; John Francis to John McClellan, Providence, 5 March 1790, McClellan Papers, Connecticut Historical Society; William Peck to Henry Knox, Providence, 15 February 1790, Knox Papers, Massachusetts Historical Society; Henry Marchant to John Adams, Newport, 7 March 1790, Adams Papers, Massachusetts Historical Society.

49. *Theodore Foster's Minutes of the Convention held at South Kingstown . . .* , ed. Robert C. Cotner (Providence: Rhode Island Historical Society, 1929).

50. William Ellery to Benjamin Huntington, Newport, 28 March and 5 April 1790, Ellery Letters, Rhode Island State Archives; Henry Marchant to John Adams, Newport, 7 March 1790, Adams Papers, Massachusetts Historical Society; John Collins to George Washington, Newport, 24 May 1790, Washington Papers, ser. 7, Library of Congress; John P. Kaminski, "Political Sacrifice and Demise: John Collins and Jonathan J. Hazard, 1786–1790," *Rhode Island History*, 35

(1976): 90–98; Daniel Owen Circular Letter, Providence, 29 March 1790, Rhode Island Historical Society.

51. William Ellery to Benjamin Huntington, Newport, 11 May 1790, Ellery Letters, Rhode Island State Archives; Ellery to John Adams, Newport, 13 May 1790, Adams Papers, Massachusetts Historical Society.

52. Providence, 20 May 1790, RG 59, Misc. Letters, Department of State Records, National Archives.

53. Providence Town Meeting, 24 May 1790, Providence Town Papers, 13:5627–28, Rhode Island Historical Society; Providence Town Records, City Clerk's Office, Providence City Hall.

54. Henry Marchant to Sarah Marchant, Newport, 9 June 1790, in Cotner, *Theodore Foster's Minutes*, pp. 26–27.

55. Daniel Updike's Minutes of the Newport Convention, Papers Relating to the Adoption of the Federal Constitution, Rhode Island State Archives.

56. 9 June 1790, Washington Papers, letterbook 7, Library of Congress.

57. "A Citizen of Pennsylvania," *Pennsylvania Packet* (Philadelphia), 12 October 1787.

58. "Landholder" V, *Connecticut Courant* (Hartford), 3 December 1787.

AFTERWORD

Wilson Carey McWilliams

The ratification of the United States Constitution was an occasion for compunction as well as celebration. Greeting the new government with hope, most Americans also felt a measure of regret. Even the Constitution's friends quarreled with this or that provision, and for others, more basic doubts inspired darker reflection.[1]

On matters of principle, the arguments against the Constitution had seemed at least as weighty as those in its favor. "Fundamental revolutionary theory," as Banning observes, was an Antifederalist talking point, and not only in Virginia. The Constitution prevailed only because its moderate critics, such as Hancock and Adams in Massachusetts, were persuaded that there was no practicable alternative and because it appealed to sometimes contradictory local interests. As Shumer argues, democrats in New Jersey felt compelled to sacrifice their political principles in order to advance the economic interests of the state. In Maryland, Onuf demonstrates, a small state's fear of having too weak a voice in national councils was overborne by the desire to lay claim to a share of the benefits of lands and resources. Austerity, an old republican watchword, rallied few supporters, and Antifederalists were not alone in wondering whether events were validating Jefferson's earlier fear that after the war, public virtue would go "down hill," until Americans would forget everything but "the sole faculty of making money."[2]

After all, the Constitution compromised the most fundamental of political principles by accommodating slavery. Even slavery's partisans

391

conceded as much, as Weir reminds us: Rutledge did not deny that "religion and humanity" are ranged against slavery, and Charles Cotesworth Pinckney observed that South Carolina could speak of natural rights, founded on human liberty, only "with very bad grace." Moreover, as Yarbrough indicates, New Hampshire delegates—already uneasy about the place of religion in the new secular order—were surely right in holding that the slave clauses, especially the provision regarding fugitive slaves, made all Americans accomplices in slavery. The conscience of any reflective citizen was bound to be troubled, shadowed by the recognition that the Republic teetered on contradictions. And while the founding fathers allowed themselves to hope that time and progress would resolve the problem, they were too shrewd to expect it.[3]

Beyond slavery, the republican foundation of the Constitution was still in question. No one doubted, of course, that republican rule rests on popular judgment and majority rule. James Wilson, as Graham makes clear, was emphatic in appealing to the "Power of the People" as a first and ruling precept, and Banning recalls Madison's equally strong insistence that government, under the Constitution, would be directed by the people at large. Jefferson expected the quality of the House of Representatives to be inferior to that of the Confederation Congress, but he thought this "evil" less important than "the fundamental principle that the people are not to be taxed but by representatives chosen immediately by themselves."[4]

In fact, this very majoritarianism troubled Antifederalists. As Tocqueville was to observe, the United States Constitution recognizes no source of public authority other than majority rule, and it acknowledges no limit on the rightful power of a majority which is sufficiently strong and determined. The Constitution checks and balances majorities, but it does not establish or even mention any other legitimate basis for rule. Unlike the Declaration of Independence or the Articles of Confederation, the Constitution does not concede that God grants or limits secular authority, and while the Framers surely believed that the Constitution rests on the principles of the Declaration, they made no explicit appeal to natural right.[5] By contrast, a great many Antifederalists called for a Constitutional affirmation of divine supremacy, and virtually all of them advocated a Constitution prefaced by a statement of fundamental principles and natural rights, a "sacred text," as Lienesch calls North Carolina's Declaration, of republican civil religion.

Compelled and persuaded to concede a Bill of Rights, Madison and his allies rejected that sort of prefatory palladium. They gave us amendments, or limitations *enacted* by positive law (and theoretically, subject to repeal), rather than the principles *declared* on the basis of natural law. Even the most sacred rights, under the Constitution, are subject to the judgment of the people. In this sense, Federalists — despite their criticism of democratic practice — were more democratic in their first principles than were their Antifederalist opponents.

The great question for any republican or democratic theory, however, is the ground for its confidence in the people's capacity for self-rule. In general, Federalists were inclined to rely on an abstract and negative case for political equality, premised on the denial that there is any natural "jurisdiction and dominion" which subordinates one to another. Human beings, by nature, are preeminently free, each having an "equal right . . . to his natural freedom, without being subjected to the will or authority of any other man." Despite our unequal merits, political equality is defensible because it is morally inescapable; legitimate authority can only be the creation of consent.[6]

Naturally independent, human beings begin as so many separate bodies, moved by instinct and passion. From that premise, however, the argument diverged. A great many Federalists were content with a second negative defense of political equality, based on the conviction that all human beings are moved by self-interest. Their ends, consequently, are equal or, at least, equally suspect; human beings differ only in their skill in choosing means. As in the Federalist appeals that Onuf describes, interest guided by reason is the standard for law.

Other Federalists were not satisfied with this negative case. Graham draws attention to James Wilson's contention that all human beings possess a moral sense or instinct which affords a universal ground for obligation and duty. Like Jefferson's similar appeal to the "heart," this doctrine follows Locke in rooting morality in the body and the inclinations of the individual. However, it gives democracy a stronger claim, a public prescription supposedly derived from private feeling.[7]

These arguments were virtually the grammar of public discourse in eighteenth-century America, and they underlie the frame and language of the Constitution. During the ratification debate, even opponents were constrained to speak a similar idiom. The Kentucky Antifederalist "Republicus" held that reason is the first law of nature, entitled to overrule both desire and self-preservation. Even so, he felt compelled to derive civil liberty from the original "freedom of mankind, in an unconnected state," although he balked at conceding more than that "some say" that such a state is natural.[8] Lienesch's fine discussion of ratification in North Carolina shows the elisions by which Antifederalists moved away from speaking of rights as "communal and constitutive" in favor of a language of private and individual liberty.

Both "enlightened self-interest" and the "moral sense" are premised on individualism, since both doctrines insist that public principles derive from and must prove themselves in the private tribunals of the self. Ordained in the language of law, such teachings shape the ways in which we speak and think about public life. For example, Madison phrased the Bill of Rights as barriers against government. Consequently, trial by jury is referred to as a right of the accused and not — which Antifederalist writers had urged — as the "democratical balance" of the judiciary.[9] And the assertion that a "free state" depends on popular service in the militia is followed, not by the proclamation of our duty to serve in the military, but by a right "to keep and bear arms" which "shall not be infringed," thus contributing to contemporary confusions.

Teaching us that "rights are trumps," or protections against politics, individualistic doctrine begins by weakening the claims of public life and duty. As Tocqueville prophesied, however, individualism gradually enfeebles all feelings of obligation, relaxing the bonds of family, friendship, and community.[10] It is no surprise, consequently, that Robert Bellah and his associates find that contemporary Americans, seeking to explain and justify their lives, are virtually confined to the languages of individualism, whether they appeal to utilitarianism ("enlightened self-interest") or personal expression (the "moral instinct").[11]

At the time of the founding, however, Biblical religion and republican theory gave Americans other articulate ways of understanding themselves and political life. In those earlier teachings, while a people's capacity for self-government derives from nature, it is realized through practice and right custom. *Federalist* 71 argues that the people are morally adequate but technically deficient; more traditional Americans—Antifederalists, but also supporters of the Constitution such as Benjamin Rush—held that the people need education to direct them to proper or natural *ends*. They distrusted instincts and untutored passions which might tempt individuals "against the *Law of Nature*, to seek a *single* and independent state."[12] As the Antifederalist "Sidney" reminded his readers, "To err is inseparable from human nature."[13] According to this view, republican rule requires that citizens be schooled to civic dignity and responsibility, a sense of their own rights and a respect for the rights of others, and, so far as possible, a devotion to the public good. "Let our pupil be taught," Rush advised, "that he does not belong to himself, but that he is public property."[14]

The principles of our government are "peculiar," Jefferson wrote in *Notes on Virginia*, since they require that personal freedom be combined with public responsibility, a "temperate liberty" which cannot be mastered without early rearing or long experience.[15] Liberty, "William Penn" argued for Pennsylvania's Antifederalists, is "the unlimited power of doing good," not simply the absence of restraint. Our natural rights presume a knowledge of the good, which can be discovered or approximated only by "painful researches" and in society. Experience is a good guide, but it is fallible, since its steps are "often interrupted," and therefore it needs the guidance of philosophy. In America, however, this higher understanding of natural right, ordinarily known only to a few, is "engraved in the hearts of every American" and expressed in the state constitutions. American custom, "Penn" was arguing, is rare and fragile, deserving both an "awful reverence" and the support of the law.[16]

The curriculum of civic virtue, after all, is a stern school, both Christian and Spartan in Sam Adams's celebrated vision. Biblical and republican teachings did not encourage a belief in disinterestedness; they held that the Old Adam persists and that the temptation to self-interest is never overcome. Custom and moral education need *force* to overcome the temptations of interest; as merely private virtues, good habits will wear away with the passing of time.[17] They need the championship of law and, since the spirit also has its needs and temptations, the sanction of religion. New Hampshire's Antifederalists were concerned for their established church; Benjamin Rush proposed to use the Bible as a schoolbook.[18] And as that suggests, many of the new government's friends shared the Antifederalist fear that the Constitution endangers civic virtue, both by neglect and by promoting the pursuit of gain.[19]

Eubanks is right to stress the importance of class issues in the New York debate, for Melancton Smith's defense of the "middling class" involves a crucial principle. Smith contended that unlike the rich, the middle classes have become accustomed to "set bounds to their passions and appetites."[20] The virtue of the "substantial yeomanry" is temperance or moderation. But for ancient political philosophy, temperance is a virtue associated with oligarchy, not democracy.[21] The ancients also associated oligarchy with commerce, because in both, the ruling principle is the pursuit of wealth. Americans, however, assumed that their republic would be more or less commercial and, consequently, that public spirit constantly would be endangered by the quest for affluence. Those who are engrossed with wealth, "Centinel" wrote, are "the last to take alarm when public liberty is threatened," and "Maryland Farmer" warned against avarice, "the cankerworm of public and private virtue."[22] Because American laws could regulate but not exclude commerce, it was necessary to strengthen the psychological barriers against commercial excess, and even oligarchic virtues had their attraction.[23] However, as "Federal Farmer" remarked in a somewhat broader context, this policy is "evidently not the natural basis of the proposed constitution."[24]

Beyond the restraint of vice, traditional republicanism aimed at a positive "confidence in and respect for the laws," hoping "to arm persuasion on every side, and to render force as little necessary as possible."[25] Republican government, if not limited to localities small enough to enable the people to assemble and deliberate, must at least be rooted in such local forums.[26] In small polities, it also is easier for citizens to aspire to office, and republicanism hoped to teach citizens, through "a general spirit of emulation," to associate personal dignity with public life and responsibility for the common good.[27] That educational strategy, of course, was the foundation of the well-established practices of jury service, rotation in office, and frequent elections.[28] A similar concern was central to the demand for a "numerous representation" and for districts small enough to make it likely that representatives would be tied to their constituents by "sympathy and fellow feeling" as well as a knowledge of their interests.[29] Political friendship, a bond of speech and sentiment, is necessary to afford citizens the strongest possible sense of being spoken for and its corollary, an equally strong disposition to abide by the decisions of representative assemblies. In large districts, "Brutus" wrote, citizens

> will, probably, not know the characters of their own members . . . and they will have no persons so immediately of their choice so near them, of their neighbors and of their own rank in life, that they can feel themselves secure in trusting their interests in their hands. The representatives of the people cannot, as they now do, mix with the people and explain to them the motives which induced the adoption of any measure, point out its utility and remove or silence unreasonable clamours against it. . . . They will not be viewed by the people as a part of themselves, but as a body distinct from them and having separate interests to pursue: the consequence will be that a perpetual jealousy will exist in the minds of the people against them; their conduct will be narrowly watched; their measures scrutinized; and their laws opposed, evaded or reluctantly obeyed.[30]

Perhaps Brutus exaggerated the immediate dangers, but it is hard, after observing contemporary American politics, not to conclude that he was right.

After ratification, the critics of the Constitution and those who shared their concern for civic virtue turned to new expedients. They attempted to use the Bill of Rights as a bastion of civic dignity, making the bearing of rights into a partial substitute for a larger sharing in rule. Or they gave devoted attention to local communities, to schools and to churches, seeking to shore up what Tocqueville would call "the habits of the heart." These strategies have enjoyed varying measures of success; if Bellah is right, however, our old habits are losing their voices if not their claims on our hearts, and they risk final defeat in their contest with the laws. But when "Federal Farmer" wrote that the "natural basis" of the Constitution is not friendly to civic virtue, he left open the possibility that the two might be conciliated somewhat by art and craft, the practice of politics. So they have been, through much of American political history, and so they can be.

Gillespie's admirable essay restores Hancock and Adams to their proper stature among the founders of the republic. And there is a special contemporary importance to the fact that Adams, like so many of his contemporaries, appreciated the ancient reasoning that associates democracy with custom and right opinion.

Ordinary citizens, caught up in the demands of daily life, cannot be expected to master changing and intricate legislation. Reformed and arcane laws make citizens dependent on — and subject to being gulled by — the "enlightened and aspiring few." The public is most competent and most autonomous when laws are as familiar as folk songs, especially where government is simple, rather than "misterious," and close at hand, subject to observation and control.

Yet, Adams was able to translate the case for the Constitution into the language of custom, suggesting that experience attested to the need for ratification. So understood, the Constitution rests on practice rather than theory, and by promoting that view, Adams also implicitly deprecated the doctrine of the Framers. Paradoxically, the republican case for custom, a vital part of the Antifederalist brief against the Constitution, is now perhaps the strongest argument in its defense. Having become commonplace, the Constitution is an invaluable bulwark of what remains of our common life.

To credit Hancock and Adams is also to recognize the bittersweet quality of their statecraft, founded as it was on the disjunction of theory and practice. Neither Adams nor Hancock regarded the Constitution as an ideal republic or even, apparently, the best possible government for eighteenth-century America. Yet they were prepared to concede that the Constitution, once proposed, might be the best practicable regime, the only chance for a "more perfect Union." Doubtless, it still is. To say this is not to forget the Constitution's flaws: it is to emphasize the need for a politics and a citizenship able to tend and mend that grand but imperfect charter.

NOTES

1. Praising Madison's contribution to *The Federalist*, Jefferson observed that "in some parts, it is discoverable that the author means only to say what may be best said in defense of opinions with which he did not concur." And Jefferson

himself raised, with approval, the possibility of a second convention. See *The Life and Selected Writings of Thomas Jefferson*, ed. Adrienne Koch and William Peden (New York: Modern Library, 1944), pp. 452, 439.

2. Ibid., p. 277.

3. Allan Nevins, *The Emergence of Lincoln*, 2 vols. (New York: Scribners, 1950), 1:392.

4. Koch and Peden, *Life and Selected Writings*, p. 437.

5. This omission was considered. Such a "display of theory," Edmund Randolph argued, would be inappropriate, "since we are not working upon the natural rights of men not yet gathered into society, but upon those rights modified by society and interwoven with what we call the rights of the States" (cited by Charles Warren in *The Making of the Constitution* [Cambridge, Mass.: Harvard University Press, 1937], pp. 392–93). Natural right might be dangerous, in other words, since the Constitution presumes the existence of, and seeks to protect, conventional right. Later, Justice William Paterson argued that the Constitution was a compromise between fundamental principles and political necessity and hence cannot be assumed to enact natural right. His view accepts natural right as a goal for policy but not as imperative for practice. And the judgment of political necessity and of the extent to which natural right can be realized lies ultimately with the people (*Calder v. Bull*, 3 Dallas 386, 1798).

6. John Locke, *Second Treatise of Government*, par. 54.

7. Koch and Peden, *Life and Selected Writings*, pp. 395–407, 430–31; Garry Wills, emphasizing this side of Jefferson's teaching and his debt—like Wilson's—to the Scottish Enlightenment, slights its Lockean foundations. See his *Inventing America* (Garden City, N.Y.: Doubleday, 1978).

8. Herbert J. Storing, ed., *The Complete Anti-Federalist* (hereafter cited as *CAF*), 7 vols. (Chicago: University of Chicago Press, 1981), 5:161.

9. Ibid., 4:200; see also 2:230, 249–50, 319–20.

10. Michael Sandel, "Morality and the Liberal Ideal," *New Republic*, 7 May 1984, pp. 15–16; Alexis de Tocqueville, *Democracy in America*, vol. 2, bk. 2, chap. 2.

11. Robert Bellah et al., *Habits of the Heart* (Berkeley and Los Angeles: University of California Press, 1985).

12. Gilbert Tennent, *Brotherly Love Recommended by the Argument of the Love of Christ* (Philadelphia: Franklin & Hall, 1748), p. 3.

13. Storing, *CAF*, 6:91.

14. "A Plan for the Establishment of Public Schools (etc.)," 1786, in *Essays on Education in the Early Republic*, ed. Frederick Rudolph (Cambridge, Mass.: Harvard University Press, 1965), p. 14 and passim.

15. Koch and Peden, *Life and Selected Writings*, p. 217.

16. Storing, *CAF*, 3:169–70; see also 2:251–52.

17. Ibid., 6:95.

18. Ibid., 4:219–20, 232–33, 5:125–28, 6:237–38; Benjamin Rush, *Letters of Benjamin Rush*, ed. L. H. Butterfield, 2 vols. (Princeton, N. J.: Princeton

University Press, 1951), 2:947, 1054; *Essays, Literary, Moral and Philosophical,* (Philadelphia: Bradford, 1806), pp. 8–9, 81–92, 94–101, 105, 112–113.

19. Storing, *CAF*, 2:114–18, 3:142–43, 4:218–19, 6:237.

20. Ibid., 6:158–59.

21. Plato, *Republic,* 551b–555a.

22. Storing, *CAF*, 2:178, 5:67–68.

23. Ibid., 6:232–33, 5:50, 264–65; see also John Agresto, "Liberty, Virtue, and Republicanism, 1776–1787," *Review of Politics* 39 (1977): 473–504.

24. Storing, *CAF*, 2:251–52; see also 4:16–20, 81–87, 93–94.

25. Ibid., 2:234–35, 264–65.

26. Ibid., 2:112, 231, 368–69, 4:251–53, 5:50–51, 6:153–55.

27. Ibid., 6:165, 2:118.

28. Ibid., 2:233–34, 288–94, 304–6, 4:63, 140–43, 236–37, 275–80.

29. Ibid., 2:379–81; see also 2:119, 230–31, 235–36, 268–69, 4:63, 5:89–91, 192, 6:157.

30. Ibid., 2:84–85.

THE CONTRIBUTORS

LANCE BANNING is professor of history at the University of Kentucky. His articles and books include *The Jeffersonian Persuasion: Evolution of a Party Ideology.*

EDWARD J. CASHIN, professor of history at Augusta College, has written extensively on the early history of Georgia. His books include *Colonial Augusta,* and his articles have appeared in such places as the *Georgia Historical Quarterly* and the *Georgia Review.*

CECIL L. EUBANKS is professor of political science at Louisiana State University and is the author of numerous articles on American political thought, which have appeared in such journals as the *American Political Science Review, Science, Political Science Reviewer,* and *Southern Quarterly.* At present he is coeditor of the *Journal of Politics.*

MICHAEL ALLEN GILLESPIE, assistant professor of political science at Duke University, has written widely on European and American political thought. He is the author of *Hegel, Heidegger, and the Ground of History* and a coeditor of *Nietzsche's New Seas: Explorations in Philosophy, Aesthetics, and Politics.*

GEORGE J. GRAHAM, JR., professor of political science at Vanderbilt University, is the author of *Methodological Foundations for Political Analysis* and a coeditor of *Founding Principles of American Government;* he has also written articles and essays on the history of democratic theory and American political thought.

JOHN P. KAMINSKI, professor of history at the University of Wisconsin-Madison, is director of the Center for the Study of the American Constitution, a coeditor of *The Documentary History of the Ratification of the Constitution and the Bill of Rights, 1787–1791*, and the author of articles on the history of the American Constitution.

MICHAEL LIENESCH is associate professor of political science at the University of North Carolina at Chapel Hill. In addition to articles on American political thought, he is the author of *New Order of the Ages: Time, the Constitution, and the Making of Modern American Political Thought.*

DONALD S. LUTZ, associate professor of political science at the University of Houston, is the author of *Popular Consent and Popular Control: Whig Political Theory in the Early State Constitutions; The Origins of American Constitutionalism;* and articles and essays on the history of American political thought. He is also a coeditor of *American Political Writing during the Founding Era, 1760–1805.*

FORREST MCDONALD is professor of history at the University of Alabama. His books include *Novus Ordo Seclorum: The Intellectual Origins of the Constitution; We the People: The Economic Origins of the Constitution; E Pluribus Unum: The Foundation of the American Republic; Alexander Hamilton; The Presidency of George Washington; The Presidency of Thomas Jefferson;* and *A Constitutional History of the United States.*

WILSON CAREY MCWILLIAMS is professor of political science at Rutgers University. In addition to *The Idea of Fraternity in America,* he is the author of numerous articles and books on American politics and American political thought.

PETER S. ONUF is professor of history at Southern Methodist University. His articles and books include *The Origins of the Federal Republic: Jurisdictional Controversies in the United States, 1775–1787.*

GASPARE J. SALADINO is professor of history at the University of Wisconsin-Madison, a coeditor of *The Documentary History of the Ratification of the Constitution and the Bill of Rights, 1787–1791,* and the author of articles on the ratification of the Constitution.

SARA M. SHUMER, associate professor of political science at Haverford College, has written articles on many aspects of modern political thought; she is presently engaged in a study of Tocqueville and the American founding.

ROBERT M. WEIR is professor of history at the University of South Carolina and is the author of *"A Most Important Epocha": The Coming of the Revolution in South Carolina; Colonial South Carolina;* and *The "Last of American Freemen,"* as well as articles on the early history of the South.

JEAN YARBROUGH, professor of government and legal studies at Bowdoin College, has written articles on the American founding that have appeared in such journals as *Polity, Publius,* and the *Review of Politics.*

INDEX

405

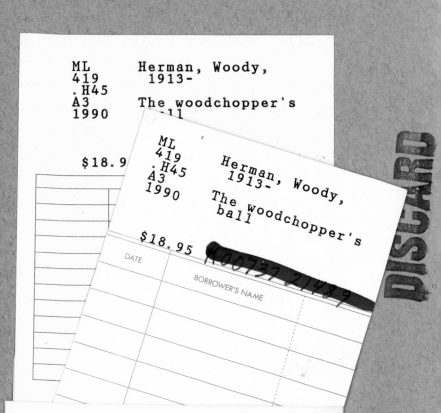

```
ML      Herman, Woody,
419       1913-
.H45
A3      The woodchopper's
1990       ball
```

$18.95

THE WOODCHOPPER'S BALL

WOODY HERMAN AND STUART TROUP

THE WOODCHOPPER's BALL

THE AUTOBIOGRAPHY OF WOODY HERMAN

E. P. DUTTON   NEW YORK

Published in the United States by E. P. Dutton,
a division of Penguin Books USA Inc.,
2 Park Avenue, New York, N.Y., 10016. R00737 21489

Published simultaneously in Canada by Fitzhenry and Whiteside, Limited, Toronto.

Library of Congress Cataloging-in-Publication Data

Herman, Woody, 1913–
    The woodchopper's ball : the autobiography of Woody Herman / Woody Herman and Stuart Troup. — 1st ed.
        p.   cm.
    ISBN 0-525-24853-6
    1. Herman, Woody, 1913–   . Jazz musicians—United States—
Biography. I. Troup, Stuart. II. Title.
ML419.H45A3   1990
781.65'092–dc20   89-37630
[B]   CIP
                                                                            MN

Designed by Margo D. Barooshian

10 9 8 7 6 5 4 3 2 1

First edition

Photographs courtesy of Ingrid Herman Reese.

Lyrics to "Early Autumn" by Johnny Mercer
copyright 1949 Cromwell Music Inc. (renewed).
Used by permission of Warner/Chappell Music, Inc.
All rights reserved.

To Jack Siefert

ACKNOWLEDGMENTS

Woody's health began to fail midway through this project. Its completion was enabled with the help of many of those who loved him; in particular, the following: Jack and Mary Siefert, Chubby Jackson, Nat Pierce, Ralph Burns, Don Lamond, Polly Podewell, Ingrid Herman Reese, Gene Lees, Erwin Sherman, George Simon, Billy Bauer, Red Rodney, Milt Jackson, Red Mitchell, Major Holley, Bill Byrne, Frank Tiberi, Alan Broadbent, Harold Danko, John Fedchock, Lynn Seaton, Richard Stolzman, Tony Outhwaite, and Peter Levinson.

CONTENTS

Sixteen pages of photographs follow page 100.

THE WOODCHOPPER'S BALL

PROLOGUE

The deputy from the Los Angeles sheriff's office drove up the steep, winding beauty of Hollywood Boulevard on Thursday morning, September 3, 1987. He stopped at the front door of Woody Herman's low-slung, deceptively simple-looking home.

He carried an eviction notice.

Woody was oblivious to the scene. He was in bed, his familiar surroundings crowded with the requirements of his condition: oxygen tanks, a wheelchair, and a full-time nurse. A tube was delivering the nutrition his seventy-four-year-old body no longer had the ability to swallow.

The deputy rang the doorbell.

Woody couldn't hear it. He was fading in and out of

consciousness, as he had since coming home a week earlier from his fifth hospital stay in seven months. The resiliency with which he survived a half-century of musical trailblazing had been overtaken by the punishing residuals of the journey, congestive heart disease and emphysema.

His daughter, Ingrid, took the envelope and read the court order. It required that the premises be vacated in five days.

Woody lay one floor below in his sanctuary, on the center level of the spacious four-bedroom home tucked against the mountainside. He and his late wife, Charlotte, had purchased the house in 1946 from Humphrey Bogart and Lauren Bacall, for cash, when the Herman band was riding its highest crest. He lost Charlotte to cancer in 1982, and he lost ownership of the house to the Internal Revenue Service in 1985. The government had seized the property and sold it at auction to mitigate the huge tax bill the IRS claimed Woody owed from the mid-1960s. He and Ingrid were permitted to remain as tenants, at $1,150 a month.

But he was no longer able to pay. The little cash he had left after the IRS began taking its weekly cut in the late 1960s had been wiped out in the past seven months by the cost of medical attention, nursing care, and medicine. Woody was four months behind in the rent.

Ingrid telephoned her lawyers, Kirk Pasich in Los Angeles and Leonard Garment in Washington, D.C. With the three-day Labor Day weekend approaching, there wasn't much time to act. The attorneys conferred and Pasich went to Superior Court the next morning, Friday, to request a temporary restraining order. Judge Ricardo A. Torres decided that the property owner, William Little, required more than a few hours of notice, and he set a hearing for Tuesday.

With their legal path stymied until after the holiday, the lawyers decided to publicize Woody's plight. By nightfall that Friday, much of the world was stunned by the news that

Woody Herman—whose dedication, droll wit, and sense of musical adventure had enabled his orchestras to survive the collapse of the big band era, the crush of rock and roll, and a twenty-year income tax battle—was impoverished, on a life-support system, and about to be unmercifully uprooted from his home.

The response was compassionate, financial, and swift. Saul Levine, the owner of radio station KKGO-FM, said he would pay the $4,600 in back rent. Help was tendered by the celebrated, among them Frank Sinatra, Peggy Lee, Tony Bennett, Rosemary Clooney, and Clint Eastwood. And spirited support, which would later be manifested in contributions and the receipts from musical tributes, was offered by the many whose love Woody had engendered during more than fifty years of relentless, swingful excursions through every city and tank town in the country.

Reporters and cameramen milled about the house throughout the weekend, searching for an update and hoping for a glimpse of Woody. But the centerpiece of the drama remained unaware. Because of her father's pride and the tenuous state of his health, Ingrid ordered those in the house to protect him from any word of the predicament.

But Woody found out somehow on Monday.

"He told his nurse he wanted to get up and come out to the living room," Ingrid said.

The cameras gave the world its first glimpse of his frail condition. Instead of traumatizing him, the news, coupled with the corresponding outpouring of love and assistance, led to a noticeable improvement in his condition and spirit.

"It made him feel good knowing that people cared," Ingrid said.

The following day, Tuesday, Ingrid and attorney Pasich went to Superior Court. Judge Torres worked out an agreement with landlord Little that, with the past-due rent paid, allowed

Woody and his daughter to remain in the house until 1989.

"I'm happy," Little was reported to say after the hearing. "I don't like problems. I'm glad they can get some help. It shouldn't be a problem in the future."

For Woody, the future was only seven weeks long.

1
EARLY DAYS

I was listening to some kind of music constantly, from the beginning. My father, Otto, was a terrible ham. He saw in me the possible fulfillment of his love for show business, and he worked with me, teaching me songs, from the time I first remember seeing him. It wasn't long after I learned to walk that he was also coaching me to dance.

He would have loved working on the stage, instead of as a shoemaker at the Nunn-Bush factory in Milwaukee. He had a great collection of recordings at home, and he sang along with them. He even bought a player piano and supplied it with all the available piano rolls.

Otto was of German descent, but born in the United States. My mother, Martha, came to Milwaukee from Poland when she was an infant. I was their only child. They were kind and beautiful. They let me try to do anything I wanted, and if it didn't work out, they were sympathetic.

During my eighth summer, Otto decided I was ready to launch the career he never had. He brought me to an audition for a kiddie revue, and I got a part with a low-budget operation that included six or seven other kids and a mature woman, an old actress who played a schoolmarm with us.

I was on the road.

The kiddie revue was part of a package that was booked into theaters with a silent movie based on a Booth Tarkington story. Our group staged a skit, with music and dancing, before the film. My high point was my comedy efforts.

We traveled around Milwaukee, moving into upper Wisconsin and Michigan, but always staying within a couple of hundred miles of our home base. The operation was booked by Ed Weisfeldt, who was the manager of a Milwaukee movie house. Weisfeldt was a talented, savvy guy who coached us. We had a good conductor who accompanied us with a fiddle, and sometimes he added local musicians.

I took a few piano lessons, meanwhile, but I wasn't much interested in that instrument. I tried the violin, too, but I didn't like it any better.

"You'd better learn to play something," my father warned me, "or I'll break your neck."

I decided to try a saxophone and, with the earnings from that first summer on the road, I bought an E-flat alto sax, silver with a gold belt.

"You're going to have to play clarinet, too," my music teacher told me. "It's much more difficult, but you'd better get one so we can start working on it." I did, but the sax was the important instrument at that time, and the one that occupied most of my concentration.

My father, meanwhile, continued to broaden my song

repertoire, even adding some risqué material. In fact, one of those tunes—"Oh Gee, Say Gee, You Ought to See My Gee Gee From the Fiji Islands"—came in handy much later. Late in the forties, we were having some problems with Capitol Records because of meager sales. During a discussion of the problem one day, I said, "Look, I'll make you a couple of sides and I won't even bring in the band." They were curious.

"Get a record date in the next couple of days," I said, "and I'll take care of the rest."

I went to the Hangover Bar and Grill, which was on Sunset Boulevard, and I picked up a few guys who weren't too loaded to speak. I took them to the studio, and we did "Oh Gee, Say Gee." Capitol shipped more records that week than they had in a long time. But by the second week, the networks banned the record because of what they considered to be risqué lyrics. The line that damned it was "She wears a lot of leaves to protect her from the air." The flip side, I think, was "Rose of the Rio Grande." I picked my own name for the recording— Chuck Thomas. Those are my two middle names, Charles Thomas, Woodrow Charles Thomas.

Along with the coaching from my father, and the music lessons, I began to study dance at a school run by Roselie Edwards, who was a friend of my parents. She once conned me into playing the part of a dancing rooster at a children's ballet recital, dressing me in a feathered costume that drove me crazy. I was more interested in tap dancing, however, and I moved to other teachers.

I loved sports, and I tried to participate in everything. But I wasn't very good at things like baseball. So while my best friend, Ray Sherman, and other buddies were at the ball field or the gym, I was usually practicing music. Ray and I were the same age and very close, like our families. Ray's mother, whom I always called Aunt Julia, assisted at my birth. Ray's brothers, Erwin and Dan, remained lifelong friends.

My folks changed houses in Milwaukee often, sometimes more than once a year. One of the more interesting places we rented was an old summer home on Humboldt Avenue, in a suburban area that was about as far north as you could go in Milwaukee. The property, owned by the Schlitz brewery family, extended about three-fourths of a mile, to the shore of the Milwaukee River. The winter there was terrible, and we had stoves in every room. But the summer was fantastic, because I slept in the tower of the building. You had to go about four flights up a big winding staircase, and then there was a special riser that took you into the tower. That seemed pretty romantic. We shared the house with another family, and I shared the tower with the other family's oldest son, who was much older than me. We could see all the huge trees throughout the property from the tower. Below the trees were zillions of wild violet plants, and at the river's edge, there was a little boat landing from which I would jump in.

My parents weren't quite as thrilled with our various housing accommodations. My mother decided we could do better if she went to work. After my father got her a job with him in the shoe factory, we got better housing. I gained some anxiety, however, being alone at home in the afternoons.

The worry disappeared with the arrival of summer, when I went off with another kiddie revue. But the tours led to a new problem. When I returned to class in the fall, the teachers and school administrators figured that my parents were nuts to let me work in show business. And I was having a difficult time getting permission from juvenile court to have working papers. I was performing only while school was out. But the school officials were nonetheless annoyed with the idea and were delaying the court's approval of my papers. Their negativity bugged me even after the working papers came through, and I decided to do something about it.

I was only ten, and in the fifth grade, but I managed on

my own to transfer to St. John's Cathedral School in downtown Milwaukee, where I had heard the administration and teachers were more interested in individuals.

By that time, my musicianship, coupled with my singing and dancing, had made me a bookable act. The kiddie-revue days were over. I was able to play theaters as a single on a year-round basis, performing locally on school nights and sometimes traveling to other towns on weekends, often with my mother along. Eventually, I even played in some vaudeville houses in Chicago, billed as "The Boy Wonder."

With me on the same bill was a comic and a four-woman chorus line, singing bawdy songs. We often played two theaters a night, two shows at each theater, week in and week out.

Being a show business act gave me some kind of glow. I tried not to be too self-impressed, but it was a gas to walk by a theater and see my name in lights, and to collect as much as fifty dollars a week—a powerful income in the early twenties. My parents held the salary for me in a bank account, and saw that I had spending money.

As my ability increased, I became more interested in musical form than in show business flavor. I began collecting a few records, one of which featured an eight-piece group called The Washingtonians, led by Duke Ellington. It was the first time I ever heard what sounded to me like jungle music, and it knocked me out. I was impressed by the originality of the sounds and the different rhythm patterns.

It was tough to find recordings then of what I considered jazz. There were some Red Nichols records that I could handle very nicely, because he had some great soloists.

I began to take saxophone and clarinet lessons from a jazz-oriented teacher who wrote out choruses for me. He had his own little band that played at one of the local hotels, and I took at least one lesson a week from him.

Jazz was becoming more of an influence also through one of my high school buddies, a piano player named Al Mack. Al's older brothers, both of them priests, were also pianists. The oldest, who later became a monsignor, was a classical player, and the middle brother was Tony, who wore straight clothes to play jazz on gigs around Milwaukee. Tony was a beautiful man who taught me some harmony and theory. He also taught Al Mack to play in the Earl Hines style. It was through Tony that I became aware of Louis Armstrong, who had cut some sides with Hines. Hearing Armstrong made you a believer in what was swing.

Tony Mack later went to Rome to serve on the Vatican staff. And if anybody had encouraged him, I'm sure he would have played a little jazz right there.

In 1925, at age twelve, I decided I wanted a career playing jazz. So I announced to my parents that I was retiring from show business and, in the vernacular of the day, I was going to be a hot player.

They almost went into a dead faint.

When they recovered, the reaction on their faces was, "How is he going to make a living that way?" For them, the connotation of playing jazz was to perform with bums. Being in the theater was fine. But being a jazz musician wasn't exactly the future they had hoped for for me. Nevertheless, they said, "Go ahead, you can try it."

In my freshman year at St. John's Cathedral High School, I got my first steady job with a band of mature guys at a gig somewhere out in the county. One of the guys picked me up and we played until four in the morning on most days of the week. The hours didn't interfere with my getting to school at eight in the morning. But the sister teaching my class wasn't happy about my nodding off during class, and she showed her annoyance by sending me to the principal's office often.

My sense of what jazz was about increased considerably

when I found recordings by the Mound City Blue Blowers. That group was led by William (Red) McKenzie, who sang and blew through tissue paper and pocket comb in trumpet-imitation style. The featured players included Coleman Hawkins, Jack Teagarden, Eddie Condon, Gene Krupa, Muggsy Spanier, Jimmy Dorsey, Pee Wee Russell, and Glenn Miller, who also arranged some of their pieces. Hawkins' tenor sax solos, in particular, were a revelation.

I studied those solos by Hawkins, listening to them over and over. Erwin Sherman would come over to the house and crank up the Victrola while I tried to emulate the licks played by Hawkins or Frankie Trumbauer.

My jazz education was enlarging, but things weren't going well at school. Then, late in my second semester, the nun who was my science teacher also became my mentor.

Sister Fabian Reilly was an angel who believed that a musician, even one who played jazz, was a very good thing to be. I was always a little behind in my work because of my musical activities. When I was sent to the principal's office, she always arrived first to cop a plea for me. Whatever my problem, she could help me work it out.

"Just stick to your music," she said. "It's the best thing for you. You'll learn the other things."

Erwin Sherman recalls:

Woody was playing the road houses that ringed the Milwaukee area. One was called the Blue Heaven, on Green Bay Avenue, which is in the heart of the northside now, but it was outside of Milwaukee then. He also played Pick's Club Madrid, and a place on Muskego Lake, about 20 miles or so out of Milwaukee. And the Modernistic, which was in the fairgrounds on the west side of Milwaukee. He'd go as far away as Oshkosh and Waupacka, but they were mainly weekend gigs because he was still going to school.

When he was about sixteen, his car broke down west of Madison, about 150 miles from Milwaukee, on the way back from a gig with a group led by Joey Lichter. He called me, because he couldn't get his folks, who were out for the evening. I kept calling his house all evening, and I finally got Uncle Otto. We went out there together—me driving and he sleeping all the way. We got there at three in the morning, and we had to tow Woody's car—it was a Whippet—all the way back to Milwaukee. After the car was repaired in a couple of weeks, he was on the road again with Lichter.

Sister Fabian supported and saved me all through my high school days. In fact, we corresponded for years after I left Milwaukee and we would get together when I would pass through. I performed for her students and once, after giving me a frantic call concerning a building crisis at the school, I brought in the band to play a benefit at the auditorium. From then on, I tried to perform there at least once a year.

Sister Fabian would have seen me through to graduation, as well, if a bandleader named Tom Gerun hadn't come along in 1931, during my last semester in high school.

2
ON THE ROAD

Tom Gerun's band was playing at the Schroeder Hotel in Milwaukee when he called me, just a couple of months before my eighteenth birthday. A few of his musicians had heard me in Joey Lichter's band, and had recommended me. I went over to the hotel, and Gerun and I talked about what I could do and what he needed, which basically was a tenor player. The deal was made.

The band left town right away for Chicago, and I followed a few days later, chugging at twenty-five miles an hour to break in the new engine in my Whippet. We played the Chez Paris there and then moved to the William Penn Hotel in Pittsburgh for a few weeks.

It wasn't long before we were headed for San Francisco, where Gerun was best known. When we got there, we played the Noon Club. Then we moved into a place called the Bal Taberin for a long stay.

We were mainly a good entertainment orchestra, rather than a jazz band. Almost all twelve members would sing at one point or another. We had some of the better players in town in the saxophone section, which eventually included Al Morris, who later became a movie and recording star as Tony Martin. I played tenor mostly, and I doubled on baritone sax and clarinet.

Coleman Hawkins, whom I had never met, had made my tenor playing impressive. Few people in San Francisco had heard of Hawkins, no less realized that I was emulating his revolutionary solos from those records with the Mound City Blue Blowers.

As a singer, I was influenced by Russ Columbo and Red McKenzie and, later, Lee Wiley. I was inspired, too, by some who weren't thought of as singers, such as songwriter Harold Arlen, who sang on dates with Red Nichols, and Jack Teagarden.

One evening at the Bal Taberin, the cast of a new musical called *Nine O'Clock Revue* came in for an opening night party. And I spotted a beautiful dancer with flaming red hair. Her name was Charlotte Neste, and we were attracted to each other from the start.

The romance continued by phone and letter after she returned to Los Angeles. When I went to visit her there about a year later, Tom Gerun asked me to try to find a new girl singer for the band. I knew a couple of music publishers there, and they helped me arrange for an audition session. More than fifty singers showed up and I listened to them all before deciding on Virginia Simms.

She joined Gerun's band and she worked out fine. But later, when we were about to go east on tour, she decided to stay in San Francisco. Tom hated to lose her, but he recommended her to the bandleader coming into the Bal Taberin—

Kay Kyser. He hired her, changed her name to Ginny Simms, and she became one of the leading pop singers of the thirties and forties.

Charlotte, meanwhile, was rehearsing in a second musical that was headed for San Francisco, with Barbara Stanwyck playing the lead. It wasn't much of a show, unfortunately, and—after it played San Francisco—it had a disastrous tour across the country. By time the show reached New York, it was in utter collapse.

Our romance, however, was going strong, despite being limited to phone conversations. But I wasn't about to consider marriage until I became a bandleader, which I had already begun thinking about.

A year or so later, the Tom Gerun band hit Chicago again for a stay at the Granada Cafe, on the South Side. It was also known as Al Quadbach's, because he was the front man for the club, which was rumored to belong to Al Capone. We followed Paul Whiteman's Orchestra in there, and we had to play for the various entertainers who were also on the bill, which included comic Fuzzy Knight.

After work one night, Fuzzy and I and Steve Bowers, the bass player with the band, went out to hear the Earl Hines Orchestra, which was playing at the Grand Terrace, a large after-hours place. Picking up on the sounds of the great bands on the South Side was the thing to do then, and we arrived at about four or five in the morning, still dressed in our band tuxedos. I was even wearing my homburg. I liked being dressed properly. I was described once in San Francisco as "the kid, drunk and dressy, and always a gentleman."

We were in a semi-hilarious mood and Fuzzy was waving his hand, a finger of which was decorated with a big diamond ring. That combination, plus the roll of more than a thousand dollars that Fuzzy flashed, didn't go unnoticed.

The trouble began while we were driving back to our hotel

in my Pontiac roadster, with Fuzzy next to me and Steve in the back. We stopped for a red light and a big black sedan pulled up next to us. Three guys jumped out and started opening our doors and banging on the car. They couldn't seem to do much with us because we were well oiled and weren't responding too well. We scuffled with them from our seats and one guy decided the noise we were making might attract attention, so he slugged me on top of the head with his fist. But the homburg saved me. The hood got frustrated, pulled a pistol, and fired a bullet toward the floorboard of the car to scare us. My right leg unfortunately was in the way, and the bullet went straight through my calf and dropped on the floor.

I got out of the car, dragging my leg behind me, and moved off to find help. I located a policeman a couple of blocks away, told him I had just been shot in the leg and that the hoods might still be back at the car with my buddies. The cop took a whiff of my breath and said, "Boy, you've been drinking. You better go home."

When I got back to the car, I found Fuzzy and Steve waiting for me. The hoods had left without getting anything. We took my car back to our hotel and called a doctor. He put me into one of those South Side hospitals that took care of things like a small shooting. And I got out the next day.

Gerun was a likeable man who treated us well. One night in Pittsburgh, he received a telegram on the bandstand that said he had been wiped out in the stock market. He stuffed the wire into his pocket and we continued playing. When we finished the last song of the evening, he threw a big party for the band. That took some kind of courage.

After about three years with the band, most of it in San Francisco, I began to get antsy to start a group of my own. In mid-1934, I left Gerun and went to Milwaukee. I knew a few agents, and I talked to people at MCA, but they weren't encouraging. The only thing left to do was hunt for another job.

I found two, one right after the other. The first was with Harry Sosnick, who had an important band that did a lot of radio work. We did broadcasts from theaters and hotels in the Midwest and Far West. Our itinerary included the Chase in St. Louis and the Cosmopolitan Hotel in Denver.

On the advice of MCA, I left Sosnick after a couple of months to join the Gus Arnheim band. It was good advice, indeed, because Arnheim's subsequent cross-country tour of theaters brought me to Pittsburgh. The Isham Jones Orchestra happened to be playing there at the same time.

3
WITH
ISHAM JONES

I got a telephone call at my hotel one day from a member of the Isham Jones band, who said I should speak to his boss.

Isham Jones was big league, and his band was more musical than Arnheim's. Jones had earned a national reputation through his compositions. I was nervous at our meeting, but Isham made it easy.

"Is it true that you can sing and dance and play good saxophone?" he asked.

"That's what I try to do," I replied.

"Well," he said, pausing for a moment, "you'd better join us."

He made arrangements for me to join the band in Denver a few weeks later. But when I got there, he had forgotten about it. The tenor player I was to replace hadn't been given notice.

I was worried plenty at first, because Isham had a reputation of being tight with the dollar, and paying salaries to two guys when only one was working was a distasteful idea to him. But he gave the tenor player an extra two weeks' pay to go home with.

My salary with Isham was in the neighborhood of $125 a week, about the same that I got with Arnheim. From that, we had to pay all of our road expenses, including travel, but the hotels were dirt cheap then. I was able to get a first-class room in 1934 for something like a buck and a half.

I did a little of everything except dancing with Isham's band—singing, playing saxophones and clarinet. He had a quite successful and identifiable tenor soloist named Saxie Mansfield, so I played baritone sax most of the time. His main singer was Eddie Stone, who was well known to Jones fans. When I was called upon to sing, I did things such as "Basin Street" and some ballads that I also recorded with the band.

Isham was a fantastic song writer. Among the hits he wrote were "I'll See You in My Dreams," "It Had to Be You," "The One I Love Belongs to Somebody Else," "There Is No Greater Love," "Swinging Down the Lane," "You've Got Me Crying Again," "When Your Dreamboat Comes In," and "On the Alamo." He cared about his charts. If you made an error in your part—missing a cue slightly, for example—he was forgiving. But you couldn't miss any notes. If you did, it would be you and him out in the back.

He loved his players, but he wouldn't interfere in any of the little problems that arise among band members on the road. If a couple of the guys got into a hassle and started fighting, he would stand by and watch them.

My romance with Charlotte was still relegated to letters and phone calls. I couldn't see marriage yet, especially after watching the difficulty married players had in the Isham Jones band, where wives were barred from traveling or from attending a lot of things. Those were the rules of the day, and only a leader could change them.

Not long after I joined the band, Isham started talking about his new ranch in Denver, where he wanted to raise turkeys. His songs had made him wealthy, and the band seemed to be only a second thought to him. He wanted to get off the road and live a new life.

Five of us, realizing that the band might be close to a breakup, began discussing the idea of forming a cooperative. Besides me, there was Saxie Mansfield, arranger and flugelhorn player Joe Bishop, bassist Walt Yoder, and Nick Hupfer, a violinist I had known in Milwaukee who had changed his name to Harper. Nick was also a pretty good arranger.

A small group including Yoder, Mansfield, and myself had already recorded for Decca, under the name of the Isham Jones Juniors. So the people at Decca were aware of me and were especially impressed with my singing. In March 1936, we had cut eight sides, five of them with vocals by Virginia Verrell or me, with a group that also included Chelsea Quealey on trumpet, Sonny Lee on trombone, Howard Smith on piano, George Wartner on guitar, and Walter Lagesone on drums.

When Isham's moment of decision occurred in the summer of 1936, while the band was in Texas, we were ready. We had a contract with Decca—a rare thing in those days—and it gave us a sense of solidity. We also took James Noble into the cooperative. Noble, whose nickname was Jiggs, was an arranger on Isham's staff, and he later prepared charts for our record dates while we were busy playing gigs. Jiggs turned out some pretty good arrangements, including "The Golden Wedding," which did well for us four years later.

The other members of the Isham Jones band picked up various jobs. Two or three of them went with Ray Noble, who was then a big hit at the Rainbow Room in New York. Gordon Jenkins got an assignment to write for a show that was opening on Broadway, and he took two or three players with him.

Our group had decided to start in New York, where we could pick up other players and begin auditioning the band for bookings. We had discussed for months exactly what we wanted to do.

We agreed to call ourselves The Band That Plays the Blues. The reason was obvious: Playing the blues was the best thing we knew how to do musically.

The guys agreed that I would be the leader, even though I was the youngest. They figured that I could handle it best because of my early show-biz background. And they knew I would be a more personable front man than Isham. He was a good musician and a great songwriter, but in front of the band he was something I had no intention of being: a flop.

4
ON OUR OWN

Being a leader was all the excuse I needed to send for Charlotte. She came to New York, where we were married by a justice of the peace on September 27, 1936. We spent our honeymoon in the city, visiting various clubs on 52nd Street—the Onyx, the Famous Door, Leon & Eddie's, Jack White's.

The band, meanwhile, needed to add seven players to our core of five. It wasn't easy to find them, with nothing to offer a player besides stock in an orchestra without a gig. But if a guy was nutty enough, he would join us. When we needed to make a decision about somebody, we held a meeting, sometimes all of us going to the men's room, where we could talk in private.

The band started rehearsing in a hall that the management of the Capitol Hotel let us use without charge. A few weeks later, The Band That Plays the Blues got its first booking, in Brooklyn Roseland, at Fulton and Flatbush Avenues—sort of a tryout for the Roseland Ballroom in Manhattan.

We opened on Election Night, 1936, with only a dozen or so arrangements in the book, so we made up tunes—so-called head arrangements—on the job. One of those head arrangements, a riff based on the blues, evolved into "Woodchopper's Ball." Everybody contributed something to it, but we didn't name it until later. And we cut our first two recordings for Decca: "Wintertime Dreams" and "Someone to Care for Me."

I was singing, playing some alto sax and mostly clarinet, which was a hot instrument during that period.

The pay scale at Roseland was $50 a week for the guys, $75 for me as leader. Big deal: leader. It was a job I couldn't afford. When somebody from the press came in, I had to pick up his drink tab. And a nut from the *Brooklyn Eagle* showed up one night and wanted to dance with the hostesses, at so much a dance. After a few of those incidents, I started making deals with the manager of the place, explaining that I couldn't pay my rent.

The main thing was that we were a hit. After three weeks there, Lou Brecker, who owned both ballrooms, moved us into the Roseland Ballroom in Manhattan. The blues were the best thing we knew how to play, but we had to do a lot of fighting to play them. The management preferred that we play mostly dance music—fox trots, rhumbas, and waltzes—to satisfy the dancers.

We stayed at Roseland for seven months, and for a while the Count Basie Orchestra was booked to play alternately with us from a second bandstand. But Basie didn't remain there very long. What may have curtailed his stay, as a matter of fact, were the dance hostesses. They would have meetings and report to the management about which bands played good music for dancing. They reported that they could dance to us, but they were having difficulty dancing to the Basie band. We were playing with a heavy two-and-four beat, and Basie was playing swing in four. The dancers of that period needed a heavy metronome; they couldn't feel the real swing of Basie.

George Simon, who chronicled the big band era, recalls:

I first heard the band in December of 1936, after they moved into Roseland in Manhattan. My review in Metronome *appeared the following month. What was very interesting was that the Basie band was on the opposite stand. And I gave the Herman band a higher rating than the Basie band, for which John Hammond never forgave me. But Bill Basie, and Buck Clayton especially, said that I was absolutely right. The Basie band played out of tune.*

I gave Woody an A — and Basie a B.

Charlotte and I, meanwhile, began married life in an apartment on Bleecker Street in Greenwich Village. Shortly after we moved in, someone gave us a wire-haired terrier, and walking that pup several times a day from a fifth-floor walkup kept us in pretty good shape. Charlotte was heartbroken when the pup died of distemper that first year, and I began shopping for another one right away. From that point on, we usually had a cocker spaniel.

We moved from there to a ground-floor apartment in Jackson Heights. By our standards then, the place was huge, with two bedrooms and a big, open area in back, which opened onto a nine-hole golf course. We were close to LaGuardia Airport, which we would visit for a meal in the main dining room when I had a day off. The guy who operated the restaurant later ran a chain of hotels around the country, including the New Yorker in Manhattan, and we eventually worked for him there.

We signed a management contract with General Artists Corporation during the Roseland engagement, but it didn't exactly signal a big break. When the gig ended, GAC told us bluntly they couldn't do much for the band. I spent a lot of time sitting in the GAC outer office, often with Glenn Miller, trying to see somebody.

I was twenty-four years old and optimistic. Glenn was a little older and sour. He had already blown a ton of money with three bands, and he was full of sad stories. GAC apparently didn't think very much of either of us at that point.

Roseland had given our band a taste of honey, but it would be a long time before things got that good again.

One of the engagements we got the following summer, however, turned up something a lot more important than an opportunity to work. It initiated my introduction to Jack Siefert, a man whose warm friendship and support would help sustain me all my life.

Jack Siefert recalls:

I was living in the Philadelphia area, and a woman from Milwaukee named Pauline Traub—Aunt Pauline, we called her—became a neighbor. I used to play my one record too loud, and one day she said to me, "You like music, don't you, Jack." And I said, "Yeah." She said, "My nephew's a musician, his name is Woody Herman."

At the time, Woody was playing with the Harry Sosnick band, which was broadcasting on a show out of Chicago every Wednesday night. So I began listening to it. I felt that I practically knew Woody because of my neighbor.

The kids in my neighborhood would do anything to get down to the Jersey shore during the summer. Money was scarce and cars were few, but somehow or other we all managed to get to the shore over the big weekends. Later on, we would run record hops during the winter, playing our own records to raise money for a place at the shore during the summer.

The first weekend that I arrived in Wildwood, New Jersey, was the Fourth of July, 1937. Woody's band was booked into Hunt's Ocean Pier on the boardwalk.

I went to see him, and said, "Mr. Herman, I'm Jack Seifert, I'm a friend of your Aunt Pauline."

"Oh, Aunt Pauline," he said. "Stick around, kid. We'll have a milk shake together."

At intermission, that's what we did.

He was five years older than me. I was just out of high school and I thought he was like God. He was booked there for about two weeks, I think, and we often went down to the beach to sit and talk. Sometimes we had softball games, with his band versus us.

Guy Hunt was a very good businessman; he owned all the theaters and amusements in Wildwood and was very generous to local charities. On Sunday afternoons, he arranged for the band to set up directly on the beach, on plywood sheets, and do radio broadcasts. That would stimulate interest and the kids, instead of going back to Philly early on Sunday afternoon, would stick around and go to Hunt's Pier and dance to the music of Woody, then drive home at night. We told people that we stayed late to beat the traffic, but the real reason was to hear the band. Woody was very popular and developed a very loyal group of fans from the Philadelphia area, a great many of whom vacationed at the Jersey shore.

Guy Hunt and Woody became very good friends, and when the engagement was about over, Guy said to him, "Where are you playing after this?"

Woody said, "No place."

"You want to play here for one more week."

And Woody said, "I'd love to."

Guy hired a plane to go up and down the beach hauling a sign that said: "Held over by popular demand: Woody Herman."

I was down there that summer for maybe four weeks with him. After that, I took my vacations and traveled with the band, wherever he was, at the Meadowbrook in New Jersey or any place in the east.

In the forties, when the band had some difficulties traveling because of gasoline rationing, I was with him at the Adams Theater in

Newark, New Jersey. Guy Hunt's Ocean Pier burned down in Wild-wood, and I showed Woody the newspaper clipping.

"Gee," he said, "I'll have to send Guy a telegram."

It said: "Dear Guy. Sorry to hear about your fire. But where the hell did you get the gasoline?"

5

THE SCHRIBMANS

Without financing, we were not going to get very far. It was suggested that we contact Charles and Si Schribman in Boston. Their operation was to finance bands at engagements in their own ballrooms or in hotels, which didn't pay an up-and-coming band what it needed to survive. But the Schribmans would arrange for air time on network radio during those appearances, and the air shots in turn provided the exposure that created bookings. When a band had enough bookings for a tour, it would move out of the New England area, take care of itself financially, and repay the Schribmans. Those hotel engagements were consequently the lifeblood of the big bands.

If it cost, for example, a thousand dollars a week to underwrite our stay at a hotel in Boston, that became the Schribmans' investment. They didn't do much of the on-the-road bookings, except for some fill-ins around New England while we were gathering enough engagements to make a road trip worthwhile. We'd be living in Boston meanwhile, and driving somewhere in the New England area every day. When we finally had enough advance bookings for a tour, we headed out of Boston to different parts of the country, playing anything we could get.

George Simon recalls:

I first heard about the Schribmans when I was living in college in Boston, leading a band called George Simon and His Confederates. That was about 1932. They were booking bands then.

I knew them both, but I knew Si better than Charlie, because he was always on the scene. Charlie Schribman was the quieter of the two, a kindly sort of guy. Si was sort of a big gruff guy. He would just barge ahead and do what he thought was right. He apparently had a tremendous instinct to do the right thing. The guys told me that he would go around at night to the various places in the Boston area and collect money for bookings. His pockets would be bulging with cash. Then he'd take what he got in one place and use it to pay a band in another place. It was unbelievable.

But he was completely honest. I never heard a bandleader ever say a word against him. He and his brother supported many of the big bands, and they saved Artie Shaw and Glenn Miller. Those air shots were terribly important.

But The Band That Played the Blues had difficulty living up to its name, especially in the South and the Southwest. At one place in Texas, the manager sent a note to me that said, "You will kindly stop playing and singing those nigger blues."

That's the way it was.

The pay on our bookings was usually based on a percentage of the house, with a minimum guarantee. With enough radio broadcasts preceding our tours, we could gross a lot of money. Radio was stronger for us than anything we've had since, even television.

Those getting support from the Schribmans included Artie Shaw, Red Norvo, and Glenn Miller. For a while, several bands were living at the Avery Hotel in Copley Square in Boston at the same time. The hotel manager was a terrific guy who would let our bills ride for weeks. He helped us a great deal, giving us gasoline money when we had to ride to a job. He was probably glad to lose us for a few days.

One night while partying in the hotel, Glenn joined us. He had made a pact with his wife that he was through drinking. He couldn't drink and he knew it; it would turn him crazy. But on this particular night, Glenn not only joined us, he brought along some liquor to supplement the little already in our possession.

It became a real roaring party. We even locked one of my guys out on the fire escape in his underpants, and it was snowing like hell. We were doing numbers like that. By three or four in the morning, everybody had just passed out or gone to bed.

The desk clerk rang Glenn a couple of hours later to remind him that he had to go three hundred miles in the snowstorm to play a one-nighter. Glenn was fuming, partly from the hangover but mostly at me. In his mind, I was responsible for his drinking and staying up most of the night. He got dressed and started beating on everybody's door. Then his guys went outside and found their cars wouldn't start.

My first realization of all this activity was when Glenn started beating on my door. I grunted a reply, and he came into the room with a bellhop, who was carrying a big tray of chipped ice and a bottle of booze.

Glenn slapped me awake. Then he handed me the bottle of booze and said, "Either you drink the booze or I give you the ice!"

I just lay there, hungover and helpless.

"Give me the ice, man," I mumbled.

He tossed it over me and the two of them stomped out. I was lying in a deep freeze, but after the night we had it felt good.

A couple of days later, Glenn called and insisted I take his lead trumpet player.

"You need this guy," Glenn said. "You need a little more power in your band."

"I do?"

"Yeah," he said, "you need him."

It didn't take long to find out why Glenn had sent him. The guy had to have a drink before he could say hello.

We had become the house unit for Decca, having to record any tune that was a hit on another label. Mary Martin sang with us for a while in late 1938, and she and the Andrews Sisters recorded with us that December and the following January in New York.

Walt Yoder, meanwhile, came up with the title for the "Woodchopper's Ball." It happened one day after he had gone to see the Sportsmen's Show at the Boston Garden. While wandering around there, he came upon a group of woodchoppers competing against the clock for prizes. That's all there was to it. And our most famous head arrangement got its name.

We recorded "Woodchopper's Ball" for the first time on April 12, 1939, and it was really a sleeper. But Decca kept re-releasing it, and over a period of three or four years it became a hit. Eventually it sold more than five million copies—the biggest hit I ever had.

The flip side of "Woodchopper's Ball" featured Mary Ann McCall on her first outing with us, singing "Big-Wig in the Wigwam." Mary Ann stayed only through the end of that year, but she returned late in 1945 on the recommendation of song-plugger Juggy Gale. During that second stint, she made many recordings with the band, including "I Got It Bad and That Ain't Good," "Detour Ahead," "Romance in the Dark," and "Wrap Your Troubles in Dreams." That last one showed that she was truly a great jazz singer.

The band was playing major rooms, such as the Meadowbrook in Cedar Grove, New Jersey. But nothing up to that time compared with the thrill of performing on Manhattan's 52nd Street at the Famous Door. There was no real bread, but the exposure and publicity were worth a fortune.

6
BROADWAY

The band's reputation was growing faster than we realized. For example, after recording "Blues in the Night" in Los Angeles on September 10, 1941, we were busy touring in the Midwest and had no idea of how the record was doing. When we returned to New York City to open at the Strand Theater, everything seemed normal until the middle of the first show. I called "Blues in the Night," and the moment I sang the first line—"My momma done told me"—the joint fell down.

We had cut that record for Decca soon after the *Blues in the Night* movie was released. Jimmy Lunceford's band played the song in the movie, with a big concert arrangement. But it didn't get much air play. We did it more simply. The writers of the song, Harold Arlen and Johnny Mercer, were there and

Johnny got into the act. In the little call-and-response thing in the middle of the song, he sang those "my momma done told me" answers. You can barely tell the difference between when I stop and he starts, because we both sounded like barroom singers.

The funny thing was, we spent more time on the flip side of that record, which was "This Time the Dream's on Me." We worked for hours on it, and had the whole band singing and making backgrounds. That side, of course, was heard maybe twice and "Blues in the Night" turned into a smash.

The reception at the Strand was cheery news, and a far cry from the way we were received on Broadway later at the Paramount Theater. We opened there with a stage show that included Bob Hope. He was making his first New York appearance since becoming a hit in Chicago, where he had set attendance records at the Chicago Theater. Hope had an act that also featured his wife and Jerry Colonna, and he was used to breaking it up.

But business was rotten because we were booked with a so-so movie. The Paramount management went crazy trying to turn things around. Between shows, they had us making personal appearances around town, trying to get our pictures into the papers. But nothing helped.

For years afterward, Hope would hiss the title of that picture. He would say: "It was called *The Magnificent Fraud.* No wonder we died."

We stayed at the Paramount five or six weeks that first time, all the while fearful that we had blown any chance of being booked there again. To add to our anxiety, Hope was on edge because his act was being punctuated by a noise that sounded like a razzberry. The noise began to occur intermittently on the third or fourth day, during one of the morning shows. A few times the razz even competed with his punchlines.

The management had security guards and cops, even schoolchildren, trying to find the culprit. Hope was certain it was sabotage, and he was going wild. Arguments broke out offstage and there was a generally nervous atmosphere. After he had suffered much humiliation, a leakage in the sound system was discovered just in back of the big screen behind us on the stage.

When the band got another chance at the Paramount later, we rewarded the management with good business. We played there often after that, sometimes accompanying a Bob and Bing *Road* picture, and wound up staying for periods of from ten to twelve weeks.

The manager of the Paramount, Bob Whiteman, made some important contributions to the well-being of my family life. Charlotte loved the theater, and when we were in New York, she would go to a different show during every free moment. She knew that getting a single ticket was easy. Whiteman changed the band's schedule at the Paramount so that I could go with Charlotte to catch opening night of *Oklahoma!*

But a new problem was developing. We were doing five, six, and sometimes seven shows a day, seven days a week, beginning shortly after nine in the morning and finishing after midnight. I was concentrating so hard on making a success of the band that I hadn't paid much attention to such logical things as food. I was suffering from malnutrition and nervousness.

My lawyer set up a couple of meetings with a psychiatrist, a European guy. He helped me a great deal. In the process, however, we transferred the anxiety to the management of the Paramount and other theaters that we played subsequently.

The psychiatrist suggested that my anxiety was being caused, in part, by my arrival an hour or so before show time.

"Stop hanging around the theater," he said. "Instead, just walk in at the last minute and jump in."

It worked. But the Paramount management almost had heart failure the first few times I stepped into the theater and onto the stage, just as it was rising out of the orchestra pit.

The news of how well we were doing on Broadway led to more theater bookings around the country. But between those theater engagements, we were still scuffling for locations, such as hotels in which we might get some radio time. Radio was everything—the single most important link to bookings and good crowds. The broadcasts sustained the bands by keeping them before the public. Without radio, we might do well in Cleveland and the following week die in Columbus.

We were headed in all directions, using cars and a converted milk van. The trips would knock us out. After the war began, however, gasoline rationing forced us to use trains, and we would get some rest between engagements. Nevertheless, we would often close in one city one night and have to open the next morning in another town. Early shows were the norm everywhere, because our music was the entertainment of youth. Kids would skip school to hear us before the prices changed after noon.

We still called ourselves The Band That Plays the Blues, but in the newspaper advertisements and on the recordings we had become the Woody Herman Band. Among the changes was the addition of a female trumpet player named Billie Rogers, a good performer from Montana who also sang very well. She stayed from 1941 to 1943, when she left to start her own band.

Beginning in 1942, we began losing guys to the Army, including some of those who co-owned the band with me. My lawyer advised me to pick up their stock.

When it came time for me to take my physical for the draft in New York City, the band was playing in Detroit. GAC, which was booking us, was concerned about losing me. One of its representatives suggested that I stop off at an Army training camp in Maryland for a pre-physical on my way to New York. I took a train to Washington, made my way to the camp, and looked up the young doctor I was told to see.

"Have you ever had anything wrong with you?" he asked.

I said, "No, not really, but I recently had a hernia operation."

He touched the wound, and said, "Boy, they did a good job on that one." Then he started me on all sorts of tests, which took the entire day to complete. I was getting fed up with it, going from one doctor to another.

Every once in a while, the first young doctor would stop by and say, "I hope we can find something, because I don't believe you should be in the Army."

"Why not?" I asked.

"I'm here doing work," he said, "but you're doing more good on the outside than you could ever do in the service."

I certainly wanted to believe him, so it wasn't difficult to.

He was upset. He said, "I'm going to shake that hernia again. Get up on that chair."

While I was standing on the chair, he lunged at me with his finger and I went right up to the ceiling.

"Well," he said, "now you've got a hernia on the other side."

When I recovered, he issued me instructions before I left for the physical in New York.

"When you get to New York," he said, "don't take a cab. Walk from Penn Station to Grand Central. And when you get there, jump up and down a little bit, to be sure it's down and hanging."

Sure enough, the doctors took one look at the hernia, and I was rejected.

The band hadn't yet become a huge financial success by early 1942, but we had carved a number of significant notches with such hits as "Woodchopper's Ball" and "Blues in the Night," a few movie shorts that helped establish our identity, and what became a major recording with Bing Crosby, "Deep in the Heart of Texas." We used the so-called Woodchoppers, a septet taken from the full band, to back Bing.

The financial insecurity didn't have much of an effect on my marriage. Charlotte and I were both experienced with the show biz roller coaster, and we anticipated the lows even while hoping for highs. When we were poor, we managed to button up. But when we had even moderate prosperity, we lived to the hilt.

One way to have Charlotte share in any success was to surprise her with something expensive. After buying her a fur stole, I decided that every successful man's wife should have a natural ranch mink coat. She was flabbergasted. So were the lawyers who managed my business affairs, Goldfarb, Mirenburg and Vallon. Their reaction was: "Has she got something on him?"

Charlotte became pregnant and she left our Queens apartment temporarily to stay with her parents in Los Angeles. Our daughter, Ingrid, was born on September 3, 1941.

While Ingrid was still very small, we arranged to have a big reunion with our parents at a Christmas party in our Jackson Heights apartment. We had all the trimmings, including a couple of bonuses. One of them arrived from Milwaukee with my parents. When I was a kid, my father had built a mechanism to keep the Christmas tree turning—it had a little motor with the revolutions geared down—and he brought along all the works and set it up with the lights and a music box.

The second surprise was for Charlotte. I had noticed a certain look on her face one day when she eyed a Russian white fur in a store window. On Christmas Eve, I bought it. When she opened the box that evening, you could hear her for miles. My lawyers really flipped out.

7
INSIDE MOVES

With the personnel changes caused by the draft, we began to play differently, and I was looking for different kinds of arrangements. Most of our charts had been done by Jiggs Noble, Joe Bishop, Nick Harper, and Gordon Jenkins. They were fine writers, but I felt that we were in a rut; we weren't progressing.

Among those I turned to were Dave Matthews, who turned out such outstanding charts as "Four or Five Times," "Do Nothin' Till You Hear From Me," "Perdido," and "Cherry." And Dizzy Gillespie wrote three or four pieces for us, including "Down Under" and "Swing Shift."

Dizzy said I was the first guy to pay him $100 for an arrangement. I remember the first time I sent him over to my lawyers' office to pick up a check. My lawyers were good business people, but they were square. Dizzy went up there in full regalia—goatee and bebop glasses and so forth. And he was cleaning his nails with a stiletto.

I got a call from Goldfarb: "What the hell have you sent us now?" He said he didn't know whether to call the cops.

"Just give Dizzy a check for a hundred dollars," I told him.

Dizzy also subbed with the band for a week when we played the Apollo. I took the liberty of advising him to concentrate on arranging and writing tunes, which was where I thought his talent really lay.

"Forget the horn, stick to writing," I said. Thank God he ignored me.

During that period of the band's transition, I moved the family to the West Coast, into an apartment at the Garden of Allah, a fancy housing complex on Sunset Boulevard, with a bar, a dining room, and a pack of resident actors.

Charlotte was wonderful and mercurial, with a mad sense of humor that was sometimes sparked by jealousy. One of her chances to display it occurred when we spent three days with friends at their Malibu beach house. The woman was an excellent chef and Ingrid played with their son at the beach every day. It was a great visit and, as we were saying our goodbyes, I kissed our hostess very gently and thanked her. That's all there was to it.

We got in the old Cadillac and started back toward Los Angeles just as a blinding fog came in. I could barely see the road, so I stopped the car at the side and jumped out to wipe the windshield. While I was out there, I could hear the engine revving up, and I moved out of the way. Charlotte had slid into the driver's seat and she suddenly drove off in a blaze.

There I was, thirty miles from nowhere. I walked to a lamppost nearby, sat down at the base of it, and lit a cigarette.

About two minutes later, a cab stopped right at the base of the lamppost. The driver stuck his head out the window and said, "Can I help you, sir?"

I jumped in and told him, "Here's a double sawbuck, and I got some more if you get me to the Garden of Allah as quick as you can."

The guy was a born race driver. The fog didn't bother him and we drove into the Garden of Allah parking area just as Charlotte was pulling the car into the other driveway. I ran into the bar and ordered a drink. The martini was in front of me when Charlotte walked in, and when she saw me she shrieked in disbelief.

It was that mad sense of humor that helped keep us together. I was very proud of her, but she could also put me in some trying positions, not all of which had laughable endings.

After playing one evening at the Sherman Hotel in Chicago, we made our usual stop at an all-night place on West Street, on the near North Side. It was about two in the morning, and the place was crowded. We went to the bar for a drink before ordering food and greeted the patrons we knew.

All of sudden a woman in back of me put her hands over my eyes, let out a shriek, and said, "Hello, Woodsy!"

Without a word, Charlotte started picking up everything she could get her hands on—glasses, ashtrays—and began tossing them at the pink-mirrored bar. Before long, she had wiped out most of the booze and made a shambles of the mirror.

I sat quietly at the bar with my drink. I wasn't about to be lured into the fray. Everyone tried to appease her, but she just kept hurling things. Finally, this heavyset man, whom we knew casually, told her, "Charlotte, you're such a lovely gal; why are you doing this?"

She turned and gave him a shot in the belly, and he fell right to his knees.

• • •

By late 1942, the draft was causing personnel changes every day or every week. A year later, such players as tenor saxophonist Vido Musso, trombonist Eddie Bert, pianist Jimmy Rowles, and trumpeter Billy May had come and gone.

Then two guys named Chubby helped turn everything around.

8
A THREE-RING CIRCUS

The law firm of Herman Gold-farb, Mary Mirenburg, and Mike Vallon were handling the band's business affairs in the early forties. Goldfarb, whose nickname was Chubby, had worked as credit manager for the Conn Company, which made musical instruments. He knew thousands of musicians.

Goldfarb was aware that I was looking for a bass player in 1943, and he kept leaving messages for me to "Call Chubby."

I called Chubby Goldfarb and said, "What's up?"

"Call Chubby," he said.

"What do you mean, 'Call Chubby.' I thought you were Chubby. Who the hell *is* Chubby?"

"Chubby Jackson," he said, "a very good bass player with

Charlie Barnet. He's a great performer and he would be good for you."

Chubby Jackson recalls:

A guy calls me one day and says, "This is Chubby. How would you like to join the Woody Herman Band?"

Chubby? I figured it was a joke, so I hung up on him.

Then one day Woody calls and says, "This is Woody Herman. Did you get a call from my lawyer, Chubby Goldfarb?"

Chubby Goldfarb was right about Chubby Jackson, of course. He was not only a terrific bassist and the band's cheerleader, he was also a great help in filling our ranks with other fine musicians. He would get out to hear everybody and come back yelling about one player or another.

Chubby first helped us get singer Francis Wayne. The two of them recommended pianist Ralph Burns, who joined us in January 1944, from the Charlie Barnet band.

Ralph Burns was an especially important acquisition—a fine piano player and a great writer. He gave me the liberty to change his charts if he thought I could improve them. But I hardly ever touched them. As late as 1986, when I was planning the Fiftieth Anniversary Concert at the Hollywood Bowl, Ralph sent me a tape of a new piece called "The Godmother," which he dedicated to Charlotte. He said once again, "If there's anything you want different, do it." He always trusted me.

Ralph Burns recalls:

I joined about a month after Chubby, but I stopped playing piano regularly with the band after a couple of years. By that time, Woody had signed with Columbia and gotten the Wildroot radio show, so I said, "Why don't I just write and follow the band around?" I would meet the band every week before the Tuesday night show and turn in my charts.

I worked exclusively for Woody for about five years, and continued to write for the band for another ten while writing for singers and other bands at the same time.

I think my first chart for Woody was "Happiness Is Just a Thing Called Joe." I had done that one for Charlie Barnet, when Mary Ann McCall was singing for Charlie. With Woody, I wrote it for Francis Wayne to sing. I have no idea how many pieces I did altogether, but it was at least two or three a week during the first few years. I wrote "Bijou" in 1945, the same year I did "Summer Sequence" while spending the summer at Chubby Jackson's house in Freeport, on Long Island.

Woody taught me so much about writing. His big thing was that it wouldn't swing if there were too many notes. A lot of stuff is overwritten when you're young and eager. Sometimes he would edit the arrangements during rehearsals or on the bandstand.

He took "Bijou" as is. But when I got a little complicated on a chart, he always tried to simplify it. Sometimes I didn't feel good about the changes, but he knew what he was doing, and that's the way you learn. It was never offensive; he would maybe take out the brass here, or something like that, so that it would swing.

The band was very headstrong, but Woody kept us under control. He was a master at pulling everything together. We were like a big pro football team, crazy and wild and one big wonderful bunch. He would let us get a little crazy because he knew the music would come out. But when things got out of hand, he'd say, "Cool it."

He always knew his limitations as a musician. It was never "I'm the king." It was more like "I'm the father." He was a master psychologist. He knew how to manipulate people, and he manipulated us into giving our all.

It was a fantasy world for us, because people thought differently about bands then, probably the way they think about rock groups now. It took me years to recover from it. If you were a jazz musician playing with Woody Herman, you were almost like a movie star. You'd get into a town and people would be lined up outside waiting for your autograph. It was a wonderful trip.

Trumpeter Neal Hefti also followed Ralph from the Charlie Barnet band. Among the great pieces he wrote for us were

"Half Past Jumping Time" and "The Good Earth." He contributed brass figures to many of our head arrangements. That was very important in such pieces as "Caldonia," where the unison trumpet part was a high point. Neal and Francis Wayne fell in love, married, and left to join Harry James in 1946.

Flip Phillips, who had subbed in the band for Vido Musso in 1943, was skeptical about joining us. He was playing tenor sax with Russ Morgan's band. Morgan had been involved with jazz musicians in New York, but he had moved to a very commercial sound. Flip felt that Morgan's was a more stable operation. Even after he first joined us, he returned to Morgan two or three times. But he joined us for good in mid-1944.

Budd Johnson, the great saxophonist who had been Earl Hines' musical director for many years, also wrote for us and subbed a few times in my band. Budd was Mister Experience as a writer and a player with a big Coleman Hawkins tone. I didn't always feel that all my men were as competent as they should have been, and Budd was the kind of guest who could help tighten things up. It was one of my wiser moves.

At about the same time, a few members of Duke Ellington's band were unhappy about not getting enough attention. I felt the complaint was unjustified. I knew how Duke operated and, if there had been reason for anybody in his band to get more attention, he would have made it possible. He was that kind of guy. They were unhappy nonetheless, and three of them—tenor saxophonist Ben Webster, trombonist Juan Tizol, trumpeter Ray Nance, and alto saxophonist Johnny Hodges—approached me about recording with us.

It didn't bother Duke. He told me: "If you can make a buck, go ahead." I jumped at the opportunity.

Ben Webster first recorded two tunes with us, on November 8, 1943: "The Music Stopped" and "Do Nothing Till You Hear From Me." We went into a studio again nine days later and cut "Who Dat Up Dere, Who Dat Down Dere," which

Duke Ellington had something to do with the writing of. We were looking for material with broad appeal. Decca was giving us more and more liberties since we proved we could sell a few records.

"Who Dat Up Dere" was an overnight success. Ben didn't get billing on the record, but those who were into music recognized his distinctive sound. Duke took some heat from the NAACP about that tune, and he called and asked me what I could do to get it off the air. I told him, "I can't do anything about it on radio. All I can do is not play it on the bandstand."

It was the second time that one of my recordings had caused a fuss. The first was in 1939, when we cut "Blues on Parade," which was written by Toby Tyler. It apparently was a takeoff on Rossini's "Stabat Mater," which had been used in the Catholic Church on Good Friday. I had no idea about that, but I began to get threatening letters from the church about playing the piece. The church wanted me to get the recording off the market, which I couldn't do. But a young friend of mine who was attending a seminary got me out of the jam. He was a big music buff and he learned, to my relief, that Rossini's music had already been banned by the church, which had decided it was too dramatic. Saved by the bell, but I sweated.

Tizol, Nance, and Johnny Hodges joined us for a World Transcriptions recording session on April 5, 1944 (later released on Coral, Decca, and Ajaz), when we cut "Perdido," which Tizol had written, and "As Long as I Live," "I Didn't Know About You," and "Blue Lullabye."

With our music more diversified in mood and sound, we were able to play the black theaters. In fact, we were one of only two white bands doing that regularly—the other was Charlie Barnet's—in Baltimore, Washington, and New York at the Apollo.

When our drummer, Cliff Leeman, decided to leave, I

decided to bring in Davey Tough, who was working in Charlie Spivak's band. Chubby flipped out when I told him. He and some of the other guys in the band remembered him as the drummer with Tommy Dorsey a few years earlier, and they felt Davey wasn't a modern-enough player. Also, they were all in their twenties, and Tough was older.

"I don't think that's what we need," Chubby told me. "We need a little sweetie who's gonna help the band."

"This guy Tough is very special," I said, but Chubby was unconvinced.

The day after Davey joined the band, Chubby came to me raving.

Chubby Jackson recalls:

I had made the biggest mistake in the world, because I became acquainted with one of the better generals of rhythm thinking. Dave Tough was totally brilliant. He tuned the drums to certain notes; he didn't believe in metronomical time; he thought we should move. Flip was right down the middle, so we stayed with him. Sonny Berman used to play behind the beat, so we'd cool under him. And Bill Harris played on top of the beat, so we'd go with him. But when it was ensemble it was Davey and myself. He insisted that I stand right next to him so I could watch his foot pedal and the movement of his hands. I learned an awful lot from Dave.

We were no longer The Band That Plays the Blues. Thanks to George Simon, the writer who chronicled the Swing Era, we were becoming known as Woody Herman's Herd. George had given us that name in *Metronome* a few years earlier, but it was just beginning to catch on.

George Simon recalls:

During the summer of 1944, as a G.I., I drove out to Pleasure Beach in Bridgeport, Connecticut, to hear Woody Herman's band. Caesar Petrillo [head of the American Federation of Musicians] had put through one of his seemingly regular recording bans. This had been a long one, so that most of us hadn't had a chance to keep up with the sounds of the bands. And even though I'd always followed Woody closely since late 1936, when I'd become a fan of his band through a friend of his, I had no idea that he'd put together the sort of group I was to hear that night. It was completely different from anything of his I'd heard before. I went absolutely out of my mind.

There was a wonderful alto saxophone player by the name of Bill Shine, and of course there were Flip Phillips, Ray Wetzel, Pete Candoli, Conte Candoli, Neal Hefti, and Dick Munson. The guy I thought was really unheralded in that band was Ralph Pfeffner. His playing was gorgeous. Because Harris was all that exciting, Pfeffner was another exceptional trombone soloist who never got the breaks he deserved.

My review in Metronome came out in September of 1944. It began:

> "Before you can have a really great band," Woody Herman once told me, "you've got to be able to play really fine music all night long. You can't just coast along on a few good arrangements and then just play average stuff for the rest of the evening." Today Woody Herman's band qualifies in terms of Woody Herman's own exacting requirements, with no reservations whatsoever. . . . It can and does do everything. It jumps like mad, with either a soloist in the lead or the entire group attacking riffs en masse. And it can play really pretty, moodful ballads . . .

Finally, after raving about the Davey Tough–led rhythm section, and about Flip Phillips, Bill Harris, Ralph Burns and others, the review concluded:

> Yes, this is truly a great all-around band, this Woody Herman Herd . . .

I called it the Herd because I was a frustrated sports writer, and I used to do alliterations: The Herman Herd, The Goodman Gang,

The Dorsey Dervishes . . . brilliant things like that. The Herd was the only thing that really stuck.

We were getting exposure in movies, although there weren't any I want to brag about. We made a number of short films, one in 1938 for Vitaphone and a few for Universal.

What's Cookin'? was our first feature film, in 1942—a routine comedy that also featured the Andrews Sisters. Two years later, we made two pictures: *Earl Carroll Vanities* and *Sensations of 1945*, with Eleanor Powell. And we played in *New Orleans*, which featured Louis Armstrong and Billie Holiday.

I had to do a little acting in some of the films, but not much. They were all nothing pictures, especially the stock Westerns we appeared in for Republic. Making the movies was hard work and the finished products were disappointing. But they helped make the band more identifiable.

Of the eight or nine feature-length films we were in, the only good-budget picture was *Wintertime* for 20th Century Fox, starring Sonja Henie, in 1943. We had an option to do a couple more for that studio, but an unfortunate incident occurred.

We had been on the picture for weeks. We recorded the music first and then sat around for a call so we could go through the motions for the camera. The guys, meanwhile, were out playing ball or doing anything to pass the time. In the evenings, we were performing at the Hollywood Palladium.

The studio suddenly decided it needed us twenty-four hours straight through for a couple of days. By the second day of that, I was worn out, and the guys were trying to amuse themselves any way they could just to stay awake.

They decided to get one of the alto players in the band loaded, a nice quiet guy named Chuck DiMaggio. In the middle of a take at four in the morning, DiMaggio heaved right into his saxophone.

That ended our options at 20th Century Fox.

By the middle of 1944, the band was a solid swing machine, beefed up in every department. Marjorie Hyams became our vibraphonist, and the rhythm section was ironclad with Chubby Jackson on bass, Ralph Burns on piano, Davey Tough on drums, and Billy Bauer on guitar.

Chubby Jackson recalls:

When I joined Woody in 1943, it was still The Band That Plays the Blues—an adequate dance band but nothing terribly impressive.

Little by little, he started leaning more toward a jazz concept. Woody was absolutely the man who gave me the full range of all my little eccentricities. And we had a devotion to him that could easily be called love. He was a great coordinator of musicians, because of his personality. He understood not to tell a new guy how to play. "Let him play," he'd say, "and adjust it." [Trumpeter] Sonny Berman, for instance, liked to play three choruses in a row. But we discovered that Sonny was best at the little shouts, the eight-bar fill, or a little chorus.

The band looked like everything we did was an ad lib. That was our reputation—"Oh, look at that, right on the spur of the moment." But each move was well planned. I was the buffoon, the first one to wear the beard, the different uniforms. I got the blame for it as years went by. I was the eccentric—"He's out of it." Nobody really knew that Woody had suggested, "Let's do this, let's do that." The numbers we did together, when he called me out front, turned into bizarre vaudeville.

For example, one of the numbers he had me doing was to put the bass across my knees while sitting down. Woody and I had a dialogue before we went into the music. My bit was always screaming, "WOODY HERMAN," and "YOWWW." I knew when to yell. Woody always said that I won the down beat *poll one year for yelling. I knew just when to yell, and the band would respond. We were all geared up to beat the Chicago Bears every night.*

We used to be in utter amazement of [trombonist] Bill Harris.

We'd wait for his chorus to come and wonder, "What is he gonna play tonight?" Every night was another challenge for him.

Ralph Burns was a genius of an arranger and a composer, very deep. Neal Hefti had a lighter flavor, but he could bounce your nose off. So we had the thrill of a very heavy symphonic classical guy who would write gorgeous things and another who would bounce you into the next state.

On one-nighters, Woody would often leave in the middle of the last set, and we would make up head arrangements. "Apple Honey," "Wild Root," "Northwest Passage," those were made up by the rhythm section playing four to eight bars to get into it. Then Flip Phillips would start to play, endlessly. Meanwhile, Neal would add figures. Then Bill Harris, and finally the ensemble.

The next night I would say to Woody, "We got one for you."

"Let's hear it," he'd say.

Little by little we were adding our own flavor. Woody never stopped us. He would be the coordinator. Sometimes it would piss us off that we had something great and he would cut the shit out of it. But we would make the record, and suddenly it was absolutely right.

He knew how to posture everybody in a very short time. He knew exactly when somebody should be playing. We started to realize that we were able to show as much genius as the boss wished. We had seven or eight guys who were winning polls every year. It was a big boost for Woody, business-wise, because the band was getting more popular.

We had a spirit on that bandstand that no other band possessed. Basie's band was a lay-back band, good ensembles. Duke's band was based on a lot of marvelous potpourri, with marvelous writing. But none of these bands had, like, the fire engines starting to go.

I was in and out of the band because the moment that I saved any money I would leave to start my own band. And I would fail miserably. Then I'd call Woody and say, "It's me." He'd say, "When do you want to come back?"

I only saw Woody get really uptight once. It was years later, in the sixties, when he was coming into the Metropole in New York.

Top: Woody (left front) as a child performer in Milwaukee.

Right: Woody at age eleven in the uniform he wore for a performance of NOLA at the Wisconsin Theater.

Top left: As a teen, Woody had already begun thinking about leading a band.

Top right: The marquee of the Oshkosh Theater in Milwaukee heralding the "Boy Wonder."

Below: Promotional poster for the Tom Gerun band in 1932 featured a clowning Woody (before he changed the spelling from Woodie) and Al Morris, the singer-saxophonist who later changed his name to Tony Martin.

Left: With his tenor sax while a member of the Gus Arnheim Orchestra in late 1934. *Maurice Seymour*

Below: Posing with his bandleader, Isham Jones, in 1935. *Progress*

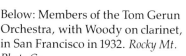

Below: Members of the Tom Gerun Orchestra, with Woody on clarinet, in San Francisco in 1932. *Rocky Mt. Photo Co.*

Above: Members of the Isham Jones Orchestra in 1936, with the leader seated at center and Woody kneeling at far right.

Below: By 1937, the Woody Herman Orchestra had grown to fourteen members. *Bill Burton*

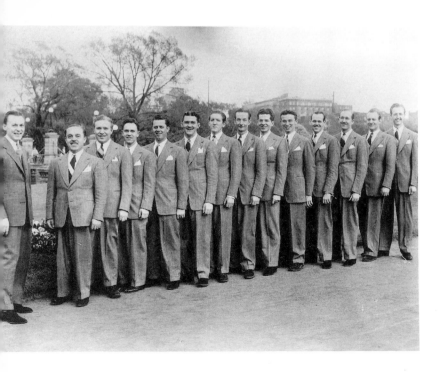

Above: Woody with Charlotte and daughter, Ingrid.

Left: Early promotion photo for Woody Herman and His Orchestra. *James J. Kriegsmann*

Below: Woody and Ingrid, age three.

Above: Woody and Benny Goodman jamming in the 1940s.

Opposite top: Tommy Dorsey (left) chatting with Benny Goodman and Woody in the mid-1940s.

Left: Benny Goodman (left) and Vaughn Monroe huddle with Woody at a Manhattan club in the 1940s. *Jack Pyle*

Above: With Tennessee Williams in the 1940s. *Albert Freeman*

Below: The Andrews Sisters and actress Claire Trevor (second from left) with Woody in the early 1940s.

Joe DiMaggio greeting Woody at a ballpark.

Woody and Tony Martin at the Hollywood Palladium in the 1940s. *Gene Lester*

Above: Bing Crosby with Woody at the recording session for "Deep in the Heart of Texas" in 1942.

Below: Woody and Charlotte (second from right) taking a break with Spade Cooley, who led a Western swing band that was booked in 1947 by Woody's office. Woman at right is unidentified. *Floyd McCarty, Warner Bros.*

Above: Woody and unidentified man watching Igor Stravinsky at work during New York rehearsal of "Ebony Concerto" in 1946.

Below: Igor Stravinsky making a point to Chubby Jackson (left), Don Lamond (center), and Flip Phillips (right) during "Ebony Concerto" rehearsal in Manhattan in 1946. *Hauser and Tischler*

Above: Woody, who was an auto-racing fan, with Mel Torme (right) and unidentified driver at a California track in the late 1940s. *Don Mohr Studio*

Below: President Lyndon B. Johnson greeting Woody at the White House in 1965.

Woody with his old high school teacher and mentor, Sister Fabian, at a benefit in Milwaukee for the Sister Fabian Scholarship Fund.

Woody and Charlotte (far right) during the South America tour in 1958.

Performing in an Armed Forces Radio show during World War II.
Armed Forces Radio Service

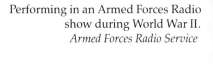

Woody greeting Johnny Mercer, with Artie Shaw (between them), George Simon, and Woody's grandson, Tom Littlefield, at right, in July 1973, opening night for Woody's band at the St. Regis Roof in Manhattan. *New Jersey Newsphotos*

Woody singing at the Vine Street club in Hollywood during a 1985 engagement. *W. G. Harris*

Above: Benny Goodman and Lionel Hampton helping Woody celebrate his opening at the King Cole Room of the St. Regis in 1986. *Richard Laird*

Right: Lawrence Berk, president and founder of the Berklee College of Music in Boston, presenting Woody with an honorary degree as Doctor of Music in May 1977. Woody, recovering from an auto accident, attended the ceremony in a wheelchair.

The Second Herd at the Century Room, Hotel Commodore, in Manhattan, on April 20, 1948.

They had hired me to be the relief band. I played the first set, and then I saw Woody down at the other end of the bar. I put down my bass, and yelled "Hey Wood," and we hugged. The boss of the Metropole was an unbelievable man. The bartenders and everybody were afraid of him. Woody and I talked while he was putting a reed in his clarinet. And the boss comes over and says, "Hey, c'mon man, let's go to work, what are you doin' here?"

Nobody talked to Woody that way.

"Excuse me?" Woody said, glaring at him.

And the guy said, "Yeah, you're Woody Herman, aren't you? Well I own this joint, so let's get on the bandstand. Talk to this guy later."

So Woody said, "I'll tell you, sir, you talk to [business manager] Abe Turchen from now on if you want to say anything to me. If you say the same thing to me again in the same tone, two things are going to occur. I'm going to turn around and tell my band to go home, and, number two, I'm gonna take this clarinet and break it over your fucking head."

I looked at Woody and, in all the years that I'd known him, I said, "Hey, is that you?"

He said, "Chubby, every now and then a man has to stand up and be a man."

Another time that he threw a great line at me was after my divorce. I was in terrible shape in Detroit, and he was coming into town. We got together in his hotel room.

He said, "All right, come on, what's the matter?"

"I really don't want to talk about it, Wood."

He said, "Look, I'm an amateur psychologist after leading a band for so many years, and you're my boy. So tell me whatever you want to tell me. Get it off your chest."

"Woody, I don't wish to talk about it."

And he said, "Thanks."

"Thanks?"

He said, "Look, I got enough going on myself. I would do it for you because of my affection for you. But being you don't want to talk about it takes a big load off my mind."

We were beefing up the band in every section.

Flip Phillips was joined in the reed section by Sam Marowitz on lead alto and John LaPorta. Pete Candoli came over from the Tommy Dorsey band to play lead trumpet. And Pete's kid brother, Conte, took a seat in the trumpet section during the summer of 1944, while he was still a teenager. I told him he could come back when he finished high school. And he did.

With some coaxing, we convinced trombonist Bill Harris to leave Bob Chester's band. Bill had also served with Benny Goodman, Gene Krupa, and Ray McKinley. He was a powerhouse who pulled the whole section with him. By the end of 1944, Sonny Berman added energy to the trumpets, and Shorty Rogers joined him the following year.

The band was like a three-ring circus. Chubby Jackson was doing his own number, jumping in the air, mugging and carrying on like crazy. And the five trumpet players paraded on the top riser, swinging back and forth.

When Tommy Dorsey was asked about the band, he said, "I don't know how they play, but they sure as hell are great dancers."

Sonny Berman finished his solo one night and, while they were swinging up there with their horns, he jumped down to the next level. His portly figure went right through the floorboard, and he was in wood up to his navel.

Sonny was a happy young man, with fire and feeling in his horn. His potential was enormous, and he might have fulfilled it if his heroin habit hadn't cut him down at the age of twenty-one, after he left our band.

Everybody in the band was trying to top each other, and Pete Candoli came up with one of our most successful gimmicks, which he initiated on his own one day. While we were playing "Apple Honey," he sneaked off the bandstand and put on a red and blue Superman outfit, cape and all, that his wife had made for him. We were playing the last chorus when he jumped out on stage in time to play his walloping passages. It brought down the house, and it remained part of our act.

Bill Harris, too, was famous for his bits. He was a great practical joker, continually finding gimmicks to use on and off stage. He had a little gizmo that would make fart sounds. I remember him in an elevator full of people, driving them mad with it at the Sherman Hotel in Chicago. And he would use it to break up the band on stage.

Bill wanted me to get a fellow in Philadelphia to make him a set of shoe cleats that locked on to the stage. That way he could bend all the way back, forward and sideways without falling, while playing trombone. But the guy in Philly was about to go out of business and didn't want to mess with it.

Once at the Paramount in New York, Bill and Sonny Berman got a monkey and put it in a dressing room on the seventh floor. Any publishers who wanted to show us songs were told they had to talk first with the new secretary in Room 702. When their knocking went unanswered, they would open the door and there was this fucking monkey swinging from wall to wall, with monkey shit all over the place.

Billy Bauer recalls:

I got there in the spring of 1944. The only guy I knew in the band was Flip, and he probably recommended me. He and I had written tunes together and we had worked together.

Woody was playing at the Meadowbrook in New Jersey. He called me and said, "I wonder if you'd come over and sit in with the band."

"Gee, Woody," I said, "you picked the wrong night." It was my daughter's birthday and we had a party going on.

So he said, "Go up to see Abe Turchen and sign a contract."

I joined the band a few days later in Detroit. The band was shrieking, and Woody let me play bombs. Davey Tough liked me. When we played in crammed quarters, he said, "You sit right here." After we got through one night, he said to me, "You know something, I only thought a Christian could play like that."

Eastwood Gardens in Detroit was an open-air place, and we were playing there once when it started to drizzle. They didn't want to cancel, so they moved the whole band under a shed, and all the people were jammed in there on top of us. The band just wailed that night. When we stopped, nobody said anything. The hair was standing up on my arms. I said to Davey, "Look." And he pulled up his sleeve and said the same thing.

I asked for raises a number of times, and got them. But one time, Woody said, "Well, let me think about it." We hit this town and Charlotte came to meet us, something she would do every once in a while. Woody said to me, "Bring the guitar to my dressing room." I did, and Charlotte was there. Woody took out his clarinet and said, "All right, come on, let's play." He started and I followed. We played away for about ten minutes. Then he looked around at Charlotte and said, "Okay, what do you think?" She didn't say anything. She just shook her head yes. I got the raise.

We had an incident once with Skippy DeSair, the baritone saxophone player. He was the kind of guy who would sleep on the floor so he wouldn't have to pay for his room. He owned a couple of apartment houses in Albany. On the road he would stop at pawn shops and pick up Conn instruments. He'd pay something like fifty dollars for them and go to the post office and mail them to Conn, and they'd send him a check for seventy-five, or something like that. Anyway, Skippy came up with this idea for guys in the band to pool their money for him to invest for us. But we didn't go for it.

Then he came up with this idea to sell little plastic penny whistles, classic black with a white mouthpiece, with Woody's name imprinted on them. He talked to Woody about it, and Woody said, "It sounds good, but I don't bother with that stuff. Speak to the lawyers who manage the band."

Skippy did, and he came back and said he had to find out how much it would cost to get a mold for the whistle. It was thousands of dollars. The lawyers called Skippy to sign a contract.

Woody said to Skippy, "Get yourself a lawyer. I don't want anything to do with it." So Skippy told us one day, "Hey, I signed a contract. I get five percent."

We didn't hear much about it after that, but we noticed later that, as we were playing, there were vendors going around with these whistles. Then we saw them in Gimbels. Skippy figured he was going to make a lot of money, but the whistle company pointed out that he was entitled only to five percent of what he sold. Woody told him again, "I told you to get yourself a lawyer." Then Woody told us, "Listen, ideas are a dime a dozen. To get them working is what counts. If Skippy had gotten a lawyer before he signed a contract he might have been all right."

Most of the guys were warm toward each other. We'd get together every night in one room or another. It was a happy band. When Roosevelt died, we were at the Sherman Hotel in Chicago. We got on the bandstand and played the Star Spangled Banner. It was a chilling moment. Then we packed up.

When we played the Paramount in New York for five or six weeks, we'd hang out in the dressing rooms between shows. Sonny Berman, Neal Hefti, and Shorty Rogers. Once we did a "Jack and the Beanstalk" recording for fun on an acetate machine for my daughter, Pam. It was Red Norvo, Chubby, and Sonny, and I was Jack. We wrote a whole skit, with Buddy Lester—the comic who was Jerry Lester's brother— narrating. Sonny did a very good Jewish accent, so on the other side they did the same story in Yiddish. I still have it.

Abe Turchen, who was the road manager, was quite a character. After we played in a fight arena in Birmingham, Alabama, one time, Abe had a big bag over his shoulder when he came on the bus. He looked like Santa Claus. And in the bag was the money.

I left the band a few months before he broke it up near the end of 1946. Chuck Wayne took my place.

• • •

Our national popularity was nourished in 1945 by our film appearances and our weekly Old Gold radio broadcasts in August and September, when we replaced the Frankie Carle band. The biggest shot in the arm, however, was signing with Columbia Records.

It was still wartime, and companies could press only a limited number of records for an artist before moving on to another artist. So I made a deal.

"Don't worry about the guarantees," I told Columbia. "Just give me as much publicity as your top two artists." The top two Columbia artists then were Frank Sinatra and Dinah Shore. Every time Columbia put an ad in a trade paper, I got one. That drove the other bandleaders crazy—Les Brown, Harry James. They couldn't figure it out. Sinatra would be on one page, Dinah Shore on the other, and I would be on the next: "Columbia Records presents . . ." We became Number One in the country because of that as much as anything. It pushed us to the very peak of popularity.

"Laura" was the first side we recorded on our first Columbia date, and it was also our first release. I had seen the movie, heard the theme and liked it. Harry James was Columbia's big band then, and he thought he had it sewed up. He recorded it a few days after us, but Columbia scrapped his and released ours.

I had arranged with Johnny Mercer to sing his lyric. We were performing at the Meadowbrook in New Jersey when we went into the studio in New York on February 19, 1945, to make the cut. It became a smash hit. Columbia had a gold record made as a special gift to me, even though the record hadn't really sold a million copies. It couldn't, because the companies weren't allowed to press that many. But Columbia gave me the gold record as a token. Over a period of years, it finally did sell a million.

On that session, we also recorded "Apple Honey," which

was one of our many head arrangements on which everybody contributed—Pete Candoli, Bill Harris, Flip Phillips, Ralph Burns, and Neal Hefti. It was based on the chords of "I Got Rhythm."

We recorded "Caldonia" and "Happiness Is Just a Thing Called Joe" a week later. I had heard about "Caldonia" through music publishing friends and some guys who had seen Louis Jordan perform at the Paramount. I sent Ralph Burns there to listen.

"Yeah! We've got to do it," he said. It was twelve bars, up-tempo, with the shout at the very end—"Caldonia, Caldonia, what makes your big head so hard!" We made up everything else in that chart with a head arrangement. We were the only band doing that sort of thing at the time, and it gave us something different to say. The kids were picking up on it and that contributed plenty to our success.

"Happiness Is Just a Thing Called Joe" was the best thing that Francis Wayne ever sang with us. She showed an awful lot on that song, which she had been doing in a nightclub act before she joined us.

Our next session was March 1, and we recorded three more of what were to become some of our biggest numbers: "Goosey Gander," "Northwest Passage," and "I've Got the World on a String."

"Goosey Gander" was completely a head arrangement. We needed a fourth side on the record date, and that's what we came up with. The beginning is based on "Shortnin' Bread," but like so many other things, it goes into the blues. The screeching trumpet over the ensemble was Pete Candoli, and that little extra drum tag that Davey Tough put on the end was one of those things we liked to do in one way or another. We hated to cut arrangements short, the way most of the big bands were doing, so we usually let about three more things fall.

"Northwest Passage," too, was a head arrangement that

evolved on the job. It began with that little thing around rhythm and vibes and we kept adding and changing it around. The ensemble shout is Neal Hefti's.

I always liked "I've Got the World on a String." It was the first arrangement that Ralph Burns wrote at Chubby Jackson's request. I used it throughout my career.

Two more of our hits were recorded in August: "The Good Earth" and "Bijou." Neal Hefti wrote "The Good Earth," and we broke it in on the job. It's a wonderfully constructed piece that every young arranger could learn from. My clarinet tag was ad-libbed, another way of not cutting our endings too short. Ralph Burns wrote "Bijou" for Bill Harris, and it really established Bill as a major instrumentalist. I gave it the "Rhumba a la Jazz" subtitle because I was trying to explain why we were abusing the Latin rhythm. I guess you could call it a "stone-age bossa nova."

Virtually every time we went into the studio, we came out with at least one hit. On the September 5 recording date, we did "Your Father's Moustache." The melody was by Bill Harris and the ensemble chart belonged to Neal Hefti. Buddy Rich did a terrific job, subbing for Davey Tough, and Red Norvo played vibes.

Almost all of our records were selling to the maximum number of wartime pressings. A number of bands were doing as well, but we were causing more excitement with the Columbia promotion and the popularity of our presentation.

In October 1945, we became the first band in years to sign for a weekly network radio show. It was sponsored by Wildroot, the hair tonic and shampoo company, and the added exposure helped us set attendance records at ballrooms and theaters everywhere.

Neal Hefti, meanwhile, composed "Wild Root," which was based on "Flyin' Home," and we played it for months before we named it after our radio sponsor.

The domino effect was incredible. The Herd was voted the best swing band in the *down beat* poll, and it won awards from *Metronome* and *Esquire*. The 1945 *Esquire* New Star awards went to Flip Phillips for tenor sax, to Chubby Jackson for bass, to Bill Harris for trombone and, the following year, to trumpeter Pete Candoli and pianist Ralph Burns. Bill, Chubby, and Davey Tough also won polls conducted by *down beat* and *Metronome*.

But by the time Tough was selected, he had become too ill to work regularly. So we sent for Don Lamond.

Don Lamond recalls:

I was in Washington, D.C., which was my home at the time, when Sonny Berman recommended me to Woody at the end of 1945. My own small band had just finished a long gig and I was jobbing around. Woody's band was in Norfolk, Virginia, when I got the call from Abe Turchen, who was the road manager. He said, "Don't bring your drums, because you can use Davey's."

I went out to the airport and got on a plane, but we were just sitting and sitting there for a long time. There was a big flood down South, from Washington all the way to Georgia. The plane couldn't take off because it couldn't land in Norfolk.

After about forty-five minutes or an hour, we got off and I went down to Union Station to get on a train. But it took us hours to get to Norfolk because the flood prevented the train from running on the regular tracks. By the time I got to Norfolk, the band had left for Raleigh, North Carolina. By time I got to Raleigh, they had left for Charleston, South Carolina.

Back on the train. The railroad had put on extra runs with steam locomotives because of all the servicemen coming home, and with the windows open we were black with soot. The train pulled into Charleston at about seven or eight o'clock at night, early enough to make the gig. But the train yards were in chaos because of all the traffic. So the train sat in the yards until it got to be about ten.

I finally got off in the train yards and walked through to the station. But by the time I got to the gig, the band had left again. I stayed overnight at the YMCA, which, like the train tickets, was at my own expense. I hadn't received any advance.

I was about ready to give up. I figured, well, Woody's probably got another drummer by now. But I took a chance and followed them to Augusta, Georgia. When I got there, I asked around for the main hotel, and I telephoned, asking if they had a Sonny Berman registered.

"Yes, he's here," somebody answered.

God almighty, I finally found them.

When I spoke to Sonny, he said, "Where the hell have you been?"

I said, "I've been trying to catch this damn band for a week."

I got to the hotel and I was black from the soot. Abe Turchen said, "Why didn't you take a private plane from Raleigh?"

I said, "Now you tell me."

When I played that night, the first tune that Woody pulled up was called "Half Past Jumpin' Time." I knew the damn thing because Neal Hefti had written the same chart for the Sonny Dunham band. The guys must have thought, this guy can really read.

Woody's was an easy band to play with. I had quite a bit of experience with Boyd Raeburn and some other big bands, so a lot of the time I didn't even look at the music; I just felt my way through it.

That band was powerful, with Flip Phillips, Bill Harris, Conrad Gozzo, and Sonny Berman. I first knew Sonny when he was seventeen, in Louis Prima's band. Then he went with Sonny Dunham, then with Boyd Raeburn. I left Raeburn to return to Washington and Sonny, meantime, went to Harry James and then to Woody. He died in 1946 at the age of twenty-one.

I had a good relationship with Woody. He never would strain you up, like Benny Goodman would. He gave me a free hand. He was a good guy to work for.

When Woody broke up that band at the end of 1946, I was living in Santa Monica, because Jimmy Rowles had talked me into coming out there. Jimmy, who was the pianist with Woody when the Army drafted him in 1943, was given his old job back when he was discharged early in 1946. It was the law. He replaced Tony Aless, who came up to me and said, "Jeez, I got my notice."

I was in the Bradford Hotel in Boston when I saw this guy walking down the corridor with dark glasses, and I said, "Who's this character?" It turned out to be Jimmy. We played a ballroom that night and all I had to hear was about eight bars before he became a real favorite of mine. A magnificent player.

Things were terrific. But the best was yet to come.

9
AT THE TOP

A young man who worked for a music publisher in New York had some conversations in 1945 with my attorney, Howard Goldfarb, about Igor Stravinsky. The young man knew the composer and Goldfarb decided he would try to interest Stravinsky in writing something for our band.

I didn't think it could happen; it seemed too impossible. But the idea was appealing.

Later that year, I received a wire from Stravinsky: "I'm writing something for you. It will be my Christmas present to you and the band."

It was one of the wildest psychological moments I ever had. Having one of the world's great composers write for me was beyond imagination.

Then Stravinsky's lawyer called Goldfarb and said, "Do you realize that Stravinsky can't afford to live, let alone be giving away music?" So we arranged to get him a fee.

Stravinsky was living in California, not far from me in Hollywood. When I met him, I found a wonderful man with a great sense of humor. We spent hours just talking about everything but music. He was amusing and amazing. His English was good, but heavily accented, and he pronounced my name more as Wood-He than Woody.

Much later, during an evening at my home, I asked him, "Mr. Stravinsky, you must tell me about French clarinetists, about German clarinetists, and the difference in their performance."

He replied, "French clarinet players: very good technique, quick tongue, very small sounds. The German players: technique not so good, tongue not so good, but very big sound . . . But you, Woody . . . Ah!"

I could have kissed him.

About Christmastime, he came to New York to rehearse the band for "Ebony Concerto." We were playing the Paramount Theater, doing six or seven shows a day, and we used a rehearsal hall upstairs. We had about an hour and twenty minutes between performances. Our brass players were all Stravinsky fans and they had been talking for days about meeting him.

The first rehearsal occurred in the morning, after the first show of the day. All the guys rushed upstairs, still wearing their uniforms—dark suits, white shirts and ties. Stravinsky arrived with a towel around his neck, wearing an old sweatshirt, grey slacks, and tennis shoes.

The rehearsal was difficult. Most of us had never received any classical training. We had to learn from each other. We fought and perspired our way through the first hour. Our nerves were completely wrenched and some of us were ready to give up. Stravinsky, sensing our collective anxiety, walked over and put his arm around me.

"Woody," he said, "you have a lovely family."

That helped reduce the pressure. We relaxed somewhat but worked like mad during the next few days.

He hummed and whistled and tapped his foot while he dragged us through it. He was only interested in whether we got it, not how we got it. It was as big a challenge for him as it was for us because he had to write out the concerto in 4/4 time. It was difficult for us to imagine, but a simple time signature like 4/4 was giving a master trouble. He told me it was torture for him, but he had to do it if he was going to write for jazz musicians.

He couldn't stay to conduct the premiere of "Ebony Concerto" in March 1946 at Carnegie Hall because of a tour that was set for him in Europe. He said he didn't care about the tour, but he had to do it to eat.

After the debut, the idea was sold as a concert and we began a tour with it across the country. Between the good receptions, there were some wacky disappointments, mainly because the tour wasn't always promoted properly. The first place we played was a hall in Baltimore. Stravinsky's protégé was conducting, and he was thrilled to death. But when we started to play the piece, the audience began to boo. They didn't want to hear it.

The concert was booked into universities, where agents figured there would be an interest in culture. Of all the schools we played, Purdue gave us the worst reception. The campus theater, which presented mostly vaudeville and show biz events, was packed. But "Ebony Concerto" thoroughly confused the audience. It was a Mexican standoff. No matter when we performed the piece—at the start of a concert, in the middle or at the finish—many of the audiences decided that the music wasn't me, that we were insulting their intelligence.

Benny Goodman, among others, was puzzled about why

Stravinsky would write a piece for me. One night I ran into him on Broadway at four in the morning, and he said, "Hey, kid, is that a hard part, that Stravinsky piece?"

"Is it hard?" I said. "Man, it's impossible."

"Oh, it can't be that hard," Benny said, making an obvious reference to how he felt about my clarinet playing.

"Listen," I said, "when I went to all the guys I could talk to at the Philharmonic and different places and had them look at it, they said, 'Jeezus, it's gonna be difficult.' "

Benny remained skeptical. "So it's a little bit difficult, but it can't be *that* hard."

I got hold of a mini-score of the concerto and sent it to his house. About six weeks later, I ran into Benny again, and he said, "Hey, that *is* a hard piece!"

From Benny, that was a big statement. He eventually did the concerto for Columbia, after we recorded it with Stravinsky conducting.

Benny had a very nutty attitude about lots of things, but it had nothing to do with his musical abilities. He was the head and shoulders of the clarinet.

We hung out socially a little bit in the forties, and once in the fifties I looked him up in Nashville after someone pointed out that he was in town. We made arrangements to meet for dinner, and I told him about a good place out in the country. But first I went to his hotel room with a bottle of gin and some vermouth. I fixed a pitcher of martinis and iced them down well.

"Hey, what's this?" Benny asked after taking a sip.

I couldn't believe he had never tried a martini. I told him what it was, and he knocked the rest of it right down. I explained that this was just a quick drink before dinner, but we wound up polishing off much of the bottle.

We never made it to the country restaurant. Instead, we held each other up and staggered into a greasy spoon across from his hotel.

10
THE HOMEFRONT

The band grossed more than a million dollars in 1946, and Charlotte and I were anxious to invest some of our earnings in a home. We moved early in 1946 to Laurel Canyon, where we leased a place for a few months while we were looking.

The house we fell in love with was being vacated by Humphrey Bogart and Lauren Bacall. It was high on Hollywood Boulevard, with a sweeping view of the valley from a large rear terrace which jutted out from the mountainside at the center level of the three stories.

Bacall was the businessperson in that real estate deal, and a pain in the ass, too.

We bought the house for about $60,000 cash, and things couldn't have seemed rosier. The band was riding high, the family was ensconced in the Hollywood Hills, and we had such sociable neighbors as Robert Benchley and Charlie Butterworth.

Beneath the surface, however, a major problem was growing. It had begun to develop a couple of years earlier, when we were living at the Garden of Allah complex. Charlotte had begun drinking and she was taking pills. As I told Gene Lees much later, you start mixing Nembutals with booze, and you're on your way home.

I suppose she was influenced by the movie crowd who lived there, and my absence for up to forty weeks a year on the road contributed to her difficulty.

I was disturbed about it, but there wasn't a great deal I could do. Like anyone with a drinking problem, she had many excuses. I even threatened to take a walk. But it was an empty gesture; we were very tight.

Charlotte suffered greatly and really tried to beat the rap. Eventually, she sought psychiatrists and other help by herself. One of the more drastic steps she took was to undergo shock treatments. Ingrid, meanwhile, was always well taken care of by Charlotte and a live-in nursemaid.

I talked to my close friends about the problem—Jack Siefert in Philadelphia, Ray Sherman and his wife in Milwaukee, and Don and Elsa Cummings. Don was a comic and Elsa had been very close to Charlotte since the early days when they had danced in shows together.

I decided that the only way I could help was to go home.

So I broke up the band.

It was just before the Christmas holidays in 1946, and I handled it with the guys as well as I could. I told them that I thought we had gone as far as we were going with the band, and I gave them sufficient notice.

I went to Alcoholics Anonymous meetings with Charlotte, to keep her company, and, the first time we arrived at one, I saw a lot of my ex-band members and many of my friends. I remember Billy May greeting me with open arms, and I told him: "I'm cool, you know. I'm just here with Charlotte." I enjoyed the meetings. It was nice to hear people bare their souls.

Being off the road was a situation I hadn't known since I was eight. It was appealing to eat dinner with my family, play with my daughter—carrying on with her out in the yard and throwing her into the bathtub.

I did a California radio show once a week with Peggy Lee and her husband, Dave Barbour, who led the band. I didn't want to be a bandleader. I was just the boy singer with Peggy. It worked out fine.

Ralph Burns put together a band, and I sang some tunes with them. I was invited to do a radio deejay show, on which we would play new releases and judge them. It was beautiful because we'd get angry phone calls.

I opened an office in what was probably the most auspicious location in the Wilshire district of Los Angeles: the former offices of Robbins Music in the Beverly Wilshire Hotel. It was on the mezzanine, which led to the outdoor pool. Anyone who wanted to reach my office was usually connected to the bar at poolside. It was a classy operation.

I installed a couple of my former road managers in that office: Jack Archer, who had worked for the band in the late thirties before marrying our female trumpet player, Billy Rogers, and leaving to start their own group; and Milton Deutsch, who had replaced Archer. With them I had Abe Turchen, who was road manager before I folded the First Herd.

Among the things they decided to do was to handle bookings for a guy named Spade Cooley, who was leading a hot so-called Western swing band in California. I knew Spade casually, and I interceded for Abe and Milton, talking him into going on the road for one-nighters. He had never done that before. He was a Los Angeles product with some minor league hits on the Victor label, and he had stuck to his home base.

Spade Cooley consented, and I advised the guys in my office: "Take him up and down the West Coast and back again. And don't go any farther east than Nevada. Anywhere else, they're not going to know him." It worked like a charm. They got good guarantees and they hit percentages every night.

They thought the boat had come in and decided to be courageous. They took him into Iowa and the surrounding area with a complete revue—horses, dancers, singers, a show biz thing. Nobody knew him, or cared, and I started to get phone calls at four in the morning. It was Spade Cooley, making soulful, moaning sounds such as, "Like, man, I'm ruined." It was a terrible fiasco. I think he had to walk back halfway to the coast.

My office quietly dissolved. Cooley wound up in jail many years later on a murder conviction.

I had fun for seven months without any urge to get back in front of a band.

11
THE SECOND HERD

One night, some friends and I went out to a little joint on Sunset near Vine Street. Phil Moore, a pianist and arranger, was leading a little group there that included trumpeter Ernie Royal and his brother, Marshall Royal, who later joined Count Basie.

When I heard Ernie play so fluently at the top of the horn, it gave me the hots for music again. Trying to make something different happen was always in the back of my mind. You hear a great player or two and the idea is replanted, as long as I could do it without having to return to what I already did.

The family problems were taken care of, and I felt I had to do something productive again.

Jimmy Giuffre, hearing that I might be organizing a band, told me he had an idea for a different saxophone sound. We started sending for guys. Most of them were at the beach, just bumming around, including Zoot Sims and Stan Getz. We sent to Boston for Serge Chaloff, because we wanted a dancer in the band. He had already fooled around with the Jimmy Dorsey band, and somebody who had heard him said, "This guy's far out." He was.

As we put together a roster of players, I kept wondering how far I could go with this new bebop sound. My fear was that we would not be able to top ourselves, that we would reach the end of the rope. I didn't want to go backwards, repeating what I had already done. When that happens, the music just becomes repetition, which is what most bands were about. I never felt that way with the First Herd.

I never wanted to sell nostalgia. Where there are certain tunes closely associated with the band, it would be unfair not to play a few on occasion to recapture memories for people. But I never considered it our big job, or our future, to delve further into the past.

Holdovers from the First Herd included Shorty Rogers on trumpet, Sam Marowitz on alto sax, and Don Lamond on drums. Walt Yoder, who had been at the core of the original Band That Plays the Blues, returned as our bassist. Along with Rogers, our writers were Ralph Burns, Jimmy Giuffre, Al Cohn, and John LaPorta.

A bandful of young, sharp players filled the rest of the lineup. With Rogers and Royal, the trumpet section held Stan Fishelson, Bernie Glow, and Marky Markowitz. Earl Swope buoyed the trombone section, with Ollie Wilson and Bob Swift. Gene Sargent played guitar, Jerry Ney doubled on vocals and vibes, and Fred Otis was the pianist.

The Second Herd was launched on the evening of October 16, 1947, at Municipal Auditorium, in San Bernardino, California.

The centerpiece of the band was the three-tenor-and-a-baritone sax section, a configuration that I kept with every big band that followed. Its anthem was Jimmy Giuffre's "Four Brothers," which soon became the band's subtitle. Giuffre's tune helped to set a style for the band. The original Four Brothers were Zoot Sims, Stan Getz, and Herbie Steward on tenors and Serge Chaloff on baritone. The sequence of sax solos on the original recording, by the way, was Zoot, Serge, Herbie, and Stan.

The Second Herd was organized with the full intent of going straight ahead with bebop. Ralph Burns and Shorty Rogers were still writing some of our arrangements, but the bebop evolution had become the core of our music. We gathered invention and diversification not only from the charts of Al Cohn and Jimmy Giuffre, but from the provocative, emotional sounds of our reed and brass soloists. After a few months, Al Cohn replaced Herbie Steward as a member of the Four Brothers, and Mary Ann McCall returned as our singer early in 1948.

Ralph Burns added a fourth movement to his "Summer Sequence," the first three parts of which we had premiered with the First Herd at Carnegie Hall, when we played "Ebony Concerto" for the first time. Ralph wrote the fourth part as an epilogue because Columbia needed more music to fill out a "Summer Sequence" album.

With a few melodic changes, the fourth part was retitled "Early Autumn," and Johnny Mercer, who was one of America's greatest poets, wrote exquisite lyrics to it. Stan Getz was the tenor soloist on the original recording, and seldom in the history of music has one record established the reputation of a player as "Summer Sequence" did for Stan. But also listen to the trombone playing of Ollie Wilson on that cut. I always thought he showed a lot of promise. And Ralph plays super piano on all four segments of "Summer Sequence."

Shorty Rogers, who helped with a lot of things in the First

Herd, was writing terrific bebop charts. He was one of the great contributors to both bands. Red Norvo, who was his brother-in-law then, was helpful in bringing him to us.

Don Lamond was playing drums, and he made that rhythm section. We had some changes in the other spots, but once it settled in, it was great. Chubby Jackson even returned after a while.

Lamond recalls:

The Four Brothers band was the best band. Maybe it wasn't quite as fiery as the First Herd, with "Caldonia" and "Apple Honey" and all. But it was the best.

The band was spectacular. But the public wasn't ready for it. Unlike the previous herd, it wasn't playing the pop music of the day.

We were getting some terrific receptions on tour, but we weren't getting enough bookings. We moved from Columbia to Capitol because Carlos Gastel, who was handling our personal management, felt he could pull some weight there. Other artists he handled, such as Peggy Lee and Nat Cole, were also recording for Capitol. But we weren't selling records like we had in the early forties. Even Sinatra had pretty much cooled off during that period.

The band's downfall was caused by a combination of things. But changing the sound was certainly a big factor. It was something I felt I had to do. The audience that could understand "Apple Honey," however, couldn't relate to "Lemon Drop" or "Four Brothers." Musically, the bebop route was magnificent. But business-wise, it was the dumbest thing I ever did. Those pieces didn't really succeed, except with a small percentage of our listeners, until the mid-1950s. If we had just continued playing "Apple Honey" and "Caldonia," we'd probably have had a fighting chance.

The band was an albatross. The first year of its operation cost me $175,000, which I didn't have. In order to keep refinancing it, I used the side-door method—doing brief tours with a small group. I would take out a sextet for a trip to keep my feet on the ground with a little profit.

Among those who came through that band at one time or another were bassist Oscar Pettiford and drummers Shadow Wilson and Shelly Manne. Replacements in the sax section included Jimmy Giuffre, Gene Ammons, and Billy Mitchell. Red Rodney joined the trumpet section in the fall of 1948.

Red Rodney recalls:

I took the place of Marky Markowitz when the band was at the Royal Roost in New York City. Chubby Jackson had called me to join when the band was being organized, but I couldn't make it. I told him I wasn't interested then in going with a big band. I was getting my feet wet on 52nd Street, and I had just been with Claude Thornhill and I wanted to be in a small band. The only reason I joined in 1948 was I needed a job; I needed the money. Woody offered good money and being with that band was an opportunity to help my career. I know that everyone says it was a financial flop, but musically it was Number One. It was the hippest and the best.

The First Herd was a unique band; it was different. But it wasn't rated by the jazz musicians as well as the Second Herd. Ours was much more musical, more subtle. Al Cohn was writing for us and Shorty Rogers, and of course Ralph Burns. He was the head writer; they all learned a great deal from him.

I had the fifth trumpet chair, which was the solo chair. Shorty, who was a soloist also, would write all the solos on my chair. I even said to him, "Shorty, why do you do this?" I was embarrassed. And he said, "Because this will be very good for you." Shorty is an unselfish guy. He really tried to make me shine. Bernie Glow was the relief lead trumpet. Stan Fishelson was the lead. Ernie Royal was the high lead. He did it beautifully. It was a dynamite band. I got a lot to play in the band. Shorty and I were the two bebop trumpet players, he the more subtle one and I the more fiery one. Woody certainly featured Ernie Royal a lot, and Ernie did a lot for that band.

Although I wasn't floored by the band when I joined, I became thrilled with it after I got there. I was really a young bebopper. I was known on 52nd Street. That was for me. But I really enjoyed playing with that big band and traveling with the guys. The adults were Bill Harris and Sam Marowitz. The rest of us were kids.

Don Lamond was our age, but he was more adult. Serge Chaloff was my roommate. He was the character of the band. Everybody was friends. We had fights among ourselves, but if anybody else was fighting us, we protected each other.

I would say that a good thirty percent of the book was modern bebop charts. A lot of times they were flexible; you could open them up. And guys would make their own backup, especially the saxophone section.

Soloist-wise, Serge and I were the two beboppers. Of course, you couldn't say that Al, Zoot, and Stan were bebop players; they were more modern versions of Lester Young.

We had all kinds of flexibility in the arrangements. Not on the ones that Ralph Burns did; he would hate when we would do it to him. He wanted everything as he had written it. But Shorty Rogers loved it. It would help him learn how to write; he used it as a vehicle for learning.

Woody was very smart to have guys in the band write for the band, because a guy writing in the band knows exactly what everybody can do and what's best for them. Shorty and Al Cohn would not write first trumpet, second trumpet, and so on. They would write Ernie, Fish, Ray. They knew which person they wanted to play each part.

It was a tremendous part of my early learning experience. It helped me learn the subtleties.

Al Cohn loved Woody. But it took a while for Woody to like him. He had Zoot and Stan, and all of a sudden Al comes in who was not as flamboyant as either of the other two. But musically, every time Al played a solo, the trumpet section and the trombone section would lean forward to listen. It didn't take Woody long to recognize Al's greatness.

Chubby knew Woody better than anybody. They were personal friends and musical buddies from the same era, the same idiom. Chubby had been part of Woody's greatest triumphs, and Woody was much more comfortable with that "Apple Honey" band than he ever was with the "Four Brothers" band. But to his credit, he knew how great that "Four Brothers" band was.

When I got there, Al was still there, but Zoot and Stan were gone. Gene Ammons came in. Shadow Wilson was there on drums, but he lasted only a second; he couldn't play. Woody gave him plenty of opportunity, and it didn't work.

Then Shelly Manne came in, and we all looked at him as a Stan Kenton drummer. We hated Stan Kenton. Don't forget, we were kids then. Today we wouldn't look at it like that. Shelly sat down and played that book from the very first note. All of us went over and hugged him and told him how great he was.

Woody must be given a lot of credit, coming out of the swing era, for putting together and keeping together that band, and getting the best out of each guy.

He was a sensitive man, and everybody loved him.

I solved the problem of being away from my family by bringing them along when I played somewhere interesting, even if it was far from home. If we were performing at a theater in New York, Charlotte and Ingrid would be backstage, talking to the people we were working with. Later, in 1955, the two of them traveled to Europe with the band.

The big band period was over. That's why all those guys who led big dance bands took their umbrellas and ran. Only the jazz bands with the nitty gritty remained—us, Duke Ellington, Count Basie. Everybody else ran for cover. Louis Armstrong went to the All-Star sextet format.

I knew Louis very well. Joe Glazer, his manager, told Abe Turchen, "I'm going to bastardize my artist," meaning Louis, "and put him on a tour with Woody's band." We did long tours on a bill with his All-Star group.

Louis was a good friend. He had all the charm, even though he felt that what he was doing then was a mere shadow of himself. You still had to give him credit because he could pull it off.

Jack Siefert recalls:

Woody had been fond of Louis Armstrong since childhood. One of his treasured possessions was Louis's recording of "Struttin' with Some Barbecue." In 1980, when Woody became the first white man to be honored and crowned as King of the Zulus at the Mardi Gras in New Orleans, he featured that tune.

When Woody and Louis were doing their tour together, Woody purchased a couple of beautiful white silk ties for Louis that would go well with his famed white handkerchief. Louis was thrilled. He thanked Woody warmly and said, "Do me a favor, Woody, and autograph these ties."

Woody just broke up.

When Louis passed away, Woody was visiting us at the Jersey shore. He received a call about the death and was asked to be an honorary pallbearer.

The band business in general had taken quite a nose dive. The future was easily foreseen, if you were alert and paid attention. But I nonetheless reinvested practically whatever money we were able to put together into the 1948 and '49 band. I felt strongly about the music we were playing and I couldn't accept the fact that we didn't have a wider audience. When I found that I was $175,000 in the hole, I became very much aware.

We rapidly lost the audience that had been ours during the First Herd. And I no longer wanted to play nursemaid to the players who were on narcotics.

12
HORSE PLAY

It was no secret that we had quite a few junkies in the Second Herd. It never became a serious problem on the bandstand, although sometimes guys missed a bus or otherwise had trouble getting to a gig on time. But the drugs didn't appear to cut into their musical ability, which is why I put up with it as long as I did.

I was so naïve about it at the beginning that I didn't know why guys were nodding out on the bandstand. On the bus, the guys who were hooked sat in a section of their own. Serge Chaloff would hang a blanket to separate his group from the rest of the band and would distribute the goodies.

My difficulties with Serge's behavior led to a confrontation in Washington, D.C. I told the story to Gene Lees, and he set down the details in his *Jazzletter*.

Gene Lees recalls:

The band not only looked bad, it sounded bad. Woody, furious at what had happened to it, had a row right on the bandstand with "Mr. Chaloff," as he called him, emphasis on the first syllable.

"He was getting farther and farther out there," Woody said. "He kept saying, 'Hey, Woody, baby, I'm straight, man, I'm clean.' And I shouted, 'Just play your goddamn part and shut up!'

"I was so depressed after that gig. There was this after-hours joint in Washington called the Turf and Grid. It was owned by a couple of guys with connections, bookmakers. Numbers guys. Everybody used to go there. That night President Truman had a party at the White House, and afterward all his guests went over to the Turf and Grid. They were seven deep at the bar, and I had to fight my way through to get a drink, man. All I wanted was to have a drink and forget it. And finally I get a couple of drinks, and it's hot in there, and I'm sweating, and somebody's got their hands on me, and I hear, 'Hey Woody, baby, whadya wanna talk to me like that for? I'm straight, baby, I'm straight.' And it's Mr. Chaloff. And then I remember an old Joe Venuti bit. We were jammed in there, packed in, and . . . I peed down Serge's leg.

"You know, man, when you do that to someone, it takes a while before it sinks in what's happened to him. And when Serge realized, he let out a howl like a banshee. He pushed out through the crowd and went into a telephone booth. And I'm banging on the door and trying to get at him, and one of the owners comes up and says, 'Hey, Woody, you know we love you, and we love the band, but we can't have you doing things like that in here.' And he asked me to please cool it.

"Well, not long after that, I was back here on the [West] Coast, working at some club at the beach. Joe Venuti was playing just down the street, and I was walking on the beach with him after the gig one night, and I told him I had a confession to make. I'd stolen one of his bits. I told him about peeing on Serge's leg, and Joe just about went into shock. He was horrified. He said, 'Woody, you can't do things like that! I can do things like that, but you can't! You're a gentleman. It's all right for me, but not you!' "

As far as their musicianship was concerned, there was no

trouble at all. But it really never affected the music or our performances. They were all excellent players. But the health of some individuals was in pitiful order. And the health problem was growing.

There was a great exaggeration of how many guys were deeply involved. But it was bad enough that we lost one or two of them, and at an early age. That was heartbreak enough—Sonny Berman and later Serge Chaloff. A couple of others were borderline cases, but fortunately some people are physically or mentally stronger.

The players in my band were pretty open to me about it. One young trumpet player from New York, Bernie Glow, confessed everything to me. But he was proud that he could handle it. When his mother and father finally got wise to him and sent him to their physician, the report was that Bernie was a twenty-one-year-old who had the body of a sixty-year-old man. He went on a long health kick and beat the rap.

A number of others recovered, including Al Cohn, Zoot Sims, and Stan Getz.

I had no personal knowledge of the actual extent of anyone's habit, such as how many things someone needed every day. That wasn't my concern, and I didn't feel I had a right to know, or enough knowledge to advise them properly.

I had tried pot as a kid, but I never liked it. When I was a sophomore in high school, about 1929, I joined a band and spent part of that summer in Tulsa, Oklahoma, where we played in a kind of auditorium that held several hundred high school teenagers. The girls were known as pigs and the boys were known as toads. Immediately, when a dance ended, they would run out into the oil fields, listen to the oil pumps and the drills make all the wild sounds, and pass a little joint, a stick of marijuana. It was universal among a great deal of high school kids in that area.

But with some guys, if grass made them feel pretty good,

they wanted something that made them feel a little bit better. It's always a big shock to them when they find they have a big, fancy, expensive habit. Early in the days of bebop, there was peer pressure. A lot of players who wanted to play in the top echelon thought there was a connection with drugs.

It was never proven. The guys who could play great could do it whether or not they were stoned. And many of them, including Charlie Parker, admitted that their playing was often inferior when they were high.

I think they also were drawn into the bag because the salesmen were out there greeting them, like it was the natural thing to do. I saw a lot of it, the connections. I was well aware of it. I saw the guys out there trying to score. But I remained the biggest square in life.

Some of the players used the difficulty of the road life as an excuse for drugs. But I don't think the road had a fucking thing to do with it. They just wanted to get high, and the contacts were everywhere, and still are. If a guy wants anything, he can get it anywhere at any time of the day or night.

Mental strain has nothing to do with it, either. The worst strain is when a guy decides to become a family person. And those guys rarely got into drugs.

Red Rodney recalls:

We were good kids even though we were doing bad things. I must clarify that. Everybody knows there was a lot of junk in that band. I was not using junk at that time. I didn't start until later. Nobody believes that to this day, because it turns out I was the more famous junky of all of them, because I continued, and I got caught a little more. With that band, however, I smoked pot, but I did not use junk.

Every once in a while, Woody would get on the bus and say, "Fellas, I got a tip that they're waiting for us in the next town." I don't think he was lying. Serge Chaloff did get busted once. But Woody got him out.

I was horrified by what these guys were doing. And all of a sudden, we became neurotic. Guys were strung out, there was no good morning, there was no high, there was no happiness. Everybody was bugged. I saw that happening.

I was concerned about the drug problem, but my overriding focus was to produce good music. I think a great deal of the music we set down for posterity at that time still lives very well today in the state in which it was put together. I found that if the players were well enough, they played extremely well. If they weren't well enough, they played adequately.

I don't think anyone ever accomplished or proved anything by saying, "You're involved in narcotics, get out of my band." If a person has ability, he must have a chance to show his ability. But I think that every young man in the band at that time, and anytime before and since, was very much aware that I didn't approve of narcotics of any kind.

The only other bandleader whose opinion I took stock in was Duke Ellington, who had some major druggies in his band as well. Duke thought pretty much like I did. "If the players could play, let 'em play." He didn't try to change them or fix them or anything else.

Chubby Jackson recalls:

Woody never did any drugs, I can attest to that. He got into his drinking and he smoked cigarettes a lot. He even quit drinking for a while. But after a while, trying to relate every night to guys coming up to him saying, "Hey man, what's happening," he would do, "Hey man, see you later." And he'd go to the bar. On the road, he rarely had anyone to talk to. It's "Hey, Woody, sign this for my sister Adrienne," and "How do you like it here in Vero Beach." His retorts got a little satirical; there was a little edge on them.

I drank whiskey, but I never felt it had me even close to whipped. There were periods when I went on the wagon or cut my intake. In the 1950s, I went down to beer. I couldn't drink that much beer, and I think it helped me. Eventually, I started feeling better. But I finally turned back to whiskey.

Alcohol was Doctor Feelgood's tonic.

George Simon recalls:

Woody and I were good friends, but I always had a feeling that he thought I was a goody-goody-two-shoes because I didn't drink. I hate the taste of it. Also it slows me down and I don't have as much fun. Woody used to kid me about it.

In the early days, I saw him and Charlotte socially. And he used to visit us in Stamford, Connecticut, in the early fifties. It was always a very warm relationship.

When the band was playing at the Cafe Rouge in the Hotel Pennsylvania, in about 1945, a waiter came over one evening and served me the most god-awful concoction of ice cream and things, from Woody.

We kept trying to make a go of the Second Herd. But it appeared that the ballgame was over, not only for us, but for big bands in general.

13
END OF
AN ERA

Several things contributed to the end of the big band era, but the most obvious was that the war hysteria had come to a close, and the emphasis shifted. The public was listening to singers rather than commercial dance bands. And simple economics had reduced the size of jazz bands, which no longer were playing the popular music of the day.

Few of the Swing Era bands, of course, ever played jazz. For each Duke Ellington, there were a hundred Mickey Mouse stylistic bands. During the height of that period, we were competing primarily with Duke, Count Basie, Benny Goodman, Charlie Barnet, Chick Webb, Andy Kirk, Jimmy Lunceford, and the Dorseys.

Sammy Kaye, on the other hand, was one of my top

choices for a band with no music. Kay Kyser was a very good showman, but his bands were contrived.

I knew Basie pretty well, but we weren't buddy-buddy. Sometimes we'd have a drink together, and once he came to my house for dinner with Joe Williams in the fifties. That was one of the very high periods for the Basie band.

I became good friends with Duke while we were both recording for Columbia, where they thought it would be a good idea if I did two vocal sides with him. I remember getting a call from Columbia to meet with Duke to work out the keys. I said, sure, and I went into Hollywood, around Vine Street, where Duke was staying. I picked him up to take him to my house, and he said he had to be back in an hour or so.

"Don't worry about it," I said. "I'll get you back."

So we drove up to my house, which hangs down a mountain and has a fantastic view of the city. We walked into the living room and Duke looked out and said, "My God, it's beautiful."

Then I remembered that he liked ice cream, and I got some out of the freezer and laid it on him. He had to be back in an hour, and he stayed for two days.

Charlie Barnet and I weren't peas of the same pod. He was a wealthy man's son and I was a struggling guy in another world, but we were friends.

Artie Shaw was probably the world's greatest natural clarinetist. He had impossible range and could play anything. But he suffered from other things. He felt it was beneath his dignity to have to sign autographs and play for dancers. He saw it as a horrible way to go through life, so he just took a walk.

I didn't feel either way about the dancers, but I was continually amazed by how few people can keep time. Standing on the stage and trying to swing, and being an ex-hoofer, it would drive me crazy to watch their feet. And when they complained to me about the tempo, I would tell them, "I'll listen to you when you learn to dance."

I respected Glenn Miller in the early days because of his arranging ability. Claude Thornhill, too, had good taste and proved it in writing for many people. He also had the good taste to discover a great singer like Maxine Sullivan.

Of the Dorseys, I liked Jimmy best because he was easy to understand. Tommy was forceful, a businessman-operator, who used every possible device to get what he wanted. He was also an excellent, meticulous musician. Jimmy was more carefree. He had an abundance of technique but he never really concentrated on sound.

Tommy was the more successful by far, but Jimmy had proven all of his points. We were both playing at an amusement park once, when Jimmy drove over to see me in a new Cadillac convertible.

"Woody," he said, "this is what 'Amapola' gave me." He had a sense of humor. If you want to hear Tommy's sense of humor, listen to Frank Sinatra. He's a complete copy of Tommy Dorsey, including the sarcasm.

Harry James decided that if he was going to win in the big band game, he had to get a ballad sound. So he made an exaggerated vibrato and pulled it off. And poor Gene Krupa paid forever for his one stupid mistake, being caught with grass.

Among the others, Boyd Raeburn's band was preposterous, overarranged. Freddy Martin had quite a good musical group, but he was never involved in jazz. Les Brown's was a good competent dance band, without room for movement. And Frankie Carle and Vaughn Monroe led stylistic or commercial bands, not unlike Sammy Kaye's or Kay Kyser's. Even among the commercial groups, however, there was some honesty and quality. But not much jazz.

14

A NEW BEGINNING

The quality of the music alone made it difficult to throw in the towel on the Second Herd. The rhythm section, with Chubby Jackson, Lou Levy on piano, and Don Lamond was cooking, and Terry Gibbs joined us on vibes, taking the place of guitarist Jimmy Raney. The arrangements by Al Cohn, Ralph Burns, and Shorty Rogers were supplemented by new charts from Tiny Kahn and Johnny Mandel.

Pianist Lou Levy recalls:

We had a great Johnny Mandel arrangement of "What's New?" that featured vibraphone. Terry Gibbs played it, and then Bags [Milt Jackson] got to play it. Johnny also wrote an original, "Not Really the Blues," that we recorded, but it wasn't the full version because we were making 78-rpm records. It was a great piece.

There was a fierce loyalty toward the music in the band, because there were so many wonderful soloists and a wonderful ensemble. The camaraderie about the music was always obvious. There was just so much talent that something would always carry the band through. Even a mediocre night would be a great night.

During the period when Oscar Pettiford took Chubby's place and Shadow Wilson and Gene Ammons were in the band, we did a ten-week tour of Loew's theaters that began on the West Coast. A few days later, I got a communiqué saying that, when we got to the Capitol Theater in Washington, D.C., we were to abide by the contract, which stipulated that we have an entire white orchestra. "And if you do not," it went on, "the entire tour will be canceled."

Weird. Here we were, a white band except for those three players, greeted wonderfully in black theaters across the country. But in the seat of democracy, in the capital's largest theater, we're told that black players weren't welcome.

I met with the three black players and explained the problem, that they had to be replaced for this one engagement, or the entire tour would be sacrificed. I gave them their pay and expense money, and they went to New York. But they returned a day later with lawyers, demanding that the blackout be protested. I told them it was up to them; they could take the time off with pay, or leave the band. They decided to wait out the engagement and they finished the ten-week tour with us.

Milt Jackson, one of the finest musicians I ever met, took over the vibes from Terry Gibbs just as the Second Herd was winding down early in 1949.

Milt Jackson recalls:

I started with the band in about February, in Chicago, and I stayed two years. We had a very good relationship. Woody respected me as an artist, and he showed it by his treatment. I never had any problems with him.

When the band was in Chicago one time, the band had some time off before we were to play in New York. Woody and Abe Turchen were flying to New York and I mentioned that I was going to Detroit. They had bought a new car, an Oldsmobile, and Abe asked if I would drive the car to New York for him. I said I would stop in Detroit for a couple of days and then bring the car to New York. He said fine.

I went to Detroit, and the next day, on Sunday, I was taking my mother to church and a cop stopped me for some thing about the out-of-town license plates. They hadn't had time to get the plates, and they had a tag stuck on the back window. I think the car was registered in Illinois, and Abe was going to get the plates elsewhere. I don't remember what the violation was, if any.

The car was brand-new, and the cops apparently thought it was stolen. They may have imagined that I had just got it off a lot somewhere. They stopped me, and we went through this routine, and they took me down to the station. They made me take out my wallet and money, and they looked through my credentials. I had about seven hundred dollars in my pocket 'cause I had just gotten paid. That only enhanced them thinking that the car was stolen. Here he is with all this money.

I explained that part, that I played with the Woody Herman band and that I had just been paid a couple of weeks pay, and that I was home for a couple of days before driving the car back to New York for them. That made the tale even more preposterous to the cops.

So they put out all kinds of bulletins and things. I said, "To simplify things, why don't you call Woody Herman, and get him to verify this, and I'll pay for the call, if necessary." Somehow, I got them to put the call through.

I explained to Woody what had happened. Then the man took the telephone to verify if it was really Woody Herman. Woody proceeded to read him the riot act. He exploded over the phone. I could hear Woody giving him hell. Evidently, it was enough to convince them that my story was genuine. And they let me go with a tremendous apology, of course, after the delay of two or three hours. Then I drove the car to New York.

There's another interesting tale about Woody. He found out some-how about me having perfect pitch and a photographic memory. It turned into sort of a game. He would try to find some music that he thought I couldn't play or didn't know. For some reason, it got to him, and he would go to a music store, get a tune he liked and have an arrangement written up, maybe by Al Cohn or Jimmy Giuffre. And it got to be interesting, because I enjoyed the challenge.

One night he came in and said, "I got you."

"OK," I said. He had had an arrangement made up of "Stars Fell on Alabama." His theory was that I was too young to know that tune. He brought out the arrangement, and we rehearsed it. The next night we played the piece, and I had a solo on it. When I played it, he was surprised that I knew the tune. It was no problem. I explained to him that, even if it wasn't a tune I actually knew, I could play it if I heard it. Those years, I could hear any kind of a tune and im-mediately play it back. That got him, and he finally gave up. He said, "Man, I won't try that anymore."

We got to be real good friends.

"Lullabye of the Leaves" was one of the tunes that I played solo with the rhythm section often. I had fallen in love with the tune from Art Tatum, who had one of the most beautiful versions of it that I ever heard. I was drawn to it. I was playing it one night, and Woody was standing next to me. He was completely enraptured, and I noticed it. And a thought came to me.

I motioned and said, "Hey man, pick up your horn—not the clarinet, the alto." And when I finished playing my solo, he played. I never heard him so inspired. To me, the whole two years I was in the band, that was the most beautiful solo I had ever heard him play on either of those instruments. That was on the job, at a concert we were doing. He got such a kick out of it.

He told me afterward, "Man, you inspired me so tremendously." Our relationship was like that.

I became good friends with Buddy Childers, who was playing first trumpet. One night in Terre Haute, Indiana, after the gig, we were invited out to a nightclub. When we got there, they refused to let me in. One of those cases of racism.

I said, "OK, I'll go back to the hotel because I know what it's about out here. And I'm not going to make any extra waves and start any trouble."

I started to leave, and Buddy said, "Uh-uh. You came with us and you're gonna go in." He called the manager, and he said, "Hey, we were invited by your management to be guests of the nightclub, and he's one of the featured members of the band and he's with us."

Buddy was getting rather insistent. I didn't want to cause any trouble, and he told me, "Hey, man, you just stand there. Be cool. Don't worry, I got this covered." Then he turned to the manager and said, "You gonna let us in or you want some trouble?" We wound up going in.

Buddy liked to play golf, and he always kept a set of clubs in the back of the bus. One day during a real hot summer month, they couldn't get a window open in the bus. So Serge Chaloff took one of Buddy's golf clubs out of the bag to pry the window open. When Buddy discovered the bent club and found out that Serge had done it, he threatened him with physical harm. Man, they had to separate them.

I finally disbanded the Second Herd in 1949. There were no hard feelings; we all knew that the band was a financial bust, that we couldn't get enough bookings.

To try to recoup momentarily, at least, I put together a Woodchoppers septet—with Milt Jackson, Conte Candoli, guitarist Dave Barbour, bassist Red Mitchell, Bill Harris, and Shelly Manne—and went to Cuba.

Milt was especially astounding during that trip. Most of the Cubans, other than local musicians, didn't know what we were playing, so I utilized Milt's graceful vibes sound as often as I could. In one show there, I asked him to play a medley and he chose standard ballads, performing them beautifully, and we won over the crowd. I couldn't upset him with a tune.

He knew every old standard, the proper bridges and all the proper changes. He was invaluable.

Milt Jackson recalls:

We stayed in Cuba for four weeks, through Christmas and New Year's. On Christmas Eve it rained and wiped us out in the outdoor nightclub. The owner went to the hospital with a heart attack. On New Year's Eve, the same thing happened. The biggest night of their whole year. I think it sent him back to the hospital.

The audiences hadn't heard of Woody's records very much in Cuba. He wasn't that well known there. Things like "Don't Cry Joe" and "Happiness Is Just a Thing Called Joe," both of which were big hits in the States, got little applause there. People reacted very casually to them. Woody was getting sort of frustrated.

So one night I called him to the side and said, "Woody, I think I ought to make you aware of something. I think the problem is that they don't know these tunes down here."

I had a collapsible set of vibes, and we were playing a tune one night when the legs gradually began to collapse. I moved down with them and never stopped playing.

Red Mitchell recalls:

I started with Woody in Cuba, at the Tropicana, in November of 1949, and stayed with him to the beginning of 1952. He was great. Needless to say, we weren't All-Stars at the time. I found him under all circumstances to be whatever we needed. He could be a leader, he could be a brother figure, or just a friend. He was there and available.

Milt and I were rooming together in Cuba. We shared an apartment. We had cockroaches and Milt used his entire Spanish vocabulary telling the owner about the cucarachas. The owner just laughed. One day we got all the poison we could buy, sprays and all, and did up the apartment. When we came back, the place was crawling with dying cockroaches. I put as many as possible out of their misery.

He had that small group for four months, and that was fun. After Cuba, we went to Philadelphia. Then we played northward, and I remember that everyplace we went it was twenty degrees colder. Then we went to the Midwest and to Texas and to California. It was a nice tour.

I remember a scene in Indiana, where we worked a ballroom of a hotel, and after the gig we went into the coffee shop to eat. The manager came over to us and said, "The boy will have to eat upstairs." We looked at him and said, "There's no boys here, we're all men. What do you mean?"

"Well, you know," he said.

Milt tried to be as graceful about it as he could. The rest of us ordered food and sent it back; ordered it again and sent it back again. The third time it came, we all got up and walked out, getting glares from the kitchen.

From California, we went back to New York and Woody reformed the big band. He wanted to have a clean big band this time. He had Ralph Burns rewrite the book. We played the Capitol Theater for a month. I remember Bill Farrell had a written routine. He was a former bass player turned singer, and he was the first singer I ever worked with. He had it written into his act that he tore up his tie at a certain point. He had certain lines, whether they worked or not. The funny part about that was they didn't work.

Gene Baylos was on the bill, and all the comedians came in to hear him. And Bill Farrell, at one point in the show, would say, "That tune happens to be on my latest record, and if you'd like a copy I just happen to have a million of them in my attic." And there would always be a long silence. He never got a laugh on that line. The next tune started with an introduction where I had to use the bow. So one time I bought caps that, put under your foot, would go off. And I put two big fat caps on the floor. When he said that line about the tune and his record, there was a long silence and—BAM! BAM!—I think Woody knew who did it. I don't think it increased his affection for me. The stage manager was running back and forth behind the stage.

After that, we did a long tour of one-nighters. The band was all white then, and we played all-white places or, a couple of times, all-black places. I remember once we played an all-white place and one of *the customers came up and liked the band, and wanted to pay me a compliment. He was shuffling his feet and looking at the floor. He wanted to tell me he liked my playing and he liked the way the band sounded, and I couldn't catch his eye. I kept ducking and trying to catch his eye. I thought to myself, Damn, this guy's sick. It's gonna be a long time before this thing heals.*

At one place, we played a white-on-white country club outside of Birmingham, Alabama. During one of the intermissions, the lady that had hired the band, the social director I guess, came up to Woody while I happened to be talking to him.

She said [in a broad Southern accent], "Mistah Herman. I just want y'all to know that I think that all the things the people are saying about the band certainly are not true. I think you're doin' a fahn job."

Talk about left-handed compliments. There was nothing worse than a white nigger. We were traitors.

Every night during that tour, people would holler, "Play Dixie." At the beginning, Woody thought they meant Dixieland. He would call down a trumpet player and a trombonist and he would play "Muskrat Ramble" or something. That wasn't what they wanted to hear. It laid an egg. Then we played "Caldonia," and they didn't get that either.

I was experimenting with the amplification of the bass, as I had from the beginning. At that point I had my own microphone sitting in front of the bass on a short stand and an amplifier on the other side of the stand. They made bass pickups at that point, but I had tried them and found fault with them. This I thought was going to be more realistic. It wasn't, it turned out. Anyway, one night between tunes, I plucked out the tune "Dixie" on the bass. And the place went wild. Woody slapped his forehead, and said, "Oh, that's what they want. Well, OK."

From then on, every night "Dixie" replaced the "Caldonia" medley as the climax of the evening. The people would give rebel yells and holler and jump up and down, and go crazy. Every night. The whole band played it in unison.

One night—and I have to give Dave McKenna some of the credit for this, because he dared me to do it—after the cheers were dying down for "Dixie," I leaned down into my microphone, and gave a long, loud Bronx cheer. There was a hush over the whole place. A lot of people didn't realize where it was coming from. But Woody did. I had never seen him like that before. He came over to me with his head literally shaking and his eyes bugging out, and he said to me in a stage whisper, "Leave the stand."

I left the stand. They only had a few tunes left, and I think they shortened the set a little bit. I found a neutral corner. Everybody was kind of looking at everybody else. We were out of there in a flash, and Woody said to me, "Do you know you could have gotten us all lynched?"

I said, "I'm sorry. I goofed."

"Goofed!" he said. "You're less than a person," which is one of the worst things anybody's ever said to me.

You never saw a big band get out of a place so fast.

Woody could be a leader on occasion, but he was more of a catalyst. He could have made a living as just a talent scout, if he had never done anything else. He always had a way of finding talent and songs while the talent was still young enough to have to go out on the road and work. We all needed leadership now and then, and he never over-did it.

On new charts, he usually had a way of opening up a solo space or whatever was required. We used to love his clarinet playing. The rhythm section used to lay for his clarinet solos. We loved it because it would be swinging, it would be on time and in tune, and the rhythm section would come together. I loved his alto playing, too.

15

THE
THIRD HERD

Music was still the only business I knew, and I regrouped a 16-piece band in a matter of weeks, retaining a few guys from the previous band—Dave McKenna, Red Mitchell, and Milt Jackson. We moved from Columbia to MGM Records.

Howie Richmond, who had done some publicity for me, came up with an idea to help us and himself. He saw the band as a great source of new material for his growing music publishing business. He was starting a new record label, called Mars, for which we began to record. One of our first releases on that label was an instrumental called "Men From Mars."

Richmond was naturally interested in finding new material to publish, and he figured we'd be a great source for that. With the recording push from Mars, business was picking up somewhat, but the fifties wasn't a good period. Even Count Basie had temporarily cashed in the big band and was touring with a small group.

The pop market was rapidly changing because of people like Mitch Miller, who was running things at Columbia, feeding the nation sing-a-long recordings. He may have set the music business back forty years. For a legitimate oboe player, he sure caused a lot of turmoil. If he had kept playing oboe, we all would have been better off.

Milt Jackson left us, returning to Dizzy Gillespie's band. But in the constant turnover that had always been part of the big band business, we caught some new winners, such as trombonists Carl Fontana and Urbie Green. One person who was fairly undiscovered in our band was saxophonist Bill Perkins, who did another "Early Autumn" with us. He played beautifully, but his rendition would always be compared with the first one by Stan Getz. Urbie Green, too, was there during a not-important time for the band. That he became known at all is a testament to his talent.

Shorty Rogers and Chubby Jackson came again and went. So did Bill Harris and Al Cohn. We were trying to hit with anything we could, and one of Al's pieces for the band was called "Music for Dancing." Even Ernie Royal rejoined us for a while, and at one point we had Kai Winding and Frank Rehak in the trombone section.

We were in there punching, but we weren't doing much better than before. We had more buyers, because we were more dependable for them; our music wasn't as flagrantly "outside" the mainstream as the Four Brothers band. We got television shots, including the Ed Sullivan show. When we appeared on "We, the People," Shorty Rogers wrote something called "We, the People Bop."

We had one, two, or more great players in every formation of every band. I tried always to get the best players with the money we had to offer, and at one moment or another in the fifties, we attracted Al Porcino, Bill Berry, and Don Fagerquist on trumpets, Wayne Andre on trombone, drummers Sonny Igoe and Chuck Flores, and bassist Red Kelly, among others.

Constant personnel changes are taken for granted in a big band. But that fact doesn't make it any easier. It's like being married and divorced a thousand times. Every two minutes there's another tenor player in the band. You break your ass and a great trombone player is leaving because his sister is having a baby.

But there's a plus side, too. To have a successful road band requires energy—the kind you get from talented young guys. They're ambitious, and they come to you with the hope that this will be the best band they ever get a chance to play with. Some stay a few weeks, most of them stay a couple of years or so, and some stay longer because they find there's something there that can't be gotten somewhere else. Not just a steady job, but being able to play music that you can hold up your head about.

Mixed in among our strong suits were some players who didn't quite measure up. But we came out with our heads up most of the time. And, of course, weaker players often play better when they perform with better players.

New musicians didn't audition. They merely joined the band when they were needed. The system worked since the recruiting network was composed of recommendations by band members or former sidemen. I've always been proud of my association with musicians because I always had a pretty good club membership with my ex-players anywhere in the world. We always hung out first class, enjoying each other, reminiscing and carrying on like idiots. What came through generally was that the best years of their lives were with the band, when it was hard and we were scuffling. They came to realize what a ball that was, when we were playing what we wanted. Maybe we didn't have a porterhouse, but we had everything else.

Perhaps the most important new member of the band during the fifties was pianist Nat Pierce, whose playing and arranging became an enormous asset. But Pierce was much more than that. Just having his spirit and his presence around was a treasure.

Nat Pierce recalls:

I learned an awful lot of things from Woody—how to pace the night, what tunes to play in what spot. He wasn't a slave driver, a Simon Legree; he kind of let things evolve. Woody always made it comfortable, more like you were working with him rather than for him. The ship was tight but it was loose at the same time.

I first joined in the fall of 1951 and stayed until the spring of 1955. And I rejoined the big band from 1961 to 1966. I did a little writing during the first period, but Ralph Burns was doing most of it. He would send in two or three charts a week, or six a month. Most of my writing for the band began in the late 1950s and, during the 1960s, I became the chief writer.

Abe Turchen saved our ass many times during the 1950s. I remember we were on TV, "The Big Show of 1952," with people like the Mills Brothers and Dinah Washington, and then we would go cross-country for about thirty days. A lot of times we bombed out money-wise. Sometimes there wasn't enough to meet the payroll, and Abe would call some bookie in New York and ask, "Who's playing tonight?" It could be basketball or baseball, it didn't matter what sport. He would bet on these games, and somehow by the time the night was over, he had all this money in his hands.

There was a lot of scuffling going on. It wasn't easy. But it's never easy.

In the fall of 1953, a rich fellow from Chicago who was interested in early jazz financed a long tour of high schools and colleges in Illinois with a package that featured the band with

Sidney Bechet and Billy Eckstine. The following year, the band went to Europe for the first time. When we went to England in 1957, however, we were an Anglo-American band—half and half—because of British rules.

What helped us stay afloat was a three-month State Department tour of South America in 1958. Musically it was great. But we had to endure some white-knuckle trips on local airlines. We seemed to have close calls every other day. It reminded me of a wild trip the band had stateside with our own Air Force near the end of World War II.

We had a movie deal coming up on the West Coast, and the Air Force offered to pick up the band in Jackson, Michigan, and fly us to somewhere in New Mexico, then to California. There was a lot of ad-libbing in the services, and they were able to send us out on a big bomber.

When we arrived at the air base in New Mexico, the commanding officer who came to greet us was so drunk that everything he said was double-talk. So I immediately played a chorus of "Straighten Up and Fly Right." Then they put us on another plane for the trip to the coast. Our pilot tried to come down three times in the Los Angeles river. He thought it was a runway. Talk about the thrill of your pants.

Some of the planes we had to take on the South American trip in 1958 were old and decrepit. We cheered when we were booked on a DC-3. The pilots didn't have the same savvy we were used to on stateside flights—the Air Force incident notwithstanding.

Major Holley, the bass player on the South American tour, recalls:

Charlotte was along on a lot of the tour and she used to like to sit next to me. When we were on Panagra Airlines, which is no longer in existence, we went all through the Andes in Chile, and I mean through those mountains, to Peru and Ecuador. Panagra supplied good planes. We liked that. When we got into the warmer climes, flying on the aircraft that belonged to various other airlines, you could actually see the ground through holes in the bottom of the planes, where seats had been removed and the holes hadn't been filled. We were flying over hostile Indians, and desert and jungle in some of those aircraft. One time, we loaded up somewhere in central South America and the plane was too heavy. The pilot tried three times to take off. It was a regularly scheduled airline. I didn't realize it at the time, but we couldn't get enough altitude, and we came back and tried it again. It still didn't work. We almost crashed on that one.

Charlotte hadn't realized that we would be flying through the mountains, and she was paralyzed by it. This was before high-flying jets. When people think about Rio and all those wonderful places we went to, they forget how we got there.

In Bolivia, they have the highest airport in the world, and we couldn't breathe up there. They had oxygen on the stage for us.

At a couple of airports, they wouldn't let me take my bass inside the cabin. I didn't have much say about it; all the business was handled by Dick Turchen, Abe's nephew, along with Woody and Al Banner, the band boy.

In some places I found some of the same apparent racism that I've found in the States. Why would a soldier pick me out while we were all sitting in an airport terminal in Colombia and take his gun butt and hit me on my feet? My feet weren't blocking the aisle. He was trying to say something to me. When he found out I was with the rest of the group, he let me alone. Being the only black man in the group, he obviously thought that I didn't belong.

At a school concert in Peru, the students wouldn't let us inside, so the soldiers had to come to open the gates for us. The school had a thing about not allowing the bad students to attend the concert, and they were upset and surrounded the place. After we got inside to play, the soldiers left. When the concert was over, we couldn't get out until they brought the soldiers back.

The receptions for the band were great, lovely. We had big press all the time, and we played every kind of location, even in bull rings and outdoors, next to swimming pools for the elite. Once in Chile we played for an audience composed entirely of men. They got me to make a speech. I have just a small working knowledge of Spanish, and people were telling me what to say. It turned out I was calling these people all kinds of names, and they were breaking up because I didn't know what I was saying.

Some of the guys in the band resented me after a while because I always had a solo. With so little big band experience, I didn't think about how important it was for guys to have solos. They didn't get a lot of space, and I was featured every night, doing my little Slam Stewart act. I got a lot of press on that trip; they called me El Bajo. *My solo was on "The Preacher," the piece by Horace Silver. It was a Nat Pierce arrangement.*

In Venezuela, soldiers surrounded the plane and wouldn't let anybody off. Americans weren't very popular there at the time. [Then–Vice President Richard Nixon had had difficulty in Venezuela, as had Secretary of State John Foster Dulles.] We weren't concerned with politics. We just did our thing. It was a great, crazy experience. I'm glad I had a chance to go.

One day I went into a store in Brazil to buy some gifts, and a black guy followed me inside. He was Brazilian and he just wanted to meet me. The saleslady called the police because she thought we were going to rob the place. Later, the consulate held a party for us after our concert, and the same chick saleslady who had called the police was there. She tried to apologize, but I wasn't having any.

Woody was very humorous. Guys in South America try to get you coming and going with gold rings, jewelry, and things. Willie Thomas, the trumpeter, bought this ring that he was proud of. We were at a consulate or embassy party after a concert one night, and Woody said to him, "Let me see that ring." Woody looked at it a moment and then set it into one of the deviled eggs on the table and handed the egg to Willie.

In Jamaica, we checked into our hotel and they took Woody to his room. He opened the door and there was a lizard sitting on the wall. Woody just closed the door and split.

The trip, which began in July, ended about October. We did Central and South America and the Caribbean Islands. And I went through that whole tour without getting a scratch on my bass. But when I boarded an Eastern Airlines flight in New Orleans, they wouldn't let me bring it into the cabin. When I got it back in New York, the bass looked like a Christmas goose, neck hanging down and broken. They paid for it.

I first joined Woody's band the year before, after I came back from living in England for five years. Nat Pierce had a band in New York that I was playing some gigs with, but it was mainly a rehearsal band. Nat was the one who introduced me to everybody in Woody's band. They had been trying different bass players, and I guess I had the big tone that they needed.

We worked around the United States in 1957, traveling by bus mostly. I had sat in with the Second Herd a couple of times in the late forties, substituting for Oscar Pettiford, when Woody had Terry Gibbs, Shelly Manne, Mary Ann McCall, Ray Wetzel, and Tiny Kahn. The last place I ran into that band was at the Apollo Theater in Harlem. For some reason, Oscar Pettiford didn't make all the shows, and I was working there with Rose Murphy, so I filled in. I found that I got along very well with Woody.

When I later joined the band, the first thing we did was make a record at the old Everest studios with Tito Puente, "Tito Meets Woody." Then we went out and played up and down the country.

I spent Thanksgiving night that year at the Fort Bragg Army base, because they still had that crap going on with segregation down south. The only place I was safe to sleep at night was at the Army base. I also got into a brief thing with prejudice when we played a concert at the University of Georgia. They didn't have anyplace for me to stay, so I stayed with a black family.

At a hall in a little town in Kentucky, I walked in with the bass on my back, wearing the old clothes that I traveled on the bus with. The people there thought I was a roadie. After I got dressed in my uniform to play, I stayed on the bandstand behind the stage during the breaks, and the cats went and got me some food.

But there were no incidents. Woody was always cool about that. He wouldn't tolerate any foolishness.

I stayed with Woody a couple of years or so. After the State Department tour, the big band toured for a while, and then Woody started taking out small groups. He had Howard McGhee one time and we went with him to Washington, D.C. Then we went out to Vegas; Seldon Powell and Gus Johnson were with us.

I used to call Woody the sheriff, because he always had that whistle. Once he blew that whistle on you, forget it, you were out the door. I only heard him call it a couple of times on players or on situations. He also would pull off his coat and rumble with you if that's the way it was. But it was a lot of fun working with Woody. He was always on an even keel. His was the best band I was ever in. I had to end it after a couple of years because I didn't want to travel in cars anymore, like we were doing with the small groups.

16
THE

DEALER

I began the sixties with a five-piece nightclub act, featuring Bill Chase, an outstanding trumpet player who had been with my big band, and charts by Nat Pierce. Our act also spotlighted tap dancer Steve Condos and singer/pianist Norma Douglas. We played for a month at the Waldorf Astoria in Manhattan.

We played dance sets at the Waldorf, and the maître d' would come over in his tux and stiff collar and say, "You can't play that music in here. The people are dancing too much." He wasn't selling any drinks.

We also performed at Freedomland, which was a rinky-dink version of Disneyland up in the Bronx. A booker tried to sell us in Las Vegas, but we got no takers.

Nat Pierce recalls:

At Freedomland, they wanted a big band, and I got some guys from New York, including Gus Johnson, Charlie Mariano, and Joe Newman—all people who'd never played with Woody before. We did that once in a while on weekends, using the big band and the five-piece nightclub act. All of us, meanwhile, were basically out of a job, including Woody, and we made trips on other weekends to Virginia, West Virginia, and Ohio for work.

When I formed the big band again in 1961, it was more of the same struggle. Despite some successes, including a Grammy Award in 1963 for the *Encore* album on the Phillips label, we were a scuffling organization.

By that time, Abe Turchen had become our overall business manager; he was installed in our office at 200 West 57th Street in Manhattan. In fact, the office of another Woody was in that building—Woody Allen—and I'd run into him on the elevator and say, "Hi, I'm the old one." He and I had to play clarinets together once on "The Tonight Show" and it was a horrible experience.

Abe had good business sense and lots of friends in the music business. He could convince people that we were saleable. Abe knew how to get things done. When he had started working with me as road manager in 1945, for example, he managed to overcome one of our biggest problems—transportation. Abe always found a way to keep us moving despite gasoline rationing.

I gave him control of everything because I felt he was qualified, despite his penchant for gambling.

Abe was quite a guy. He was about five-foot-nine, and weighed about 200, which was his weight when he was a sergeant in the Marine Corps. Out of shape, he was about 250. He was a man about town who loved the show business world and had a particular fondness for certain comics, such as Fat Jack E. Leonard. He knew that I knew all of them, and that became his entry into hanging out with them.

At the office, he was wheeling and dealing alone. Well, almost alone. He had a habit of inviting everybody in who needed a job. That's how he would show kindness, by giving them office space. The whole outer office was usually loaded with bookmakers, money lenders, and others he was doing business with.

Nat Pierce recalls:

When I was road manager in the sixties, we had a contract for a while at Harrah's in Reno and Lake Tahoe, six weeks each. Basically it was just cowboys and Indians there, but there was gambling.

Abe would get fifty percent of our money up front, so I was operating with the fifty percent we collected at the engagements, and I would put a little money in a bank account we established in Reno. One night, I was totally out and playing craps, just throwing hundred dollar bills on the field. I think I lost about four or five thousand that night. I was sick, and I called Abe in New York. All he could do was laugh. Even Woody laughed.

"You've got to be kidding," Woody said.

I wrote plenty of arrangements for years to make up for it.

A few times Abe came out and played at the blackjack table. When I lost some of the band's money, I said to him, "I need twenty-five hundred." He said, "Don't worry about it. You stand here and I'll call you over." He called me over and gave me about seven hundred. Then he said, "How much more you need?" I told him, and later he called me back and gave me more. "You got enough now?" Yeah.

They finally barred him he was winning so much.

In Los Angeles, we played a place called Basin Street West, where we made the record that won the Grammy. Our engagement was an unqualified success. We came back there six or eight months later, and business was still pretty good. But I couldn't get any money. There were these strange people coming in and out of the club every evening, some of them carrying paper bags. They were apparently siphoning off the money. When I went to get the pay, there wasn't any. Woody was up in his house, and I called him and said, "What should we do?"

We bounced a few checks for gasoline money, so we could get to the next gig in Tahoe. When I didn't have money to get us out of Tahoe, everybody came up with a little cash to put gasoline in the bus.

Later on, Abe was taking all the money and I wasn't able to operate the band. I called him from a phone booth in the desert in Texas, and told him that if the money wasn't where we were going, we weren't going to be able to operate. Sometimes the money was there.

Besides being the business manager, Abe tried to get us jobs because, during the fifties, Joe Glazer and, later, Willard Alexander weren't getting us enough bookings.

Abe also had other business things going. Early on, he had bought land on an island off San Diego. He built three luxury houses there and lived in one of them himself. But that wasn't fast-enough action for him. He had many different things that he became involved in for short periods. We set up a personal management office in New York once, in which I tried to work with him to help develop people. But he became bored with that, too. Not enough action.

Gene Lees recalls:

While I was editor of down beat, *from 1959 to the fall of 1961, Wood came through Chicago with the only sloppy band I ever heard him have. The band was ragged and he was in a profound depression. I got drunk with him.*

It was the first time I had formally met him. When I was fifteen, I tried to get his autograph in Toronto. I tried to strike up a conversation with him, which can be very annoying to a person in a position of public celebrity. He sloughed me off, and I was very hurt. I carried a small resentment for years over it.

Now here I was at down beat *in Chicago, and I had an interview with him, and we ended up getting plastered. I began to sense a different person than the impression that I'd had. Woody could be abrasive, never cruel. But he had a tough streak in him along with the sweetness. He was road-hardened.*

Sometime after that, I left down beat *and came to New York.*

Woody had a septet at that time with Zoot Sims, Nat Adderley, Jake Hanna, and Nat Pierce. They were playing upstairs at the Metropole, and I went there with Marian McPartland. We sat with him and the guys, and he made a remark that stuck in my mind like glue. He said, "I never was much of a clarinet player." And I absolutely fell in love with the man in that split second. It's that vivid in my mind.

I was having a difficult time getting established in New York— living at the West Side Y and getting locked out of my room regularly, when I couldn't pay my rent. It was late in 1961. Woody and Abe Turchen said to me essentially: "You shouldn't be living like this, this hand-to-mouth existence. Wood suggested that I come to work for them.

"Doing what?" I asked.

"Who cares," Wood said. "Doing the publicity."

So I went to work for him doing publicity. By this time, he had organized the band that recorded for Phillips, the band with Bill Chase, the band that played standing up at the Metropole. It was one of the great bands he had, rich in soloists like Bill Chase and Sal Nistico. It was wonderfully disciplined.

He built that band but I built its image. I started out writing pieces for publications in which it was easy to plant stories. I did the second-line publications first, then I went after the biggies. It worked. It wasn't a hard sell. It might have happened without me, but I think Wood always felt that what I did that year was very important.

We all loved Abe Turchen. He was a pessimistic realist. He reminded me of Jack E. Leonard. He talked like Jack; he was very friendly, very overweight, homely, diabetic, and he chewed his fingernails. He used to try to tell Jewish jokes with a New York accent, and he couldn't do it. He was from the Midwest. The jokes were awful, and Abe was inadvertently funny.

He was a chronic gambler. He used to sit in that office, with piles of papers on his desk, picking up the phone, watching television, playing solitaire, and booking the band all at the same time.

Lou Singer, the songwriter, shared the office in the other room of the suite. Abe had his office in the front of the building, and he'd *be placing bets on the phone. Once I had to take his car and go out to Brooklyn and collect an envelope of money for him. I went to Lundy's in Sheepshead Bay and I sat there at the bar waiting, as instructed, and this guy comes up to me and hands me an envelope and says, "Count it." I took it back to Abe.*

Sometimes the envelopes of cash went out, too. I assumed that it was Abe's money, and maybe it was.

Woody called the office one day and asked me to get so-and-so's address from the files. I laughed. "The files? What files?"

That was the sloppiest operation in history. But I understood Woody's feeling about the man. Abe would find him supermarket openings to play—the weirdest gigs in the weirdest places—and he kept that band working; he kept those salaries flowing.

Abe would sit back in his chair with his damn TV set going all day long. His cards and his phones and his betting were going on in a kind of soup of activity. I didn't pay any attention to it. All I knew was that the band worked. I was busy trying to get stories done on the band.

Sometime in 1963, I wrote lyrics for Bill Evans' "Waltz for Debbie," at Bill's request. A woman in Sweden named Monica Zetterling recorded it. I was sent a copy of the record and I gave it to Mort Fega, the disc jockey, and Mort started playing it on the air, mentioning who had written the lyric. Woody happened to hear it on the radio while riding in from the airport in a taxi.

He walked into the office and said to me, "Why didn't you tell me you could write lyrics like that?"

"You didn't ask me," I said.

He called Howie Richmond and within forty-eight hours I was signed to a nice sustaining contract, which is how I came to write all the things with Charles Aznavour, who was doing a lot of stuff for Howie. That gave me enough money to live on. Then a few things happened for me in succession: A novel of mine was published, Tony Bennett recorded two or three of my lyrics, including "Quiet Nights." I was getting really busy, doing a lot of freelancing. And Woody didn't need me anymore. The publicity was beginning to generate itself.

He came in off the road to work the Metropole in 1963, after I had been with him a year or so. I went to lunch with him, and I explained that I was having a problem.

"What's the problem?" he asked.

I said, "Essentially, you don't need me anymore. And I, on the other side of the coin, am up to my eyes in work."

He said, "What's the problem? What are you trying to tell me?"

"I don't have time to do it anymore," I said.

"I still don't understand what the problem is."

"I really hate to leave you and the band."

"If that's all there is to it," he said, "I'll make it simple for you. You're fired. Now let's have lunch."

He went around for years afterward introducing me as the only man he ever fired.

I didn't think Abe Turchen's yen for gambling would get in the way. But there were plenty of clues, if I had been more attentive. While I was playing somewhere in Europe in the late fifties, for example, Abe telephoned to say we had to sell my music publishing company, Charlin, because he needed more financing for what we were doing.

"Forget it," I told him. "Charlin is my legacy to Charlotte and Ingrid."

But Abe had power of attorney as business manager, and he sold it out from under me.

By the mid-sixties, I had fallen into a financial stranglehold from which I would never recover.

17
THE IRS DEBACLE

The first I learned of how much trouble I was in was when the Internal Revenue Service sent me a letter ordering me to appear in person. Until then, the IRS had been corresponding with my office, and Abe Turchen never gave me a clue about it.

I arrived at the tax office with Abe and learned that, not only had my personal income taxes been unpaid for 1964 through 1966, so had the withholding taxes on the musicians' salaries. The punishment was a tax bill of about $750,000, with interest and penalties over the years bringing the figure to $1.6 million.

I sat there, stunned.

I never believed their figures. All the years in which we had big grosses—not big profits—we paid taxes to the hilt.

Here I was down and out in the sixties, and the IRS was basing its estimate of my debt on years when our revenues had been high.

Charlotte was appalled at how stupid we had been in our judgment of Abe. But I felt as responsible as Abe for the mess.

Gene Lees observes:

Woody was the oddest mixture of shrewd perception and pure naïveté. He could be almost cunningly observant of people. Yet I believe he was utterly unaware of what Abe had done. What Woody was guilty of was not paying attention. That was the nature of the problem.

I never went into a state of shock over it. I was depressed for a moment or two, but I knew that I had to get back to the business of music in order to take care of it as best I could. We worked out an arrangement to pay the government $1,000 a week through whomever was booking us. But we couldn't always afford it; we had to renegotiate.

My lawyers worked hard to help get me off the hook somehow. I saw what the government had done to Joe Louis, forcing him to wind up as a handshaking shill for a Las Vegas hotel. I would have preferred going to jail than to finish like that. But I never considered imprisonment as a threat. I always figured the IRS would have less to gain with me behind bars.

For some unearthly reason, I kept Abe on the job. But by August 1968, I couldn't take any more.

Bill Byrne, who joined the trumpet section of the band in 1965, recalls:

Nat Pierce and Bill Chase were the road managers, splitting the duties, when I arrived. Abe Turchen got me to do it in 1967, when we were playing the Riverboat in the Empire State Building for a month. I left for a while, and Woody, meanwhile, got rid of Abe.

Every week a bus company would come up to the band with a subpoena, because Abe hadn't paid. And they would try to take the band's music library. Woody just got fed up with it.

Abe died in San Diego some years ago. All that time Woody didn't say anything publicly about Abe. Woody liked characters, and Abe was a Damon Runyon classic.

When I fired Abe Turchen, I took on Hermie Dressel as business manager. He was the only guy who would accept it. I had talked to others who could handle the job. Norman Granz, for example, said, "Thanks, I think it's a great honor. But no thanks."

Willard Alexander's office was booking the band, but he had no faith in us. He had his favorites, such as Count Basie and the Glenn Miller ghost band.

Funny thing was that in 1966, one of the tax years in contention, we made another State Department tour, this one to Algeria, Morocco, the Congo, Uganda, Tanzania, Yugoslavia, and Romania. Among the guys in that band were Ronnie Zito on drums, Marvin Stamm and Bill Chase on trumpets, Carl Fontana on trombone, and Nat Pierce on piano.

Nat Pierce recalls:

On the way, we landed in Madrid for an overnight stay, and they took all the music and Woody's alto sax, put them in a big cage and padlocked it. We went into town and had a nice dinner. At the airport the next morning, the cage was empty.

"What happened?" we asked. They said they put it on the plane. But when we got to Dar es Salaam, there was no music and no alto sax. We were able to borrow an alto down there, but Woody couldn't even get a noise out of it. We got the music back a few days later, but the alto didn't come back for a couple of years.

We were playing a reception for the second vice president of Tanzania, and I had to write out the Tanzanian national anthem for the band. I thought I'd doctor it up a little and put some flashy things in for Bill Chase to play. We were rehearsing it in the room in which we were to play while workers were up on step ladders decorating the place with crepe paper and banners. When we started to play it and Bill started playing the flashy stuff, the workers started coming down off the ladders and coming toward the band. I said, "Uh-oh, we'd better leave out that Bill Chase part."

The band sounded the worst during that gig, because we had no music and there were some new guys in the band. Also, Woody couldn't play the same things on clarinet that he could play on alto.

Bill Byrne recalls:

Beginning in 1966, we also started making annual European tours, mostly to England, for about ten straight years. When we first started going over there, we played double concerts, with full houses most of the time—one at six and one at nine. As years went along, it dwindled to one concert a night, which was easier on us.

In 1970 we went to Japan for George Wein. We also hit Hong Kong, Singapore, and Bangkok. Great receptions. In 1966, we did a European and English tour, and then to Africa.

We used to have a booker in Sweden named Boo Johnson, and he took us to Poland for about five years in a row during the mid- and late seventies. Woody was treated like royalty because his mother was born there. We also played Finland, Norway, Sweden, Denmark, East Germany, for Boo.

Among other notable foreign trips was one to South America in 1980, and a couple of tours of Europe and Australia in 1985 with the big band and with small groups—one that included Harry (Sweets) Edison, Buddy Tate, Al Cohn, Jake Hanna, John Bunch, and a bass player from Toronto, and another with Nat Pierce replacing John, and without Tate.

I was tired, but I kept plugging away because I loved the music, I had an overwhelming need to make a living, and the government wouldn't have looked kindly on my retirement.

18

A NEW PUSH

I had a speech I gave to all kids in junior high schools, high schools, and sometimes in colleges. I told them to be as independent and together about their music as they possibly could be. And to find some other way to earn a living, because they would have a better life. I would suggest possibly a career in electronics or computers, so they could get into the swim of what's happening today. I told them to use their music as something to help keep their minds and their hearts straight.

Weird. Here I was making an appeal to youngsters and ignoring the music that moved them. The emergence of rock and roll was making it tougher to get bookings, but I wasn't going to be bulldozed by it. The secret, I figured, was to explore its most inventive offerings and make them swing.

And I got some timely help from a young pianist.

Alan Broadbent recalls:

I was twenty-one when I left the Berklee School of Music in Boston and joined Woody's band in 1969. Woody was just starting to get guys from schools like North Texas State and Berklee. Bill Byrne was there and Frank Tiberi was there. Sal Nistico rejoined the band a couple of times.

It wasn't really that glamorous when I first joined the band. All we were doing were Army bases and Elks clubs. We weren't yet doing college things. It was kind of a slump period.

But Woody was doing some contemporary things like "Mac-Arthur Park" and "Light My Fire." I had to find a way to introduce myself to Woody as a writer. The hot group of the time was Blood, Sweat and Tears, and they did a tune called "Smiling Phases," which featured jazz soloing. I did a chart on it and we rehearsed it without Woody. We had a prom coming up. Woody wanted to hear it at the prom, and the kids went wild. We also did "Proud Mary," a Creedence Clearwater Revival piece.

Then I figured I'd do another tune, a ballad, and we tried it again without Woody at a rehearsal. I tried to use all my Berklee training and my Gil Evans voicings, and mutes and woodwinds. Well, it just didn't work, acoustically or any way when we played it on the bandstand. It started falling apart. The band sort of petered out at the end. Woody looked at me as if to say, "Is that it?" And I said, "Yeah." That was a major lesson for me.

After that, we had a big Las Vegas gig, which gave me a regular place to stay, because I lived on the bus.

Woody was kind of intrigued by "Smiling Phases" and all this Blood, Sweat and Tears stuff. He said, "Why don't you do something with 'Blues in the Night?' " I spent the next month or so thinking about it, writing out little sketches and things. I threw in everything I could think of, including the bridge. I put in baroque things; I always had this flair for the grandiose; I knew the ending was going to be big. When I had pieced it together, and we rehearsed it, Woody just loved it. The best recording of it was when he did it in 1976 at Carnegie Hall for the Fortieth Anniversary concert.

Then we did an album with Mike Bloomfield, a blues guitar player, for Fantasy records.

I did about fifteen or sixteen charts altogether for the band. The major charts Woody left as is. There were a few things he suggested. But I think there were a couple of rock charts in which he put different motifs in different places. He knew exactly what it was that would make a chart sound good.

In 1970, we made a tour of the Far East and we played a high-falutin businessmen's club in Tokyo. There was another band performing on the other stage, and we alternated sets. We had this thing on the ending of "MacArthur Park," a big show biz ending with the five trumpet players going into different corners of the room, and there would be this big improvisation. Buddy Powers, the second trumpet player, went out with the others to the corners for this big climax, and suddenly they started improvising. Buddy was standing halfway back in the room near some tables. This Japanese businessman was so affronted by the trumpet playing near him that he took his drink and threw it in Buddy's face.

One of the guys on the bandstand watched it happen and said, "Did you see that?" Buddy came back to the bandstand all flabbergasted and wet. Woody went over to Buddy, while we were still playing the ending, and asked him what happened. Then he took his clarinet, removed the cap from the mouthpiece, and slowly walked out into the audience, smiling at everybody. He came up to the table of the guy who threw the drink and squawked and squeaked his clarinet directly at him. We were in hysterics. The gigantic ending had to last an extra few minutes while Woody did his thing at that table.

Woody was very protective of us. I guess it was a real paternal thing, which is why he's always been called the Road Father.

I was young and I wasn't taking care of myself too well. By the end of the third year, I just didn't want to be part of the road anymore. Woody understood that. I gave him a lot of notice. But it was always hard for him, I think, to let that go. He saw it so many times with guys he really felt for. I could sense that he was hurt, letting a son go. It was the same way he felt about Sal Nistico.

It was a very special thing. He always knew when you were up, when you were creating. He could always make that intense moment yours. If you were improvising, having a good time, he never stomped on you.

But I don't have very fond memories of being on the road. Bill Byrne was the saviour for us all, Woody included. All the shit would just roll off his back. He'd get pissed off, but it was such an honest pissed off, and two minutes later it would be gone and he'd be so apologetic. Somehow he managed to keep everybody going.

I continued to write for Woody for two years after I left the band. My favorite charts were "Bebop and Roses" and "Far In." And a few of the ballads, one that I did for [trumpet player] Tom Harrell, "A Time for Love."

Gene Lees recalls:

Woody had an astonishing capacity to spot talent before it was particularly obvious to anybody else. Two fine examples were Kenny Ascher and Alan Broadbent. Woody asked me to work with both of them. Ascher, who was arranging and playing piano in the band in the sixties, and I wrote one or two songs together, but they didn't go anywhere. With Alan, I had listened to some of his charts and playing and I couldn't see it for sour apples. But Woody kept telling me how gifted this guy was, that this was a guy I should write with.

Today I consider Alan Broadbent one of the greatest pianists in jazz and a marvelous composer. Woody saw that talent when it was in a very germlike stage.

He made careers; he had a lot to do with mine. But the list of careers that he either made or advanced is staggering.

We gathered new strength in 1973 from the *Giant Steps* album on Fantasy, which earned us a Grammy. Most of the arrangements were made by trumpet player Bill Stapleton, including the title cut, composed by John Coltrane. It also contained Alan Broadbent's "Bebop and Roses" and an arrangement of "La Fiesta" by Tony Klatka.

When Broadbent left the band, our drummer, Joe La-Barbera, recommended Harold Danko to replace him.

Harold Danko recalls:

I joined the band in April 1972, and stayed through October. I was in the Army when I got the call from Bill Byrne. I was discharged on April 3, and I joined the band April 6. I had had no idea what I was going to do after I got out of the Army. All of a sudden I had a great gig.

Al Johnson was on bass, Al Porcino was on lead trumpet, Bobby Burgess was lead trombone, Frank Tiberi on sax. I think everyone who went through the band learned a lot from Frank.

I had good coaching from drummer Joe LaBarbera for getting on with Woody. He briefed me and gave me tapes. He said, "Don't bother saying hello to Woody. Just go out and do the gig." And he hipped me to a couple of Woody's tests for incoming pianists. Joe said, "Do you know Duke's intro to 'Satin Doll' and 'A-Train'?" I said yes. He said, "Well, Woody's liable to call them, and if you play just a normal intro, he knows you don't know the shit."

Sure enough, on the first gig I didn't bother saying hello to Woody. He came on the bandstand and said to me, " 'Satin Doll,' intro." So I played it.

Shortly after I joined, we went into the studio to record "The Raven Speaks." It was my first record date, and I was thrilled. Thinking aloud, I felt that this was a piece of history, recording with Woody Herman. The session was in New York City. Some of the stuff we were reading for the first time. One of the pieces we did was "Bill's Blues," a blues in A-flat, written by Bill Stapleton. He was a great trumpet player and writer in the band. I had two choruses on it up front. So of course I tried to tell my whole life's story in these two choruses of A-flat blues, playing whatever I felt I knew. The band came in not quite right. Take one didn't quite work. I don't know if I played a horrible solo. Maybe I did.

We did another take, and I think I tried even harder at that point. I felt, Jeezus, I gotta play my ass off. Again the band didn't come in quite right. And Woody came up to me and said, "Harold, it's only an intro."

The band was another powerhouse. When Harold Danko left, we formed a new rhythm section with Andy LaVerne on piano, Ed Soph on drums, Wayne Darling on bass, Joe Beck on guitar. We also had some crackling horn soloists—Stapleton on trumpet, Jim Pugh on trombone, and Greg Herbert on tenor sax.

The following year, we collected another Grammy, this one for *Thundering Herd* on the Fantasy label.

Considering the climate for big bands, even one that was experimenting with electronic piano and some jazz-rock charts, we were getting good receptions, particularly at colleges, where we had begun to do combination concerts-clinics.

The University of Houston honored me by establishing the Woody Herman Music Archives at its School of Music. Initially, I gave them record albums, original scores of "The Woodchopper's Ball" and other hits, along with some instruments. The man who made the biggest contribution to the archives, however, was my longtime friend Jack Siefert, who had collected and chronicled material on me and the bands since we first met in 1937.

Jack Siefert recalls:

I took off the entire summer of 1974 to put together the Woody Herman archives. I did it in chronological order—every single tune, every version, cross-indexed. My wife, Mary, did the typing and my kids did all the indexing.

I took thirty-three reels of tape to Houston; and I made a bound volume of the index. When I got to Houston, I went to Neiman-Marcus with these suitcases full of tapes and asked to have them gift-wrapped. The store clerk asked, "Were they bought here?" I said no. And he said, "Well, that's against our policy."

123

"Mr. Herman is donating this to the University of Houston," I said. "I'm just a courier."

"Oh," he said, "in that case . . ." and he wrapped up the book and the suitcases in gold. He charged me the minimum of about two dollars.

There was a big ceremony at the University of Houston. Woody was so proud. I felt so good. He hadn't expected it to be that amount of work. But I said, "Woody, this is your life."

He was the kind of friend for whom there was nothing I wouldn't do. When he would go to Europe, say for six weeks, he would park his Corvette at our house near Philadelphia, rent a car for the drive to the New York airport, and dump it. Meanwhile, we'd have his car serviced. When he would return, and he'd have a day or two off, he used to go to the school to pick up our kids. The kids just loved him. They'd get in his Corvette, sometimes with their friend who was crazy about the car, and he would drive them home. That's the real Woody Herman.

He was at our house one night during the sixties, and tried to telephone his father, who was in a nursing home. He called and called, and finally a nurse answered and said, "I'm sorry, but we can't rouse your father. He doesn't know who you are."

Woody hung up and he had tears in his eyes. "Dad didn't know who I was," he said. In an effort to comfort him, I said, "That's a shame, you went to all that trouble." Woody put his arm around me and said, "Jack, the important thing is that I knew who he was." He had a keen understanding of what was important.

And nobody realizes what a lady Charlotte was.

Mary Siefert recalls:

One of the many times Charlotte came to the house was when Woody was being honored at the White House by Lyndon Johnson. She stayed here to get her wardrobe ready while Woody was doing one-nighters in the area. It happened to be around Christmas time. Jack and I had been invited to several parties.

I said to Charlotte, "I have to find another something to wear."

She said, "Well, what would you like to wear?"

It was the time when long skirts were beginning to come back in fashion. I said, "I would like a nice long skirt, a nice red velvet skirt."

She suggested we go to a store, because she wanted to buy some material. She made me this gorgeous red velvet skirt. She was marvelous with her hands.

And Woody was probably the Duncan Hines of the music business. He could tell you the best restaurant in any big city or small town, and invariably he was right. He remembered where they were and exactly what he ate in every one of them.

Jack Siefert adds:

When I was traveling for my company, I used to say to Woody, "Hey, I'm going to Cincinnati."

"Three places," he'd reply. "This one's the best." Same thing whether I was going to Chicago or to Denver. He knew every restaurant.

Sometimes I would be amazed to see someone come up to him at an engagement and ask for a Glenn Miller tune. Woody never did that even when he was recording cover tunes. If he was in the right mood, he'd lean over and say, "I'll tell you what, next time I see Glenn Miller I'll tell him you requested that."

He was sick as a dog one day at our house and he had to go play at a place about a hundred miles away. We had a station wagon with a four-inch mattress in the back, and Mary added a pillow. I drove down there, with Woody lying in the back. We had some medicine for him. He made the performance, and a lady came up to him and said, "You know, I remember you from Old Orchard, Maine, back in 1940, and you don't look the same." He looked at her, and he said, "You know, I remember you from Old Orchard, Maine, too . . ."

Before he could say anything else, she turned to her husband and said, "He remembers me?"

Then Woody turned to me and said, "I guess I'm losing my touch. I was gonna say I recognized the dress."

Right after that he went to Annapolis to play a dance. He was really sick. After the first set, he started sweating, and he announced, "Is there a doctor in the house?" There was a doctor—a man who coincidentally had played in the band briefly in the forties. So he took Woody backstage to lie down. Woody said to me, "I want them to know that I'm not on drugs, that I'm sick. I want the doctor to tell them; he's one of theirs."

The doctor came back and said, "You have a 102 temperature. You have the flu." The doctor announced to the crowd: "Ladies and gentlemen, I have known Woody for years. In the true show business tradition he came out here tonight. But he has no business being here with the flu. He should be in bed."

The whole place roared. We flew him to New York, and he was out for about a week.

In the house that I had, we set aside a suite of rooms for him. I had a room downstairs with a piano and bar and a jazz room with all the stuff. We called it Wood's Hole. Woody considered our home his eastern pit stop.

I'm a working engineer, so my hours were different than his. When he would visit, I'd try to keep up. But by the fourth night in a row, I'd just fall down. We were coming home at one-thirty in the morning, Mary would make something to eat, and we'd sit and talk until four. And I got up at five-thirty. He would sleep until eleven-thirty or noon, and have long conversations during the day with Mary. She said it was like talking to your brother. Woody would talk about his mother, about Charlotte, and about Ingrid. He was just a warm human being, the warmest I ever met. He had the right sense of values.

We stopped numbering the Herds after the third one, but we were still thundering across the country nicely in the seventies, me by car, the band by bus and plane—until fatigue on one bright summer afternoon in 1977 almost ended it all.

19

OF FREEDOM

Driving across the country, from tank town to city to tank town, gave me the feeling of independence I had enjoyed since I first left Milwaukee in my Whippet to join Tom Gerun's band in Chicago.

I made practically all the jumps by car. If the band had to travel 7,000 miles, I drove 7,000 miles, sometimes alone, sometimes with Charlotte. In the late fifties and sixties, with Bill Chase, who was an avid motor fan.

But the law of averages caught up with me in March of 1977. I was alone in a rented car—my Corvette was being worked on somewhere—and on my way to Kansas State University from somewhere in central Kansas. I had left central Kansas around ten in the morning and it wasn't long before

I realized I was sleepy. It was cumulative tiredness, fatigue. I stopped two or three times to walk around the car.

It was a lovely summer day, about two in the afternoon. I was driving along a regular two-lane highway near Fort Reilly, which is an old Army camp. Maybe fifty or a hundred yards from the main gate of the camp, I fell asleep. I crashed head-on into another car.

No one was hurt seriously in the other car, thank God. But the wreck practically demolished my leg. They took me to St. Mary's Hospital in Manhattan, Kansas, where they had to put steel pins in my leg up to my hip. I stayed there about four weeks and went home for therapy.

The band continued to tour with Frank Tiberi at the helm, and Buddy DeFranco fronted the band on a few dates.

On May 14, 1977, just a couple of days before my sixty-fourth birthday, I was still in a wheelchair when I took a flight to the Berklee College of Music in Boston to receive an honorary degree as Doctor of Music.

By the first week in June, I was back in front of the band. My driving days were over. I missed the freedom of making my own schedules. But in the long run, it was less tiring to take buses and planes or have someone drive me in a car from location to location.

I had recovered pretty well, but Charlotte was in the midst of her own major health crisis.

She had always been a very healthy woman. But she began to suffer from cancer in the early seventies. It started as breast cancer and then went through her body. She was operated on several times, but she was able to handle the situation well, between her spirit and the chemotherapy.

Gene Lees recalls:

Charlotte was an extremely beautiful woman, with flaming red hair, a crepe paper skin and gorgeous bone structure. The underlying structure of the face was so exquisite that even when her face became lined she remained beautiful.

She achieved a remarkable balance in her behavior toward the band. She had a sixth sense about how friendly to be. She was warm to the guys, never forbidding, never inaccessible. But she did not encourage people to get too close. She was very supportive of the musicians. She was diplomatic and knew exactly how to handle her situation with the band members.

I knew, of course, how bad she was. I had talked to her doctors and to my own, Dr. Stanley Levy in Detroit. He was losing his wife to cancer at about the same time. We had a lot in common. I knew Stan for about twenty-five years. I met him when I had an emergency while playing in Detroit. It was a blockage in my esophagus. I liked the way he handled my situation. He had put me in a hospital immediately and found the problem. After that, anytime I had a problem of any sort I would consult with him. He would advise me about surgeons or medication, or whatever I needed. He became more like a brother than a doctor.

Jack Siefert recalls:

Stanley Levy was one of the finest men I ever met in my life. He took care of Woody for twenty years. Wherever Woody was, he'd call Dr. Levy and Dr. Levy would call him back in twenty minutes.

He loved Woody. Dr. Levy made three-thousand-mile house calls. When I was operated on for a hernia, Woody was staying at our house. I came home, took some of the medication the doctor had given me, and I passed right out. I fell in the tub and cracked my ribs. Woody came in and said, "Let me get ahold of Dr. Levy."

He got through to him faster than I could have gotten a doctor in Philadelphia. Dr. Levy called back and said, "Let me talk to Jack." He told me, "Get off that medication." Here was Dr. Levy on the phone telling me what to do through Woody.

In 1976, we decided to arrange to celebrate my fortieth anniversary as a bandleader. We were trying for a date at Avery Fisher Hall in Manhattan when a cancellation at Carnegie Hall, for November 20, fit right into our plans. We managed to attract an all-star package of alumni. Flip Phillips, Chubby Jackson, Sam Marowitz, and Don Lamond came up from Florida. Nat Pierce and Jimmy Rowles shared piano duties with Ralph Burns, who took time out from a road tour for the reunion.

For the "Four Brothers," we had Stan Getz, Zoot Sims, Al Cohn, and Jimmy Giuffre. Jake Hanna, who had been a driving force in the band in the early sixties, played drums.

Pete and Conte Candoli added sparkle, along with Billy Bauer and Gary Anderson, who had written our arrangement of "Fanfare for the Common Man." Trombonist Jim Pugh, who played in the band in the early seventies, delivered a warm reading of "Everywhere," which Bill Harris had composed. Phil Wilson took the trombone choruses on "Bijou," which Ralph Burns had written for Harris. And Mary Ann McCall sang "Wrap Your Troubles in Dreams."

The concert was a smash, and was recorded by RCA. I was starting my fifth decade as a coach—a title I've always preferred over bandleader—on a high note.

20
NEW ORLEANS
EXPERIMENT

Among the unusual honors I've received occurred when the Zulu Society named me King of the Zulus for the New Orleans Mardi Gras parade in February 1980. Louis Armstrong was accorded the same tribute in 1949, but I was the first white person to be so named.

Afterward, Tom Gaskill of the Hyatt Regency Hotel in New Orleans came to see me. He loved our band, and he had approached a couple of outside people about building a room adjoining the hotel, and installing the band in it. I think that jealousy was among the reasons for wanting to do it. Pete Fountain's band was having great success attracting people to the Hilton.

It sounded like a dream idea to me, even a turning point

for helping big bands to survive. If we were able to repeat the kind of success Pete Fountain was having, hotel people around the country might say, "Hey, what's this?" What a way to cap off my later years.

Best of all, it would give us a home base from which to operate and help us reduce the constant traveling. That, in turn, would cut the normal, steady turnover of young musicians. And the bonus was having the time and place to rehearse. From that base thirty-six weeks a year we could arrange tours for the other months and have our pick of the best engagements. The reason for that is that when you're not available most of the time, the demand and the price go up.

The Hyatt Regency had a 9,000-foot shell that had been left unfinished next to the hotel, on the mall level of Poydras Plaza. The room, when it was completed, could hold 500 people, with theater-style seating. We opened Woody Herman's late in 1981.

A few problems accompanied us. Many of the fixtures and lights weren't yet in place, and the hotel had no budget for advertising; the funds had been used to build the room. If there had been sufficient publicity, everything might have been great. Instead, Woody Herman's was the best kept secret in New Orleans. We were performing six nights a week and I would run into locals on the street who asked me, "What are you doing in New Orleans?"

We stayed there a few months before going off on tour for a while. When we returned, we found the room the way we had left it—unfinished. The idea of having entertainment there during our absence, to solidify the place, went by the boards.

The backers never came up with the money they had promised, so we were operating at a loss from the beginning. And I wasn't able to depend on people I needed, such as Hermie Dressel, who was our business manager then.

It was a great disappointment, and not the only one. The bottom dropped out of what looked like a great deal to do three television shows with lots of guest stars. We shot it all in New Orleans, and it looked wonderful. Those shows are lying in a can somewhere in Florida. The whole thing was in litigation. Nobody got paid. I doubt if the shows will ever be shown, because of the money involved.

By the spring of 1982, the dream in New Orleans was failing. More important, Charlotte's condition had worsened. She had apparently given up. She stopped taking the chemotherapy, and she didn't want to go to the bedroom on the bottom level of the house any longer. She decided to spend her days and nights on a soft leather lounge on the second level, off the living room.

I was on the phone with her every day. Not a lot of people, outside of our personal friends, knew how sick she was. She tried to cover it; she wasn't the kind of person who would have wanted anyone to know that she was ill.

I had to go to her.

Jack Siefert recalls:

He told the guys in the band that he was going home and that the club was going dark. They understood.

As he was leaving from the airport the next day, some callous reporter approached him.

"Mr. Herman," he said, "I understand the club has gone dark and you're going home. What's the greatest record you ever made?"

Woody replied, "I've been married and in love with the same woman for forty-six years. Can you match that record?"

I went to see her at the hospital in Los Angeles and stayed at her bedside. One afternoon when Ingrid and I were visiting her, I was sitting on the edge of her bed, holding her hand, and I saw that she was failing. I started to sob. She summoned up what strength she had left, reached up, and punched me on the arm.

"Straighten up, Wood," she said. "We've been through tougher times than this."

I was with her in the hospital room when she died two weeks later.

A week later, I was back at work. It was the only therapy I knew, and I was sure the government wouldn't look kindly on a long hiatus.

Staying in one place too long isn't good for a man with a band. Being on the road gave me a certain kind of freedom to concentrate on the music and to play what I wanted. If you stay in one place too long, pretty soon you begin to play the music that someone else wants you to play. And you become nostalgic.

Nostalgia never appealed to me, spiritually or musically. In terms of the latter, there naturally were certain tunes closely associated with the band. That's often what people came out to hear, to stir their own memories. By the same token, I never felt the band's future was tied to delving into the past.

If I had to be confined to what I did when I was a young man, if I felt there weren't any more challenges besides doing that over and over again and polishing it a little more, I would have thrown in the towel. I couldn't have continued, because I was not built for the vaudeville era. I started that way, but I couldn't live by that kind of rule book.

Young players helped us to keep a fresh approach. They're better educated in music today, and they have all the experience that the older guys amassed to fall back on. I wouldn't tell any section of the band, "Do it this way." But I might say, "Don't do that, try it another way, is there another way you might like to try it."

When we would do our old tunes, we tried to stretch out and have individual players add their own concepts. How much room I gave someone on a tune depended on the player.

I would extend anybody's solo if they had something to say.

Sometimes the whole pattern of an oldie would change. In the case of "Woodchopper's Ball," we developed so many versions that we had to send out and get a stock arrangement to see how the thing was done to begin with. I think it's part of growing and living.

John Fedchock, the trombonist who played and arranged for the band from 1980 to 1987, recalls:

Woody didn't like to do the old stuff, and sometimes he would get bugged when people would request it.

One time at an old dance hall in Iowa, some guy who had a little too much to drink was angry that we weren't playing all the old hits. We weren't playing Glenn Miller, we weren't playing Tommy Dorsey, everything wasn't two-beat, he couldn't sing along. He went up to Woody and they exchanged words. Then I heard Woody say something like, "What did it cost you to get in here?" The guy told him, and Woody just whipped out a twenty and gave it to him, and said, "See you later, pal."

I started on the same day as Mike Brignola and John Oddo and a trumpet player, Steve Harrow. I took the place of Nelson Hines. I had been at the Eastman School of Music in Rochester, New York, doing master's work, and I met a few people there who knew some of Woody's players who had gone to Eastman. We went out to hear the band a couple of times and I gave a tape to Gene Smith, who was then the lead trombone player. When Nelson left the band, they gave me a call. As a matter of fact, it was about four in the morning, while they were in California playing Disneyland.

I got an official leave of absence from school and it worked out great. I returned in 1985 while Woody was doing a small group tour, and I squeezed everything I had left to do in five months. When the band went back out in May, I took a week off from school, joined them for some important gigs, and returned to school for my finals.

My first gig with the band was in Chicago—a three-hour concert in a park. I can't remember why, but I didn't have any chance to warm up all day. We went straight to the gig, and I had something like six solos that night. Nelson, the guy I replaced, played a lot of plunger and real funky type stuff. I knew how he played, but I figured I'd do my thing.

At the end of the evening, Woody came over to me and he was really angry. He said, "It's not funky enough. It's gotta be funkier or we'll have to do something about it." Here's this guy I always revered, this legend I always wanted to play with . . . It could have really made me apprehensive and nervous. Instead, it got me pissed off. I knew I could do what he wanted. It's just that I didn't know what he wanted before then.

The next night, I just bluesed out on every solo—I played every blues lick I'd ever learned or heard—and tried to make it swing real hard. Woody came up to me later that night, when we were hanging out at a bar, and said, "Sounds good." He just wanted to see if I had the roots for it. From then on, I was able to play however I wanted. It was on that second gig that he dubbed me Too Tall John, and he continued to call me that every night. Afterward, guys came up to me and said, "He must really like you, because he doesn't do that for everybody." Things were great from then on.

I did about sixteen or seventeen charts for Woody, but I didn't write for the band at first. I had taken one year of beginning arranging at Eastman. I had written one or two charts in my life. John Oddo had sort of taken over the writing chores in the band and I was apprehensive to even try. With this great band that I always wanted to play with, with all the great charts that had been recorded, I was more concerned with playing.

After about two-and-a-half years, I tried a chart. We were in the club in New Orleans for six months and I had an apartment. I figured it was a good time to do one. I wrote an arrangement on a Lou Donaldson tune called "Fried Buzzard." It featured Mike Brignola on baritone sax and myself. Woody said, "Maybe you ought to write it so that the melody is just unison saxophones." I didn't want to do that because there are three or four other charts in the book like that.

If I wrote it that way, he'd probably call those other charts. I stuck to my guns and he was cool about it. He started calling it every night. We recorded it later on the fiftieth anniversary album.

It was about eight months before I tried another. I was just sort of feeling my way around. The luxury was that every night you're playing great stuff and you're getting a feel for what voicings sound good. Also, the charts in Woody's book are paced very well; from beginning to end they have a nice shape to them. When you're studying in school, sometimes you don't get that because you're too worried about the mechanics; you lose the overall. But just playing that music night after night, you get a feel for the phrasing, for how much rest you need to leave for a brass section after you give them a hard blow.

The second chart was an original called "The Great Escape," which we recorded on the "Woody's Gold Star" album. It didn't go over as well as the first. We used it on jazz gigs, but not at dances. Then, after John Oddo had left the band, Woody said he wanted me to write something. I was all excited. My first assignment from Woody Herman. Later, at a private party for us after a gig in Baton Rouge, Louisiana, Woody said, "I want you to write a new funky version of Herbie Hancock's 'Watermelon Man.' "

That was the last thing I wanted to hear. There was already a "Watermelon Man" chart in the book by Nat Pierce. It was a funky jazz thing that the band recorded in the sixties. I really didn't want to update that. The guys were giving me a hard time about it because I was trying to let it lay. But Woody wouldn't let up. Every night he'd say, "You working on that chart? 'Cause I got some ideas for it." I finally decided to write it, and it came out OK. But it took a couple of years before he was comfortable with it because, as soon as I wrote it, he said it wasn't what he expected. I thought of funk in the modern sense, and he thought of funk as real bluesy. He had us add a trumpet solo at the beginning in kind of the old feel. He did that to a lot of charts.

On some of the older charts in the book, he might add a chorus of melody or add a chorus of rhythm in front, or just four bars in front. He wasn't really an arranger, per se, but he had the ears for it.

On his very last recording date, we had some Latin percussion players, and Woody said he wanted to try the "Watermelon Man" chart. The percussion players couldn't read music, so while I played my parts I'd be standing to wave them in or wave them out of passages. It was wild. I was almost a nervous wreck. But it came off great, and Woody was adamant about putting it on the album.

Woody never told us in advance what tunes we would play. But the band would know what the upcoming number was after a couple of words of the little rap he gave the audience. When he'd say, "Here's something from 1948," you knew it was "Early Autumn"; or something to feature the four saxophones, you knew it was "Four Brothers."

Woody would ride on the bus occasionally, but he didn't interact too much with the guys. He'd hang out in the bar after the gig sometimes. His only rule was to get on the stand and swing and play great. That was it.

There was always that sort of thing where guys were afraid to approach him. It wasn't like just talking to another guy in the band. He was sort of set up a little higher. On the bandstand, even though he wouldn't say anything, you could tell from how he was looking at someone in the band if he wasn't digging it. There were times when he might have been thinking only about the next tune, but if he happened to be looking in your direction, you were playing for Woody. Sal Nistico told me in 1984 that he still got nervous with Woody watching him. If he really liked your playing, you'd play more, be featured in concerts. If he didn't like the way you played, he wouldn't call tunes that you played on. There were occasions when he didn't like the way someone played a solo, so he'd open up the tune and bring down a guy he liked. On "Woodchopper's Ball," for instance, someone would come down front to play the solo. If Woody didn't dig it, he'd bring forward a second guy to play it, just to show the first guy "Hey, you're not making it." He didn't have to say anything.

We once played a huge dance in Canada for the Sylvania company, in a big hotel ballroom. It was obvious that this engagement was paying a lot of money. One of the guys from the company requested "Tie a Yellow Ribbon." At any other place, Woody would have had this guy beheaded. But Woody knew that this was one of the guys paying for the gig. The trouble was Woody didn't know the tune. He turned to the rhythm section and asked if anyone knew it, and they shrugged their shoulders. Then he turned to the rest of us, and none of us would have wanted to play it even if we knew it. The reason is that you have this great book lying in front of you and you're wasting five minutes of playing time.

Finally Woody said, "Fifty dollars to whoever will play 'Tie a Yellow Ribbon.'" Dave Riekenberg, the tenor player, stood up and played it. The rhythm section was kind of iffing it through the changes. Dave made fifty bucks.

At a policemen's ball outside of Boston, nobody was really listening to the band. We were positioned sort of off to the side, background music. Nobody cared that it was Woody Herman, living legend, up on the stage. As the night wore on, one of the guys in the band broke out a whoopee cushion, and started screwing around with it. When somebody went up for a solo, the cushion was on his seat when he returned. Eventually Woody started getting into it, and he would motion to put the whoopee cushion on somebody's seat.

The party was winding down, people were leaving, nobody was listening. Steve Harrow went out to play some blues on "Cousins," with a Harmon mute. Woody sent one of the guys up to the microphone with the whoopee cushion to trade fours with Steve. And Steve started making those same kinds of sounds with the horn. The band was roaring. But nobody was listening.

I started digging Woody's band when I was a junior in high school in Cleveland. The band actually came to my school to do a clinic and concert. It really made an impact; it was one of the things that helped me decide to go into music—wanting to play on that band, and to play trombone as well as Jim Pugh. It was inspiring. I sat in the front row, and got everyone's autograph on a record that I still have.

That's when I really started collecting the Woody Herman records and getting into all the charts. When I came on the band, I had two or three ninety-minute cassettes full of anything that Woody might call. So as far as reading the book when I got there, I even had some of my parts memorized. I knew on certain tunes where the trombone section had to stand up and play a passage. Reading the arrangements wasn't any worry for me.

The thing I always noticed about Woody's playing—especially after being on the band for a while and then looking at old films and listening to the old records—was that he really swung. Even when he was playing with minimum chops and minimum ideas, everything felt good. Every other clarinet player is so preoccupied with what notes he's playing and how many he can play. But Woody's main thing was swinging. Even if he just played something simple, it would come off because it really felt good. That came off in the band; you'd pick up on it. Woody's swing feel was something I have yet to find in another clarinet player. It was very relaxed, very flowing.

We did an album with clarinetist Richard Stolzman, and I wrote a chart on "Come Sunday" for Richard to play. The chart builds up at the end; I wrote it so that he would play over the band, the way Woody did. He had a heck of a time relating to the concept of having to play over this massive sound with just a clarinet. His manager said, "You can't do that with a clarinet." Mike Brignola said, "Well, you better talk to Woody, 'cause he does it every night."

Woody once asked Byron Stripling, who was our lead trumpet player at the time, to play a high G at the end of "Things Ain't What They Used To Be." Byron said, "I'll give it a try." And Woody replied, "Well, if you can do it, I can still top you by a third."

I always wanted our material to come from within the band, which is why I sought pieces from my players. That was the secret of our freshness. And that's why I always told interviewers that my favorite herd was the one I'd have next year.

We always had guys in the band who would write charts, from the beginning. I felt that the most constructive way to write was for a certain group of musicians. If you could make those guys become profound as soloists with what you wrote as background for them, it was a stepping-stone for the players and the writers alike.

Besides Joe Bishop, Ralph Burns, Neal Hefti, Al Cohn, and Nat Pierce, there was always someone who contributed. Jimmy Rowles didn't do charts for me, but he always had great suggestions about tunes and ideas.

When I needed something, there was Bill Holman. I rarely requested a chart, but usually someone would do something and bring it in. Gary Anderson did many great things for us— "Fanfare for the Common Man" and "Don't You Worry 'Bout a Thing." He came out of Berklee and has since done everything from movie work to television.

And, of course, there was Alan Broadbent and John Fedchock. David LaLama was another pianist who could take direction very well. He was very important to the band, and Alan Broadbent, in the seventies. I would tell him what I needed and he would do it.

With writers like that, and the kinds of players we managed to find and help develop, I never considered myself a bandleader. I was a coach.

21

ANYPLACE I
HANG MY HAT

The Internal Revenue Service was getting the lion's share of our earnings. But few people were aware of it, aside from close friends. I refused to go public with it while Charlotte was alive. She was fiercely proud, and there was no point in causing embarrassment.

I managed to live very well on the road, taking enough expense money as I needed to ensure good accommodations and good meals. But I was also keenly aware that it would end if we missed a payment to the government every week. We'd be out of business, without any material goods other than the house and the clothes on my back.

Suddenly, in 1985, my ownership of the house was in jeopardy as well. The government notified me that it would be auctioned off to help satisfy the tax debt.

It all happened with little fanfare. I feel there wasn't

enough public notice, and that only certain people knew about it. If you were into buying properties, I guess you could find out easily. The person who wound up with it, William Little, was apparently doing a lot of business with the government on properties.

Little got the house for 99,000 some-odd dollars—an astoundingly low price, considering that we had a legitimate estimate that the house was worth around $350,000. I presented the government with the fact that my wife and I had signed a will leaving the house to Ingrid. Charlotte's death, in effect, had given Ingrid half of the house. The document, however, had been drawn up during the last few days of Charlotte's life, and the government apparently doesn't like last-minute wills. After much fighting, it was decided that Ingrid owned 50 percent of the house and that 50 percent of the purchase price paid by Little was to be held in escrow for her. But she wouldn't pick up the money because we were still trying to work out something to make it possible to keep the house.

An arrangement was negotiated in which we would pay rent to Little for half of the house—a home that I had paid cash for almost forty years earlier. Only the government could have thought of something like that.

When the public learned of the situation concerning my debt and the status of my home, I tried to gloss over it with humor. "Having the IRS in on my house has fringe benefits," I said. "One IRS guy shows up twice a week to mow the lawn. Another one cleans and trims the bushes."

But I was not amused. Being a man without credit was difficult enough for me, and I had been in that position for more than twenty years. I had to have cash on me at all times. I was without a personal bank account or credit cards—a tough existence for a man constantly on the road. I usually had to pay my hotel bills in advance.

I figured that, with the visits I had made to other parts

of the world for the State Department, they might at least leave me something to hang my hat on. The government had put liens on everything I had touched. I felt that I should be looked upon as a human being who had tried very hard to be correct.

But I didn't expect any miracles. If the IRS had taken some of the rigor mortis off me, there were lots of things I wanted to do, such as be able to pay for a vacation in which I wasn't confined to the home I was in danger of losing.

Those problems, however, didn't affect the music we were playing or my desire to continue playing it. I was able to shunt off a lot of stuff because of the way I was educated. The schools did a good job of teaching me a philosophy of staying alive, which is why I have never truly been depressed.

Just when I was becoming accustomed to being a tenant in my own home, William Little informed us of his intention to sell the place and of our need to vacate. But a judge granted us a six-month extension to remain and, meanwhile, my lawyer was attempting to resolve the situation. Ingrid, who had followed Hermie Dressel as the band's business manager in 1981, was certainly not about to give up the house for half of $99,000.

22
THE CODA

I was weary. It became harder each day to gather strength for another hike to another town, to another hotel room, to another guy asking me, "Hey, Mr. Herman, how do you like it here in Decatur?" or wherever the hell we were.

On the bandstand, things were fine, we were swinging. Tom Cassidy, our booker, was keeping us busy; Bill Byrne, our road manager, was taking care of details; and trombonist/arranger John Fedchock and Frank Tiberi, who had been an anchor in the sax section for many years, were keeping our music fresh and exciting.

But off the stage I was dragging my ass. Most of the time, I couldn't remember where we had played yesterday. I still loved the music, but being reduced to a government serf was gnawing at me.

We nonetheless had a reason to celebrate. It was 1986, my fiftieth year in front of a band. We hadn't merely survived the collapse of the big band era, the crush of rock and roll, and a twenty-year income-tax battle which kept me at the brink of poverty. We had also managed to keep the music adventurous and ensured the requisite energy by keeping the ranks filled with energetic and talented young men.

Fifty years called for a helluva celebration.

Through George Simon, meanwhile, I had met and heard a great young classical clarinetist named Richard Stolzman, who was to play a key role in the anniversary concert we were preparing.

George Simon recalls:

I met Richard Stolzman on the West Coast sometime in the early eighties at the Grammy Awards, and he told me that he loved to play jazz. I told him, "Why don't you sit in with us sometime at Twilight Jazz," which was the early evening gig I was doing with writer Bill Simon and other musicians each Wednesday in New York. At that time we were installed at Eddie Condon's.

One Tuesday, I came home and listened to my answering machine. One of the messages was a voice that said, "Mr. Simon, this is Richard Stolzman. I play the clarinet. When we met in Los Angeles, you said some time when I came to New York I might be able to sit in with your group. I'd love to come in tomorrow evening. But if you don't want me to, just put a sign outside that says to stay away."

I called him back and he came in. And so did Woody Herman.

Richard Stolzman recalls:

I played a little blues and one reckless chorus of "Take the A-Train." Then George said to me, "There's somebody over in the corner who wants to talk to you."

I couldn't believe it—Woody Herman.

He talked to me about my playing and asked if I were interested in playing "Ebony Concerto" with his band at the fiftieth anniversary concert at the Hollywood Bowl.

I had first heard the piece when I was in college, and I wasn't particularly impressed with it. I guess I thought at that time that I was going to hear a jazz piece and, when I didn't, I ignored it. Later on, I learned that the sounds, harmonizations, voice leadings, and such in the piece were really special—jazzlike and ahead of their time. Stravinsky had a fondness sometimes for rather reckless intervals, odd leaps, and kind of jagged, quirky lines. But after having played "Ebony" many times, it seems to me to be exactly right.

The fiftieth anniversary concert, on July 16, 1987, was a highly emotional day for me. Between the rigors of assembling the program, I was preoccupied constantly with thoughts of my parents, of Charlotte, and of Sister Fabian, who had given me support in school—all those who had been as incremental in feeding my musical fire as Duke Ellington.

Finally, there was the music itself, lush and punchy, delivered by the herd and a second band, packed with alumni: Pete and Conte Candoli, Bill Berry, Don Rader, and John Audino on trumpets; Dick Hyde, Buster Cooper, and Carl Fontana on trombones; Dick Hafer, Med Flory, Bob Cooper, Jack Nimitz, and Herman Riley on saxes, and a rhythm section of Nat Pierce, Monty Budwig, and Chuck Flores.

More than 12,000 people heard us play not just the expected revivals—"Blowin' Up a Storm," "Bijou"—but a new composition that Ralph Burns wrote in honor of Charlotte, called "Godmother." Rosemary Clooney sang "My Buddy," and Jimmy Rowles, with his daughter Stacy on flugelhorn, were elegant on "Old Folks" and Billy Strayhorn's "Lotus Blossom." Rowles returned for a duet with Stan Getz, playing Jimmy's "Peacocks," which they had recorded years earlier.

Before Richard Stolzman came out to play "Ebony Concerto," I told the audience: "Since we first played this piece at Carnegie Hall forty years ago, I have been hoping and wanting dearly to hear it—particularly my solo—as it should be played."

Then I took a seat on the stage.

Stolzman gave it the kind of justice a work of art deserves.

At the end of the concert, the party continued through the night at my home with a couple of hundred friends.

Two days later, the band was back to business as usual. But my body wasn't. Pain from the steel pin in my leg made walking a hardship. It was difficult to get through an airplane terminal or to climb stairs. Just the thought of packing and unpacking, of hopping from hotel to hotel, from city to tank town, was awesome.

For the first time, I looked for help, and I found it in Ed Dye, who began accompanying me on the road as valet, aide, nurse, and general man Friday. But the fatigue of living on the road was relentless, like the tax and house problems. The nightly music was the only payoff and my failing health was making it difficult to perform for more than an hour. By November 1986, while playing an engagement outside of New York City, I collapsed and was taken to Bellevue Hospital in Manhattan, where they pumped at least a pint of water from my lungs. Lying in a crowded hospital ward didn't make for much of a Thanksgiving.

Stuart Troup recalls:

Woody lay in bed in a noisy ward when I arrived with Polly Podewell, the singer who had performed with him from time to time during the previous few years.

He looked more frail than usual. In a weak voice, he admitted that his body wasn't up to what little spirit he had left. Just before I was leaving, he smiled, took my hand, and motioned for me to come closer.

"You know," he said, "Igor Stravinsky was right. He said that growing old is just a series of humiliations."

Frank Tiberi fronted the band in my place. When I left

the hospital, I went to Jack and Mary Siefert's home outside of Philadelphia to recuperate.

I rejoined the band after a few weeks, but my energy was minimal. I don't know how I put together the strength to record early in March 1987, when we made the *Woody's Gold Star* album for Concord.

Shortly afterward, we played an engagement in Denver, and the altitude was getting to me. I got some medicine for it, but I felt noticeably weaker.

John Fedchock recalls:

In Denver, Woody started to get really sick. Some of the decisions about the Gold Star *album hadn't been made yet—we just had the rough tapes—and he told me, "Come by my room tomorrow and we'll talk about the record and decide what to do." I went up to his room at about four in the afternoon. He answered the door in his underwear, and his hair was sticking up all over the place. He had been in bed all day, and he said, "Sorry, all I can do is sleep." He wanted to conserve his energy for the two hours of playing each night. I remember him sitting down very slowly in a chair next to the desk, and he said, "OK, what have we got here?"*

I showed him a piece of paper with the names of the tunes, but he had trouble reading it, so I read it to him. He said, "I want to make sure that they put some extra tunes on the CD." That was very important to him. If someone was going to spend the extra money for a CD, he wanted to give them something extra.

About three weeks later he went into the hospital in Detroit, and they said that he had only about 25 percent of his lung capacity. So he played on that last album date with virtually no air. And he still sounded good.

After the Denver engagement, the tour took us to Grand Meadow, Minn., for a concert at the high school. By the end of the evening, I had nothing left. The next stop was Dr. Stan Levy in Detroit.

EPILOGUE

Woody was hospitalized in Detroit. "Dr. Stan Levy worked on him around the clock," Jack Siefert said. "He practically gave up his private practice."

His body was under attack from emphysema and heart disease, and his health continued to fail after months in the Detroit hospital. After a transfer to Cedars-Sinai Medical Center in Los Angeles for several weeks, he went home to his Hollywood Hills bedroom for a while, where he remained tied to a life-support system, with oxygen, a wheelchair and a nurse at his bedside. His daughter, Ingrid, and singer Polly Podewell tried to comfort him, but his periods of consciousness and coherence kept diminishing. He had to return to the hospital several times.

With his lungs and his heart becoming increasingly weak,

Woody was taken again to Cedars-Sinai, where he died on October 29, 1987.

Four days later, at ten o'clock in the morning, Jack Seifert was a solitary figure sitting in a forward pew at St. Victor's Catholic Church in West Hollywood—the same church in which a funeral mass was celebrated for Charlotte five years earlier. He was composing a eulogy when he was interrupted by my arrival. He knew that Woody and I were writing a book, but we had never met. We had a couple of hours before the funeral was to begin, and we talked, first at the church and then over a snack at a nearby restaurant.

"Woody was not a gift-wrapped empty box," Jack said. "He was a modest musician, never a wiseguy. And he had a fantastic sense of humor."

I told him how one night, while Woody and I were taping some history at our usual corner in a Manhattan lounge, someone began to play the spinet piano. My back was to it, and the sound came as a shock, since I had never seen anyone go near the piano before. The player, obviously aware of Woody's presence, was delivering a feeble reading of "Early Autumn."

"What the hell is this?" I said.

Woody was somber-faced, but with a twinkle in his eyes—the look that often preceded one of his droll remarks. He said, "They have a song demonstrator here."

"He had a special way of phrasing everything," Jack responded. "If he addressed someone as 'pal,' for instance, you knew he had no use for the guy."

I remembered Woody using that term the first time I met him, in 1945, after the band had just finished a matinee performance at a Broadway theater. I was eleven and couldn't afford to go inside, but I was among a group of about fifteen awaiting Woody at the stage door. When he appeared, autograph books were thrust toward him. I was smaller than the others, and last.

Long before he got to my book, an insistent fan began

noisily elbowing others out of the way. Woody looked up from the book he was signing and said, "What's your problem, pal?" His inflection reduced the bully to a lamb.

"C'mere, kid," Herman called to me. I gave him my book and, as he was writing, he said, "You know your way around the city?" I nodded.

"Want to do me a favor?"

Holy mackerel, sure. He took out a piece of paper, wrote a note, and stuffed it into an envelope. "Take this over to the Lincoln Hotel on Eighth Avenue," he said. "It's for Horace Heidt."

Woody reached into a pocket and gave me a five-dollar bill, a fortune for a kid in 1945.

Thirty-seven years later, while sitting at a rehearsal in Fat Tuesday's in Manhattan, I asked him, "Why did you give me so much?"

"I was trying to make a paying customer out of you," he replied.

A crowd was gathering when Jack and I returned to the church. Among Woody's friends were Henry Mancini, Les Brown, Ray Anthony, and Stan Kenton's widow, Audrey. Gene Lees was chatting with members of Woody's alumni, who included Ralph Burns, Jimmy Rowles, Nat Pierce, Bill Holman, Ross Tompkins, Bill Perkins, Cappy Lewis—whose trumpet was heard on the original recording of "Woodchopper's Ball"—and Cappy's son Mark, who became a second-generation trumpet player in the band; Mary Ann McCall, John Fedchock, Terry Gibbs, Pete Candoli, Don Rader, Dave Riekenberg, and others.

Ingrid arrived with her children, Polly Podewell, and Charlotte's mother, Inga Neste.

Only trumpeter Bill Byrne was there to represent the then-current Herman Herd. The band, he explained, was on the road, having played a concert the night before at Oklahoma State University, with Frank Tiberi leading.

"Woody wanted a simple, traditional mass," Jack said, "in tribute to his parents." Monsignor George Parnassus complied after the carnation-and-rose-covered casket was wheeled down the center aisle.

"Woody, the one word that means so much to so many," Jack Siefert intoned to the two hundred or so assembled mourners. "As a bandleader, he defied the laws of physics because of his unique talent of being able to make the whole greater than the sum of its parts. . . . Above all, he was a role model for the young people of today, for he proved that you can still reach your artistic goals and be a nice guy. . . . Woody was the rarest of all human possessions: he was a true friend."

Jack's eulogy was brief and particularly poignant when he summoned the words to "Early Autumn." The appropriateness was astonishing.

"Woody always felt that Johnny Mercer was one of America's greatest poets," he said, and he began to read:

> *When an early autumn walks the land*
> *And chills the breeze,*
> *And touches with her hand*
> *The summer trees,*
> *Perhaps you'll understand*
> *What memories*
> *I own.*
> *There's a dance pavilion in the rain*
> *All shuttered down,*
> *A winding country lane*
> *All russet brown,*
> *A frosted windowpane*
> *Shows me a town*
> *Grown lonely . . .*

INDEX

Miller, Glenn, 11, 25, 29, 30–31, 88, 125, 135
Miller, Mitch, 99
Mills Brothers, 101
Milwaukee, 6, 8, 11, 16
Mirenburg, Mary, 43
Mitchell, Billy, 76
Mitchell, Red, 93, 94–97, 98
Monroe, Vaughn, 88
Moore, Phil, 72
Morgan, Russ, 46
Morris, Al, 14
Mound City Blue Blowers, 11, 14
Munson, Dick, 49
Murphy, Rose, 105
"Music for Dancing," 99
"The Music Stopped," 46
"Muskrat Ramble," 96
Musso, Vido, 42
"My Buddy," 147

Nance, Ray, 46–47
Neste, Charlotte, 14–15
Neste, Inga, 152
New England, 28–29
New Jersey, 25–27, 32
New Orleans, 50, 131–33
New York City, 33–34, 52–53, 107–108, 129–30
Newman, Joe, 108
Ney, Jerry, 73
Nichols, Red, 9, 14
Nimitz, Jack, 147
Nine O'Clock Revue, 14
Nistico, Sal, 111, 119, 121, 138
Noble, James (Jiggs), 20, 39
Noble, Ray, 20–21
"Northwest Passage," 52, 59–60
Norvo, Red, 30, 57, 60, 75
"Not Really the Blues," 89

Oddo, John, 135, 136, 137
"Oh Gee, Say Gee," 7
"Old Folks," 147

"On the Alamo," 19
"The One I Love Belongs to Somebody Else," 19
Otis, Fred, 73

Paramount Theater, 34–36
Parker, Charlie, 83
Pasich, Kirk, 2, 3
"Peacocks," 147
"Perdido," 39, 47
Perkins, Bill, 99, 152
Petrillo, Caesar, 48
Pettiford, Oscar, 76, 90, 105
Pfeffner, Ralph, 49
Phillips, Flip, 46, 49, 52, 54, 59, 61, 62, 130
Phillips Records, 108
Pierce, Nat, 101, 104, 105, 107–108, 109–10, 111, 115, 116–17, 130, 137, 141, 147, 152
Podewell, Polly, 148, 150, 152
Porcino, Al, 100, 122
Powell, Eleanor, 50
Powell, Seldon, 106
Powers, Buddy, 120
"The Preacher," 104
Prima, Louis, 62
"Proud Mary," 119
Puente, Tito, 105
Pugh, Jim, 123, 130, 139

Quealey, Chelsea, 20
"Quiet Nights," 112

Racism, 90, 93, 103, 105
Rader, Don, 147, 152
Radio broadcasts, 29–30, 36, 44, 60
Raeburn, Boyd, 62, 88
Raney, Jimmy, 89
"The Raven Speaks," 122
Rehak, Frank, 99
Reilly, Sister Fabian, 11, 12, 147
Republic Pictures, 50